The Government and Politics of the Middle East and North Africa

"No doubt this is the best and most comprehensive textbook on the Middle East in the English language. It provides the student with all the basic knowledge needed to acquire an understanding of this highly important and dynamic region of the world. An interesting feature of the book is its departure from the traditional concept of the Middle East in that it does include the states of North Africa and it devotes a special chapter to the Palestinians."

Raymond Habiby
Oklahoma State University

"The best of the general, state-by-state studies of the Arab world, Israel, Turkey, and Iran. The country chapters are a good starting point for comparison; their breadth is also useful to complement more specialized studies. The book is an excellent anchor for a comparative course on the region."

Martin W. Sampson
University of Minnesota

About the Book and Editors

A new and fully revised edition of the most comprehensive text available in the field, this multiauthor volume meets the need for a broad introduction to the politics of the states of the Middle East and North Africa and of the Palestinians as well. All chapters—including bibliographies and tabular material—have been reviewed and revised, many extensively.

Written by specialists from both academic and policymaking worlds, the text has been completely updated to reflect the evolution of the area up to 1986. This new edition includes discussion of the effects of the Iranian Revolution, changes in the oil situation, the Iran-Iraq War, and the new government in Sudan. The war in Lebanon and its impact upon regional politics is assessed, and an entire chapter on the politics of the Palestinians has been added.

While reflecting the latest developments in the Middle East, the text also focuses on the inherent and continuing features of each political system and the factors that influence them—cultural and political heritage, social attitudes, and economic realities. Multiple authorship has allowed the advantage of depth of expertise for each of the countries, and though the chapters follow a common outline, the approach reflects the individuality of each government, political system, or movement.

David E. Long is in charge of the Near East and South Asia in the Office of Counter Terrorism and Emergency Planning of the Department of State. He was formerly executive director of the Center for Contemporary Arab Studies at Georgetown University. **Bernard Reich** is professor of political science and international affairs and chairman of the Middle East Studies Committee at George Washington University.

Northern Africa and the Middle East

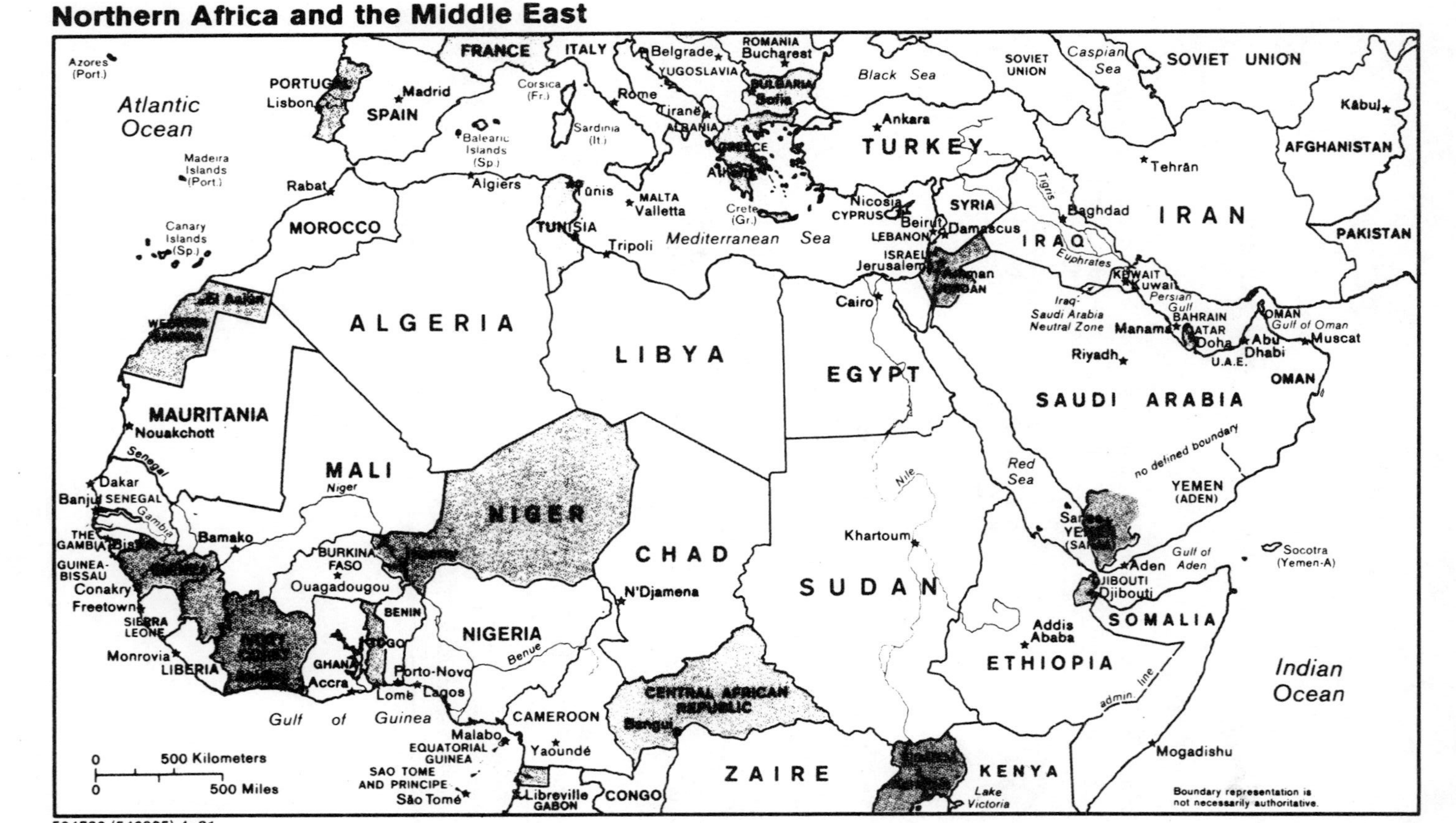

504736 (546325) 4-81

Second Edition, Revised and Updated

The Government and Politics of the Middle East and North Africa

edited by David E. Long and Bernard Reich

Westview Press • Boulder and London

Published in 1986 in the United States of America by Westview Press, Inc.; Frederick A. Praeger, Publisher; 5500 Central Avenue, Boulder, Colorado 80301

Library of Congress Cataloging-in-Publication Data
The Government and politics of the Middle East and
North Africa.
Includes bibliographies and index.
1. Near East—Politics and government—1945-
2. Africa, North—Politics and government. I. Long,
David E. II. Reich, Bernard.
DS62.8.G68 1986 320.956 86-4102
ISBN 0-8133-0336-2
ISBN 0-8133-0337-0 (pbk.)

Printed and bound in the United States of America

The paper used in this publication meets the minimum requirements of the American National Standard for Permanence of Paper for Printed Library Materials Z39.48-1984.

10 9 8 7 6 5 4 3

Contents

Maps and Tables

Maps

Tables

Preface to the Second Edition

Much has happened in and to the states of the Middle East and North Africa since the completion of the first edition of this book in 1980. Coups, revolutions, and wars have occurred side by side with dramatic changes in regional economic and social conditions. These changes have added to the already complex nature of the politics of this variegated and complicated region. At the same time, many of the major features of national life and political development have remained constant. In revising this work we have retained, after careful review and where it continued to be appropriate, substantial portions of the material from the first edition. Additions and modifications have been made to reflect the changes that have occurred, and the bibliographies have been revised to include more recent literature.

The reader will note that a chapter dealing with the Palestinians has been added. This addition reflects the editors' views that separate coverage is warranted by the size and significance of the Palestinian movement in the politics of the Middle East. Although the Palestinians were discussed in several country chapters of the previous edition, our decision to create a single chapter on the subject permits more systematic coverage. Moreover, some new authors have joined the original team in order to ensure even more specialized coverage of the themes in the volume. We hope that this new edition will continue to serve a new generation of students of the Middle East, just as the earlier one did for thousands of their predecessors.

As in the previous edition numerous people, especially the several authors, have ensured the timely completion of this work. Frank Ricciardone's knowledge of Iraq, Christine Arden's skillful copy editing, and Jeanne Campbell's editorial talent (once again) have been extraordinarily helpful to the editors. Without the assistance and understanding of our wives, Barbara and Madelyn, none of this would have been possible.

David E. Long
Bernard Reich

Preface to the First Edition

In recent years considerable attention has been devoted to the Middle East by people in all walks of life, from the layman to the student to the policymaker. Writing about the region has continued to grow in quantum leaps. Books and articles by serious scholars exist in large number and cover many aspects of the region, especially its history, politics, and economics. Many have been fascinated by what they see as a newly discovered region of the world. Student interest has also increased. Despite this interest and the large number of specialized works on the area, no introductory work on the politics of the states of the region that is both comprehensive and up-to-date exists for the general student. It was with this in mind that the editors sought the assistance of a diverse group of Middle East specialists with academic and policy-oriented experience to produce a current, comprehensive, and general book that focuses on the politics (and especially political dynamics) of the region known as the Middle East. To ensure its comprehensiveness, we have included the states of Arab North Africa. Multiple authorship has the advantage of providing greater depth of expertise on the individual countries and political systems than can be provided by a single author. Although all authors have followed a common outline, each chapter differs according to the peculiarities of the particular political system being examined and the approach of the author.

The preparation of a book of this type requires the cooperation and assistance of many people, including, of course, each of the authors listed. In addition, the editors wish to acknowledge the assistance of all those without whom the work would not have been seen in print. Brian Flora, Callie Gass, and Sally Ann Baynard have been particularly helpful. Our wives, Barbara and Madelyn, ensured completion of the work.

David E. Long
Bernard Reich

1

Introduction

David E. Long
Bernard Reich

For centuries the Middle East has fascinated scholars and observers and has been the focal point of great-power attention. The region's strategic significance and the variety and importance of its political, social, and cultural heritage have generated this concern. Through the years the Middle East has had intense religious meaning for the peoples of the Western world. Judaism, Christianity, and Islam all originated in the area, and the most sacred holy places of these three monotheistic faiths are located there. In the mid-twentieth century occasional wars and superpower rivalry have added to the region's strategic dimension. The overall importance of the region, however, is broader and is tied to its location and to its primary resource—oil.

Situated at the hub of Europe, Asia, and Africa, the Middle East is a crossroads and a bridge. Historically it linked the trade routes connecting Europe with Asia and Africa. Today its location makes the Middle East a critical link in the communications network joining Western and Eastern Europe with Eastern Africa, the Indian subcontinent, Southeast Asia, the Far East, and Australasia. The Middle East's military importance is a direct result of its location and has long fascinated the powers interested in greater control of that portion of the world and the adjacent areas.

Oil is the major resource of the Middle East. Middle Eastern oil is abundant, is of unusually high quality, and is exported in huge quantities. It is an essential energy source for the industrialized West and for many of the developing states. The export and sale of Middle Eastern oil, at high prices, has generated a surplus of "petro-dollars" in many of the oil-producing states, has contributed to area-wide economic growth, and has provided the leading producers with increased potential in the international financial community. The importance of Middle Eastern oil and the oil-producing countries' economic potential have combined to increase the concern shown for the Middle East by outside commercial and strategic-political interests.

This interest in the Middle East seems unlikely to abate. The ongoing and intensified efforts to achieve a settlement of the Arab-Israeli conflict continue to involve the superpowers in the Middle East. Further, it seems likely that the dependence of both the industrializing and the industrialized world on Middle Eastern oil will persist for the foreseeable future.

The states of the Middle East have a variety of political systems that reflect their differing historical backgrounds, colonial experiences, social and economic conditions, religions, geographical settings, climate, and population pressures. There is no single category that can include all of these systems. They run the gamut of alternative political structures and dynamics. Personalized one-man authoritarian regimes coexist with Marxist regimes, monarchies, and democratic regimes. However, the Middle Eastern governments perform the various functions of the standard political system, albeit with varying degrees of ability or success and in numerous and diverse ways. These differences in background and in existing conditions provide for variations in political life, structure, and style.

The very real differences that exist among the states of the Middle East should not obscure the similarities, such as the heritage of Islam, the presence of foreign influences, and the concentration of leadership in the urban upper and middle classes and the rise of new elites of technocrats and military officers that link them. Throughout the Middle East, political life in the past few decades has been characterized by the shift from traditional to modern activity. The traditional elite of kings and landowners is either declining in power or has already been replaced in most of the political units in the area. A new salaried middle class is emerging as the most active political, social, and economic force, and leadership is increasingly passing into their hands. This group of salaried civilian politicians, organizers, administrators, and experts is supplemented by growing numbers of secondary and university students and by the military. In many of the states the military forms the core of this new politically conscious middle class striving to modernize the state. They have assumed this role as a result of their training, skills, and motivation. The great majority of the population—the peasants and the workers—are only now beginning to enter the realm of politics.

Pan-Arabism and the Islamic revival are integral parts of contemporary activity in the Middle East. In a sense they are complementary movements that have rekindled an Arab and Muslim identity among the diverse peoples of the area. This in turn has affected both the foreign and domestic policies of the Middle Eastern states. In the postwar era, for instance, pan-Arabism has helped to determine the Arab response to Israel and has led to attempts at federation and economic cooperation among several of the Arab states. The Islamic heritage and revival have acted simultaneously as both a revolutionary and a conservative force. In such countries as Saudi Arabia this force has helped to shape the response to modernization and westernization by advocating an Islamic way of life in the face of change. At the same time, Islam has been a divisive force as differences between and among the various sects and traditions surface and intrude into politics.

This book has been planned in keeping with the general view of the Middle East just described. We provide not only a comprehensive discussion of the politics of each of the states, within the context of each system's unique characteristics, but also a view of the basic factors affecting politics so that comparisons across national boundaries can be made. The book reflects our view that certain commonalities exist in Middle Eastern political systems that can provide a basis for the comparison of their politics.

Understanding the politics of the Middle East requires more than an examination of the institutions of government. It is particularly important that the student of the Middle East understand the context in which politics is played. Accordingly, this book examines the political systems in terms of their approach to the problems confronting them. The machinery of government is examined not only in terms of what it is but also in terms of why it is the way it is; why and how it works; and what it has done, or attempted to do, in confronting the state's problems.

Consideration of the legislative, executive, and judicial machinery of politics is thus complemented by study of the elements that affect the actual translation of goals and policy into action. To convey the full flavor of each individual system and its operation, we have examined several components of each system, such as its historical setting, its available resources, its economic and social structure, and its ideologies, as well as the more traditional topics such as political parties, and/or other instruments of mobilization elites, and leadership. While these elements operate in each of the systems, they do so with differing results. Thus the factors are considered differently in each of the studies in this book. This, in itself, provides a useful means of comparison of systems and can be illuminating.

Obviously, a detailed investigation of all of the influences on the politics of any country would require more space than can be allotted in one volume. Therefore, the authors have isolated the most important elements for examination and discussion. This system concept is reflected in the structure of each of the studies. Each country is examined in terms of its

- historical background,
- political environment,
- political structure,
- political dynamics, and
- foreign policy.

Historical Background

The Middle Eastern sense of history is strong, and comprehension of the political systems of the region is almost impossible without an understanding of the historical background of each of the states. Tangible evidence of ancient systems can be found not only in archaeological ruins but also in functioning political systems. The origins of contemporary problems often can be traced back to the ancient civilizations that developed in the region. Throughout the region, history tends to be of such importance that there is little attempt to divorce contemporary developments from historical events and little sense of time to suggest that they should be separated. Thus the origins of Judaism, Christianity, and Islam provide a working context for twentieth-century politics. Specific historic events, such as the Jewish exodus from Egypt and the subsequent establishment of a Jewish state, the Ottoman Turkish conquests, and European colonization and domination continue to affect the political systems of the Middle East in profound ways.

The style of politics often emulates or responds to ancient methods and conflicts. In many of the countries, centuries of history have helped to determine the roles of the elites and the masses and the present-day interaction between them. The form and style of decisionmaking is also the result of historical development as well as of the modern demands placed upon the system. Nowhere is this more apparent than in the continued importance of the kinship group in the decisionmaking process. Ancient rivalries and boundary disputes still affect the relations among the states of the region. In the Middle East the past tends to provide the parameters for the systems operating today.

Political Environment

Despite its crucial role in developing an understanding of the modern Middle East, history alone cannot completely explain modern politics. Geography, demography, climate, and economics have all contributed to the emergence of the Middle East as we know it. The individual environment of each state provides a further understanding of the special and unique forces operating in it. Environment can help to explain the diversity of politics that exists in the face of shared historical background. The geopolitical uniqueness of the region and of its component states is essential in any explanation of political behavior. Geography partially determines the wealth or poverty of a nation and indicates its potential for development. It can also point to a nation's strategic value and to the problems it may face. Such problems, and the means and the methods used to deal with them, provide much of the substance of modern politics and policy.

Demography, too, must be considered. Wars, famines, and religious and national upheaval have led to large-scale immigration and migrations throughout the region. These migrations have left many of the states with substantial ethnic minorities as well as chronic problems of overpopulation or underpopulation. Regional, national, and religious minorities abound. In most areas these minorities have been relegated to second-class status, but in some they have become the ruling elite. In either case, the social structure that determines the weight and merit of minority groups as well as the problems that result from over- or underpopulation can tell us much about the nature of politics.

Economics also plays a key role in determining the political environment of the Middle East. All of the states are undergoing some form of economic and social development, and the governments are very much involved in the process by which such development will be achieved. Here too, however, there is diversity, for the states of the Middle East range from some of the wealthiest in the world to some of the poorest. Oil is a prime factor in explaining this disparity, but other conditions are involved as well. The population size, education, the human resource endowment, and the state's ability to mobilize modernization all affect the context in which policy is made. The different states have adopted different methods to meet the challenge presented by economic and social development. These methods reflect their own economic needs, resources, and capabilities.

Political Structure

The description and analysis of the formal governmental institutions, their powers, and their decision-making processes traditionally have been the initial step in the study of a state's politics. The Middle East is characterized by a wide range of diverse political institutions—some of which have no match anywhere in the world.

The systems of the Middle East can be examined in terms of the presence, or absence, of such political institutions as constitutions, political parties, judicial systems, and modern bureaucracies. Examination of these institutions helps to provide some insight into the decision-making process and to identify both the decisionmakers themselves and the locus of power within the system. This insight, in turn, provides a framework for making comparisons between and among the states of the region. It should also provide the ability to assess the differences and similarities between the systems and to understand the nature, extent, and direction of political development and modernization.

Political Dynamics

Identifying the institutions of politics and the constitutional methods, if any, by which they are supposed to work provides only a partial picture of a political system. In any state there is a dichotomy between theory and practice. The methods by which a state really operates and the interaction between and among its institutions can be appreciated only through an assessment of its political dynamics. Essentially this assessment would involve an attempt to view the government in action. To the Western student (especially the American) who resides in a country where political systems operate relatively openly and in an orderly and systematic fashion, the complexities of the more closed systems and the Byzantine methods of the Middle Eastern systems may seem unduly complicated. These Middle Eastern systems have their own dynamics conditioned by history and environment. To know only the institutions of government, without understanding the political dynamics involved, is to know only how the system ought to work—not how it does work. The examination of the dynamics of Middle Eastern politics must be undertaken with the particular viewpoint of the Middle East in mind, if the student is to understand Middle Eastern politics.

Foreign Policy

To help the reader understand the interaction of the history, environment, structure, and dynamics in the states, each study concludes with an examination of the foreign policy of that state. Examination of the totality of international relationships for each state is impossible, but the main directions of that policy are looked at in order to develop a picture both of the concept of politics at work in each system and of the methods of operation. These overviews of foreign policy provide insight into the decision-making process and into the views of the decisionmakers. Foreign policy thus acts as something of a summary of state concerns, capabilities, and actions, as well as of the processes by which politics is played within the political system.

Ultimately, this multifaceted examination of the more than twenty independent states of the Middle East and North Africa reveals a good deal not only about the politics of the individual states but also about the region as a whole and about Third World developing states in general. Because of their diversity and the wide range of patterns and approaches they represent, the states of the Middle East provide a useful case study of the examination of politics in Third World states. By examining the basic factors affecting politics, the organization of the political system, and its dynamics and foreign policy, we will come to understand more about the complex and important part of the world known as the *Middle East.*

2

The Land and Peoples of the Middle East

David E. Long

The Land

One of the most difficult tasks in studying the Middle East is to agree upon the lands that it comprises. In some respects, it is like defining a mirage. From a distance, the region appears as a coherent whole; but the closer one approaches, the faster it disappears. One difficulty is that no single demographic factor is uniformly applicable throughout the area. For example, the single most unifying factor is the cultural heritage of Islam. Yet the Islamic world extends far beyond the Middle East, from the Far East to sub-Saharan Africa; and there are also a number of very important non-Muslim groups in the Middle East.

The Middle East is often equated with the Arab world, but to make this equation is to exclude other important ethnic groups, such as the Turks, Persians, Jews, Kurds, Berbers, Nubians, and Armenians. On the other hand, Arabic-speaking Mauritanians are more often included in studies of sub-Saharan Africa than in those of the Arab states to the north.

Even history is not always the best guide. The term *Middle East* was coined at the turn of the century to refer to the Gulf area lying between the Near East and the Far East.[1] Since then, it has come to incorporate the older term, *Near East*, and *North Africa* as well. Politics has led to the inclusion and exclusion of various countries over time. For example, in the nineteenth century, the Balkan countries were regarded as a part of what is now known as the Middle East, whereas today they are studied in the context of Eastern Europe. Few people unfamiliar with Middle Eastern history realize that the founder of the Egyptian monarchy overthrown by Colonel Nasser was an Albanian, and that Albania as well as other Balkan states have significant Muslim populations.

One way to define the Middle East is to begin with those countries that are virtually always considered to be within the region, and then to move outward to those on the periphery. Egypt, Israel, the Arab states of the Fertile Crescent, the Arabian peninsula, and Turkey thus constitute the core area. The rest of North Africa, particularly the Maghrib (Tunisia, Algeria, and Morocco), is sometimes considered separately, and the Sudan is often grouped with sub-

Saharan Africa. Because of their close Arab ties, however, we have chosen to include them in this study. Likewise, Iran is sometimes grouped with Afghanistan and Pakistan as an extension of South Asia, but its location in the Gulf area and its identity as a major Middle East oil producer dictate its inclusion.

Several countries that could have been included were not. Mauritania, which has been accepted into the Arab League, is one. Given the extension of Arab politics into the Horn of Africa, Somalia (which was also accepted into the Arab League) and Ethiopia have some claim to inclusion. By the same token, Greece, because of its relations with Turkey, could have been considered, as could Afghanistan (which came under the original Middle East designation) and Pakistan. Although we realize that our choice of countries is somewhat arbitrary, we feel that it best represents the broadest group of countries exhibiting sufficient commonality to constitute a single region.

Topography

The topography of this vast area is diverse and complex. Physically, the Middle East can be described as a large, generally arid area dissected by several large inland seas that radiate from the center like spokes in a wheel: the Mediterranean, the Red, Black, and Caspian seas, and the Persian (Arabian) Gulf. The northern reaches of the Indian Ocean, including the Arabian Sea, the Gulf of Oman, and the Gulf of Aden may also be added.

The land itself is further divided by large sand "seas" and mountain ranges. The mountains of the Middle East are geologically young and tend to be rocky, jagged, and difficult to traverse. In the Maghrib countries, the Atlas Mountains, reaching 4,000 meters (13,000 feet), form a barrier between fertile coastal areas and the Sahara to the south. Further east, the Sahara extends all the way to the coast, except in eastern Libya, where the highlands of Jabal al-Akhdar, which jut out into the Mediterranean at the tip of Cyrenaica, bring some moisture into the area.

The Sahara, which in Arabic means desert, stretches from the Red Sea Hills to the Atlantic in a belt that extends nearly 2,500 kilometers (1,500 miles) south into Africa. This expanse is broken up into great sand "seas" such as the Nubian desert of Egypt and Sudan, the Libyan desert, and the Great Eastern and Western Ergs of Algeria. Interspersed throughout the area are high massifs such as Jabal Marra in the Sudan (3,000 meters, 9,800 feet), the Tibesti-Toda region of Chad and Libya (2,500 meters, or 8,200 feet), and the Ahaggar (Hoggar) massif in Algeria (2,300 meters, or 7,500 feet).

In the north, mountain ranges stretch in a line eastward to the Himalayas. In Turkey, the Pontus Mountains, which rise along the Black Sea in the north, and the Tarus Mountains, which begin on the Mediterranean coast in the south, join near Mt. Ararat (5,165 meters, or 16,945 feet) close to the Iranian border. From there the Elburz Mountains continue eastward across northern Iran, reaching their highest point at Mt. Demavand (5,600 meters, or 18,400 feet) near Tehran.

Running roughly perpendicular to these mountains are several less imposing highland areas. Two of them flank both sides of the Great Rift Valley, a geological fault system that runs from Turkey through the Jordan Valley and the Red Sea

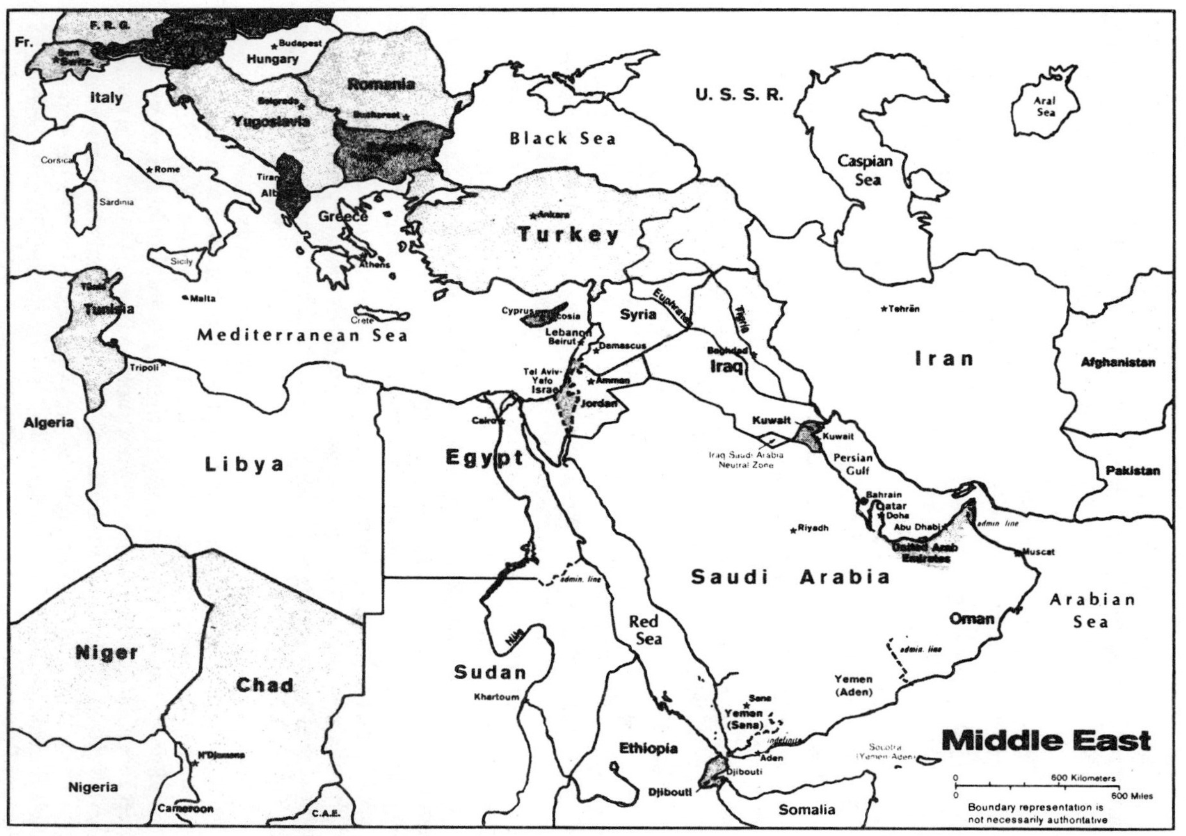
Fr.
F.R.G.
Italy
Corsica
Sardinia
Rome
Sicily
Malta
Hungary
Budapest
Romania
Yugoslavia
Bucharest
Greece
Athens
Crete
U. S. S. R.
Black Sea
Aral Sea
Caspian Sea
Turkey
Ankara
Tunisia
Tripoli
Mediterranean Sea
Cyprus
Syria
Lebanon
Beirut
Damascus
Tel Aviv-Yafo
Amman
Jordan
Euphrates
Tigris
Iraq
Tehrān
Iran
Afghanistan
Pakistan
Algeria
Libya
Cairo
Egypt
Kuwait
Iraq Saudi Arabia Neutral Zone
Persian Gulf
Bahrain
Qatar
Doha
Abu Dhabi
admin. line
Muscat
Riyadh
Saudi Arabia
Arabian Sea
Oman
Red Sea
Nile
Niger
Chad
Sudan
Khartoum
Yemen (Aden)
Sana
Yemen (Sana)
Aden
Ethiopia
Djibouti
Somalia
Nigeria
Cameroon
C.A.E.
Middle East
0
600 Kilometers
600 Miles
Boundary representation is not necessarily authoritative

before branching into the Indian Ocean and East Africa. In the north the Great Rift Valley divides the Lebanon Mountains from the Anti-Lebanon range, which rises to 3,000 meters (9,800 feet) at Mt. Hermon (Jabal al-Shaykh) on the Syrian-Lebanese border.

Further south, on the African side of the Red Sea, the Red Sea Hills stretch southward from Egypt, rising abruptly as they reach the Ethiopian highlands to peaks over 4,000 meters (13,000 feet). On the Arabian side, the Hijaz Mountains also gain in altitude as they extend southward to the Asir Mountains and finally to the Yemen highlands, where altitudes reach 3,700 meters (12,000 feet). From the Yemen the mountains curve back to the northeast along the south Arabian coast. They gradually lose altitude except for the Qara Mountains of western Oman, which reach 1,500 meters (5,000 feet). In easternmost Arabia the Hajar Mountains separate the coastal area of Oman from the interior. The highest elevation, Jabal al-Akhdar (Green Mountain), exceeds 3,000 meters (9,800 feet).

Across the narrow Strait of Hormuz, the broad Zagros Mountains of Iran extend southeast from the Tarus and Elburz ranges, down the eastern shore of the Persian Gulf and eastward along the Gulf of Oman. The highest peak, Zard Khuh, is 4,500 meters (14,800 feet). Finally, on the eastern frontier of Iran, the less imposing eastern Iranian highlands branch southward from the Elburz to the Arabian Sea, where they connect with the Zagros.

Juxtaposed between these mountain ranges are a number of high plateaus and two major river systems. The high, arid central plateau of Iran is totally enclosed by the Zagros, the Elburz, and the eastern Iranian highlands. In its center are two huge, shallow, saucer-like salt deserts that serve as drainage basins for the plateau. They are the Dasht-e-Kavir in the north and the Dasht-e-Lut in the south. In Turkey, the Tarus and Pontus mountains ring the high Anatolian plateau. Central Anatolia is less arid and better drained than Iran. While salt flats and dry lake beds do exist, several river systems cut through the northern mountains to the Black Sea. In a sense, nearly the entire continent of Africa can be considered a relatively high plateau area that drops abruptly as it nears the coast. Along the Mediterranean, this drop is much more gradual than elsewhere in the continent, particularly in the east where the Nile River gradually descends some 6,500 kilometers (4,000 miles) from the East African and Ethiopian highlands.

The Nile is one of the Middle East's two great river systems. As it leaves the swamps and grasslands of the Sudan, its banks are confined to a narrow valley that winds like a great serpent through the brown expanses of the Sahara. The second great river system is formed by the Tigris and Euphrates rivers, which meet about 150 kilometers (95 miles) north of the Persian Gulf to form the Shatt-al-Arab River. Their watershed extends southward from the Tarus Mountains of Turkey. The Tigris and Euphrates provided water for the development of ancient civilizations in the otherwise flat, arid Iraqi plain, just as the Nile had done in Egypt.

Further south, central Arabia drops gradually toward the Gulf from the western Arabian highlands. The area is bisected by occasional westward-facing escarpments such as Jabal Tuwaiq, which extends for some 1,000 kilometers (620 miles) in a shallow arc. Although arid, central Arabia contains several large, dry river-drainage systems. Riyadh, the Saudi capital, is located along one of them, the Wadi Hanifa. There are also two great sand "seas" in Arabia—the Great Nafud in the north and the Rub'al-Khali in the south. These are connected by a narrow strip of sand dunes east of Riyadh known as the Dahna. Passing through the Dahna between Riyadh and the Gulf coast, the traveler can envision the Rub'al-Khali, where some of the great dunes reach over 2,000 meters (6,600 feet) in height.

Geology

For the layperson, geology is a subject so technical that it generally seems best left alone. In the Middle East, the problem is compounded by the fact that the geology is particularly complex. At the same time, however, its geology is the primary source of interest in the contemporary Middle East and has made it a region of major political and economic importance to the rest of the world. For the same quirk of fate that produced vast deserts and steep barren mountain ranges also produced the world's richest oil reserves.

In the last dozen years or so, geologists have developed new theories of continental drift. Continental landmasses, according to these theories, rest on huge plates that slide over the denser material beneath the earth's crust. As the plates separate, they cause the seafloor to spread and create new seas. When plates collide, they create crush zones that cause mountain ranges to push up. The surface of one plate can also be dragged beneath that of another.[2]

During the Mesozoic period, the Afro-Arabian landmass began to drift northward. As it came in contact with a similar northern landmass, probably in the Tertiary period, a crush zone was created. This gave rise to a line of mountains that extends from the Alps to the Himalayas.

Along the leading edge of this Afro-Arabian landmass, a number of smaller plates were created. Three of these, the Aegean plate, an adjacent Turkish plate, and a central Iranian plate, have been the source of considerable earthquake activity in recent years. The three major plates in the Middle East are the African plate, the Eurasian plate, and the Arabian plate. Once part of the African landmass, the Arabian plate moved northeast and is now separated from Africa by the Red Sea. As the Arabian plate moved, it collided with the Iranian plate and created a crush zone. The leading edge of the Arabian plate was pushed downward under the Persian Gulf, and the Zagros Mountains were thrust up on the other side. As a result of this collision, the rock strata in Arabia tilt downward from west to east. The pre-Cambrian, or basement complex, rock that is found on the surface in western Arabia is buried deep underground in the Persian Gulf. In eastern Arabia, the basement complex is covered over with younger sedimentary rock formed by the broad ancient sea that used to separate Arabia and Iran and of which only the Gulf remains. As the Arabian plate was pushed down, marine matter from this ancient sea collected in pockets called domes or anticlines. These domes now constitute the Gulf's oil and gas fields. Similarly, in North Africa, older pre-Cambrian formations are found on the surface only on the Red Sea coast. Further west, newer sedimentary rock was formed by marine deposits in the large prehistoric sea between Africa and Europe. These deposits have become the source of African oil and gas.

Climate

One hears much about the Middle East as the crossroads of three continents: Africa, Europe, and Asia. It is no less a climatic crossroads, falling almost entirely into a transitional or subtropical zone between the tropics of sub-Saharan Africa, and the temperate zone of Europe and Asia. One common characteristic of subtropical zones approximately 30 degrees in latitude is aridity, whether on land or at sea.[3] Although the reasons are not entirely clear, aridity appears to be related to the prevailing wind systems.

The wind systems of the Middle East are characterized by prevailing westerly winds called cyclones, which are generated along the front of polar air, separating it from tropical air masses. These cyclone winds are the primary determinants of the weather conditions throughout the Middle East. In the summer they blow across the northern portions of the region so that scarcely any air movement occurs further south, and the hot, dry air masses of North Africa and Arabia prevail. The low pressure systems that develop during the summer months generate strong, hot local winds that scourge the entire region. For example, in southern Iraq, they are called the *shamal* ("north wind"), and in southeast Iran, the *sad-ou-bist* ("120-day wind"). Maximum temperatures can average 40°C in some places, with absolute temperatures approaching 50°C. After sunset, temperatures can drop 30°C because the dry air does not retain heat. The effect on the body, however, is even more pronounced. I once saw a man shivering in an overcoat in Saudi Arabia at a mild 20°C. The temperature, however, had dropped from 45°C in less than three hours.

In the winter the cyclones move south, creating prevailing westerly winds from the Atlantic Ocean to Pakistan. Moist air from the North Atlantic is drawn into the region, bringing most of the rain that falls in the Middle East. Extremely cold, dry polar air can also be drawn from Siberia into Anatolia and central Iran, causing temperatures to plummet below zero in mountain areas. Warm air from the Red Sea, the Gulf, and the Indian Ocean can also be drawn northward, and as frontal systems pass eastward, strong, hot desert winds are occasionally funneled northward. They are known as the *khamsin* ("50-day wind") in Egypt, the *ghibli* in Libya, the *shlur* in Syria and Lebanon, the *sharqi* in Iraq, and the *simun* in Iran.

As the winter westerlies travel eastward they lose more and more moisture, so that by the time they reach Arabia, Iraq, and Iran, the rains can be extremely fickle. Indeed, if the mountains of Iran were not high enough to capture the remaining moisture, most of Iran would be virtually uninhabitable. Average annual rainfall figures for this area can be deceiving as an indication of climate because torrential downpours do occur in the deserts, only to be followed by droughts of perhaps several years' duration.

This weather system does not reach the southernmost regions of Sudan eastward to southern Arabia. There the monsoons of the Indian Ocean govern the weather. The Qara Mountains of Dhufar province in Oman and the Yemeni and Ethiopian highlands all receive rains in the summer from moisture-laden winds blowing up from the Indian Ocean. In Dhufar, the traveler is struck by the sight of coconut palms growing in place of the more common date palms of the Middle East because there is too much rain. In the Sudan, which also experiences cool winters, the summer monsoon winds bring moisture to the southern part of the country. By the time the monsoon winds reach Khartoum, however, most of the moisture is expended. Occasionally in the summer, these now-dry winds blow across central Sudan, driving huge clouds of dust (called *habubs*) thousands of meters high.

In the winter the monsoons shift direction, blowing steadily southward. The cause of this semiannual cycle is not precisely known. It seems to be related to seasonal shifts in a westerly jet stream in the upper atmosphere that flows north of the Himalayas in summer and to the south of them in winter. Although as a weather determinant the monsoons are only peripherally important to the Middle East, they have had a major impact on society in the Gulf region and southern Arabia. For centuries Arab mariners have sailed their dhows southward to India and Africa on the winter monsoons and back home again on the summer monsoons. Thus, until recent politics intervened, people in this part of the world looked south and east as much as they looked west toward the more traditionally accepted "centers" of the Middle East.

The Peoples

The peoples of the Middle East are extremely heterogeneous, and, as a result of massive, oil-funded economic and social development, their societies are changing practically overnight. Yet despite heterogeneity and social change, Middle Eastern peoples are still predominantly traditional in outlook. Among the uneducated, this is fairly obvious. Among the sophisticated classes, however, traditional attitudes are often obscured behind a facade of westernization and reappear only in times of great stress or crisis.

Social Organization

Race and Language. Contrary to popular belief, racial distinctions mean relatively little in the Middle East. In fact, what are often taken by outsiders to be major racial distinctions—as between Jews and Arabs, Turks and Persians—are not racial at all, but linguistic and cultural. Nevertheless, major racial differences do exist.

A number of racial types can be identified, none of which coincide exactly with any one country or subregion and all of which are found outside the Middle East as well. The most prevalent by far is the Mediterranean race, which originated within the region. Mediterranean types are found from the Atlantic to Afghanistan, and, as a darker-skinned and finer-boned variation, are the major racial element in the Indian subcontinent as well.

Mediterranean types vary in size and color. Though generally white, their skin color ranges from cream colored to olive. They are usually medium in height and build but can also be quite tall. Their hair is usually dark brown or black but can be red or even blond. Blondism is noted more frequently in the form of blue or green eyes than in skin or hair color, although brown eyes are more usual. Among the Berbers of North Africa, one can find blond, blue-eyed Nordic-looking types, whereas Circassians who emigrated south to Syria and Jordan could double for redhaired Scots.

Mediterranean faces are generally long and their noses prominent, the stereotype being an Arab bedouin or a Jewish merchant. Arabs and Jews together possess the highest concentration of Mediterranean racial characteristics.

In Turkey and the Levant, people of a different racial stock can be observed. Dark, short, and stocky with large chests and round heads, they have a tendency to baldness. These are Alpine types. A similar group, the Armenoids, are found in northern Iran and eastern Turkey. They generally have heavier body hair, very prominent wide or aquiline noses, and high foreheads.

Along the southern reaches of the Middle East, Negroid strains from sub-Saharan Africa are found. Finally, in eastern Iran, western Afghanistan, and the adjacent Soviet Union, Mongoloid types can be observed—small, round-headed, and possessing folds of skin over their eyes that make them appear slanted. Ironically, they no longer speak a Mongolian language; Persian is now their tongue. The Turks were originally Mongoloid, but centuries of mixing with the larger indigenous population of Anatolia have all but obliterated these traits.

Language is far more important than race as a distinguishing characteristic. There are two major language groups in the Middle East—Semitic and Indo-European. Semites are those who now speak or who spoke in ancient times a Semitic language. Arabic and Hebrew both belong to this group.

Semitic languages are characterized by a triconsonantal root system. Typically, each word is identified by the placement of three consonants that form a root. Words with the same root tend to have similar or related meanings, and different words are formed by adding vowels, suffixes, and prefixes around these root sounds. For example, the Arabic root, K-T-B, is found in *kitab* ("book"), *maktab* ("office"), *maktaba* ("library"), and *kaatib* ("secretary"). Over time, of course, many non-Semitic words have entered the vocabulary. Consider the consternation of a beginning Arabic student trying to find the triconsonantal root in "shurshyl," only to discover that it is the Arabic transliteration of "Churchill." In Israel, many three-letter acronyms have been transformed into Hebrew verbs and nouns, leaving the uninitiated with no idea of the meaning or origin of the word.

Akkadian is the earliest known Semitic language. From it developed Babylonian and ancient Assyrian. (Assyrian is not to be confused with the language of contemporary Assyrians in Syria and Iraq, who speak a dialect of Syriac.) These ancient languages, all dead, constitute the "eastern Semitic group."

The "western Semitic group" is more pertinent to the modern Middle East. It is generally divided into northern and southern subgroups. The northern subgroup includes ancient Canaanite, from which developed Phoenician, Aramaean, and Hebrew. Phoenician speakers, who may have originally come from the Gulf area, brought their maritime skills to present-day Lebanon. They also perfected the alphabet, begun earlier by the Canaanites, who borrowed the idea of writing consonantal signs from the ancient Egyptians. As masters of the sea, the Phoenicians spread the concept throughout the ancient Middle East. Semitic script has usually been written right to left.

From Aramaean have come Aramaic and Syriac. The former was the prevalent language of the Levant during the time of Christ and is still spoken in a few isolated villages in Syria. Another derivative, Syriac, has been preserved as the liturgical language of several eastern churches and as so-called Assyrian, mentioned above.

Hebrew also survived as a ritual language of the Jewish faith. In recent years it has been revived as a modern living language in the state of Israel. Ironically, many Jewish tourists in Israel have become frustrated when they cannot communicate in Yiddish, a Germanic language, to Sabras (native-born Israelis) who speak Hebrew.

The southern subgroup of western Semitic languages includes Arabic, ancient south Arabian, and the closely related dialects of Ethiopia, just across the Red Sea. South Arabian dialects were spoken by ancient city states that reached their zenith during the Roman empire, growing rich in their monopoly over the supply of frankincense and myrrh. These spices, found only on the coasts of south Arabia and Somalia across the Gulf of Aden, were used to sweeten the smoke of Roman funeral pyres. The south Arabian languages are collectively called Sabean after one of the city states, Saba, thought to be the ancient Sheba of King Solomon's day. With Christianization and the decline of pagan Rome, demand for the spices declined, undercutting the economies of the city states. The final collapse of south Arabian civilization is generally dated at 450 B.C., when the famous dam at Ma'rib, in what is now the Yemen Arab Republic, broke for the second and last time, rendering irrigated agriculture no longer possible.

South Arabian languages survive on the Arabian side of the Red Sea only in isolated pockets, such as Socotra Island off South Yemen, and among the Qara and Mahra tribesmen in eastern South Yemen and western Oman. In Ethiopia, however, descendants of Sabean languages survive as Amharic, Tigre, and Tigrina. The historic link between Ethiopians and south Arabians via Sheba and the ancient Jewish kingdoms of the Yemen was the origin of the late Emperior Haile Selassie's title, "Lion of Judah."

The latest Semitic language and probably the most influential of all languages in the Middle East is Arabic. At the time of Muhammad, it was spoken in central Arabia between the Aramaic areas in the north and Sabean areas in the south. Arabic's principal political importance originated during the Muslim conquests, when it was spread throughout the Middle East. Moreover, neighboring languages such as Turkish and Persian have borrowed heavily from Arabic vocabulary. In East Africa, Swahili originated as a trade or contact language using a largely Arabic-derived vocabulary on a Bantu grammatical base.

The importance of Arabic transcends politics. Even before the time of Muhammad, Arab tribes, while speaking different but mutually intelligible dialects, used a single literary language. The Arabic of the Quran, because of its holy inspiration, represents to this day the highest form of the literary language. Though understood by few, it is the holy language of hundreds of millions throughout the Muslim world.

Many changes have occurred in Arabic over the years since Muhammad. Spoken dialects have changed so greatly that Maghribi dialects and eastern Arabic dialects are no longer even mutually comprehensible. Pride of dialect is so great, however, that one can virtually guarantee a vociferous argument over which dialect is closest to classical Quranic Arabic. Since nearly all dialects have some elements closer to and others farther from the classical, there is no winning of this argument on literary merits alone.

Between classical Quranic and spoken dialects, a modern literary language that is universal to the entire Arab world has developed. Actually a simplified form of classical Arabic, it is not mutually intelligible with spoken dialects and is therefore known only to the educated classes. This is generally the language of the media as well as of literature, as spoken dialects are considered too inferior to be used on such occasions. As a result, the uneducated masses often do not understand what is being spoken or written in the media.

Arabic is also the major art form throughout much of the Middle East. For the nomadic people who originally developed the language, the spoken word was logically the primary means of artistic expression. Even the graphic arts were largely devoted to calligraphy—the Arabesque. Oratory and singing are also highly regarded. One of the highest compliments ever paid to Christian missionaries in the Arab world in the last century occurred when the Muslim community was asked to attend services in order to rapture over the beauty of a gifted preacher's command of Arabic. And when the Arab world's premier singer, an elderly grandmother named Umm Kalthum, died a few years ago, more people wept for her than for any Middle Eastern political figure in modern times.

Next to Semitic, Indo-European languages are probably the most important in the Middle East. This same group includes English and most of the European languages. The largest group of Indo-European speakers in the Middle East speak various dialects of Iranian. These include Persian and the closely related dialects of the Bakhtiari and Lurs tribes of Iran; Kurdish, which is spoken by tribes living in the area where Iran, Iraq, and Turkey meet; and Baluchi, the language of southeastern Iran and neighboring Afghanistan and Pakistan. Another Indo-European language of note in the Middle East is Armenian. Although the Armenians, originally situated along the Iranian-Soviet-Turkish frontier, have been scattered all over the world by political upheavals in their former homeland, they have striven to preserve their language and culture.

Two other language groups are also found in the Middle East. The Ural-Altaic group, which includes Mongolian, Siberian, and the Turkic or Altaic languages, as well as Finnish and Magyar (Uralic), is represented by several Turkic languages. By the seventh century, Turkic speakers had moved westward to the lands east of the Caspian Sea and soon thereafter were converted to Islam. One group, the Seljuk Turks, moved west into Anatolia and established the sultanate of Rum. The Mongol invasions of the thirteenth century put an end to this sultanate, and it was superseded by a new sultanate of Ottoman Turks. Neither Seljuks nor Ottomans were ever in the majority in Anatolia, as evidenced by the virtual disappearance of Mongoloid racial features, but Turkish became the language of the entire area.

Farther east, there are also Turkic speaking tribes in Iran: the Azeris of Azerbaijan in the northwest, the Qashqa'is in the eastern Zagros, and Turkomen tribes in northeastern Iran who have kinship ties across the border in the Soviet Union.

Hamitic, the other group of languages in the Middle East, is apparently of African origin. Within this group are ancient Egyptian, the Berber dialects of North Africa, and the Kushitic dialects of the Horn of Africa, including Somali Beja and others. Modern Coptic, the last surviving descendant of ancient Egyptian, is the liturgical language of the Coptic Christian church in Egypt and Ethiopia.

The Role of Religion: The Impact of Islam. Throughout history, religion has played an important, often crucial, role in politics. Yet nowhere has religious force had a stronger impact on the politics of an area than Islam has had on the Middle East. More than just a religion, Islam is an entire way of life, with no distinction made between the secular and the sacred.

The theological aspects of Islam are quite simple. They are embodied in the *shahada* ("profession of faith"): *la ilaha illa llah wa muhammadun rasula llah* ("there is no god but God and Muhammad is the messenger [prophet] of God"). The word *Islam* itself refers to the total submission of the believer to God. The requirements of Islam are also simple: the five pillars of Islam. In addition to the profession of faith, they consist of prayer, alms giving, fasting during the Muslim lunar month of Ramadan, and the *hajj*, or great pilgrimage to Mecca, to be made once in the lifetime of all believers physically and financially able to do so. *Jihad*, or "holy war," to defend the faith is sometimes considered a sixth pillar.

The many writings and treatises of Islamic scholars are more juridical than theological in nature, for Islam is in essence a system of jurisprudence. Muslims believe that God revealed himself to man in Judaism and Christianity as well as Islam. The followers of these faiths are called "people of the book." It may be noted that because Judaism is respected as a revealed religion, Arab Muslims invariably characterize Zionism, which they oppose, as a political rather than a religious doctrine.

For Muslims, God's final revelation of himself to man is embodied in Islam. The revelation was brought by God's messenger, Muhammad, in the form of holy law, called the *Shari'a.* The law is based on the Quran and the Sunna. The Quran is the revealed word of God expressed in the recorded preachings of Muhammad. The Sunna is a compendium of the "Traditions" (teachings and sayings) attributed to the Prophet. Each tradition is contained in a *hadith* ("short narrative"). Collectively they are called "the Hadith."

The Quran and the Hadith do not constitute a codified system of law but, rather, are the sources of the law. These sources are applied to everyday problems through an elaborate system of analogy developed by early Muslim scholars and accepted by the consensus of the Muslim community. Where there was no consensus, individual interpretation was allowed. As consensus over the interpretation of the law increased through the years, however, individual interpretation was restricted and finally disallowed altogether by orthodox or Sunni Muslims. To this day, orthodox Islamic law is applied on the basis of interpretations and consensus formed prior to the ninth century.

Four major orthodox schools of jurisprudence were established, each generally recognized by the others. They are the Hanafi school, named after Abu Hanifa (d. 767); the Maliki school, founded by Malik ibn Anas (d. 795); the Shafi'i school, founded by al-Shafi'i (d. 820); and the Hanbali school, founded by Ahmad ibn Hanbal (d. 855). The Hanafi school was used in the courts of the Ottoman Empire and is prevalent in lower Egypt, India, and most orthodox Muslim areas in Asia outside Arabia. Malikis are found in North Africa, upper Egypt, and the Sudan. The Shafi'is are found in the lowland areas of the Yemen, South Yemen, and Indonesia; and the Hanbalis are found in Saudi Arabia and Qatar.

In addition to orthodox or Sunni Muslims, there are several groups of heterodox, or Shi'a, Muslims. Most of the inhabitants of Iran as well as large numbers of Iraqis, Bahrainis, and Yemenis are Shi'ites. The Sunni-Shi'a schism first arose in a dispute over who would succeed the fourth caliph, Ali, and juridically there is little difference between the two. Over time, however, other differences developed. For example, a relatively greater element of mysticism crept into Shi'ism than into Sunni Islam. Shi'as believe that the views of an imam ("commander of the faithful") should predominate over the consensus of the Islamic community as a whole. A Shi'a imam, therefore, was the absolute authority on doctrine, unlike the Sunni caliph, who, while being the absolute political and religious leader, could not interpret or define dogma. Because Shi'as were not prohibited from individual interpretation of Islamic law, Shi'a scholars have continued to reinterpret the law in light of social and political changes over the years.

Three main groups of Shi'as have survived. The Imami sect, which is the state religion of Iran, is the largest and generally the most liberal. It is also found in Iraq, where it originated in the oases of the Gulf region, in Syria, and in southern Lebanon, where a branch, the Matawila, live. Imamis trace the line of imams from Ali, whom they consider the first, through twelve imams. The last, Muhammad al-Mahdi, disappeared around A.D. 873 and is expected to return at a propitious moment.

The Ismailis, a more radical sect, believe that the eldest rather than the second son of the sixth imam succeeded him, and that his son was the last "visible" imam. Ismailis under the leadership of the Aga Khan are found mainly in Pakistan, India, and Iran. There are a few Ismaili remnants of a once terrifying branch, the Assassins, who are now farmers in the hills of central Syria.

The third major group of Shi'as is composed of the Zaydis of the highlands of the Yemen. They trace a separate line of succession from the fifth imam but do not believe that any successors are concealed or have supernatural powers. The last Zaydi imam to rule in the Yemen was the Imam Ahmad. Soon after his death, his son Badr was overthrown in a revolution in 1962.

An even earlier schism in Islam involved the Kharijites, who broke with the orthodox Muslim consensus that the leader (caliph) should be a descendant of the Prophet. They insisted that he be popularly elected by the community. Although the movement all but disappeared, it still survives in Oman, where a majority of the people are Ibadi Muslims, and also in southern Algeria.

In the twentieth century most Muslim states have incorporated Western legal codes. In order to maintain that they have not broken with the Shari'a, or Islamic law, they accomplished this transition through the use of legal distinctions within Islamic law itself. The Shari'a goes further than distinguishing between right and wrong, employing instead a five-stage system. There are acts that are mandatory, recommended but not mandatory, forbidden, discouraged but not forbidden, and a last category concerning which the law is indifferent. It has been through the placement of Western legal codes in this last category that their adoption has been justified in legal reform throughout the Muslim world. Rather than calling them laws, however, since only God can make a law, Muslims generally refer to them as regulations.

In sum, Islam is essentially a system of legal norms for human behavior. Because Muslims believe that the law is of God, it is theoretically unchangeable. Moreover, since the prohibition of independent interpretation in the ninth century, orthodox Islam has become a closed system in which conformity with the teachings of the great classical jurists is required. Later scholars have been able merely to comment on the work of their predecessors.

Within this system, God's will as revealed in God's law inevitably determines whatever happens. This doctrine has enhanced if not created a highly developed sense of the inevitable, which is often referred to as Islamic fatalism. It is expressed in the widely heard Arabic phrase, *insha'allah*, or "God willing." Against God's will no man can prevail. This sense of the inevitability of life beyond man's will to change it pervades Middle Eastern culture in general, is shared by Muslims and non-Muslims alike, and is experienced even by those who no longer practice any religion.

The fixation on the omnipresence of divine will has enabled Middle Easterners to view events as separate exercises of God's will or fate, having little or no association with related events. This view has made it relatively easy for them to hold more than one position on the same issue that Westerners might find too contradictory. It has also tended to keep problems over conflicting loyalties or interests to a minimum. For example, hostile political relations in the Middle East need not rule out good commercial relations, for the two are viewed quite separately.

There is also a tendency to view political and economic relationships in highly concrete, personalized terms rather than abstract or ideological terms. A conspiratorial explanation of events involving specific people, for example, is quite common, and the conduct of business or government is viewed more in terms of specific persons or interest groups than as a system or a process. Thus political parties and organizations, even those with highly developed ideologies, are usually little more than confederations of personal followings. Each contender for power within the party or organization tends to be in competition for leadership, and each party is in competition with other parties for national leadership—winner take all. A classic example of personalized politics in the Middle East is the rapidity with which "Nasserism" died after the death of Nasser, for Nasserism amounted to little more than the ideological trappings of Arab nationalism.

There are other religions in the Middle East. In fact, probably every major schism of Christendom still extant is present there. Christianity, however, has not had the cultural impact that Islam has. So it was with Judaism as well, until the rise of Zionism and creation of Israel. Because Judaism as a cultural-political force is almost exclusively linked to Israel, discussions of Judaism will be deferred to the chapter on Israel itself.

Group Identification and Social Stratification. Middle Easterners, like peoples everywhere, profess multiple loyalties. Among their principal loyalties are the nuclear and extended family, clan and tribal affiliation, the professional group, the hometown or region, ethnic origin, religious confession, state nationalism, pan-Arabism, pan-Islam, identification with the developing countries, and, for some, the Organization of Petroleum Exporting Countries (OPEC). Of these, primary loyalty is to the extended family. Traditionally, it includes the father and mother, the sons and their families, and unmarried daughters. This unit is the glue that holds together Middle Eastern society.

Strife and tensions are often rife within the extended family, but to outsiders the family presents a unified front. Although its cohesion has been under assault by the forces of modernity, the extended family still has major influence on such basic decisions as choosing a spouse, a residence, or a career. Certain benefits also accrue from membership in an extended family. For example, the strategic location of relatives can be vital to the success of a young businessman or bureaucrat.

The existence of compartmentalized multiple loyalties and intense personalization of behavior has tended to limit the degree of social and political institutional cohesion. Most of the major decisionmaking in the Middle East takes place in small, informal groups. Membership in such groups, whether revolutionary command councils, palace cliques, or gatherings of business people, bureaucrats, or junior army officers, is usually based on similarity of interests. Called *shilla* ("informal group") in Egypt, *jama'* ("group") in Saudi Arabia, and *dowrah* ("circle") in Iran, these groups are quasi-social and totally unstructured. Typically, members of the group gather in the evenings to talk, play cards, and discuss the business of the day. As a reflection of the favor-oriented Middle Eastern society, each member is expected to aid and support each other member as the need arises.

The impact of these perceptions, loyalties, and social attitudes on Middle East politics cannot be underestimated. At the same time, they are seldom consciously considered by the decisionmakers. Like politicians everywhere, Middle East political leaders are primarily searching for solutions to day-to-day operational problems. Their cultural heritage, however, serves as the filter through which all problems are viewed.

Notes

1. See Roderic H. Davison, "Where Is the Middle East?" *Foreign Affairs* 38 (July 1960), pp. 665–675.

2. See Peter Beaumont, Gerald Blake, and J. Malcolm Wagstaff, *The Middle East: A Geographical Study* (New York: John Wiley & Sons, 1976), pp. 19ff.

3. Ibid., pp. 49ff.

Bibliography

Two articles have attempted to capture the elusive confines of the Middle East: Roderic H. Davison, "Where Is the Middle East?" (*Foreign Affairs* 38 [July 1960], pp. 665–675); and Nikki R. Keddie, "Is There a Middle East?" (*International Journal of Middle East Studies* 4 [1973], pp. 255–271). For longer works, see Peter Beaumont, Gerald Blake, and J. Malcolm Wagstaff, *The Middle East: A Geographical Study* (New York: John Wiley & Sons, 1976), and W. B. Fisher, *The Middle East: A Physical, Social, and Regional Geography*, 7th ed. (London: Methuen, 1978), which offer excellent and comprehensive overviews of the region's geography.

A number of social scientists have endeavored to identify the common traits and values of Middle Eastern peoples. Raphael Patai's *The Arab Mind* (New York: Charles Scribner & Sons, 1973), Sania Hamady's *Temperament and Character of the Arab* (New York: Twayne Publishers, 1960), and Morroe Berger's *The Arab World Today* (Garden City, N.Y.: Doubleday, 1962) present interesting descriptions on how Arabs live, work, and think. Though dated, Carleton Coon's *Caravan: The Story of the Middle East* (New York: Henry Holt, 1951) is still a classic; it should be recommended to every beginning student, as should Stephen H. Longrigg's *The Middle East: A Social Geography*, 2d ed. (Chicago: Aldine Publishing Company, 1970).

Louise E. Sweet, ed., *Peoples and Cultures of the Middle East: An Anthropological Reader*, 2 vols. (Garden City, N.Y.: Natural History Press, 1970), focuses on urbanization, the status of women, the development of Islam, and the family, as does Daniel G. Bates and Amal Rassam, *Peoples and Cultures of the Middle East* (Englewood Cliffs, N.J.: Prentice-Hall, 1983). Finally, David Lerner, in *The Passing of Traditional Society: Modernizing the Middle East* (London: Free Press, 1958), discusses the universal modernizing role of literacy and the media, their development, and their relationship to the emergence of modern institutions.

3

Republic of Turkey

George S. Harris

Historical Background

Modern Turkey differs profoundly from most of the nations that have emerged in the past century. Its distinctive quality stems directly from the fact that it had long and deep roots in an imperial past as an independent state. Of cardinal significance is the fact that it inherited from its Ottoman forebears a highly developed system of institutions and traditions. To be sure, Turkey was only one of a number of countries that came into being in the lands once ruled by the Ottomans. But while all betrayed influences of the six centuries of Ottoman rule, Turkey alone embodied the continuation of both the empire's institutions and the ruling class that had run one of the most successful multiethnic and multireligious states in world history.

The Ottoman structure offered the fledgling state an experienced, functioning, and strong central administration. A flair for bureaucratic organization distinguished the Ottomans from the earliest days of their existence; this talent may have provided the critical edge over the other Turkish principalities that were vying to displace the Byzantine Empire in the fourteenth and fifteenth centuries. Organizational ability remained characteristic of the Ottomans, even though the state suffered from periods of misrule and insurrection. Indeed, the reorganizations of the nineteenth century (the so-called Tanzimat reforms) played a significant part in keeping the empire from collapsing during increasingly difficult days.

Initially, the government apparatus was dominated by the armed forces; construction and expansion of the state were first of all military ventures. But once the era of conquest was over, the problems of administering the huge Ottoman territories demanded increased attention. In response, the civilian hierarchy, already impressive in the earliest Ottoman period, expanded in prestige, size, and complexity. By the time the empire neared its end, the Ottomans had evolved machinery of government capable of handling far-flung domains in such areas as taxation, justice, and, to a lesser degree, education. Thus, while the army always played an important role, the Ottoman Empire was far more than a praetorian state run by a dominant military caste.

The lengthy Ottoman experience with state-directed reform left a valuable legacy for the Turkish nation. The impetus for persistent efforts at self-improvement was defensive. By the end of the eighteenth century the Ottoman leaders recognized that Europe was clearly outstripping the empire in power. Hence, the tradition of reform did not grow out of efforts to satisfy popular pressures within the Ottoman state, but instead represented a conscious policy of the top leadership to galvanize the populace in ways that even violated popular will and custom on occasion. This elitist approach, predicated on the notion that the rulers know best, has remained an enduring hallmark of Turkish reform through the centuries.

At the same time, the effort to keep the Ottoman state competitive triggered an important conflict within the ruling group. Secular modernizers, who came into ascendance by the nineteenth century, saw the adaptation of European technology as the sole means of coping with the intrusions of the West. On the other hand, traditionalists looked toward a return to religious purity and a rejection of Western materialism as the recipe for staving off the European challenge.

By the end of the empire, however, the religious branch of the government class had lost the battle and the argument had shifted significantly. The idea of utilizing European technology was accepted, and the nub of dispute centered on whether wholesale cultural borrowings from the West were essential to complement technology or whether science and hardware from Europe could be implanted in Turkish society without disturbing traditional patterns. This debate has not yet been resolved.

The Ottoman Empire embraced peoples of sharply differing languages and religions. In the era before national consciousness had been awakened among its subject peoples, the Ottoman system of working through existing religious communities was a cost-effective method of rule. But the persistence of communal identity, which the Ottoman way fostered, provided a fertile ground for separatist movements once the seed of nationalism had been planted. These ethnic separatists threatened to dismember the empire from within, while the European powers were pressing from without.

Turkish nationalism did not emerge full-blown until the fall of the Ottoman Empire. But as early as the Young Turk period, powerful protagonists of Turkism were in evidence. After the 1908 revolution, Committee of Union and Progress Central Committee member Ziya Gok Alp spearheaded an effort to celebrate Turkish achievements and to turn the Ottoman Empire into a Turkish state. In reaction to the financial controls imposed on the Ottomans by European creditors through the Public Debt Administration, the Turkists also espoused economic nationalism. Yet, although Turkey's World War I political leader Enver Pasha was a convinced exponent of assembling the world's Turks in a single state, neither he nor his fellow Young Turks ever abandoned their hopes of maintaining the empire, especially its Arab Islamic elements.

The political structure erected by the Young Turks also set the stage for modern Turkey. The parliamentary mode instituted after 1908 led to the wartime assembly in Ankara and the facade of parliamentary process that ensued.

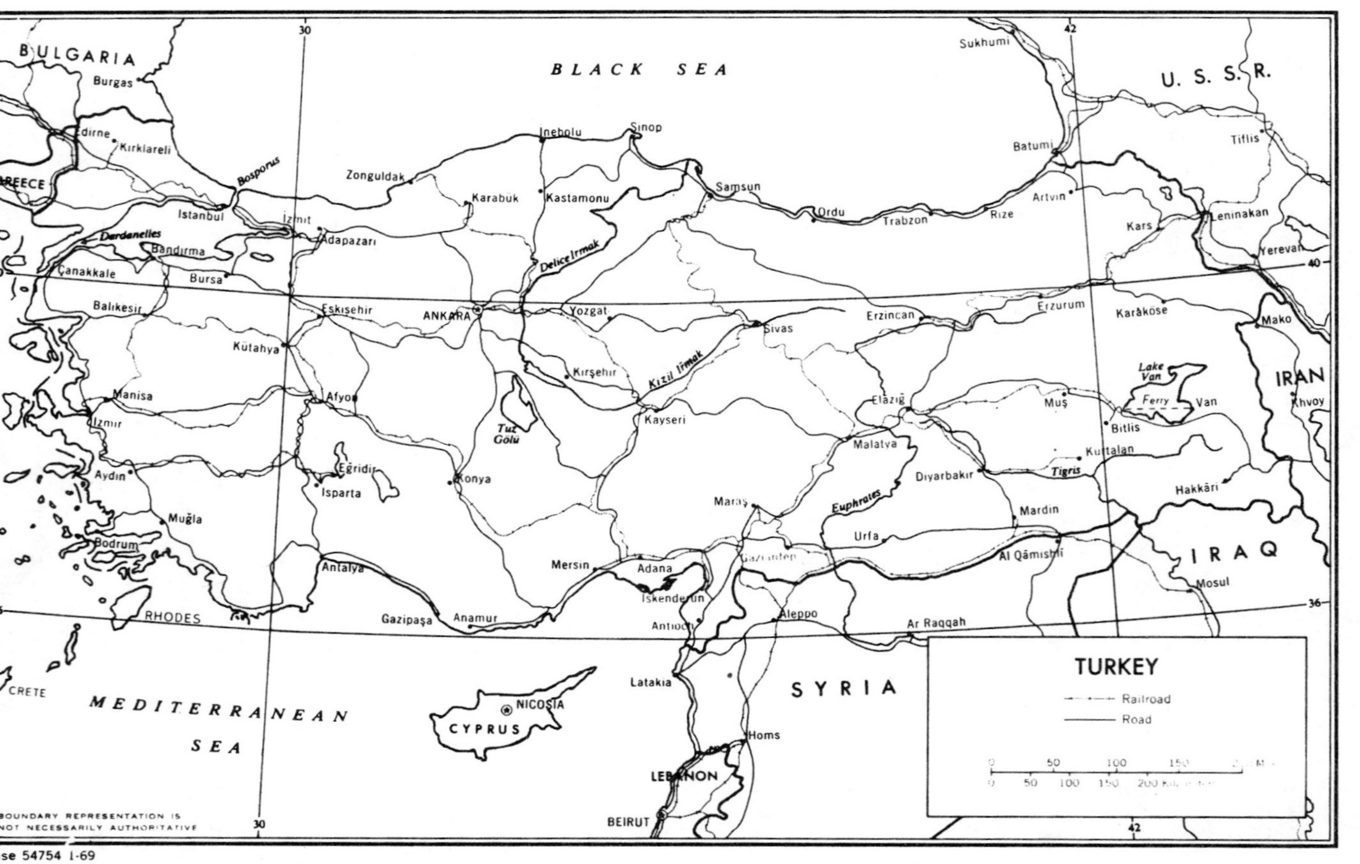
BULGARIA
BLACK SEA
U. S. S. R.
GREECE
IRAN
IRAQ
SYRIA
LEBANON
CYPRUS
NICOSIA
BEIRUT
RHODES
CRETE
MEDITERRANEAN SEA
TURKEY
Railroad
Road
Burgas
Edirne
Kırklareli
Istanbul
Bosporus
Dardanelles
Bandırma
Çanakkale
Bursa
Balıkesir
Kütahya
Manisa
Izmir
Aydın
Muğla
Bodrum
Zonguldak
Izmit
Adapazarı
Eskişehir
Afyon
Eğridir
Isparta
Antalya
Gazipaşa
Anamur
Karabük
Inebolu
Kastamonu
Sinop
Samsun
Delice Irmak
ANKARA
Tuz Gölü
Konya
Yozgat
Kırşehir
Kızıl Irmak
Kayseri
Sivas
Mersin
Adana
Iskenderun
Antioch
Latakia
Homs
Aleppo
Maraş
Ordu
Trabzon
Rize
Artvin
Batumi
Sukhumi
Tiflis
Leninakan
Yerevan
Kars
Erzincan
Erzurum
Karaköse
Mako
Khvoy
Lake Van
Ferry
Van
Muş
Bitlis
Kurtalan
Tigris
Elazığ
Malatya
Diyarbakır
Euphrates
Mardin
Urfa
Al Qāmishlī
Hakkâri
Mosul
Ar Raqqah
BOUNDARY REPRESENTATION IS NOT NECESSARILY AUTHORITATIVE
Base 54754 1-69

The Committee of Union and Progress, which was the dominant political party during much of the Young Turk period, served, in addition, as a model and precursor of Mustafa Kemal Ataturk's own political organization. Likewise, some of the patterns of political controversy carried over into the modern Turkish state.

The First Republic

Ataturk is rightly credited with having established Turkey out of the ruins of the Ottoman state. Yet his resistance movement was not the first revolt against the European plan to carve up the Turkish heartland after World War I. The Committee of Union and Progress had sought to perpetuate itself through local "defense of rights" organizations in Anatolia and Thrace before Ataturk's move was actively under way.

Kemal Ataturk did, however, play a critical role as a rallying point for the resistance effort. His charisma was essential in filling the vacuum left by the departing Young Turk leaders and in resisting the invading Greeks who landed in Izmir in May 1919, just as Ataturk was on his way to Anatolia. Thanks to his leadership, Turkey regained its independence, expelling the Greek army and convincing the Western powers to end their occupation of Istanbul and other major points.

Ataturk then began a thorough modernization of Turkish society. For Ataturk nationalism was the key to this endeavor. One of his major contributions was to recognize the folly of trying to retain a multiethnic state (the only significant exception being the retention of the Kurds, who shared a segment of the Anatolian core area that Ataturk considered essential for modern Turkey). To boost pride in being Turkish, he sought to translate attachment to religion into patriotic fervor for the new state.

Ataturk's approach was in many respects evolutionary. Far more a political than a social revolution, the reform movement was based on the Ottoman elite, expanded through the slow process of education and co-option. Social mores were adjusted by fiat at times, but no sizable group was expelled to create a nucleus thirsting for the old regime.

The new Turkish state was a parliamentary republic in form, though an autocracy in practice. The basic slogan of the republic was "Sovereignty Belongs to the People"—a sovereignty that was formally exercised by a single-house Parliament. Yet Ataturk chafed under opposition. He thus created the Republican Peoples party as his tool to dominate the political scene, despite the merely symbolic powers accorded the presidency by the constitution. Backed by a parliamentary majority, he closed down rival political organizations, starting with supporters of the caliph in the 1923 elections, the Progressive Republican party in 1925, and even his own tame creation—the "opposition" Free party—when it threatened to get out of hand in 1930. Thereafter, he attempted to fuse his single party with the state in a system that left no room for legal opposition. This effort at a corporate state, however, led to the atrophy of the party and the clear dominance of the government organs.

The concentration of power in the hands of one man could not long survive Ataturk's death. In fact, his successor, Ismet Inonu, gave notice almost immediately upon taking office that he would liberalize the regime. And as soon as the dangers of World War II had passed, opposition parties were permitted, partly in order to cast Turkey's lot with the victorious democracies in solidarity against the aggressive Soviets.

Four prominent defectors from the Republican Peoples party took advantage of the liberalization to form the Democrat party in 1946. Headed by Celal Bayar, Ataturk's last prime minister, this party scored creditably in the July 1946 general elections, although it was not allowed time to finish its organization in all of Turkey's provinces. By 1950, it won handily, capitalizing on the widespread discontent generated in decades of Republican Peoples party rule. Inonu thereupon gracefully surrendered power.

The smoothness of this transition concealed deep flaws in Turkey's democratic experiment. Lacking a tradition of tolerance of dissent, the Democrats soon began to retaliate against the opposition. In 1953 they sequestered the assets of the Republican Peoples party, claiming that the latter had misused its state connection during the single party era, and in 1954 the Nation party was closed for exploiting religion. In 1957, as opposition to such acts rose, election coalitions were banned to head off a combination of the Republican Peoples party and the small Freedom party, which had split from the Democrats in protest against autocratic actions.

A climate of oppressive political tension developed in Turkey. Clashing socioeconomic interests of the rising business elements backing the Democrats, on the one hand, and the bureaucrats favoring the Republican Peoples party, on the other, added a special bitterness to the political contest. The persistent efforts of the Democrat party to use foreign aid for partisan purposes and to enlist those upset by Ataturkist zeal in religious and social reform also increased the fervor of the combat. Finally, by the end of the 1950s, the Democrat party appeared to be moving to quash the opposition in an attempt to return to a one-party system.

The Second Republic

In this situation, the middle levels of the officer corps led a revolt in 1960 to arrest mounting political tension. The legality of this move has never been seriously questioned. Yet an important faction within the junta, aided by the senior generals who saw the dangers of politicizing the armed forces, viewed their proper role as merely to put the political process "back on the tracks" and to return power to responsible politicians. The presence of Ismet Inonu (Ataturk's closest collaborator and a former general) as head of the party that had been in opposition during the decade before the military revolt offered the officers an attractive alternative to staying in power.

Thus, after dissolving the Democrat party and after presiding over popular ratification of constitutional checks and balances (including creation of a Senate and a Constitutional Court), intended to prevent the excesses of the earlier concentration of power, the junta held elections. But revanchist sentiment led a substantial number of voters to back parties that campaigned more or less openly as continuations of the former ruling Democrat party. As a result, Inonu's Republican Peoples party received merely a plurality in the lower house. With the military ostentatiously looking over his shoulder, he formed a series of coalitions that served to reassure the officers that there would be no retaliation for the 1960 intervention.

Inonu's three years in office were a period of dexterous maneuver. On the one hand, the supporters of the former regime among his government partners constantly agitated for immediate amnesty. At the same time, two abortive coups by restive military elements signaled distress in the armed forces at the possibility of pardon for political prisoners. Torn between these opposing tendencies, the Inonu governments of the early 1960s were weak, unstable, and short-lived. Moreover, by early 1965 Inonu's last cabinet was brought down during the budget debate.

In the ensuing election, the Justice party, whose name reflected a demand for fairer treatment of the old regime, won a decisive majority. Suleyman Demirel, representing the moderate wing of the party, took over as prime minister. His administration granted amnesty to the Democrat party members sentenced after the military takeover. Although Demirel made few economic departures, a rapidly rising tide of remittances from workers in Europe ensured unaccustomed prosperity for Turkey. As a result, the Justice party scored a second victory at the polls in 1969, although its proportion of popular vote declined somewhat.

Demirel was challenged, however, by the growth of extremism. Rapid politicization of the universities led to violence as right-wing youths disrupted meetings of the small but active Turkish Labor party; left-wing students used strong-arm tactics against their conservative opponents. Government indecisiveness in dealing with the growing disorder led the senior military commanders in March 1971 to issue an extraordinary public demand for more effective rule. They warned that if a stronger government were not speedily forthcoming, the armed forces would use their "legal rights and seize power directly."

Demirel resigned on the spot, and Parliament voted into power a series of cabinets of technocrats under nonpartisan prime ministers. These governments imposed martial law, banned the Turkish Labor party (Turkey's only legal Marxist party), and made widespread arrests to suppress terrorism. Political prisoners, some charged with offenses as nebulous as encouraging sedition through textbooks, filled the jails.

Constitutional forms were preserved during the ensuing two years of nonparty governments. Indeed, in the interests of permitting regularly scheduled elections, controls were relaxed somewhat to allow campaigning in 1973. The vote produced a standoff among the major parties as the right-of-center constituency behind the Justice party fragmented. A religious party (the National Salvation party) wooed Islamic fundamentalists; a group of conservatives also left the Justice party in a dispute over cabinet representation. These splinters ended up in the swing position between the Justice party and the Republican Peoples party, now led by Bulent Ecevit, who had replaced the aging Ismet Inonu in a final showdown.

The next seven years were difficult ones of coalition government as Ecevit and Demirel alternated in the position of prime minister. Each in turn relied on support from the National Salvation party, which extracted concessions in policy and personnel placement as its price. Ecevit's first coalition sent Turkish troops to Cyprus in July 1974, following a Greek-inspired putsch against President Makarios. But when Ecevit resigned in an effort to force early elections to cash in on the popularity of this move, he was stymied by parliamentary arithmetic. Demirel took over the government.

Both major parties increased their share of the vote in the 1977 elections at the expense of the minor factions. In fact, Ecevit's party nearly won a majority, thanks to his personal popularity and the fact that Demirel had failed to deal effectively with both renewed political violence and the international oil shock that hit Turkey in the mid-1970s. But Ecevit's tactics of luring defectors from the Justice party by the offer of posts in an expanded cabinet heightened tensions. Bitter personal rivalry between Ecevit and Demirel contributed to political paralysis as nearly equal alignments faced each other in Parliament. Ecevit's failure to do better than Demirel in another stint in office starting in 1978 rapidly eroded his party's standing. After it ran far behind the Justice party in the Senate elections in a third of the provinces in 1979, he abandoned the prime ministry to Demirel.

Although the Justice party minority government led off with bold economic departures to satisfy the International Monetary Fund (IMF) and restore Turkey's external creditworthiness, the parliamentarians remained deadlocked in the contest to elect a president of Turkey, despite months of voting in 1980. The opposition ignored repeated warnings from the ranking generals to cooperate with the government in granting additional authority to the military so as to impose order. Instead, the National Salvation party demonstrated open disrespect for the constitutional provisions against exploiting religion; Kurdish dissidence mounted in the east; and the government's existence was challenged by motions of no-confidence against cabinet ministers.

The generals cut through the deepening political impasse on September 12, 1980, ousting the civilian government, proroguing Parliament, and rounding up hordes of suspected terrorists. On the economic front, the generals co-opted Demirel's financial team under Turgut Ozal, who had served as undersecretary for state planning. Although General Evren, the chief of staff who headed the new military junta, soon promised an eventual return of power to the civilians, he made no secret of the need for extensive changes to ensure Ataturk's reforms before party politics could resume.

It would be three years before a new constitution, election law, and political parties act could be put in place and elections held. During the first two years of this period, party propaganda was prohibited, the old parties were soon abolished for failing to cooperate with the military rulers, and institutions such as the universities and unions were fundamentally reformed. Moreover, the generals banned from political participation for ten years all officials of the previous parties before permitting new political organizations to be established. To prevent backsliding, the new constitution provided that Evren would be the first president for a seven-year term. And the parties eligible to run in the first election were limited to three: the conservative Nationalist Democracy party, headed by a retired general; the free-enterprise Motherland party under Ozal; and the left-of-center Populist party, led by a trusted functionary.

The Third Republic

Against this background, the Motherland party won a solid majority in Parliament in the November 1983 elections. Ozal had shown himself to be a capable political performer, and his lengthy experience gave promise that he could handle Turkey's always precarious economy.

Ozal used his parliamentary majority to enact more radical and rapid economic liberalization than ever before tried in Turkey. In the political realm, he overturned President Evren's veto of a bill speeding nationwide municipal elections in which parties not qualifying for the general elections in 1983 could compete. His judgment was resoundingly vindicated when the results in March 1984 showed the Motherland party to have kept its previous margin of popularity, thus stilling complaints that it was not truly representative of popular desires. Throughout 1984, Ozal moved slowly, but steadily, to reduce the number of provinces under martial law, while avoiding any provocation of the military establishment by taking steps toward amnesty for those sentenced during the years of military rule.

If the municipal elections strengthened the position of Ozal's Motherland party, they undermined the legitimacy of the Nationalist Democracy party and the Populist party. They ran well behind two competitors: the Social Democracy party of Erdal Inonu, son of Turkey's second-ranking political hero after Ataturk; and the True Path party, whose initials in Turkish (DYP) suggested that it was Demirel's New party (Demirel'in Yeni Partisi). On the basis of their strong showing, these two parties claimed that they, and not the parliamentary opposition, were the legimate spokesmen of the popular opposition to the Motherland party. The anomaly of a strong out-of-parliament opposition contributed to periodic agitation to hold early general elections without waiting for the end of the normal five-year term. The apparent shift in voter sentiment toward the Social Democracy party and the True Path party also intensified the bickering among the various opposition parties. And in hopes of currying favor with the voters, some opposition politicians even agitated for changing the constitution to eliminate disqualifications of the parties and leaders of the former regime.

Political Environment

Turkey is a land of pronounced physical contrasts. Stretching over 780,576 square kilometers (301,380 square miles, or over 40 percent larger than France), it ranges from sea level to the 5,165-meter (16,945-foot) peak of Mt. Ararat, higher than any European mountain. The western part of the country, bordering on the Aegean and Marmara seas, is a region of developed communication and easy access to the inland plateau. Well-watered farming areas produce cash crops, such as cotton, tobacco, and raisins. Eastern Turkey, abutting on the USSR, Iran, and Iraq, is mountainous, cut by rivers into more or less isolated valleys. Its thinly covered lava terrain, which produces sparse vegetation except in the river corridors, and the relatively severe climate encourage pastoral pursuits in much of the area. The more arid central Anatolian region supports dry farming as well as sheep and cattle raising. From the Mediterranean on the south and the Black Sea on the north, the land rises sharply to the rim of the Anatolian plateau. In the narrow coastal strips, tea and hazelnuts are grown in the north, and citrus fruits and early market vegetables are grown in the south.

A country of about 50 million people in 1985, Turkey's inhabitants are increasing at a rate of slightly over 2 percent a year. Population density generally declines from west to east and from the coast to the interior. Istanbul, the former Ottoman capital on the Bosporus, remains Turkey's largest city, with a metropolitan population of some 3 million. Ankara, the capital in west-central Anatolia, is a magnet second only to Istanbul in drawing power; it boasts about 2 million inhabitants. Izmir, on the Aegean coast, and Adana, on the Mediterranean, complete the roster of major urban foci. The east, on the other hand, has the sparsest population; moreover, its inhabitants lead in migration to other parts of the country or abroad.

Modern Turkey is far more homogeneous than the multinational Ottoman Empire had been. Yet the population is still divided by significant religious and ethnic differences. Census records indicate that Turkey is currently about 99 percent Muslim. The Sunni version of Islam clearly predominates in the country as a whole; but especially in central and northeast Anatolia, the heterodox Shi'ite interpretation finds many adherents. Although census data do not distinguish between these two forms of Islam, some experts allege that Shi'ites number up to 25 percent of the total population.

Most of the Shi'ites in Turkey, generally called Alevis, favor a politically reformist, secular approach by the government. In the past, they backed the left-of-center stand of Ataturk's Republican Peoples party, except for a brief dalliance with the tiny left-leaning Turkish Unity party. In the 1983 elections, the Alevi vote seems to have split between the Motherland party and the Populist party; many of those who voted for the Populists evidently transferred their support to the Social Democracy party in the 1984 municipal elections.

Kurds constitute the second largest minority in Turkey, numbering some 10 to 15 percent of the population. Speakers of the Indo-European language Kurdish, they form the overwhelming majority in Turkey's southeast provinces. Indeed, Diyarbakir remains a largely Kurdish-speaking city and has the largest urban concentration of Kurds—although Istanbul's squatter communities are increasingly becoming a mecca for this minority.

Most of the Kurds in Turkey lead a pastoral, transhumant, tribal life under traditional chiefs. The latter are frequently also leaders of dervish orders (Nakshibandi and Kadiri) or belong to religious sects (such as the Nurcular), to which Kurds seem particularly drawn. This tight social organization both perpetuates an identity quite separate from that of the rest of the Turkish population, and divides the various tribes and clans into sharply rival units nourishing ancient feuds over grazing rights and marriage partners. Thus the restiveness in eastern Turkey (given three tribal uprisings in the 1920s and 1930s) remained limited in scope and did not lead to general revolt; some Kurdish loyalists even cooperated with Ankara in opposing this defiance. Although small, clandestine separatist groups roiled the eastern provinces in the late 1970s, their activities were tinged with banditry and social protest against traditional tribal leadership practices. No charismatic political leader emerged, and it is not even clear that most Kurds in Turkey desire more than greater cultural and economic advantages.

But the Kurdish problem will not soon be resolved. Kurdish bands, apparently aided and encouraged by their ethnic brothers in Iraq, harassed Turkish security forces in frontier provinces in the fall of 1984. As long as safehavens in neighboring countries allow dissidents freedom of action, such incidents will be hard to prevent. More generally, Kurdish distinctiveness is fed by grievances over the lack of development of eastern Turkey. During the Second Republic, Kurdish students were prominent in demanding more investment for their region. Some Kurds joined the small, now defunct, socialist parties that wooed them by calling for greater rights for Kurds. The outlawed Turkish Communist party still seeks to play on this appeal in its quest for recruits through propaganda broadcasts into Turkey.

Turkey's political parties solicit support from tribal leaders by offering them prominent places on the ticket. Thus the Populist party and the Nationalist Democracy party won their greatest electoral successes in the 1983 elections in various Kurdish provinces by forming powerful local alignments. But the price Kurdish notables pay for the freedom to represent their constituencies in Parliament is to eschew all overt appeals to ethnicity.

Another important cleavage is the sharp rural-urban divide. In effect, there are still two distinct Turkeys. Living conditions and social customs have changed only slowly in the more remote villages, which lack the rudimentary accoutrements of modern life. By contrast, rural settlements near urban centers are rapidly becoming modernized; many serve as bedroom communities for workers in the larger cities. In between are villages seeking to become part of the market economy. Peasant demands for roads and water form the grist for political campaigning. Many of the more modern peasants have voted for parties that promise material improvements without challenging time-honored social patterns. But as peasants become exposed to city values, their willingness to follow their traditional leaders in voting is eroding.

Peasants moving off the farm typically head for Istanbul as their first choice. But rapidly growing squatter communities of rural migrants now surround all of Turkey's larger cities. Sprawling mushroom housing, usually grouping people from the same geographic locality or region, forms a transitional stage between the traditional life of the village and the more modern style of the city. Unemployment is high in these relatively primitive ghettos. But those who come see the city as offering more amenities and hope than can be found in the villages.

Turkish culture is highly status conscious: Age and position elicit respect. Traditionally, government and the military were the most honored careers; education and the free professions ranked next. In recent years, business has increased in esteem as industry expanded and began to offer far better salaries and perquisites than did the traditional occupations. University education is the dividing line between the elite and the rest of the population. But the expanding numbers of educated urban dwellers are fragmented in political allegiance. The elite no longer proceeds in lockstep along a commonly agreed path.

Turkey has brought urban women into the mainstream of political, professional, and cultural life. The educational level of women is rising steadily, and females have not faced legal discrimination since the 1930s. In the villages, however, custom has maintained the traditional male-dominated pattern of life.

The government has been the pacesetter in employing women. More than token numbers serve as senior officials. Although females are well represented in the free professions as well, their role in politics has declined somewhat in recent years. During the one-party era, Ataturk used Parliament as a showcase of women's progress, securing the election of 16 women to the then 339-seat Parliament in 1935. But with the advent of competitive politics, the ranks of female deputies thinned. Despite the activities of women's organizations in all of the parties of the Second Republic, only 4 females—all representing major urban constituencies—won deputyships in the 450-seat lower house in 1977. From this nadir, and despite the banning of women's organizations as divisive in the Third Republic, 12 women were elected to the 400-seat Parliament in 1983. Yet this rise does not suggest that women either will be strongly represented in future assemblies or will serve at top levels in political parties.

Economic development is a major engine of transformation of Turkish life. The state has led in fostering economic advance; indeed, the responsibility for national planning was assigned by the 1961 and 1982 constitutions to the State Planning Organization. Nonetheless, Turkey has always had a mixed economy (even though the largest enterprises have been state or quasi-public economic enterprises).

Since World War II, foreign aid—mostly from the United States—fueled a great expansion of Turkey's infrastructure. Radio and television have brought knowledge of the outside world in; roads have added a flexibility in communications that has revolutionized the daily lives of the populace. This mobility fed a large-scale migration of laborers in quest of work, of untutored people in search of education, and of ambitious persons seeking advancement. In the 1960s, this migration extended outside of Turkey as well; at present there are about 1.5 million Turks in Europe, mostly in West Germany. Their remittances have helped ease Turkey's perennial balance-of-payments deficits.

Turkey has undergone something of a green revolution. As a result of the introduction of new seeds and techniques, the country has turned from being a net importer of large amounts of food in the 1960s to becoming a significant exporter. Wheat is the main export crop, but market vegetables, cotton, tobacco, and dried fruits find ready markets in Europe and the United States.

Another major factor in Turkey's economic progress has been the continuing effort to create an increasingly sophisticated industrial base. It is still an open question whether the proliferating steel and aluminum mills, oil refineries, and other major facilities can produce economically against European and Japanese competition. Yet such industries provide experience with modern technology that augurs well for the future. The growing industrial sector, however, cannot now, nor for the foreseeable future, soak up the substantial unemployment. Nor can domestic industry come close to meeting Turkey's needs for continuing development and fulfill consumer expectations at the same time.

Of great promise for Turkey's future has been the rise of large contracting firms operating mostly in the Middle East. Emerging in the 1970s, these firms gained the expertise to compete successfully for petrodollars in Libya, Saudi Arabia, Iraq, and Iran. And by the mid-1980s, Turkish companies had over $15 billion worth of foreign contracts on the books.

Turkish development, however, has been threatened by surges of hyperinflation in each decade since World War II. These intense convulsions resulted from overexpansion of public-sector spending and excessive money creation by the Central Bank. At bottom, this course reflected partisan efforts to use state machinery for short-term political advantage. Especially after the world oil crisis began in 1973, Turkey entered a period of wild domestic inflation, unmanageable balance-of-payments deficits, and a sharp fall in imports. As a result, the gross national product was in decline by the end of the 1970s.

To cope with this economic challenge, the Turkish leaders finally accepted IMF urging to liberalize the economic structure, dismantle the system of subsidies on energy and other basic commodities, maintain a realistic exchange rate, reduce budget deficits, and stimulate exports. Indeed, in reducing the advantages enjoyed by the state economic enterprises over private firms, the stabilization plan represented a total reorientation of the economic structure away from the state-directed approach that had prevailed for over fifty years. The electorate unmistakably approved this change in bringing its architect, Turgut Ozal, to power in the Third Republic.

Political Structure

Turkey's rich variety of political mechanisms has endowed its multiparty structure with vitality. Except when the whole system is overturned, Turkey follows its constitution with considerable precision. Even with military interventions (to be discussed in a later section), Turks have demonstrated a strong commitment to restoring constitutional practices. This restorative trend gives the democratic order considerable permanence. Elected government is what almost all Turks clearly associate with Ataturk's reforms.

The 1982 constitutional structure is centered on a 400-seat unicameral legislature, introduced in an effort to ensure effective government. The members are elected for five-year terms, although elections may be held earlier by consent of the assembly. It can also pass legislation over the veto of the president by a simple majority; the prime minister is responsible to this body.

Executive authority is explicitly subordinated to the legislative in the Turkish construct. The cabinet can issue decrees with the force of law only if explicitly authorized for a specific period by the assembly. Cabinet ministers are "jointly responsible" for the execution of the government's general policy as well as personally liable for their ministries' acts. The prime minister, however, ensures that the ministers operate according to the law; he can dismiss them as he sees fit, by the terms of a provision first used in October 1984 to relieve the minister of customs, who publicly criticized a cabinet colleague.

A striking characteristic of the new system is the strengthening of the powers of the presidency over those that pertained in the Second Republic. The president is to ensure that the constitution is carried out and that the organs of state function smoothly. To this end, he can veto legislation and refer proposed constitutional amendments to popular referendum. For the first six years, constitutional amendments can be passed over his veto only by the vote of three-quarters of the total membership of the assembly.

The president can refer laws to the Constitutional Court for a ruling on their constitutionality. He also appoints senior officials and heads the National Security Council. To assist him for the first six years, he is aided by a Presidential Council, composed of the four ranking generals who shared power with him during the most recent period of military rule.

The 1982 constitution provides for the National Security Council to revert to its status in the Second Republic as a body to assist in "taking decisions and ensuring necessary cooperation" in national security policy. The cabinet is enjoined to "give priority consideration" to the decisions of the National Security Council, which is no longer the ultimate authority of the state (as it had been between 1980 and 1983).

An independent judiciary remains integral to the Turkish system. As an innovation, the 1982 constitution institutes State Security Courts to handle offenses against the integrity of the state, the democratic order, and the internal and external security of the country. Although superior administrative and military courts have final jurisdiction over cases within their competencies, the system also provides for a Constitutional Court to rule on the constitutionality of laws and decrees. Charges against the president of the republic and other senior officials would be considered by the Constitutional Court in its capacity as the Supreme Court. The Constitutional Court also decides all cases relating to the closure of political parties.

Several additional administrative organs play prominent roles in the government of the state. The State Planning Organization, continued from the 1961 constitution, fulfilled the desire for more regular economic projections. This body, however, has lost significance in recent years, inasmuch as the prime minister has kept basic economic responsibility in the cabinet. As a further control, Motherland party Prime Minister Ozal appointed his younger brother to head the Planning Organization.

An innovation carried over from the period of military rule is the Higher Education Council, whose central supervision of the various universities is confirmed in the new constitution. This council, established in 1981 under Ihsan Dogramaci, was accorded authority to appoint university governing boards, which in the past had been elected by the professors of the institutions involved. In the last days of the military regime, Dogramaci used the council's power to purge the universities, dismissing some professors and inducing others to resign.

The interest of the drafters of the constitution in preventing social strife is reflected in the provisions regulating labor activities. The right to form unions without prior permission is recognized, but labor groups are prohibited from extending their activities into the political realm or from having ties with a political party. Although strikes are legal, the union shop is not; nor can labor action be carried on "to the detriment of society." Collective bargaining is also permitted, but it is subject to extensive government supervision. From these limitations, it is clear that there will be no return to the freewheeling labor practices of the pre-1980 period.

Well-organized political parties are the basic units of parliamentary activity. Ataturk's original single party spawned most of the parties of the First and Second republics. The right-of-center and left-of-center constituencies that came into being by the end of the First Republic persist. But the contest to represent them continues.

The Motherland party has thus far demonstrated the strongest claim to dominate the right-of-center voting bloc. Its profile in the 1983 elections shows it to be an amalgam of important elements of the former Justice party, National Salvation party, and National Action party rather than a successor to the Justice party alone. Its heart lies in central Anatolia. Yet its supporters gave their votes in the expectation that Ozal's economic program would succeed. If it does not do so to their satisfaction, these votes could shift—probably to the True Path party, which seeks to assert itself as the rightful successor to the Justice party. The Nationalist Democracy party, which also competes for some of the same voters, has declined to the point that its long-term survival appears doubtful. Similarly, the Prosperity party seems unlikely to succeed in its bid to attract enough of the past supporters of the National Salvation party to be a viable contender.

The left-of-center constituency seems on the way to being captured by a single organization, the Social Democracy party. In the past, the left-of-center vote rarely exceeded 40 percent of the total electorate. The Social Democracy party commands only about two-thirds of this bloc, as shown in the 1984 municipal elections. Yet the tendency to go with a major contender rather than to waste votes on a minor party is likely to help this organization in the future.

The challenge of the Populist party, which ran second in the 1983 general elections, may well fall short in the competition for the allegiance of the left of center. It lost much of its electoral support when confronted by the Social Democracy party and is now torn by bitter factional rivalries. A Democratic Left party, which has been in the process of formation for over a year, is gearing up to vie for the extreme left votes, but its potential seems limited.

The new political parties law is designed to discourage sectional or limited-issue parties. Political oganizations are not permitted to promote class, religion, race, or language distinctions of one group over another. They can have no international ties, nor can they advocate repeal of the basic secular reformist laws of the Ataturk era. In addition, they cannot question the legitimacy of the 1980 military takeover.

Political parties must present a slate of at least thirty founding members in order to begin operations. Before a party can enter national elections, it must complete its organization in one-third of the districts (including the provincial capital) in more than half of Turkey's sixty-seven provinces. To guard against the partisanship in administration seen before 1980, the constitution prohibits professors, civil servants, and members of the armed forces from becoming members of political bodies.

The membership of political parties was accorded rights that diluted the power of the national leadership to determine candidates or otherwise dominate the party. The party chairmen are elected by a majority at the party national convention to serve a total of no more than twelve years without a break of at least four years before being eligible for reelection. The new law also restricts the right of the national headquarters to place candidates on the ticket.

The mechanism for funding party activity has also been amended to limit the power of special-interest groups. Donations are restricted in amount, and deputies may not contribute more than their salaries to their parties. As in the recent past, state aid to parties is limited in total to 1/5,000th of the national budget for the previous year. These subventions are distributed in proportion to the votes received in the latest national election to those parties that elected deputies. As a special exception, all parties participating in the 1984 municipal elections were included in the money-sharing arrangements.

Turkey's electoral constituencies are based on the province. But for cases in which the number of deputies to be chosen exceeds seven, electoral districts are constructed to ensure that no more than that number of seats is in contest in any district. The number of deputies to be elected currently ranges from two in sparsely populated Hakkari to the thirty-six of Istanbul, which is divided into six electoral districts.

Anyone not constitutionally barred from being a candidate may run for election either on a party ticket or as an independent. But electors who vote for an independent lose the right to mark their ballot for any other candidates, thereby wasting part of their electoral mandate. Otherwise, voting is by straight party ticket, a fact that makes party affiliation a distinct benefit.

In the Third Republic, as in the Second, Turkey's election law is based on the d'Hondt system of proportional representation. To elect a deputy, a party must win more than the quotient of the number of valid votes in an electoral district divided by the number of seats to be awarded. An additional national barrier of 10 percent of the nationwide vote has been added, however, to increase the bias in favor of the larger parties. As a result, in the 1983 elections under the combined national and provincial barrier system, the Motherland party got thirty-one additional seats beyond its proportion of the total vote. In fact, with only 45 percent of the votes, it won 53 percent of the seats.

Position on the ticket becomes a major determinant of electoral success in this system. In the future, candidates will be placed on the list through primary contests in which voting is confined to the membership of the party in each electoral district. The party's national leaders can dictate 5 percent of the candidates nationwide but cannot put them ahead of locally selected figures who received at least three-quarters of the primary vote. Nor can the national headquarters put party switchers on the ticket unless the new adherents win in a primary.

In theory, voters can use a complicated mechanism to indicate individual preference among a party's nominees to select the candidates irrespective of their position on the ticket. The primary system is designed to produce a party list with twice the number of candidates as there are seats in the districts. If the voters are to exercise their preference, at least 25 percent of the ballots for the party must contain preference marks and the voters must not mark either more or less than the exact number of seats to be awarded in the voting district. But this procedure will probably prove too cumbersome to be effective in changing the order of candidates.

Interest groups that in the past have had political roles will find it more difficult to participate in politics. Both politicians and labor leaders are likely to want to erode the ban on political activity by unions. But movement in this direction will necessarily be gradual. And it may take a subsequent Parliament to be able to amend current prohibitions before labor can play a political role.

There is even less likelihood that student organizations will soon be permitted to resume political activity. Since students were in the forefront of the disorders that produced both the military ultimatum of 1971 and the 1980 military takeover, the authorities will be strongly resistant to easing the tight restrictions on the political activities of youth, despite the interest of some politicians to lower the voting age.

Political Dynamics

The patterns of politics in Turkey show remarkable continuity in spite of military interventions. The conduct of party leaders, voting patterns, and the issues of political debate all bespeak a large debt to the past, thus reflecting the fact that Turkish parties are not emanations of charismatic personalities but, rather, that they represent aggregations with differing approaches to social issues. Hence politics in the Third Republic still revolve around the contest to represent the right-of-center and left-of-center constituencies. This competition has been the bedrock of political life in Turkey since the latter days of the First Republic.

The persistence of political patterns and the tenacity of the commitment to elective parliamentary rule also reflect the quality of Turkish leadership. The Turks were fortunate that the high status and prestige of government service meant that virtually the entire personnel resources of the country were at the disposal of politics. Until recently, business or private careers did not attract the "best and the brightest." Ataturk may have delayed the advent of multiparty competition by his autocratic behavior. But Inonu's consistent dedication to building democracy made his steady hand available even in his 80s to help over the rough spots. Beyond the top leaders, the second- and middle-echelon politicians were often also of uncommon ability. There were always phalanxes of choices for the cabinet; "musical chairs" between a limited pool of ministerial talent has not been common in Turkey. Nor has it been difficult to secure competent personnel to staff the bureaucracy and judiciary.

The political parties have operated with relative efficiency in mobilizing voters. Participation in elections has generally been high (ranging between 92 and 64 percent of the eligible voters). Starting from the tradition of universal voting as the duty of citizenry in the one-party era, however, the percentage of those actually going to the polls declined until 1973. Turkey's experience was thus contrary to the expectation of those who theorize that greater education, involvement in the political process, and development should be accompanied by rising interest in voting. The prevailing explanation of Turkish experience ascribes the falling participation rate to the decline in bloc voting as Turkey became more modern. It seemed reasonable to assume that as individuals became responsible for their own voting decisions, there would be natural fall in the number going to the polls. The generally higher rate of voting in the 1960s in eastern Turkey, where clan and tribal ties were strongest, was taken as additional substantiation of this hypothesis.

The rebound in the participation rate since 1973 calls this explanation into question and suggests that the process went far beyond a simple link to modernity and the breakdown of bloc voting. On the one hand, reaction to each military intervention (1960, 1971, and 1980) spurred participation. At the same time, changes in political alignments and the increasing urgency of the issues at stake in the 1970s had a clear impact on voting. For example, the lower turnout in 1965 and 1969 appears to have reflected the fears of the traditional rural notables in the Republican Peoples party over the "left-of-center" stance that the party introduced in 1965 and the bitter internal dispute that it triggered. In protest, these voters may simply have stayed at home on election day.

By the 1970s the parties were running spirited campaigns that piqued voter interest. Republican Peoples party leader Bulent Ecevit showed a certain charisma. His appearances at times galvanized crowds of tens of thousands of sympathizers. Moreover, these were years when radio and television was bringing election activities more intimately into the lives of Turks. The confluence of these trends produced a steady upswing in voting by 1973. This rising tide was most apparent in western Turkey. By 1983 the major centers of Istanbul, Ankara, and Adana had been left behind by the Aegean, Mediterranean, and western Black Sea provinces, which all scored over the remarkably high 92 percent national average.

Since World War II, the political contest in Turkey has generally been a "two-party affair." In the First Republic, with its majority voting system, one party usually (though not always) swept the entire slate in a province. Under these circumstances, the larger parties with their nationwide organizations ended up with the lion's share of the seats. Under such conditions, the future of minor parties was unpromising.

The dominance of the two major parties was not as marked in the Second Republic (see Tables 3.1 and 3.2). The introduction of proportional representation in 1961 faciliated the survival of splinter groups. In the freer political climate of the past two decades, personality conflicts, coupled with disputes over philosophy and course by rival aspirants to top leadership positions, contributed to the defection of parliamentary factions from both major parties. These fissiparous tendencies went so far that in 1973 and 1977, neither major party could muster a majority in Parliament. Turkey entered its second period of precarious coalition politics, a course that this time led to the downfall of the Second Republic and to its replacement in due course with the Third Republic.

Yet even as splinter groups were proliferating, there were already signs in the 1970s of strong underlying tendencies favoring the two major parties. In fact, despite the mushrooming of small entities in the 1970s, the overall record of survival of minor parties in the Second Republic was not impressive. With one exception, these splinters all lost support, often dramatically, in every general election after their first appearance. The New Turkey party faded away after declining steeply in three successive general elections; the National Salvation party declined from forty-eight seats in 1973 to twenty-four in 1977; and other right-wing contenders were nearly wiped out by 1977. Only the extremist National Action party managed to buck this trend, rising from one seat in 1969 to sixteen in 1977 in the lower house. Thus, although from 1973 to 1980 the minor parties occupied the swing position between the relatively evenly matched majors, their total bulk was receding by the end of the period.

The performance of the parties in the Third Republic suggests that a similar dynamic may be at work (see Table 3.3). Indeed, after the shaking-out process in the next elections, there will likely be no more than two major rivals on the right of center and perhaps one on the left. The others may have to merge with the more successful parties or go out of business.

The splinter groups have fared so poorly for a number of reasons. Their survival depends directly on the degree of proportional representation in the system. Yet even when electoral provisions are relatively favorable, minor parties suffer disadvantages. Turks, like most people, value strong national leadership. Indeed, given the urgent economic and social challenges of recent years, the yearning for a decisive hand on the tiller is quite understandable. That fact has only reinforced the long-standing desire in Turkey to avoid

TABLE 3.1 Election Results in the Second and Third Republics: 1961–1984 (in percentages)

	Second Republic					Third Republic		
	450-member lower house					400-member national assembly	Mayoral election	Provincial Assembly
Years	1961	1965	1969	1973	1977	1983	1984	1984
Participation rates	81.0	71.3	64.3	66.8	72.5	92.3	85.6	91.0
Left-of-Center Totals	*36.7*	*31.7*	*32.9*	*34.3*	*41.9*	*30.5*	*32.6*	*32.2*
Republican Peoples party	36.7	28.7	27.4	33.2	41.4			
Turkish Unity party			2.8	1.1	.4			
Turkish Labor party		3.0	2.7	closed	.1			
Populist party						30.5	7.8	8.8
Social Democracy party							24.8	23.4

Right-of-Center Totals	*62.5*	*65.1*	*61.5*	*62.8*	*55.6*	*68.5*	*64.3*	*66.9*
Justice party	34.8	52.9	46.5	29.8	36.9			
National Salvation party				11.9	8.6			
National Action party	14.0	2.2	3.0	3.4	6.4			
Republican Reliance party			6.6	5.3	1.9			
Democratic party				11.8	1.8			
New Turkey party	13.7	3.7	2.2					
Nation party		6.3	3.2	.6				
Motherland party						45.2	43.2	41.5
Nationalist Democracy party						23.3	5.4	7.0
True Path party							11.9	14.0
Prosperity party							3.8	4.4
Independents Totals	*.8*	*3.2*	*5.6*	*2.8*	*2.5*	*1.1*	*3.2*	*1.6*

TABLE 3.2 Election Results in the Second and Third Republics: 1961–1984 (in seats)

	Second Republic					Third Republic		
	450-member lower house					400-member national assembly	Mayoral election	Provincial Assembly
Years	1961	1965	1969	1973	1977	1983	1984	1984
Left-of-Center Totals	*173*	*149*	*153*	*186*	*213*	*117*	*378*	*564*
Republican Peoples party	173	134	143	185	213			
Turkish Unity party			8	1				
Turkish Labor party		15	2					
Populist party						117	94	58
Social Democracy party							284	506

Right-of-Center Totals	*277*	*301*	*284*	*258*	*233*	*282*	*1,243*	*1,721*
Justice party	158	240	256	149	189			
National Salvation party				48	24			
National Action party	54	11	1	3	16			
Republican Reliance party			15	13	3			
Democratic party				45	1			
New Turkey party	65	19	6					
Nation party		31	6					
Motherland party						211	883	1,420
Nationalist Democracy party						71	106	99
True Path party							238	188
Prosperity party							16	14
Independents Totals			*13*	*6*	*4*		*80*	*21*

TABLE 3.3 Election Results in the Second Republic: The Senate

	1961	1964	1966	1968	1973	1975	1977	1979
Participation Rates	*81.4%	60.2%	56.2%	66.3%	*65.3%	58.4%	*73.8%	70.6%
Left-of-Center Totals	*37.2%*	*40.8%*	*33.9%*	*31.8%*	*35.7%*	*44.3%*	*42.3%*	*33.0%*
Republican Peoples party	37.2%	40.8%	30.0%	27.1%	33.6%	43.8%	42.3%	29.1%
Turkish Unity party					2.1%	.5%		1.2%
Turkish Labor party			3.9%	4.7%				.7%
Socialist Workers party of Turkey								1.3%
Socialist Revolutionary party								.7%
Right-of-Center Totals	*63.0%*	*56.5%*	*66.4%*	*66.5%*	*62.3%*	*55.9%*	*57.6%*	*65.6%*
Justice party	35.5%	50.3%	56.3%	49.9%	31.0%	40.8%	38.3%	46.8%
National Salvation party					12.3%	8.8%	8.4%	9.7%
Democratic party					10.4%	3.1%	2.2%	
National Action party	13.5%	3.0%	1.9%	2.0%	2.7%	3.2%	6.8%	6.6%
New Turkey party	14.0%	3.5%	2.3%					
Nation party			5.9%	6.0%				
Republican Reliance party				8.6%	5.9%		1.9%	2.5%
Independents Totals	*.3%*	*2.3%*	*.5%*	*1.7%*	*2.0%*	*.1%*	*.1%*	*1.3%*

*coincided with general elections to the lower house

drift. In this situation, it is clear to most voters that only by backing a major party can the requisite leadership be found. It is the main parties, moreover, that have the reservoir of impressive talent; splinter groups have at most one or two well-known figures. And, finally, the inability of most minor parties to carve out a well-defined constituency prevents them from growing and makes their survival difficult.

Turkish parties also reflect a blend of national and local interests. In Turkey, reformist politics have always been national; local groups, on the other hand, have been opposed to far-reaching social and cultural reform. The accommodation of these conflicting approaches, while preserving the essence of Ataturk's pragmatic modernizing thrust, has been one of the major achievements of Turkey's political life. Thus the political contest has focused especially on tactics to achieve development and on the issue of how much disruption of traditional social mores is necessary for advancement.

In the one-party era, little moment was attached to local desires in selecting parliamentarians. Deputies were assigned to provinces, frequently without regard to their ties to these localities. Indeed, the top leadership of the Republican Peoples party was always singularly unconcerned with identification with a particular locality. Ataturk, after all, was born in Salonika, a place not even within the bounds of modern Turkey. Although originally from Izmir and brought up in Sivas, Inonu did have family associations with Malatya, his eventual electoral constituency; he maintained his home in Ankara and Istanbul, however—not in Malatya. Despite the fact that Bulent Ecevit was a native of Istanbul, he never represented this province; he ran from Ankara before shifting to Zonguldak in 1965 to emphasize his solidarity with the workers of this labor center.

Bias against localism on the part of national politicians has been enshrined in all republican constitutions. Deputies represent not their local district but the nation as a whole. Hence, in the Third Republic, prominent figures run in districts with which they are not intimately associated. For example, Motherland party leader Ozal was born in Malatya and was elected from Istanbul. But in the current Parliament, the Nationalist Democracy party has shown itself to be the party most disdainful of local sensitivities. About one-fifth of its deputies were born outside the provinces they represent.

Nonetheless, the multiparty era brought concern with selecting popular candidates, though party—not personality—remains the key to politics in the more developed regions of Turkey. The Democrat party sought to emphasize its democratic nature as early as 1949 by prohibiting the national leaders from choosing more than 20 percent of the candidates on the local provincial slates. The Republican Peoples party also moved in this direction, even though its leadership retained the right to name 30 percent of the party's candidates in the 1950s. Far tighter legal restrictions against dictating candidates for the local lists were imposed in the election laws of both the Second and Third republics. But candidate selection has always been controversial. In the 1977 general elections, for example, placing figures not native to the province at the head of the local tickets affected the outcome in several smaller constituencies. In eastern Turkey, the failure of aspirants with strong local bases to get places at the head of the lists led them to abandon the party altogether after the primaries and to run on their own. All four successfully elected independents in 1977 had quit major parties when denied choice spots on their party's tickets.

With this impetus, politics in the multiparty era has assumed a character increasingly responsive to local interests. One of the principal ways in which localism has modified Turkey's course has been in the realm of policy toward Islam. Ataturk, like many of his generation, saw attachment to religion as the main impediment to westernizing Turkey. He therefore disestablished Islam as the state religion and imposed rigorous restrictions on its practice. He closed the dervish lay orders that formed a separate hierarchy outside the control or guidance of the orthodox religious establishment, which itself had been a wing of the government. He also closed the religious schools and banned clerics from wearing religious garb outside places of worship. In addition, he imposed Turkish in place of Arabic in religious services.

Multiparty competition worked to relax these restrictions. Optional courses on religion were added to the curriculum in the 1940s; a faculty of divinity was reopened; Arabic was restored in worship; and a proliferation of local training schools for religious leaders was eventually permitted. Moreover, as local pressures mounted, the public observance of religious festivals increased. A binge of mosque building began, including a huge and prominent structure dominating the skyline of new Ankara—a development inconceivable in Ataturk's lifetime. It became fashionable for officials to fast during Ramadan, and many educated people attended Friday noon prayers—even before the rise of the National Salvation party, which encouraged this trend.

The resurgence of Islamic practice gained such momentum that even the strongly secular Kemalist revival of the generals after 1980 did not stop it. Ozal is himself religiously observant, and his piety may have attracted votes. In any event, the Motherland party's moves to encourage greater conservatism in dress in the May 19 athletic celebrations in 1984 added to the impression that religious custom would be more respected than in the past.

Localism has also fostered changes in the socioeconomic interests represented in Parliament. Ataturk's one-party regime ran heavily to military and civilian officials in his hand-picked single chamber assembly. Once the transition to multiparty competition was under way, the character of the assembly began to change. Professionals, especially lawyers, became deputies in rising numbers. They were joined by businessmen, who had been scarce in the Ataturk era. At the same time, the contingent of officials declined. This transformation, reflecting the emergence of a middle class, came slowly. At first it affected the lowest levels of power, but gradually new elements infiltrated the higher ranks.

Entry of these new men had its effect on deliberations concerning domestic policy above all. Economic approach, the role of central planning, and the place for private enterprise were debated with rising intensity as the new arrivals challenged the older notion of state-directed reform. Clustered around first the Democrat party, later the Justice party, and now the Motherland and True Path parties, these elements, with their nongovernmental focus, have been attacked as seeking to dismantle the Ataturk reforms. But the dispute has in fact been a question more of nuance than of principle. Even the new men accept a heavy state involvement. Although the Motherland party has embarked on a program of "privatization" to sell shares in some profit-making enterprises to the public, Ozal is not seeking to dispose of essential public services.

Just as the rise of the center-right constituency was associated with the burgeoning of the middle class, the emergence of a sizable industrial labor force in recent decades has been seen as favoring the left of center. Indeed, the rebound of the Republican Peoples party from its low point in 1969 was attributed to this cause. From just over 27 percent of the votes in that year, this party managed to rise to over 41 percent in the 1977 elections.

Some investigators saw in this experience a "critical realignment" of voter support away from territorial and cultural cleavages and toward voting along class lines. They credited such a realignment with the gains scored by the Republican Peoples party in the last two general elections of the Second Republic. That party's socialist approach gave it claims to represent the interests of workers in the urban areas. Although this theory was comforting to the reformist elite, it appears to contain a large dose of wishful thinking. The evidence is convincing that sectional, ethnic, linguistic, religious, and cultural factors continue to affect voting patterns in Turkey. And no class-based realignment has yet taken place.

Indeed, it is apparent that the improvement in the fortunes of the Republican Peoples party in the 1970s reflected factors unrelated to economic development or social change. First was the shock that the Justice party suffered from the military ultimatum in 1971. In the ensuing election Demirel was at a disadvantage in projecting the image of a man who could govern effectively. His loss of confidence clearly discouraged his normal constituency, which was badly fractured by the defections of the Democrat party and the National Salvation party.

In 1977, although Demirel ran a much more confident campaign, having returned to office as prime minister, he faced Ecevit, who had emerged in the interim as something of a popular hero. Ecevit's appeal was based on oratorical ability to project a populist aura as a modern-day Robin Hood (*Karaoglan* in Turkish), coupled with the remnants of the national exultation he had earned from ordering the Cyprus intervention in 1974.

But Ecevit's ability to profit from national euphoria did not last. When his coalition proved unable either to contain political violence and terrorism or to relieve the pressing economic pinch, the popularity of the Republican Peoples party dropped precipitously in the 1979 senatorial elections, whereas that of the Justice party rose sharply. This turnaround in the right-of-center vote, maintained in the Third Republic, convincingly shows that Turks do not cast their ballots on a class basis. Indeed, these ups and downs in major party performance appear to confirm not so much a "critical realignment" as the fact that Turkish politics is essentially a struggle between the ins and outs. The desire to change the party in power seems to grow in Turkey after two terms. Although experience is far too short to tell whether a similar limit will operate in the Third Republic, there is no reason to doubt that it is the ability of the ruling party to govern effectively and find solutions to major problems that will ultimately determine its staying power.

The Role of the Military

The armed forces have a special position in Turkey. This political weight enters into a broad range of government calculations. In part, this influence comes from their monopoly of legal force and their status as the last recourse in domestic conflict. In part, their role derives from the peculiar history of the military in the Turkish reform movement and its centrality in the creation of the republic.

Ataturk and his chief lieutenants were career officers when they launched the struggle for independence. The armed forces, with their secularist schools, were the main window on the West at the end of the Ottoman Empire. As a result, officers were the reformists par excellence. Indeed, the fact that Ataturk's outlook was archetypical of the army's approach helped him rally military support for his cause.

The difficult days of the struggle for independence and of the founding of the republic were not times to separate military and political careers. In accord with the needs of the moment, senior commanders served in Parliament, on diplomatic missions abroad, and as government administrators without resigning their commissions. Ataturk depended on the military command structure as an essential prop for his move to abolish the Ottoman royal house.

It was not until the political scene began to clarify early in the republic that the problem of mixing politicians and military officers became acute. When some of Ataturk's closest collaborators defected to the mounting civilian opposition in 1924, the threat of military disloyalty imparted urgency to a separation of the military and political tracks. In 1927, when the dissident generals requested to return to active army commands, Ataturk retired his opponents. At the same time, he and his associates gave up their active-duty status.

Yet Ataturk and Inonu maintained close ties with the armed forces, even after retirement. Marshal Fevzi Cakmak ran the military establishment on their behalf, keeping the forces out of day-to-day politics. Nonetheless, Ataturk continually cited the army as the ultimate guardians of the republic, making clear that it was to defend the reform effort as well as to protect against foreign foes.

As part of the move to expand democratic practice, the armed forces were removed from the president's purview in 1944 and put under the direct control of the prime minister. Five years later, the general staff was placed under the control of the Ministry of National Defense. The top generals, however, remained loyal to Inonu. There are credible reports that senior commanders sounded him out on whether to prevent the Democrats from taking over after they won the 1950 elections. But Inonu was categoric in opposing a military move.

It took a complex of pressures to lead the armed forces to overturn the Democrats in 1960. Loss of status and prestige by officers during the Democrat party's decade in power prepared the ground. Prime Minister Adnan Menderes was seen as deliberately denying the military its position as the ultimate guarantor of the state. Nonetheless, the officer corps might have remained loyal if the Democrats had not threatened the parliamentary system. Even the Republican Peoples party wished the military not to obey partisan commands by the Democrat party administration. Of course, the line of disobedience was hard to draw. In the end, a group of colonels and younger officers led a revolt that brought the entire military apparatus along.

The military move was readily accepted in Turkey as necessary to prevent perversion of the political process. Trials of the Democrat leaders helped discredit Menderes. The execution of the three main defendants and the incarceration of many others, however, were harder for the body politic to swallow. Yet, although civilian politicians sought amnesty for the jailed Democrats, there was no serious effort to deny the legality of the Second Republic or to seek punishment for the military junta, whose members were accorded life membership in the Senate.

Thanks to the general acceptance of the legitimacy of the military move, the junta could arrange to surrender the reins of government to a civilian regime after only sixteen months. But the stint in power had disrupted the chain of command, damaged discipline, and deeply politicized the officer corps. It took two abortive coups in 1962 and 1963 to teach officers that plotting carried severe risks. Talat Aydemir's execution for leading the 1963 putsch virtually ended efforts by those below the level of the senior commanders to overturn the civilian government.

In the 1960s, the National Security Council, presided over by the president of the republic, provided a forum for the armed services to convey political messages. Hence, although the senior commanders and the president (himself a former top general) did occasionally make their views known—for example, in objecting in 1969 to the restoration of parliamentary rights to former President Celal Bayar—their actions were accepted as falling within the bounds of constitutionality. Even the "coup by memorandum" that brought down the Demirel government in March 1971 was never subjected to legal challenge. The care of the generals to remain behind the scenes, working through the constitutional system, limited the resentment expressed over their intervention.

Nonetheless, Demirel's downfall lent the armed forces an aura threatening to the normal operation of the political process. Parliament continued to function, but the deputies formed cabinets of technocrats in order not to offend the generals. This deference evidently whetted the appetite of the chief of the general staff, General Faruk Gurler, for political power. Gurler made his bid in the presidential election in the spring of 1973. Since the constitution barred the incumbent from reelection, Gurler sought to present himself as the military's candidate. Demirel, recognizing that the new president would name the prime minister after the following general elections, wished to make sure that a neutral figure, not associated with the 1971 ultimatum, would be chief of state. The Republican Peoples party, under Ecevit's leadership, also wanted to break the precedent that would automatically make the chief of staff president when a vacancy occurred. Military backing for Gurler seems to have wavered, perhaps because of interservice rivalries. As a result, the otherwise badly divided Parliament rejected Gurler and settled instead on long-retired Admiral Fahri Koruturk.

This outcome marked a significant turning point in the relations between the military and civilians. It was widely read as a retreat of the armed forces before determined civilian opposition. It thus sent the misleading message that the military establishment was a "paper tiger" lacking the will to insist on its demands. This signal was reinforced by the ease with which first Demirel and then Ecevit purged the upper ranks of those each considered unsympathetic to his respective party. And military patience during lengthy party bickering over the formation of cabinets confirmed the impression that military intervention was a thing of the past.

Notwithstanding these indications that the civilians were in charge, the regime was becoming ever more dependent on the armed forces. After the outbreak of communal violence in Kahramanmaras in December 1978, the civilians turned to martial law. But the divided Parliament could not agree to grant the commanders enough authority to stem rising political violence. More significant, the civilians could not elect a successor to President Koruturk, when his term ended in March 1980. Even retired officers proposed by the Republican Peoples party were rejected by the Justice party. This parliamentary paralysis was compounded by the injection of religion into politics by the National Salvation party—a situation that particularly alienated the secularist generals. Disrespect for the state shown at a party rally in Konya in September 1980 was the final straw in that it brought the senior generals under Chief of Staff Kenan Evren to take power in a bloodless coup in September 1980.

The new military regime with General Evren as chief of state set up a government of technocrats, drawn mainly from civilian experts but headed by recently retired Admiral Bulend Ulusu. The National Security Council became the organ for policy decisions and issuance of laws. The cabinet was reduced to a body serving to administer the country under the guidelines of the Security Council.

Although General Evren recognized Turkey's constitutional inadequacies as well as its partisan failings, it was clear that the commanders wanted to return to an elected democratic system. In order to give Turkey a breathing spell free of violence in which to make necessary changes, Evren announced a six-point program to preserve national unity, restore security, reinvigorate state authority, ensure social peace, apply social justice, and reinstate civilian rule within a "reasonable" time. In short, Turkey was to be saved through institutional reform.

In addition to constitutional adjustments, the commanders concluded that new parties and new leaders were needed as were new rules for political behavior. Thus, in the process of banning old political organizations and ruling the former political leaders out of politics for ten years, the generals sought to ensure the dominance of elements committed to a return to Kemalist principles. To this end, they encouraged former General Turgut Sunalp to form the Nationalist Democracy party. And General Evren sought to assist this organization by appealing—albeit largely in vain—to voters to favor this party in the 1983 general elections.

Concern over establishment of the legitimacy of the 1980 move was integral to the transition to civilian politics. The constitution affirmed the legitimacy of the takeover and banned legal questioning of the acts of the military rulers. Popular acceptance of the intervention was high in any event, as the populace welcomed the respite from violence. There was wide agreement in Turkey that the political process had broken down to the extent that the military had to move. What was less accepted was the abolition of the parties of the old regime. And efforts to recreate the old parties or to take over the new have persisted.

With the civilians back in office after 1983, the role of the military has reverted to that of an influential pressure group. Its interests are defended by the president, although he no longer has active-duty status. The revamped National Security Council serves as a watchdog over security and especially the applications of martial law, which is still in force in most of Turkey's sixty-seven provinces. And the president has used the Council to direct such operations as the moves against Kurdish rebels in southeastern Turkey.

On the other hand, President Evren has found dealing with the politicians to be a challenging task. The overturning of his veto of the bill speeding municipal elections demonstrated the limits of civilian independence. Moreover, in economic affairs the military establishment clearly has left the field entirely to Ozal. But the civilian leaders are still wary of changing the political rules set during the period of military rule, although there is pressure to do so from the rank and file as well as from the leadership of the banned parties. On many practical questions, the working out of the limits of military influence continues, and it will be some time before a clear answer on the role of the military has been established.

Foreign Policy

Ataturk set the basic Turkish goals for international relations. The corollary of his determination that Turkey be accepted as a powerful modern state was Western orientation. To the Kemalists, and soon to virtually all of Turkey, therefore, the foremost design of the republic was to become identified as European. This state of affairs, in turn, implied close ties with England and France in the interwar years and with the United States in the era after World War II. There were deep roots in Turkish thinking that caused membership in NATO to be seen as confirmation of the Kemalist dream. Although joining the Common Market occasioned debate over proper timing, it was not a goal to be easily rejected in principle. In short, Turkey's Western alliance is solidly based on the wellsprings of the modern Turkish state.

For Ankara there was, moreover, little alternative to grasping the West as tightly as possible after the war's end. Defense against Russia was a deeply ingrained response in Turkey, despite the era of revolutionary cooperation between the new Turkey and the Soviet state in the 1920s and 1930s. It was a cardinal tenet of the Kemalist regime not to be caught in a position that would give Moscow either the opportunity or the provocation to confront Turkey. Turkish neutralism during World War II spared it the burdens of active military operations or military destruction. It also seemed to offer a way to prevent being forced into the embrace of the Soviet Union. Yet with the defeat of the Nazis, Turkey was left highly exposed to pressure from Moscow.

Although the issue of whether or not the Soviets would invade Turkey had already been settled by 1947 as a result of the Turks' stout resistance and Stalin's concern lest he provoke U.S. retaliation, Ankara was eager to secure military aid from the United States. Once NATO came into being, first a Republican Peoples party government and then a Democrat party government worked earnestly to gain admission. In those days of cold war intensity, foreign policy was bipartisan in Turkey, and the U.S. connection was welcomed by virtually everyone.

The Turks thus entered the Atlantic alliance without reservations. The Democrat party regime was willing to make whatever diplomatic moves (such as setting up the Baghdad Pact) it judged pleasing to Washington. Military cooperation between the United States and Turkey was highly successful. Ankara's creaky armed forces were revitalized and upgraded. U.S. strategic interests were well served by a number of bilateral endeavors conducted with the Turks under the NATO umbrella. More difficult, however, were efforts to mesh Democrat insistence on using aid for partisan purposes with the desire of the World Bank and Washington to structure assistance on reasonable economic criteria.

The overthrow of the Democrat party regime in 1960 did not immediately usher in changes in Turkey's foreign relations. The military rulers were too preoccupied with domestic problems to devise major foreign initiatives. Moreover, coming out of Turkey's military tradition, they were reasonably satisfied with the U.S. performance.

More important over the long run for Turkey's foreign orientation were the repercussions of the broader political debate permitted in the Second Republic. The rise of the socialist movement in the early 1960s was accompanied by a changing spirit in Turkish foreign policy. Symptomatic in this connection was Turkey's move to show sympathy for the Algerian independence struggle against France.

But the main foreign issue confronting Turkey was Cyprus. In December 1963, violence between the small Turkish and much larger Greek Cypriot communities led Ankara to send planes over the island to demonstrate its commitment to the Turkish minority. Continuing communal troubles brought the Turkish Cypriots to group themselves in enclaves and the Turkish government to consider landing troops, using the authority provided in the Treaty of Guarantee that established the Cypriot state in 1960. Before the Turks could dispatch forces to the island, however, U.S. President Lyndon Johnson in June 1964 sent Prime Minister Inonu a harsh letter warning him that NATO might not protect Turkey if the Turks took military action on Cyprus. Turkey desisted under this pressure. But public resentment against this U.S. intervention was strong; the incident marked the end of the era of unquestioned diplomatic cooperation with the United States.

Under pressure from leftist extremists—who took up the cry of moving Turkey out of NATO—the Turkish authorities began to reinspect the alliance. A new agreement restricting the scope of U.S. privileges and activities was hammered out in 1969 after several years of negotiation. That stabilized relations for a time. But the new pattern of cooperation had more limited bounds, reflecting the now somewhat divergent interests of Turkey and the United States.

Coincidentally, Turkey's position in the East-West confrontation had changed. In the aftermath of the Cuban missile crisis of 1962, medium-range surface-to-surface missiles had been removed from Turkish soil. This move significantly diminished the likelihood that Moscow would make a first strike on Turkey in the event of war with NATO. At the same time, the Turks became drawn into the process of East-West détente, with a noticeable increase in diplomatic exchanges with the USSR. Against this backdrop, the failure of the Western allies to support Turkey on Cyprus spurred normalization of Ankara's relations with the Soviet Union. In the mid-1960s, the Soviets concluded a program of major economic projects, including an aluminum plant and a steel mill. But the Turks refrained from seeking arms from the USSR in order not to risk disrupting NATO ties.

The Cyprus controversy also induced Turkey to broaden its contacts with the Third World in general and with the Arab states in particular. In an effort to prevent adverse votes in the United Nations over Cyprus, Turkish policymakers dispatched missions to Africa and the Middle East to explain the Turkish position and sought to appeal to common religious ties of solidarity with other Muslim states. But except for Central Treaty Organization (CENTO) ally Pakistan, the Turks were not notably successful in getting diplomatic support.

Turkey's foreign position faced an even greater challenge from events in Cyprus in July 1974. After some years of gradually warming communal relations on the island, an initially successful coup against Archbishop Makarios was mounted by the military rulers in Athens. Although this action was not directed against the Turkish community in the first instance, the man who seized power in Nicosia, Nicos Sampson, was known as a long-time protagonist of joining Cyprus with Greece and as a dedicated foe of the Turks. In response, Ankara landed troops on the island, claiming that it was exercising its treaty rights to repair a clear violation of the Cypriot constitution. Under strong international pressure, however, the Turks halted their military action after two days, having secured a foothold in the Kyrenia region, north of Nicosia. Peace talks were held in Geneva. But when the new regime in Athens asked for a delay in negotiations in August, Turkey resumed military operations and speedily secured control over slightly more than the northern one-third of the island.

Although Ankara insisted that its actions were sanctioned by the Treaty of Guarantee with Cyprus, Turkey found itself largely isolated in the international community. The U.S. Congress imposed a complete embargo on all deliveries of arms to Turkey in February 1975, a ban that lasted until September. It was then lifted partially after the Turks closed all U.S. installations and abrogated the 1969 Defense Cooperation Agreement. The continuing limited embargo also prevented deliveries of U.S. weapons by all NATO countries, thus impeding the ability of other allies to supply Turkey's military requirements. Moreover, the European powers lent their combined influence to urging Turkey to offer concessions to the Greek side with respect to Cyprus.

In this context, Turkey's relations with Greece took a decided turn for the worse. Tensions generated by Cyprus were further inflamed by an emerging dispute over the continental shelf and air rights in the Aegean Sea. The geography of this body of water, with numerous Greek islands hugging the Turkish coast, presented complex problems in apportioning the seabed. Following discovery of oil in commercial quantities in Greek waters in 1973, the Turks issued licenses for exploration in international waters on their side of the median line, but in areas that Athens claimed were above the continental shelf of its islands.

Neither Turkey nor Greece, however, wished to see the dispute escalate into war. After Turkish seismic exploration in the Aegean raised tensions to the boiling point, both sides agreed to avoid inflammatory tactics and to pursue active negotiations. But the death of Archbishop Makarios in August 1977 set back progress on Cyprus. And despite the desire of Ecevit's government (which came to power in January 1978) to resolve differences, little could be accomplished. Turkey did drop its objections to Greece's return to the military wing of NATO; yet, regarding Cyprus, neither side was prepared to make sufficient concessions to allow a settlement. And particularly after Andreas Papandreou's Socialist party came to power in Athens in 1981 on a platform of intense suspicion of Turkey, relations with Greece deteriorated anew.

Behind the difficulties in dealing with Greece and Cyprus in the 1970s lay a new and painful fact for Turkey: The U.S. Congress, and not the executive branch, had become the focal point for Turkish-American problems.

Whereas presidents of the United States were understanding of the compulsions that led Turkey to act in Cyprus, the U.S. Congress was far less willing to credit Turkish arguments. This contest of wills in Washington slowed renegotiation of defense cooperation arrangements. But after Congress finally lifted the remaining limitations on arms to Turkey in September 1978, U.S. facilities were reopened and hard bargaining began on a new Cooperation on Defense and Economy Agreement. This accord was signed in March 1980.

It was in this context that the generals took over in 1980. That situation immediately added new complexities in relations with Europe, which was already showing disenchantment with the large influx of Turkish workers. The north Europeans, in particular, were critical of military rule as well as of the treatment of former politicians. So hostile was the Council of Europe that the Turkish parliamentary delegation withdrew. This rejection by some of Turkey's European allies pushed the Turks again toward the Middle East, this time with manifest success in establishing commercial relations and in winning lucrative contracts. Trade with Iraq and Iran spurted after the two became involved in prolonged conflict in the fall of 1980. And to cement these favorable trade trends, Turkey deepened its involvement in the politics of the Islamic world while lowering the level of diplomatic ties with Israel.

The legacy of foreign difficulties left by the generals was made all the more trying by the unilateral declaration of independence of the Turkish Cypriot legislature in November 1983. This so-called Turkish Republic of Northern Cyprus was recognized by Ankara alone of all nations of the world. Even though the military rulers went out of office within weeks, Ozal's refusal to repudiate this step earned sharp criticisms from the United States, which had otherwise shown understanding of the period of military rule. Members of Congress demanded heavy cuts in aid to Turkey unless progress was recorded in resolving the Cyprus dispute.

Turkish sensitivity to such pressure boiled over into widespread public distress against the United States. Although the failure of congressional critics to prevent a sizable increase in aid to Turkey in 1984 limited this unhappiness, the readiness of Turkish politicians and journalists to vent hostility demonstrated afresh how close to the surface grievances against the United States remained. And this bitterness was clearly visible in the Turkish anger at congressional interest in commemorating "genocide" against Armenians during World War I.

Renewed difficulties with Washington also impelled the Turks to redouble efforts to smooth out their tangled relations with Europe. But it was only after the municipal elections in March 1984 revalidated Ozal's legitimacy and vindicated the genuineness of Turkey's return to democratic procedure that the steam went out of European criticism. Turkey was allowed to resume its seat in the Council of Europe.

Finally, the Turks moved cautiously, but with limited success, to try to repair the relations with the USSR that had been strained by the period of military rule. Moscow had seen the generals' regime as a willing collaborator with Washington and charged that Ankara was falling in with U.S. plans to intervene in the Gulf area. These charges did not disturb trade arrangements; indeed, the visit to Ankara of Soviet Premier Nikolay Tikhanov at the end of 1984 apparently spurred the expansion of some large joint economic projects and a significant increase in trade. Yet Moscow pronounced the Ozal regime unwilling to make substantial changes from the policies followed by the generals. And differences evidently prevented the issuance of the usual communiqué on Tikhanov's departure.

The panoply of problems with friends and foes confirmed the difficulties of a relatively small state in following the self-reliant pattern that the Turks had desired since the start of the republic. But interdependence was not devoid of painful challenges. The literal, rather mechanistic, application of treaty instruments that the Ankara regimes would have preferred also ran up against the refusal of treaty partners to conform to such expectations. And as the international environment became more complex and the cold war receded, the levers that had produced so successfully for the Turks in the immediate postwar era no longer yielded fully satisfactory results. As 1985 progressed, Ankara found itself no nearer than it had been at the end of the Second Republic to resolving these problems. Although a multidimensional foreign policy with greatly expanded trade with the Third World offered benefits, Turkey's dependence on its main alliance partners remained central to its foreign policy. Nor was there any obviously beneficial way to change that strategic fact, even had the Turks wished to do so.

Political Prospects

Turkey's future is fraught with more than the usual uncertainties. Its political system is in transition. The return to completely normal civilian politics is proceeding, but important questions remain to be resolved before the transition will be finished. The departure from Turkey's traditional economic direction has been so sharp that the past offers little guide to the future. These challenges come at a time of increasingly rapid social change, which will test the flexibility and adaptability the Turks have customarily shown in periods of crisis.

How long the political transition will take is set in one sense by the temporary provisions in the constitution and legal structure. Most of these will go out of force by the end of 1988, although the ban on political leaders of the former parties returning to politics will not expire until late in 1992. A natural milestone in the process will be the next general elections, which are due by 1988. Ozal stands a good chance to keep his parliamentary majority in these contests, if his economic program proves relatively successful. Whoever wins, the elections will end the abnormality of having the strongest opposition parties not represented in Parliament.

The question of the role of the military is clearly among the most important issues overhanging political development. The military's lock on the presidency is likely to remain solid for some time to come, inasmuch as the function of the chief of state to be commander of the armed forces and to serve as presiding officer of the National Security Council suggests an intimate connection with the military establishment. Indeed, the wording of the constitution might even permit Evren to be elected for a second term.

As long as the regime can maintain law and order, the chances do not seem high that the senior commanders would press for direct political power. Beyond maintaining law and order, the armed forces have a strong interest in protecting national unity, ensuring a sufficient share of national income to undergird a credible defense effort, and preventing the politicization of the officer corps through civilian interference. The officers have also demonstrated their concern over egregious backsliding against Ataturk's secular reforms and over extreme bickering among the politicians threatening political paralysis. Absent such challenges, the Turkish armed forces seem unlikely to use their residual power to intervene; the senior officers, like the rest of the Turkish population, still basically appear to accept the principle that multiparty politics and elected parliaments are the sole legitimate system for governing Turkey over the longer run.

One of the issues that will be of most concern to the military is amnesty for those jailed for participation in illicit causes. About half of the over 40,000 arrested for membership in leftist, Kurdish, or rightist organizations are still in jail. The constitution prohibits relief for those who engaged in terrorist acts or sought the breakup of the Turkish state. But continuing interest even by Motherland party deputies indicates that limited pardons are eventually likely to be enacted, at least for those guilty of propaganda offenses.

Within the system there is also continuing pressure to broaden the political spectrum. Already the Prosperity party is pushing to the limits its appeal to the religiously oriented. More important may be efforts to restore the voting bloc that backed the National Action party, even if necessarily shorn of its "commando" auxiliary and not led by Turkes. Similarly, the place to the left of the Social Democracy party will attract contenders. A Democratic Left party came into being in 1985, although it seems doubtful that such an organization can win parliamentary seats.

Whether the new order will run into major difficulties probably depends in the first instance on whether there is a renewed upsurge of political violence. Politicians, however, are by now so sensitized to the consequences of failing to respond forcefully that they would probably cooperate across party lines to strengthen security. On the other hand, there is little chance of being able to go beyond resolute police action to reach a consensus on basic approaches to the root causes of violence. Given that, in view of the sanctuary and support from abroad, incidents of terrorism are likely to continue, vigilance for a long time would seem to be required.

The state of Turkey's international relationships will also influence the country's course. As in the past, the unresolved Cyprus issue poses complications to relations with Turkey's allies in general and with the United States in particular. A sharp turn in the diplomacy of this problem could cause a cycle of action and exaggerated reaction, thus engaging national pride on all sides in a destructive downturn.

Turkey also cannot escape links to the global economic structure. Not only are imports vital to the continuing operation of its economy, but Turkey will be extremely sensitive to changes in export quotas, remittances, and contracts for work abroad. Shifting world energy prices, to single out the most salient example, will have a strong, direct, and immediate impact on the Turkish scene. Although the shift to export orientation is likely to persist even under a left-of-center regime, other changes by such a government could affect Turkey's economic growth. Undoubtedly, economic policy will continue to form a central issue of Turkish political debate.

In dealing with these challenging problems, Turkey must also cope with rising social dynamism. Migrants to the city are not able to find the economic satisfaction they crave. Politicians are under increasing pressure to meet the expanding needs of the rural sector. Yet over time, rural-urban differences will narrow and eventually a truly national Turkish culture will come into being.

In this process, the competition between Western and Islamic values will grow. But, although Islam is more evident in the daily life of the city than in Ataturk's day, the elite no longer seems as threatened by Islamic practice as it was in the past. One battleground concerns dress; but that is clearly going to be a losing battle for Islam. Topless bathing is spreading, and most of the city-born generation will not follow their mothers' bundled-up style of apparel. Indeed, it seems evident overall that the main direction of change is not toward the pervasive Islamization of the elite, but toward the modernization of traditional Islamic mores of the remainder of the populace.

In sum, although Turkey faces manifold problems, there is reason for optimism. The Turks are flexible in their approaches and show an ability to try new ways when the old ones are blocked. They have the resources in talent and material to succeed in the challenging business of modernizing their society and polity. The smoothness with which they have come back from political chaos and military rule is impressive. It indicates a permanance to the commitment to develop under representative government that augurs well for the future, however many uncertainties remain.

Bibliography

For a broad survey of the current Turkish scene and its background, see George S. Harris, *Turkey: Coping with Crisis* (Boulder, Colo.: Westview Press, 1985). Stanford J. Shaw's detailed two-volume *History of the Ottoman Empire and Modern Turkey* (London: Cambridge University Press, 1976-1977) contains a mine of data on the events it chronicles. Lord Kinross (Patrick Balfour) wrote a somewhat fictionalized portrait of Turkey's great leader, including dialogue that was mostly invented, in *Ataturk: A Biography of Mustafa Kemal, Father of Modern Turkey* (New York: William Morrow & Co., 1965). The Second Republic has been studied intensively in Feroz Ahmad's *The Turkish Experiment in Democracy, 1950–1975* (Boulder, Colo.: Westview Press, 1977). The military regime that ended the Second Republic and its preparations to return to civilian rule are covered by C. H. Dodd, *The Crisis of Turkish Democracy* (North Humberside, England: Eothern Press, 1983), and in Frank Tachau, *Turkey, the Politics of Authority, Democracy, and Development* (New York: Praeger Publishers, 1984).

Richard F. Nyrop, ed., surveys physical and cultural geography in *Turkey, a Country Study* (Washington, D.C.: Government Printing Office, 1979), as does John C. Dewdney, *Turkey: An Introductory Geography* (New York: Praeger Publishers, 1971). The dynamics of population movement are analyzed by Brian W. Beeley, *Migration: The Turkish Case* (Milton Keynes: Open University Press, 1981), and the fundamental matter of women's changing roles is evaluated in Nermin Abadan-Unat, ed., *Women in Turkish Society* (Leiden: E. J. Brill, 1981).

Z. Y. Hershlag, *Turkey, the Challenge of Growth* (Leiden: E. J. Brill, 1968), is thoroughly out of date. Bertil Walstedt, *State Manufacturing Enterprise in a Mixed Economy: The Turkish Case* (Baltimore: Johns Hopkins University Press, 1980), brings the story closer to the present. For a later view, see the series of OECD surveys: *Turkey* (Paris: OECD, 1984). Ergun Ozbudun and Aydin Ulusan, eds., *The Political Economy of Income Distribution in Turkey* (New York: Holmes & Meier, 1980), argue that growing inequities in income distribution may be incompatible with participatory democracy.

For aspects of recent politics, see Ergun Ozbudun, *Social Change and Political Participation in Turkey* (Princeton, N.J.: Princeton University Press, 1976); Binaz Toprak, *Islam and Political Development in Turkey* (Leiden: E. J. Brill, 1981); and the U.S. Senate, Committee on the Judiciary, Subcommittee on Security and Terrorism, *Terrorism, the Turkish Experience* (Washington, D.C.: Government Printing Office, 1981).

Military developments are surveyed in Kemal H. Karpat, "Turkish Democracy at an Impasse: Ideology, Party Politics and the Third Military Intervention," *International Journal of Turkish Studies* 2 no. 1 (Spring-Summer 1981), pp. 1–43. For a discussion of foreign policy see George S. Harris, *Troubled Alliance: Turkish-American Problems in Historical Perspective, 1945–1971* (Washington, D.C.: American Enterprise Institute, 1972). Decisionmaking is considered in Ferenc A. Vali, *Bridge Across the Bosporus: The Foreign Policy of Turkey* (Baltimore: Johns Hopkins Press, 1971). For a more recent treatment, see U.S. House of Representatives, Committee on Foreign Affairs, *Turkey's Problems and Prospects: Implications for U.S. Interests* (Washington, D.C.: Government Printing Office, 1980).

4

Islamic Republic of Iran

David E. Long

On April 1, 1979, Ayatollah Rouhallah Khomeini announced the creation of the Islamic Republic of Iran. Thus ended a dynasty in power a little over 50 years and a monarchical form of government stretching back 2,500 years in Persian history. The root causes of the Iranian revolution will be debated for some time to come. What is beyond debate is that the downfall of the monarchy was the result of a bona fide, grass-roots, social as well as political revolution and not the more typical coup engineered by a small group, usually of military officers, that generally spells the end of a Middle Eastern regime. In a very real sense, the Islamic Republic is history in the making. While thoroughly Persian in its historical, ethnic, and political antecedents, it is also the first and as yet only regime representing the new strain of militant Islamic fundamentalism that has gained adherence throughout the Muslim world. As such, Iran will be an important country to watch for some time to come.

Historical Background

In the first half of the sixth century B.C., Cyrus the Great united the Medes and the Persians into the first great Persian Empire. Cyrus and successive rulers of the Achaemenid dynasty ushered in a golden age of Persian civilization. Persian culture, its Zoroastrian religion, its statecraft and military science all left an indelible imprint on the course of ancient history. The carved stone wall friezes at Persepolis attest to the magnificence of the Persian Empire, which stretched from present-day Afghanistan to Egypt and Anatolia.

The Achaemenids were beset with wars against the Greeks. In 490 B.C., they suffered a major defeat at Marathon and ten years later were defeated again at Salamis. Finally, the dynasty was overthrown by Alexander the Great, who defeated the Persian army at Arbelia in 331 B.C. and burned the capital at Persepolis. Alexander, who regarded himself as the head of the Persian Empire, began the first period of alien imperial rule that was to alternate with native Persian rule down to modern times.

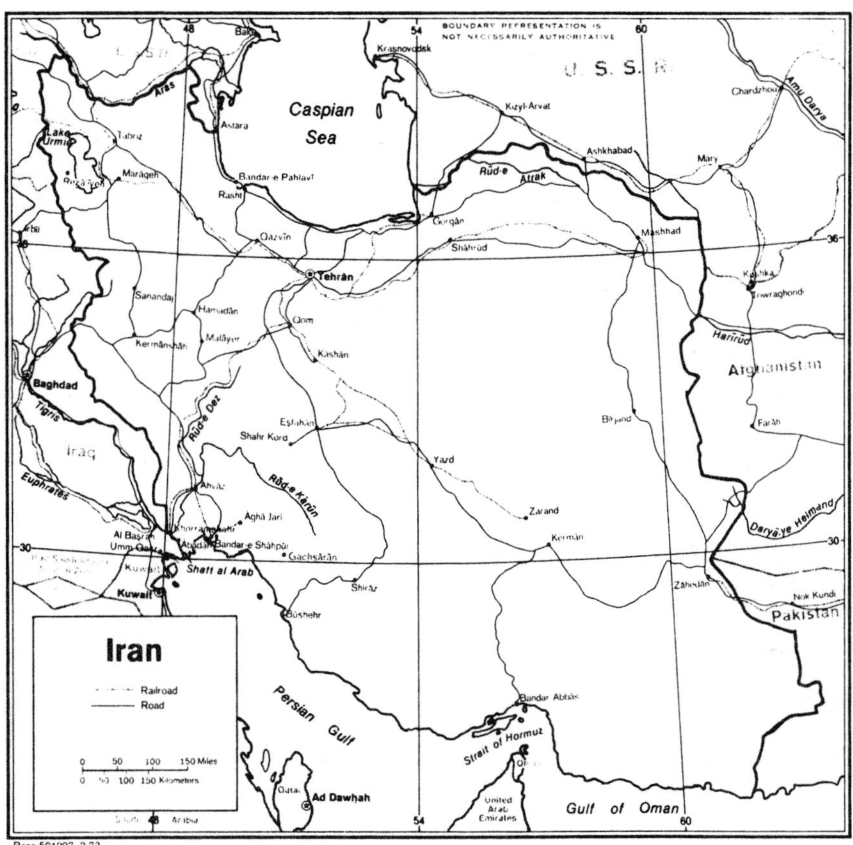

After the death of Alexander, his empire was divided among his generals. Seleucus became heir to Persia, founding the Seleucid dynasty. This dynasty ruled until 247 B.C., when it gave way to the Parthian Empire of the Arsacids, who ruled for nearly 500 years.

In A.D. 22, another Persian dynasty, the Sassanids, came to power. Although never reaching the glory and power of the Achaemenids, the Sassanids (who were also from the region of Fars) restored Zoroastrianism and made great strides in civil administration. As with past dynasties, its chief military threat was from the west—in this case, Byzantium. So exhausted were the Sassanids by their numerous wars with Byzantines that when the Arab hordes came surging out of the desert, propagating the new religion, Islam, Persia was like a ripe plum free for the taking. In A.D. 642, the Arabs defeated the Persian army at the battle of Nehavend. The empire was dismembered and ruled from Damascus and later Baghdad by various Arab and Persian provincial governors. Zoroastrianism was banished and Islam introduced as the state religion.

In some respects, the Persians conquered the Arabs as much as they themselves were conquered. With the transfer of the caliphate from Damascus to Baghdad in A.D. 750, Persian culture became a major influence on Arab-Muslim civilization, which was then reaching its zenith. With the decline of the Abbasid Empire, Seljuk Turks made their appearance in the north, introducing a system of feudal land tenure and civil administration to Persia. The Arab period came to an end in the thirteenth century with the Mongol invasions under Hulagu Khan, who sacked Baghdad in 1258. For the next 250 years, Persia was again under foreign rule.

Modern Persia originated with the rise of the Safavids in the sixteenth century. Under Ismail Safavi (r. 1502–1524), the country reemerged with the same general boundaries that exist today, although some territories were lost to Russian conquests in the eighteenth and nineteenth centuries. Ismail made Shi'a Islam the state religion. The Safavid dynasty also introduced a new golden age that reached its apogee under Shah Abbas I the Great (r. 1558–1629). Isfahan, the Safavid capital, became one of the most beautiful cities in the Middle East.

The Safavids remained in power until 1750. Following an interregnum under Karim Khan Zand (r. 1750–1779), the Qajar dynasty came to power at the end of the century. It remained in power until it was replaced by the recent shah's father in 1925. The Qajars, however, were weak, and their reign was characterized by intrigue and foreign domination.

During the nineteenth and first half of the twentieth centuries, Persia became a pawn of great-power rivalries. For most of this period, Russia and Britain were the two main antagonists. Since the time of Peter the Great, the Russians had desired a warm-water port on the Persian Gulf. The British interest in Persia stemmed from its desire to protect its imperial lines of communication with India. The British desired a relatively strong and independent Persia as a buffer against Russian southern expansionism but did not, however, wish to add Iran to their imperial domain.

In the early nineteenth century, Napoleonic France threatened British hegemony in the area by seeking political and economic concessions from the shah. There ensued a four-way series of intrigues involving Britain, Russia, France, and Persia. The Congress of Vienna ended the French threat, but soon thereafter Russia extracted from Persia territories to and beyond the Aras River. For the next several decades, Russia expanded southward down the east side of the Caspian Sea, touching off several crises involving Britain, Persia, and Afghanistan. In the meantime, the British sought commercial advantages. In 1872, a naturalized British businessman-adventurer, Baron de Reuter, obtained a sweeping concession from Nasir ed-Din Shah. Under Russian pressure it was canceled, but a British-owned Imperial Bank of Persia was chartered with exclusive rights to issue bank notes. The Russians, however, from whom Persian rulers had borrowed heavily for their personal extravagances, obtained in return the right to collect customs duties over much of Persia.

The most important concession of all was obtained by an Australian. On May 28, 1901, Alfred M. Marriot signed an agreement with Shah

Muzafaar ed-Din on behalf of an Australian financier, William Knox D'Arcy, which granted D'Arcy the first Middle Eastern oil concession. In January 1908 oil was discovered, and in the following April D'Arcy's interests were reorganized as the Anglo-Persian Oil Company (APOC). The strategic importance of oil was just being felt. When Winston Churchill became first lord of the admiralty in 1911, the Royal Navy was rapidly converting from coal to oil. Churchill, aware that Britain had no oil resources anywhere in the empire, set about to acquire some. On June 14, 1914, barely two months before World War I broke out, Churchill passed an act through Parliament authorizing the British government to purchase a 51 percent controlling interest in APOC. In 1935, APOC was renamed the Anglo-Iranian Oil Company (AIOC). When Iran subsequently nationalized its oil in 1951, the name was changed to British Petroleum (BP).

Domestic Persian politics during the first decade of the twentieth century were exceptionally turbulent. Not only were the Qajar shahs weak and despotic, but a movement of political liberalism gained a hold on the intelligentsia and growing middle class. In 1906, the newly formed Democratic party organized riots in Tehran, the capital, that ultimately forced Muhammad Ali Shah to grant a Western-styled constitution and a parliament (Majlis). Muhammad Ali Shah repudiated the constitution in 1908, but in the following year he was forced to abdicate in favor of his minor son, Ahmad, who restored the constitution.

By that time the clouds of war were already gathering over Europe. Britain and Russia, long rivals in Persia, found themselves allied against Imperial Germany. When World War I broke out, the young and ineffectual Shah Ahmad could not maintain Persia's declared neutrality. Turkish, British, and Russian troops were active inside Persia, and German agents were successful in stirring up tribal unrest.

By the war's end, Persia's internal affairs were in chaos. The Russian menace, however, had receded at least temporarily as a result of the Russian revolution. Soviet troops on the Caspian did back a Persian rebel leader, Kuchik Khan, in proclaiming a republic of Gilan, but the troops were withdrawn following a Soviet-Iranian treaty of friendship in February 1921. The British also made a bid for primacy in Persia, but, after failing in 1919 to obtain a treaty guaranteeing them that position, they began to withdraw the troops that had been stationed there during the war.

In February 1921 the commander of the Persian Cossack Division, Reza Shah Pahlevi, and a young nationalist intellectual, Zia ed-Din Tabatabai, engineered a coup. Reza Shah became minister of war and commander-in-chief and Zia became prime minister. By 1923, however, Reza Shah split with Zia and forced him into exile, assuming the premiership himself. Soon after, he forced Shah Ahmad to take a "long vacation" in Europe, and in 1925 was himself proclaimed "shah-in-shah" (king of kings).

Reza Shah was a very astute and farsighted politician. Working his way up through the ranks of the Cossack Division, he engineered the dismissal of its Russian officers corps in 1920, temporarily used British officers to fill the gap, then converted the force to an all-Persian unit. From this base, he rapidly moved up, ultimately becoming the shah.

Having first set out to pacify the country, Reza Shah then turned to internal reform. In this endeavor, he wished to emulate his contemporary, Kemal Ataturk, the great reformer and creator of modern Turkey. Although Reza Shah's reforms never reached the scope of Ataturk's, they were impressive in their own right. He began to link the country through modern communications and was particularly proud of the entirely locally financed trans-Iranian railroad, which was completed in 1939. In education, he laid the groundwork for a modern school system and set up the Iranian Academy of Literature to purge the language of foreign, and particularly Arabic, influences. To reflect this new mood, he changed the Hellenistic name of Persia to Iran (meaning Aryan) in 1935.

In the field of law, Reza Shah introduced the French judicial system, challenging the reactionary religious establishment's hold on the legal system through Islamic law. He did not provoke an open confrontation, however, and explicitly championed Islam as the state religion. In fact, reformer though he was, Reza Shah was no democrat. He did not believe democratic institutions could work in Iranian society and admired efficient, benevolent government administered from the top, as he thought was the case in Nazi Germany. His affinity with the Germans (who before World War I had provided Iranian nationalists with a great-power alternative to the British and the Russians) ultimately led to his downfall. For the Allies, Iran was the only practical route of resupply to the Soviets. Thus, when he refused to accede to Allied demands to expel German expatriates in 1941, the British and Soviets forced him to abdicate in favor of his son, Muhammad Reza. For Iran, the abdication required a total reassessment of its foreign relations. At the war's end, Iran turned to the United States as its major great-power ally. For the rest of Muhammad Reza Shah's reign, the United States remained his foremost ally.

Muhammad Reza Shah's reign began inauspiciously with his father's abdication. In 1953 he weathered a severe threat from Prime Minister Muhammad Mossadeq, who attempted to seize control of the country. In May 1951 Mossadeq, backed by Iranian nationalists, had nationalized the country's oil resources. AIOC immediately threatened to sue any company that bought Iranian oil. Lacking the technical expertise to operate the oil fields, and with world marketing in the hands of the oil companies, Iran witnessed an abrupt reduction in oil production. As government oil revenues dried up, Mossadeq soon began to encounter discontent. He became increasingly more dictatorial as prime minister.

In July 1953 Mossadeq dissolved the Majlis (the lower house of Parliament) and in August tried but failed to seize all powers of the government. On August 12, Reza Shah had ordered his dismissal and had appointed General Fazzollah Zahedi in his stead. Mossadeq defied the order and arrested the messenger that delivered it; thereupon, the shah and his family fled the country.

In the following days, however, military units loyal to the shah plotted a counter coup with the covert support, it is widely believed, of the United States. On August 18, the loyalists attacked, and, after a brief but sharp fight in Tehran, defeated military units loyal to Mossadeq. The next day, General Zahedi, who had been in hiding, reemerged to take over the government. On August 20, Mossadeq surrendered, and a few days later the shah returned, ending a period of strife in Iranian political history that was to be a harbinger for events that would occur a quarter century later.

From then until the Iranian revolution, Iran remained closely tied to the United States and the West. It joined the Baghdad Pact in 1955 (later CENTO) and looked to the United States as its major arms supplier.

Iran's oil resources remained nationalized, under the control of the National Iranian Oil Company (NIOC). In 1954, an agreement was worked out in Washington and London whereby Iran agreed to pay compensation to AIOC (renamed British Petroleum or BP), and a consortium of seven international oil companies was created to run former AIOC operations in the country. BP held 40 percent of the stock in the consortium; Royal Dutch Shell had 14 percent; Compagnie Francaise de Petrols held 6 percent; and Jersey Standard, California Standard, Mobil, Gulf, and Texaco each had 8 percent. In reality, the consortium operated very much the way companies with concessions in the region did, and under similar comparable financial terms. However, when other Middle Eastern oil-producing countries sought to take ownership of their oil resources in the 1970s, Iran had already done so.

During the 1960s the shah launched his own reform program, known as the White Revolution. The program was originally announced in late 1961, with land reform as the central focus. In January 1962, after ceding all his own personally held land to the nation through the Pahlevi Foundation, the shah decreed the Land Reform Act, which was to give land tenure to the largely landless peasants. A year later, the shah's reform program was submitted to public referendum as the first six Points for Progress of the Revolution of the Shah and the People: land reform, nationalization of forest lands, sale of equity in state-owned factories to the private sector to raise revenues for land reform, provision for sharing with the workers 20 percent of the net profits of industrial establishments, emancipation of women, and creation of a literacy corps. By 1978 thirteen additional points had been added, including the creation of the Health Corps, the Development and Agricultural Extension Corps, and an equity corps for legal aid. Other points called for nationalization and development of water resources, urban and rural reconstruction, and reform of the civil service.

In 1967 the shah's long-awaited and often-delayed coronation took place. After crowning himself, he crowned Queen Farah, the first time in Iranian-Persian history that a woman had been so honored. This event, however, marked the pinnacle of the shah's power. By 1977 economic and social conditions had begun seriously to deteriorate, and opposition to the regime began to mount. Religious sentiment, led by the exiled Shi'ite religious leader Ayatollah Rouhallah Khomeini, spurred large-scale political unrest. In an attempt to counter discontent, the shah relaxed somewhat the tight grip of the government over the people and intensified a campaign against corruption in high places, which had become a major issue.

These moves, however, did not satisfy growing discontent with the shah. Antigovernment demonstrations broke out in Qom on January 9, 1978, setting the stage for the growing political turmoil that was to bring down the shah a year later. Demonstrations marking the end of a forty-day period of mourning for those killed in the previous riots provided the impetus for continued strife.

As the situation deteriorated, the shah's efforts to placate the people became more desperate. In June, he dismissed General Nemetollah Nassiri, head of the dreaded SAVAK, the secret police. His efforts, however, were too little and too late. On August 19, at least 377 people perished in Abadan when an arsonist, suspected of being a part of the Muslim opposition, set fire to the Rex theater. Unrest followed, and on August 27 Prime Minister Amouzegar was replaced by Jafar Sharif Emami. Finally, after massive demonstrations on September 7 and 8, martial law was proclaimed.

A semblance of order was restored with martial law but proved to be only the calm before the storm. In November Sharif Emami was replaced as prime minister by General Gholam Reza Azhari, but the latter's government survived only into December. The month of December 1978 roughly coincided with the Islamic lunar month of Muharram, held particularly holy by Shi'a Muslims. Popular emotions rose to a fever pitch. Last-minute efforts by the shah to meet with opposition leaders failed. Rioting again broke out that virtually shut down the oil industry by December 27.

As the year ended, Shahpur Bakhtiar, a leader in the opposition National Front (a descendant of Mossadeq's political organization), was asked to form a cabinet. The Bakhtiar cabinet, sworn in on January 6, 1979, was destined to be the last one under the monarchy. The shah left the country on January 16, and on February 1 Ayatollah Khomeini returned triumphantly from Paris, where he had been in exile. On February 5 Khomeini announced the creation of a new provisional government under Mehdi Bazargan, who was sworn in the following week. The demise of the monarchy was completed six weeks later. Following a plebiscite on March 30, Khomeini announced the creation of an Islamic republic on April 1.

The Iranian revolution is virtually unique in contemporary Middle East history. Most so-called revolutions in the region are really coups, usually by the military. Far from popular movements, they are generally imposed from the top down. The Iranian revolution was truly a grass-roots movement, spreading from the bottom up and gaining support from every class of society. The causes were many—social, political, and economic.

Ironically, while many in the West decried the shah's huge military expenditures, his economic and social development expenditures were probably more destabilizing. In his efforts to create a Western European–styled industrial society and economy, the shah invested far more in the domestic economy than it could absorb in terms of increased productivity. The result was massive inflation, creation of noncompetitive industries, and the destruction of the agricultural sector as peasants rushed to the cities. The social dislocations of a traditional Islamic society colliding headlong with Western secular influences were equally destabilizing. What kept the whole system afloat were oil revenues. When the oil glut of the mid-1970s reduced revenues and forced the government to adopt austerity measures, Iranians from all walks of life became disaffected with the shah.

As the process of disaffection intensified, the charismatic Ayatollah Khomeini, whose fiery anti-shah sermons were being sneaked into Iran, provided the people with an ideological rationale and a political focus that transformed disaffection into revolution. Thus Khomeini provided a moral justification for overthrowing the shah's secular regime as well as for opposing all Western, particularly U.S., influences as secular and hence immoral. The xenophobia that was unleashed quickly built up into an irresistible force that ultimately toppled the monarchy.

The groups that initially took over the reins of power had little in common other than their mutual distaste for the Pahlevi regime and all who were associated with it. In broadest terms, the loci of political power and organization were divided between the secular nationalists and the clerics. The secular nationalists encompassed various groups including the National Front and its various affiliates, which were political heirs of Mossadeq. For the most part they were Western-trained and generally left of center in political orientation; but, most of all, they were nationalists. Also included among the secularists were the Marxist Tudeh party (the Communist party of Iran) and the Fedayeen-i-Khalq (the Organization of the People's Devoted Guerrillas). The clerics, represented in Khomeini's Iranian Republic party (IRP), were very parochial, generally ignorant of the outside world, stridently conservative in their adherence to the tenants of Shi'a Islam, and more loyal to the Islamic concept of nation than to the more recent Western concept of nationalism. Distinctions between the two groups were not all that clearcut, however. Many Western-trained Iranians held strong religious convictions; and in the case of one guerrilla group, the Mujahidin-i-Khalq, its ideology was an amalgam of Islam and Marxism.

Almost from the start, the clerics under Khomeini began to isolate the secular political groups and to consolidate power in their own hands. The process of consolidation was uneven, however; it was also complicated by the hostage crisis, which the Islamic radicals eventually used to gain full control of the political system. On November 4, 1979, militant Iranian students occupied the U.S. Embassy, taking its personnel as hostages. After long, difficult bargaining and an abortive U.S. rescue effort, an agreement was signed in Algiers on January 19, 1981, calling for their release as well as settling outstanding claims of U.S. and European banks and firms against Iran. As a parting expression of spite, Iran waited until after President Reagan's inauguration to release the prisoners, thus denying outgoing President Carter the opportunity to receive them officially.

During virtually the entire period of the hostage crisis, Iran operated without a formal government. Provisional Prime Minister Mehdi Bazargan resigned on November 5, and presidential elections were not held until January 25, 1980. By this time, the National Front had lost out entirely, and the remaining secular politicians were clearly supporters of Khomeini's Islamic revolution. One of them, Abu al-Hasan Bani Sadr, was elected president. In the months that followed, however, Bani Sadr became engaged in a power struggle with the militant clerics.

On September 22, 1980, Iraq invaded Iran, beginning the protracted Iran-Iraq War. With the Iranian armed forces in total disarray in the wake of the revolution, Bani Sadr, as commander-in-chief, spent a great deal of time reorganizing the armed forces, including many visits to the front. Politically, it was a no-win situation for him. To the degree that armed forces were successful against Iraq, his political rivals complained to Khomeini that he was attempting to build up an independent power base; at the same time, Iran's initial failure to drive Iraq from Iranian soil was also blamed on the president. In June 1981, the Majlis (Parliament) instituted impeachment proceedings against Bani Sadr. With IRP control, the outcome was never in doubt, and even before Khomeini formally ordered his dismissal, Bani Sadr went into hiding. On July 28, in the company of Mujahidin leader Massud Rajavi, the ex-president escaped to France in an air force plane flown by Colonel Behzad Moezzi. With his departure, the clerics were in complete control.

Ousting the lay politicians was not the only step by the clergy in consolidating power. At the same time, any clerics who dared voice opposition to government policies were also suppressed. The most noted was the Grand Ayatollah Muhammad Kazem Shariatmadari, whose opposition to the shah and religious reputation both rivaled, if not exceeded, those of Khomeini. It was Shariatmadari who persuaded the shah to spare Khomeini's life after a religious uprising in 1963, and it was from his native Tabriz that the first major anti-shah uprising occurred in February 1978, beginning the process of the shah's downfall. Nevertheless, as his public concern for the increasingly autocratic activities of the government increased, Shariatmadari was ruthlessly silenced and, until 1985, was under virtual house arrest. Other ayatollahs suffered similar fates. Indeed, as the clerics succeeded in institutionalizing their rule, it was the most politicized rather than the most distinguished clergy, from Khomeini on down, who survived as wielders of power. The latter retain considerable potential influence, however, and will be an important factor in the succession struggle when Khomeini leaves the scene.

Political Environment

Population and Social Structure

Accurate statistical data on Iran since the revolution has been extremely difficult to obtain. By the mid-1980s, the estimated population exceeded 40 million, and the median age was believed to have dropped to under twenty years. In any event, it is a young population with the potential to continue the population explosion of the past two decades (over 3 percent population increase per year).

The process of urbanization is also continuing apace. At the turn of the century, the rural population accounted for roughly 80 percent of the total. Now greater Tehran alone has an estimated population of over 8 million.

Chaotic economic and political conditions and the continuing Iran-Iraq War have doubtless had a major demographic impact on Iran, but in the absence of reliable data it is next to impossible to know precisely how great the impact has been. For example, the war has devastated the oil-rich Khuzistan province and has been responsible for hundreds of thousands of Iranian casualties. The rural migration to the cities has also continued, despite government measures to stop it. By 1984, stemming the rural migration had become a major government concern.

Iranian society is extremely heterogeneous in that it is divided both by class structure, occupation, and income, and by ethnic identification. Slightly less than half of the population is composed of native Persian speakers, although Persian is the official language. With the emphasis on Persian language, history and culture in the schools, public media, and government operations, Persian cultural predominance is gaining ground. Nevertheless, the hold of non-Persian ethnic identification remains strong and has been given added impetus by the overthrow of the monarchy.

In the northwest, Turkic-speaking Azeris of Azerbaijan still cling to their old cultural patterns, and in the regional capital, Tabriz, Azeri is heard even in government offices, where anything but Persian would normally be frowned upon. The Azeris are kinspeople of those in neighboring Soviet Azerbaijan, and in 1946 the Soviets tried unsuccessfully to gain control of the Iranian Azeris through the creation of a so-called Azerbaijan Republic with Tabriz as the capital. On the east side of the Caspian Sea live Turkomen tribes who also have blood ties to the north in the Soviet Union. The Qashqa'is constitute the other major Turkic-speaking ethnic group. Their tribal homeland is located in the southern Zagros Mountains.

Two important ethnic tribal groups actually speak dialects of Persian. The Bakhtiaris inhabit the central Zagros near Isfahan, and their cousins the Lurs are located immediately to the west along the Iraqi border. To the north of the Lurs are the Kurds, whose homeland spills over into Iraq, Turkey, and the Soviet Union. The Kurds have a long, proud ethnic heritage, and, unlike most Iranians, they are Sunni Muslims. The Soviets also tried to promote a Kurdish "republic" after World War II. Prior to 1975, the shah's support of Iraqi Kurds in their demands for political autonomy had been a major irritant in Iraqi-Iranian relations. Although this support was withdrawn, the potential for both countries to become involved in Kurdish irredentist movements across the border remains. Within Iran, the collapse of the monarchy also rekindled irredentist Kurdish aspirations, leading to several incidents of violence.

In the oil-rich province of Khuzistan, at the head of the Persian Gulf, and in the region southward along the Iranian coast, most of the population is Arabic speaking and generally Sunni Muslim. When Reza Shah first came to power, one of his first tasks was to curb the semi-independent powers of Shaykh Khazal of Muhammara, whose feudal domain included Khuzistan. There remain today occasional cries of irredentism by Iraqi-supported local dissidents who call the area Arabistan. Though a potential cause of concern in Tehran, their political significance is virtually nil. Because much of the fighting in the Iran-Iraq War has centered in Khuzistan, the area has witnessed significant devastation, but the population's loyalty to Tehran appears to be relatively intact.

A final major ethnic area is located in the far southeast, where Baluchistan spills over into neighboring Pakistan and Afghanistan. The Baluchis, who inhabit this barren, hard-bitten land, are known for their warlike qualities and are often contracted as mercenaries by neighboring armies. For centuries, Baluchis have crossed the Gulf of Oman to settle along Oman's Batinah coast. More recently, they have been attracted by relatively good wages as manual laborers in the oil-rich but labor-short Arab shaykhdoms of the lower Gulf. The Baluchis are also Sunnis.

There are some smaller groups to be noted as well. The Jewish community, which dates from the fifth century B.C., is mostly urban and comparatively prosperous. There are small communities of Armenian Christians and Assyrians that date from the beginning of the Christian era. Zoroastrians, who still follow the pre-Islamic religion of Persia, are also found in small numbers.

Social class structure in Iran is complex. At the top of the social order is the elite class. Family ties continue to be a major source of Iran's social order, headed by the so-called first forty families. The actual number is much larger and is augmented by perhaps 150 to 200 prominent provincial families. Although changes in family fortunes have both added and removed families from the political elite over the years, there has been an impressive continuity among the group. As Iranian development programs have taken hold in the last ten to fifteen years, however, the need for top-level skilled technocrats and the rapidly expanding educational system have made membership in the elite more competitive. It is increasingly possible for the most humbly born Iranians with sufficient skill and ability to aspire to positions of major influence.

The middle and working classes are for the most part traditionalist, religious, and conservative in outlook. There is also a growing modern class of new middle-level technocrats who, though playing an increasingly important role in the country's economic development, have not yet become a major political factor. Those young professionals who do show an interest in politics generally aspire to join the elite.

Among the traditional middle class are the bazaar shopkeepers, the middle- and lower-level bureaucrats, and the Shi'a Islamic clergy, or ulama. A great majority of the population is Shi'ite, the established religion of Iran.

Broadening the educational system has introduced modern concepts and ideas to this group, but old ideas die very slowly. In fact, Shi'ism has undergone a renaissance that became a primary contributing factor to the overthrow of the shah. By the mid-1970s the Shi'a leadership, called ayatollahs, began rapidly to expand the number of their followers while preaching a return to the fundamentals of Islam. Their often violent opposition to the social development programs of the shah helped undermine the stability of the regime. Ayatollah Khomeini, exiled in 1963, was considered by many to be the spiritual leader of the Shi'ite community and was venerated by the mass of Shi'ite faithful. It was under the aegis of Khomeini that the new Islamic republic was created.

The working classes in Iran include peasant farmers, tribesmen, artisans, servants, and a small but growing industrial labor force. Farmers still constitute a major element in Iranian society, with 40 percent of the population engaged in agriculture. In recent years, however, thousands of peasant farmers have swelled the populations of the cities, particularly Tehran, further exacerbating social and urban problems. Living conditions in the cities can be harsh for the working class, particularly for those flocking in from the countryside, but, like the middle class, the peasants are basically conservative in outlook and, in more tranquil times, are generally apolitical.

One other group that has a great influence on politics is composed of university students, teachers, and other intellectuals. Though not directly participating in the political process, they are an articulate indicator of political and economic conditions generally. Historically, those with a higher education (in earlier times, the monopoly of the elite) could expect prestigious jobs on the completion of their studies. As the number of graduates increases each year, however, competition for jobs is becoming more intense. In fact, one of the greatest challenges confronting the government in the coming years will be to assimilate effectively the graduating students and highly skilled and educated professional classes into the political process.

A large part of social intercourse in Iran revolves around highly unstructured and informal groups of men of roughly the same age, background, and social status. These groups, called *dowrahs* (circles), are essentially social in nature. However, many of the day-to-day decisions of business and government both in high places and low are made under the aegis of a *dowrah*. The institution of *dowrahs*, therefore, tends to reinforce further the high degree of personalization in Iranian society.

One great unanswered question concerns the degree to which the Islamic revolution and the ongoing Iran-Iraq War will permanently alter Iranian society. In all probability, the society will not change very greatly or very rapidly. Basic social patterns tend to change slowly over time. There is no doubt, however, that short-term effects will be felt. The greatest casualty appears to be the emerging middle class, the very group upon which the shah had hoped to depend in pursuing his White Revolution. Many of this group either fled the revolution or dared not return. By 1984, the government, faced with an acute shortage of technicians and skilled manpower, had begun a policy of attracting emigres back to Iran, but with little success. Ironically, the shortage is to some degree assuaged by the virtual stagnation of the modern sectors of the economy.

Economic Conditions

The shah's dream of quickly and forcefully creating a modernized, industrial state was unrealizable. Even if government investment policies had not undermined the agricultural sector, had not created a noncompetitive industrial sector and, through overinvestment, had not produced massive inflation, and even if the softening in the oil market had not forced austerity, the society was too lacking in a work ethic and entrepreneurship to sustain rapid economic development in a basically freemarket economy.

However bad the condition of the economy during the last days of the shah, it has continued to deteriorate under the Islamic Republic. In the wake of the Iranian revolution, world oil prices shot up as consumers feared a cutoff of Iraqi and Iranian oil. Iranian production quickly recovered, albeit not to previous levels of around 5 million bpd, but have remained at between 2 to 3 million bpd. Unfortunately, however, the oil glut of the 1980s softened the price, lowering Iran's real oil income. This occurred at a time when the Iran-Iraq War had increased Iran's revenue needs and also, due to a loss of refinery capacity, actually forced it to import refined products at the same time it was exporting crude oil. When combined with the exodus of technical expertise, the Islamicization of the banking system, and the decline in government services, the overall decline in the Iranian economy has been so severe that it could take decades to reverse.

Political Structure

The political structure of the Islamic Republic is still emerging. Whatever its final form might be, it is clear that the political institutions, as they are evolving, are a direct result of attempts to put Shi'ite political theory into practice. Islam makes no distinction between church and state. All people are under divine (i.e., Islamic) law. Shi'ite Islam, in particular, has always found it difficult to rationalize secular rule, ultimately recognizing no authority but that of God. The Ja'fari, or "Twelver," sect, the major sect of Iran, believes that Imam Muhammad al-Muntazar, twelfth in line from the Caliph Ali, mystically disappeared about A.D. 873. Ultimate political authority is vested in this "hidden imam," or *mahdi,* who is expected to return one day.

One school of thought claims that until the hidden imam's return, all his secular as well as spiritual responsibilities can be carried out by the Shi'ite clergy, generally known as *mujtahids,* meaning interpreters of the law (literally, those who exercise *ijtihad,* or the application of human reason to the application of Islamic law). The most distinguished *mujtahids* are accorded by acclamation the title of ayatollah, and if there is one who is clearly without equal, he is recognized as the *marja-i-taqlid* (source of emulation). According to this school of thought, such a man is looked to as the principal spiritual and secular leader as, in effect, an agent of the hidden imam. The concept of a principal theologian-jurist is termed *vilayat-i-faqih* and was espoused by Khomeini and other political activists among the lesser clergy.

The other school of thought believes that the clergy should concentrate on maintaining the purity of Islam within government rather than seeking directly to rule. It was the predominant school of thought before Khomeini and is even today espoused by most of the leading senior clergy, including Ayatollah Shariatmadari. It had also found expression in the constitution of 1906, which provided for guardianship over secular legislation by the clergy.

The constitution of 1979 (ratified in a referendum on December 2 and 3) incorporated the guardianship theory in Principle 91, which sets up a Council of Guardians to ensure that all laws passed by the legislature conform to Islamic law. Nevertheless, the maximalist view predominates in the constitution. Principle 5 embraces the *vilayat-i-faqih* concept, stating that in the absence of the twelfth imam, "he will be represented in the Islamic Republic of Iran as religious leader and imam of the people by an honest, virtuous, well-informed, courageous, efficient administrator and religious jurist, enjoying the confidence of the majority of the people as a leader." This principle gave Ayatollah Khomeini constitutional legitimacy as well as the personal acceptance of the vast majority of the population as the supreme leader of Iran. All other political institutions were clearly subordinate to him.

The other institutions provided in the constitution represent an amalgam of Islamic and Western, generally French, political theory. They include a president, a National Consultative Assembly of 270 members, and an independent judiciary under a High Council of the Judiciary. As Islamic law is the law of the land, the judiciary was dominated by the clergy from the start. Zoroastrians, Jews, and Assyrian and Chaldean Christians, all recognized by Islam as "Peoples of the Book," are also granted representation in the legislature. The constitution also refers directly to the armed forces, which are to be wholly Iranian, and legitimizes the Revolutionary Guard, or Pasdaran, which sprang up during the revolution. Private individuals, on the other hand, are denied the right to bear arms.

Political Dynamics

As more and more components of the original coalition that overthrew the monarchy fell out with the new regime and ultimately came to oppose it, there was hope in some quarters that, particularly following the death of the octogenarian Khomeini, the rule of the clerics would collapse. But the opposition is too splintered and too disorganized and the regime too well organized for an immediate collapse to occur. The only other group that could possibly topple the regime is the armed forces, which are currently too heavily engaged in the Iran-Iraq War to consider such a move.

The consolidation of power under the clergy does not equate with cohesion, however. Not only are a number of the most distinguished clerics out of sympathy with the regime, but there are different factions within the ruling group as well. So long as Khomeini remains active, his charisma and force of personality can maintain unity within the government. Yet Khomeini is by inclination and background not a strong administrator. Islam is basically a legal system, and Khomeini sees himself more in the role of chief judge than in that of chief executive. It is a role totally consonant with *vilayat-i-faqih*. Under Khomeini, the clerics share power in informal coalitions, deriving power from their control over the legislature, the judicial system, and the Pasdaran. The latter is not a tightly disciplined force but, rather, a collection of local armies loyal to particular clerics.

Because of Khomeini's age, the question of his successor must be a constant consideration in Iranian politics. According to the constitution, if a single leader does not emerge, Khomeini would be succeeded by a leadership council. Several candidates have been informally mentioned, including Ayatollahs Ali Rafsanjani, Speaker of the Consultative Assembly; Ali Khamanah'i, President of the Republic; and Husayn Muntaziri, Khomeini's "presumed" successor. Yet regardless of whether these or others emerge, it is not likely that Iran will or can be ruled collectively for very long. If clerical rule is to continue, a strong single leader must emerge. If one does not, the regime will decline and ultimately collapse. How long that might take, however, is anyone's guess.

Foreign Policy

Under the Islamic Republic, Iran has shown antipathy toward both the United States and the Soviet Union. The United States, particularly as a close friend of the shah, is viewed as the personification of evil—in the form of Western secularism and neo-imperialism. But the godless Marxist regime of the Soviet Union is seen in little better light. In 1984 the regime systematically executed many of the leaders of the Marxist Tudeh party in Iran. Although both superpowers are pleased with the Iranian antipathy expressed toward the other, they are both powerless to exploit or channel it in pursuit of their own interests.

At the root of republican Iran's foreign policy is a conviction of moral superiority and an avowed intention to spread its brand of morality to others. Principle 154 of the constitution asserts that Iran "will protect the struggle of the weak against the arrogant in any part of the world."

"Exporting the revolution" has been a major concern particularly to Iran's neighbors in the Gulf region, but also to the victims of Iranian-supported Shi'ite terrorism in Lebanon, the so-called Hizballah (Party of God). The Hizballah, which has its counterparts inside Iran, is an amorphous, undisciplined collection of Shi'ite terrorists, thugs, and theologues. Because it exhibits little or no organizational cohesion, one would find it next to impossible to ascribe Iranian official participation in specific Hizballah acts of terrorism beyond the general moral and material support the various groups undoubtedly receive.

Iran's militant foreign policy has been felt mainly in the Gulf area. Since the revolution began, daily Arabic broadcasts from Radio Iran have spewed out invectives against the Sunni regimes in the Gulf, aimed primarily at the Shi'ite minorities (in Iraq and Bahrain, the Shi'ites are in the majority). In December 1981, a coup attempt was staged from Iran against the ruling Al Khalifah in Bahrain. Despite these activities, however, the Iran-Iraq War has become the major arena for Iran's fanatical, doctrinaire foreign policy.

The Iran-Iraq War was initiated on September 22, 1980, by Iraq, apparently seeking to smash the Islamic revolution before it could get fully organized. The effort failed. By late 1982 the reorganized Iranian army had pushed out of Iran the Iraqi troops established to carry the war into Iraq. The Iranian success was aided to a great degree by the use of thousands of shock troops, many of them teenagers, in what amounted to suicidal attacks. Since 1982 the war settled down into a stalemate.

Iran's "terms" for ending the war are unconditional Iraqi cessation of hostilities, admission of guilt, payment of war reparations, and the demise of Saddam Hussein's Iraqi regime. In fact, the war has become for Iran and particularly for Khomeini a virtual holy war. So long as Khomeini remains in power, there is little hope that he will accept anything less than the ouster of the Baathist regime of Iraqi President Hussein in agreeing to a negotiated settlement. And so the war goes on, despite the mediation efforts of Algeria, Japan, Turkey, and other countries with access to both sides. Iran also considers the Arabian peninsula states supporting Iraq to be accessories, and one can only surmise that if the war were to end, or even merely to taper off, the threat of Iranian-supported subversive activities in the Gulf area would greatly increase.

As a result of its militant foreign policies, Iran has become extremely isolated not only in the region but throughout the world as well. If anything other than the death of Khomeini can mitigate Iranian foreign policy in the next few years, it will probably be an emerging sense that such isolation goes against Iran's national interests. Toning down its policies will probably be the reflection not of a shift in convictions, therefore, but merely of a shift in tactics.

Bibliography

Over six years after the revolution, there are still very few good books on contemporary Iran. Hassein Bashiriyeh's *The State and Revolution in Iran* (New York: St. Martin's Press, 1984) is a short, pithy description of the revolution and its impact on the Iranian state. Sepehr Zabih's *Iran Since the Revolution* (Baltimore: Johns Hopkins University Press, 1982) and Shaul Bakhash's *The Reign of the Ayatollahs: Iran and the Islamic Revolution* (New York: Basic Books, 1984) provide insightful accounts of the rise of the clerical government. Cheryl Bonard and Zalmay Khalilzad, in *The Government of God: Iran's Islamic Republic* (New York: Columbia University Press, 1984), offer a balanced, objective, and well-documented study set in an insightful theoretical context. This is a source that can be used with great benefit both by students and by serious scholars of the Iranian revolution. Another major contribution to the literature is Eric Hooglund and William R. Royce, *Triumph of the Turban*, published by the Middle East Institute in Washington, D.C., in 1985. A great deal, mostly apologia, has been written about the Iranian revolution from the diplomatic point of view. John D. Stemple's *Inside the Iranian Revolution* (Bloomington: Indiana University Press, 1981) is probably the best of this American diplomat's books. It gives an excellent overview of the unfolding revolution and of the U.S. reaction to it in an appropriate theoretical context. Anthony Parsons's *The Pride and the Fall: Iran 1974–1979* (London: Jonathan Cape, 1984) is a provocative memoire by the British ambassador of the period and provides a candid look at his own mission. One of the best, if most critical, treatments of the hostage crisis is Christos P. Ioannides's *America's Iran: Injury and Catharsis* (Lanham, Md.: University Press of America, 1984). Ioannides provides the Iranian side of the story as well as the American side.

Good theoretical works on the religious bases of the regime, or on Shi'ism in general, are hard to come by. One of the best treatments of Shi'ite political thought, though not for the casual reader, is Hamid Euagat's *Modern Islamic Political Thought* (Austin, Tex.: University of Texas Press, 1982). Farhang Rajaee's *Islamic Values and World View: Khomeini the Man, the State and International Politics* (Lanham, Md.: University Press of America, 1983) relates Shi'ism to Khomeini's political doctrine. Chapter 2 provides an excellent analysis of the concept of *vilayat-i-faqih*. For those who wish to hear directly from the source, there is Khomeini's *Islam and the Revolution*, translated and annotated by Hamid Algar (Berkeley, Calif.: Mizan Press, 1981).

Though much has been written about Iranian foreign policy, no definitive theoretical work as yet exists. In Chapter 9 of James A. Bill and Carl Leiden, *Politics in the Middle East* (Boston: Little, Brown, 1984, 2d ed.), Bill gives an excellent overview of Iran and the Gulf region, with a focus on the regime and its concept of exporting Islamic revolution. Finally, a good short treatment of Iran's war with Iraq is Stephen R. Grummon's *The Iran-Iraq War: Islam Embattled*, vol. 10, Washington Paper No. 92 (New York: Praeger Publishers, 1982).

5

Kingdom of Saudi Arabia

David E. Long

Few countries encompass so many anomalies as Saudi Arabia. A major power in international oil affairs, Arab politics, and Islamic world affairs, it has only recently begun to build a modern army commensurate with its economic power. Its rulers have spent billions of dollars on the material and social welfare of their people, yet strive to maintain a spiritually based society reflecting the earliest years of Islam. It is a country with a strong free-market philosophy, but because of its vast oil reserves and the paucity of its other resources, the Saudi economy's public sector overwhelms the private sector. It is a country dominated by the royal family, but technocrats have a major influence on policymaking. Although the leading princes are very visible, the royal family as a whole is highly secretive and avoids publicity. An indication of the complexity of the Saudi political system is that despite Saudi Arabia's prominence in world and regional affairs, it remains one of the least known and understood countries in the Middle East.

Historical Background

Early History

Saudi Arabia has the rare distinction of being named after a family. It was created in 1932 by the ruler, King Abd al-Aziz bin Abd al-Rahman Al Saud, who united the kingdoms of Najd and the Hijaz to form the kingdom of Saudi Arabia. The history of the country is basically the history of the Al Saud (House of Saud), which has ruled from the desert fastness of Najd, as central Arabia is called, for over 200 years. The founder of the dynasty was Amir Muhammad bin Saud (c. 1703–1704 to 1792), the amir (ruler) of Dir'iyyah, a small oasis town located on the Wadi Hanifah, a usually dry streambed in central Najd.

In 1744–1745, the Amir Muhammad came under the influence of a zealous religious revivalist, Muhammad bin Abd al-Wahhab, from the neighboring town of Uyainah. When Shaykh Muhammad bin Abd al-Wahhab was driven

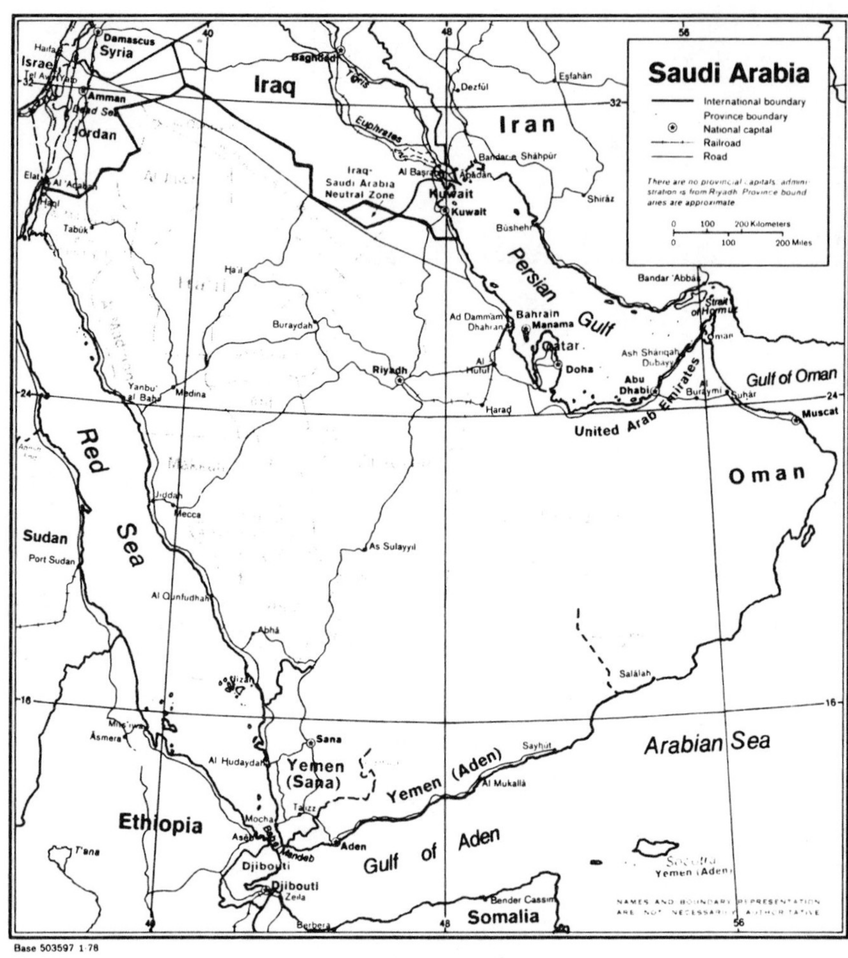

Base 503597 1-78

from his own town because of his religious beliefs, Amir Muhammad bin Saud became his patron.

The revival movement of Abd al-Wahhab was drawn from the writings of an early Islamic jurist, Ibn Taymiyyah (c. A.D. 1262–1328). It was based on the Hanbali school of Islamic jurisprudence, the most conservative of the four schools in Sunni Islam. Abd al-Wahhab stressed a return to the fundamentals of Islam and condemned many of the religious practices that had cropped up since the time of Muhammad. Calling for adherence to strict monotheism, he condemned the followers of these practices as idolators and polytheists. Abd al-Wahhab particularly condemned the practice, then in vogue, of making pilgrimages to the tombs of holy men. To this day, the followers of the revival bury their dead in unmarked graves lest their tombs become revered as religious shrines. These followers call themselves

"Muwahhidin" (Unitarians), denoting their strict monotheism. To outsiders they have become known as Wahhabis, after the name of the founder, Muhammad bin Abd al-Wahhab, although his followers rejected this name because it could possibly imply worship of Abd al-Wahhab rather than God.

Muhammad bin Abd al-Wahhab was known as the teacher, or shaykh (*shaykh* has many meanings in Arabic, including teacher, leader, ruler, and elder statesman). His descendants are still called Al al-Shaykh (House of the Shaykh), and as they still provide the religious leadership of the country, they are second in prestige in Saudi Arabia only to the Al Sauds. The spiritual fervor of the Wahhabi revival and the temporal power and statecraft of the Al Sauds proved to be a powerful combination, and by the end of the eighteenth century, Al Sauds had subdued nearly all of Najd and were preparing to expand even further.

Saudi expansion in Najd was carried out almost unnoticed by the outside world. In 1801, however, the Al Sauds and their Wahhabi warriors forced themselves into world consciousness, particularly Islamic world consciousness, when they sacked the Shi'a holy city of Karbala in southern Iraq. They destroyed the tombs of a number of holy men, including the tomb of Husayn, the grandson of the Prophet Muhammad. Husayn's large domed tomb was venerated by the Shi'as as a destination of religious pilgrimage second in importance only to Mecca and al-Madinah.

In 1806 Wahhabi forces defeated the Ottoman garrisons in the Hijaz and seized Mecca and al-Madinah. In the east, another army pushed into Oman, forcing the sultan at Muscat to pay annual tribute to the Al Sauds. Gulf sailors, newly converted to the revival, sent privateers against British and local merchant vessels, deeming the former to be nonbelievers and the latter to be heretics. Thus, in a few short years, Saudi domains had expanded from little more than an oasis to most of the Arabian peninsula.

It is interesting to speculate how far the armies of the Al Sauds would have marched had they not run into superior military technology, for it was just this kind of holy army sweeping out of Arabia that first flung the banners of Islam from Spain to Indonesia a thousand years before. The Wahhabis soon met their match, however. With the fall of the Muslim holy places of Mecca and al-Madinah, the Ottoman sultan in Constantinople was roused into action. He bid his viceroy in Egypt, Muhammad Ali, to send an army against the Wahhabis. Muhammad Ali appointed his son, Ibrahim Pasha, to lead an army dispatched to invade Najd. It took Ibrahim seven years to march through the inhospitable sands of Najd and attack the Al Saud capital of Dir'iyyah. But finally, in 1818, Dir'iyyah fell. Ibrahim laid waste to the city, whose ruins can still be seen today, cut down the palm groves, and took the amir, Abdallah bin Saud Al Saud, fourth in the line, in exile back to Cairo along with many other Al Sauds and Al al-Shaykhs. Abdallah was later sent to Constantinople, where he was ultimately beheaded. During the next four years the Ottoman-Egyptian occupiers set out to destroy the Al Sauds' base of power so that they could no longer threaten the holy cities of the Hijaz. In 1822 the Ottomans withdrew to the Hijaz after concluding that Mecca and al-Madinah were no longer under the threat of renewed Wahhabi attack. Najd was again free of foreign influence.

As the Ottoman-Egyptian garrisons in central Arabia were drawn down, several local leaders moved to fill the vacuum. One was Mishari, a brother of the last Saudi amir, who ruled briefly and unsuccessfully in 1820. In 1823–1824 a cousin, Turki bin Abdallah, consolidated power and reestablished Saudi rule. He moved the capital about twenty kilometers south of Dir'iyyah to the town of Riyadh, where it has remained the seat of the Al Sauds ever since. By the time of Turki's assassination in 1834, he had reasserted Saudi rule throughout Najd and eastward to the Gulf area.

Turki was succeeded by his son, Faysal. In 1837, however, Faysal was ousted by Khalid, brother of Amir Abdallah and Amir Mishari. With the help of the Egyptians, Khalid had Faysal exiled to Cairo. Khalid was himself overthrown in 1841 by yet another cousin, Abdallah bin Thunayan; but in 1843 Faysal escaped from Cairo and returned once again to become the undisputed ruler of Najd. During his second reign (1843–1865), Saudi leadership reached the zenith of its powers in the nineteenth century. Faysal restored peace in Najd, extended his rule to Jabal Shammar in the north and laid claim to Buraymi Oasis in Oman. This claim was the basis of a territorial dispute with Oman and Abu Dhabi that extended to the 1970s.

Faysal's death in 1865 signaled another eclipse in the fortunes of the Al Sauds. He was succeeded by his son Abdallah, but Abdallah's leadership was almost immediately challenged by a second son, Saud, who became amir in 1871. After Saud's death in 1875, Abdallah again became amir, but by this time, the Al Sauds' hold over the countryside was slipping. The eastern province (al-Hasa) was reconquered by the Ottomans in 1871, Buraymi Oasis was lost, and the Jabal Shammar tribes rose in revolt. In 1887 the Saudi state again collapsed. This time, Muhammad Ibn Rashid, amir of the Shammar, seized Najd and ruled it from the Jabal Shammar capital at al-Hayil.

A younger brother of Abdallah and Saud, Abd al-Rahman, served briefly as Rashidi governor of his family's capital at Riyadh; but failing in an abortive revolt, he was forced in 1891 to flee with his family to Kuwait, where he lived off the hospitality of the ruler, Mubarak the Great.

The rise of the Al Sauds from humiliating exile to leadership of the world's foremost oil state was due primarily to the accomplishments of Abd al-Rahman's son, Abd al-Aziz bin Abd al-Rahman Al Saud, who became known in the West as "Ibn Saud." Abd al-Aziz struck an imposing figure. Well over six feet tall and handsome, he had the natural grace and poise of a true desert aristocrat, which enabled him to deal effectively with tribal shaykh and oil executive alike. From his mother's family, the Al al-Shaykhs, he was well grounded in Islam. His prowess with the opposite sex was also legendary in the best Arabian tradition. Abd al-Aziz's true measure of greatness, however, was in his breadth of vision. Even though he did not fully comprehend the revolutionary changes that his acts would ultimately produce, he brought his country out of the desert confines of Najd to take its place in regional and world political and economic councils.

The first step on the way to recovery of the lost patrimony was to recapture Riyadh in 1902. The nearly legendary tale of how Abd al-Aziz retook Riyadh sounds like the plot for a Hollywood thriller. Having left Kuwait the previous year, the young prince and a band of forty followers stole over the city walls. Once inside the city, they lay alternately sleeping and praying all night long while waiting for the Rashidi governor, Ajlan, to emerge from his stronghold, the Mismak fortress. He slept there as a security precaution. The next morning, as Ajlan left the fortress for home, he was set upon by Abd al-Aziz and his men. Ajlan ran with his retinue back to the fortress, where a brief tussle occurred as both sides tried to pull him through the postern gate. During the retreat, Abd al-Aziz's cousin Abdallah bin Jaluwi threw a spear that landed in the gate, where the broken spear tip remains to this day. Ajlan was finally pulled through the gate, but before it could be closed, Abdallah bin Jaluwi forced his way in and slew the governor. All resistance then ended.

It took two decades from the January morning that Abd al-Aziz retook Riyadh to accomplish the conquest of the Ibn Rashids. His success was greatly facilitated by the fratricidal jealousies that split his rivals much as the Al Sauds had been split a generation earlier. By the time Abd al-Aziz finally captured al-Hayil in 1922, he had also recovered eastern Arabia from the Ottomans. He named Abdallah bin Jaluwi the governor of the Eastern Province, and upon Abdallah's death his son Saud bin Jaluwi became governor. At the latter's death, a second son, Abd al Muhsin, became governor, a position he still held in 1978.

Abd al-Aziz might have defeated the Ibn Rashids sooner with his bedouin force, the Ikhwan (the Brethren), which was composed of tribesmen newly converted to the Wahhabi revival. World War I, however, temporarily brought the Arabian peninsula into the arena of great-power politics, with the British and the Turks competing for the support of the peninsula's three major rulers, Abd al-Aziz of Najd, Saud Ibn Rashid of the Jabal Shammar, and Sharif Husayn of Mecca. Ibn Rashid chose the Turks and the Germans; the other two chose the British. It was during this period that two Britons came to fame in Arabia. Colonel T. E. Lawrence (Lawrence of Arabia) was sent to the Hijaz to encourage Sharif Husayn to revolt against the Ottoman sultan and to lead raiding parties to disrupt Turkish supply routes along the Hijaz railway. In 1917 the British also sent a mission to Abd al-Aziz to persuade him to side with Sharif Husayn and the Allies and to attack the Ibn Rashids. One member of the British mission was H. St. John B. Philby, who stayed on in Arabia as an explorer, writer, and confidant of Abd al-Aziz.

With the war's end, Abd al-Aziz finally conquered the Ibn Rashids. In the meantime, relations with the Hijaz had begun to deteriorate. After revolting against the Ottomans, Sharif Husayn had proclaimed himself "King of the Arabs" and claimed precedence over the Al Sauds, whom he regarded as mere desert chieftains. In 1912 Husayn seized Abd al-Aziz's brother Sa'd, and released him only after he forced Abd al-Aziz to accept humiliating terms. In 1919 Abd al-Aziz's son (and later king), Faysal, traveling through Paris on his return from an official visit to London, was snubbed by Husayn's son Faysal, who was there for the Versailles peace convention. In the same year Abdallah, another of Husayn's sons, set out east of al-Taif to claim the oasis of Kurmah. While camped at nearby Turabah, his army was virtually wiped out by the fierce Saudi Ikhwan. Only those with horses escaped, including Abdallah.

Abd al-Aziz did not press his advantage. However, in 1924 the Ottoman caliphate was dissolved, and King Husayn proclaimed himself the new caliph. This was more than Abd al-Aziz could accept, and he set out to invade the Hijaz. Al-Taif was taken without resistance, but for a still-unexplained reason, a shot rang out and the zealous Ikhwan sacked the city. The Hijazis panicked when they heard of al-Taif's fate and forced Husayn to abdicate in favor of his son Ali. Ali's fortunes were no better, however, and in January 1926 he, too, set sail from Jidda to follow his father into exile.

In a quarter century, Abd al-Aziz, starting with forty men, had regained the Saudi patrimony. In 1934, after a brief war with the Yemens, the Saudis acquired the Wadi Najran, rounding out the present frontiers save for some subsequent boundary settlements. When Abd al-Aziz first captured Najd, he chose the title amir and, later, sultan of Najd. After the conquest of the Hijaz, he took the title king of Najd and the Hijaz. Finally, in 1932, he consolidated the two kingdoms into the kingdom of Saudi Arabia.

With the restoration and consolidation of Saudi domains, peace came to Saudi Arabia as it seldom had throughout recorded history. Abd al-Aziz's tribally organized military force, the religiously zealous Ikhwan, became restless. In 1929, the king was forced to put down an uprising of the Ikhwan at al-Sibliah. This became the last great bedouin battle ever fought. Abd al-Aziz disbanded the Ikhwan, and, with the exception of the brief campaign in the Yemen in 1934, Saudi Arabia was one of the very few countries to have no regular standing army during the turbulent 1930s and 1940s. The king did, however, declare war on Germany during World War II, and Saudi Arabia became a charter member of the United Nations.

The Postwar Era

The history of Saudi Arabia since World War II has been one of unprecedented economic and social development. The enabling factor has been oil, first found in commercial quantities in 1938 but not exported in commercial quantities until after the war. By the time of his death in 1953, King Abd al-Aziz had constructed a firm foundation on which subsequent leaders could build the modern oil kingdom that is Saudi Arabia today.

King Abd al-Aziz was succeeded by his eldest surviving son, Saud. (His eldest son had died in the influenza pandemic of 1919.) Saud had been groomed for rulership as viceroy of Najd under his father. More at home among the tribes, however, he lacked the breadth of vision required to propel Saudi Arabia from a desert kingdom to a major oil power. His reign was characterized by intrigue and lavish spending. Despite oil income, the treasury was often virtually empty. In 1964 the royal family withdrew its support from King Saud in favor of his brother Faysal. Saud departed Saudi Arabia, choosing to remain in exile until his death in Athens in 1969.

King Faysal came to the throne with nearly a half-century's experience in public affairs. In 1919, at the age of fourteen, he represented his father on an official visit to England. After his father conquered the Hijaz, Faysal was made viceroy in 1926, and when the Ministry of Foreign Affairs was created in 1930, he became foreign minister—a post he held for the rest of his life with the exception of a short period during the reign of Saud.

King Faysal was dedicated to the preservation of a conservative Islamic way of life both in Saudi Arabia and the Muslim world, while at the same time introducing material and technological progress. His domestic development policies proceeded from a ten-point reform program, which he designed in 1962 while still crown prince and prime minister, and were built upon the foundations already laid by his father. The measure of his success can be explained in large part by his capacity to be ahead of his people, introducing economic and social development programs, but never so far out in front that the essentially conservative Saudi public would not follow. By proceeding carefully and with deliberation, for example, he was able to win over even the most conservative segments of the population to such innovations as public radio and television and education for women. In order to dispel religious opposition to radio and television, for example, Faysal ordered that large portions of programming time be devoted to religious instructions and readings from the Quran.

Foreign affairs, however, held Faysal's greatest interest. As foreign minister, he became one of the most widely traveled Saudi officials of his time. For example, he attended the 1945 San Francisco conference that established the United Nations. Faysal's primary focus was on the Muslim world and the preservation of its values. Because of Saudi Arabia's key position as an oil exporter, Faysal's ability to act as a force for moderation both in the Arab world and the world at large was greatly enhanced by the shift in the control of oil prices from the oil companies to the producing countries in the early 1970s and from the dramatic oil price rises in 1973.

King Faysal was assassinated by a nephew on March 25, 1975, and was succeeded by his half-brother, King Khalid. Another half-brother, Fahd, was made crown prince and attended to much of the day-to-day administration of the Saudi government. In June 1982, Khalid died of a heart attack and Fahd became king and prime minister in a smooth transition. A half-brother, Prince Abdallah, who was the head of the National Guard, became crown prince and first deputy prime minister. Fahd's full brother, Sultan, the minister of defense, became second deputy prime minister. Under Khalid and now Fahd, Saudi domestic and foreign policies have generally followed the lead of Faysal and Abd al-Aziz in their emphasis on economic development and social welfare within the framework of Islamic values.

Political Environment

Population and Social Structure

Saudi Arabia has an estimated population of between 4 and 5 million, probably one-fifth of whom are expatriates. The population is scattered throughout the country in cities and towns, oases, mountain villages, and nomadic tribal concentrations. Saudi Arabia has no predominant metropolis such as Cairo, Baghdad, or Tehran. The major cities—Riyadh, Jidda, and Mecca—still have populations of less than one-half million. At the same time, the process of urbanization is accelerating rapidly, particularly since the oil boom in 1974. City skylines are changing overnight, and, in one instance, a new city with a projected population of 250,000 is being planned at the Gulf port of Jubail, little more than a fishing village a few years ago.

Oasis and mountain villagers, however, still constitute a major portion of the population. The yeoman farmers of central Arabian oases were the traditional backbone of political support for the Saudi monarchy in the nineteenth century and are beneficiaries of considerable agricultural development. The nomads, still an important segment of the population, are nevertheless no longer a potent political force; their influence has been steadily undercut through the process of modernization. Tribal ties and extended family loyalties, however, are still of primary social importance.

Saudi Arabia is one of the more homogeneous states of the Middle East. Virtually all of the native population is Arab and Muslim. There are, however, significant regional differences. Najd, as central Arabia is called, is not only the geographical center of the country but the political heartland as well. The harsh environment of Najd has had a major impact on the Najdis' perceptions of the world around them. Isolated by vast stretches of desert and never dominated by Western colonial powers, these peoples have developed a strong sense of self-reliance and, ironically, an equally strong fear of encirclement by enemies. They also have a strong sense of pride in their lineage, believing themselves to be the only racially pure Arabs. Their belief in the superiority of their bloodlines is so secure that they seldom feel the need to prove it with the regal trappings more common elsewhere in the Middle East. Thus, despite their aristocratic demeanor, Najdis display an easy desert egalitarianism, for even the meanest nomadic tribesman can claim that his lineage is every bit as good as that of the house of Saud.

In contrast to the insular character of Najd, the Hijaz has a highly cosmopolitan society. For centuries, the Muslim pilgrimage (the *hajj*) to its two holy cities, Mecca and al-Madinah, have annually drawn peoples from all over the Muslim world. In earlier years many stayed on in the Hijaz for extended periods, often permanently, making Hijazi society an ethnic melting pot. Though thoroughly Arabized, the Hijazis reflect origins from western Africa to Indonesia. With the pilgrims came commerce and the development of great, old mercantile families that are now mainly located in Jidda. In recent years Riyadh has become the banking and financial center of the kingdom, with the concentration of national income in the form of government-held oil revenues. The Jidda merchants, however, having created nationwide operations, still dominate commerce. Other Hijazis have entered public service as technocrats, administrators, soldiers, and diplomats. Because of the more cosmopolitan background of the Hijazis and the political predominance of the Najdis, a rivalry has developed between the two regions, exacerbated by the fact that the Hijaz was once an independent kingdom. With great advances in social and economic development, however, this rivalry has abated to a great degree in recent years.

South of the Hijaz is Asir, a semimountainous region that has the highest population density in the country. Asiris are hardworking people who till terraced hillside farms and live in villages constructed of stone. Less conservative than Najdis, the women seldom wear veils. The region is also one of the most isolated and least developed in the kingdom. The new road system being constructed by the government, however, will bring change, introducing the positive as well as negative influences associated with rapid development.

The other major region in Saudi Arabia is the Eastern Province, located along the Persian (Arabian) Gulf coast. It is here that the oil deposits are located. Formerly known as al-Hasa (or al-Ahsa), it consists of two major oases—al-Hasa somewhat inland and al-Qatif along the coast—and a number of coastal towns. The largest, Dammam, is the provincial capital. Just south is al-Khubar. Inland a few kilometers from al-Khubar is Dhahran. Not a city at all, Dhahran is the location of the Dhahran air field, the American Consulate General, the Petroleum and Minerals University, and the major headquarters of the Saudi oil-producing company built by ARAMCO (the Arabian American Oil Company). The oil terminal at Ras Tanura is some distance north of Dammam, and further still are the new city and naval base being built at Jubail.

The Eastern Province was traditionally an area of oasis farmers, fishermen, and mariners. With the discovery of oil and the influx of workers from all corners of the kingdom and indeed the world, the Eastern Province lost much of its homogeneity and cohesion. Yet, close by the oil facilities at Ras Tanura, one can still picture an earlier age at the quiet village among the date palms of Tarut Island. However, with much of the Saudi economic-development expenditures being made in the Eastern Province, such serenity may soon be a thing of the past.

Nearly all Saudis are Sunni Muslims and most follow the teachings of the great revivalist, Muhammad bin Abd al-Wahhab. In the Eastern Province there are some groups of Shi'a Muslims, notably at al-Qatif Oasis, who are akin to Shi'a communities in nearby Bahrain and northward to Iraq. The impact of Islam on the society can be seen everywhere. The Muslim lunar calendar is still used because it marks the Muslim holy days, particularly the annual *hajj*, or pilgrimage to Mecca, that absorbs the energies of virtually everyone in the kingdom for about two months a year. Since the lunar calendar is eleven days shorter than the solar calendar, holidays fall nearly two weeks earlier each year. Strict compliance with Islamic social norms is required in Saudi Arabia and enforced by a religious police force: Shops close five times a day for prayers, women still go veiled in public, and alcohol and public cinemas are illegal.

It is difficult to overestimate the influence of Islam on Saudi society. Old patterns are extremely hard to break, and what are often taken for changes in social values are in reality changes in the social environment to which the society is merely reacting. In Saudi Arabia, the environment is changing almost before one's eyes. As late as the 1940s, Westerners were required to wear Saudi garb in Riyadh to call on the king, and as late as 1967, there were fewer than 100 Westerners in Riyadh, compared to about 15,000 today—an indication of the rapidity of change in the social environment. Traditional values and perceptions, however, are changing much more slowly.

Wahhabism, moreover, has for the past two centuries given the society purpose and moral strength and created a sense of homogeneity among the people. One of the interesting aspects of the revival has been the ability of its adherents to adapt to social change and still maintain their conservative principles. The psychological strains and identity crises often associated with the introduction of Western-style education into a traditional society do not appear to be prevalent among Saudis. This is probably a reflection of strong Islamic-oriented values and extremely strong family ties. Thus, while modernization will undoubtedly create increasing social strains, traditional Saudi social values should on balance remain a stabilizing force in the country.

Economic Conditions

Saudi Arabia has one of the most laissez-faire economies in the world. The same Hanbali school of Islamic law that is so strict on social behavior is ironically the most liberal on business and economic matters. Likewise, there are few political restrictions on commerce. Although diplomatic relations with communist countries are prohibited, goods from China and Eastern Europe are plentiful throughout the country.

The freewheeling laissez-faire philosophy based on Islam has in turn created a business ethic that is quite different from that known in the West. Stealing is considered a very serious crime and is harshly dealt with. The traditional Islamic punishment is to cut off a hand. In business dealings, a man's word is his bond regardless of what formal legal commitments he may have acquired. At the same time, it is considered permissible to charge for a service rendered, even in circumstances that might be considered a conflict of interest by Western business ethics. This ethic, which is endemic to the entire Middle East, is best typified by the phrase "buyer beware."

Looking at Saudi Arabia's huge oil wealth today, we may find it difficult to visualize just how poverty-stricken the country was fifty years ago. When still confined to Najd, the Saudi realm required few financial resources but seldom possessed enough even then. Ottoman and British subsidies provided a major prop for its meager economy. When the Saudis conquered the Hijaz, government expenses increased greatly. But by taking the Hijaz, the Saudis also gained what was to become the major foreign-exchange earner for the kingdom prior to oil—the annual *hajj*. When the world economic depression and political disorders that preceded World War II combined to reduce greatly the number of pilgrims in the 1930s, the Saudi economy was badly hit. Economic necessity forced the Saudi government to seek to maximize *hajj* revenues despite its commitment to lowering expenses and halting the economic exploitation of the *hajjis* (pilgrims) that had so long been the norm.

The coming of oil has changed all of that. The psychological impact of the years of poverty, however, is still felt on economic policymaking. Most of the present leadership reached manhood before oil had made an impact on the kingdom's economy and society. Thus, despite the billions of dollars in foreign exchange, the laissez-faire capitalism, and the freewheeling traditional business ethic, Saudis tend to be tenacious in negotiating contracts with foreign firms for their many economic development plans.

The first Saudi oil concession was sold to Major Frank Holms, an entrepreneur from New Zealand, in the 1920s, but it was subsequently allowed to lapse. In 1933 Standard Oil of California (SOCAL) obtained a new concession with the good offices of Karl Twitchell, an American geologist who had explored for water in the kingdom, and H. St. John B. Philby, the British explorer and writer who had become a confidant of King Abd al-Aziz. Oil was first discovered in 1935; in 1938, when "Dammam No. 7" was spudded in, Saudi Arabia's future as a major oil-producing country was secured.

To produce the oil, SOCAL created a subsidiary, CASOC (California Arabian Standard Oil Company). In 1936, TEXACO became a joint owner when the two companies combined their overseas operations as CALTEX. In early 1944, CASOC was changed to ARAMCO (Arabian American Oil Company), and in 1948, Exxon and Mobil also bought into ARAMCO.

For almost three decades ARAMCO was the major owner and producer of Saudi oil (Getty and the Arabian Oil Company [Japan] had concessions in the Saudi-Kuwaiti neutral zone). By 1970, however, the market was changing to the advantage of the oil-producing countries, which were by then organized into the Organization of Petroleum Exporting Countries (OPEC). Several years earlier Saudi Petroleum Minister Ahmad Zaki Yamani had announced a scheme for the eventual Saudi control and ownership of its own oil production. He called the scheme "participation." By 1974 the Saudis had bought 60 percent equity in ARAMCO and had begun negotiations to acquire full ownership of the oil-producing company.

With its huge oil revenues accruing directly to the government, Saudi Arabia's economy is dominated by the public sector despite its laissez-faire economic philosophy. Over 90 percent of the Saudi gross national product is oil-related. Government development schemes are ambitious. The first five-year plan (1970–1975) concentrated on diversification of the country's single-commodity (oil) economy. In 1975, the second plan was announced with a budget expenditure of $149 billion. Continuing along the lines of the first plan, it has emphasized agriculture; industrialization, particularly petrochemical industries; and social and economic infrastructure.

The second plan was ambitious, providing general guidelines more than a fixed policy. Moreover, the very successes of the development plan have created a serious manpower bottleneck. With rapidly expanded responsibilities involved in implementing the many projects, the bureaucracy's decisionmaking ability has been greatly strained, and sustained public spending has created inflationary pressures. Thus, in 1977 the government began to reduce the pace of development in order to allow the economy to consolidate the gains already made. The third plan, begun in 1980, was designed to continue consolidation and to ensure the maintenance of Islamic values in Saudi society.

By 1986 the oil glut had appreciably reduced Saudi Arabia's income and caused a slowdown in economic development. Oil production was down from over 10 million barrels per day (bpd) to less than 3 million, and the Saudis were in the ironic position of running a current-account deficit. With a small population and most of the economic and social development infrastructure in place, however, the economic "crisis" was only relative. But government efforts to diversify the economy are not likely to reduce the country's overwhelming dependence on oil, and the government will thus continue to be the prime mover in economic development. With its strong traditional business ethic and Islamic concept of the social good, Saudi Arabia appears to be developing a unique form of Islamic state capitalism.

Political Structure

Saudi Arabia is an Islamic monarchy. Indeed, Islamic law, according to the Hanbali school, serves as the constitution. Islamic law is considered to be divinely inspired, and there is no room in classical Islamic political theory for man-made laws or a legislature. However, there has long been on the books a consultative assembly for the Hijaz, and in recent years there has been talk of reviving it on a nationwide basis.

Operational regulations can be distinguished from holy Islamic law: The former are called *nizams* ("royal decrees"). Disputes involving administrative regulations are heard by administrative tribunals such as the labor and commercial courts and by a special tribunal called the *diwan al-mazalim* ("board of grievances"), which hears cases brought against the government. All other cases are heard in the *quda* (Islamic courts). The chief legal official is the minister of justice, traditionally a member of the Al al-Shaykh. The highest legal official is the king, who serves as imam ("commander of the faithful"). Since the law is higher than the king, he can theoretically be sued in his own courts.

Under the king are a council of ministers and various independent agencies. He is not an absolute monarch, however, for in addition to Islamic law, the royal family serves as a constraint on his actions.

Political Dynamics

Saudi politics revolves around two distinct though closely related sets of dynamics: royal-family politics and national politics. The country is one of the few in the area in which the military does not play a decisive role.

Royal-Family Politics

The royal family serves as the constituency of the kingdom in that, in order to rule, the king must secure and maintain a consensus of support from the family. No one outside the family is quite sure how it creates such a consensus or even how large the family is, probably several thousand in size. Very secretive in family dealings, the Al Saud always tries to maintain the image of unity and harmony.

The choice (or, as in 1964, the ouster) of a king is made by an ancient Islamic institution, "the people who bind and loose" (*ahl al-aqd wal-hall*), which is dominated by the royal family. The decision is given legal sanction by a *fatwa*, or formal Islamic legal opinion. In practice, however, the process of reaching a consensus on the choice of a king or any other matter is much more complicated.

The locus of power in the family centers around the sons of the late King Abd al-Aziz. Kings Saud, Faysal, Khalid, Fahd, and Crown Prince Abdallah are all sons of the old king. Since Abd al-Aziz had many wives, the sons are of different mothers, and full brothers tend to work together. King Khalid and his older brother, Muhammad (disqualified by poor health from taking the throne), form such a sibling group. As senior living son, Muhammad is very influential in royal-family affairs although he holds no government position. King Fahd and his six brothers, including Defense Minister Sultan and Interior Minister Nayif, are another influential group. They are sometimes called "the Sudayri Seven" from the maiden name of their mother. There are also two surviving brothers of King Abd al-Aziz (uncles of the king). Belonging to an older generation, they are quite influential in the family. Several collateral branches also have a voice in family affairs. Muhammad Saud al-Kabir, the head of the Saud al-Kabir branch, actually ranks second behind the king in royal-family protocol because the founder of the branch was an older brother of the founder of the ruling branch. Because of his rank, Muhammad and other older and senior princes constitute an informal senior statesman grouping, sometimes called the "Council of Elders."

National Politics

At the head of the government is the king, who is also prime minister. Royal princes hold all the major national security-related positions. This does not mean that royal-family politics dominate national politics, however, for there are very powerful members of the family not in government and at least one powerful member of the cabinet, Saud al-Faysal, who is still a junior member of the family.

Despite the high representation of the royal family in government, the leadership has insisted on qualified technocrats being placed in all key public service- and development-oriented ministries. Government decisionmaking, therefore, reflects a combination of royal-family and developmental concerns.

Equal in importance to the makeup of the government leadership in the decisionmaking process is the structure of the bureaucracy. Historically, the Saudi regime relied on personalities rather than institutions, and the rulers drew from the advice of trusted advisers to create a consensus in policymaking. These advisers came from many walks of life, including a number of influential foreigners. When the Hijaz was conquered in 1926, King Abd al-Aziz inherited a cabinet government and consultative assembly that he maintained in Jidda, but in Riyadh he continued his personalized system of rule. Gradually, however, as the need was perceived, national ministries were created, the Hijazi ministries disappeared, and by the time of Abd al-Aziz's death in 1953, the first Saudi Council of Ministers had been formed. Since many of the ministries predate the cabinet, considerable power remains at the ministerial level, and prerogatives are guarded like feudal fiefdoms. Major decisions affecting the kingdom as a whole are taken at the cabinet level.

The creation of a government bureaucracy has not greatly diminished the personalization of government decisionmaking however. Rather, it has rechanneled the traditional personalized system through more modern bureaucratic institutions. Delegation of authority through a chain of command is still highly limited. Many seemingly minor decisions must still be made at the ministerial level, and high-level decisions are still made by only a handful of men. Although measures are being made to upgrade the efficiency of the bureaucracy, the burden of Saudi Arabia's ambitious development programs has continued to strain the country's bureaucratic resources.

Foreign Policy

The Saudi perception of the world draws heavily on the classical Islamic world view. The central position, according to this concept, is occupied by the Muslim community. The Christian and Jewish communities—the other revealed monotheistic religions recognized by Islam as "peoples of the book"—are allied to the Muslim community, and all of them are surrounded by unbelievers. In its more modern setting, this translates into the Muslim community allied with the United States and the rest of the free world against atheistic and antireligious states espousing communism and kindred radical ideologies. The Saudis, as guardians of the Muslim holy places—Mecca and al-Madinah—feel a special responsibility to protect the Muslim community and the Islamic way of life. Reinforced by the tenets of the

Wahhabi revival, this commitment has become the primary determinant of Saudi priorities in foreign affairs.

A second determinant is pan-Arabism. Unlike most of the Arab world, which rediscovered its Arabness only in the last century, the Saudis derive a great degree of their sense of identity from the purity of their ancient Arabian bloodlines. Saudi pan-Arabism, however, is closely associated with pan-Islamism, and the two serve to reinforce each other.

The late King Faysal was convinced that communism and political Zionism were the two greatest threats to the Muslim way of life. The current leaders, though no longer emphasizing Faysal's formulation of a communist-Zionist conspiracy, essentially share his world view. Communism is antireligious and therefore a threat to Muslim society. Political Zionism (as distinct from religious Judaism) is also perceived as a threat. Israel, which is the embodiment of Zionism, has in the Saudi view not only denied access of Jerusalem's Aqsa Mosque to millions of Muslims but, by displacing the Palestinian population, has also created frustrations among Arabs that have served to radicalize them. In policy terms, the Saudis view the United States as both the ultimate defender of the free world against communism and the ultimate defender of Zionism. To overcome this anomaly, the Saudis have made a major effort to persuade the United States to use its influence to bring about a fair solution to the Arab-Israeli problem and to be diligent in protecting the free world from communist expansion.

Saudi Arabia's role in world affairs is derived from its position as the world's key oil-exporting country. Thus, its foreign economic and oil policies will make the greatest impact on regional and world affairs. Saudi foreign economic and oil policies are also greatly influenced by the Saudis' world view. The Saudis view a strong United States and free world as the underpinning of the West's will and ability to contain communist and other radical forces. Moreover, with foreign exchange holdings of $60 billion, the Saudis realize that whatever adversely affects the world economy will hurt them also. At the same time, the Saudis have shown themselves willing to use oil as a political weapon. It was King Faysal who led the Arab oil embargo in 1973–1974 after feeling betrayed by the announcement that the United States was committing $2.2 billion in military aid to Israel.

The Saudis have also been concerned about the adverse effect of rising oil prices on the Third World and, as a result, have greatly increased their development aid programs. Their aid programs show a clear distinction between God-fearing and godless states. In order of priority, the recipients of Saudi aid have been the non–oil producing Arab states, the non-Arab Islamic states, and finally the other less-developed countries.

Bibliography

An increasing amount of literature has been written on Saudi Arabia in recent years. Much of it is of very mixed quality, however, and definitive works are comparatively few in number. R. Bayly Winder's *Saudi Arabia in the Nineteenth Century* (New York: St. Martin's Press, 1985) is the standard work on earlier history, and Christine Moss Helms' *The Cohesion of Saudi Arabia: Evolution of Political Identity* (Baltimore: Johns Hopkins University Press, 1970) is an excellent study of the creation of the present-day state.

There are a number of older books about Saudi Arabia that are considered classics. These include T. E. Lawrence's *The Seven Pillars of Wisdom* (Garden City, N.Y.: Doubleday, 1935), which is about the Hijaz in World War I, and H. St. John B. Philby's many works, two of which are *Arabian Jubilee* (London: Robert Hale, 1952) and *Saudi Arabia* (London: Benn, 1955).

A growing number of works are being written on Saudi society and internal dynamics. David E. Long's *Saudi Arabia*, vol. 4, Washington Paper No. 39 (Beverly Hills, Calif.: Sage, 1976), is somewhat dated but provides a concise overview of Saudi political dynamics. John A. Shaw and David E. Long, in *Saudi Arabian Modernization: The Impact of Change on Stability*, vol. 10, Washington Paper No. 89 (New York: Praeger Publishers, 1980), analyze the impact of social and economic development on the kingdom. Some of the same problems are addressed in Tim Niblock, ed., *State, Society and Economy in Saudi Arabia* (New York: St. Martin's Press, 1982); Ragaei El Mallakh, *Saudi Arabia—Rush to Development: Profile of an Energy Economy and Development* (Baltimore: Johns Hopkins Press, 1982); and Fouad Al-Farsy, *Saudi Arabia: A Case Study in Development*, rev. ed. (London: Kegan Paul International, 1982). Readers interested in how Saudi Arabia administers the *hajj* should read David E. Long's *The Hajj Today: A Survey of the Contemporary Makkah Pilgrimage* (Albany, N.Y.: State University of New York Press, 1979).

On the early days of the oil industry, George W. Stocking's *Middle East Oil: A Study in Political and Economic Controversy* (Nashville, Tenn.: Vanderbilt University Press, 1970) is a classic. ARAMCO, *The ARAMCO Handbook* (Dhahran: ARMACO, 1968), and the more recent *ARAMCO and Its World: Arabia and the Middle East*, by Ismail I. Nawwab, Peter C. Speers, and Paul F. Hoye, eds. (Dhahran: ARAMCO, 1980), are also worth looking into. On the policy side, there is Aaron David Miller's *Search for Security: Saudi Arabian Oil and American Foreign Policy, 1939–1949* (Chapel Hill, N.C.: University of North Carolina Press, 1980); William B. Quandt's *Saudi Arabia's Oil Policy* (Washington, D.C.: Brookings Institution, 1981); and Ali D. Johany's *The Myth of the OPEC Cartel: The Role of Saudi Arabia* (New York: John Wiley, 1982).

On political and strategic issues, an increasing amount of material is appearing. Anthony H. Cordesman's *The Gulf and the Search for Strategic Stability: Saudi Arabia, the Military Balance in the Gulf, and Trends in the Arab-Israeli Military Balance* (Boulder, Colo.: Westview Press, 1984) is the most comprehensive study of strategic matters. William B. Quandt's *Saudi Arabia in the 1980s: Foreign Policy, Security and Oil* (Washington, D.C.: Brookings Institution, 1981) is somewhat dated as a policy monograph but still insightful. David E. Long's *The United States and Saudi Arabia: Ambivalent Allies* (Boulder, Colo.: Westview Press, 1985) analyzes U.S.-Saudi political, military, oil, and economic relations in their entirety.

There are also some nonacademic books worth mentioning. Robert Lacey's *The Kingdom* (London: Hutchinson, 1981), though somewhat gossipy and occasionally misleading, provides an impressionistic view of contemporary Saudi Arabia. A similar and somewhat more sophisticated book is David Holden and Richard Johns, *The House of Saud* (London: Sidgwick & Jackson, 1981). Finally, Richard F. Nyrop ed., *Saudi Arabia: A Country Study*, one of the American University Foreign Area Studies handbook series (Washington, D.C.: Government Printing Office, 1984), provides a compendium of information as well as an excellent bibliography.

6

Republic of Iraq

David E. Long
John A. Hearty

Historical Background

Between the Tigris and Euphrates rivers lies a land with an exceptionally turbulent history. Known as Mesopotamia ("land between the rivers") until the Arab conquests in the seventh century A.D., Iraq has been a battleground of strategic importance and a land of internal strife from ancient times to the present. The geography of the region has been a significant feature in the history of Iraq. Bordered by deserts in the south and a multitude of passes in the north, Iraq is virtually without natural defenses against any invasion. Indeed, the country has been occupied by the Persians, Greeks, Romans, Arabs, Mongols, Ottomans, and British. Each of these incursions has left its mark on the people and culture, thus fashioning a very complex and heterogeneous society.

Arab Conquests

The Arab conquest of Iraq began in A.D. 634 under the successor to Muhammad, Abu Bakr, who was the first caliph (632–634). A few years later, the fourth caliph, Ali, was assassinated. His rival, Muawiya, declared himself caliph and established the Umayyad Empire in Damascus. In the meantime, Ali's son Husayn, who had fled to Iraq, led a revolt in Karbala, Iraq, and was killed there by the Umayyads in 680. Those events initiated a rivalry that has become an important theme in present-day relations between Iraq and Syria and also initiated a religious schism in Islam that led to two main contending branches, the Shi'as and Sunnis, who disagreed on the succession of the caliphate.

During the sixth and seventh centuries, the Muslim Empire under the Damascus-based Umayyad dynasty expanded politically, economically, and socially, extending from southern France to China. Nonetheless, the seeds of discontent had been sown. The Shi'ites, primarily located in Iraq and Persia, continually challenged the legitimacy of the Umayyads. In 747, Abu al-Abbas embarked from Iraq upon a military campaign that resulted in the collapse of

Base 502879 1-76

the Umayyad dynasty and the rise of the Abbasid dynasty. The Abbasids moved the capital of the Islamic world from Damascus to Baghdad. The era that followed, from 750 to 1258, was known as the "Golden Age of Islam" and brought tremendous advances in literature, art, and the sciences.

The decline of the Abbasid period was gradual, generated by internal strife. The ultimate destruction and collapse of the Abbasid Empire, however, came at the hand of a foreign invader. In 1258, Hulagu, the grandson of Genghis Khan, unleashed his forces on Baghdad and destroyed, in a relatively short period of time, what had taken five centuries to build. To this day, Iraq has been unable completely to recover or to rebuild what the Mongols destroyed.

However violent the downfall of the Abbasid rule, the Arab conquest of Mesopotamia altered the consciousness and character of the inhabitants of the land between the rivers. Politically and socially, the indigenous population was Arabized to the extent that, many centuries later, a strong Iraqi pan-Arab movement would attempt to join into a series of unions with Jordan, Syria, and Egypt.

Ottoman Rule

From 1258 to 1534, when it was captured from Persia by the Ottomans, Iraq existed in a political vacuum. There was constant turmoil between the Sunni tribes of northern Iraq, Kurdistan, and parts of Baghdad on the one hand, and Shi'ite-dominated southern Iraq and Baghdad on the other. In 1623 the Safavid dynasty of Persia under Shah Abbas was able to seize Baghdad from the Ottomans. The Ottomans regained control thirteen years later and were able to hold Iraq from that time until after World War I.

The Ottoman rule of Iraq was both inefficient and corrupt. What little was left of the splendor of the Abbasid period was allowed to fall into ruin. The Ottomans were able to exercise little political control over Iraq until Sultan Mahmud II asserted direct rule in 1831. Prior to this, Iraq was divided into three *vilayets* (districts)—Baghdad, Basrah, and Mosul—each directly linked to Istanbul. The central government was concerned only with the collection of taxes and some form of political control. This was accomplished by appointing the strongest tribal chiefs as governors of the provinces. Instead of politically and economically integrating the country, this form of political institutionalization fragmented Iraq, perpetuating constant local uprisings from less powerful tribes in the south and the Kurdish tribes in the north.

Mahmud II was partially successful in extending more direct Ottoman control over Kurdistan and the Persian frontiers, but his gains were soon lost by inept successors. Most Ottoman attempts at administrative and social reforms were failures, and, as the people were mercilessly exploited by their Ottoman overlords, the Ottomans came to be generally hated.

During the later stages of the Ottoman rule, Iraq was drawn into international politics, culminating with World War I. Because of its strategic location astride British routes to the latter's Asian empire, Iraq attracted increasing British concern. Britain's interest in Iraq was threefold. First, the Turkish-German alliance and the approach of World War I threatened Britain's Middle Eastern colonies and protectorates. Second, the British perceived a potential strategic threat to their oil interests in Iran. Third, India, the gem of the British Empire, was thought to be endangered by the possible German occupation of either Iraq or Iran. Thus, when war broke out, British troops invaded Iraq and occupied the city of Basrah. Later they captured Baghdad and northern Iraq.

In summary, the Ottoman rule of Iraq was more significant for what it did not accomplish than for what it did accomplish. By not developing unified political institutions or a central administration, Iraq became fragmented. This facilitated a domestic situation and created cleavages among the Sunni and Shi'ite Muslims, the urban and rural populations, the Arabs and the Kurds. Although these feuds were not initiated by the Ottoman occupation of Iraq, the Ottoman administration was a decisive factor in their remaining a feature of Iraqi politics to the present day.

The British Mandate

As early as the Sykes-Picot Agreement of 1916, Great Britain obtained tacit Western consent to the occupation of Iraq. British control was formalized at the

San Remo Conference in April 1920. This conference, in effect, granted the British mandatory powers over the region they had already militarily occupied. There were, however, several considerations that placed serious constraints on the role the British could play in effectively ruling Iraq. First of all, there were conflicting demands made upon the British by a myriad of groups and associations within the mandate. For example, the tribal shaykhs wanted grants of new land, whereas the villagers wanted the tribal incursions stopped. At the same time, there was within Great Britain a growing demand to cut back the financing of any commitment to Iraq. This current of opinion became more pronounced after the anti-British revolt in 1920, which cost nearly 40 million pounds sterling to quell. There was growing evidence, especially after the 1920 revolt, that Britain would incur domestically unacceptable costs to maintain any significant military force in Iraq. Another constraint concerned the mandate itself. It was formally designed to prepare the country for independence rather than colonization. Thus, at the very least, the British were under some legal constraints.

The British understood that there could be no colonial status for Iraq. They were faced with finding someone to rule Iraq who would allow them to preserve a predominant role in both the internal and external affairs of the country. They finally chose Prince Faysal of the Hashimite house of Mecca, the son of the former sharif and newly named King Husayn of Hijaz. The Hashimites were loyal supporters of the British during World War I. In 1921 Faysal became the first of three kings from the Hashimite family to sit on the throne of Iraq. The British and Iraqis subsequently signed, in 1922, the first of three treaties that were to govern their relations with each other until 1968. The treaty of 1922 allowed for indirect rather than direct control and was the first sign that the mandate would soon end.

The British structured the political system so that they could maximize their position and influence. Modeled on the British constitutional system, Iraq's government had an independent parliament and judiciary. However, to ensure a friendly government, the constitution reserved for the monarch considerable powers, including the right to appoint the prime minister and the right to dismiss parliament. The king was commander-in-chief of the armed forces and had considerable veto power over legislation. These powers enabled the king to wield virtual dictatorial authority.

The problem for Faysal and his successors was to manage a balance between British interests and those of the strong Iraqi nationalists. A significant gain for the nationalists came in 1929, when the British negotiated a treaty with Iraq to end the mandate upon Iraq's acceptance into the League of Nations. Finally, in October 1932, the league admitted Iraq. The Anglo-Iraqi treaty went into effect, the mandate was ended, and Iraq became an independent state under the protection of the British.

Constitutional Monarchy

The internal stability of the newly independent state continued to be plagued by traditional Sunni-Shi'a religious conflicts. In addition, its borders, created at San Remo, contained a number of separate ethnic groups with little or no loyalty to the new state. The most important of these groups were the Kurds. Constituting about one-fifth of the population of Iraq and located in the northeast, with kin in Turkey, Persia, and the Soviet Union, the Kurds had fought a losing battle with Persia and Turkey and now Iraq for an independent state of their own.

Another source of instability was the untimely death of King Faysal I in September 1933. Respected by almost everyone, Faysal had the capabilities and personality to control the internal cleavages, as well as to carry out a delicate balancing act between the British and the nationalists. Faysal was succeeded by his son Ghazi, a well-liked but inexperienced nationalist.

Great Britain itself proved to be a source of instability. Although the British were originally interested in Iraq's strategic location, the discovery of oil in 1923 and the commercial exploitation of oil in 1930 greatly intensified their interests. With the approach of World War II, the significance of Iraq to the British became even more apparent. As the British stake in maintaining control in Iraq grew, anti-British groups sprang up throughout the country and, more portentously, within the army.

It was during Ghazi's reign (1933–1939) that a distinctive pattern for future Iraqi politics became evident. In 1936 a successful coup d'état was executed by the army. The first of five coups in as many years, it was aimed at the cabinet, not at the king.

Two important consequences ensued: institutionalization of the coup as a method of changing governments, and the splintering of Iraqi politics into two blocs—a pro-British group headed by Nuri al-Said and an anti-British group whose leading spokesman was Rashid Ali al-Gaylani. Because it was anti-British, this group was supported by the Germans.

In 1939, with war on the horizon, the accidental death of King Ghazi placed the prime minister, General Nuri al-Said, in a very tenuous situation. Ghazi was succeeded by King Faysal II, his four-year-old son, and a brother, Abdul Illah, became regent. Two years later, Rashid Ali led a successful coup and ousted Nuri. As the new prime minister was pro-Axis and attempted to alter the Anglo-Iraqi treaty in order to make Iraq neutral in the war, the British reciprocated by invading Iraq, suppressing Rashid Ali and placing Nuri and the monarchy in power again. From 1941 to 1958, the power structure of Iraqi politics remained relatively stable, with King Faysal II assuming full powers from Abdul Illah in 1953. Nuri al-Said was thirteen times prime minister during this period, but even when not occupying a formal position, he maintained his strong influence on decisionmaking. Nuri developed a framework for policymaking early in his career that remained consistent until he was assassinated in 1958. A military man, he placed great emphasis on discipline, loyalty, and integrity. He was also firmly convinced that foreign powers had a role to play in the development and security of Iraq, and, thus, he favored close cooperation with the West, relying heavily on Great Britain to provide assistance in the security of his country.

In Nuri's view, pan-Arabism encompassed economic and political cooperation, but not necessarily federation or unity. Nevertheless, in 1946 he was influential in the creation of the Arab League, and in 1958 he reacted to the Egyptian-

Syrian union by proclaiming a federal state between Iraq and Jordan. The union never had much of a chance for development because of a coup that overthrew the monarchy five months later.

Nuri and the monarchy were overthrown for a number of interrelated reasons. Although Nuri concentrated on such internal long-term development programs as flood control, the majority of the population remained destitute, especially those in the rural regions. Although the programs would have ultimately benefited them, these people were convinced that they were being exploited for the benefit of the wealthy merchant and land-owning classes.

The political institutions of Iraq offered little public participation in the political process. The legislative process, although electoral laws were reformed numerous times, was controlled by the executive. The Parliament, moreover, did not represent the varied economic, religious, or social classes; nor was it a check on the executive's power. Although Nuri had allowed five political parties to organize after World War II, he effectively restricted party activity and finally outlawed parties in 1954. The suppression of the parties left little room for opposition. Any individual who voiced concern over the government's decrees was jailed. It was estimated that at one time Nuri had jailed ten thousand political prisoners.

Nuri himself also contributed to the collapse of the Hashimite kingdom. His penchant for public order justified in his mind the need for coercion. His methods of terrorizing all opposition made him one of the most hated men in the country. Even his friends were frustrated by his intransigence and his forceful personality.

Nuri and the monarchy were also vulnerable to the charge of being tools of imperialism. With nationalism strong, the population had been consistently anti-British. The cordial relationships between Iraq and Great Britain widened the rift between Nuri and the people he ruled. Moreover, when the Baghdad Pact was signed in 1955 by Iraq, Pakistan, Turkey, Iran, and Great Britain, with the United States as an observer, Nuri was attacked by the leaders of a great many other Arab nations. President Gamal Nasser of Egypt was so outraged that he called for the Iraqi people to overthrow the prime minister. Relations with the more radical Arab states were further strained when France and Great Britain sided with Israel and invaded Egypt in 1956.

Disaffection with the regime came to a head in 1958. On July 14, troops under General Abd al-Karim Qasim and Colonel Abd al-Salam Arif moved on Baghdad, and a bloody revolution ensued that did not cease until the entire royal family and Nuri al-Said had been killed.

Republican Iraq

Following the overthrow of the monarchy, Iraq became a republic and the ruling Council of Sovereignty was established. Qasim became acting prime minister and minister of defense. Arif was given the positions of deputy prime minister and minister of interior. Within two weeks after the revolution, a provisional constitution was enacted, placing all executive and some legislative authority in the Council of Ministers, subject to the approval of the Council of Sovereignty. In addition, Qasim released all political prisoners and granted amnesty to all exiled opponents of the old regime. This included the release and return of the communists and other dissidents, including Mustafa Barzani, the leader of the Kurdish rebellion.

In September 1958, an agrarian reform law was enacted that transferred large tracts of land owned by the upper class to the landless *fellahin* (peasant farmers). The new regime also abrogated the Baghdad Pact and recognized the Soviet Union and the People's Republic of China. Finally, differences between Nasser and the Iraqi government were reconciled to the extent that there was even talk of union between Egypt, Syria, and Iraq.

The tremendous amount of enthusiasm and support generated for the new regime could not cover up the power struggle that surfaced as early as September 1958. Four major political factions quickly appeared. At one pole were the communists, who tended to follow the Soviet line. At the other were the Arab nationalists, including the currently ruling Baath ("renaissance") party, who supported either union or at least very close ties with Egypt. The Kurds constituted a third group. For tactical reasons, they sided with the communists and were thus also considered pro-Soviet. Finally, the more moderate National Democrats and the Istiqlal (Independence) party upheld Iraqi independence but were inclined toward closer relations with Egypt.

Qasim erroneously believed he could play each faction off against the others and thus maintain power. In September 1958 he dismissed Arif as deputy prime minister and assigned him as ambassador to West Germany. Arif never arrived at his new post, however, for he was arrested on charges of conspiracy and imprisoned. Arif's dismissal provoked a rift between Qasim and Nasser, with whom Qasim had just signed a protocol pledging closer cooperation. In March 1959 a rebellion broke out in Mosul. The leaders called upon all Arabs to help overthrow the Qasim regime and to form a union with Egypt. With the assistance of the Kurds and the communists, the rebellion was suppressed, thus crushing the Arab nationalist movement and at the same time providing a greater role for the communists. Qasim then proceeded to reduce the communists' influence by restricting their political activities. Because of his use of terror, however, Qasim's victory over the nationalists resulted in a considerable loss of public support for the regime.

The Kurdish revolt of 1961 further undermined the stability of the Qasim regime. The Kurds felt that Qasim had not fulfilled his promises for some form of regional autonomy. Having revolted in 1919, 1937, and 1946, they again rebelled; with military aid from the Soviets, they effectively engaged a large segment of the Iraqi army, greatly intensifying the divisions within the country.

Another problem facing Qasim was the Iraqi claim to Kuwait, which he renewed in 1961 when Kuwait became independent. His position alienated virtually every Arab country and left Iraq hopelessly isolated. It also cost him domestic support that he could ill afford to lose.

On February 8, 1963, Qasim was ousted in a coup led by the Iraqi Baath party, together with sympathetic army officers and pan-Arab groups. Colonel Arif was appointed president, but the real power was exercised by a Baathist general, Ahmad Hasan al-Bakr. The Supreme Revolutionary Council was formed, with the Baathists in control of all important positions, and the first action it took was the execution of Qasim, followed by a purge of the army and government of all communists and their sympathizers. Although the new regime was devoted to Arab unity, a split occurred between moderate Baathists and Nasserites who wanted unity with Egypt, and more radical Baathists who favored closer ties to Baathist Syria. The Nasserites appeared to win out in November 1963. President Arif wrested full powers from the Baathists and established the Revolutionary Command Council.

Arif, who was an admirer of Nasser, had already taken steps toward union with Egypt beginning with integration of military, economic, political, and information policies. In May 1964 Arif and Nasser issued a number of joint statements. They provided that over the next three years a provisional government headed by a joint Presidency Council would begin to merge the two countries. In July 1964 Arif decreed that all political parties would join one organization, the Iraqi Arab Socialist Union. In effect, Iraq was attempting to emulate the Egyptian Arab Socialist Union, thus facilitating movement toward total union.

Although President Arif desired union with Egypt, he differed with elements in his cabinet who thought he was moving too slowly, and six members of his cabinet subsequently resigned. One of Arif's reasons for slowness was his conviction that Iraq's internal problems should be resolved before the union could be consummated. As time went on, however, plans for the union began to recede. After an unsuccessful coup attempt in September 1965 by the pro-Nasser premier, General Arif Abd al-Razzak, all thoughts of union disappeared. Al-Razzak and his supporters fled to Cairo.

Despite his differences with the Baathists, Arif was firmly committed to a socialist program for economic development. At the same time that he announced the formation of the Arab Socialist Union, he also nationalized many of Iraq's leading business firms as well as all Iraqi privately owned banks and insurance companies. The one noticeable exception was the oil industry. Arif realized that he needed the oil companies to ensure revenues for his development plans.

Like his predecessors, Arif continued to have problems with the Kurds. They remained in a continuous state of rebellion over demands for autonomy from 1962 to 1964, despite an offer of limited autonomy made in 1963. In February Arif obtained a cease-fire from the Kurds, but it lasted less than a year.

Arif's accidental death in a helicopter crash on April 3, 1966, led to a power struggle between the civilians, led by Premier Abd al-Rahman al-Bazzaz, and the military. The cabinet and the National Defense Council were charged with selecting a suitable replacement. In a compromise solution Arif's brother, Major General Abd al-Rahman Arif, became president, and Dr. Bazzaz remained as prime minister. Following an attempted coup by pro-Nasser military officers, the new President Arif consolidated his position and forced Bazzaz to resign in August 1966.

Prior to his ouster, Bazzaz had negotiated yet another settlement with the Kurds. It was based on a twelve-point declaration that allowed the Kurds a limited degree of autonomy and equal representation in the government. But many key provisions had not been honored, and by 1968 war had broken out again. After two years the government again negotiated a settlement. The 1970 Kurdish agreement was more comprehensive than any previous agreement and, it was hoped, would be permanent. After a few years, however, when it became obvious that the Kurds would not receive the degree of autonomy they sought, Kurdish leader Mustafa Barzani again raised the standard of revolt, this time with military aid from Iran. The rebellion was crushed in 1975 after Iran agreed to refrain from aiding the Kurds in return for Iraqi recognition of Iranian sovereignty over half of the Shatt al-Arab River where it forms the border between the two countries. Another result of the agreement was to force Barzani into exile in the United States, where he later died.

On July 17, 1968, the second Arif regime was overthrown in a bloodless coup by General Hasan al-Bakr. The Kurdish rebellion, the humiliating Arab defeat in the 1967 Arab-Israeli war, and Arif's inability to get the country's domestic development moving all contributed to his overthrow. The coup brought the Iraqi Baath party back to power.

In the years since the Baath returned to power, Iraq has known a greater measure of stability than at any time since the overthrow of the monarchy. In July 1973 an abortive coup was attempted by the security chief, Nazim Kazzar, which resulted in the creation of the National Front to broaden the regime's political base. Although the National Front also included the Communist party of Iraq, relations between the Baathists and the communists were never good and in recent years have actually become worse. It was originally hoped that Barzani's Kurdish Democratic party would also join, but that quickly proved illusory. During the second half of the 1970s Saddam Husayn al-Takriti rose to the position of strongman behind President al-Bakr. For several years Saddam maintained a low profile as vice-chairman of the party regional (i.e., Iraqi) command and vice-chairman of the Revolutionary Command Council. On July 17, 1979, the eleventh anniversary of the current Baath regime, Saddam succeeded to the presidency as al-Bakr, stating reasons of ill health, handed over to him the full reins of power.

Saddam's tenure as president has been notable for several reasons. First, he has continued and strengthened the grip of the Baathist regime on Iraq, both through his personal charisma and through ruthless suppression of all forms of dissent. Second, he has shown a remarkable ability to act decisively in pursuit of perceived national interests, unfettered by ideological or rhetorical contraints. For example, Saddam has increasingly aligned Iraq with the conservative Arab states and has led the way for Arab rapprochement with Egypt. Also, despite Iraq's wartime reliance on the Soviet Union for military equipment, Saddam, in late 1984, implemented a decision reportedly taken as early as 1980 to resume diplomatic relations with the United States.

The third and most significant development of Saddam's tenure thus far is the continuing war with Iran, into which he led Iraq. Iraq dates the war's beginning from September 4, 1980, when Iran shelled Iraqi border points. Iran cites the Iraqi invasion of Iran on September 22 as the beginning of the war. Iraq's principal stated reasons for invading were to halt the Khomeini regime's support of subversion in Iraq, to force Iran to observe the terms of the 1975

Algiers Accord regarding the Shatt al-Arab and disputed points along the land border, and to return several strategic islands in the Gulf to Arab sovereignty. Iraq has consistently disclaimed territorial ambitions, although most outside observers believe that wresting the oil-rich Khuzistan province from Iran was a major motivating factor. Called Arabistan by Iraq, it has a predominantly Arab ethnic population. Claiming that its military objectives were limited, Iraq accepted the first United Nations resolution in late September 1980 calling for a cease-fire, negotiations, and succeeding resolutions.

Evidently expecting immediate capitulation by Iran, the Iraqi military adopted a defensive strategy after the initial thrust, designed to minimize losses. Iraq quickly lost the initiative, however. Iranian forces, badly disorganized after the revolution, regrouped more quickly than anyone had thought possible, and with the aid of "human waves" of suicide troops—consisting of old men and teen-aged "volunteers"—they drove the Iraqis out of Iran by June 1982.

The strategic situation has remained relatively unchanged since 1982. Iraq has repulsed several major invasion attempts, in some cases using poison gas in contravention of Iraq's obligations as a signatory of treaties banning the use of chemical warfare.

Both sides have attacked civilian population centers in what has devolved into a very dirty, if limited-action, war. The impasse on land has caused the spread of hostilities to the Gulf. In the first weeks of the war, Iran closed the Shatt al-Arab, Iraq's only access to the sea, and destroyed Iraq's strategic offshore oil-export terminals. In 1984 Iraq stepped up attacks on ships serving Iran, and in 1985 began stepped-up air attacks against Iran's major offshore oil-loading facilities at Kharg Island. Iran retaliated by attacking neutral ships serving nonbelligerent Arab states in the Gulf and has threatened to close the Gulf to shipping entirely.

In the meantime, Iraq has been seeking land-based oil pipeline alternatives to get its oil to market. It has more than doubled the capacity of its pipeline through Turkey and has been working on a hookup with Saudi Arabia's pipeline to the Red Sea.

Both countries have suffered terrible human and economic losses. Iraq has mounted a diplomatic campaign to bring international political and economic pressure on the Khomeini regime to accept a cease-fire and negotiations toward a settlement. Iran, however, has refused all of the numerous mediation efforts by such parties as the United Nations, the Organization of the Islamic Conference, the Nonaligned Movement, and several states with access to both capitals. Iran's essential condition for peace is the removal of Saddam Husayn and his secular Baathist regime. Hence, after over a half-decade of military stalemate, a diplomatic solution appears no more likely than a military one, at least until the departure of either or both Khomeini and Saddam.

Political Environment

The present borders of Iraq date back only to 1920 and were created with more of a mind to great-power interests than to ethnic unity. This fact explains, in great part, the chronic lack of political cohesion that has plagued all Iraqi governments since that time. Thus, despite oil wealth and other natural resources, a potentially productive agricultural sector, and a population that is not out of proportion to its resource base, Iraq has been an extremely difficult country to govern, regardless of the ideological professions of the regime in power.

The People

The population of Iraq is estimated to be 11 million, with an annual growth rate of 3.3 percent. The capital and largest city is Baghdad with a population of 3.5 million. It is followed by Basrah with a population of around five hundred thousand, and Mosul with four hundred thousand. The population of Iraq is divided into several ethnic groups: The two largest are the Arabs, who make up 75 percent, and the Kurds, who constitute 15 to 20 percent. Iraq is predominantly an Arab country, but in no way should this fact be equated with homogeneity. Differences among the Arabs and between them and the non-Arabs are pronounced.

The Arab population is split along religious confessional lines. Almost three-fourths of the Arabs are Shi'ites. This fact stands out all the more when one considers that the Iraqi government has traditionally been dominated by Arab Sunnis. Most Shi'ite Arabs are farmers, shepherds, or unskilled laborers who live in central and southern Iraq. Because of their religious heritage and their traditional way of life, they tend to be conservative in outlook and resistant to change. This explains in great part their ambivalent attitude toward Arab nationalism. Before the Iranian revolution, many Iraqi Shi'ites had a closer affinity with their co-religionists in Iran than with Sunni Arabs in Iraq. Nevertheless, Iraqi Shi'a, who constitute a disproportionate majority of the armed forces, have overwhelmingly supported the Saddam regime in the Iran-Iraq War.

The Sunni Arabs are found in all strata of Iraqi society. In the larger cities like Baghdad they dominate the professional classes. Because their level of education is generally higher than that of the rural and village-dwelling Shi'ites, they have been better able to assimilate modern secular political concepts and ideologies. Arab Sunnis are also found in agrarian villages, particularly in northern and central Iraq, and in the deserts of the southwest.

One fascinating though politically insignificant group of Arabs inhabits the marshes and deltas in the south between the Tigris and Euphrates rivers. The so-called marsh Arabs are a seminomadic people who have adapted to life in the marshes. For the most part they are Shi'ites, although some are Sunnis. The marsh Arabs are tribally organized, and engage in fishing and agriculture. Their population is estimated to be between three and four hundred thousand.

The Kurds are the largest non-Arab minority group in Iraq. They occupy the mountainous regions of the northeast and are also found in contiguous areas of Iran, Turkey, and Syria. Because of their separate cultural heritage and language, the Kurds persist in the dream of self-determination. Thus they continue to be a destabilizing element to Iraq's Arab-dominated political system. Predominantly nationalists, they have been willing to side with the Soviets or with Iran to further their aim of autonomy. By no means, however, are the Kurds united on what form autonomy should take.

The Kurds are generally Sunni Moslems and primarily seminomadic, but they are increasingly moving to such urban areas as Mosul and Kirkuk. Nonetheless, the Kurds still maintain a traditional life-style, which includes patterns of seasonal migration for some and tribal animosities for all—the latter tending to divide them.

Iraq has a number of other smaller minority groups, many of which have bonds with neighboring states. Turkomens inhabit parts of northern Iraq bordering Turkey. They constitute about 2.5 percent of the population and are about two-thirds Sunni and one-third Shi'ite. Persians and Lurs (who speak a Persian dialect) are found in eastern Iraq along the Iranian border. They are generally Shi'ite Muslims. In 1980 thousands of Iraqis of apparently Persian origin were expelled to Iran under suspicion of being sympathetic to Iran's call for the overthrow of the Baathist regime in Baghdad.

Finally, about 5 to 7 percent of the population are non-Muslims. Among them are Christians, Yazidis (the so-called devil-worshippers), Mandeans (a pre-Christian religion), and a small community of Jews. Although the Jewish population of Iraq numbered close to one hundred and fifty thousand in 1950, most living in Baghdad, today there are less than a few thousand. The rest have immigrated, mostly to Israel.

Social Structure

The highly diverse nature of Iraqi society and the primary loyalty of the individual to his or her extended family and ethnic group has inhibited the growth of a purely Iraqi nationalism. This is especially the case in the rural areas, where resistance against change is most prevalent. In fact, the gap between attitudes in the cities and the outlying areas is immense and is further exacerbated by the overwhelming concentration of political power in the capital city, Baghdad. Although the distribution of income has improved since the prerevolutionary days of city-dwelling absentee landlords and landless peasants, there is still a disparity between the rural areas and the more affluent urban areas. The government has been trying to redress this difference through land reform, expanded education, and rural infrastructure development. Since 1958, there has been a sixfold increase in the total number of new graduates from both secondary and higher educational institutions. As the Baathist regime is committed to a socialist economic structure and has limited the size of the private sector, the burden of placing the growing number of graduates has fallen mainly on the government. This problem has been greatly alleviated in recent years, however, due to the manpower requirements of the war. The war has also greatly aided the entry of women into professions traditionally reserved for men. Moreover, since 1982 the government has eased up on its socialist doctrine and has begun to expand the private sector.

Economic Conditions

The political constraints placed on private enterprise by Iraq's socialist government and the predominating position of the oil sector in the economy place upon the government the main responsibility for the management of the economy. Despite the oil-based economy, agriculture is the largest employer, taking up over half the labor force. Mesopotamia was the breadbasket of the ancient world, with an elaborate network of canals for irrigated farming. But the Mongol invasions of the thirteenth through the sixteenth centuries utterly destroyed the system, and it has never been fully restored.

Modern Iraq has expended a great deal of energy on improving agriculture, but it still suffers from inefficient land-tenure practices, resistance of the farmers to more modern techniques, and undercapitalization. Republican regimes since 1958 have endeavored to solve the land-tenure problem by stripping the absentee landowning class of their large holdings. Over four hundred thousand farmers have received title to their land. These measures, more politically than economically inspired, actually lowered agricultural productivity. Moreover, they did not address the system of freeholds, religious endowment (*waqf*) land, and three kinds of government land, which further complicate land tenure. In 1982 the government took the major step of abandoning its policy of consolidating agriculture into collective farms, and began to encourage private-sector agriculture.

Iraq is one of the few Middle Eastern countries with the potential for a balanced economy. During the 1960s, the country was not only undergoing political upheavals but, owing to a dispute with the largely British-owned Iraq Petroleum Company (IPC), oil revenues were down and the government was having a difficult time economically as well. Much of the external financing of Iraq's economic development during that period came from the Soviet Union. During the 1970s, Iraq's financial position greatly improved, and the government has increased much-needed capital investment in the agricultural sector, including construction of dams, canals, and adequate drainage facilities to prevent salinization.

One additional agricultural problem still to be addressed is the control of the Euphrates River waters. Owing in part to bad relations between Syria and Iraq, there is no Euphrates water agreement, and in 1975 Iraq accused Syria of cutting the flow of the river behind its new dam, causing Iraq severe crop damage. Although control of the Euphrates waters will probably never lead to an outright war between the two countries, it remains a potentially threatening problem.

The oil industry is capital-intensive, employing relatively few Iraqis, but it nevertheless dominates the economy. Oil has long been known to exist in Iraq. For centuries the residue of oil seeps was used to fuel lamps, and natural gas was ignited to create the "everlasting sacred fires of Kirkuk." The original modern oil concessionaire was an Armenian from Constantinople named Calouste Gulbenkian who organized German, Dutch, and British interests in the Turkish Petroleum Company in 1912. After World War I, the French took over the German shares and the company was renamed the Iraq Petroleum Company (IPC).

The dispute with IPC that had so adversely affected oil revenues in the 1960s was never resolved, and in June 1972 IPC was nationalized. The owners agreed to an arbitrated settlement over compensation in January 1973 that also included the transfer of assets to Iraq of a small sister company, the Mosul Petroleum Company. Two years later, another sister company, the Basrah Petroleum Company, was also nationalized. All of Iraq's oil is now in the hands of the state-owned Iraq National Oil Company (INOC). Brazilian and French companies are currently employed by INOC on service contracts and are conducting major exploration and expansion programs. Iraq had hoped to increase production from roughly 3 million barrels a day in 1978 to 4 million by the mid-1980s.

However, as noted previously, the Gulf war disrupted such plans. Iran destroyed one of Iraq's three oil-export routes when commandos blew up the offshore loading terminal at Fao. In April 1982 Syria closed the Iraqi pipeline through Syria to the Mediterranean. Coupled with the drop in world oil demand and prices, Iraq's foreign exchange earnings dropped drastically at a time when its war expenses were increasing. In response, Iraq has expanded the capacity of its pipeline through Turkey and, in 1985, completed the first phase of a pipeline route across Saudi Arabia. With planned increases in throughput of both pipelines and the possibility of another route through Jordan, Iraq could maintain secure export capacity regardless of what happens in the Gulf war or in Iraqi-Syrian relations.

Nonoil industry has never played a major role in Iraq's economy. The government is concentrating on industrialization, utilizing its strongest economic sectors—oil and agriculture. Ultimately it hopes to develop both agri-industry and petrochemicals, and to reduce its dependence on crude oil exports.

Economic development is closely monitored through economic planning, which is based on socialist models. The earliest planning, however, occurred under the monarchy. The main accomplishment of that period was the progress made in controlling the flood-prone Tigris and Euphrates rivers.

Iraqi development plans followed Soviet planning philosophy until the late 1970s, when the government made a determined effort to acquire more Western technology in all areas of economic development. During the 1970s emphasis was on industrial development; in 1982 the Iraqis refocused on the agricultural sector, abandoning collective farms and encouraging private farming.

Although the government refuses to allow foreign private investment, much of the work on Iraq's development programs is actually performed by Western private firms through turnkey projects that are turned over to the government upon completion. With increased revenues to fund these projects after the quantum jump in oil prices in 1973, and with excellent agricultural potential and less population pressure than many of its neighbors, Iraq's economic prospects could be bright if it maintains political stability and can find a way to end the war with Iran.

Political Structure

Iraq is a republic dominated by the Socialist Arab Baath party. Technically, the Iraqi Baath party is a branch of the same party that rules Syria, but due to strong ideological and political differences, the two regimes are on bad terms. The titular head of the party's "National Command" ("National" here refers to the Arab nation as a whole) is Michel Aflaq, a Christian Arab who helped found the Baath in Syria in 1943. At the state level, the Iraqi "Regional Command," theoretically under the National Command, is headed by President Saddam Husayn. In actuality, Iraqis dominate both the National Command and the Regional Command since Syria does not recognize the authority of either.

The Baath party maintains a separate identity from the government. In this way, there is less conflict of loyalty among party workers who maintain an extensive party organization. Below the Regional Command level are provincially based unit commands that are further subdivided into branches (*far*); sections (*shu'bah*); divisions (*firqah*); and circles or cells (*halaqah*).

In November 1971 the National Action Charter was promulgated in an effort to broaden the Baath's political base by integrating other parties into the party structure. Following negotiations and in the wake of the Kazzar coup attempt in 1973, the Progressive National Front was created to include the Communist party of Iraq, Barzani's Kurdish Democratic party, and two smaller leftist groups, the Independent Democrats and the Progressive Nationalists. As relations with the Kurds deteriorated, Kurdish participation never materialized, and, at any rate, the Baath never intended to give the National Front any real participation in the political process. Non-Baath political views, however, are represented in the council of ministers.

Since the 1958 coup, Iraq has been ruled under several constitutions. The most recent to date, promulgated in July 1970 as a provisional constitution, delineated legislative, executive, and judicial branches of government. The constitution called for a National Assembly, to be initially appointed by the Iraqi Revolutionary Command Council (RCC) and representing all political, economic, and social groups in the country. The National Assembly held elections for the first time in 1980 and again in 1984. Its powers are fairly limited.

Executive powers are shared by the RCC and the national government. The RCC possesses ultimate control. It not only enacts legislation but also oversees all foreign and domestic policies and chooses (by two-thirds vote) the president and vice-president of the republic. The RCC is composed of nine members elected by simple majority from the Regional Command and, in turn, chooses its own chairman and vice-chairman. It is also empowered to relieve any of its members or members of the government and, if need be, to prosecute them. It is by far, therefore, the most powerful governmental institution in Iraq.

The national government consists of the president, the vice-president, and the cabinet ministers. According to the constitution, the president is the chief executive and commander-in-chief of the armed forces. He is empowered to nominate the vice-president and chooses his own council of ministers. He is also responsible for choosing and dismissing judges. Under his direction, the government prepares the annual budget for presentation to the RCC.

The 1970 constitution also provided for an independent judiciary. Above the courts of first instance are five courts of appeal and, at the top, a court of cassation. The judiciary also includes religious courts and revolutionary courts. The latter are convened to hear political cases. The legal system of Iraq is based primarily on the French code.

At the local level, Iraq has sixteen provinces administered by governors who are appointed by the president and are responsible to the minister of interior. Because Iraq is a unitary system with all powers reserved at the national level, the governors' powers are relatively limited.

The four Kurdish provinces are theoretically an exception. The 1970 Kurdish settlement (the so-called March Manifesto approved by the RCC on March 11, 1970) granted a degree of autonomy to the Kurds. Although it has never been fully implemented, it does grant proportional Kurdish representation in the RCC and the government and a degree of cultural as well as political autonomy.

Political Dynamics

Baathism professes to be socialist and pan-Arab, and takes a revolutionary approach to foreign policy. Baathist ideology, however, is difficult to define in theoretical terms. It is basically an amalgam of anti-imperialistic xenophobia, nostalgia for the ancient glory of the Arab empires, and a commitment to redistribution of wealth to benefit the poorer classes. The 1970 constitution, which serves as a statement of Baathist principles and goals, upholds socialism but appears to reject the socialist concept of the collective good in favor of the individual, who should be able "to develop his personality, cultivate the Arab heritage and live in freedom unfettered by social and economic differentials"[1] It acknowledges the important role of Islam in Arab society but emphasizes the secular nature of the state—a key point in the ideological conflict with the Islamic fundamentalist regime in Iran.

Baath ideology has appealed mainly to Sunni Arab urban classes (though many have originally come from villages) at the lowest and least secure levels of the middle class. Since party membership is almost a necessity for career advancement, party roles are probably larger and more representative of all segments of Iraqi society than is the number of ideologically committed. By any standards, the latter group represents a small minority of the population. Despite the urban and revolutionary character of the party, traditional family and village ties can still be important. For example, both al-Bakr and Saddam Husayn al-Tikriti, as well as a number of lesser political figures, came from the same hometown, Tikrit, a small village on the northern Tigris. Saara', a town near Tikrit, and Anah, near the Syrian border, have also supplied a disproportionate number of men to the leadership structure.

The party dominates the political process in Iraq, all the more so because of the traditional weakness of formal political institutions. The government, likewise dominated by the Baath, serves more of an administrative role, formulating operational policies based on guidelines set down by the party. The distinction between the party and the government, however, can be overdrawn since all Iraqi politics are personality oriented and the party and the government are dominated by the same personalities.

Civilians dominate the Baath party of Iraq. In turn, through the party's military wing, it dominates the military establishment, which is charged with defending the regime but is at the same time kept under close surveillance to guard against coup plotting among the officer corps. As an additional check on the armed forces, the party has organized its own paramilitary units, the popular militia.

President al-Bakr was the head of the military wing, which was predominant when the Baathists seized power in 1968. In recent years, the civilian wing of the party under Saddam Husayn has gained ascendency in Iraqi politics. Saddam ruthlessly outmaneuvered his political rivals (many of whom are now deceased), but he would not have been able to do so without the full support of al-Bakr. He also developed a reputation as a pragmatist. He has never allowed his Baathist principles to be interpreted in so doctrinaire a fashion as to interfere with the needs of his country. Thus, despite the internal Kurdish problem, the endemic lack of legitimacy facing the regime, the war with Iran, and the many other foreign policy problems he must deal with, Saddam has brought a considerable degree of political stability to Iraq. Given the political as well as military threat of the war with Iran, however, one cannot rule out the possibility of a coup attempt.

Foreign Policy

Particularly since Saddam Husayn's emergence as president, Iraqi foreign policy has been based more upon analytical assessments of Iraqi national interests than upon purely ideological precepts. Nonetheless, the ideological concepts of Iraqi nationalism, nonalignment, and pan-Arabism remain important features of rationales provided by the regime for its foreign policy decisions. Iraqi nationalism, already the dominant force in foreign policy considerations, has been even further strengthened by the war with Iran. The war has also further diminished the weight of ideological considerations in Iraqi foreign policy, which since 1980 has been almost totally focused on extricating the country from the war.

From the overthrow of the monarchy in 1957 until the late 1970s, the predominant concern of Iraqi governments with domestic issues left Iraq relatively isolated in regional and world politics. This isolation meant that Iraqi leaders had progressively less extensive experience of the outside world and also that few Westerners had intimate dealings with Iraq. One result of Iraq's isolation was that its radicalism appeared to deepen in the mid-1970s. A founding member of OPEC in 1960, Iraq had often played a hawkish role within that organization in support of price increases. The post-1968 Baathist regime had a reputation for harboring and using international terrorists even against fellow Arab states as a means of political influence. Although, or perhaps partly because, Iraqi forces made little more than symbolic contributions to Arab military action against Israel in the wars of 1948–1949, 1967, and 1973, Iraq has been one of the most strident rhetorical enemies of Israel. Baghdad hosted Arab summit conferences in 1978 and 1979 to impose sanctions against Egypt for its negotiations and peace treaty with Israel at Camp David. In 1972 Baghdad's signing of a treaty of friendship and cooperation with Moscow further set it apart from most other Arab states by appearing to confirm a view of Iraq as a Soviet stalking-horse in the region.

Nonetheless, Iraq's foreign policy had begun to reflect more practical considerations of the national interest by the late 1970s. As relations with Moscow cooled with the growing Baathist concern over the subversive activities of the Moscow-backed Communist party of Iraq, Iraq began to purchase major weapons systems from Western Europe, including French-built Mirage aircraft. Baghdad promptly and forcefully condemned the 1979 Soviet invasion of Afghanistan and successfully sought to burnish its image as a leader among the nonaligned countries. Iraqi plans to assume formal leadership of the Nonaligned Movement (NAM) were thwarted when the continuing war with Iran precluded the convening of the September 1982 NAM summit in Baghdad as planned at the previous 1979 NAM summit. Baghdad remains highly suspicious of both superpowers. It suspects that the United States seeks regional hegemony through its "agent," Israel, yet is aware that the Soviet Union and its allies are primary conduits for arms to Iran, including the Soviet-made Scud missiles that Iran began to launch at Baghdad in 1985.

Iraq's relations with its immediate neighbors are also motivated to a large degree by ideological considerations. Baghdad considers the Syrian Baath regime to be heretical and a traitor to pan-Arabism in its support of Iran in the Iran-Iraq War. Relations with Iran had been bad even under the shah, and, of course, they deteriorated into war after the Iranian revolution. It would be a mistake, however, to view the war as simply one of fundamentalism against secularism. Iranians and Iraqis have been separated for centuries by ethnic, national, religious, tribal, and many other rivalries.

Largely as a result of the war, Iraq has encouraged a rapprochement with its conservative Gulf neighbors, which collectively have contributed billions of dollars to the Iraqi war effort. In a part of the world where personal diplomacy is so important, the new ties are not likely to be quickly erased after the end of the war. Moreover, since 1982 Iraqi leaders have avowed their support for any settlement of the Arab-Israeli dispute that is acceptable to the Palestinians, and have stated that a "condition of security" is necessary for both the Israelis and the Palestinians. Iraq has also publicly condemned international terrorism and, in 1983, expelled the Abu Nidal organization, one of the deadliest of the Palestinian terrorist groups.

Pragmatism has also been manifested in relations with the West. For example, Iraq has for years been one of the bitterest foes of U.S. policy in the Middle East. Nevertheless, Iraq has always preferred U.S. technology over Soviet technology, and even its political antipathy underwent a change when the exigencies of the Iran-Iraq War necessitated a new direction in Iraqi foreign policy.

Bibliography

The three studies written over a period of years by Majid Khadduri are among the better studies of modern Iraq in English: *Independent Iraq: A Study in Iraqi*

Politics from 1932 to 1958 (New York: Oxford University Press, 1961); *Republic Iraq: A Study in Iraqi Politics Since the Revolution of 1958* (New York: Oxford University Press, 1969); and *Socialist Iraq: A Study in Iraqi Politics Since 1968* (Washington, D.C.: Middle East Institute, 1978). Khadduri's approach is historical, and much of the material is based on personal interviews with leading Iraqi politicians such as Saddam Husayn. Christine Moss Helms, *Iraq: Eastern Flank of the Arab World* (Washington, D.C.: Brookings Institution, 1984), has written one of the best books on current Iraqi politics. Her discussion of the goals and theories of Baathism and the problems confronting the decisionmakers is perhaps the only work largely based on primary sources. She also includes a section on the war and its ramifications on Iraqi politics.

A comprehensive book appearing in 1978, and up-dated in 1984, is Edith Penrose and E. F. Penrose, *Iraqi International Relations and National Development* (London: Ernest Benn; and Boulder, Colo.: Westview Press). An interesting shorter study on Iraqi politics is Phoebe A. Marr's "The Political Elite of Iraq," in George Lenczouski, ed., *Political Elite in the Middle East* (Washington, D.C.: American Enterprise Institute, 1975). Still relevant today, the study is concerned with locating factors in the formation of political attitudes by the Iraqi leadership. Marr has also just published an excellent history, *The Modern History of Iraq* (Boulder, Colo.: Westview Press, 1985). Three other interesting and informative books that deal primarily with domestic politics are Lorenzo Kent Kimball's *The Changing Pattern of Political Power in Iraq, 1958–1971* (New York: Robert Spiller & Sons, 1972); Edgar O'Ballance's *The Kurdish Revolt, 1961–1970* (Hamden, Conn.: Archon Books, 1973); and Edmond Ghareeb, *The Kurdish Question in Iraq* (Syracuse, N.Y.: Syracuse University Press, 1981).

Jasim Abdulghani's *Iran and Iraq* (Baltimore, Md.: Johns Hopkins University Press, 1984) examines the origins of the Gulf war, including a discussion of the war itself and its regional and global implications. David Long presents a brief discussion of Iraq's domestic and foreign policies in *The Persian Gulf: An Introduction to Its People, Politics, and Economics*, rev. ed. (Boulder, Colo.: Westview Press, 1978). Finally, the American University's *Area Handbook for Iraq* (Washington, D.C.: Government Printing Office, 1979) offers a valuable overview of the political, social, and economic institutions and dynamics of Iraq.

7

Eastern Arabian States: Kuwait, Bahrain, Qatar, United Arab Emirates, and Oman

John Duke Anthony
John A. Hearty

Before the discovery of oil, the eastern Arabian states eked out a subsistence-level existence from pearling, fishing, seaborne commerce, and, among the nomads, animal husbandry. The sudden and dramatic change from relative austerity to oil-generated affluence has characterized nearly all of these states and lent a fairy-tale atmosphere to their capitals, each with its own new international airport and luxury hotels. Beneath the glitter, however, each state remains locked in an ongoing struggle with the awesome tasks of social, economic, and political transformation. This struggle has been made all the more difficult by changing military, political, and economic conditions. The fall of the shah in 1979 led to a hostile Islamic fundamentalist regime in Iran. In 1980 war between Iraq and Iran broke out and has been going on ever since. Finally, the oil glut of the 1980s has significantly lowered the real income of the Gulf states. In the face of these destabilizing conditions, the Gulf states have displayed a remarkable degree of resiliency.

Historical Background

Little is known of eastern Arabia during prehistoric times. In the north, the ancient civilization of Mesopotamia extended along the shores of the Persian (Arabian) Gulf as far south as contemporary Saudi Arabia. From around 4000 to 2000 B.C., much of eastern Arabia was controlled by the ancient civilization of Dilmun, centered in the Bahrain archipelago. A later civilization, called Magan, arose in Oman.

Because most of the hinterland of eastern Arabia has always been ecologically inhospitable, the ancient inhabitants turned primarily to the sea for their livelihoods. The ancestors of the Phoenicians are believed by some to have first learned their maritime skills in the Gulf. Inland, nomads

began to develop animal husbandry, and at the large oases, irrigated farming was also developed. In Oman there was farming in the Hajar Mountains. Moreover, despite the isolation of communities in the Gulf region, fairly regular intercourse has existed between the interior and the coastal towns since ancient times.

Indigenous Gulf maritime trade reached its zenith during the reign of the Abbasid caliphs in Baghdad (A.D. 750–1258). Like spokes from the hub of the Abbasid Empire, routes followed by the Gulf seafarers extended to India and Africa, supplying goods from the east and the south to the center of the Islamic world. With the fall of the Abbasid capital of Baghdad to the Mongols in 1258, the region's trade declined and politics became increasingly chaotic, producing a situation that changed very little until the first European penetration of the Gulf two and one-half centuries later.

The first significant European incursion into the Gulf was made by Vasco da Gama of Portugal in 1497. The Portuguese objectives and administrative practices in the Gulf area were subsequently adopted by the Dutch and English, who followed Portugal's prime objective—paramountcy in the trading of eastern luxury goods to which Europe had grown accustomed during the time of the Abbasid and Umayyad empires. Another concern was the security of the maritime routes to and from India.

As the Portuguese Empire faded so did its control over the Gulf. A successful English-Persian attack on Portuguese-held Hormuz signaled the decline of Portuguese hegemony and the advent of the Dutch, who had begun to establish trade links to the east. By the middle of the eighteenth century, however, the Dutch began to yield to the British. With the abandonment of Kharg Island (offshore contemporary Iran) in 1765, the Dutch presence in the Gulf area was effectively ended.

The British, like the Portuguese and Dutch before them, became interested in the Gulf for both strategic and commercial reasons and, like their predecessors, adopted an administrative policy based on indirect rule, with a minimum of interference in local affairs. British trade with the Orient was obstructed by piracy and civil war in the Gulf region and was threatened from outside the area by the French.

These impediments to British interests motivated the British government to enter into a number of special treaties with the littoral states. The first such treaty was concluded with Oman and coincided with the French invasion of Egypt in 1798. The pact was designed to deny the Gulf to the French and to improve the system for protecting Britain's lines of communication with its increasingly important Indian Empire.

As the French Revolution caused the challenge that France had represented to recede, another challenge presented itself in the form of Arab privateers. Sailing from such shaykhdoms as Sharjah and Ras al-Khaymah, Gulf mariners would strike at European shipping. Even though a number of military expeditions were dispatched to the Gulf from England's Indian dominions, the British were unable to halt such attacks until 1819 when, after heavy fighting, they successfully defeated the Arab fleet based in Ras al-Khaymah. A treaty signed the following year with the local shaykhs became the cornerstone of Britain's political, strategic, military, diplomatic, economic, commercial, and administrative presence in the Gulf area for the next 150 years.

Although Arab harassment of British shipping in the Gulf and Indian Ocean ceased thereafter, a major problem remained in the sense that the shaykhdoms had not been prohibited from engaging in war with one another on land. Hence, in 1835, the British prevailed upon all the ruling shaykhs to sign a second agreement. The latter treaty prohibited the tribes under the ruler's jurisdiction from raiding each other during the fishing and pearling seasons, which in time came to be called the "trucial period." Taken together, the two pacts marked the beginning of a long series of treaties between the British and what became known as the Trucial States, and were the principal means by which Britian legitimized its administration of the latter's defense and foreign affairs.

From the beginning, British authority in the Gulf was exercised indirectly through the local rulers in the area. In fact, control of domestic affairs remained largely in the hands of indigenous, albeit traditional, leaders throughout the long period of British protection. By 1916 Britain was able to assume direct control over the shaykhdoms' external relations and indirect control over domestic affairs. Most rulers acceded to official British "advice"; those who refused or resisted risked almost certain exile, ouster, or British naval bombardment of their principalities. In this manner, Britain introduced an unprecedented degree of stability to the region.

After World War II, and especially following the independence of India and Pakistan in the late 1940s, British interests in the Gulf area changed significantly. Although the strategic need to protect the Indian Empire had ceased, oil interests in Iran, Iraq, Kuwait, and other states had not only continued but increased. In the minds of U.K. policymakers, the extent of British involvement in the Gulf region's petroleum resources was sufficient to warrant the continued stationing of military forces in Oman, Sharjah, and Bahrain. In time, however, the costs to British taxpayers of maintaining a military presence in the Gulf area became an issue of increasing controversy in British domestic politics. As but one indication of growing disenchantment at home with the country's imperial policies, the British decided three years after the 1958 coup in Iraq to grant full independence to Kuwait, a decision that would be repeated ten years hence when the last of the protected-state treaties with the nine remaining Gulf shaykhdoms was terminated.

Britain's greatest impact on the Gulf area was to introduce and develop modern administrative and legal practices into the region, as exemplified by the establishment of municipal governments and the application of Western-style legal codes. A more pervasive consequence of British influence was the promotion of English as the area's language of international trade, defense, and diplomacy. Rooted in more than a century and a half of cooperation between individual British officials and the indigenous inhabitants, Great Britain's legacy in the Gulf area is deeply imbedded in the emirates and gives every indication of remaining a prominent feature of life in the area for some time to come.

The Gulf Cooperation Council

The founding of the Gulf Cooperation Council (GCC) in 1981 was of considerable political, economic, and even strategic importance for the region. The six GCC member states—Saudi Arabia, Kuwait, Bahrain, Qatar, the United Arab Emirates (UAE), and Oman—had discussed creating such an organization for almost a decade, following the departure of the British from the Gulf area; but owing mainly to Iran's and Iraq's desires to be a part of it, the idea did not materialize. From the Gulf states' point of view, Iraq was too radical and Iran too large and not entirely trusted by the Arab Gulf states. The fall of the shah in 1979 and the outbreak of the Iran-Iraq War in 1980 changed all that. Because of the perceived threat of the war, and with both Iran and Iraq too involved in the war to try to insinuate themselves into a regional security organization, the GCC was born.

Security was not the only factor in the creation of the GCC; cooperation in economic and political affairs was also important. Indeed, Kuwait initially emphasized these areas, while Oman emphasized security. With the war dragging on, however, and given the military and terrorist attacks on Kuwait and an aborted coup attempt linked to Iran in Bahrain, the security aspects of GCC cooperation gradually took on primary importance. In 1983 the GCC held its first joint military maneuvers and began to develop the concept of joint military planning.

The GCC's principal policymaking body is the Supreme Council, which comprises the six heads of state. It meets at least once a year. There are also a number of ministerial councils that meet as often as necessary to coordinate and collaborate on economic, foreign, and military policies. A secretary-general, appointed by the Supreme Council, deals with day-to-day affairs. At this writing, the secretary-general is Abdallah Bishara, former Kuwaiti ambassador to the United Nations.

Modern Gulf States

There are ten Gulf emirates and one sultanate constituting five states: Kuwait, Bahrain, Qatar, the seven-member United Arab Emirates, and Oman, respectively. The governments of these states are all conservative politically and each, save the UAE, which is a federation headed by a president, has a dynastic form of rule. Even in the UAE, the local administrations of the various dynastic emirates have a greater impact on the daily lives of the citizens than that of the federal government. The relatively stable political conditions that prevailed in the Gulf throughout most of the 1970s stood in marked contrast to the previous, often violent histories of a number of these states. Even the strains of the Iran-Iraq War and the sharp decline in national incomes due to the oil glut of the 1980s have not thus far significantly affected the remarkable degree of resiliency exhibited by the Gulf states' regimes.

KUWAIT

Historical Background

The Kuwaitis trace their history back to the late seventeenth and early eighteenth centuries, when several tribes of the great Unayzah tribal confederation emigrated from their famine-torn homeland in central Arabia. Calling themselves the Bani Utub ("the people who wandered"), roughly half of the emigrés settled in Bahrain. In 1716 the remainder founded present-day Kuwait.

Over the years, several leading clans of the original wave of emigrés—the Al Sabahs, the Al Ghanims, the Al Khalids, the Janaats, and the Al

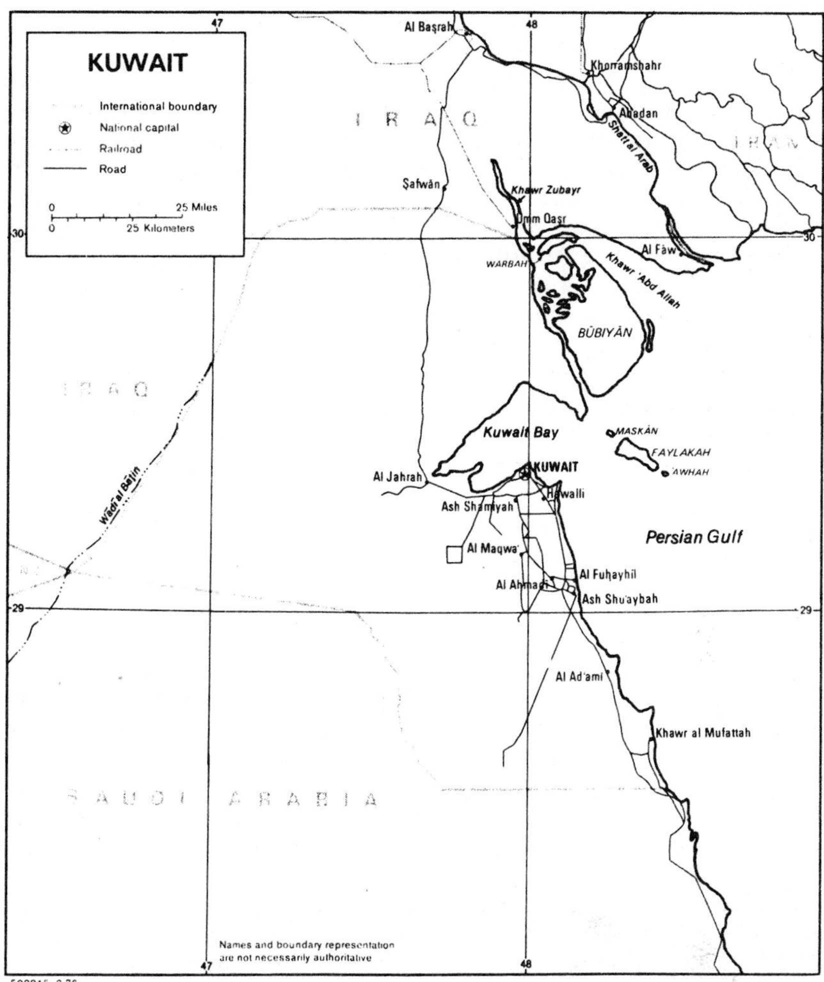

Salihs among others—combined to create an oligarchical merchant principality presided over by the Al Sabahs.

In 1899 Mubarak Al Sabah, subsequently referred to as "Mubarak the Great" (r. 1896–1915), who had expanded Kuwaiti influence along with Al Sabah preeminence, allowed the principality over which he reigned to enter into a protected-state relationship with the British. Shaykh Mubarak's reason was his fear that the Ottomans, who claimed nominal suzerainty over the shaykhdom, might try to implement political control. At his death Mubarak had succeeded in expanding Kuwaiti rule to about twice its present size. In 1922 Kuwait's British protectors negotiated half of the principality's enlarged territory back to the Saudis and to Iraq in the Treaty of Uqayr.

The treaty also created the Saudi-Kuwaiti Neutral Zone, the landward side of which was split equally between the two parties in 1970.

The British allowed the bulk of domestic administration to remain in Kuwaiti hands, although in time they would provide advisers to help create and staff the beginnings of a modern bureaucracy. As would occur elsewhere in the Gulf and especially throughout eastern Arabia, British interests in Kuwait underwent a dramatic transformation following the discovery of oil. The Kuwait Oil Company, jointly owned by Gulf Oil Company and British Petroleum (formerly the Anglo-Iranian Oil Company), received a concession in 1934 and discovered oil in 1938. The first commercial quantities, however, were not exported until after World War II.

In 1961 Kuwait regained full independence from the British. At the time, Iraq made threatening gestures, claiming sovereignty over the emirate based on old Ottoman claims. Britain, under treaty provisions, sent troops to Kuwait and the crisis subsided. In 1963 Kuwait became a member of the United Nations, and later the same year Iraq recognized Kuwait's independence.

Even so, in 1973 Iraq laid claim to the Kuwaiti islands of Warbah and Bubiyan, which command the approaches to the Iraqi naval base at Umm Qasr. In May 1973 Iraq occupied the Kuwaiti border post of Samitah on the mainland, and a military clash ensued. Although the Iraqis withdrew late in 1974, additional incidents subsequently occurred.

Iraq has offered to lease the islands, but Kuwait still considers this offer too dangerous. Notwithstanding Iraqi overtures to improve the situation in the late 1970s, relations between the two states remain uneasy on territorial as well as ideological grounds.

Three factors have had a telling impact on Kuwaiti stability in the 1980s: the Iran-Iraq War, terrorism, and the oil glut. The proximity of Kuwait to the war was brought home dramatically in the fall of 1981 when Iran bombed two Kuwaiti border areas, and in 1982 when Iranian aircraft attacked a Kuwaiti oil facility. Iran's major aim appears to be to so intimidate Kuwait that it will cease to be a conduit for money and materiel for the Iraqi war effort. Iran has also supported terrorist activities in Kuwait.

In December 1983 Shi'a terrorists of the Da'wa party bombed a number of government and foreign installations, including the U.S. Embassy. The release of those tried and convicted of these acts became the major demand of the Lebanese Shi'a, who subsequently kidnapped seven Americans and whose kin are among the convicted. In December 1984 Shi'a terrorists hijacked a Kuwaiti airliner, killing two American passengers and landing the plane at Tehran. At the time of this writing, they have yet to be brought to justice. In the spring of 1985, two popular Kuwaiti restaurants were bombed and an attempt was made on the amir's life. Although the role of Iran was never directly proven in any of these cases, strong evidence links them to Iranian support, in line with its general support of terrorism in the furtherence of its brand of Islamic revolution.

Though less dramatic, the oil glut has also affected Kuwaiti stability to the degree that jobs have become more scarce and the government has been forced into austerity measures. The brunt of the belt tightening is being felt not only by nonresident aliens but also by resident aliens—particularly Palestinians, many of whom have been residents in Kuwait for almost forty years.

Political Environment

Population and Social Conditions

Kuwait lies at the northeast end of the Gulf and contains some 16,000 square kilometers (ca. 6,200 square miles). The emirate's land borders Iraq to the north and Saudi Arabia to the south. In addition, Kuwait shares a de facto maritime boundary (as do all the emirates) with Iran. The terrain is mostly flat, sandy desert with occasional ridges and rock outcroppings, particularly to the west.

The population of Kuwait is roughly 1.79 million, most of whom live in the capital city, which, as in most of the other Gulf emirates, carries the same name as the state itself. Approximately 85 percent of the inhabitants are Arabs; the remaining 15 percent are mainly made up of Iranians, Indians, Pakistanis, and Europeans. More than 85 percent of the native Kuwaiti population is Sunni Muslim; the remainder are Shi'ite. It is significant, however, that more than half the total population is composed of aliens. This expatriate and immigrant population is almost entirely the result of requirements by the oil industry and ancillary enterprises for skilled manpower resources in excess of what can be produced by the Kuwaiti educational system.

The largest nonindigenous group is the Palestinian community, which constitutes approximately a quarter of the total population, or, according to unofficial estimates, about 300,000 people. The Palestinians began arriving in Kuwait after the first Arab-Israeli war in 1948. Although many of them are well-educated and have lived and worked in Kuwait long enough to attain high positions in business and government, relatively few have attained full Kuwaiti citizenship. Like their compatriots in other countries, they have maintained strong ties to their homeland.

Other foreign groups have come to Kuwait to make their fortunes and then return to their native lands, a phenomenon that accounts for the disproportionate ratio of males to females. Except for Palestinians and Europeans, many workers leave their families behind while sending a high percentage of their earnings back home.

Kuwait's "cradle-to-grave" welfare system, supported by oil revenues, is one of the most distinctive in the world. In the day-to-day administration of the system there is little distinction made between resident aliens and native Kuwaitis. The government provides medical, educational, and welfare services, and even domestic telephone calls are free. Kuwait's educational establishment is comprehensive, compulsory for all children, and modern. It includes a tuition-free university and numerous vocational schools, all of which are subsidized by the state. The generous welfare program has been credited with reducing substantially the basis for social and economic unrest in the emirates. Nonetheless, owing to the limited opportunities for Kuwaitis and non-Kuwaitis alike to participate in the governing process and, in the case of the latter, to obtain citizenship, various forms of political dissatisfaction have been a recurring phenomenon. As a result, the government was prompted in 1982 to tighten immigration controls.

Economic Conditions

Prior to the production of oil, most Kuwaitis were engaged in economic activities typical of many other areas in the Gulf region, such as pearling and fishing along the coast and pastoral nomadism in the interior. Before development of cultured pearls by the Japanese, Kuwait had a fleet of over eight hundred pearl boats and some thirty thousand divers. Kuwaiti trading dhows also sailed annually to Africa and India carrying cargoes laden with limes, dates, and other items exported from Iraq, and returning with timber, textiles, and many other essential items not readily available locally. Since World War II, however, Kuwait has become a major world oil producer. Oil revenues have allowed Kuwait to evolve an advanced welfare system and have provided job opportunities for well over a half-million expatriates. Under the "participation" policies first enunciated by Saudi Arabian Petroleum Minister Shaykh Ahmad Zaki Yamani in the late 1960s, Kuwait bought 100 percent equity in the Kuwait Oil Company (KOC). In 1980–1981, Kuwait completely reorganized its oil sector. A new holding company, the Kuwait Petroleum Corporation, was formed to consolidate the upstream (oil production) operations of KOC, and the downstream (refining, marketing, and shipping) operations of the Kuwait National Petroleum Company.

Like all Gulf Arabs, the Kuwaitis are greatly concerned about the future of their emirate's economy "after the oil runs out." As but one expression of this widespread anxiety, conservation measures were adopted in 1972, which restricted maximum production to 3 million barrels per day. Subsequently, the Kuwaitis have increasingly adhered to the view that oil left in the ground is worth more than money in the bank, especially in view of inflation and, in the late 1970s, the rather bleak prospects for the discovery of alternate energy resources elsewhere in the world. In the positions they have adopted vis à vis these and other issues for which conventional economic wisdom has posed few answers, the Kuwaitis are not that much different in their thinking than many other Gulf Arabs.

Concern about the depletion of oil reserves has resulted in accelerated attempts to modernize and diversify the economy, particularly in the fields of petrochemicals, fertilizer production, and shrimping. Agriculture remains practically nonexistent because of a lack of suitable soil and sufficient quantities of potable water. Indeed, Kuwait's chronic water shortage was resolved in the 1950s only by the installation of costly desalinization plants. Before that, Kuwaiti divers collected fresh water in earthen jugs from various springs that bubbled up from the floor of the Gulf.

The emirate's success to date in diversifying its economy has been limited owing to the paucity of nonpetroleum resources, the small size of the domestic market, and duplication of industries and projects by other Gulf states. Thus far, most industrial enterprise is in state-owned corporations, with the private sector active mainly in retail marketing and investment banking.

By the late 1970s an estimated 1 billion dollars annually was being accrued as a result of astute public and private investments made over the years since oil production began. The Kuwaitis, considering their experience in this area thus far, foresee returns from capital investments, handled through their own banks and investment firms, as a major source of their national income when oil runs out. Although they have been generous to most developing countries, most of their investments are in Europe and the United States. Much more than any of the other emirates, Kuwait has exhibited a willingness to invest a proportion of its assets in foreign real estate holdings, as evidenced by its investment in a major resort island in South Carolina and by its acquisition of Santa Fe International (a U.S. oil-drilling company).

Kuwait's economy experienced some setbacks in the 1980s, owing in large part to the oil glut and declining oil revenues. On the other hand, because of earlier production cutbacks, the decline in oil income did not result in the shock to the economy that it otherwise might have. Kuwait also has to worry that its oil production does not decline so far that the natural gas associated with the oil production is insufficient for the domestic energy requirements for which it is used.

In 1982 Kuwait experienced another kind of economic crisis when the Suq al-Manakh (the Kuwaiti stock market) collapsed. The collapse was the result of worsening economic conditions and inadequate regulation. A new stock market was subsequently opened with substantially more government supervision.

Political Structure

The constitution, inaugurated in 1962 under Amir Abdallah al-Salim Al Sabah, provides for the establishment of a legislature, an executive branch, and an independent judicial system.

The legislature, called the National Assembly, was granted significant powers, including the right to petition the amir (ruler) concerning cabinet appointees and the prime minister. The electoral base has remained narrow and is limited to citizens of Kuwait who are male, literate, and over twenty-one years old. Although political parties have yet to become legal in the emirate, the National Assembly had become an increasingly vocal force in Kuwaiti politics by the time of its dissolution in August 1976 amidst government concern over the prospects for regional and domestic instability. This concern was due, at least in part, to tensions generated by the Lebanese civil war and an inability of the parties concerned to address the Palestinian dimension of the Arab-Israeli conflict. In 1981, following redistricting and general elections, the National Assembly once again convened. In the elections, some of the older radical personalities lost out to younger men, and the entire assembly shifted to the right with the election of religiously conservative members.

The executive branch is headed by the amir, who is usually designated by the preceding amir with the consent of the ruling Al Sabah family. The only formal constraints on the selection process are that the prospective ruler be of age and a descendant of Mubarak the Great. The amir rules through a prime minister, who usually holds the post of heir apparent simultaneously, and a council of ministers. According to the constitution, the council of ministers is responsible to the National Assembly, but, in fact, it is responsible to the amir who selects and may remove its members as well as other government and judicial officials. The council of ministers numbers about twenty members. The amir also serves as the commander-in-chief of the armed forces.

The judiciary is based on the Egyptian model and is an amalgam of Islamic law, English common law, and the Ottoman civil code. The highest court is the Supreme Court of Appeal, although the amir himself can act as the final court of appeal. There are also permanent courts of appeal and a number of courts of first instance that hear such cases as those involving divorce or inheritance. More recently, a State Security Court was established in 1975, to handle political cases deemed to be in violation of specific Kuwaiti laws.

Kuwait is divided administratively into three districts (Kuwait City, Al Ahmadi, and Hawalli), each of which is headed by a governor appointed by the amir. The governor (*wali*) is charged with maintaining and supervising the work of the municipalities, and he himself is responsible to the ministry of interior.

Members of the military have been prohibited from participating in the governing process per se and, for the most part, have remained depoliticized. The Kuwaiti army is relatively small, consisting of some ten thousand men, but is relatively well trained, equipped, and paid. There is also a National Guard and a National Security Force under the direction of the ministries of defense and interior, respectively.

Political Dynamics

Kuwait is a constitutional monarchy whose rulers have traditionally been chosen from the Al Sabah family. In recent years, the rulership has alternated between two branches of the dynasty that include the descendants of two sons of Mubarak the Great: "the Salims" and "the Jabirs." This sequence was broken by Shaykh Sabah al-Salim Al Sabah, a Salim who became amir in 1965, succeeding a Salim.

The sequence was restored on January 1, 1978, when Shaykh Sabah, in turn, was succeeded by Shaykh Jabir al-Ahmad Al Sabah, a Jabir. The new ruler maintained the tradition by choosing a Salim, Shaykh Sa'd bin Abdallah, as heir apparent.

Despite the monarchical structure of government, Kuwait is actually an oligarchy. The power of the amirs is shared both with the rest of the Al Sabah family and with the other old, established families of the Bani Utub tribe. With such a small population base, Kuwait, like all other emirates, has had to rely heavily on the services of expatriates to aid in the administration of government. Many key positions have been filled by able Palestinians who have been resident in Kuwait for decades. In some instances, they and other long-time residents have been granted citizenship. Even so, the number involved is very limited, and assimilation of long-time resident aliens remains a major problem confronting the regime.

Foreign Policy

Because of insufficient military and population capabilities to defend itself against such countries as Iraq, Kuwait has long used its oil revenues as its principal foreign policy instrument. Kuwait has attempted to utilize systematic foreign-assistance programs to neutralize potential opposition. With this and other purposes in mind, the Kuwait Fund for Arab Economic Development was established in 1967. In the aftermath of the June 1967 war, moreover, Kuwait, along with Saudi Arabia and Libya, became a major contributor of financial aid to Jordan and Egypt. The emirate has also significantly aided the Palestinians through financial contributions. More recently, Kuwait has been a major contributor to Iraq's war effort against Iran. The Gulf states have collectively contributed over $30 billion to Iraq. Kuwait has also been a major conduit for military supplies being shipped to Iraq.

Kuwait's realization of its limitations in defending its foreign policy interests have caused it to pursue a policy of trying to accommodate all sides, both in regional and in global political arenas. In regional politics, Kuwait stridently supports Palestinian rights and is an activist in its public policy support on Arab issues, despite the fact that its conservative political system places it closer to the Arab conservatives than the Arab radicals. At the same time, the Kuwaitis strive never to be too far out in front on any issue for which there is no solid Arab consensus. In global politics, even though its market economy and conservative political system give it a closer affinity to the West than to the East, its public diplomacy often seems closer to that of more leftist, radical Arab states.

BAHRAIN

The state of Bahrain consists of an archipelago of some thirty islands, located between Saudi Arabia and the Qatar peninsula. The largest island, Bahrain (al-Bahrayn), is 48 kilometers (30 miles) long and 15.5 kilometers (9.6 miles) wide, and contains the capital, Manamah (population 110,000). The second largest island is Muharraq, which is nearby and accessible by a four-mile causeway. It contains the state's second largest town, also called Muharraq, and the international airport. The total land area of the emirate is about 662 square kilometers (ca. 256 square miles) and the population is about 400,000.

Historical Background

In the mid-eighteenth century a branch of the Bani Utub tribe, which had settled Kuwait, moved to the northern tip of the Qatar peninsula and established a fishing and pearling ministate at Subarah. In 1782, the Al Khalifah and other families crossed over from Qatar to the nearby Bahrain archipelago, where they formed a ruling merchant oligarchy over the local oasis farmers, fishermen, pearl divers, and seafarers. The Al Khalifahs have remained the ruling family to this day. Initially, although Persians contested Al Khalifah rule, they had little choice but to acquiesce to the de facto state of affairs when Bahrain came under British protection in the early nineteenth century. The claim was reviewed periodically in the nineteenth and twentieth centuries, and especially during the reign of the Pahlevi dynasty in Iran, which used the occasion to advance the claim once more in 1968 when the British announced their intention to withdraw by the end of 1971. In 1970, however, Iran acceded to the findings of a special UN fact-providing mission sent to Bahrain and formally recognized Bahrain's right to independence. This was granted in August of the following year.

Iran again raised its claim to Bahrain in 1979, following the Islamic revolution. Although it has not pushed the claim, at least two coup attempts have been uncovered in Bahrain since that time, both with strong evidence linking them to Iran. The most serious attempt, which was discovered in December 1981, led to the arrest of seventy-three people.

The British exercised indirect control in Bahrain and the lower Gulf shaykhdoms (the terms *shaykhdom* and *emirate* are synonymous) through political agents serving under a single British "Resident." From 1763 to 1946 these Residents had their headquarters in Bushire (Iran), after which the Residency was moved to Bahrain. Until they received independence in 1971, Bahrain, Qatar, and the seven Trucial States (now the UAE) all came under the purview of the Resident.

Political Environment

Population and Social Conditions

The population of Bahrain is primarily Arab, although a great many of the local inhabitants are of Persian descent. The proportion of natives to resident aliens is much greater than in the other Gulf states like Kuwait or the UAE. The vast majority of the population is Muslim—half Shi'ite and half Sunni. The Al Khalifahs and other Bani Utub families are Sunnis, whereas the older indigenous population has a large proportion of Shi'ites, many of whom have centuries-old ties to Iran. Persian is often spoken alongside other tongues in the markets, although Arabic is the official language.

Some Bahrainis with Iranian ties hail from the south Iranian coastal town of Lingeh, and are called Lingawis. Others, claiming to be the descendants of Arabian migrants to Persia who later returned to the southwest side of the Gulf, are called *muhawwalahs*. Still others are Persians from the north, sometimes called Red Iranians.

By Gulf standards, Bahrain has a sophisticated society, with one of the oldest oil industries in the region. Bahrain has an articulate labor force and in the past has experienced labor unrest, although no unions are permitted. The country is also noted for its intellectual tradition and boasts some of the region's leading poets, artists, and authors.

The Bahraini school system is over fifty years old, the oldest in the Gulf area. School attendance is compulsory for children between the ages of six and sixteen. This has made possible a highly technical work force of native Bahrainis. There are also free health and social services.

Economic Conditions

Once the center of the pearling industry in the Gulf region, Bahrain's pearl industry, like that of all the other emirates, suffered heavily from the introduction of Japanese cultured pearls several decades ago. The emirate's agricultural and fishing sectors have fared better; but future prospects for farming are bleak owing to heavy Bahraini and Saudi industrial use of the underground water (Bahrain and Saudi Arabia's Qatif Oasis are connected) that has lowered the water table. Excessive and unregulated exploitation of the region's marine biology resources, especially by the Gulf's lucrative shrimping industry, could also threaten fishing.

Bahrain's present economy is oil based. Petroleum production began in 1932—the operating company, Bahrain Petroleum Company (BAPCO) was originally owned by Standard Oil of California (SOCAL) and the Texas Company (TEXACO)—and has been declining for some years. Nowadays 85 percent of the production at BAPCO's refinery on Bahrain is based on Saudi crude, which arrives through an underwater pipeline.

The emirate has also been and remains a leading entrepôt center. The overall volume of trade passing through the archipelago has been enhanced by the new port, Mina Salman, and the new Bahrain International Airport, which is heavily used because of its central location in the Gulf region and on the route from Europe to the Far East and Australia. There is also a successful aluminum smelter, Aluminum Bahrain, Ltd. (ALBA), which uses natural gas resources, and a large drydock under the Organization of Arab Petroleum Exporting Countries (OAPEC) sponsorship known as the Arab Shipping and Repair Yard (ASRY). The emirate is also the headquarters of Gulf Air, the flag carrier of the Arab states of the lower Gulf region. The completion in 1985 of a causeway connecting Bahrain and Saudi Arabia should also enhance the economic prospects for the emirate, particularly if (as is suspected) it increases tourism by residents of nearby Eastern Province of Saudi Arabia. Finally, Bahrain has built up a considerable offshore banking sector, especially following the energy crisis of the 1970s and the collapse of the Lebanese banking industry as a result of the Lebanese civil war.

The oil glut has adversely affected Bahrain as it has other oil states in the Gulf, but because Bahrain did not have the same abundance of oil resources in the first place, and because it was more conservative in economic develoment, austerity has not been so disruptive as it might have been. The offshore banking industry—numbering more than sixty banks by the 1980s—has felt the economic squeeze, but Bahrainis have always been ambivalent about this largely foreign-owned sector of their economy.

Political Structure

Bahrain has developed a constitutional form of government that administers the emirate under the amir, a member of the Al Khalifah family. The constitution provides for separate executive, legislative, and judicial branches of government.

The first parliamentary elections were held in December 1973, shortly after the constitution had been ratified by popular referendum. The National Assembly was composed of thirty elected and fourteen appointed cabinet members. Although the assembly had fewer powers than that of Kuwait, its electorate was more widely based. The cabinet resigned in 1975 over the issue of alleged assembly interference in the administrative affairs of the government. The ruler, in response to the resignations, issued a decree that dissolved the legislature for an indeterminate time.

The executive branch of government has been headed by the prime minister. As of 1980, the prime minister was Shaykh Khalifah bin Salman Al Khalifah, the brother of the ruler. Shaykh Khalifah, who has held that position since 1973, is charged with managing the fifteen-member cabinet. Since the adjournment of the legislature, the cabinet has performed both legislative as well as executive functions. The ruler, Shaykh Isa bin Salman Al Khalifah, is advised by the cabinet but has long been personally active in tending to the day-to-day affairs of state. He is also assisted by other members of the ruling family, who hold most of the eight important cabinet portfolios. The heir apparent, Shaykh Hamad bin Isa Al Khalifah, Shaykh Isa's son, holds the post of minister of defense.

The Bahraini legal system is based on Western civil law and Islamic (Shari'a) law. The Shari'a court system accommodates the religious divisions within Bahraini society by establishing separate courts for Sunni and Shi'a sects. The amir has final power of review and pardon. The civil court system is organized much the same as the Shari'a system; that is, there are courts of first instance, courts of appeal, and a supreme court (high court of appeal). The supreme court not only hears appeals from lower courts but also rules on the constitutionality of laws and decrees.

Political parties are not permitted in Bahrain, although the loosely organized "Popular Bloc" of the left won ten seats in the first elections to the National Assembly. In addition, there is a radical subversive group of long standing known as the Bahrain National Liberation Front, but it has never been recognized by the government.

Political Dynamics

The ruling family wields the preponderance of influence within the Bahraini power structure despite the constitutional form of government. This pattern has at times enhanced and on occasion endangered the political stability of a country in which relatively sophisticated labor and leftist intellectual groups exist. Such groups have provided an impetus for a great many of the political and social reforms implemented by the government, but they have also spearheaded much of the emirate's labor unrest over the years. The leftist reform movement, now more than three decades old, suffered a serious setback when the National Assembly was dissolved. As a consequence, the ruling family has relied increasingly on the security forces to maintain its internal security.

The merchant community has generally been content to adopt a position of political neutrality so long as their commercial interests did not appear to be threatened. For example, despite the fairly large electoral base at the time of the 1973 elections, the merchants were not widely represented nor did they apparently care to be.

The Bahraini armed forces, consisting of about fifteen hundred men, and a public security force of roughly the same size, are headed by the amir. Both contingents have been loyal to the government. The public security forces are charged with maintaining internal order, a problem that periodically has plagued Bahrain more than any other emirate in the Gulf region. These forces are primarily responsible for controlling demonstrations and collecting intelligence on radical individuals and groups within Bahrain.

Foreign Policy

In keeping with its status as a small, militarily weak state, Bahrain has taken care to remain on good terms with its immediate neighbors. The historic territorial dispute with Qatar over the Hawar Islands, located off the coast of Qatar, briefly flared up again in 1982 when Bahrain named one of its naval vessels "Hawar"; but before the dispute could get out of hand, Saudi Arabia negotiated a "freeze" of the situation. In general, the nature and orientation of the emirate's external policies are conservative, pro-Arab, and, though not without reservations on specific issues, pro-Western. In regional matters, it generally follows the lead of Saudi Arabia. Like the latter country, and indeed like all the emirates of eastern Arabia, it also has close ties with the West. Until independence in 1971, the British maintained a naval base at Jufair (near Manamah). The United States, which since 1949 had rented space from the British to establish a headquarters for its Middle East Force (MIDEASTFOR), leased much of the former British facility directly from Bahrain from 1971 to 1977.

The Bahraini government was generally pleased to have the U.S. facility as an overt, official symbol of U.S. support for the regime. At the same time, a growing number of Bahraini officials began to view the U.S. presence as a potential liability in terms of the opposition it could engender from local and regional radical groups. Primarily for this reason, Bahrain decided to terminate the lease. Since 1977, MIDEASTFOR has ceased to use Jufair as its home port, although the U.S. admiral who commands MIDEASTFOR's flagship still makes his residence there when he is not at sea, and MIDEASTFOR ships continue to make frequent use of the local facilities.

QATAR

The state of Qatar is situated on a peninsula that extends for about 170 kilometers (ca. 106 miles) north from Arabia into the Gulf. The emirate's territory encompasses approximately 10,360 square kilometers (ca. 4,000 square miles), and of its population of 260,000 more than 150,000 live in the capital at Doha on the eastern coast. The peninsula is low lying and consists largely of sandy or stony desert.

Historical Background

Like Bahrain and the United Arab Emirates, Qatar was under British protection until independence in 1971. The protective status was based on treaties signed in 1869, 1913, and 1916. Apart from its having been admitted into the Arab League, OAPEC, OPEC, and the United Nations, the principal political development since independence was a nonviolent palace coup in 1972. On that occasion, Shaykh Khalifah ibn Hamad al-Thani, long known as one of the most forceful and development-oriented personalities in the Gulf area, ousted his cousin, Shaykh Ahmad.

Political Environment

Population and Social Conditions

Prior to the production of oil in 1949, the population of Qatar was one of the poorest of any in eastern Arabia. The great majority of the inhabitants lived at subsistence level, with most of their income derived from fishing and pearling. Most of the indigenous population is Arab, and a large percentage of this group ware *muhawwalah* Arabs with ties of varying strength and duration to their kinfolk along the south Iranian coast. The Arabs of Qatar are largely Sunni Muslims and generally subscribe to the fundamentalist teachings of the same Hanbali school of Islamic jurisprudence as that practiced in Saudi Arabia.

There is also a large foreign population of Iranians, Pakistanis, Indians, and Palestinians. The Iranians constitute the majority of the small merchant class, while many Indians and Pakistanis are employed as manual laborers, artisans, and clerical staff in local banks and businesses. The Palestinian population occupies the lower and middle levels of the bureaucracy and equivalent white-collar positions in the private sector.

Prior to the discovery and export of petroleum three decades ago, Qatar was devoid of even the remotest semblance of a modern school system, hospitals, clinics, piped water, electricity, and many other government services. Great strides have been made in all of these services in recent years, however. In education, for example, all of the emirate's primary school teachers are Qataris, and the first of what will ultimately be several colleges of the new Gulf University has been opened in Doha.

Economic Conditions

Petroleum production and export, together with the leadership of reform-oriented members within the ruling family, have been responsible for much of the dramatic transformation that has taken place in the country's social and economic life. In 1975, both major oil producers, Qatar Petroleum Company and Shell Oil of Qatar, were nationalized by the government. The emirate's extensive reserves of natural gas have much potential, and a plant has been built at Umm Sa'id (south of Doha) to utilize this resource, with a pipeline paralleling the oil pipeline from the fields at Dukhan on the opposite side of the peninsula. With petroleum providing the emirate's principal export, and nearly everything required beyond basic foodstuffs being imported, the government has been the source of considerable investment in economic infrastructure. The capital city is serviced by paved roads linking Qatar to its neighbors; a new international airport has been built in addition to a modern port that is constantly being expanded.

Qatar is attempting to modernize and diversify its economy as rapidly and efficiently as possible in order to lessen its dependence on oil production. In 1973, it began to manufacture fertilizer. The country has also built a cement plant and flour mills and has expanded its shrimping industry.

As with the other Gulf states, the oil glut has adversely affected Qatar's economy. By 1983 Qatar had entered a negative cash flow position and was forced to rely on its considerable hard currency holdings to avert a crisis.

Political Structure

In 1970, a year before it achieved independence, Qatar became the first of the lower Gulf states to promulgate a written constitution. The constitution provided for a council of ministers and an advisory council, and stipulated that the former was to be appointed by the ruler and that the majority of the latter were to be elected by the general population. A decade later, elections had not been held and there was little indication when the event itself might occur. The council of ministers (or cabinet) is led by the prime minister, who is theoretically appointed by the ruler, although in practice, the ruler himself has served in the post. The cabinet is responsible for proposing laws that must be submitted to the ruler for ratification and is also technically accountable for supervising the state bureaucracy and the financial affairs of the emirate.

The advisory council, finally established in 1972 after the coup, consisted exclusively of members appointed by the ruler. The council, although designed to represent major social and economic interest groups in Qatar, has little more than recommendatory authority and, by itself, is not empowered to initiate legislation. Nonetheless, the council has consistently convened every year since it was promulgated.

In keeping with the time-honored practice of legitimizing leadership in eastern Arabia, the ruler is selected by a careful process of consensus within the family dynasty and, like his predecessors since time immemorial, may and indeed can be expected to be replaced by the same process. He is charged with ratifying all laws, commanding the armed forces, appointing governmental officials, and conducting foreign affairs. The constitution also calls upon the amir to select a deputy ruler, who, depending on the consensus of the family at the time the choice is made, may or may not be also designated as heir apparent.

The judicial system includes five secular courts and religious courts. A court of appeals exists, but the function of a supreme court is vested in the ruler, who has the power to reduce or waive penalties.

Finally, although Qatar is a unitary state, progress has been made toward decentralizing the administration. Nevertheless, because the majority of the population lives in Doha, the government has met with only limited success in its efforts to expand the allocation of political authority among the emirate's component political units.

Political Dynamics

The al-Thanis constitute the largest ruling family in the region, numbering in the thousands. To a considerably greater extent than any of its counterparts elsewhere in the region, it has traditionally dominated most of the important functions of government. The primary constraints on the ruler are Islamic law and the influence of what is undoubtedly the most conservative religious establishment of any of the emirates. The al-Thanis, although close-knit and secretive like all the other dynasties in the area, harbor within their midst a great many factions and rivalries based on different personalities and genuine disagreements over what, among various options, should be the most efficacious approach to the emirate's development.

The family holds around ten of the fifteen cabinet portfolios, including all of the vital ones such as interior, defense, finance, and foreign affairs. Shaykh Khalifah ibn Hamad al-Thani has maintained close control over the country's affairs while granting to select members of the family a sufficient number of governmental positions to assuage their political ambitions. In much the same way as his counterpart in the ruling family of Saudi Arabia, Shaykh Khalifah is strongly anticommunist and maintains an ongoing vigilance against potential subversion within his borders.

The merchant class has traditionally exerted less influence on government affairs than its larger and older counterparts in Kuwait, Bahrain, Dubai, or Oman. The power of the merchants is primarily exerted on the commercial aspects of the emirate's developmental projects. However, as oil revenues accumulate and as many members of the ruling family have become more interested and involved in business themselves, the traditional separation of al-Thani–dominated government and merchant class–dominated business has begun to disintegrate. The dynasty and the business community, by symbiotic process, have increased their cooperation and collaboration in a great many areas pertaining to the emirate's economic growth.

Foreign Policy

The emirate's foreign policy has been consistently conservative, pro-Arab, and pro-Western in the process of being, above all, dedicated to the pursuit of Qatari national interests. The focus of its policy has been primarily on Gulf affairs, with the exception of its broader oil interests. On many external policy matters, Qatar has been prone to follow the lead of Saudi Arabia. The continuation of traditional forms of rule in the Gulf area is of no less concern to Qatar's dynasty than it is to other ruling households in the region, and for this reason, if no other, Qatar has sought to remain on friendly terms with all the littoral states of the Gulf.

Although it still has some commercial ties with Iran, Qatar nonetheless supports Iraq in the Gulf war. With a sizable Shi'a community and a maritime border with Iran that lies astride potential reserves of significant energy resources, it is important that warm relations are once again established.

Qatar has managed to maintain remarkably good relations with most other Arab states. Although it has consistently supported the Arab cause on the Palestinian issue, Qatar fully realizes, as does its neighbors, the threat to its own interests from the radical proclivities of various elements within the Palestine liberation movement. Qatar has also been generous with financial aid, in keeping with the traditional Arabian ethos whereby those with bountiful resources feel an obligation to extend a helping hand to their less fortunate neighbors. Foreign aid programs are also a means of maintaining good relations with possible domestic and Arab critics.

On oil matters, Qatar is an active member of both OPEC and OAPEC. Considered a moderate in contrast with some of the more militant OPEC members, the emirate has nevertheless pursued a considerably more activist role regarding oil price rises than either its Saudi or its UAE neighbors.

UNITED ARAB EMIRATES

Historical Background

In 1820, in an attempt to protect maritime trading routes from privateers operating from ports along the lower Gulf, Great Britain devised and in rapid succession imposed by force on the littoral emirates the first of what were to become a series of truces designed to put an end to what had previously been practically incessant naval warfare. As a result, the area, formerly known as the Pirate Coast, came in time to be called the Trucial Coast and the seven small principalities that dotted its shores the Trucial States.

The international status of these principalities as British-protected states continued until 1971, when Great Britain terminated its special treaty relationships with Bahrain, Qatar, and the Trucial States. For the previous three years, following the announcement of its intention to withdraw from the Gulf, Britain tried to create a federation that would have included all seven of the Trucial States plus Qatar and Bahrain. Until 1970 Iran's territorial claim over Bahrain prohibited these efforts from being realized. Thereafter, Bahrain took the initiative and lobbied for representation in the new federation in accordance with population size (it had the largest number of inhabitants). When refused, it elected to withdraw. Qatar, which not only contested Bahrain's drive to dominate the new state politically but also remained in conflict with Bahrain over the latter's claim to both the Hawar Islands and the village site of Zubarah on the Qatar peninsula, then also decided to withdraw, leaving only the Trucial States to form the new UAE. On December 1, 1971, Abu Dhabi, Dubai, Sharjah, Ajman, Umm al-Qaywayn, and Fujayrah joined the union. Ras al-Khaymah joined in early 1972.

At the outset, the UAE faced numerous difficulties. Abu Dhabi had an unresolved dispute with Saudi Arabia and Oman over the Buraymi Oasis, which lay in the eastern region of the emirate. There were, moreover, strong traditional rivalries among the rulers that dampened an otherwise favorable atmosphere conducive to achieving a measure of functional integration among the member states. Finally, on the eve of independence, Iran, resurrecting a claim to the Greater and Lesser Tunbs islands claimed by Ras al-Khaymah, and Abu Musa, which was claimed by Sharjah, occupied all three islands. Iran's occupation of Abu Musa was in accordance with an eleventh-hour agreement arrived at between the shah and the ruler of Sharjah, but no such understanding had been reached with Ras al-Khaymah regarding the Tunbs. As a result, Ras al-Khaymah's troops forcibly resisted the Iranian invasion, and there was loss of life on both sides. The islands problem contributed directly to a coup attempt in February 1972 that cost the life of the ruler of Sharjah. Another long-standing territorial dispute involved a number of villages in the Buraymi Oasis region, which were claimed by Saudi Arabia. In 1974, an agreement between Abu Dhabi and

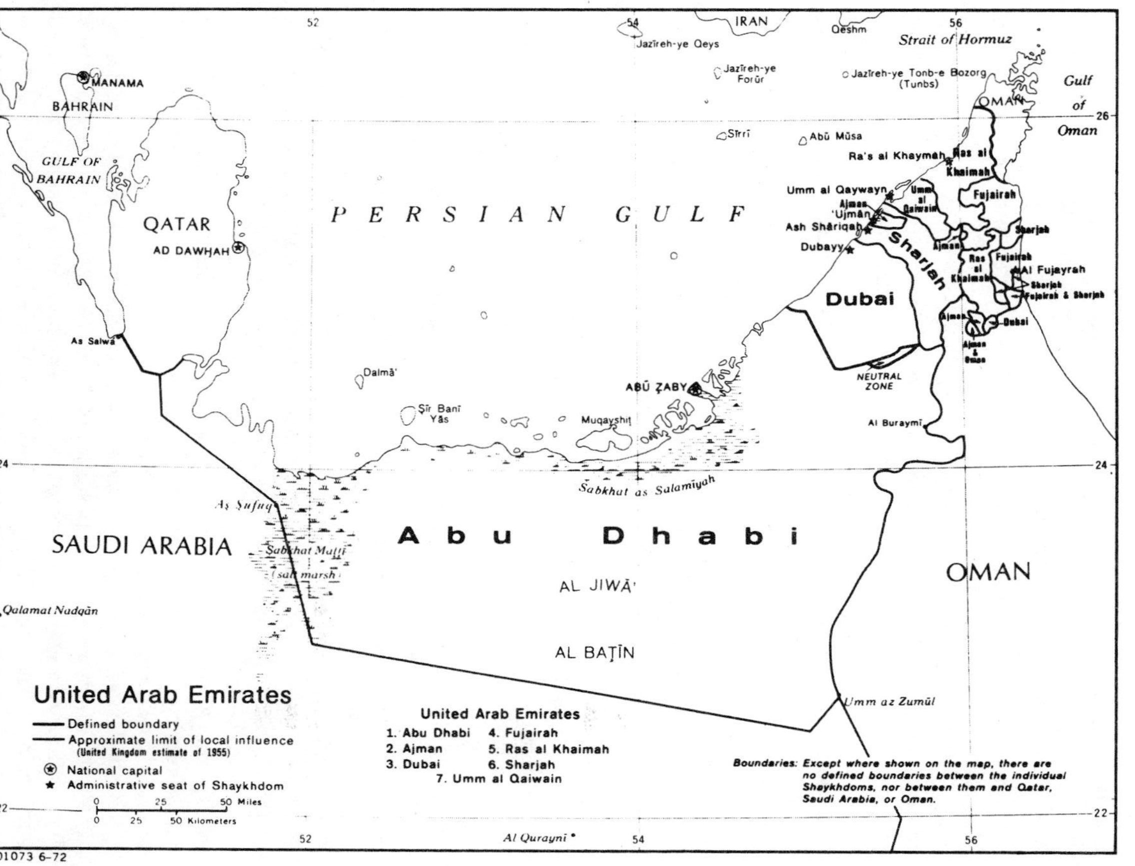
United Arab Emirates
Defined boundary
Approximate limit of local influence (United Kingdom estimate of 1955)
National capital
Administrative seat of Shaykhdom
0 25 50 Miles
0 25 50 Kilometers
United Arab Emirates
1. Abu Dhabi
2. Ajman
3. Dubai
4. Fujairah
5. Ras al Khaimah
6. Sharjah
7. Umm al Qaiwain
Boundaries: Except where shown on the map, there are no defined boundaries between the individual Shaykhdoms, nor between them and Qatar, Saudi Arabia, or Oman.
IRAN
Qeshm
Jazīreh-ye Qeys
Jazīreh-ye Forūr
Jazīreh-ye Tonb-e Bozorg (Tunbs)
Strait of Hormuz
Gulf of Oman
OMAN
MANAMA
BAHRAIN
GULF OF BAHRAIN
QATAR
AD DAWḤAH
PERSIAN GULF
Sīrrī
Abū Mūsa
Ra's al Khaymah
Ras al Khaimah
Umm al Qaywayn
Umm al Qaiwain
Ajman
'Ujmān
Ash Shāriqah
Dubayy
Fujairah
Sharjah
Al Fujayrah
Dubai
NEUTRAL ZONE
Al Buraymī
As Salwā
Dalmā'
Şīr Banī Yās
Muqayshiţ
ABŪ ẔABY
Sabkhat as Salamīyah
Aş Şufuq
Sabkhat Maţţī (salt marsh)
SAUDI ARABIA
Abu Dhabi
AL JIWĀ'
AL BAṬĪN
OMAN
Qalamat Nadqān
Umm az Zumūl
Al Qurayni
501073 6-72

Saudi Arabia ended this long-standing dispute and paved the way for the establishment of Saudi-UAE diplomatic relations.

Political Environment

Population and Social Conditions

The UAE is a federation of seven emirates extending for some 1,200 kilometers (746 miles) along the southern coast of the Persian Gulf and another 250 kilometers (155 miles) on the Gulf of Oman. Consisting of approximately 83,650 square kilometers (32,300 square miles), the country has a population of nearly 1.26 million. Abu Dhabi is almost as large as the rest of the shaykhdoms combined and contains more than half the total population. Six of the emirates—Abu Dhabi, Dubai, Sharjah, Ajman, Umm al-Qaywayn, and Ras al-Khaymah—have territory on the Persian (Arabian) Gulf, with Sharjah having additional, noncontiguous territory along the coast of the Gulf of Oman. Only Fujayrah is located wholly in the latter portion of the federation.

The indigenous inhabitants account for only about one-quarter to one-third of the union's total population. The UAE citizenry is in many ways similar to its counterparts in other countries, which, like it, are caught up in the throes of administrative, social, and economic modernization. Basically tribal and familial in terms of social organization, the native population ranges from an ever-dwindling number of bedouins, who remain basically illiterate and traditional in outlook, to a largely Western-educated and well-traveled elite.

One of the most distinguishing characteristics of the various shaykhdoms is not so much geography as tribal affiliation. Six principal tribal groups inhabit the country: the Bani Yas, a confederation of nearly a dozen different tribes, two branches of which (the Al Bu Falah and the Al Bu Falasah, respectively) provide the ruling families of Abu Dhabi and Dubai; the Manasir (singular: Mansuri), who range from the western reaches of the UAE to Saudi Arabia and Qatar; the Qawasim (singular: Qasimi); the Al Bu Ali in Umm al-Qaywayn; the Sharqiyin in Fujayrah; and the Nu'aym in Ajman. All the native tribes are Arab and Sunni Muslims. In the nineteenth century, many of them espoused the teachings of the Wahhabi revival that spread from Saudi Arabia.

Of all the tribal groupings, those that can still be classified as bedouins constitute no more than 15 percent of the local population. They usually live around oases and for some years now have been migrating to and settling in urban areas. Numerous UAE citizens of bedouin stock are to be found in the police and military forces, upon whose loyalty the government heavily depends.

A highly sophisticated merchant class has developed, particularly in Dubai. It has maintained and, where possible, expanded, what for several decades now has been a rather extensive relationship with the Indian subcontinent and, until the Gulf war, with Iran. Most of the merchant families are Sunni Arabs, but allied with them are a substantial number of Persians and Indians who have been resident in the lower Gulf area for generations. For much of the period following World War II and prior to the emergence of oil as the dominant factor in the region's economies, among the most colorful merchants were those "free traders" in gold and other luxury items whose picturesque dhows concealed powerful engines capable of outrunning curious coast guard vessels of half a dozen countries.

The period of the 1960s and 1970s brought a new kind of entrepreneur: Western contractors and bankers who have played an important role in the oil revenue–financed development boom. Because of the long-standing ties between the emirates and Great Britain, U.K. firms have remained in an especially strong position. In addition to Europeans, thousands of Indians, Pakistanis, Persians, Baluchis, and third-country Arabs have flocked to the Gulf region as clerks, accountants, and manual laborers.

Economic Conditions

Before the discovery of oil in Abu Dhabi in 1958, only Dubai and Sharjah had developed an extensive entrepôt trade. The oft-reported rivalry between these two shaykhdoms stems in part from the fact that Dubai began to eclipse Sharjah both politically and commercially when Sharjah's harbor began to silt up in the 1940s. The conditions for perpetuating the former's economic edge over the latter were practically ensured in the 1950s, when Dubai succeeded in dredging its own estuary (or "creek" as it is called locally).

Abu Dhabi Town, by contrast, was situated on an island and was little more than a mud-brick village prior to the petroleum discovery. Today, however, it is a major city, by far the most advanced in terms of administrative and social welfare services of any in the UAE. Dubai and Sharjah, which possess oil in lesser amounts than Abu Dhabi, have also undertaken extensive development projects. The contrast between these three affluent shaykhdoms and the other four remains substantial, although the gap has been lessened somewhat in recent years by the fact that the federal government, using largely Abu Dhabi money, has funded numerous development projects in the poorer states. The abundance of new income; the lack, to date, of a strong, centralized planning authority with power to veto or modify individual emirate developmental ventures; and, most important, the continuation of intense competition among the various rulers for prestige and preeminence in the area inevitably have resulted in the duplication of many facilities, such as "international" airports and harbors in Abu Dhabi, Dubai, Sharjah, and Ras al-Khaymah.

Dubai, because of both its long-standing position as the major trading center of the lower Gulf region and the commitment of its ruler to developing the maritime sector of its economy, has by far the largest port facilities in the region. Attempts have been made to diversify the economies of the individual emirates in order to lessen their dependence on the petroleum industry. Toward this end, a huge drydock was constructed at Jebel Ali in Dubai. An aluminum smelter and several cement plants have been constructed, tourism has been encouraged, the local fishing industry has been modernized and expanded, and agricultural improvements and experimentation continue to be encouraged in Abu Dhabi and Ras al-Khaymah. In addition, ongoing consideration is given to the establishment of various kinds of light to intermediate industries, for which the principal energy source would be gas that has traditionally been flared (i.e., burned off).

The emirates have also been affected by the oil glut and the reduced demand for oil and petrochemicals. Large development projects and consideration of new projects are either being scaled down, delayed, or abandoned. Many expatriates are leaving and residence and immigration regulations are being tightened, with deportations on the rise. This situation is creating some tension and some repercussions. The UAE ambassador to France was assassinated in 1984 by a group called the Arab Revolutionary Brigade, allegedly over the UAE's treatment of its "guest workers." There have also been some local demonstrations by workers against government labor policies.

Political Structure

The UAE's provisional constitution, which dates from 1971, provides for federal legislative, executive, and judicial bodies. The legislature, called the Federal National Council (FNC), is, in reality and in keeping with the norms of traditional tribal and Islamic rule in this part of Arabia, more nearly akin to a consultative assembly. The FNC is composed of forty members nominated by the president and approved by the rulers of the seven member states who constitute the Federal Supreme Council. In accordance with the relative size of their constituent populations, eight of the seats are apportioned to Abu Dhabi and Dubai, respectively; six each to Ras al-Khaymah and Sharjah; and four each to the remaining three members. The FNC's duties are limited mainly to its discussion and approval of the budget, to its authority to draft legislation to be presented for action by the Council of Ministers, and, of no small significance owing to the absence of political parties, trade unions, and various other kinds of voluntary associations familiar to Westerners, to its role as forum for discussion and debate of policies and programs under consideration by the government.

The Council of Ministers was composed of twenty-six ministers in early 1980, but its size and composition does change from time to time, with ministries being added, merged, or disbanded. Although together with the Federal Supreme Council (FSC) and the presidency it forms a key part of the executive branch, two of its primary responsibilities are to draft laws and to act as a legislative body when the FNC is not in session.

The greatest concentration of authority within the federal structure is in the FSC. The seven-member council is charged with formulating and supervising all federal policies, ratifying UAE laws, approving the union's annual budget, ratifying international treaties, and approving the prime minister, the president, and the members of the supreme court. In procedural matters, a simple majority vote is sufficient for passage of any resolution. However, in substantive concerns, Abu Dhabi and Dubai have a veto power. Thus, on any substantive vote, five members, including the two veto powers, must approve a resolution in order for the motion to have the force of law. This constitutional allocation of a preponderance of political power to Abu Dhabi and Dubai has been a major point of contention among most of the other emirates.

Since independence, Shaykh Zayid of Abu Dhabi has been president of the UAE, a post to which he was reappointed for a second five-year term in 1976 and a third in 1981. Shaykh Rashid of Dubai has been the union's vice-president for the same period of time and, in 1979, became its prime minister as well. Although the powers of the presidency are in theory subordinate to the FSC, Shaykh Zayid has been relatively successful in keeping together what has become in this century the Arab world's foremost example of regional political integration. His success has been due in part to Abu Dhabi's preeminence as the most profederation state in the union and Zayid's own strong personal dedication to the UAE's development. Many of the federation's operations are almost completely funded by Abu Dhabi.

Foreign policy decisionmaking is vested in the federal executive branch. However, although articles 120 and 121 of the constitution stipulate that foreign affairs decisions are the responsibility of the union, article 123 states that the individual shaykhdoms may conclude limited agreements concerning local matters, as, for example, in the granting of concessions—including the right to explore for, produce, refine, and export oil—to foreign economic interests. Thus, to some extent, the individual shaykhdoms have considerable latitude and power in the conduct of foreign affairs.

The federal judicial system established by the constitution has both a supreme and lower court. The judges are appointed by the president with the approval of the FSC. To date, however, the function of administering and applying UAE laws through the union's court procedures has remained one of the least developed of UAE government activities owing to the scarcity of local citizens who have received legal training and to the as yet relatively small accumulation of a body of federal laws that the courts might apply.

Consequently, the bulk of cases submitted for adjudication in the UAE are dealt with by the lower courts in each of the shaykhdoms.

The powers reserved to the shaykhdoms, as stated in article 122, imply that the individual emirates remain responsible for all matters that do not fall under the domain of the federal authorities. In addition, the emirates retain a few expressed powers.

Political Dynamics

Since the inception of the federation, the strongest cohesive force within it has been Shaykh Zayid of Abu Dhabi followed by Shaykh Sultan of Sharjah. Shaykh Rashid of Dubai has always been in a position to play a role in federal affairs. However, in the eyes of his critics he did not seriously begin to perform such a function until he accepted the post of prime minister, having previously concentrated most of his attention and energies on Dubai.

Within the shaykhdoms, politics traditionally have been tribally based and autocratic, even if tempered by such age-old concepts as social democracy, consultation, consensus, and adherence to the principles and norms as enshrined in Islamic law. The ruler, or shaykh, is usually the oldest son of the immediately preceding ruler, although there are instances in which his uncle, a brother, a nephew, or a cousin has been the one to accede to power. To remain in power, the shaykh must maintain the support of the inner circles of the ruling family and numerous other groups (e.g., religious leaders, merchants) within the emirate.

The past history of internal politics of the ruling families has been replete with intrigue and jockeying among real and potential contenders for the limited number of positions of official power. Prior to the establishment of the UAE, numerous local rulers were assassinated, in many cases by their brothers, cousins, or sons. As recently as 1966 a palace coup in Abu Dhabi brought a new ruler to power; and in February 1972 the UAE's minister of education, Shaykh Sultan bin Muhammad al-Qassimi, of Sharjah, assumed the rulership in his home emirate following the abortive palace coup in which his predecessor was murdered. In 1981, however, Shaykh Humaid of Ajman peacefully ascended the throne when his father Shaykh Rashid passed away.

Popular participation in local government along lines or in accordance with organizational forms familiar to Westerners is limited. In the early 1980s there were no trade unions, political parties, or popularly elected bodies through which local demands could be articulated. Neither was there a free press—again, as defined by Western standards. Political power continued to be maintained and effectively wielded at the top by cousins, sons, brothers, and uncles of semihereditary tribal rulers, although an increasing number of foreign-trained technocrats were to be found in such sensitive areas as national defense, internal security, foreign relations, developmental planning, and communications.

Delegation of responsibility between the federal and local levels, like that in the United States for decades after its establishment, is not in every instance as well defined as modern practitioners of public administration would prefer. Theoretically, the federal government has control over defense, finance, and foreign affairs. In practice, however, the dual capacity exercised by the rulers as both members of the federal government and rulers of member states, yields additional opportunities for control to the various shaykhdoms. The integration of the shaykhdoms into a federation, therefore, has been no simple or easy task and, for the reasons delineated herein, remains a challenge fraught with myriad difficulties for the members of UAE officialdom.

In 1976 continued dissension among the various members of the federation prompted a crisis when Shaykh Zayid refused election for another five-year term as president unless fundamental changes were made. After considerable negotiation and accommodation, he finally changed his stand, was reelected, and the temporary constitution was extended for five more years.

Undoubtedly one of the most important steps taken toward integration occurred in May 1976, when all external and internal military forces were united and placed under the single command of the Union Defense Force. Previously there had been a separate and independent army for nearly every emirate, plus the union force. Although constitutional in formulation, each emirate competed to have its local contingent form an important component of the larger and more modern military force. Abu Dhabi's oil revenues—at more than $5 billion annually, somewhat prodigious in comparison with the income of the other emirates—gave Shaykh Zayid an obvious advantage in pressing for unification of the UAE's armies. Even so, as with most administrative reforms, total integration of the military has been evidenced sooner on paper than in practice. The logic behind the process, however, remains unassailable: Its major internal task of preventing or pacifying local, tribal disputes would have remained an infinitely more difficult task had the armed forces themselves, as had been the case for the first four years of the union's existence, remained organized along tribal lines.

Despite all the centrifugal forces inherent in a traditional society in which parochial tribal interests are paramount, federal cooperation is increasing in the UAE. It will be interesting to note how the next generation responds to federalism when it takes over leadership. Unlike the current leadership, this younger generation has been exposed to more formal education and, in many cases, has a greater understanding of the fact that without interdependence, neither the UAE nor its individual members can survive in their present form.

Foreign Policy

In its external relations, the UAE is conservative and anticommunist, and strives to maintain friendly relations with its neighbors. It is sometimes difficult for the outsider to understand UAE foreign relations inasmuch as each individual shaykhdom has considerable latitude in conducting its own economic and, to a lesser extent, political relations with outside states. Oil relations are less complicated because Abu Dhabi so dominates the UAE's oil production.

In peninsula politics, the UAE is an active member of the GCC and increasingly uses the GCC as the medium for Gulf regional issues. It also has close relations with the Yemen Arab Republic (YAR). Shaykh Zayid has always had a warm place in his heart for Yemen, for it was there that the Nuhayan family is believed to have originated centuries ago.

In Arab politics, the UAE supports the Palestinians' right to self-determination as the sine qua non for bringing an end to the Arab-Israeli conflict. As a small country, the UAE generally keeps a low profile in regional politics, following the Saudi-led conservative lead on most issues. It supported the Fahd Plan of 1981 and the Fez proposals of 1982, for example. It also contributed funds and troops to the Arab Defense Force in Lebanon in the late 1970s.

The heart and soul of UAE foreign policy, however, is its position as a major oil producer, not only in OPEC affairs but also in its capacity as a major aid donor (foreign aid being the principal foreign policy instrument at its disposal). Thus, the oil glut of the 1980s has not only reduced the UAE's ability to maneuver in foreign policy but has contracted its economy as well.

The main focus of UAE foreign and security policy in the 1980s has been the Iran-Iraq War. The UAE has contributed over $.5 billion to Iraq since 1982 but still tries to maintain normal relations with Iran. These efforts are made more difficult by Iran's militant revolutionary foreign policy, and are further exacerbated by the continued dispute over the Tunbs and Abu Musa, three islands claimed by the UAE but occupied by Iran since the early 1970s.

OMAN

Historical Background

Oman has a proud history dating back many centuries. It has maintained its independence since the expulsion of Portuguese garrisons from its coastal towns in the seventeenth century. A Persian occupation in the mid-eighteenth century was ended under the leadership of Ahmad bin Sa'id Al Bu Sa'id, who was subsequently elected imam. The imamate was a combination of religious and political leadership uniquely developed by the Ibadi Muslims of Oman. The Ibadi are part of the Kharijite schism, dating from the earliest days of Islam, and broke with the main body of Muslims over their insistence that the caliph should not be determined in accordance with genealogical considerations but should be elected on the basis of merit. Ahmad's successors, however, abandoned this procedure and, in time, became purely secular rulers with the title of sultan. This development created a political schism between the coastal areas administered from Muscat and the more conservative interior ruled by the imam. The sultans in Muscat, as a security measure, developed a close association with Great Britain that has continued to the present. Assisted by British forces, the country was reunified during the 1950s after the military defeat of the imam of Oman at his interior stronghold, Nizwa. Unification was completed under sultan Qabus, who in a nearly bloodless coup d'état in 1970 replaced his father, Sa'id bin Taymur (ruler

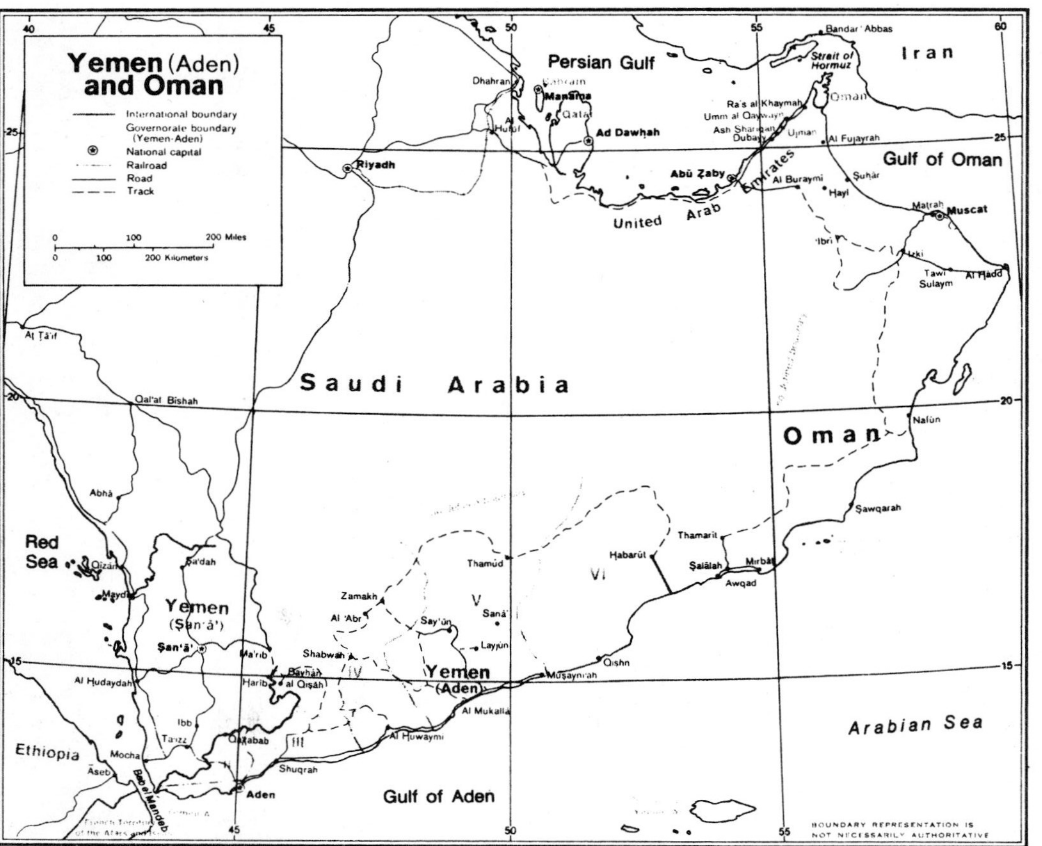
Yemen (Aden)
and Oman
International boundary
Governorate boundary
(Yemen-Aden)
National capital
Railroad
Road
Track
0 100 200 Miles
0 100 200 Kilometers
Persian Gulf
Iran
Strait of Hormuz
Bandar 'Abbas
Dhahran
Manama
Al Hufuf
Ad Dawhah
Riyadh
Ra's al Khaymah
Umm al Qaywayn
Ash Shariqah
Dubayy
Ujman
Al Fujayrah
Abū Zaby
United Arab Emirates
Gulf of Oman
Al Buraymi
Hayl
Şuhār
Matrah
Muscat
'Ibri
Izki
Tawi Sulaym
Al Hadd
Saudi Arabia
At Ta'if
Qal'at Bishah
Abhā
Red Sea
Qizān
Maydi
Oman
Nalūn
Şawqarah
Thamarit
Şalālah
Mirbāt
Awqad
Habarūt
Thamūd
Zamakh
Al 'Abr
Say'ūn
Sanā'
Layjūn
Shabwah
Yemen (Şan'ā')
Şan'ā'
Şa'dah
Ma'rib
Bayhān al Qişāb
Harib
Yemen (Aden)
Qishn
Al Mukalla
Al Huwaymi
Al Hudaydah
Ibb
Ta'izz
Mocha
Ethiopia
Āseb
Bab el Mandeb
Aden
Shuqrah
Gulf of Aden
Arabian Sea
BOUNDARY REPRESENTATION IS NOT NECESSARILY AUTHORITATIVE

since 1932), and changed the name of the country from the Sultanate of Muscat and Oman to, simply, the Sultanate of Oman.

The southernmost province of Dhufar, annexed in the late nineteenth century after years of quasi-autonomous existence, became the site of another insurrection in the early 1960s. By 1968 leadership of the rebellion had been seized by the Marxist-oriented Popular Front for the Liberation of the Occupied Arabian Gulf (PFLOAG), the same group that subsequently changed its name, first to the Popular Front for the Liberation of Oman and the Arab Gulf (also PFLOAG) in 1971, and, in 1974, to the Popular Front for the Liberation of Oman (PFLO). Supported by Soviet and Chinese aid channeled through South Yemen, the PFLO had occupied large areas of the province by the early 1970s. Ideological affinity existed with South Yemen. Both had espoused the radical doctrines of the Arab Nationalists Movement, whose leaders included George Habbash of the Popular Front for the Liberation of Palestine. The rebellion was finally put down in late 1975 through the combined efforts of mainly British advisers and Iranian combat troops. Under Sultan Qabus the heretofore isolated country has been opened to the outside world on a scale unprecedented in its history, while the government has simultaneously embarked on an equally unprecedented and ambitious program of socioeconomic development. For the first time, an impressive array of modern government services has been extended to even the most remote regions of the interior of the country.

Political Environment

Located on the eastern reaches of the Arabian peninsula, the Sultanate of Oman is a country of some 212,000 square kilometers (82,000 square miles). The estimated population is around 1.18 million. The capital, Muscat, has a population of 20,000 and is neighbored by the somewhat larger commercial center of Matrah. The largest single town is Salalah, capital of the southern province of Dhufar. This province consists of three ranges of low mountains surrounding a small coastal plain and is separated from the rest of Oman by several hundred miles of desert. Oman proper consists of inner Oman and the coastal plain known as the Batinah. Inner Oman contains a fertile plateau and the oldest towns in Oman, including the religious center of Nizwa. Separating this region from the Batinah is the Hajar mountain range, which stretches in an arc from northwest to southeast and reaches nearly 3,000 meters (9,800 feet) at Jabal al-Akhdar (Green Mountain). The majority of Oman's population is found along the Batinah coast, which has the greatest agricultural potential in the country. An important fishing center and traditional port is at Sur, southeast of Muscat.

Population and Social Structure

Most Omanis are Arab, although many Baluchis who were originally from the coastal area of Iran and Pakistan live along the Batinah coast. Many of the merchants of the capital region and the coast are Indians, either Hindu or Khoja (a community of Shi'ite Muslims). There are also Persians and other groups of Shi'ite Muslims, including some originally from either Iran or Iraq. Dhufar and the surrounding desert is the home of several peoples whose primary language is South Arabian. In the Musandam peninsula to the north, wild Shihuh tribesmen, legendary descendants of the Biblical Shuhites, speak their own language. In recent years, Oman has experienced an influx of migrant labor, principally from other Arab states and the subcontinent.

With the change in government in 1970, Oman entered a new era. The accumulation of oil revenues over several years of production (exports began in 1967) was quickly put to work in an effort to modernize the country. Within a few years, the number of schools increased from three in 1970 to 431 in 1983, and the number of government employees from several hundred to over nine thousand. Fortunately, the country was able to rely on the manpower and expertise of a number of Omanis who had migrated to Saudi Arabia and various Gulf countries for work and education in the years prior to 1970. Another important source of manpower were the "Zanzibaris"—Arabs of Omani origin whose ancestors had migrated to the former Omani dominion of Zanzibar over the last two centuries. With the Africanization of Zanzibar, many of them returned to Oman.

Before 1970, the population was fairly evenly distributed throughout the country. With the rapid pace of development in the past few years, however, urbanization is beginning to occur, particularly in the capital area.

Economic Conditions

Economic development was totally neglected in Oman until the accession of Sultan Qabus. Since that time, economic development has progressed steadily. In the early 1980s construction was completed on copper mining and refining facilities, and two cement plants began operations in 1984. By the mid-1980s Omani development policies for diversifying its economy were beginning to take shape, thus further strengthening the economy.

Oil is Oman's most important natural resource. However, its reserves are modest by Gulf standards, and the oil is located in small and scattered fields. Production is expected to decrease unless new reserves are found. Although the oil sector has also been adversely affected by the oil glut, it has not suffered so much as in some of the other gulf states. Modest oil supplies had forced Oman to moderate the pace of development in the 1970s, and reserves are greater than earlier projected. By 1983 oil revenues had gone up to $3.9 billion, almost four times those of 1975.

Plans have been made for a natural-gas pipeline paralleling the oil pipeline from the interior to Muscat, and GCC members are still considering a strategic pipeline to Salalah that would bypass the Strait of Hormuz. It is not likely that such a line will be built in the near future, however, owing to the oil glut.

Limited water supplies in most areas prevent wide-scale agriculture. Traditionally, Omani cultivation has been at the subsistence level, the only significant cash crops being dates and limes. In Dhufar, where monsoon rains fall, coconuts are also grown.

Political Structure

The sultan's father maintained a basically traditional, personalized rule. Modern political institutions in Oman are therefore new and still in a relatively embryonic stage. There is no constitution or modern judicial system, and there are no political parties or elections. Islamic law is still the law of the land and is administered through traditional Islamic courts. Judges are appointed by the sultan. In the most remote regions, tribal law still functions in a rough-and-ready manner.

Final legal and administrative power in the country is vested in the sultan. Sultan Qabus is head of state, and all authority emanates from him. Since coming to power, however, he has created a formal council of ministers to carry out the administrative and legislative operations of the government. The council is headed by the prime minister, who is appointed by the sultan. Although all important decisions must have the approval of the sultan, the ministers have a great deal of latitude in formulating day-to-day policy.

In 1976, the sultan reorganized regional and local government by establishing thirty-seven divisions (*wilayats*), one province, and a municipality of the capital. The *wilayats* are administered by governors appointed by the sultan, who collect taxes, provide local security, settle disputes, and advise the sultan. The province, Dhufar, was historically a separate sultanate and still has more local autonomy than other regions. The municipality of Muscat was also considered important enough to warrant special status.

In 1981, Oman established an advisory council to advise the sultan on matters of social, educational, and economic policy (defense and foreign policy are excluded). The members, drawn from the tribal, merchant, and government communities, are appointed by the sultan. The number of council members was originally forty-five, but this total was raised to fifty-one in 1985.

Political Dynamics

There are four politically important groups in Oman: the royal family, the tribes, the expatriate advisers, and the merchant class. In many respects the royal family is still the most important group. Among the sultan's most influential advisers are his cousins and uncles. They occupy a number of key ministerial and governorial posts. The importance of the royal family can be illustrated by the fact that Sultan Qabus married the daughter of his uncle, Tariq bin Sa'id, and any male offspring from this marriage will most probably be named heir apparent.

Traditionally the tribes have also played a key role in the Omani political process. Under Qabus' father, Sultan Sa'id bin Taymur, manipulation of tribal rivalries was a major element in ruling the country. Qabus, on the other hand, has made attempts to decrease the power of the tribes by decentralizing the government through political reforms such as the establishment of local government councils.

Because of long, close relations with Great Britain, many of the expatriate advisers are British. In the past, Britons held key posts in the government and especially in the military. Today they still direct and train the army, but Qabus has made moves to bring more Omanis and other expatriates into other governmental positions—including the army, which for the first time in 1984 found itself with a Omani commander. The process of Omanization is accelerating as the Omani educational system turns out more qualified personnel. Nevertheless, for some time to come, Oman will have to rely on foreigners to assist in developing the country.

The merchant community has traditionally been the sultan's link to the outside world. In addition to old Omani trading families, there is still a sizable number of non-Omani merchant families from India and Pakistan, reflecting Oman's traditionally stronger ties with the Indian Ocean countries. In recent years, however, there has been a more Westward orientation. Oman has participated in both Arab and world politics. It has strengthened ties with the Western industrial world to gain goods and services for Oman's development programs. As a result of oil revenues, many less-established Omanis are being induced to enter into commerce, a position once monopolized by the merchant families. This process is beginning to dilute the power of the traditional merchant families.

Foreign Policy

Prior to the reign of Sultan Qabus, Oman was one of the most isolated countries anywhere. It relied on the British for protection and in return granted the British air and naval bases in Salalah and on Masirah island in the Arabian Sea. Qabus brought Oman out of its isolation by both necessity and design. He was forced to seek outside support against the Dhufar insurgency, and he also sought to gain international and Arab acceptance for the Omani regime. Qabus succeeded in reestablishing relations with Saudi Arabia, estranged since 1955 when the Saudis (and other Arabs) backed the Imam of Oman's challenge to the regime. Qabus also established a close security relationship with the shah, who sent Iranian troops to help in the fight against the Dhufar rebels. After the fall of the shah, Oman's relations with Iraq, which had formerly supported the insurgents, quickly improved. In addition, Oman joined the GCC and became a leading advocate of closer military cooperation among its members in the face of the Iran-Iraq War. Qabus also strengthened ties with the United States, particularly in defense-related matters. He signed an agreement with the United States in 1980, granting it access to Omani military facilities, and since then the two countries have participated in several joint military exercises.

Throughout the period, Qabus also maintained traditional close ties with Britain. As he has gained confidence in international relations, he has continued to broaden Oman's foreign affairs horizons. In 1985, for instance, he established diplomatic relations with the Soviet Union.

Bibliography

During the last decade a plethora of books have been written about the states in the Gulf region. This literature ranges from works suggesting how to conduct business in Arab shaykhdoms to travel guides pertaining to the Duhfar province in Oman. Although some works are quite good, much of the literature is weak and of a mass-market quality.

One of the more useful books offering an overview of the Gulf is David Long's *The Persian Gulf: An Introduction to Its People, Politics, and Economics* (Boulder, Colo.: Westview Press, 1978). Although this work is to some extent outdated, Long provides a good introduction to the politics and stability of the area. Another useful but also somewhat outdated introduction on domestic, regional, and international aspects of the Gulf states can be found in M. S. Agwani's *Politics in the Gulf* (New Delhi: Vikas, 1978). Agwani's review of the area is brief and competent; moreover, as an Indian he is able to provide insight into the dynamics of the Gulf from a different but important perspective. J. B. Kelly's *Arabia, The Gulf and the West* (London: George Weidenfeld, 1980) is a well-documented (though not entirely objective) review of Gulf history.

The International Institute for Strategic Studies (IISS) has published four volumes collectively entitled *The Security of the Persian Gulf*: Shahram Chubin, *Volume I: Domestic Political Factors* (Farnborough, England: IISS, 1982); Robert Litwak, *Volume II: Sources of Interconflict* (Farnborough, England: IISS, 1981); Avi Plascov, *Volume III: Modernization, Political Development and Stability* (Farnborough, England: IISS, 1982); and Shahram Chubin, *Volume IV: The Role of Outside Powers* (Farnborough, England: IISS, 1982). The first volume deals almost exclusively with domestic issues pertaining to the Gulf states. The second volume is concerned primarily with the roles of the regional powers—Iran (postrevolution), Iraq, and Saudi Arabia. The third volume is probably the most useful, in that Plascov discusses the rapid change that has occurred in all the Gulf states and emphasizes the nature and degree of transformation brought about by massive amounts of oil revenues. Finally, the fourth volume reviews U.S. and Soviet behavior toward their respective clients.

John Duke Anthony's *Arab States of the Lower Gulf: People, Politics, Petroleum* (Washington, D.C.: Middle East Institute, 1975) deals with the internal politics of the United Arab Emirates, Qatar, and Bahrain. There is a section on each of these countries exploring the history, constitutional structure, and political dynamics. A more recent work on the UAE is Frauke Bey's *From Trucial States to United Arab Emirates: A Society in Transition* (New York: Longman, 1982). Here, the author analyzes the wealth of the emirates as well as their culture, including discussions of religion, tribes, and historical traditions. A book by Emile Nakhleh, *Bahrain: Political Development in a Changing Society* (Lexington, Mass.: D. C. Heath, 1976), presents a straightforward account of the political problems Bahrain is encountering and how the leadership is attempting to resolve them. Rosemarie Said Zahlan's *The Creation of Qatar* (New York: Barnes, 1979) is probably the best study on historical and political development in Qatar.

Robert Landon's *Oman in the Late Nineteenth Century and After* (Princeton, N.J.: Princeton University Press, 1967) offers an informative guide to Omani politics. In addition, the reader can refer to Lies Graz's *The Omanis: Sentinels of the Gulf* (New York: Longman, 1982), which discusses all aspects of Oman including its second five-year plan and the U.S.-Omani agreement. A book that deals with Omani society is Michael Darlow and Richard Fawkis' *The Last Corner of Arabia* (London: Namara Publishers, 1976).

There is no comprehensive work on Kuwait. One can refer to Zahra French and Victor Winestone, *Kuwait: Prospect on Reality* (New York: Crane and Russak and Co., 1972) for a more general historical survey of Kuwaiti politics; and Soliman Demir, *The Kuwait Fund and the Political Economy of Arab Regional Development* (New York: Praeger Publishers, 1976) for Kuwait's role in regional and international politics. Robert Stevens, *The Arab's New Frontier* (London: Temple Smith, 1973; and Boulder, Colo.: Westview Press, 1977) discusses the Kuwait Fund for Arab Economic Development. John B. Kelly's *Eastern Arabian Frontiers* (New York: Praeger Publishers, 1964) offers a general history of the Persian Gulf shaykhdoms, focusing on Kuwait. One will also find the American University's *Area Handbook for the Persian Gulf States* (Washington, D.C.: Government Printing Office, 1977), valuable as a resource not only on Kuwait but also on the other Gulf shaykhdoms.

8

Yemen Arab Republic

David McClintock

Historical Background

The Yemen Arab Republic (YAR), sometimes called Yemen, North Yemen, or Yemen (San'a), is situated on the southern Red Sea coast of Arabia and extends eastward, encompassing most of the south Arabian highlands. To the south is the People's Democratic Republic of Yemen (PDRY), and to the east is the vast Rub' al-Khali (Empty Quarter) of Saudi Arabia.

The YAR's strategic location at the southern end of the Red Sea has been the main source of its regional political importance for more than two millenia. In the present day, the YAR, while lacking oil resources itself, has also played a significant but little-publicized role in the development of its oil-rich neighbors in the Arabian peninsula. It has provided a work force that now totals more than 1 million—a major segment of the regional manpower base. The Yemeni civil war of the 1960s and the resultant foreign intervention brought notoriety of a different kind. Even earlier, in the 1930s, Britain and Italy vied for support of the xenophobic imam of Yemen in a quest for control of the Strait of Bab al-Mandab. Similar strategic interests prompted Turkish military and political control from the sixteenth century up to World War I.

The fact that Yemen has made so little impact on the Western world for a period of many centuries and yet was so famous in antiquity as the home of the Queen of Sheba provides a fitting commentary on the long decline in its political and economic fortunes. If there has been any single dominant influence shaping the events of these three millenia of recorded history, it is that of comparative physical isolation. Significantly, however, Yemen has enjoyed a surprisingly high degree of civilization from ancient times to the present despite geographic and other handicaps.

The beginning of southwestern Arabian civilization occurred some time prior to 1200 B.C. with the influx of Semitic peoples from the Fertile Crescent—perhaps from the area of Palestine and east of the Jordan. It is unclear whether this migration resulted from displacement through overpopulation or warfare, or whether frankincense and myrrh served as an economic lure. These products, which were greatly prized in the ancient world, are actually resin from rare thorn bushes found only in southwestern Arabia and the adjacent Somali coast.

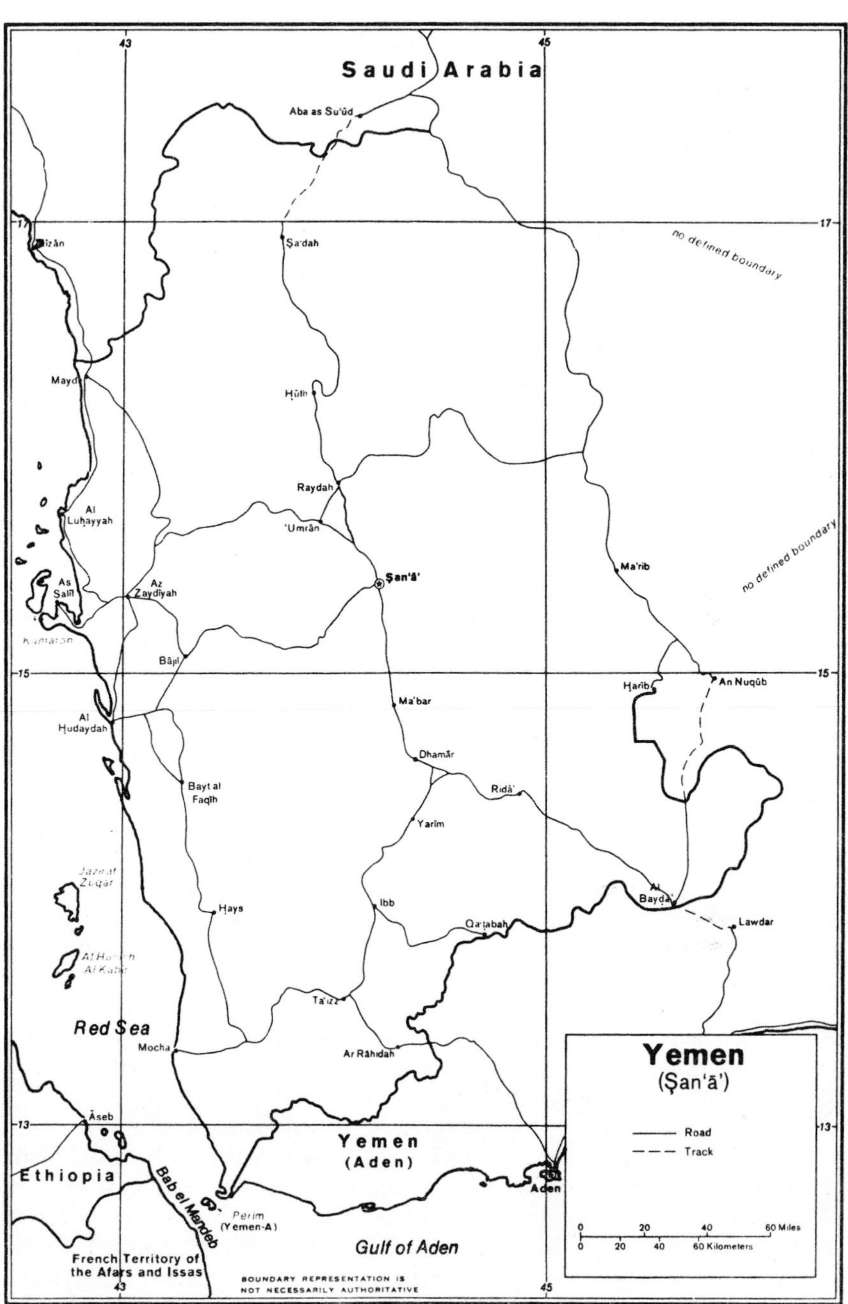
Saudi Arabia
Aba as Su'ūd
Ṣa'dah
Ḥūth
Raydah
'Umrān
Ṣan'ā'
Ma'rib
Al Luḥayyah
As Salīf
Az Zaydīyah
Bājil
Al Ḥudaydah
Ma'bar
Dhamār
Ḥarīb
An Nuqūb
Bayt al Faqīh
Riḍā'
Yarīm
Ibb
Al Bayḍā'
Lawdar
Ḥays
Qa'ṭabah
Ta'izz
Red Sea
Mocha
Ar Rāhidah
Āseb
Ethiopia
Bab el Mandeb
Perim (Yemen-A)
Yemen (Aden)
Aden
Gulf of Aden
French Territory of the Afars and Issas
no defined boundary
no defined boundary
Yemen (Ṣan'ā')
Road
Track
60 Miles
60 Kilometers
BOUNDARY REPRESENTATION IS NOT NECESSARILY AUTHORITATIVE
Base 501038 4-73

Frankincense had a ritualistic use in cremations, and myrrh was used in cosmetics. These valuable substances could be transported northward either by sea, with attendant risks from storms or piracy, or by caravan through the south Arabian highlands. It was the latter trade that enriched the small kingdoms that successively rose and fell in regional importance. The most significant among them were Saba (Sheba), Qataban, and Ma'in, with respective capitals at Ma'rib, Timna, and Qarnaw.

In addition to foreign trade, these ministates also developed a high degree of agricultural self-sufficiency based on terracing and irrigation. Near Sheba's capital of Ma'rib, a great stone-faced earthen dam functioned until the fifth century A.D., irrigating an area of approximately 2,000 hectares (4,942 acres). Although local tribal rivalries persisted then as now, the region enjoyed comparative peace and benign isolation until approximately the fourth century A.D.

Ironically, the formal adoption of Christianity by the Roman Emperor Constantine in A.D. 323 dealt a telling blow to the south Arabian kingdoms. Economically, it destroyed the frankincense trade, as the custom of cremation soon gave way to burial. Ethiopia became Christian within a matter of decades and began a series of regional conquests. Between this time and the advent of Islam in the seventh century, control of various portions of the south Arabian highlands shifted among Coptic and Nestorian Christians, local Jewish rulers, and Sassanid Persians. Since the latter occupiers brought with them Zoroastrian worship, the previously pagan population was exposed almost simultaneously to three major foreign religions. Disruptions emanating from military conquest and religious upheaval, coupled with the collapse of the valuable caravan trade, set the stage for the Muslim conquest in A.D. 631 that linked Yemen to the neighboring Arab world.

The first Muslim adherents followed Shafa'i teachings and carved a permanent niche for themselves in the southern area of the highlands as well as in the coastal lowlands. In A.D. 893, however, a group of Shi'a, or heterodox, Muslims arrived under the leadership of Hadi Yahya, who claimed descent from the Prophet's daughter Fatima. Specifically, this group embraced Zaydism, a Shi'ite sect that originated in Persia and paid homage in name to Zayd, the great-grandson of Fatima's husband, Ali. Settling in the more northerly mountainous areas, the Zaydis soon came into conflict with their Shafa'i (Sunni) neighbors. Their rivalry, which has lasted to this day, has been based not so much on mutual religious intolerance as on political competition. More tribally oriented and warlike, the Zaydis have tended to predominate politically over the more sedentary and agriculturally oriented Shafa'is.

The Muslim conquest brought about a significant change in the role of the monarch. Whereas earlier rulers had been the equivalent of tribal paramount chiefs, the Zaydi imams were spiritual as well as political leaders who ruled over a larger and more politically unified Yemen. Successful imams were adept at capitalizing on both the religious power derived from their title (prayer leader) as well as the tactical advantage of being able to play off one tribe or tribal confederation against the other. Although the principle of "divide and rule" normally worked, the tribes periodically would have the opportunity of deposing a weak or unwise imam by temporarily banding together. This historical phenomenon should be remembered by any observer who wishes to understand the political dynamics of the postrevolutionary era.

If Yemen had suffered geographical remoteness since its earliest times, it sank even further into oblivion between the tenth and sixteenth centuries. In 1568 the Ottoman Turks arrived as conquerers. Under Ottoman occupation, Yemen derived a marginal importance from Turkish rivalry with the European powers and Turkish interest in acquiring secure trade routes to the East. With European circumnavigation of Africa and the later development of Indian Ocean commerce, control of the lower Red Sea became more important to the Turks. They ruled Yemen directly only from 1568 to 1630 and again from 1849 to 1904, but here as elsewhere in the Arab world the Turks' impact on legal and governmental institutions was significant. Ironically, the Ottomans were isolated, if not prisoners, within their own satrapy, since their military control tended to be confined to the fortress towns and the few communications routes that their armies could hold. From the sixteenth through nineteenth centuries, religious and tribal authority of the imamate ebbed and flowed in opposition to alien Turkish rule. These unique circumstances in effect molded a nation that was to undergo violent revolution and civil war in the mid-twentieth century. The popular description of contemporary Yemen as a medieval state that has run headlong into the modern era ignores this important evolutionary process.

The fluctuating struggle between the Ottomans and the indigenous Yemeni rulers did not occur in isolation. In fact, it influenced the course of events in Aden and adjacent south Arabian territories that came under British rule in 1839. Britain's arrival not only checked the southern expansion of the Turks but, more important in terms of local political history, set the stage for mistrust and periodic conflict between Yemeni imams and a goodly number of sultans in the Aden Protectorates whose authority and territorial claims were supported by the British. Although the southern border of modern Yemen thus became a dividing line between two nominally hostile imperial states, it also came to symbolize indigenous rivalries that have persisted to the present day.

Finally rid of the Turks as a result of their defeat and consequent withdrawal at the end of World War I, Yemen's Imam Yahya not only faced potentially hostile petty rulers to the south but also came into conflict with the Saudis and the then-independent ruler of Asir to the north. This situation eventually precipitated a war with Saudi Arabia in 1934. The Saudis won handily but made few territorial demands, and a large part of the present Yemeni-Saudi border was thus definitively demarcated. An agreement with the British in 1935 fixed the southern border with somewhat less certainty.

His status as an absolute monarch impelled Yahya probably as much as the foregoing external conflicts to maintain his kingdom in virtual isolation. He implemented this policy in part by restricting his subjects' travel abroad. He also attempted to prevent the introduction of outside influences, even by restricting the ownership of radios. This resistance to modernization succeeded temporarily, but physical isolation proved to be an increasingly difficult objective in the interwar years. France, Britain, and Italy occupied key colonial territories around the strategic Strait of Bab al-Mandab at the southern entrance to the Red Sea. The British and Italians in particular became anxious to win the imam's favor at the others' expense so as to expand their geographical foothold. Neither fully succeeded, and Yemen thus survived World War II in its traditional isolation. However, dissident exiles sowed the seeds of change with the creation of a free Yemeni movement in Aden in 1944. Imam Yahya was assassinated in a coup attempt in 1948, but his son Ahmad managed to retain control on behalf of the Mutawakkilite dynasty. Nonetheless, he remained so fearful of the intrigues in the traditional capital of San'a that he moved the seat of his own government to the southern (Shafa'i) town of Ta'iz.

In 1958 Yemen joined with Egypt and Syria in the ill-fated United Arab States, largely through the influence of the imam's son, Crown Prince Badr. This act produced no significant political or economic advantages for Yemen, but it managed to intensify the natural suspicions of the neighboring south Arabian sultans who, along with Britain, were fearful of the intentions of Egypt's Nasser. At the same time, the crown prince also initiated a more active Yemeni foreign policy—primarily in an Eastward direction. He brought in development aid from China and East Germany and military assistance from the USSR and Czechoslovakia, which further compounded the concerns of the pro-British sultans. The United Arab States dissolved in 1961 with the rift between Egypt and Syria, but Nasser remained interested in Yemen, in large part because of its proximity to British Aden.

Imam Ahmad died—rather surprisingly of natural causes after surviving many assassination attempts—in September 1962. On September 26, only days after he had assumed power, the new Imam Badr (Ahmad's son) was driven from San'a in a military revolt. The insurgents, led by a heretofore obscure colonel, Abdallah al-Sallal, abolished the monarchy and established the Yemen Arab Republic. Badr fled San'a and mustered tribal warriors loyal to the royal family. The ensuing civil war lasted eight years.

Ironically, the imam—who shortly before had engineered Yemen's entry into Nasser's United Arab States and had established relations with Eastern Europe and China—received his principal support from Saudi Arabia and Britain, both of which were strongly opposed to Nasserist adventures in the Arabian peninsula. Al-Sallal, on the other hand, received his principal support from Nasser, who ultimately sent an Egyptian military force in support of the republic.

As time went on, the Yemen adventure became increasingly disastrous for Nasser, whose military and political problems in this remote corner of Arabia were roughly analagous to those that later confronted the United States in Viet Nam. Egyptian problems were further compounded by the deficient leadership of President al-Sallal.

The United States recognized the revolutionary republic on the tacit understanding that the Egyptian force would soon be withdrawn. The United States attempted, through a special diplomatic mission led by Ambassador Ellsworth Bunker, to bring an early end to hostilities. This effort, along with those of a United Nations peacekeeping mission, failed in the face of increasingly bitter fighting. As the situation reached an impasse, republican Lieutenant General

Hassan al-Amri usurped the authority of al-Sallal during the latter's absence in Cairo in 1965. Al-Amri's move laid the original groundwork for an eventual republican rift with the Egyptians. Nasser was able to reinstate al-Sallal in mid-1966, but the regime collapsed again when the June 1967 Arab-Israeli war necessitated withdrawal of the Egyptian troops from Yemen.

During 1968 and 1969 the republican-royalist conflict was complicated further by intrarepublican fighting in which the more moderate General al-Amri solidified his control within the army. Muhsin al-Ayni, a former Baathist, became prime minister in February 1970 and skillfully negotiated with exiled royalists in Saudi Arabia for their return to republican Yemen. Since the returnees were accorded a place in the government as well as restoration of their property rights, the assimilation proceeded with extraordinary ease considering the bitterness engendered by the just-concluded civil war.

Although the republic had at last achieved peace, chronic problems remained. General al-Amri's involvement in a bizarre shooting incident in 1971 and his resultant exile indirectly provided a suitable climate for a series of civilian governments whose tenure was determined more by economic than ideological challenges. Under the constitution of December 30, 1970, political power was neatly balanced between a three-man republican council chaired by the nominal chief of state, Abd al-Rahman al-Iryani, and the prime minister and his council of ministers. The flow of development aid from both Eastern and Western donors and the United Nations gradually increased, but the most politically significant assistance began to arrive from Saudi Arabia, which previously had backed the royalist counterinsurgency. However, as relations with the Saudis became more normal, relations deteriorated with the Peoples' Democratic Republic of Yemen—the Marxist-oriented state that replaced the British protectorate (including the crown colony of Aden) in 1967. The conflict with Aden soon degenerated into border raids and alleged PDRY-staged terrorist attacks on prominent Yemenis living abroad. The PDRY was perceived both in San'a and Riyadh as a threat, and this mutual perception tended to hasten the process whereby the revolutionary republic became a moderate one, and by which traditionally conservative Saudi Arabia could cooperate with its former Yemeni republican adversaries.

Notwithstanding the civilian role in the post-civil-war normalization process, army Colonel Ibrahim al-Hamdi successfully challenged the leadership of President al-Iryani and assumed power in 1976. His revolutionary command council replaced the troika-style republican council. Al-Hamdi was a strong and popular leader and went far in healing old sectional, religious, and tribal cleavages. Resulting from motives that are still somewhat unclear, al-Hamdi was assassinated in October 1977 and was replaced by Ahmad al-Ghashmi. In June 1978, al-Ghashmi was assassinated by a PDRY agent ostensibly bringing a message from PDRY President Salim Ruba'i Ali, who was himself killed in Aden two days later when the resultant binational crisis degenerated into a domestic coup. Lieutenant Colonel Ali Abdallah Salih was chosen to succeed al-Ghashmi. As President, Ali Abdallah Salih survived an attempted coup in October 1978 and was reelected by the People's Assembly to an additional four-year term in May 1983. Although these recent events underscore the volatility of the YAR leadership struggle, the fact of the growth in political sophistication that the republic has attained between the mid-1970s and the mid-1980s should not be overlooked.

Political Environment

The Zaydi-Shafa'i dichotomy that has pervaded Yemen's Islamic history continues to be a significant factor in the political environment. While the two groups constitute roughly equal halves of Yemen's estimated population of 7.5 million, approximately two-thirds of the nation's tribes are Zaydi. The latter are concentrated in the central and northern highlands and the eastern interior region. They are composed of clans and in turn are sometimes grouped into confederations. The most prominent tribal confederations are the Hashid and Bakil. Not surprisingly, these mountain tribes have warred periodically for centuries, usually as a result of internal leadership challenges or external shifts in alliances. Adroit imams would pit one Zaydi tribe or confederation against another under the time-honored concept of divide and rule; however, when tribal adversaries temporarily united, they could overthrow an imam.

Despite the tribal orientation of the Zaydis, they have not followed the nomadic existence so common in similar mountainous terrain elsewhere in the Middle East. On the contrary, Zaydi culture is rooted in permanent villages composed of fortresslike stone buildings. These are frequently situated on hilltops, cliffs, or other defensible sites. The title of shaykh is given to the tribal headman. Theoretically it should pass down through the male line of the same family, but a shaykh can be deposed if deemed incompetent or weak by the members of the tribe.

On an economic as well as social plane, Yemeni society continues to be semifeudal. Despite the nominal socialist orientation of the early republican regime, central government authority within the tribal hinterland has never been sufficiently strong to alter landlord-tenant relationships on the land or traditional intratribe allegiances. What the government has not been able to do, however, might ultimately be accomplished by the large-scale emigration of adult males to the oil-rich countries of the Arabian peninsula. These workers are sending large remittances to Yemen, which, in turn, are underwriting new economic and social patterns. Meanwhile, the government is gradually extending its control into the hinterlands.

The Zaydis have tended to dominate Yemeni government both in republican as well as monarchial times. This is due partly to the aggressiveness and military prowess of their tribes, and partly to their dispersion throughout the strategic central and northern highland regions. This political preeminence, rather than religious intolerance, is the primary irritant in Zaydi-Shafa'i relations.

Although village-oriented culture also predominates in the Shafa'i areas of southern highlands, clan and tribal affiliations are less pronounced. Rainfall is generally more abundant here, and agriculture thus is more rewarding. The more outgoing Shafa'is have nurtured not only a farming mentality but also a greater penchant for trading than the Zaydis of the north. Prior to the development of the port of Hodayda in republican times, imports traditionally passed overland from Aden through the Shafa'i city of Ta'iz and on to the Zaydi north. Their contact with the outside world also encouraged the Shafa'is to emigrate to more distant lands long before petroleum wealth in nearby Arabian peninsula states served as a more universal lure. As a consequence of earlier twentieth-century Shafa'i emigration, there are small Yemeni colonies even in the United States—for example, in Brooklyn and Buffalo, New York; in Lodi, California; and in Dearborn, Michigan.

The inhabitants of Tihama, the coastal plain, constitute Yemen's third population group. Primarily Shafa'is, many of these people are of African origin and construct rounded thatch houses and wattle fences reminiscent of the East African coast. Though not discriminated against on racial grounds, they tend to occupy lower economic and social strata than the two major highland groups. Ironically, their land has the greatest agricultural potential, subject to mechanization and development of group water resources.

A small but highly distinctive Ismaili (Shi'ite) community is situated in mountainous regions around Manakha, about halfway between San'a and the port city of Hodayda. The Ismailis follow a variation of Shi'ite doctrines and regard the Aga Khan as their spiritual leader. Favorable relations with their Shafa'i and Zaydi neighbors presumably have been aided by their isolation in what amounts to a semi-arid Shangri-La.

A few hundred Jews remain in and around the northern town of Saada, all that is left after the departure of approximately fifty thousand Yemeni Jews to Israel in 1949 by means of the then-famous "Operation Magic Carpet." The Jewish community, which had resided in Yemen for millennia, not only left a considerable architectural and handicraft heritage to their homeland but also injected a unique Oriental note into Israeli culture.

Yemen's population mosaic thus is the product of both religion and geography. Not surprisingly, long isolation from foreign influences and tenuous internal communications have tended to reinforce particularism and a certain degree of xenophobia. The latter is especially characteristic of the Zaydi highlanders. Significantly, the Shi'ite-Sunni dichotomy has not posed the same obstacle to national unity as it has elsewhere in the Muslim world. Likewise, cultural and attitudinal differences among the four major population groups have proved less divisive than might have been expected during the brief but traumatic transition from imamate to republic.

Social Conditions

Despite the turbulent nature of Yemeni politics, political change on balance has been more evolutionary than revolutionary. The pace of economic change has likewise been restrained, primarily because of limited resources and massive developmental problems. It is not surprising, therefore, that social change is not occurring in Yemen as abruptly as elsewhere in the Arab world. This is further explained by the fact that Yemen is predominantly rural. Considering that the total national population is probably between 7 and 8 million, it is significant that San'a, Ta'iz, and Hodayda have a combined population of less than one-half million. The emigrant work force, situated mainly in the oil-producing Arabian peninsula states, is estimated at about 1.25 million. As a result, the bulk of the population is scattered in hundreds of isolated villages and consists of a disproportionate number of women, children, and elderly. Although there is some urban movement, the attraction of the cities is offset by higher prices, scarce housing, and minimal job opportunities. For the villagers, life is neither wretched nor especially comfortable. The stone and mud-brick housing is good if an outside observer were to consider that per capita income is only in the area of $100–$200 per annum. Likewise, food supplies in most years are adequate and reasonably varied. On the other hand, health facilities are almost nonexistent outside the three urban centers. Annual population growth, estimated at between 2 and 3 percent, occurs in the face of a staggeringly high infant mortality rate in the neighborhood of 50 percent. Schools exist mainly in urban areas, so it is not surprising that the overall literacy level is extremely low—probably around 10 percent. In Tihama, rural life is similar, differing only in terms of the hot, humid climate of the coastal plain and African cultural influences.

Hodayda, Ta'iz, and San'a have amenities that are approximately on a par with provincial towns in, for example, Syria or Egypt. Here there is a high demand for consumer goods, fueled by emigrant remittances that could be running as high as $1 billion annually. The economic significance of these remittances can be misleading, since rising living standards are being financed by an exported human resource rather than though comparable expansion in domestic agriculture or industrial productivity. Emigrants work at the sufferance of host nations.

Prior to the recent upsurge in emigrant remittances, income disparity was not pronounced. The majority of the populace was poor (and still is) and few individuals could be considered wealthy by virtue of land ownership or profitable trading ventures. To a Western observer, the life-style of a rich family was not markedly different from that of a poor one. A middle class was nonexistent during the imamate; however, there existed a class of feudal bureaucrats known as *sayyids*—literally, descendants of the Prophet but, more important, with connections more royal than religious. Almost universally detested for their role as tax collectors and extortionists, many of these *sayyids* were killed in the early days of the revolution.

In the current republican era there is a small but growing middle class of government bureaucrats and an expanding merchant community living from the import trade. Qualified college graduates are still few in number, but externally funded scholarship programs and local educational facilities eventually will bring a few thousands of professionals into the economy. Nevertheless, shortages of trained personnel in the essential public-service areas will remain chronic for the indefinite future. The gap can be filled only through the imported expertise of international organizations and foreign aid missions.

Economic Conditions

Discounting momentarily the peculiar economic relief afforded by emigrant remittances, Yemen has been and remains a poor agricultural country. Repeated attempts to find petroleum have failed, and mineral surveys have failed to locate deposits that would be economically feasible to develop. In the mineral sector, copper might offer limited export possibilities, but extraction and transportation costs are currently too great. In the eighteenth and nineteenth centuries Yemeni coffee found lucrative markets in Europe and even in the United States. There are nineteenth-century accounts of New England merchant ships setting sail for the Yemeni port of Mocha as a primary destination, and of British and Dutch complaints that the Americans had outbid their resident buyers. Unfortunately, the middle-elevation coffee slopes proved equally suitable for the cultivation of qat, a leafy plant with high tannin content that the Yemenis chew for its mildly narcotic effects. Today, while premium grades of Yemeni coffee could be earning needed foreign exchange, the substitute crop of qat is being consumed in-country with deleterious effects not only on its users but also on the agricultural economy. Because qat must be chewed while fresh, the distribution process places unnecessary demands on the fledgling truck transport system that is needed for the distribution of market crops. Qat in effect represents an economic opportunity lost since it is not exported and diverts labor and land resources from crops that could be either exported or consumed domestically.

The geographical determinants of Yemen's population zones also differentiate roughly analogous agricultural zones. The Tihama coastal desert runs north and south along the Red Sea and is physically separated from the interior by an abrupt curtain of mountains situated approximately thirty miles inland and parallel to the coast. Rising in a series of ridges separated by deep valleys, these mountains cradle a high interior plain that slopes gently eastward to the undemarcated portion of the border with Saudi Arabia's Empty Quarter. Intermittent ranges longitudinally intercept this plain and on the south provide a natural frontier with the PDRY. The moisture-laden monsoon winds blowing from the Indian Ocean strike these successive ranges and normally produce a fairly heavy precipitation for this otherwise arid region. The soil is especially fertile in the central highland plain of Yarim, and in the rainy season this plain is checkerboarded with green fields. Rainfall there ranges from 400 to 1,000 millimeters (16 to 40 inches).

In many highland areas terraces have been developed over the centuries to hold soil that otherwise would be washed by the 400- to 600-millimeter annual rains through deep wadis (dry river beds) to the Red Sea. All of the highland areas are cool for these latitudes by virtue of the elevations, which range from 750 to 3,500 meters (approximately 2,500 to 12,000 feet). The somewhat warmer and moister valleys and mountainsides in the Hujarriyah region south and west of Ta'iz are especially fertile. Rainfall in the mountains provides ample groundwater for the Tihama Desert, which itself receives only about 150 millimeters per year. This is supplemented by periodic flooding of the wadis that bisect the plain.

As might be expected, each geographic region poses special agricultural problems. In Tihama, the flat terrain favors mechanization, and the water resources may be fully exploited only with mechanical pumping or elaborate catchment schemes. By contrast, the mountain terraces efficiently capture the rainfall but are poorly suited to mechanical cultivation. The northern and eastern highlands are semi-arid and will require irrigation development. The fertile topsoil is a fragile resource in most areas and in some instances has been damaged by too-heavy plowing with oversized tractors.

Although Yemeni statistics are of doubtful accuracy and in any event often fail to describe this uniquely underdeveloped economy, it is reasonable to assume that less than 10 percent of the approximately 195,000 square kilometers (75,000 square miles) of national territory is under tillage. Nonetheless, agriculture provides roughly three-quarters of the gross domestic product. Only about 20 percent of the cultivable lands are irrigated, leaving the remaining majority dependent on monsoon rainfall. As the Sahel drought revealed in Africa, these monsoons may be becoming less dependable as a result of increasing fluctuations in the global climate.

Yemen's agricultural production is surprisingly diversified. In addition to the primary crops of millet and sorghum, wheat, maize, potatoes, dates, and grapes are produced. Coffee could be reintroduced in quantity at medium elevations, and long-staple cotton acreage in Tihama could be increased. Ironically, however, Yemeni imports are running at a level almost ten times as high as exports; food and beverages constitute approximately half of these imports and probably total more than $30 million annually. Even if agricultural development failed to stimulate a more favorable export trade, at least import requirements could be reduced.

The present trade imbalance is compounded by the rising expectations of the new urban classes who are now living within a new cash economy. Whereas sorghum and millet provide about 70 percent of the food requirements of the village inhabitant, city dwellers are no longer satisfied with this diet. Demand for domestically produced raw foods is low by comparison, and the resultant low market prices offer little incentive for the farmers to produce more. It is apparent, therefore, that international development aid will have to be meshed with government incentives, and that import policies will have to be developed to discourage the squandering of remittance income in this direction. Likewise, the government will have to develop an adequate system of rural credit, discourage qat production by taxation or other penalties, and generally ensure that the fledgling cash economy is not confined to the three urban centers. This is a difficult task, but Yemen cannot live indefinitely on the earnings of its expatriate labor force.

The task of developing Yemeni agriculture and the broader economic infrastructure thus far has fallen to external aid programs operating on both grant and loan bases. Unfortunately, bilateral foreign aid has tended to reflect the political motivations of the donor nations. Consequently, there has been a lack of coordination among and attention to specific Yemeni priorities. International aid, primarily through the United Nations, was inefficiently administered in the civil war years but increased in quality and quantity in the 1970s. Even a partial list of development schemes indicates the mixed results of what has been a massive external financial effort to raise Yemen from its position near the bottom on the world development scale.

As noted earlier, China and East Germany were among the earliest bilateral aid donors. In contrast to rather lackluster East German agricultural and telecommunications projects, the Chinese projects involved successful construction of a high-quality paved highway between the port of Hodayda and the capital at San'a, a cotton textile mill and a technical school in San'a, and extension of the Hodayda-San'a road northward to the Saudi frontier. Although the textile mill appeared at first glance to be uneconomical by virtue of its high water consumption in the semi-arid capital, it may have represented a deft politicoeconomic maneuver to disrupt East German plans for development of Tihama cotton for a bilateral barter trade. Most foreign observers have given the Chinese high marks for efficiency, good local relations, and programs that have been free of visible "strings."

The United States embarked on its aid programs shortly before the revolution with two major projects: a municipal water system in Ta'iz and a road between Ta'iz and San'a. Work continued after the revolution until 1967, when diplomatic relations were broken as a result of the Arab-Israeli war. The opening of an American Interests Section in the Italian Embassy in 1970 permitted U.S. food donations in the famine of 1970, and the resumption of full relations in 1973 enabled the U.S. Agency for International Development (AID), formerly based in Ta'iz, to initiate new projects—for example, in water supply and sanitation—from new headquarters in San'a. The Americans in their turn have received high marks for their water projects but were previously criticized for not paving the Ta'iz-San'a road. Ironically, this project was taken over by West Germany, and the road has since become in Yemeni eyes a "German" one. West Germany also reconstructed the airport at San'a.

The USSR's very diverse aid efforts have had mixed results. The San'a airport actually was first constructed by the Soviets, but the runways proved inadequate for heavy commercial aircraft operations. Like the U.S.-built road, this became a "German"airport. A more successful effort involved the construction of a trans-Tihama road south from Hodayda to the east-west U.S.-built road from Mocha to Ta'iz. Other projects included a hospital at San'a, a cement plant at Bajil in Tihama, and the dredging of a new port at Hodayda. The USSR also extended a series of large trade credits and provided a full range of military equipment including tanks, jet aircraft, weapons, and spares. Soviet aid has carried more obvious "strings" than the Chinese aid, with which it apparently has been competing. Although Soviet economic development projects no doubt have been fairly well received, considerable resentment was incurred in the mid-1970s as a result of withholding ammunition and military spares for purposes of political leverage at a time when Yemen was strengthening its Saudi ties and clashing with the radical Aden regime. A 1979 border clash between the two Yemens resulted in the definitve supplanting of the Soviet Union by the United States as the principal arms supplier to the YAR.

Other bilateral aid has come from such diverse sources as Britain, Hungary, Italy, Kuwait, and Saudi Arabia. Kuwaiti aid has been funneled in large quantities through the Kuwait Fund for Arab Economic Development, and has been especially helpful in terms of rural development and the educational infrastructure. Even more massive Saudi aid has assisted the central government in San'a in meeting its budgetary deficits, and (more recently) in acquiring Western arms to replace the obsolescent Soviet inventory. Considering that Yemen now relies extensively on Saudi loans as well as on indirect support through tolerant foreign labor and remittance policies, political relations have come almost full circle since the civil war days, when the Saudis supported the royalists against the Egyptian-backed republican regime.

International organization aid has changed both qualitatively and quantitatively since the United Nations began its peacekeeping operations shortly after the outbreak of the civil war. Although the peacekeeping effort failed, subsequent development projects by various UN agencies touched many areas neglected by individual foreign aid missions. Most important, the United Nations has served to focus international attention on Yemen by listing it among those nations most in need of development aid.

The most significant current international development assistance is being extended by the World Bank. Spanning such project areas as textiles, irrigation, and road building, this financial assistance is accompanied by more careful planning than heretofore available.

Political Structure

The formal structure of Yemen's government has changed greatly since the revolution. Form, however, has been altered more than substance.

The imamate was thoroughly autocratic and feudal. While in theory any male citizen of good character was eligible to become imam, the office actually was the preserve of a few aristocratic families and clans. The accession of one or another of these families would depend on the shifting allegiance of the key highland Zaydi tribes. Provided the imam could correctly manipulate this tribal support, military, legal, spiritual, and fiscal power could be concentrated in his own hands. Mention already has been made of the *sayyid* class, which filled in the entire pyramid of civilian authority. Military power on the other hand was exercised by Zaydi tribal levies answerable to the imam through a separate hierarchy of shaykhs. To ensure this military support, imams frequently would resort to the medieval practice of holding hostages from the principal tribes. The prison system also could be used to eliminate challenges from within the imam's own family. The legal system represented a combination of Islamic structures and Ottoman legal forms. Administration tended to be divided according to the provincial governorates established by the Ottomans.

Not surprisingly, in creating the Yemen Arab Republic the revolutionaries substituted a modern Arab socialist governmental structure not unlike that of Egypt, the major source of external political and military support. Exercising authority through the revolutionary command council, President al-Sallal placed military officers in many key ministerial posts. Each ministry in turn had an Egyptian adviser, and thus received guidance not only from the presidential palace but also from Egypt's military headquarters and embassy. A presidential council was created by the provisional constitution of April 1964. A subordinate executive council was composed of cabinet ministers, who functioned in this second capacity as substitute legislators. With the departure of al-Sallal in 1967,

Abd al-Rahman al-Iryani became chief of state, functioning as head of a three-man republican council. In 1969 a forty-five-member national council was created to function as a legislature. Its membership was drawn primarily from the tribes. With the return of the royalist exiles following the agreement negotiated by Premier Muhsin al-Ayni in 1970, the republican council was expanded to five seats and the national council to sixty-three. However, the national council exercised only token legislative authority as real political power remained with the republican council, the council of ministers, and the army.

Further systemic changes occurred with the introduction of a new constitution in December 1970. The republican council was allowed to fluctuate between three and five members, with the chairman still functioning as a chief of state. However, the national council was abolished in favor of a consultative council of 159 members. This in turn has been replaced by a 140-member People's Constituent Assembly, created in 1978.

In 1976 the eight-year process by which Yemen's political structure had evolved following the departure of President al-Sallal changed abruptly with the accession of Lieutenant Colonel Ibrahim al-Hamdi. By creating a revolutionary command council, he reversed the process by which power was gradually shifting from the presidency to the prime minister and cabinet and—to a very limited extent—the variously named legislative councils. Even more significant, he reforged the linkage between the army and the central government that had weakened in the early 1970s. This trend has been maintained by his successors.

Political Dynamics

Under Colonel al-Sallal's military coup in 1962, Yemen became nominally another revolutionary Arab socialist republic. While this formal title might be appropriate if applied to the formal political structure or to proclamations of official policy, an examination of the nation's political dynamics suggests that the revolution has been a limited one and that socialism relates more to tribal egalitarianism than to actual economic practice.

Yemen's political structure has been highly centralized in both pre- and postrevolutionary times, but central authority in power terms actually has diminished during the republican era. The leadership in both eras has relied heavily on sanctions or threatened sanctions in the exercise of power. Control over urban centers has always been relatively easier in Yemeni history, but the significance of this has been diminished by the fact that the population is predominantly rural. Therefore, the tribes have held—and continue to hold—the key to control of the hinterland areas. This control is crucial because, with the exception of the remittance factor, rural agriculture is the prime contributor to the national economy. Both the imams and the republicans have depended on favorable tribal alignments for critical support, but in this endeavor the republicans have proved weaker than the imams. The tribes have been relatively immune to military control owing to the difficulty of the terrain, and have been less than fully supportive of the republican central government as a result of their belief that funding for development and social services has favored the few urban areas.

It remains to be seen whether the tribal areas will continue to play the same dynamic political role that transcended imamic times and the early republican years. In terms of simple population statistics, the countryside holds—and most likely will continue to hold—the larger constituency. The key unknown, however, is the extent to which burgeoning employment in the adjacent oil-rich areas of the Arabian peninsula will continue to siphon off working-age males and thus indirectly shift a significant portion of the remaining population to the cities and into more urban life-styles based primarily on remittances. The new economic realities cannot be overlooked, but it would be premature to write off the fundamental tribal conservatism that prevades Yemeni political culture and that, to date, has made the Yemeni revolution a very cautious one by Third World standards.

Although population and wealth may shift, leadership patterns in the tribal areas most likely will remain relatively stable. At this late date in the twentieth century, authority is still vested in the tribal shaykh ("old man"). As noted previously, a shaykh who lacks leadership abilities can be replaced through the connivance of various elders and the passive consent of the tribe as a whole. Yemeni tribal politics are complicated, especially in the pivotal Zaydi areas, because the principal tribes are affiliated with either the Hashid or Bakil confederations, headed by paramount shaykhs. Rivalries exist among the tribes and between the two confederations, but these are balanced by shifting alliances. While temporary alliances could topple a universally unpopular or incapable imam, postrevolutionary regimes are more likely to stand or fall on the basis of San'a politics and/or the disposition of the more secular republican army.

Leadership patterns in the republican era have been remarkably varied. Former President al-Iryani and many senior officials occupying republican council and cabinet posts have been traditionalists both in physical appearance and political outlook. Either simultaneously or alternately, modernist civilian intellectuals and military officers have rotated in and out of the prime ministry and key cabinet posts. Personal affiliations and political philosophies have counted, whereas party affiliations have not. With the advent of al-Hamid and his successors Lieutenant Colonel al-Ghashmi and Ali Abdallah Salih, the pendulum appears to have swung back to the military side. In comparison with the intrigues and violence that characterized the imamate, the postrevolutionary era has been much calmer, despite the violent overthrow of two presidents in less than a year in 1977–1978. This was especially true in the early and mid-1970s, when civilian prime ministers held sway. Political opposition was a riskier business in the preceding regime of Lieutenant General al-Amri and again appears to be so in the new military era.

In the absence of meaningful electoral processes, power tends to accrue through a coalition-building process involving—in various degrees—key military officers, youthful technocrats, a few key tribal leaders, and urban traditionalists with acceptable republican credentials. The leverage of the military is obvious in view of its potential for forceful action. However, the civil war proved that even tanks and jet aircraft cannot control an uncooperative hinterland. The youthful, educated technocrats have no comparable power base but are an increasingly essential human resource in the irreversible process of political modernization. Tribal leaders represent the other side of the political coin—they control remote areas that the military cannot.

Finally, the traditionalist politicians provide something of a human link between the old and new political cultures, neither of which yet predominates. Political change can occur (and has occurred) by violent means such as assassination or military coup, but it is just as likely to occur through a shifting consensus among these power-sharing coalitions. For example, civilian prime ministers until recently rotated in and out of power according to their relative success or failure in dealing with omnipresent economic problems. The mood of the power-wielding constituencies cannot be quantified in the absence of a legitimate electoral process, but the number of governments that have come and gone since September 1962 attests to the efficiency of this system. Now that the pendulum has swung again to the military side, outside observers should look not to the constituent assembly for signs of confidence but within the officer constituency that is now ascendant.

Foreign Policy

As indicated earlier, Yemeni foreign policy during many centuries of the Zaydi imamate was xenophobic in the extreme. The only successful foreign intruder was Ottoman Turkey, and success is a quite relative term if the costs of conquest and two periods of military dominance are compared with the negligible commerce and dubious political benefits that accrued from this remote imperial outpost. In the nineteenth century Britain became the potential intruder through its alliances with the sultans of South Arabia, and in the early twentieth century the nascent Saudi state constituted a disturbing presence to the north. Ironically, the more worrisome British threat never materialized, whereas the Saudi one escalated into war and temporary military occupation in 1934. Although King ibn Saud's peace terms were magnanimous, this overt conflict and the earlier, more deeply seated cultural differences fostered a Yemeni mistrust that has lasted to the present day. Equally ironic, the Arab revolutionaries who eventually drove Britain from South Arabia quickly became republican Yemen's principal adversaries. During all but the final years of the imamate, a successful foreign policy meant being left alone. Since the revolution of 1962, foreign policy priorities have been aimed—reasonably enough—at obtaining foreign aid for massive development needs with the minimum of political strings.

Considering the history of Arab nationalism in the late 1950s and early 1960s in the context of East-West regional posturing, it is hardly surprising that Yemen—as an admitted client of Nasser's United Arab Republic—depended heavily on direct and indirect Soviet military support and simultaneously entered into extensive economic aid agreements with the USSR, its Eastern European allies, and China. Unlike Britain, the United States and West Germany recognized the republican regime. However, their aid programs earned only minimal influence in the face of Nasserist distrust. Relations with West Germany were severed in 1965 when previously secret German military aid to Israel became public knowledge, and U.S. ties were severed equally abruptly as a result of the 1967 Arab-Israeli war. By this time, however, the republic had become a restive client of Nasser; the withdrawal of Egyptian forces in late 1967 amid growing local hostility marked a new period of what might be termed "political introspection."

After two years of quasi-isolation, there emerged a republican Yemen free of the Egyptian-client image and ready for a rapprochement with Saudi Arabia and the royalist exiles. Relations with West Germany not only resumed but also blossomed into a large-scale aid program. Ties with the United States partially resumed with the opening of the American Interests Section in the Italian Embassy in 1970 and expanded with the establishment of a full-fledged U.S. Embassy in 1973. Almost concurrently, relations with the USSR deteriorated—not as the result of overt Western moves but rather because of Yemeni dissatisfaction with what was perceived as Soviet favoritism toward South Yemen in the area of arms transfers. Prime Minister Muhsin al-Ayni's 1970 agreement, which permitted the peaceful return of the royalist exiles, paved the way for a gradual improvement in Yemeni-Saudi relations. By the mid-1970s, successor regimes had begun to depend so heavily on Saudi economic aid that this wealthy northern neighbor became the most influential foreign actor on the local political scene. Ironically, although Yemeni foreign policy was dramatically reoriented in terms of friends and adversaries over this short span of years, relations with China continued in the same positive vein. No doubt the Soviets were extremely frustrated to witness a succession of successful Chinese aid projects dispensed without discernible political strings at a time when many of their own projects were falling short of Yemeni expectations. Relations with the United States have followed an upward course since 1970, undoubtedly boosted by a residue of goodwill engendered by the favorable interpersonal relations that have accrued with a series of aid projects that began in the final years of the imamate. Unlike the Soviets, Americans have been personally popular even when their government's policies have been unpopular.

Yemeni external relations during the remainder of the 1980s most likely will continue to be conditioned by the economic reality of the YAR's proximity to its incomparably rich oil-producing neighbors, and by the seemingly perpetual hostility of the Aden regime—notwithstanding the equally perpetual efforts on the part of the San'a and Aden governments to hold "unity" talks.

The massive development problem already has engendered extensive relationships with international entities—the United Nations from the first days of the republic and more recently the World Bank. Saudi Arabia remains, of course, the most important external factor in Yemeni political and economic affairs. Budgetary support, emigrant remittances, and subsidies for military weapons are all vital to the YAR government, and this northern neighbor is a unique source for all three. However, cultural differences and political sensitivities on both sides probably will continue to complicate this otherwise symbiotic bilateral relationship.

YAR-PDRY relations cannot help but be perplexing to the outside observer. Even since the emergence of the latter as an Arab nationalist state in the late

1960s, the two neighbors have engaged in propaganda battles, periodic border confrontations, and perpetual mistrust. However, unity talks aimed at eventual political merger occur almost as regularly as border warfare. These intermittent negotiations represent a peculiar sort of political safety valve, since actual unification on terms acceptable to one clearly would be unacceptable to the other.

Tensions between San'a and Aden reached a crisis point in early 1979, when an escalating border fight prompted the Saudis to consider active military intervention on the YAR side. This train of events, in turn, involved the United States, the Soviet Union, and the Arab League in a complex set of maneuvers. Perceiving the evolving pattern of PDRY infiltration, subversion, and—finally—military probes as an element of Soviet adventurism in the area as well as a simultaneous test of Saudi confidence, the United States agreed to sell the YAR modern weapons worth $390 million (underwritten by Saudi Arabia) and to dispatch a naval task force to the area. Although the immediate crisis subsided when PDRY forces withdrew from the frontier, the potential for even greater future crises increased by mid-year as peninsula oil soared in political and economic value in step with the latest events in the global energy crisis. Once-remote Yemen is now situated near the focal point of world rivalry for a critical resource.

In the 1980s YAR-PDRY relations normalized as the PDRY focused most of its attention on internal affairs. The bloody coup overthrowing President Ali Nasir Muhammad in January 1986, however, may result in a return of tensions. The new leaders were particularly dissatisfied with Ali Nasir's moderate foreign policies. On the other hand, the new acting president, Haidar Abu Bakr Attas, the former prime minister, said that the PDRY government will continue to seek good relations with its neighbors.

Bibliography

The most comprehensive recent work on Yemen is Robert W. Stookey's *Yemen: The Politics of the Yemen Arab Republic* (Boulder, Colo.: Westview Press, 1978). J. E. Peterson's *Yemen: The Search for a Modern State* (Baltimore: Johns Hopkins University Press, 1982) is also a valuable reference. Two journalistic treatments of the civil war period are Edgar O'Ballance's *The War in the Yemen* (Hamden, Conn.: Archon Books, 1971), and Dana Adams Schmidt's *Yemen: The Unknown War* (New York: Holt, Rinehart & Winston, 1968). A more scholarly treatment of the latter days of the imamate and the advent of the republic is found in Manfred Wenner's *Modern Yemen: 1918–1966* (Baltimore: Johns Hopkins University Press, 1967). Roughly the same period, with a helpful explanation of the complex relations between imamate Yemen and British South Arabia, is found in Harold Ingrams's *The Yemen: Imams, Rulers and Revolutions* (London: John Murray, 1963). Eric Marco treats Yemen's earlier history in his *Yemen and the Western World Since 1571* (New York: Praeger Publishers, 1968). There is also a chapter on the Yemen by the author of this chapter in Abid Al-Marayati et al., *The Middle East: Its Government and Politics* (Belmont, Calif.: Duxbury Press, 1972). A useful study aid is the American

University's *Area Handbook for the Yemens* (Washington, D.C.: Government Printing Office, 1977). Finally, an excellent analysis of Yemeni emigration may be found in an article by Jon C. Swanson, "Some Consequences of Emigration for Rural Economic Development in the Yemen Arab Republic," *Middle East Journal* 33 (Winter 1979), pp. 34–43.

9

People's Democratic Republic of Yemen

David McClintock

The People's Democratic Republic of Yemen (PDRY), which is also known as South (or Southern) Yemen or Yemen (Aden), extends along the southern coast of Arabia from the Strait of Bab al-Mandab at the lower entrance of the Red Sea to the Sultanate of Oman in the northeast. To the north is the Yemen Arab Republic. The two countries have antithetical regimes ideologically, but both claim a common south Arabian cultural heritage. The peoples of western PDRY are ethnically Yemenis, although some of the eastern tribes are not.

In recent times, the two Yemens have had many common experiences, though not concurrently. North Yemeni exiles from the imam resided in Aden, where much of the plotting of the 1962 coup took place; many South Yemeni exiles resided in the YAR during British control of Aden, and a new generation of antiregime exiles has moved there since PDRY's independence in 1967. Under the imamate, North Yemen was one of the most isolated countries in the region; and in recent years, South Yemen has slipped into comparable obscurity. For over a decade, it has had the only avowedly Marxist regime in the entire Arab world without exciting more than a small fraction of international interest. Despite its isolation, it is situated astride an important international sea-lane. Accordingly, it deserves more attention in the West than it has received in the past decade.

Historical Background

There has been a symbiotic relationship between the two Yemens culturally, politically, and economically that has prevailed since ancient times. Frankincense and myrrh, the export of which made the highland domains of the Queen of Sheba and neighboring ministates rich, actually grew in the coastal areas of south Arabia and the nearby African coast. Both highlanders and lowlanders in much of the area occupied by the present-day YAR and PDRY claimed descent from one of the two great ethnic divisions of Arabian peoples, the Qahtanis. The other division, the Adnani Arabians, were mainly found further north. In pre-Islamic times, these distinctions often had great political significance. Although perennial feuds among the petty states throughout the region prevented the development of a larger Qahtani polity, the Zaydi conquest of the Yemen highlands in the ninth century A.D. installed a Shi'ite ruling elite in an otherwise Sunni Muslim area. Henceforth the isolation of the highlands was to a great extent a self-imposed political one.

South Arabia, which was roughly coterminous with the present PDRY, was susceptible to the intrusions of foreign powers pursuing their maritime strategies. The Turks were sufficiently interested in Aden to fortify it in the 1500s as a check on the European powers who were beginning to use the Indian Ocean as a new route to the East.

In 1839 the British seized Aden and the nearby hinterland in order to secure the now highly developed Indian Ocean "lifeline." By that time Turkish power in the region had declined, but Muhammad Ali's Egypt was rapidly becoming a new threat. At the turn of the nineteenth century, Britain had entered into a protective treaty with the sultan of Lahej; after the annexation of nearby Aden, this treaty set the pattern for a succession of similar agreements with other sultans in the south Arabian hinterland. The city of Aden itself was governed from British India as a dependency of the Bombay presidency.

The strategic importance of Aden increased markedly with the opening of the Suez Canal in 1869, since the excellent natural harbor offered ideal naval basing facilities. A short distance to the west, fortifications on Perim Island in the Strait of Bab al-Mandab allowed effective control of the southern end of the Red Sea. The development of large steam vessels also favored the development of Aden as a principal coaling station between Europe, South Asia, and the Far East, and this fact in turn necessitated the eventual construction of one of the world's largest bunkering facilities. Cable and Wireless Ltd. constructed a relay station here for its undersea cable from India, thus adding another facility of strategic value.

The importance of this British foothold in Arabia was not lost on other European powers. Rival French and Italian colonial ventures in the nearby Horn of Africa underscored the importance of Bab al-Mandab in the later nineteenth century; however, the Somali colonies and Eritrea never matched British Aden in military value. The deeply ingrained consciousness of Aden's strategic importance influenced British policies and actions in the difficult preindependence era almost a century later. Similarly, Mussolini's efforts to win the allegiance of the Yemeni imam in the 1930s reflected Italian preoccupation with the southern Red Sea.

The history of British Aden in the first half of the twentieth century is a complex one, but the principal themes were the further development of Aden as a port and dominant urban economic center within the region; the simultaneous struggle to impose uniform political authority over the backward and potentially rebellious hinterland sultanates; and the growth

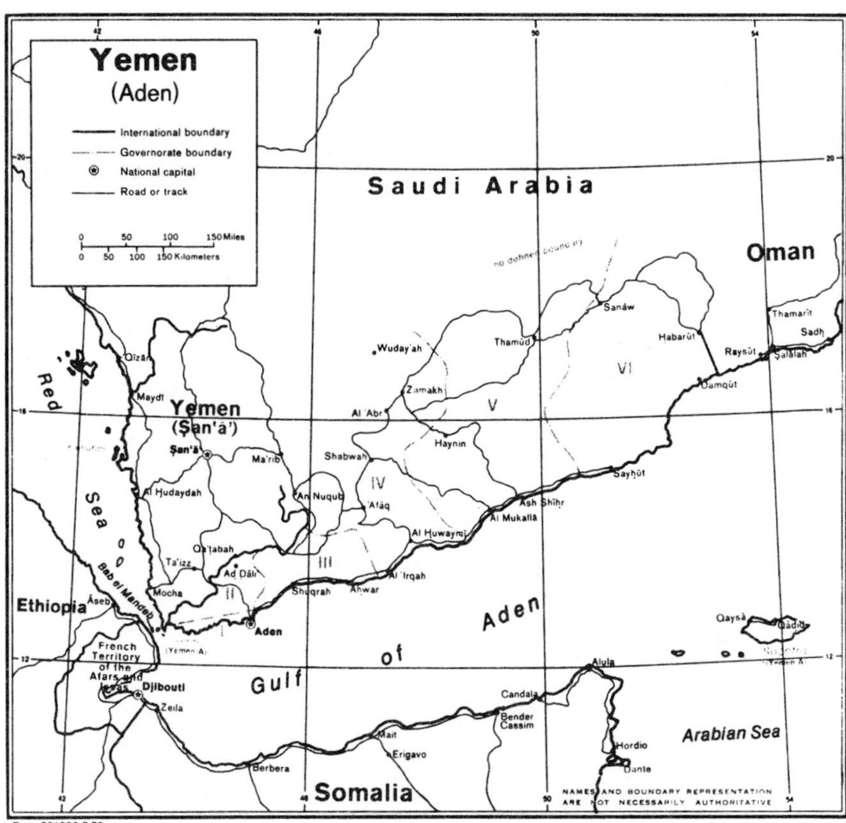

of mutual suspicion on the part of northern Yemen's imam and the pro-British sultans in the south. Four years before their departure from Yemen at the end of World War I, the Turks had demarcated the frontier between the two regions by means of a convention with Britain. The line as drawn was unacceptable to Imam Yahya, but his disastrous encounter with the Saudis in 1934 compelled him to agree to a partial settlement with Great Britain the same year.

For Britain, the principal problem was not the latent hostility of Yemen's imam but the dubious loyalty of the disunited sultans who provided a territorial buffer on three sides. Significantly, aerial bombardment of tribal villages in the 1930s proved to be the most effective means of eliminating dissidence.

The colonial development of Aden increased the cultural and political differences between this urban area and the remote sultanates. Certain changes in administrative philosophy occurred in 1937 with the transfer of Aden to Colonial Office control. The port city became Aden Colony, and the sultanates were divided into the Western and Eastern Aden Protectorates. Wisely, the Yemeni imam resisted Italian overtures on the eve of World

War II, and his neutrality afforded Britain a more comfortable position in this strategic location.

Not surprisingly, Aden figured early and prominently in the postwar debate about a British withdrawal east of Suez. In the early 1950s the British political agent Kennedy Trevaskis submitted a plan favored by Conservatives in Parliament to link the sultanates in a federation that could serve as a vehicle for eventual independence. This failed to attract enthusiastic support from the sultans but succeeded in arousing further suspicions on the part of the Yemen's Imam Ahmad. (Imam Yahya had been assassinated in 1948, and his son and successor Ahmad felt so insecure that he moved his capital from San'a to the southern town of Ta'iz.)

Reciprocal misunderstandings were compounded by other regional developments in the mid-1950s. Britain became increasingly unpopular in most Arab eyes as a result of the 1956 Suez fiasco, which in turn paved the way for Yemen's bizarre affiliation with Nasser's United Arab Republic (UAR), consisting of Egypt and Syria, in the short-lived United Arab States (UAS). During this time, Imam Ahmad's son Crown Prince Muhammad al-Badr pressed successfully for expanded foreign relations. The first foreigners through this slightly opened door were the Soviets, East Germans, and Chinese, who promptly initiated military and economic aid projects. (U.S. aid also began at this time, but on a less visible level.)

If these Yemeni actions were a defensive reaction to a perceived threat from the British and their sultan clients, they produced a mirror-image reaction in the south. Heretofore, the sultans had been indifferent toward the federation scheme, but by 1959 six leaders in the Western Protectorate agreed to join an entity called "The Federation of the Amirates of the South." For the time being, no formula could be found to bring in Aden Colony and the eastern protectorates. The latter area contained the exotic Wadi Hadhramaut, an ethnically distinct region that for centuries had close contact with the East Indies. The Hadhrami merchants were not anxious to dissipate their wealth in this federation scheme, nor were the eastern protectorate sultans anxious to risk the loss of any petroleum wealth that might result from the then-active exploration effort on the part of the Pan American Petroleum Company.

The republicans who overthrew the Mutawakkilite dynasty in Yemen in September 1962 were more actively negative toward the British. With the prompt arrival of a massive Egyptian expeditionary force, the stage was set for Yemen-based subversion of the new south Arabian federation. At the same time, the British on the southern border and the Saudis on the north welcomed the formerly hostile royalists in their forced exile and provided two bases for countersubversive action against the republic. After the failure of the Bunker peace mission to obtain early withdrawal of Egyptian troops from Yemen, the United States found itself in the unenviable position of maintaining its close relationship with Saudi Arabia, recognizing the Yemen Arab Republic, and wishing success to British efforts to create a viable preindependence state in south Arabia.

If the British had found the situation of the 1950s less than propitious for building a viable south Arabian political entity, the Yemen civil war made the task infinitely more difficult in the 1960s. Nevertheless, a formula finally was found to allow the merger of Aden with the sultanates, and in January 1963 the South Arabian Federation was born.

Although the British and their sultan clients were understandably fearful of the course of events in the YAR, it is fair to assume that similar fears and suspicions motivated the Egyptians and their republican Yemeni clients when the conservative federation came into being. Suspicion soon escalated into overt hostility; the Egyptians and Yemenis began to experience difficulty in maintaining the allegiance of many conservative tribal leaders. None could be permanently "bought" with the newly printed YAR paper riyals, and imposition of military control proved difficult because tanks and jet aircraft were ill-suited to the craggy highland terrain. Thus, the British and Saudi-backed royalist tribesmen in the YAR had a tactical advantage in the countryside. By contrast, the British were highly vulnerable in urban Aden, where there was significant anticolonial sentiment. The Egyptians took full advantage of the dissident, antifederation political forces on hand. By 1965 bombings, grenade throwings, and sabotage operations were almost daily occurrences. Although the British presumably had hoped that the federation would enable Britain to exercise its influence in economic and defense matters while promoting gradual self-rule, the demand for complete and immediate independence spread from these militant opposition factions to the more conservative ones.

Political coalitions in south Arabia had become well defined by the 1950s. These groups articulated their political demands with a surprising degree of sophistication, considering their lack of experience with anything except colonial rule. The spawning ground for many of these aspiring politicians was the well-developed Aden Trade Union Congress (ATUC). Under the leadership of Abdallah al Asnaj, the ATUC formed the Peoples Socialist party (PSP). Sharing its anti-British sentiments were the South Arabian League (SAL) and the National Liberation Front (NLF). The SAL drew its strength primarily from the Lahej area. The NLF was essentially an Egyptian creation operating from across the Yemen frontier, though its ideology was closely akin to the Arab Nationalists Movement (ANM), which included such leaders as George Habbash of the Palestinian resistance movement. The most conservative group was the United National party (UNP), which represented pro-British business interests.

The NLF struck the first serious blow to the new federation scheme in 1964 by inciting tribesmen in the Radfan district to revolt. The NLF not only solidified its position through this operation but also gained strength through the defection of Qahtan al-Sha'bi and some of his followers from the SAL. Al-Sha'bi was to become the future nation's first president.

All but the most conservative factions competed among themselves in efforts to undermine the federation. They not only attempted the mobilization of public support (primarily in Aden) but also resorted to paramilitary and terrorist actions in both the port and the hinterland. In the meantime, a shift in British policy doomed the original federation plan. The British Labour government, which came to power in 1964, was inclined to reduce (or eliminate where possible) British commitments east of Suez. Accordingly, it favored the establishment of a unitary state in south Arabia that could serve as a vehicle for an early and complete independence. This set the stage for markedly increased infighting among the local political factions.

The British Labour party's resolve to rid itself of the troublesome south Arabia problem was strengthened by anticolonialist pressure in the United Nations. The latter had actually begun as early as 1948 and had been reiterated at the 1955 Bandung Conference of Afro-Asian states. In 1963 a UN committee focused on the "Aden problem," and did so again in 1964 as the new Labour government was attempting to develop a constitution for a postindependence entity. Even the Security Council became involved in the spring of 1964, when Yemen charged that the Aden-based Royal Air Force had bombed the border town of Harib. Throughout 1965 the British were frustrated both by escalating terrorism and the resultant need to respond with greater military force, and by the refusal of the competing factions to agree on a constitutional design for a new state. Having lost patience with the continuing impasse, the British announced in February 1966 that all military forces would be withdrawn by December 1968.

During the next two years the already chaotic situation deteriorated even further as the anti-British factions competed for dominance. The NLF continued to grow in strength but at the same time found its Arab opposition more virulent. At about the time that the British set their withdrawal date, the NLF merged with a rival group, the Organization for the Liberation of the Occupied South (OLOS), to form the Front for the Liberation of the Occupied South (FLOSY). Internal rivalries were too keen, however, and the NLF withdrew to become the chief rival of the remnant FLOSY, which then fielded a commando unit called the People's Organization of Revolutionary Forces (PORF). Terrorism became even more pervasive than in the preceding years, when the several factions had been loosely united against the British. United Nations mediation efforts failed completely since neither the NLF nor FLOSY was interested in a compromise or in sharing control of the postindependence state.

Britain now moved the departure date to the end of 1967 and in essence marked time while the NLF and FLOSY struggled for domination. Both organizations were perceived by London as unpalatable, but FLOSY's now closer ties to the UAR were probably a factor in the British tilt toward the NLF, given Britain's antipathy toward Nasser. However, considering the years of debate that had taken place on the subject of how to minimize the impact of a reduced British presence east of Suez, it is ironic that the south Arabian struggle was won by the faction that was fundamentally the most anti-Western. During the final military showdown in November 1967, the British-equipped and -trained south Arabian Army—which had been attempting to maintain a modicum of public safety—also threw its weight to the NLF, allowing this group to inherit formal authority from the departing British on the last day of the month. On November 30, the independent People's Republic of Southern Yemen came into existence under its new president, Qahtan al-Sha'bi.

After independence, the ruling NLF was renamed the National Front (NF), and many FLOSY supporters went into exile in Yemen. There was no doubt by this time that the NF was leftist, but the more extreme aspects of its ideology appear to have been muted to accommodate negotiations with London over the terms of its promised budgetry support. Despite this ploy, the NF was disappointed on that score. The economy was dealt a worse blow, however, by the closure of the Suez Canal during the June 1967 Arab-Israeli war and by the resultant diversion of world shipping around southern Africa. This maritime traffic and the related profits from bunkering and local trade had made preindependence Aden a mini-Hong Kong.

Through perceived necessity and no doubt political inclination as well, President al-Sha'bi attempted to strengthen ties with the USSR, Eastern Europe, China, and the more radical Arab nationalist regimes. These sources did provide various types of aid, ranging from developmental to military assistance.

South Yemen's relations with its conservative neighbors were predictably poor. The Saudis were distressed by the increase in both communist and Arab nationalist influence on its southern border. Yemeni republican leaders had similar qualms. Resentful of their treatment by Nasser between the 1962 revolution and the withdrawal of the UAR expeditionary force in December 1967, they had become more conservative. They also were disenchanted with Soviet economic and military support. To the east, the conservative Sultanate of Muscat and Oman (redesignated the Sultanate of Oman in 1970) shared Saudi and Yemeni antipathy toward the political philosophies of the National Front regime in Aden.

The South Yemeni regime began to turn progressively more radical. Al-Sha'bi was severely criticized by the militants under the secretary-general of the National Front. At the first party congress in Zinjibar in 1968, an aspiring leader named Abd al-Fattah Ismail framed the Zinjibar Resolutions for leading the country to Marxism. In June 1969 al-Sha'bi was overthrown and replaced by Salim Ruba'i Ali, a militant but also an archrival of Ismail. As a reflection of this further shift to the left, the country was renamed the People's Democratic Republic of Yemen in 1970.

Differences between San'a and Aden were exacerbated when Yemeni Premier Muhsin al-Ayni reached accommodation with the Saudis in 1970 and subsequently readmitted those exiled Yemeni royalists who were willing to accept the republic. Although both Yemens officially espoused some form of political unification of the two countries, attitudes in the north were becoming increasingly more conservative, whereas in the south they remained doctrinaire and radical. Accordingly, during the 1970s the two nations presented the curious spectacle of calling periodically for unity and equally as often hurling invectives at each other.

Relations with San'a approached a crisis stage on several occasions during subsequent years. In October 1972, YAR forces seized Kamaran Island, which had formerly been a British dependency linked to Aden and was thus claimed by the postindependence PDRY despite its remote location north of the midcoastal port of Hodayda in the YAR. Also in 1972, border skirmishes in the south led to a state of near-warfare that necessitated an Arab League peacekeeping mission. The most bizarre event in this saga of conflict occurred on June 30, 1978, when emissaries from President Salim Ruba'i Ali and from YAR President al-Ghashmi were both killed in San'a by a bomb hidden in the PDRY envoy's briefcase.

Domestic politics throughout most of the 1970s reflected not only a shift to the left but also the rivalry between Ismail and Ali. Early on, Ismail, who was more pro-Soviet, was labeled by outsiders as more pragmatic than Ali, who was called a Maoist. In fact, Ali was much more pragmatic, as seen in his dialogue with the Saudis in 1976–1977. The rivalry, however, was less ideological in nature than personal, and it culminated in the overthrow and execution of Ali in June 1978. Although Ismail appears to have engineered the plot against YAR President al-Ghashmi, he convened the National Front's politburo on July 1, apparently to implicate Ali in the assassination. Ali refused to attend and, in a showdown that night, shooting broke out, Ali was captured and executed, and Ismail seized virtual control of the government. The following day he had Prime Minister Ali Nasir Muhammad al-Hasani also appointed president, but in the fall he took over the presidency again in a major party reorganization. Ismail, with the help of Soviet advisers, reorganized the National Front into the Yemeni Socialist party (YSP).

On April 21, 1980, the situation was again reversed when Prime Minister Ali Nasir Muhammad took over as chairman of the YSP Presidium and party secretary-general, thereby reducing Ismail to the nominal position of party president. This move apparently resulted from growing discontent with Ismail's perennially close ties with the Soviet Union, which precluded the establishment of potentially profitable economic and political relations with other Arab states.

Ali Nasir Muhammad focused on internal problems, and, as a result, relations with his neighbors improved. These pragmatic policies and a steadily deteriorating domestic economy led to opposition to him within the government, however, and on January 13, 1986, Ali Nasir attempted to preempt his opponents, who were planning a coup. His attempt failed, and, following heavy fighting, a new government under former Prime Minister Haidar Abu Bakr Attas was established in Aden. Whether or not the new government will abandon the pragmatic policies of Ali Nasir remains to be seen. In any case, the new government is even more closely aligned with the Soviet Union than its predecessor had been, and Soviet toleration of PDRY adventurism will probably be an important factor in its foreign policy direction. On January 31, Haidar, as acting president, announced that the new government would continue to seek good relations with its neighbors.

Political Environment

Population and Social Conditions

With a population estimated at only 1.5 million, the PDRY presents a strikingly different demographic picture from the neighboring YAR. On the other hand, Aden, with a population of approximately 250,000, provides an urban focus that is missing in the north. In the considerably more prosperous preindependence era, Adenites were more cosmopolitan than their isolated geographic situation would have suggested. Ship chandlering, bunkering, the oil refinery, and other large-scale economic operations generated a certain affluence that in turn favored a better education by regional standards and the development of a skilled labor force. The next largest towns, Mukalla and Sayun, have populations only a fifth and a tenth as large, respectively, as Aden's, and were never so sophisticated as the capital.

Outside the cities, the PDRY is sparsely populated, with a tribal social structure not markedly different from that in North Yemen. However, since they are predominantly Shafa'i Muslims, the Sunni-Shi'ite dichotomy found in Yemen is missing. The sultans formerly represented a rural aristocracy but of course disappeared with the advent of the radical Marxist regime. The inhabitants of the Wadi Hadhramaut in the former Eastern Aden Protectorate developed a relatively advanced town and village culture based partly on local agriculture and partly on emigration to (and trade with) the East Indies. Intermarriage with Javanese and other Indonesian peoples has given many Hadhrami families a distinctive physical appearance. At the other end of the rural social scale, some tribes remain purely nomadic. At the eastern end of the country, wild Mahra tribesmen predominate. Closely related to Mahras in neighboring Oman, they speak a non-Arabic language.

With the advent of the National Front and its collectivist economic policies coupled with the virtual collapse of the preindependence economy, most of the foreigners who gave Aden its polyglot character have fled. Somalis previously were the principal foreign laborers; Indians and Pakistanis worked as merchants and clerks; and Europeans, primarily British, filled managerial and high-technology positions. Many indigenous south Arabians have departed as well, for both economic and political reasons. The tens of thousands of northern Yemenis who once found employment in bustling Aden also are gone. By a perverse twist of economic history, many southerners found sanctuary in the YAR, where their managerial skills have been put to good use. Several have even been appointed to cabinet positions in the YAR. The combined exodus may have approached one-half million. The PDRY thus is demographically weak in terms of population size as well as in terms of its diminished, trained adult work force.

Social patterns in the PDRY roughly approximate those of the preindependence era as far as the dichotomy between Aden and the hinterland is concerned. However, there is little doubt that living standards have declined in both areas as a result of collectivization and other governmental incursions into the socioeconomic sphere. The tribal elements reportedly have been resistant in many instances to these policies. Nomads here as elsewhere have found it difficult to adapt to a sedentary agricultural life, and the sedentary tribes with established agricultural traditions have been resistant to collectivization. The regime made early efforts at land redistribution, but this fact did not lead to the erection of a radically different rural society inasmuch as poverty prevailed both before and afterward. In both the rural and urban spheres, employment opportunities have diminished. On the other hand, the PDRY appears to have accelerated women's liberation, primarily through the General Union of Yemeni Women, which has operating branches in all governorates. Since the union is an appendage of the Yemeni Socialist party, its vigorous activities reflect government interest in this aspect of modernization. Similar efforts have been made to mobilize the country's youth.

Health conditions were never adequate in the countryside and remain substandard. Although adequate statistics are lacking, disease rates and infant mortality are believed to be high. Severe nutritional problems complicate the health picture. There have been intermittent reports of famines, food shortages, and rationing.

By regional as well as world standards, the PDRY society is in a peculiar state of transition. Living conditions both before and after the revolution naturally have been driven by economic realities. However, the National Front appears to have gone out of its way to stifle any vestige of political opposition and to impose a doctrinaire economic system where there were insufficient resources to make it work. As a result, a basically traditional people continues to live in traditional poverty with new, contrived societal norms. Its youth eventually can be acculturated; for its adults, however, the effects cannot help but be stifling.

Economic Conditions

Mention already has been made of the coincidence of the closure of the Suez Canal with the advent of independence. The concurrent British military pullout also eliminated large quantities of hard currency, previously funneled into the local economy through the air and naval bases. Whereas the Yemen Arab Republic received developmental aid from both East and West as well as international organizations, National Front leaders in Aden found only token aid in the West and less help from the radical Arab nationalist camp and communist world than they had hoped. Indeed, the major Soviet aid effort has been a military one, which has exacerbated relations between the two Yemens. This Soviet tie also raised the apprehensions of the moderate, oil-rich Arab regimes that could have granted many times as much developmental aid in exchange for a less-menacing external posture.

Post-independence emigration, proportionately heavy in relation to the small total population, could be considered both a product of the politico-economic situation and a negative influence on the economy. In the latter instance, the fledgling nation lost its principal entrepreneurial talent with the departure of key Adeni business leaders. Some relocated in the Yemeni port city of Hodayda and continued operations on a small scale commensurate with post-Suez Red Sea trade, while others—particularly the Indian merchant families—went farther afield. Some business even shifted to Djibouti, which subsequently became independent of France under considerably more stable economic and political conditions. The economic impact on South Yemen was inordinately great, because most trading firms were extremely diversified in their business operations.

Steadily deteriorating political relations between San'a and Aden also worked to the economic disadvantage of the PDRY, since frequent border closures effectively served to redirect the Yemen trade through Hodayda. Although this trade was comparatively less important in preindependence times, the implied loss was considerably greater with the cessation of the Suez traffic and the benefits derived from it: bunkering, tourism, and general brokerage. Ironically, when Suez reopened in 1975, considerable bulk transport had shifted to wider, deeper-draft supervessels unable to transit the canal. Aden was thus unable to recapture the entrepôt trade it had once enjoyed and has no immediate prospects of doing so. It must be remembered that Aden developed a complex economic infrastructure as a result of unique advantages accruing from the British military presence, port activity, and east-west communications. With the removal of not just one but all three underpinnings, along with the Marxist policies of the government, disaster was inevitable. The once-great entrepôt is now on more even economic terms with its impoverished agricultural hinterland.

Even with official encouragement, the agricultural sector has a limited potential owing to the low percentage of fertile land, water shortages, and poor transport facilities. Nonetheless, the area around Lahej retains some potential for cotton production, and fertile but remote noncontiguous wadi areas such as the Hadhramaut could produce more in the way of grains and garden crops. In the absence of even more ambitious foreign aid projects, it is unlikely that productivity can be increased to a significant degree. On the other hand, the development potential for fisheries could be more encouraging in view of the PDRY's extensive coastal waters and established port and handling facilities. Petroleum remains a question mark. Prior to independence, the Pan American Oil Company was engaged in extensive exploration in the interior. New concessions with sufficient financial incentives and investment guarantees would make a renewed search feasible. At present, the great irony confronting both Yemens is that although the rest of the Arabian peninsula virtually "floats" on oil, both countries must import all of their fuel requirements.

Political Structure

Political structures not directly related to the ruling Yemen Socialist party have little practical significance in the PDRY. Government functions are therefore essentially party functions. Understanding these, however, is a difficult task in view of the secretive, totalitarian character of the party.

The party system was designed with the help of Soviet technical advisers, presumably according to the principles of "democratic centralism" that have been applied in the communist world. The emphasis, of course, is on centralism and vertical control. Notwithstanding the existence of a pro-Chinese faction, the party has never embraced a "hundred flowers" philosophy that might offer opportunities for innovation.

Until the dramatic events of June 1978, real power was divided between the president, Salim Ruba'i Ali, who controlled the armed forces as commander-in-chief, chaired the Presidential Council, and served simultaneously as assistant secretary-general of the National Front. The secretary-general of the National Front, Abd al-Fattah Ismail, was in a constitutional sense subordinate to the president. As events proved, he was able to muster critical military support when the showdown came. In the pre–June 1978 period, the prime minister clearly occupied third place.

As subsequently restructured, the PDRY's paramount legislative body is the People's Supreme Council, which consists of 111 members elected to five-year terms. The council in turn elects, Soviet style, a Presidium of eleven to seventeen members and a prime minister. The Presidium president is chief-of-state. Other state ministers are selected by the prime minister and approved by the council. YSP membership is not an essential qualification for election to the council.

Reminiscent of the Soviet Communist party, the YSP has a Central Committee and a Political Bureau and controls subordinate women's, youth's, and laborer's organizations as well as an independent People's Militia. Through this structure the YSP secretary-general is able to wield decisive ideological and political authority.

In the PDRY, as elsewhere in the Arab world, the gap between formal governmental authority and personality-oriented sources of power is fairly great. As the events of June 1978 demonstrated, control of the military establishment is the decisive element of power. The only thing that distinguishes the PDRY from other, more typical Middle Eastern examples is that political-military power is divided between the regular armed forces and the People's Militia.

Political Dynamics

In the absence of normal electoral processes, participation in national political life obviously can occur only through participation in some activity sanctioned by the Yemen Socialist party. Although the party has resorted to the familiar expedient of "mobilizing" women, youths, "workers," and farmers, it must be remembered that these groups were not as readily distinguishable as their counterparts in other more truly revolutionary societies, such as the Soviet or Chinese. Aden became modern in late British times only in an economic sense. Here and in the hinterland, society remained traditionalist and conservative until (and into) the postindependence period. It has not been possible to dismantle this traditionalist society to the extent that the National Front leadership presumably would have desired because the regime has continually lacked the material resources to make the new order function. Consequently, the regime has found it easier to invoke sanctions against nonconformism than to offer political or economic rewards for supportive behavior. In this latter sense, political rewards can be defined as influential jobs, and economic rewards as pay or perquisites. As a result, political processes necessarily are elitist despite the egalitarian philosophy of the ultra-leftist regime. This situation can remain viable over the relatively short term—that is, measured in years rather than decades. Sanctions have worked during the first decade of National Front rule, but rewards will become increasingly necessary if the regime is to achieve political participation on a scale that will ensure its own survival.

In theory, economic and political demands are articulated in pyramidal fashion by local people's councils, operating at a local level and reporting through the regional governorates. Assuming council members are elected by popular will, this offers one democratic element in an otherwise totaltarian governmental process. However, it is questionable whether the councils have exercised any real influence to date, or whether a meaningful electoral process has occurred even at this grassroots level. Since the front leadership reportedly has taken pains to place party members at all levels for purposes of surveillance and control, it is also questionable whether the people's councils can either articulate popular demands or provide meaningful feedback to what the central government has initiated. Considering the extent to which even the more traditionalist Arab societies are participatory through their ability to extend or withhold confidence in shaykhs at the local level, or in monarchs at the national level, the system espoused by the Yemen Socialist party and the National Front before it is very alien to the region. Likewise, it is somewhat alien even to other nations in the Arab nationalist world, where old and established societies have continued to function with only minor adaptations to new—primarily military—governing elites and rather permissive socialist economic rules. Considering societal realities, the PDRY's political system is running greater risks in the political sphere than it has incurred in its rigid economic planning.

Foreign Policy

As indicated in the preceding historical sketch, the National Front did not immediately turn away from Britain and the West after inheriting its governing authority. Nevertheless, circumstances prompted the establishment of early links with the Soviet Union, Eastern Europe, and China. While this was politically logical as well as economically necessary, the results—as evidenced by the PDRY's situation vis-à-vis the YAR—must have been disappointing to the National Front. While it is true that the USSR openly favored the PDRY by granting it military hardware and withholding the same from the YAR during various phases of the Yemeni conflict, developmental aid has failed to restore even a portion of preindependence prosperity. Chinese aid, oriented more to the hinterland through such means as medical teams, probably scored more comparative success in terms of grassroots goodwill. In recent years, however, and particularly with the ascendancy of Ismail, Chinese influence has waned.

These primary alignments with the two major powers in the communist world have had interesting repercussions in other areas of PDRY foreign relations. During the late 1960s and early 1970s, Western nations periodically suspected that the PDRY had offered the Soviets Indian Ocean base facilities—perhaps on the offshore island of Socotra. While reports of actual base construction thus far have proved unfounded, the fact remains that Aden itself has become a useful Indian Ocean haven for the Soviet fleet. Thus there are new strategic implications for the area of Bab al-Mandab.

During this period, the PDRY was actively involved in efforts to overthrow the sultan of Oman through guerrilla forces of the Popular Front for the Liberation of the Occupied Arab Gulf and the earlier Dhufar Liberation Front. The political affinity of Aden and the Dhufar rebels lies in the fact that both espouse radical doctrines of the Arab Nationalists Front. By the mid-1970s South Yemen support for the Dhufar rebels had tapered off for the dual reasons that the guerrillas were gradually being defeated by Oman with the help of Iranian, Jordanian, and British military aid, and that cessation of active PDRY support was the price asked for financial support from the oil-rich peninsula regimes, particularly Saudi Arabia.

The PDRY also actively supported the Eritrean dissidents in their struggle against the conservative regime of Haile Selassie and against the non-Eritrean military leaders who overthrew the emperor. Ironically, this traditional support for the Eritreans became an issue in the final struggle between Ali and Ismail in 1978, since the president reportedly favored its continuation whereas the secretary-general preferred to support the Soviets, who by then had switched support to the new Marxist Ethiopian central government.

In 1976 the Saudis made quiet overtures to Ali, offering financial aid if the PDRY would moderate its militant foreign policies. Some progress appeared to have been made; but as the PDRY gave wholehearted cooperation to the Soviet-Cuban military effort by Ethiopia against Somalia, the Saudis began rethinking their strategy. Nevertheless, Ali was deemed far more reasonable by the conservative Arabs than Ismail. This, coupled with the long-standing personal rivalry and the crisis conditions brought on by the assassination of the YAR president, led to the confrontation in which Ruba'i Ali perished and Ismail emerged triumphant. In retaliation, the Arab League declared an economic boycott of the PDRY in July 1978. It was, however, only marginally successful.

It has been previously popular to interpret PDRY foreign policy in terms of Ali's alleged preferences for China and Ismail's support for the USSR. To the outside world, both leaders were long considered radical ideologues. Ironically, as the dramatic events of June 1978 unfolded, the world press began to portray Ali as the "moderate" and Ismail as the extremist. This was accurate in the context of recent antecedent events, but it overlooked the extent to which the rival leaders had pursued radical foreign policies that had made the PDRY a pariah as far as other Arab neighbors were concerned. Ali apparently had moderated in his last years and might well have won passive if not active Saudi support as well as improved relations with the West had not events in the Horn of Africa dictated a show of support for the Soviet Union. This in turn might have brightened the foreign-aid picture.

With the downfall of Abd al-Fattah Ismail in 1980, presumably as a result of his unswerving close ties with the USSR, Ali Nasir Muhammad has been able to pursue somewhat more conciliatory policies. Most significant, the PDRY established relations with Oman on October 27, 1983. In addition, periodic "unity" talks have been held with the YAR, and the YAR-PDRY "Joint Military Committee" has been convened. Although genuine unity is as elusive as ever and relations between the two nations remain tenuous, these meetings would at least suggest that a modus vivendi is being reached. Any loosening of PDRY-Soviet ties and concurrent friendlier relations with peninsula neighbors would, of course, be welcome news to Saudi Arabia in particular and the West in general.

Bibliography

The best and most definitive work on South Yemen is Robert W. Stookey's *South Yemen: A Marxist Republic in Arabia* (Boulder, Colo.: Westview Press, 1982). A fairly complete but rather dated survey may be found in the American University's *Area Handbook for the Yemens* (Washington, D.C.: Government Printing Office, 1977). My chapter in Abid Al-Marayati, *The Middle East: Its Governments and Politics* (Belmont, Calif.: Duxbury Press, 1972), gives an overview of its first few years. For the British and earlier periods, a number of works exist. Harold Ingrams, author of *Arabia and the Isles*, 3d ed. (New York: Praeger Publishers, 1966), is one of the leading authorities on south Arabia's tribes and the problems of pacifying them. Ingrams is the man who engineered peace in the Hadhramout. Three books on the period of transition from British rule to independence are Tom Little's *South Arabia: Arena of Conflict* (London: Pall Mall Press, 1968), Sir Kennedy Trevaskis' authoritative *Shades of Amber: A South Arabian Episode* (London: Hutchinson, 1968), and Gordon Waterfield's *Sultans of Oden* (London: John Murray, 1968). In addition, the Yemen bibliography in the previous chapter should be consulted.

10

Republic of Lebanon

M. Graeme Bannerman

Historical Background

Although the modern state of Lebanon is a creation of the twentieth century, the people of Lebanon have had a long and distinctive history. The coastal plain was the home of Phoenician merchants whose ships sailed throughout the Mediterranean world more than a millennium before Christ. While the Lebanese of today have only an indirect connection with the ancient Phoenicians, many Lebanese who wish to emphasize their uniqueness as a people reach back to the past and stress their "Phoenician heritage."

In the seventh century A.D., when Muslim armies swept out of the Arabian peninsula, the rugged Lebanon mountains gradually became a refuge for Levantine Christians, predominantly Maronites, and other dissident groups who opposed the Islamic establishment. Under both the Umayyad (660–750) and the Abbasid (750–1258) caliphates, the Lebanese mountaineers retained a degree of political autonomy. Although the Muslim rulers easily controlled the coastal cities, their total domination of the mountain was never fully achieved.

The Muslim Arabs who surrounded the mountain nevertheless had considerable impact on its inhabitants. Many customs and social values of the surrounding region penetrated the mountain fastness. Symbolic of these changes was the slow growth in the use of Arabic. By the thirteenth century, Arabic had replaced Aramaic as the dominant language, although Syriac, a branch of Aramaic, was spoken in some villages well into the seventeenth century and remains the liturgical language of the Syrian (Syrian Orthodox) church until the present.

By the end of the eleventh century three groups of dissidents—Maronites, Shi'ites, and Druze—dominated in the Lebanese mountains. The Maronites were predominant in the northern region of Jubayl, Batrun, and Bsharri. Shi'ite Muslims formed the majority in the remainder of Lebanon. During the eleventh century, however, the followers of Egyptian Fatimid Caliph al-Hakim (985–1021) entered Lebanon. Led by the disciple Darazi, the followers joined with local Lebanese to form their distinctive community, which is widely known as the Druze.

The crusaders overran Lebanon in the early twelfth century, capturing Tripoli in 1109 and Beirut and Sidon in 1110. Tyre held out until 1124. The crusades

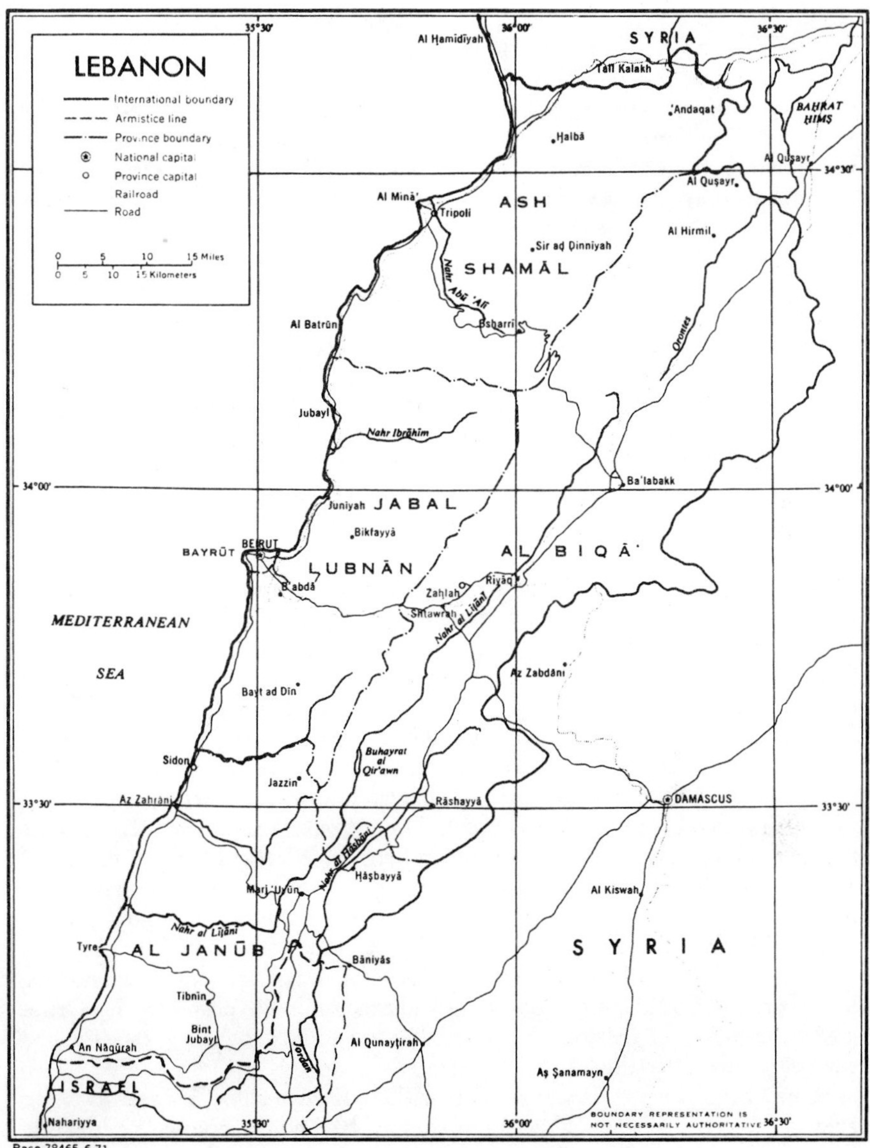

Base 78465 6-71

had a profound effect on the Maronites, for it was at that time that they were brought into union with the Roman church, establishing a link that still endures. In addition, the large French component among the crusaders established ties with the Maronites that later generations would view as the basis of a special relationship between France and Lebanon. Moreover, Maronite assistance to the crusaders further alienated their Muslim neighbors.

The crusades also had devastating impact on Lebanese Shi'ites. Before the crusades, Muslim Lebanon was predominantly Shi'ite rather than Sunni. The growth of Shi'ite influence was largely due to the Shi'ite Fatimid caliphate in Cairo, which had successfully competed for control of Syria with the faltering Abbasid (Sunni) caliphate in Baghdad. The failure of the Fatimids to adequately protect Muslims from the Christian invaders, however, contributed to the decline of Fatimid power and influence in Syria. Without the protection of the powerful Shi'ites in Cairo, the fortunes of Lebanese Shi'ites also declined. In the absence of effective Shi'ite leadership, a succession of Sunni dynasties initiated the countercrusade that ultimately led to the defeat of the crusaders and to the decline of Shi'ite influence in Lebanon and Syria.

In Egypt, the Fatimids were succeeded by the Sunni Ayubids. They in turn were replaced by Sunni Mamluk dynasties, which dominated Egypt, Syria, and Lebanon until the sixteenth century. The Mamluks were originally slaves and descendants of slaves who had been brought from the Caucasus region to support the sultans in Egypt, whom they eventually overthrew. Under Mamluk domination, Sunni Islam became firmly entrenched along the eastern shore of the Mediterranean. Less tolerant than their predecessors, who allowed other religious communities to live in peace, the Mamluks pressed their subjects to convert to Sunni Islam. In Lebanon, the Shi'ites and the Druze suffered most. An abortive Shi'ite rebellion in the late thirteenth century brought widespread devastation to central Lebanon. For the most part, however, the Mamluks were not intent on dominating Mount Lebanon directly but were content to rule indirectly through local leaders. Thus, Lebanese autonomy continued to be preserved.

In 1516 the Ottomans defeated the Mamluks in northern Syria, establishing Ottoman control over the Arab Levant. The Ottomans dominated this area for the next four centuries. The Ottomans continued the Mamluk policy of recognizing a local Lebanese notable as ruler of a semiautonomous state. Two great dynasties, the Druze and the Shihabs, reigned in the mountains of Lebanon until 1843. The Druze house of Ma'an was paramount until 1697, reaching its zenith under Fakhr al-Din II (1586–1635). His efforts to obtain total independence for Lebanon led ultimately to his defeat and execution. Nevertheless, this Druze leader did much for Lebanon by reopening the country to the West as it had not been since the crusades.

A one-time exile in Tuscany, Fakhr al-Din II later allied himself with the rulers of that Italian state. These ties extended beyond the political realm. The Druze leader emulated his allies in attempting to create a modern army. He also imported engineers and agricultural experts to promote better land use. These efforts, however, had only a minimal long-term impact on Lebanon. Of greater significance was Fakhr al-Din's encouragement of the Maronite peasantry to move south. Over the subsequent centuries, the Maronites spread from their northern Lebanese strongholds and slowly expanded their numbers and influence throughout the Lebanon mountains.

In 1697 the Ma'an family was replaced by the Shihabs as the amirs (princes) of Mount Lebanon. Under Bashir II (1788–1840), the Shihabs pressed for full independence. The early nineteenth century was a time when the Ottoman state was being torn apart by local rulers who, playing upon the weakness of the central government, strove to break away from the authorities in Istanbul. Bashir made an unfortunate miscalculation, however, by supporting Muhammad Ali of Egypt against the Ottomans, who, in turn, were supported by the British. As a result, when the Egyptian leader was obliged to give up his claims to sovereignty in the Levant, his ally Bashir was forced into exile in 1840.

The next twenty years were marked by strife and turmoil. Internal Lebanese rivalries were exacerbated by Ottoman weakness and European intervention. During the preceding two centuries, the fundamental economic and political balance of Mount Lebanon had been upset by the growth in the Maronite population and their gradual migration southward from traditional strongholds in North Lebanon. Druze preponderance had been seriously eroded. The Ottomans, in an attempt to ward off potential intercommunal difficulties, in 1843 divided Lebanon into two districts (*qaim maqaimyyah*). A northern district was placed under a Christian subgovernor and a southern district under a Druze.

This system proved unsatisfactory. The Druze and Christian populations were already too intermingled and antagonistic to permit such a simple solution. Despite Ottoman efforts, tensions between the communities increased. These tensions were made worse by French protection of the Maronites and British protection of the Druze. Moreover, the Ottomans were not satisfied with the status quo. Istanbul desired to limit the traditional autonomous status of the inhabitants of Mount Lebanon and resented European interference in Ottoman internal affairs. Another problem was the growing resentment of the industrious Maronite peasantry toward their oppressive feudal aristocracy. In 1858 a peasant revolt broke out. In the northern district, the Maronite peasantry turned against Maronite shaykhs; in the southern district, the Maronite peasantry rose against the Druze aristocracy. Because the Druze peasantry in the south felt closer bonds with their co-religionists than with the Maronite peasants, the hostilities south and east of Beirut became more a religious war than a peasant revolt. Thousands of Maronites were massacred by Druze and other Muslims. These massacres have contributed to Christian and Muslim suspicions and animosities that have yet to be assuaged.

Following direct European intervention, Mount Lebanon was reunited and made a semiautonomous governorship (*mutasarrifyyah*). The governor was a non-Lebanese Ottoman Christian who was appointed by the Ottoman sultan with the consent of the five great European powers. He was aided by an elected administrative council, which ensured representation to each of the major sects, and a locally recruited police force. This system remained in force until World War I.

The period from 1860 to 1914 was marked by increasing contacts between the Lebanese and the West. Intellectual activity increased, largely through the efforts of foreign missionaries. Presbyterians from the United States founded the American University of Beirut in 1866, and French missionaries founded Saint Joseph University in 1875. Economically, however, Lebanon held little prospect of supporting its own growing population. The Maronites, who had been expanding their area of settlement for over two centuries as a way of providing for their growing population, found further expansion of their community in Lebanon limited. Late-nineteenth-century Ottoman attempts at reviving their state often were colored with Islamic overtones and were politically repressive. At the same time, many nations appeared to offer greater opportunities. Consequently, thousands of Maronites and other Christians emigrated, seeking their fortunes in the United States, South America, and elsewhere. Although some Muslims and Druze also went to these areas, many more traveled to other areas of the Ottoman state or Egypt.

Four centuries of Ottoman rule came to an end in Lebanon with World War I. Through wartime agreements, Lebanon was mandated to the French, who created Greater Lebanon; this area included not only Mount Lebanon but also Beirut, Sidon, Tyre, southern Lebanon, the Biqa valley, and the Akkar plain in the north. The French hoped that a larger Lebanon would make Lebanon economically viable and a more influential friend. This expansion, however, altered the demographic balance by including large numbers of Sunnis and Shi'ites in the new state and diluting the Christian preponderance.

Under the French mandate the Lebanese made slow progress toward full independence. Lebanese nationalists kept pressure upon the French, gaining greater and greater independence. In 1926 a constitution was promulgated. The Lebanese nationalists were not satisfied with this document, however, for the French high commissioner retained final authority. For example, in 1932 and again in 1939 the French suspended the constitution. Despite the French hold, the Lebanese were permitted to choose their first presidents and to assume greater responsibility for their own political destiny. Differences with the French led many Lebanese to examine alternate political philosophies, including Arab and Syrian nationalism, socialism, and others. Nevertheless, the French continued to receive significant support from large numbers of Lebanese, particularly the Maronites.

The French mandate authorities were also instrumental in building the economic and governing infrastructure of modern Lebanon. Roads were constructed, electricity was brought to numerous villages, and Beirut harbor was enlarged and repaired. A bureaucratic structure that continues to be the foundation of Lebanese public administration was established. In 1943, during World War II, the mandate came to an end, and Lebanon was granted its independence.

Political Environment

The Land

Lebanon has a total area of 10,400 square kilometers (4,015 square miles) and is divided into four major geographical regions: a coastal plain, the Lebanon mountain range, the Biqa valley, and the Anti-Lebanon Mountains. The coastal plain varies in width from more than a dozen kilometers (ca. 7.5 miles) in the north to almost nothing at some points. Most of the major towns and cities of Lebanon are situated on this plain, including the three largest—Beirut, Tripoli, and Sidon. Rising abruptly from the plain are the Lebanon Mountains. Their highest peaks are within 20 kilometers (12 miles) of the coast, creating a situation whereby one can be skiing on the slopes and still see the Mediterranean below. The mountains are highest in the north, where the tallest peak is more than 3,000 meters (9,842 feet), and lower to the south, although Jabal Sanin, which is east of Beirut, is still more than 2,600 meters (8,350 feet).

To the east, the fertile Biqa valley lies between the Lebanon Mountains on the west and the Anti-Lebanon range on the east. It is the breadbasket for the country. To the north of Baalbek, where the valley is widest, it is watered by the Orontes River, which flows north into Syria. For most of the valley, however, the Litani River provides the main source of water. The Litani flows north to south for most of its length, but about 20 kilometers north of the Israeli border it makes a 90-degree turn and flows westward to the Mediterranean.

The Anti-Lebanon Mountains form the eastern frontier with Syria. They are not as high as the Lebanon Mountains and receive considerably less rainfall. At more than 2,000 meters (6,561 feet), Mount Hermon, on the Syrian, Lebanon, and Israeli border, is the highest peak. In south Lebanon, the geographical regions are less distinct as the Lebanon mountain range degenerates into the undulating hills of northern Galilee. A small line of hills divides the Biqa valley from the northern drainage of the Jordan River.

The People

The mountains of Lebanon have provided refuge for threatened minorities throughout history. Fleeing from conquering invaders or religious persecution, minority communities have found relative security in the isolated valleys and mountain hillsides of Lebanon, making it a patchwork nation with a mosaic of various groups. Almost all Lebanese now speak Arabic, although some speak another language in the home. The distinctions among the numerous factions within Lebanon remain great, however. The focus of these differences is religion. But religion in Lebanon is more than solely a belief system. It represents a major element of self- and family identity and of communal values as well.

The approximately 3 million Lebanese are divided into two major communities—Christian and Muslim. Each constitutes about half the population. The Christians are further fragmented into more than a dozen sects. The largest such sect is that of the Maronites, a Catholic sect that makes up more than half the total Christian community and has dominated Lebanon since the modern state was founded.

For the past four centuries, the Maronite population has been growing faster than the ability of this mountainous area to provide a living for the people. As a result, migration has occurred. During the eighteenth century and the first half of the nineteenth, the Maronites moved southward through the mountains until their movement was blocked by the hostile reaction from the Druze community. With this avenue closed, many Maronites emigrated. With independence in 1943, however, the majority of those who previously might have left the country congregated in Lebanon's urban centers. Beirut and its eastern suburbs soon had the largest concentration of Maronites in Lebanon.

The Greek Orthodox community forms the second largest Christian sect. Unlike the Maronites, who retired to the mountains for security after the Muslim conquest of the Levant, the Greek Orthodox remained in urban centers in Syria, Jordan, Israel, and Lebanon, where they lived under benevolent Muslim rule. The largest rural concentrations of the Greek Orthodox in Lebanon are in the Koura district southeast of Tripoli, where they form the majority of the population, in the Marjayoun area in southern Lebanon, and in several villages in the upper Metn. The Greek Orthodox generally have more contact with the Muslims than do the Maronites, owing not only to the daily commercial exchanges in urban centers but also to the wider distribution of the Orthodox throughout the Levant.

These differing approaches to minority status have greatly influenced the political outlook of both communities. The Greek Orthodox rarely deny their Arabness, as do many Maronites. On the contrary, the Orthodox have been in the forefront of those who assert that being an Arab is quite different from being a Muslim. Many leading late-nineteenth-century Arab nationalists were Greek Orthodox. By asserting and stressing the non-Islamic cultural and political heritage of being an Arab, these Orthodox were establishing a basis for giving their community equal standing with their Muslim neighbors. For most Arabs, however, Islam is a vital element of Arab nationalism; therefore, early Orthodox hopes of fostering Arab nationalism without a strong Islamic emphasis have proven fruitless. For similar reasons, Greek Orthodox have been active in ideological movements that transcend national and Islamic borders. The Syrian Nationalist party, which promotes a greater Syrian state including Syria, Lebanon, Jordan, and Israel, has always been predominantly Orthodox. Similarly, intellectually active individuals who were drawn to Western ideologies such as socialism and communism were often from the Orthodox community.

In Lebanon, although many Greek Orthodox have been active in such organizations, a majority appear to have been politically quiescent or to have chosen to ally themselves with the larger Maronite community. Even in the latter case, however, the Greek Orthodox generally have exhibited greater willingness to reach an accommodation with the Muslims than have the Maronites.

The Greek Catholics constitute the third largest Christian community in Lebanon. They are generally inclined to follow the Maronite lead but as a community do so with little zeal. Greek Catholic villages are more often found in areas that are considerably less defensible than are those of the Maronites. Moreover, the Greek Catholics do not dominate any particular areas, such as Mount Lebanon. Their villages are scattered from the Syrian border in the north to the Israeli border in the south. The only rural area with a concentrated Catholic population is in the hills southeast of Sidon. With the urbanization of Lebanon since World War II, the Catholics have increasingly congregated in Maronite-dominated areas of East Beirut.

The most recent Christian immigrants to Lebanon have been the Armenians. Fleeing the Turks during and after World War I, they were welcomed into Lebanon, mainly Beirut. Of all the non-Arab groups the Armenians have most ferociously maintained their cultural identity. At the same time, they have been active participants in the Lebanese political scene. Six of the ninety-nine members of Lebanon's last parliament were Armenian. The Armenians have generally avoided becoming overly identified with one political faction or another and have usually supported the forces of power. In this manner, they have ensured the maximum freedom to run community affairs with a minimum of government interference. In recent years, however, because their community is concentrated in Christian Beirut and its suburbs, the Armenians have been under increasing pressure from various Christian political factions to take a more active role in Christian Lebanese affairs. In addition to the major Christian groups, there are numerous other identifiable sects, but none has a large impact on the Lebanese political system.

On the Muslim side of the political ledger, there are three major groups: the Sunnis, Shi'ites, and Druze. The Sunni community has tended to predominate to a greater degree than their numbers would suggest. The Sunnis are highly urban, probably the most urbanized of any major Christian or Muslim sect. They are concentrated in the large coastal cities of Beirut, Tripoli, and Sidon. There are scattered Sunni villages elsewhere in Lebanon—near Sidon, in the Biqa valley, and northwest of Tripoli toward the Syrian border—but most Sunnis are urban dwellers, and as a result they have been more politically active than other Muslims.

The Sunnis also have closer ties to the Arab world at large than do other Lebanese groups. They have been more aware of and in tune with trends in the predominantly Sunni Arab world. The Sunnis traditionally have desired Lebanon to play a greater role in Arab affairs, resulting in sharp differences with the Christians.

The Shi'ites, who according to estimates may well be the single largest religious group in Lebanon, are economically and politically the most backward of all the major religious sects in Lebanon. They are predominantly rural and are concentrated in the Lebanese hinterland—south Lebanon and the Biqa valley. They lack the European connections of the Maronites and the Arab ties of the Sunnis. One of the attractions of Khomeini's Iran, no doubt, is the desire to have a strong external ally as do the other Lebanese sects. The Shi'ites have generally lacked the political influence necessary to get their opinions heard. Their villages are isolated and poor, and those who have migrated to Beirut tend to be poor laborers. Moreover, the Shi'ites have been generally ill-served by their traditional leaders. In recent years, some young Shi'ites have turned to radical ideology to solve their problems. The growth of influence of the Shi'ites since the Iranian Revolution, and even more so since the Israeli invasion of Lebanon in 1982, is the most significant shift in the balance of power in Lebanon in more than a century.

Although the Druze are historically an offshoot of Shi'ite Islam, their beliefs have evolved to the point where they neither consider themselves Muslims nor are they so considered by other Muslims. Nevertheless, in the political spectrum of Lebanon the Druze are generally placed on the Muslim side of the equation. Despite their relatively small number—something less than 6 percent of the population—the Druze have political influence. They are the Maronites' neighbors in Mount Lebanon, mainly living in scattered villages in the mountains to the east and southeast of Beirut. As a well-organized, tightly knit community and by dint of their reputation as fierce fighters, the Druze have been able to retain considerable political influence despite the relative decline in their numbers.

In addition to religion, Lebanese individuals traditionally consider their extended families and villages to be the principal sources of self-identity. Because one usually does not marry outside one's religion, family and religious identification are mutually reinforcing. The extended family in Lebanon imposes a sense of mutual obligation and commitment that extends to distant cousins. The family is vital to the success of the individual, giving protection and support to its members in return for their loyalty. The success of one member reflects well on the family as a whole, just as disgrace reflects poorly.

The family has traditionally been the vehicle for political advancement. In order to achieve success, one must have the full backing of his or her family, and the family that can best muster its total resources is likely to be the most successful in the political arena. The family has also retained many of the welfare functions that in more advanced nations have been taken over by the state.

Economic Conditions

The Lebanese have a long tradition of being clever merchants and craftspeople. The entrepreneurial spirit, which some date back to the Phoenicians, historically has thrived in the towns of Lebanon. Small shopkeepers, artisans, and the service industries have flourished under Lebanon's free-enterprise economy. Despite the number of large firms in existence, the self-employed family enterprise or small business continues to be the rule.

Since independence and before 1975, Lebanon's regional economic role was enhanced by the ability of the Lebanese to benefit from economic and political developments elsewhere in the area. The independence of Israel and the hostile Arab reaction resulted in the cutting of economic ties between the Arab states of the Middle East and most of the former British mandate of Palestine. The break left a large gap that the Lebanese filled. For instance, the terminal for the Iraq Petroleum Pipeline was transferred from Haifa to Tripoli. More important, overland transport and communications that might have traversed mandated Palestine were funneled into Beirut. Avoidance of the Israeli ports in combination with the natural advantages of Lebanon created a boom in the Lebanese economy. Scores of international corporations and banks established regional headquarters in the Lebanese capital.

The Lebanese were also able to take advantage of the growing wealth of the Arab oil states. Beirut supplied a source of entertainment and investment as well as a transit point for goods and services. Arabs from the Gulf states, Syria, Iraq, and Jordan flocked to Beirut and the neighboring mountain villages each summer to escape the heat. The Lebanese provided these visitors with entertainment and European shopping in an Arab environment. Many of these Arabs purchased homes in the mountains or invested in Beirut.

In the decade prior to the 1975 civil war, Lebanon experienced a rapid growth of the industrial sector. The large oil refineries at Zahrani and Tripoli had been the primary industry for years. In the 1960s an industrial belt began to grow in the poor suburbs that surrounded the city. Most of the enterprises were small and engaged in the production of light consumer goods or textiles and in food processing. Nearly 10 percent of the population was involved in such industry in 1975.

The agricultural sector of the economy remains very important. The distinction between rural and urban living is diminishing, however. Most Lebanese have easy access to a large town or city. Nevertheless, nearly half of the Lebanese earn part or all of their incomes from the land. Apples, citrus fruit, olives, olive oil, and grapes remain major items of export. The Biqa valley is a breadbasket that supplies the cities with much of their agricultural needs. Most Lebanese farmers are small landholders, although there is a large element of tenant farming in some areas.

One of the more interesting aspects of the Lebanese economy is its perennial trade deficit. Year after year imports are five times as great as exports. In the past, this deficit was offset in a variety of ways. Lebanese emigrants—both long-time emigrants to the West and temporary residents in the oil-producing states—remitted money. Large numbers of tourists and foreign residents also contributed substantially to the flow of capital to Lebanon.

The industrial and commercial sectors of the economy have been devastated by the civil war, however. Many of the new industries were destroyed in the fighting. Communications facilities were also damaged. But the real loss has been the loss of confidence in the state. Lebanon formerly provided a safe haven of freedom and abundance in a sometimes inhospitable region. This has been lost. Rebuilding the economic structure of Lebanon is possible, but a complete economic revival is not—until the political issues that plunged the nation into civil war are solved and the international community once again has faith in Lebanon.

Political Structure

The system of government bequeathed to the Lebanese by the French at the time Lebanon gained its independence was modeled after that of France but took into account the peculiarities of the Lebanese situation. The two principal pillars on which the Lebanese governing system is based are the constitution and the informal National Covenant. Although the constitution generally establishes a three-branch governmental system, article 95 gives it a peculiarly Lebanese flavor by providing that religious communities shall be equitably represented in government, employment, and key ruling bodies including the cabinet and the Chamber of Deputies.

The unwritten National Covenant of 1943, however, was the vehicle through which this idea has been elaborated and the unique political system fashioned.

The system was one in which each of Lebanon's independent-minded religious communities felt its interests were adequately defended and a fair share of government largesse—bureaucratic positions, public works projects, scholarships, and so on—was received. The impact of this confessional system was felt throughout society.

The unicameral legislature, the Chamber of Deputies, is the primary vehicle used for preserving communal interests. Ninety-nine deputies are elected to the chamber, with seats distributed on both a confessional and a geographical basis. They are allocated to the various religious communities on the basis of the 1932 census. A new census has not been taken primarily because several groups fear that their influence might be reduced by the redistribution of power that would follow a new census. There are currently fifty-four Christian seats compared to forty-five Muslim and Druze. The Christian seats are allocated as follows: thirty to the Maronites, eleven to the Greek Orthodox, six to the Greek Catholics, five to the Armenians, and the remaining two seats to other Christians. Among the Muslims, the Sunnis have twenty, the Shi'ites nineteen, and the Druze six.

The deputies who are elected to fill these seats are chosen from each of twenty-six geographical districts. Each district has a specified number of seats allocated by religion. For instance, from the district of Jubayl north of Beirut, two Maronites and one Shi'ite deputy are elected. All citizens in the district vote for candidates for all three seats. In some districts, however, a religious confession may not have representation. For example, in Bint Jubayl in south Lebanon, the two representatives are Shi'ites, despite the existence of a significant Christian minority. In other districts, Muslim minorities are similarly not represented by a co-religionist.

The question of minority representation has not been a serious problem because, as a rule, the various religious sects tend to be concentrated in specific areas. Tripoli, Sidon, and Akkar are overwhelmingly Sunni; Batrun, Bsharri, Zghorta, Kasrawan, Jubayl are similarly Maronite; Nabatiya and Baalbek have Shi'ite majorities; and the Koura is predominantly Greek Orthodox. Even in areas of mixed population (with the exception of the Shouf), villages tend to be composed almost exclusively of a single religious group. In towns, mixed villages, and cities in which more than one religious sect is present, each group tends to live in its own neighborhood or quarter. The representative system that was established under the departing French was thus an attempt to adapt democracy to Lebanese demography.

The distribution of higher offices in the government and much of the bureaucracy also reflects the religious balance. The presidency, the most powerful office in the land, has thus become the preserve of the Maronites. The president is chosen by the Chamber of Deputies for a six-year term. He, in turn, selects a Sunni Muslim prime minister who then forms a cabinet. The ministerial portfolios, as well, are allocated along confessional lines. Both senior and many minor governmental positions in the executive, legislative, and judicial branches are also distributed on a sectarian basis. Even judges and teachers in schools and universities are recruited with an eye on quotas for each sect.

In addition to confessionalism, the National Covenant deals with the issue of the conflicting political, economic, and social orientation of the diverse religious groups. On the whole, the Christians, particularly the Maronites, look toward the Western nations as their protectors. They have often considered themselves to be a part of the Mediterranean community rather than of the Arab world. This attitude was expressed in a virulent form of "Lebanese" nationalism in sharp contrast to "Arab" nationalism. The Muslims, on the other hand, have considered this Western orientation unnatural and have viewed "Lebanese" nationalism as a denial of Lebanese Arabness and Lebanon's rightful position in the Arab world. The Christian desire to be something other than Arab appeared to the Muslims to be harmful to long-term Lebanese interests. To the Christians, on the other hand, the pan-Arab orientation of the Muslims seemed to sacrifice Lebanon's, and particularly Lebanese Christian, interests to broader Islamic and Arab goals.

The National Covenant thus was designed to reach a compromise between the "Lebanese" and the "Arab" nationalists. In the unwritten agreement, the Christians committed themselves not to attempt to alienate Lebanon from the Arab world or to draw Lebanon too close to the West. At the same time, the Muslims recognized Lebanon's uniqueness and agreed not to pressure the government to become overly involved in the affairs of the Arab states.

On top of this peculiarly Lebanese system, the constitution provided the framework for the freest democracy in the Arab world. All Lebanese were guaranteed basic rights that included equality before the law, equal aid, and political rights. Personal liberty and freedom from arbitrary arrest were provided. Freedoms of press, association, speech, and assembly were also guaranteed.

The Lebanese central government was given only limited powers. The system of checks and balances whereby each of the religious communities was secure in the belief that its interests were protected also guaranteed a very weak central government. In contrast to most modern states, the central Lebanese government provided only a minimum of services. It was truly laissez-faire. Private organizations, mainly religious, provided welfare, health services, and, given the paramilitary forces, even internal security.

Political Dynamics

The Lebanese constitutional system was designed to preserve the existing social order, and initially it did so very effectively. Political control was concentrated in the hands of traditional leaders of the various religious communities. The replacement of the mandatory regime by the Lebanese government reinforced the position of these traditional leaders. The electoral districts were generally small, permitting traditional leaders to call upon village and family loyalties to win elections. Local and personal ties thus far outweighed national or foreign commitments. The key elements of a traditional leader's political strength were his ability to form a coalition with other traditional leaders that could draw the widest popular support and his ability to provide services to his constituency.

In each electoral district, parliamentary seats were divided by religious sects that in a general way approximated the religious makeup of the district's population. The district of Zahlah in the Biqa valley provides an example.[1] The population of the Zahlah district is one of the most mixed in Lebanon, and therefore its parliamentary representation is also. The population breaks down approximately as follows: 23 percent Greek Catholic, 19 percent Maronite, 10 percent Greek Orthodox, 8 percent Armenian Orthodox, 5 percent other Christian minorities, 24 percent Sunni, 19 percent Shi'ite, and 1 percent Druze. The district's parliamentary seats were thus distributed one each to the five largest religious groups—Greek Catholic, Maronite, Greek Orthodox, Sunni, and Shi'ite.

During an election, competing lists were formed by traditional leaders. Each list was composed of one candidate for each seat; thus, in Zahlah, each list had both Christians and Muslims. Other districts were either all Muslim or all Christian, so this multiconfessional listing was not necessary. Nevertheless, in most cases, competition for political influence in a district was between co-religionists. In Zahlah, for example, the dominant local leaders have been two Greek Catholics—Joseph Skaff and Joseph Abu Khatir. Each of these men have headed competing lists pitting Maronite against Maronite and Sunni against Sunni.

If the system had been designed so that Christians competed against Muslims, a district such as Zahlah would probably have elected five Christians. In several other districts, a large Muslim minority would also likely have been disenfranchised. Conversely, Christian minorities in other districts would probably also have been unrepresented.

Another consequence of the list system has been that a minority candidate tended to reflect the views of his fellow list members to a greater extent than those of his co-religionists. For example, a Christian elected from a predominantly Muslim district was more likely to support Muslim pan-Arab aspirations than Christian aspirations for close ties with the West. On the other hand, Muslims elected from preponderantly Christian districts would be Lebanese nationalists. As a result, votes in Parliament rarely broke purely along religious lines.

Although support for a candidate was in part due to political, religious, and historical considerations, another important factor was the services he could render. Because the central government was weak and impoverished, the parliamentary deputy often became the vehicle through which public services were distributed. The local leader also provided direct assistance in the form of loans and subsidies to his constituents from his own personal funds. In this way, he could build up a solid base of support.

Deputies and party lists also maintained support by the direct distribution of funds at election time. Expenditures included payments to political agents, general expenses, buying bloc votes, occasional bribes, and the transportation to the polling places of supporters residing outside the district. The greatest single expense, however, was the purchase of individual votes. Since most of this money went to those who in all probability would have voted for the list in any case, these payments were more in the nature of a subsidy. Few voters actually searched for the highest bidder.

Independent candidates rarely did well. An independent usually had neither the family ties nor the financial backing to challenge established lists. Another important result of the political system was the failure of truly national parties to take root. Politics remained local, not national. Those few parties with a truly national following, as a rule, were not so much national political parties as nationwide lists led by a prominent politician. For instance, the National Liberal party, founded by Camille Chamoun, tended to be a coalition of local leaders who were personally loyal to Chamoun. Rank-and-file members often had little contact with one another. Thus, a Shi'ite supporting the National Liberal party from Tyre was probably a follower of Shi'ite leader Kazim Khalil, who was allied with Chamoun. The individual Shi'ite would have little in common with a National Liberal from the Maronite area in the Shouf and even less contact with him.

A few parties were based on a definite political ideology. These included the Lebanese Communist party, the Syrian Nationalist party, and the pro-Iraqi and pro-Syrian factions of the Arab Baath Socialist party. These parties had little electoral success. On the whole, traditional Lebanese leaders were successful in preventing ideological parties from establishing a strong regional base. The very few members of Parliament who have represented these parties were often elected because of family ties rather than party affiliation.

Some parties have combined traditional leaders with a party organization. For instance, the Progressive Socialist party has two very distinct elements: those who are moderate leftist in outlook and the traditional Druze following of party leader Walid Jumblatt. Whereas the former have tended to dominate the party hierarchy and have certainly had the most articulate spokesmen, the latter have formed the backbone of support for the party. Similarly, the Phalange party has combined traditional loyalty to the Gemayel family with a virulent form of Lebanese nationalism. The Phalange has probably been the most successful of all parties at gaining a truly national following. However, although membership is more than the personal following of the Gemayels, the Phalange remains overwhelmingly a Christian party.

Even most successful alignments and political parties could not come close to dominating the Parliament. A bloc of fifteen members was considered very large. Perhaps a third of the deputies did not consider themselves committed to any coalition or bloc affiliation whatsoever. Alliances were made and broken; a one-time ally could easily become a political foe.

For the most part, the Lebanese political system worked—at least until the civil war. Most Lebanese were reasonably satisfied that their basic concerns—security and a fair share of government largesse—were provided. Many of the younger Lebanese grumbled about the anachronistic system and felt that they were held back by the rigid quota system; but when the time came to vote or to seriously alter the system, most preferred the status quo.

The one great crisis of the first twenty years of Lebanese independence occurred in 1958. In that year, Camille Chamoun was to relinquish the presidency of the republic, because the constitution prohibits an individual from serving more than one term. Chamoun, however, attempted to force a change in the constitution so that he could succeed himself. He appears to have been motivated mainly by personal ambition. Nevertheless, he was also greatly concerned over the growing influence of Nasserism throughout the Arab world and the strong influence of the Egyptian leader on Lebanese Sunni Muslims; he therefore wished to move Lebanon closer to the West in order to protect it from regional trends.

Despite Chamoun's attempt to focus on these latter concerns, the key issue in the 1958 crisis became his violation of the National Covenant in which the Christians had agreed not to disassociate Lebanon from the Arab world in favor of the West. In 1958 each community believed the other was breaking the agreement, and intercommunal conflict erupted.

By the compromise that ended the fighting, Chamoun agreed to step down when his term expired. The new president was General Fuad Chehab, Maronite commander-in-chief of the army. Chehab and his chosen successor, Charles Helou, governed Lebanon for the next twelve years by reestablishing the principles embodied in the National Covenant. Despite the relative political calm and the economic prosperity of this period, however, the fatal flaw in the system began to be uncovered. Though carefully balancing the country's many factions in order to ensure security for all, the designers of the system made it too inflexible. Modification was nearly impossible. As a consequence, the political system became less and less responsive over time to the changing political needs of the country.

The 1960s were marked by a rapid acceleration of social change in Lebanon. This change occurred in three areas—population growth, urbanization, and the political awakening of the resident Palestinians. Lebanon's population was growing rapidly, with some sects increasing faster than others. Nevertheless, political representation was still based on the 1932 census. Fearing that the delicate sectarian balance would be upset, no agreement on how to conduct a new census could be reached. The Christians insisted that overseas (emigrant) Lebanese be included, since they were mostly Christians. Many Muslims also had doubts as to how their own community would fare. Thus, although nearly everyone agreed that a census was necessary, no one was anxious to press for one, and, as a result, parliamentary representation became less and less representative.

Urbanization and all of its related problems brought major changes to Lebanon during the 1960s as Muslim and Christian villagers flocked to Beirut. The capital's metropolitan area expanded to include between one-third and one-half the country's population. A belt of poor suburbs soon ringed the prosperous core. In each suburb, one religious confession tended to predominate. For example, Ayn Rummanah, Hadath, and Furn al-Shebak were Christian strongholds. Others such as Shiyah and Naba were predominantly Shi'ite.

As elsewhere in the Third World, the poor workers and unemployed of these areas were courted by the ideologues—socialists, communists, and rightists. Most nevertheless retained traditional loyalties. They still returned to their villages whenever possible. Families continued to be an important source of support, and communal identification remained strong. Finally, what little influence these people had on the government depended on the traditional deputy who represented their home village. A person, even a second- or third-generation resident in Beirut voted, by law, in the village of his family's origin.

With growing economic prosperity in Lebanon in the early 1960s, disparity in the distribution of income became more apparent, resulting in the alienation of many of the urban poor. The Shi'ites, who fled from the south to Beirut fearing Israeli raids and looking for work, in particular became disaffected. The Shi'ites were greatly influenced by Palestinian neighbors in the crowded districts in which they lived. Indeed, the Palestinian community proved to be a catalyst for social change in Lebanese society. The more ideologically oriented and militarily powerful Palestinian commando groups provided an umbrella under which Lebanese leftist organizations received direct financial assistance and training.

The transformation of the Palestinian community in Lebanon was another development with which the Lebanese system was incapable of coping. Following the 1948 Arab-Israeli war, more than 100,000 Palestinian refugees fled to Lebanon. Relatively less constrained in Lebanon than in other Arab states, this community grew and to a large extent prospered. The poorer Palestinians, however, never escaped the squalid refugee camps.

Even most of the well-off Palestinians were never fully integrated into Lebanese society. Some took Lebanese citizenship, but these were a distinct minority. Most did not want to be Lebanese; nor did the Lebanese want the Palestinians to remain. Although they were welcome guests with whose plight the Lebanese sympathized, most Lebanese considered them aliens. Moreover, a wholesale granting of citizenship would have upset the delicate confessional balance and created severe economic strains. In addition, the absorption of the Palestinians into the Lebanese political system would permit the international community to forget its obligation to the Palestinians, leaving the burden of providing for them totally on the Lebanese.

For the most part, the Palestinian community in Lebanon caused little difficulty until the 1960s. Hope of returning to their homeland rested with the Arab states. The Palestinians were politically docile. But in the early 1960s, the realization began to grow among the Palestinians that the Arab states were not fully committed to assisting the Palestinians' return to their homeland. Increasingly, young Palestinians came to believe that if they were ever to see their homeland they must rely on themselves and not the Arab states. These young men formed the backbone of the nascent commando groups. The form of Palestinian nationalism espoused by the commandos, however, did not attract large numbers of active supporters until after the 1967 Arab-Israeli war. The humiliation of the Arab armies at that time convinced even the doubters that the Palestinians had no one to rely on but themselves.

This transformation of attitudes radically changed the Lebanese-Palestinian relationship. The Palestinians armed themselves and exerted pressure on all Arabs for more active support. For the Palestinians, the liberation of Palestine became the central aim of the "Arab struggle." According to their view, all Arabs must direct their energies to this struggle, and any act designed to reach this goal was justifiable.

For many Lebanese, particularly the Christians and rightists, the Palestinians became overbearing. Armed Palestinians on the streets of Beirut became the symbol of Palestinian arrogance. The weak Lebanese government and undermanned army, itself made impotent by sectarian politics, were incapable of dealing with the Palestinian militants. The inability of the government to cope with the situation was underlined by a growing cycle of Palestinian attacks on Israel, followed by Israeli retaliations against Lebanon.

The Palestinians were able to use the inflexible Lebanese political system to gain allies among the Lebanese. For many Muslim Lebanese, a political alliance with the Palestinians gave them not only the mantle of Arab nationalism but also the military support of the commandos. For the Palestinians, an alliance with the Lebanese left gave them a foot in the Lebanese political system without becoming part of it. Even a small Palestinian foothold was sufficient to prevent a concerted Lebanese effort to limit Palestinian autonomy in Lebanon. Following a series of inconclusive clashes between the small Lebanese army and the Palestinians, an agreement was reached in Cairo in 1969 between the Lebanese government and the Palestinians that regulated Palestinian-Lebanese relations. The Cairo Accord, in fact, recognized Palestinian rights to operate outside Lebanese sovereignty in some areas of Lebanon.

Because of the failure of the government to assert Lebanon's interests over those of the Palestinians, Lebanese rightists built or expanded their own militias. Of all the Lebanese parties, the Phalangists were the most determined to provide sufficient military force to counter the Palestinians. The rightists also moved to strengthen their influence in the Parliament in order to force the government to take a firmer stand against the Palestinians. In August 1970, by a fifty to forty-nine vote, a hard-line Christian rightist, Sulayman Franjiyah, was elected president. The election was generally regarded as a victory for the pro-Western "little Lebanon" supporters of former President Chamoun and as a defeat for the coalition of General Chehab that had run Lebanon for the previous twelve years. The rightists counted on Franjiyah, who had the reputation of being very tough, to use the Lebanese army to control the Palestinians.

The Jordanian army crackdown on the Palestine Liberation Organization (PLO) in 1970–1971 had a tremendous psychological impact on all Palestinians. Lebanon had become the only Arab state in which the commandos could still organize and operate freely. Consequently, thousands of armed Palestinians fled from Jordan to the relative security of Lebanon. This influx of armed Palestinians further upset the military and political balance in Lebanon.

Thus, by the early 1970s the stage was set for the Lebanese civil war. The rigid political structure that had proved so effective at preserving the status quo was incapable of adjusting to the changes that had been caused by maldistribution of wealth, uneven population growth, rapid urbanization, and the growing militancy of the Palestinians. Attempts to reconcile the differences failed because the consensus that had been embodied in the constitution and the National Covenant was no longer accepted by a sufficient number of Lebanese and Palestinians.

The years of fighting that have devastated Lebanon since the spring of 1975 have further exacerbated political differences. Moreover, some of the old restraints that had at least prevented the society from disintegrating were ignored.

Palestinian commandos became intimately involved in Lebanese politics and fought for one faction against another. Leftist Muslims openly demanded that the National Covenant be dropped. The Lebanese army became involved in sectarian struggles and disintegrated. The Syrians, who many believed wanted to absorb Lebanon into Syria, were invited into the country to bring order. Finally, many Lebanese Christians and rightists allied themselves with the Arabs' primary foe, the Israelis.

The Israeli invasion of Lebanon in June 1982 shattered the illusion of the military strength of the Palestinians and freed the Lebanese, for a short interlude, to address their own problems. Quite surprisingly, the election of Bashir Gemayel, Phalange military chief, as president of the republic gave hope to a wide spectrum of Lebanese. Christians obviously saw order being restored by a strong, confident leader. Many Muslims and Palestinians, however, also welcomed the election. They saw in Bashir a person who could control the most extreme Christian elements and make a commitment and stand by it. Immediately after his election, Bashir made several conciliatory gestures to the Muslims and the Palestinians that raised hopes that Lebanon was finally ending its ordeal. But these hopes were an illusion. Bashir Gemayel was assassinated, and some of his supporters struck down hundreds of Palestinians and Lebanese residents of the Israeli-controlled neighborhoods and camps—Sabra and Chalilla—outside Beirut. Sectarian feelings were inflamed, and a brief opportunity to stabilize the political balance in Lebanon was lost. Subsequent attempts to reestablish the traditional Lebanese leaders have failed. Bashir Gemayel's elder brother Amise was elected president by an overwhelming majority of Parliament. These men, however, did not represent the younger generation of Lebanese who had matured during the seven and one-half years of strife. Ten years of bitter fighting had weakened, if not destroyed, the basis of traditional leadership.

The undermining of the traditional sectarian political and social leadership in favor of those who better represent popular attitudes will make political reconciliation more difficult. Traditional leaders, Muslim and Christian, have generally enjoyed fairly good relations. Their followers, embittered by years of bloody war, have become hardened against compromise. The new sectarian leaders, therefore, have also come to reflect this hostility. The new leaders, moreover, are increasingly outside the framework of the old parliamentary leadership, who last stood for election in 1972. With virtually no prospect for new elections, few Lebanese believe that the elected government represents their views, and they are increasingly unwilling to follow its unrepresentative and discredited leadership. If the Lebanese can rebuild their shattered political system, they must first build a new political consensus, based on the common interests that link the various communities.

Foreign Policy

Lebanon's foreign policy has been determined by geography. Bordering the Mediterranean, Lebanon has been a meeting place for the East and the West. To play this role successfully, the Lebanese have had to maintain their neutrality.

They have avoided taking sides in Soviet-Western disputes or in intra-Arab politics. As much as possible, they have attempted to avoid becoming involved directly in the Israeli-Arab dispute. The Lebanese realized that, in order to maintain their neutrality, they had to be either a powerful regional state, thereby discouraging neighbors from interfering in Lebanese neutrality, or so weak as to make any move against them a blatant act of aggression. The Lebanese chose the latter course.

Despite the difficulties in reaching a domestic consensus on foreign policy, Lebanon played an active role in international affairs. It was a founding member of the Arab League and generally placed itself in the moderate range of the Arab political spectrum. The Lebanese supported anti-Israel measures by the Arab states in the past but not quite so virulently as some of their neighbors. As Palestinian influence within Lebanon has increased, however, the Lebanese attitude has hardened. In the early 1960s it was often said that Lebanon would be the second Arab state to recognize Israel; this is no longer the case.

Lebanon has also provided a key regional center for educational institutions, international organizations, and diplomatic activity. Given its good relations with the Soviet bloc states, the West, the Third World states, and the Arabs, Beirut constitutes a center of international communication. The Lebanese have taken their international role very seriously. They are founding members of the United Nations and view themselves as a bridge between East and West.

The formulation of Lebanese foreign policy has nevertheless been hindered by the same disagreements that have marked Lebanese domestic affairs. The Christian community has tended to stress the non-Arab Lebanese ties and Lebanon's long-established relations with the West. Moreover, they have emphasized the enduring links that Lebanon maintains with its large emigrant communities in the United States, Canada, Australia, and Latin America. The Christians have usually preferred to emphasize the differences between Lebanon and its Arab neighbors rather than the similarities. In contrast, the Muslims, as a rule, have preferred to enhance their role and that of Lebanon in the Arab world. Lebanese foreign policy was therefore a compromise, as embodied in the 1943 National Covenant. The Christians agreed to recognize Arabness, and the Muslims agreed to recognize Lebanon's unique position between East and West.

The first great crisis in Lebanese international relations occurred in the late 1950s when elements of both communities broke faith with the covenant. Many Muslims, greatly influenced by Arab nationalism as espoused by Egypt's President Nasser, agitated to move Lebanon closer to the Arab world. Some even advocated joining with Egypt and Syria in the United Arab Republic. At the same time, many Christians led by then-President Chamoun attempted to move Lebanon into the Western camp, possibly even joining the Baghdad Pact. The clashes of these two trends were a primary cause of the 1958 Lebanese civil war. Only when a more moderate coalition of Muslims and Christians took control of the government and agreed to the reestablishment of the former accord was peace restored.

Neither the Christians nor the Muslims have yet abandoned the hope of someday prevailing. During the current civil war, the same issue came to the fore. Unable to prevail on their own, many Muslims have looked for outside assistance from the Arab states, and more recently some Shi'ites have turned to Islamic Iran. Some Christians have turned to the international community, to the West, and, as a last resort, to Israel.

It is in this context that the introduction of U.S. Marines and other members of the multinational force must be viewed. The U.S. view of its role differed sharply from that of both Muslim and Christian Lebanese. The United States attempted, by the introduction of its troops, to provide a force for stability that would provide the Lebanese a foundation upon which they could rebuild their society. Lebanese factions, however, viewed the U.S. pressure more in terms of how it affected their position within Lebanon. Christians generally viewed the Americans as supporting them and the status quo. Muslims and Palestinians accepted the Americans as their best hope of getting the Israelis to withdraw from Beirut and Lebanon. Few Lebanese considered national reconciliation their first priority.

Following the Israelis' unilateral withdrawal from the Beirut area in August 1983, the U.S. presence was viewed quite differently. Muslims and Palestinians, relieved of Israeli pressure, no longer had a need for the U.S. Marines. In fact, the Marines were viewed as merely a force supporting the Christians, and forcing their withdrawal was believed to be imperative. Conversely, Christians and traditional conservative Muslims opposed the withdrawal because it would weaken them.

All foreign forces have been used, and continue to be used, by the Lebanese to strengthen their own faction against the others. As circumstances and the balance of forces shift, so do Lebanese attitudes toward foreigners. Syrians can intervene to save the Christians at one moment only to find themselves being attacked at another. Palestinians can be fighting the Syrians one year only to be allied the next. Israelis were welcomed by Shi'ite villagers one year only to be the target of their attacks the next. Until Lebanon places national reconciliation above factional interests, any foreign intervention—no matter how noble the motive—is likely to have the enmity of one or another faction.

Notes

1. See Peter Gubser, "The Zu'ama of Zahlah," *Middle East Journal* (Spring 1973), pp. 173–189.

Bibliography

Of all the Arab Middle Eastern states none has received more attention than Lebanon. There are dozens of excellent works on Lebanon, and the number has increased significantly in recent years as international interest has grown during the past decade of the turmoil. A few representative samples are mentioned here. For an understanding of Lebanese history, Kamal S. Salibi's *The Modern History of Lebanon* (New York: Praeger Publishers, 1965) should be the starting point. This modern history is concise, well written, and not overwhelming in detail, and Salibi is perhaps the finest historian of Lebanon. Since the first publication of *The Precarious Republic* (New York: Random House, 1968), by Michael C. Hudson, it has become the measure by which other works are judged.

Lebanon's political and social development are analyzed in a series of more specialized works. Samir G. Khalaf, in "Primordial Ties and Politics in Lebanon," *Middle Eastern Studies* 4 (April 1968), pp. 243–269, discusses the basic personal, family, village, and religious identification of Lebanese and how this self-perception affects politics. Khalaf's work is based on years of experience analyzing Lebanese society while he was a professor at the American University in Beirut. A most sympathetic explanation of the traditional Lebanese political system is found in Elie Adib Salem, *Modernization Without Revolution: Lebanon's Experience* (Bloomington: Indiana University Press, 1973). Although this work has obviously been overtaken by events of the last several years, it provides a rare glimpse of the positive aspects of the traditional system. Halim Barakat offers the best short study of the Lebanese political and social systems in "Social and Political Integration in Lebanon: A Case Study," *Middle East Journal* 27, no. 3 (1973), pp. 301–318. Barakat's analysis of Lebanese society provides an excellent framework for a better understanding of the former Lebanese political system and the difficulties involved in creating a new one. A fine study of the functioning of the Lebanese political system at the village and district levels is presented by Peter Gubser in "The Zu'ama' of Zahlah: The Current Situation in a Lebanese Town" *Middle East Journal* 27, no. 2 (1973), pp. 173–189. Here, the author analyzes the function of local political leadership in pre-civil war Lebanon. John P. Entelis discusses the formation and growth of the Phalange (Al-Kata'ib) in *Pluralism and Party Transformation in Lebanon: Al-Kata'ib, 1936–1970* (Leiden: E. J. Brill, 1974). This work offers insights into how the Phalange has managed in recent years to begin the transformation from a traditional personality-oriented organization to a more Western-style political party.

The 1975–1976 period of the Lebanese civil war has generated considerable literature. Completed in the middle of the conflict, Kamal Salibi's *Crossroads to Civil War, Lebanon 1958–1976* (Delmar, N.Y.: Caravan Books, 1976) provides an excellent study of the trends and events that led to the crisis. In Michael Hudson's short article, "The Palestinian Factor in the Lebanese Civil War," *Middle East Journal* 32, no. 3 (1978), pp. 261–278, is presented a concise and well-developed analysis of the Palestinian dilemma in Lebanon. In P. Edward Haley and Lewis W. Snider's *Lebanon in Crisis* (Syracuse, N.Y.: Syracuse University Press, 1979), a series of participants discuss the Lebanese crisis from a variety of perspectives. The book emphasizes the international aspect of the conflict. Among the more recent studies that examine the civil war is Walid Khalid's *Conflict and Violence in Lebanon: Confrontation in the Middle East* (Cambridge, Mass.: Center for International Affairs, Harvard University, 1979).

As the crisis has become more internationalized with the protracted Syrian occupation of Lebanon, the Israeli invasion, and the brief interlude of the multinational force, a number of excellent works have been published. *The War for Lebanon, 1970–1983*, by Itamar Rabinovitch (Ithaca, N.Y.: Cornell University Press, 1984), provides a scholarly presentation written with a high degree of objectivity. A series of journalistic accounts are also available. The best of these is Jonathan C. Randal's *Going All the Way: Christian Warlords, Israeli Adventures and the War in Lebanon* (New York: Viking Press, 1983). Randal displays considerable knowledge of the Lebanese scene—a knowledge that he developed during many years of reporting from Beirut. He makes little attempt, however, to present an objective study. In Randal's view, among the many villains the Lebanese Christians and the Israelis are by far the most responsible for Lebanon's problems.

11

Syrian Arab Republic

M. Graeme Bannerman

Historical Background

Syria's history is long and varied. Its capital, Damascus, is one of the oldest, continuously inhabited cities in the world. The country has been ruled during different periods by Assyrians, Babylonians, Persians, Greeks, Romans, and, more recently, Ottomans and the French. Modern Syria traces its unique heritage as an independent state to the seventh century Umayyad caliphate. Two years after the death of the Prophet Muhammad in A.D. 632, his followers captured what is now Syria from the Byzantine Empire. The Christian majority apparently welcomed the conquering Muslims, who put little pressure on them to convert. In fact, from the perspective of government revenue, it was preferred that they did not.

Following the Muslim war over succession to Muhammad during the 660s, Muawiyah, the governor of Damascus, was recognized as the fifth caliph, or leader, of the Islamic community. He transferred the capital of the expanding empire from the Arabian peninsula to Damascus. Syria thus became the hub of an empire stretching from Spain to India. This empire achieved a glory hitherto unknown. The regime, however, remained a military elite superimposed on a non-Muslim majority. The rulers lived aloof from the general population. Islamic law applied only to the Muslims, whereas the Christians, as long as they paid taxes, were allowed to follow their own customs and laws.

In theory, Syria could have remained indefinitely a Christian state with an Islamic ruling elite. In reality, there were great economic and political advantages in converting. However, the *mawala*, as converts were called, were not treated as equals by the Arab Muslim conquerors. The failure of the *mawala* to achieve parity with their fellow Muslims was a primary cause of the overthrow of the Umayyad dynasty in 750 and its replacement by the Abbasids, who moved the capital to Baghdad. Damascus, once the proud center of the empire, became a provincial capital—a status it continued to hold until modern times.

Following the Abbasid revolution, Syria became a political pawn of more powerful neighboring states. Invading armies entered from Mesopotamia, Anatolia, and Egypt. All left their imprint, but none more than the Shi'ite Fatimid dynasty of Egypt. Conquering the eastern Mediterranean shore in the tenth

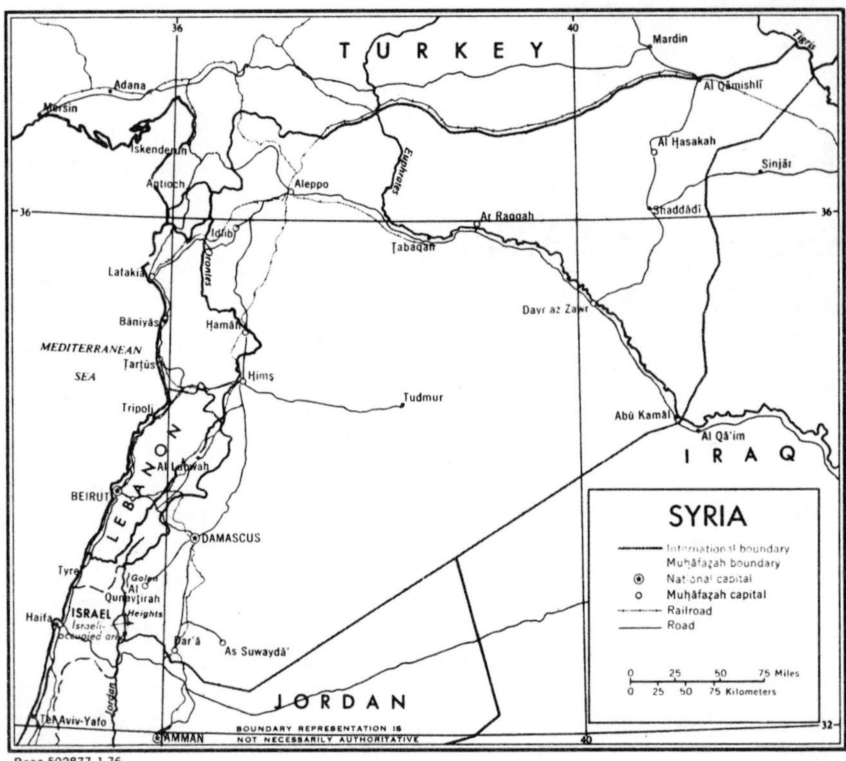

Base 502877 1-76

century, the Fatimids, more than any other Muslim rulers over Syria, propagated Islam by forcing conversion and persecuting Christians. In response to their increasingly difficult position, many Levantine Christians assisted the invading European crusaders, thus contributing to confessional divisions and strife. This tactical error further harmed their relations with the Muslim majority. Thus, in the mid-twelfth century, when Saladin (Salah ad-Din) reconquered the area held by the crusaders, many indigenous Christians were considered traitors and were treated harshly.

Relative stability returned to Syria when it was conquered by the Ottomans in 1516. During the four centuries of rule from Istanbul, the foundations of modern Syria were laid. The Ottomans ruled not only Syria but most of the Arab world. They gave autonomy to local governors and the various religious groups. Under the millet system, personal law and certain civil functions were placed under the purview of a hierarchy in each recognized religious community. In addition, governors of major provinces had great latitude of action as long as taxes were paid regularly to the Sublime Porte in Istanbul. What is today modern Syria was not one province but several. Aleppo and Damascus were competing regional centers. This regional and communal autonomy has plagued the Syrians throughout their modern history.

As the Ottoman state declined, Western economic, political, and military penetration increased. The growth of Western interests in Syria exacerbated divisions. Christians and other minorities developed close associations with the Europeans and benefited greatly. The French established particularly close ties with the Catholics, while the Russians took a protective interest in the Orthodox. The British, for their part, were the protectors of Protestant converts and the Druze. By the middle of the nineteenth century, European interference in Ottoman affairs had become direct and persistent. French troops, for instance, landed in Lebanon in 1860 to protect the Christian Maronites. The European powers compelled the Ottomans to establish an autonomous region in Mount Lebanon in order to guarantee Maronite security.

The Arab Muslim majority in Syria supported the Ottoman sultans and resented the advantages enjoyed by Christian minorities. When in the last decades of the nineteenth century Sultan Abdul Hamid II called upon Muslim Ottomans to support the revitalization of the Ottoman state, most Syrians readily gave him their support. As Ottoman territories were lost in Europe, Syria became increasingly important to the Ottoman rulers. Thus, by the end of the nineteenth century much attention was being paid to the development of Syria's commercial and agricultural wealth. These interests offered added reasons for Syrians to remain loyal to Istanbul.

The key to Ottoman success at that time was the sultan's appeal for pan-Islamic solidarity. Islam as a force that captured Syrian minds, however, was soon challenged by the emergence of Arab nationalism. During the last decades of the nineteenth century, a few Arab intellectuals began to discuss what they called their Arab heritage. They did not deny the importance of Islam to the Arabs or that of the Arabs to Islam, but they emphasized that being an Arab was something more. Among this group were a considerable number of Christian Arabs who either consciously or subconsciously were striving to find a common identity with their fellow Arabs that transcended religious differences. Despite the fanfare given to this early Syrian pan-Arabism by subsequent historians, most Syrians remained loyal Ottomans, hoping to gain a greater role for themselves and the Arab provinces within the Ottoman state.

The Arab nationalists did not begin to gain widespread support until after the Ottoman revolution of 1908, when the "Young Turks" began to implement policies that discriminated against Arabs in favor of Turks. Wider acceptance of Arab nationalism was, to a great degree, a reaction to the overzealous advocates of Turkish nationalism. Many Arabs, however, still clung to the hope that the Young Turk regime would be based upon Turkish and Arab cooperation. Despite their continued support in the Arab provinces, the Ottoman authorities feared that Arab nationalism in Syria, Lebanon, and Palestine might lead to a revolt. Moreover, the Christians were notoriously pro-French. Thus, when World War I broke out, Jamal Pasha, a member of the ruling Ottoman triumvirate, was sent to Damascus to strengthen Ottoman control over Syria. His harsh policies, however, drove the population further into the anti-Ottoman camp. In the spring of 1916 the Syrian people were receptive to Sharif Husayn of the Hijaz—a Hashimite—who proclaimed himself king of the Arabs. This he did as a means to end Ottoman rule in Arab lands—an action few would have supported several years earlier.

Both the Arab nationalists in Syria and the Hashimites believed that if they rose against the Turks, the British would support the establishment of an independent Arab kingdom. When Amir Faysal, son of Sharif Husayn, led the triumphant Arab army into Damascus in 1918, he was greeted as the liberator of Syria. With the assistance of Syrian nationalists, many of whom had served in the Ottoman bureaucracy, Faysal established an Arab administration in the interior cities of Damascus, Homs, Hamah, and Aleppo. A French force controlled the coast, and the British were in Palestine.

There followed a bitter disappointment that few Syrians have forgotten to this day. The Arab nationalists believed that when the Western nations spoke of freedom, self-determination, and the will of the people, these ideas were meant for all people—including Arabs. Therefore, after the war, when wartime secret agreements dividing the Arab east into British and French spheres of influence were revealed, the Arabs felt betrayed. In a futile attempt to thwart the European plan, Faysal called a general Syrian congress in July 1919. The assembled delegation expressed its wish for a sovereign and free Syria with Faysal as king. However, in April 1920, at the San Remo Conference, the European powers, ignoring the wishes of the Syrians, placed Syria under French control, and in July, after limited Arab resistance, French troops entered Damascus. Faysal and many Syrian pan-Arabists fled. Two years later the League of Nations recognized France as the mandatory power over Syria.

The hostility of the Syrian Sunni Muslim population to French rule led the mandatory authorities to adopt a policy that played upon the divisions within Syrian society. Of all the groups in the Syrian mandate, the Maronites in Lebanon were most friendly to France. Therefore, the French expanded the border of the Ottoman district of Mount Lebanon and administered the area as a separate entity, although the first three Syrian governors-general simultaneously held the same office for Lebanon. The remainder of French-mandated Syria was then divided into five zones. Each division was chosen to play upon traditional rivalries. Latakia was carved out for the Alawites, Alexandretta for the Turks, and Jabal Druze for the Druze. The Sunni Muslims, the majority population, were divided between Aleppo and Damascus. Moreover, many Circassians and Alawites were brought into the local military force in numbers far exceeding their percentage of the population. Thus the Sunni Arab nationalists, who were primarily members of the urban educated classes, were isolated from much of the country.

French rule was generally regarded by Syrians as oppressive. Many of the early administrators had previous experience in North Africa or the sub-Saharan colonies and drew heavily on this background, which proved to be inappropriate in Syria. French was introduced in the schools at the expense of Arabic. Singing the French national anthem, the "Marseillaise," was required, and the French franc became legal tender. Embittered Syrian nationalists played upon these obvious symbols of the French presence and won widespread support in their opposition to French rule.

It was not the nationalists, however, who caused the most difficulty for the French. Traditional ethnic and religious leaders led a series of minor rebellions.

Shaykh Salih ibn Ali led the Alawites, Shaykh Ismail Harir rose in Hawran, Mulhim Qasim led a dissident movement near Baalbeck, and the Druze appeared to be in constant revolt. The most serious rebellion began in the summer of 1925, when rebel Druze tribesmen drove the French out of the towns and villages in Jabal Druze. Ironically, the Druze were not motivated by Arab nationalism but, rather, opposed the efficiency of the French administration in governing their community. Under the Ottomans they had managed to maintain their communal autonomy. The Arab nationalists in Damascus, seeing an opportunity to rid themselves of the French, called upon the Druze to liberate Damascus and initiated their own demonstrations in the capital. Despite the alliance between the nationalists and the Druze, overwhelming French military superiority, symbolized by a bombardment of Damascus, extinguished the revolt by the end of the year.

Thereafter, Franco-Syrian relations remained tense, but differences were generally played out in the political arena rather than on the battlefield. The next decade and a half was marked by slow progress in Syria's attempts to establish a political framework under which it could move toward full independence. A constituent assembly was elected in 1928, but efforts to draft a constitution foundered over the French high commissioner's refusal to accept several proposals and the assembly's refusal to compromise. One area of controversy was the Syrian insistence that all the territories controlled by the French be considered part of Syria, thus denying the autonomy of Lebanon, Alexandretta, and Jabal Druze. In 1930 the high commissioner dissolved the assembly and promulgated a constitution based on the constituent assembly's draft, but without the offending articles.

The evolution of Franco-Syrian relations took another major step in 1936, when a Treaty of Alliance was worked out. This agreement followed considerable unrest in 1935 and a general strike in the year after that. The assumption of power in France of Leon Blum's liberal-socialist government also facilitated movement toward the agreement. Although the French Parliament never ratified the treaty, it served as a basis from which future ties evolved.

Nevertheless, Franco-Syrian relations were continually soured by the issue of autonomous government in Lebanon. A series of weak French governments also created difficulties. The cession of the province of Hatay (the Syrian province of Alexandretta) to Turkey in 1939 further incensed the Syrians. Nearly all Syrians believed that Turkish neutrality in World War II had been bought at Syrian expense.

The turmoil of World War II, however, provided the opportunity for the Syrians to gain full independence. Some progress toward independence was made by the Vichy government, which established partial self-government in 1941 after riots in Damascus. When the free French arrived in the summer of 1941, they promised full independence in order to win popular support. De jure independence was in fact granted that September, but the French still acted as a mandatory power. Although an elected nationalist government came to power in 1943 under President Shukri al-Kuwatly, full independence was not achieved until 1946, when the last French soldiers withdrew. Even then, the British had to prevail upon France to leave gracefully.

Political Environment

The Land

Syria in a geographical sense includes all the states of the eastern Mediterranean shore. Jordan, Lebanon, Israel, and the Turkish province of Hatay (Alexandretta) are part of geographic Syria. To the Syrians, the modern state of Syria is the remnant of the geographical area that the European nation builders left after carving out special-interest areas. Palestine and Jordan were first separated in order to form a British mandate. Lebanon was taken to protect its Christian minorities, and Hatay was turned over to the Turkish minority because of French political considerations.

The boundaries of the modern Syrian state, therefore, have been determined more by political expedience than by geography or by the wishes of the Syrian people. For the most part, Syria's southern and eastern borders are arbitrary lines in the desert. In the west, the Syrian frontier with Lebanon generally follows the Anti-Lebanon Mountains northward until it turns west to the sea. Syria's coastline marks its only true natural border. Most of the historical Syrian coast, however, has been given to Lebanon or to Turkey. Syria's northern border with Turkey was drawn at the end of World War I. A key consideration of the great powers at that time was that the only east-west railroad in the region was located mostly in Turkey.

The area of the Syrian republic is 185,180 square kilometers (ca. 71,000 square miles). Syria can be subdivided into five geographic zones: a narrow coastal plain, a high mountain range, a deep flat-bottomed valley, another range of hills, and an eastward-sloping plain. The eastern four-fifths of Syria is a large plain that gradually declines from west to east. The Euphrates River valley, which diagonally crosses the plain from the northwest to the southeast, and the line of occasional mountain peaks running from the southwest to the northeast are the only distinctive features of the plain.

The key element in the economic development of Syria has been the supply of water. Sixty percent of the country is desert or semi-arid steppe receiving less than 20 centimeters (8 inches) of rain a year. Heavier rainfall is concentrated in the west and north. This rain is seasonal, with nearly all falling in the winter. Nevertheless, Syria, by Middle Eastern standards, has an abundant supply of arable land and a considerable potential for dry-land and irrigated farming. This land is in the west and, to a lesser extent, in the Euphrates and Tigris river basins to the north and east. Nearly 80 percent of all Syrians live in the western 20 percent of the country—hence the situation in which western districts are overpopulated while manpower is needed in the east. The Syrians are engaged in a constant struggle to push back the edge of the desert.

All of Syria's largest cities—Damascus, Homs, Hamah, and Aleppo—are located on the inland side of the two coastal mountain ranges. They have been both regional agricultural centers and entrepôts, situated on the traditional east-west and north-south trading routes. In a sense, they are like coastal ports, but on the edge of the large Arabian desert instead of the sea. Historically, each has a special relationship with a Mediterranean coastal city. Each could reach the coast through passes in the two coastal mountain ranges. However, political divisions in the twentieth century have created problems for the two largest Syrian cities. Aleppo has been cut off from its principal port, Alexandretta, now Iskenderun, Turkey; and Damascus, to a lesser extent, has been cut off from Beirut in Lebanon and Haifa in Israel.

The People

In spite of numerous ethnic, religious, social, and geographic divisions, Syria's culture is fairly homogeneous. Ninety percent of all Syrians are Arabs, and most are Sunnis. The Sunni Arabs have generally been most conscious of their Islamic-Arabic cultural heritage and are the dominant cultural group in Syria.

The Alawites, an offshoot of Shi'ite Islam, constitute between 11 and 15 percent of the Syrian population. They form a majority in the coastal Syrian province of Latakia and have vigorously maintained their religio-cultural identity. Many Muslims believe that the Alawites have strayed so far from Sunni (Orthodox) Islam that they are no longer truly Muslims. The Alawites have the reputation of being rugged mountaineers and, as such, have maintained a high degree of regional autonomy through much of history. In recent years, however, the Alawites have played a role in Syrian politics and the armed forces that far outweighs their number.

The Druze, a sect that may have strayed even further than the Alawites from Sunni Islam, constitute perhaps 3 percent of the Syrian population. They make up a majority in the area in southwestern Syria known as Jabal Druze, and are numerous on the Golan and in Damascus. They, too, have maintained their autonomy and independent outlook. In addition to the Druze and Alawites are other schmismatic Muslim sects, including Shi'ites, Ismailis, and Yezidis, but their numbers and influence are limited.

Christian Arabs, who compose about 8 percent of the population, are themselves divided into several groups. Most are Greek Orthodox, but also present are Syrian Orthodox, Greek Catholics, Maronites, Syrian Catholics, and others. The Christians generally live in the urban centers of Damascus, Homs, Hamah, Aleppo, and the coastal area near Tartus. The Greek Orthodox have been active in the development of Arab nationalism and have contributed much to the ideological development of several political parties, including the Baath.

The non-Arab portion of the population includes Kurds, Armenians, and less significant numbers of Turkomens, Circassians, Assyrians, and Jews. Perhaps 5 percent of all Syrians are Kurds, who mainly inhabit the mountainous regions along the Turkish border. A significant number, however, live in the Kurdish quarter of Damascus. Like most Syrians, the Kurds are Sunni Muslims. To a limited extent, they have involved Syria in Kurdish problems with Iraq and Turkey. Tribal identity remains relatively high among the Kurds, although most live in small villages and towns.

The Armenians are the next largest ethnic group but make up less than 3 percent of the population, and their number appears to be static or declining.

Most arrived in Syria in the early part of the twentieth century, having fled from maltreatment at the hands of the Turks. They had lived in neighboring Anatolia for centuries. Nearly all the Armenians have settled in Syrian cities, with nearly three-fourths of their number residing in Aleppo. The rest are scattered throughout Syria—many in the small towns along the Turkish border. They are Christians, primarily Armenian Orthodox, but perhaps 15 percent of them are Catholics. The Armenians generally are merchants and craftspeople. They have resisted assimilation, clinging to their families and Armenian identity. Their failure to identify with Syria and their role as merchants have often strained the community's relations with the Arab majority. Many Armenians have emigrated, frequently going to Beirut's large Armenian quarter. The Armenian community in Syria is divided, as elsewhere, into two primary political groupings—Hunchaks and Tashnaks.

The Turkomens, who number less than one hundred thousand, originally migrated to Syria from central Asia. They speak a Turkic language and are Sunni Muslims. The Turkomens live primarily in the eastern region of Syria, although some live in and around Aleppo.

The Circassians are Sunni Muslims who fled from the nineteenth-century Russian invasion of their traditional homeland in the Caucasus Mountains. The Ottomans offered them asylum in the Arab provinces. In Syria, most Circassians settled in the vicinity of Qunaytrah in the Hawran region, occupied in large part by the Israelis in 1967. In recent years, the Circassians have increasingly assimilated into Syrian Arab Sunni society.

The Assyrian Christians and the Jews are two additional minority communities in Syria, each of which is declining in population owing primarily to emigration. The Assyrians are Nestorian Christians from extreme eastern Syria. They were settled there by the French in 1933 to help them escape persecution in Iraq. Since then, many have emigrated to Lebanon. Most of the Jewish community emigrated from Syria after 1948. The once-prosperous community of perhaps forty thousand has been reduced by emigration to roughly three thousand.

The Syrians are also divided by social cleavages—urban dwellers, villagers, and bedouin. The urban dwellers consider themselves to be the true purveyors of Arab civilization. The cities are the seats of economic and political power. The city dwellers believe themselves to be superior to the villagers and to the bedouin. The bedouin, nevertheless, are widely considered to embody traditional Arab virtues even though their number and influence are small. In the view of most urban Syrians, the villagers have few redeeming characteristics. They toil on land that they may own but that is more often owned by a leading figure in the village or by an absentee landlord. Recent Syrian governments have given more land to the peasants.

Syria has also been plagued by competitive regionalism. The major cities of the interior are centers of regional activities. Homs, Hamah, Damascus, and Aleppo each serve as a commercial center and market place for their own hinterlands. Aleppo and Damascus, moreover, have engaged in an intense rivalry for centuries. At one time, Aleppo was the second most important city of the Ottoman state. In recent years, with Damascus assuming an increasing prominence as the capital of all of Syria, Aleppo has been losing ground and is now definitely Syria's second city. Damascus is also drawing away from other regional centers. The Jazira area of eastern Syria, Jabal Druze, and the Alawite Mountains of the coastal range are also becoming integrated into the Syrian state.

Despite the fragmented nature of Syrian society, there are a growing number of bonds that tie the Syrian people together. To most Syrians the family forms a central place in the social organization. Duty to family overrides nearly all other obligations. Kinship ties are somewhat less in the city than in either the village or tribe; nevertheless, relations among most individuals continue to be governed by family ties.

Since the period of the French mandate, pressure has grown on most Syrians to raise their national identity above traditional particularisms. Family, ethnic, religious, and regional loyalties have been challenged by a wider identity. The concepts of Arabism, Islamism, Syrian nationalism, Baathism, and socialism have forced many Syrians to reevaluate their loyalties. Even more important than these ideological movements in breaking down the barriers among Syrians has been the functioning of a state government centered in Damascus. As greater numbers of Syrians are touched by the central government through conscription, taxes, and the provision of services, or through better communications, a sense of loyalty to Syria has begun to take root. Many Syrians are now focusing on their Syrian nationality more than they had done previously.

The growth of Syrian national identity, however, has created strains within Syrian society. All Syrians feel this new pressure, but the minorities seem to be under the greatest strain because the Syrian national identity has developed a strong Arab-Islamic tone. The emphasis on Islam is natural and has occurred throughout the Arab world. Defense of one's minority status has become increasingly difficult. Some groups, such as the Circassians, the Kurds, and the Alawites, have found such defense to be easier than have some of the Christian minorities. Many Armenians, Assyrians, and some of the Catholic groups have emigrated, in many cases to Arab (but Christian) Lebanon. Among the Christians, the Greek Orthodox as a group have had the least difficulty in adjusting.

The process of identifying oneself as a Syrian first is by no means complete. Even among some of the most fervent nationalists, traditional ties remain very strong. Many continue to fear that someday Syria could be torn apart by the traditional cleavages. Many were concerned that sectarian tensions in Lebanon could have spilled over into Syria. Others predict that the Sunni majority will someday turn against the dominant Alawite minority. There have been few signs, however, that the Alawite presidents have favored their sect. In fact, they usually have performed well as nationalists, with Syrian national interests as their guideposts.

Economic Conditions

With a population of roughly 10 million and given that slightly less than half of its 185,180 square kilometers are arable, Syria is fortunate among Middle Eastern states to have a strong agricultural sector. The greatest boon to agriculture in recent years was the completion in 1975 of the dam on the Euphrates, which may lead to the eventual irrigation of some 650,000 square kilometers of land. Most of Syria's labor force is in agriculture, although agriculture accounts for only about one-fifth of the gross domestic product. Cereal grains are the major crop, and bread is the staple of the Syrian diet. Cotton, however, has replaced grains as the largest export earner. Syria also produces fruits, vegetables, meat, and wool for export.

Despite years of internal political strife, the Syrian industrial sector has grown significantly, although not at a steady pace. The first industry to take hold was textiles, after World War II. Since then, there has been considerable economic diversification, including agribusiness, food processing, and tobacco. Syria produces a very small amount of petroleum. The closing of oil pipelines from Iraq and Saudi Arabia that traverse Syria has reduced revenues. Iran reportedly compensates Damascus for the economic hardship created by the closure of the Iraqi pipelines.

Perhaps the greatest blow to the industrial sector occurred with the massive Israeli bombing attacks during the 1973 war, in which damage was estimated at $1.8 billion. The economy bounced back, however. With the period of political tranquillity under President Hafiz al-Assad, Syria has experienced something of an economic boom. This boom is due largely to the pragmatic policies of the current regime and, in part, to luck. In the past, philosophical commitments to socialist ideologies or to economic warfare with other states seriously harmed the economy. Although Syria's economy remains state-directed, al-Assad has shown greater flexibility in his policies. Syria has moved to open new links to the Western states despite political differences. The vast increase in subsidy payments from the oil-rich Arab states has also helped. Declining revenues in these oil-producing states, however, could adversely affect the Syria economy.

Political Structure

Syrian history has been marked by considerable political turmoil, which has resulted in frequent changes in the Syrian system of government. Nevertheless, since the collapse of the Ottoman state, the Syrians have appeared determined to create for themselves a Western-style republic. At times they have strayed off course and have had a long series of easily replaceable constitutions, but their overall search for a responsive, representative government has not ceased. The Arab nationalists made the first attempt during the brief rule of King Faysal. They wrestled with the same problems Syrian leaders still face today: the need to blend Western and Islamic legal systems in such a way that minorities are protected and the majority is not harmed; and the need to have an executive branch with sufficient authority to maintain order but without creating a dictatorship. These problems and others have yet to be solved, and Syria today remains a strongly authoritarian state under the control of the Baath party leadership.

In 1919 the first Syrian constitution created a limited monarchy. Because of the almost immediate collapse of the Arab kingdom, however, it was never fully implemented. The next constitution was promulgated in 1930 by the French high commissioner. It created a form of government modeled on the French republic that remained in force with modifications until 1950. In that year, Syria elected a constituent assembly, which studied numerous Asian and European constitutions and drafted Syria's first indigenous constitution. It protected the rights of all citizens, although the president was required to be a Muslim and Islamic law was established as the law of the land. In the 1950s and 1960s, the many coups d'état in Damascus promulgated a series of new constitutions and sometimes revived former ones. Typically, when a coup first occurred, the new rulers would suspend the constitution for ostensible "security reasons." In all cases, however, they expressed an underlying need to return to constitutional government.

In January 1973 a draft constitution was approved by the People's Council and confirmed by a referendum in March. Many Sunnis, however, objected to the exclusion of the traditional article making Islam the state religion. After some agitation, the critics were satisfied by an amendment that declared that the president must be a Muslim—a claim that President Assad, an Alawite, has made for himself despite the uneasiness of many Sunnis. Islamic jurisprudence was retained as the primary source of legislation, and the Arabic character of the state was confirmed. Freedom of religion was confirmed for all groups, however.

The Arab socialist orientation of Syria is retained in the current constitution. The state maintains a great role in the economic sector, as has been the case under previous constitutions. Nevertheless, in response to traditional Syrian reliance on the family and the individual, a nonsocialist tradition has been maintained through the securing of inheritance rights, patents, and copyrights.

The role of the president remains dominant. The president appoints the People's Council on the basis of the will of the Baath party. The members of the Baath party Regional Command are elected. The president also appoints the prime minister and the cabinet, who are responsible to him and not to the People's Council.

The People's Council, which serves as the national legislature, has limited powers. It is, at best, a watchdog that monitors the actions of the prime minister and his government. In theory, it can withdraw its confidence from a minister or the entire cabinet. In practice, however, this is not done, for the president may dismiss the People's Council at any time and then appoint a new one.

The constitution has also theoretically established an independent judiciary. The appointment, transfer, and dismissal of judges are all determined by a higher judiciary council, which is composed of senior career civil judges. There are three tiers of courts, the highest being the supreme court in Damascus. On the whole, however, legislation passed by the various regimes since independence remains in effect. No attempt has been made to restructure the entire legal system. Therefore, law in Syria is based on a combination of Western (mostly French) and Islamic concepts. Many personal cases are still handled by the Shari'a (Islamic) courts.

The Syrian civil service has, for the most part, remained outside politics, and no regime has specifically attempted to politicize it. There are indications, however, that after twenty years of Baathist rule, loyalty to the party has become a key to advancement. Within that framework the general practice has been to employ and advance the most professionally qualified people, although repeated government changes and the transition in leadership from the traditional leaders to the Baath party in the 1960s caused some exodus of qualified personnel.

At the local government level, Syria is divided into twelve provinces. Damascus is an independent city that, in status, is the equivalent of a province. The provinces are divided into districts that, in turn, are subdivided into localities. In Syria's highly centralized system of government, appointment to the subdistrict level or even to village positions must be approved by the Baath Regional Command Council. Local administration, therefore, has become an instrument for the Baath party to maintain its control at the grass-roots level. In the village, the headman (*mukhtar*) is usually the leading figure or is approved by the village leaders personally. In either case, the Baath party must approve the choice.

Political Dynamics

Syria has undergone a major political transformation since independence. The rapid turnover in regimes has led to fundamental changes in the Syrian ruling elite. The clubby traditional leadership has been replaced by the Baath party structure and the military. At independence, political power was monopolized by the traditional Sunni leaders of the major interior cities—Aleppo, Hamah, Homs, and particularly Damascus. These leaders were generally from traditional landholding or mercantile families. Many had reached political maturity at the time of King Faysal, and nearly all had been active in the struggle for independence.

These leaders were divided into two principal groups representing different wings of the elite. The National party was heavily Damascene, with a substantial representation of lawyers and industrialists. This party traced its origins to the National bloc that formed a majority in the constitutional convention of 1928. In inter-Arab politics it favored maintaining Syrian autonomy and allied itself with more distant Egypt and Saudi Arabia. The People's party (originally the Constitutional bloc) formed the opposition. It represented the landed class and merchants of Aleppo. Because of trade ties with Iraq, its members favored a union with Hashimite Jordan and Iraq. Neither group was sufficiently concerned with the Syrian masses, being more occupied with regional international events—particularly the leadership of the Arab world.

In the nine years following the first Syrian coup in 1949, when Colonel Husni Zaim established a military dictatorship, the strength of the National and People's parties eroded. Zaim began the process by disbanding Parliament and banning political parties. Zaim's was the first in a long series of military coups that thoroughly enmeshed the Syrian armed forces in politics. A military career became the primary means for political advancement. The politicization of the military has had several significant consequences for Syria. First, the Syrian armed forces became torn by competing political factions, thus greatly reducing the country's military effectiveness. This was particularly so in the 1950s and 1960s, when many qualified officers were sent into exile and others were promoted on the basis of political loyalty rather than competence. Second, the minorities have been heavily represented in the military. Consequently, minority groups—Alawites, Druze, and Christians—have had a disproportionate influence on government policy. Zaim's coup was welcomed by most Syrians, and he was cheered in the streets of Damascus. Syria's poor showing in the Palestine War, quarreling among the political leaders, rising prices, and a general feeling of discontent all contributed to the popularity of the coup. The weakness of the military government, however, resulted from the fact that the army reflected all the divisiveness of Syrian society. After only four and one-half months, Zaim was overthrown by Colonel Sami Hinnawi, who appeared to be a proponent of the old order. Hinnawi, however, was quickly overthrown by another colonel, Adib Shishakli.

Shishakli managed to be either the head of state or the power behind the government for the next four years. His relative success was due in part to his association with one element of the old order—Akram Hourani and his Republican bloc, an offshoot of the old National bloc. Hourani not only gave legitimacy to the regime but also induced Shishakli to introduce a number of social reforms. Moreover, it was under Hourani's guidance that the relatively liberal constitution of 1950 was promulgated. The Parliament created by the new constitution, however, gave the old-line politicians a forum from which they could undermine the colonel's authority. Sensing the rising tide of opposition, Shishakli staged a second coup in November 1951 and struck at his opponents. He dissolved Parliament and outlawed all sources of opposition, including political parties, student organizations, and trade unions.

Even then, Shishakli felt a need to maintain at least a veneer of traditional legitimacy. He replaced the political parties with his own Arab Liberation Movement, replaced the liberal constitution with one putting more power in the hands of the president, and had himself elected president for a five-year term. Shishakli's heavy-handed rule, however, solidified all factions of Syrian society against him. A coalition of dissidents overthrew him in February 1954.

Although the coalition was dominated by the old-line politicians, a new element had emerged on the Syrian political scene in the form of ideological political parties. Three were of particular note: the Baath party, the Syrian Nationalist party, and the Syrian Communist party. Over the longer term, the most important was the Arab Socialist Resurrection party, or the Baath, which was established in 1953 from the merger of Akram Hourani's Arab Socialist party and the Arab Renaissance (Baath) party, led by Michel Aflaq and Salah Bitar. Hourani's party began as a youth group in Hamah, and most of its members were personally loyal to Hourani. During the early 1950s, however, Hourani began to espouse more socialist beliefs. He thus brought to the Baath a socialist commitment, experience as a political leader, and a committed following, particularly among the Sunnis in Hamah. Aflaq, the founder of the Baath, was strongly influenced by the French leftist philosophy to which he had been exposed as a student in Paris. He rejected Marxism, however, but hoped to adapt his leftist social doctrine to an Arab society.

Aflaq, a Greek Orthodox, became close friends with Salah Bitar, a Sunni Muslim from Damascus. Together they had founded the Arab Resurrection party in 1940. The Baath ideology was not geared solely to the intellectual elite. Three key elements had much broader appeal. First of all, its program of social reform and economic justice appealed to a wide spectrum of the lower classes. Second, the Baathists stressed the idea of a greater Arab unity by pressing for political merger. They opposed any form of regional unity that did not have as its ultimate goal a union of all Arabs. Finally, the Greek Orthodox Aflaq recognized the unique relationship between Islam and Arabism. Aflaq structured his ideas upon the common memory of all Arabs of the glory of the golden age of Islam. Nevertheless, the Baathists asserted that discrimination against other religions was unacceptable and thus promoted religious tolerance as a basic tenet.

The Baathists considered their party to be not merely a Syrian party but, rather, a pan-Arab party. Much of the leadership's effort was spent winning support elsewhere in the Arab world. They had large followings in Iraq, Jordan, and Lebanon. The strength of the Baath rested in its organization. Bitar was the specialist in administration. The Baath party in each Arab state was designated a "regional command." Regional in this instance referred to each individual state within the larger Arab nation. The supreme body was the National (pan-Arab) Command.

In Syria, the Baathists took particular care to organize young military officers. They promoted revolution rather than evolution, and in Syria the army remained the key to power.

The chief Syrian rival of the Baathists in the early 1950s was the Syrian National party (PPS). This party, founded in the 1930s by Antun Saadah, a Lebanese Greek Orthodox, favored unity of all geographical Syria, meaning Lebanon, Palestine, Syria, and Jordan. Later, Iraq, Kuwait, and Cyprus were added as part of the scheme to unite the entire Fertile Crescent. The PPS was tightly organized and conspiratorial in nature, but it never gained power. It failed for several reasons. First of all, on a practical level the execution of Saadah by the Lebanese government in 1949 deprived the party of his leadership at a crucial moment. Second, the concept of specific Syrian nationalism was not as strong as pan-Arab nationalism. Moreover, the PPS favored close relations with the West at a time when the Arab world was genuinely attracted to Nasser's policy of leading Egypt and the rest of the Arab world away from the West. Finally, the PPS made some serious tactical errors. In April 1955 a PPS army sergeant assassinated Major Adanan Makki, deputy chief of staff and a prominent Baathist. Swift Baathist retribution overwhelmed their rivals. The PPS was accused of plotting a coup d'état, and its influence in the officer corps was eradicated. The PPS was never again an effective force in Syria.

In its attack on the PPS, the Baath party was aided by the Syrian Communist party. Founded in 1933, the Communist party, like the PPS and the Baath, had attracted many of its adherents from the minorities—Druze, Kurds, Alawites, and Christians. Moreover, like the other two ideological parties, it was well organized and in 1955 was probably the preeminent Communist party in the Middle East. Party leader Khalid Bakdash, a Kurd, was elected to Parliament in 1954 and became one of its most powerful members. The Communists, however, were handicapped in several ways. First, they were considered anti-Islamic atheists by most Syrians. Second, their loyalty to Syrian and Arab nationalism was placed in doubt by ties to Moscow and international communism. Because of these liabilities, Communist fortunes became dependent upon the party's ties to the left wing of the Baath and how that wing fared in intraparty squabbles. The Communist role was also a function of Syrian-Soviet relations.

In 1956 the Baath entered the government for the first time. Shortly thereafter, Akram Hourani became speaker of the House. For the next several years, the Baathists, though outnumbered by the traditional Sunni ruling elite, dominated the government through party discipline and ideological commitment. The Baathists and the traditional leaders were united in their opposition to a shift in Syrian policy toward the Soviet Union and away from Arab nationalism. When, under the growing influence of the Communists and other leftist elements, Syrian policy moved sharply to the left, the Baathists and their allies among the traditional leadership appealed to Nasser to merge Syria with Egypt to forestall what they believed was a possible takeover by pro-Soviet elements. Reluctantly, Nasser agreed. In January 1958 Syria and Egypt formed the United Arab Republic (UAR).

The merger of the two states turned out to be very unpleasant for Syria, as Nasser sought to make Damascus subservient to Cairo. Both the Baathists and the Arab nationalists soon regretted their push toward union. The Baathists, who had been riding a wave of success, found their activities increasingly restricted. Political parties were replaced by the National Union, an instrument designed to promote the interests of Nasser. When elections were held in 1959 for ten thousand local committee officers, the Baath party received less than 2.5 percent of the votes. In protest over Egyptian control of Syrian affairs, the five Baathist ministers resigned in December 1959. The traditional Arab nationalists of the ruling elite, who had been losing ground to the rising middle class, found the last remnants of its power base destroyed by Egyptian-sponsored policies, which included land reforms.

Elements of the traditional elite, however, managed to foster a coup in 1961 that threw out the Egyptians. In the Syrian nationalist fervor that followed, the traditional parties—the People's party and the Nationalist party—won the two largest blocs in Parliament. The election, however, was an aberration. The leadership represented only a small element of society that was of decreasing importance. As the anti-Egyptian feeling waned, political squabbling and governmental paralysis led to popular discontent. This brief interlude was the last hurrah for the traditional Syrian Sunni leadership.

In 1963 a Baathist-supported junta seized control, and the Baath party has dominated Syrian politics ever since. Initially broad based, with a wide spectrum of political opinion and ideology, the party has become increasingly dominated by military members of the Baathist National Command. One aspect of the Baath party that did not change was the disproportionate number of minority members. As a result, Baathist leadership, and consequently Syrian leadership, has been dominated by the minorities who have been drawn to ideological parties and have been active in the military. The Alawites have been particularly influential.

For the most part, the struggle for power within Syria has become a struggle for control of the Baath party and the army. This struggle has been both personal and ideological. At times, it has not been possible to separate the two. Generally speaking, there are two wings of the party—a "progressive" wing and a "moderate" wing. When in power, the progressives have pressed for closer ties with the Soviets and greater socialization of society. Their domestic policy has at times precipitated violent antigovernment demonstrations by the conservative Sunni community. The moderates have been more pan-Arabian in outlook and have a more cautious approach to social reform.

Since November 1970 Hafiz al-Assad, current president of the Syrian Arab Republic, has dominated the Baath regime, bringing a high degree of political stability to Syria. He has ruled with the pragmatism of the moderate wing of the party, dominating the Baathist Regional Command and the army. In order to broaden his political base, he established a National Front within the People's Council with a range of moderate leftist Syrians represented, including such organizations as the Arab Socialists, the Communists, trade unions, and others. In this way, al-Assad appears to have made his potential opponents on the left responsible for government actions without sacrificing Baathist dominance. His policies have done much to transform the Baath from the small, ideological, and closely knit party of the 1950s to an instrument of mass political mobilization.

The most serious challenge to Baathist political dominance in recent years has come from the Islamic fundamentalists. Between 1976 and 1982, anti-Baathist sentiment was focused in a clear revolt of these fundamentalists. The heart of the movement was the urban Sunni population. Terrorist attacks were common in every major urban center. The movement failed, however, to win widespread support in the countryside or among the minorities. As a result, the Baathist-dominated military was able to suppress the revolt with considerable brutality. The last gasp was the leveling of much of the city of Hamah in February 1982. Since then, no serious challenge to the regime's authority has been mounted.

Foreign Policy

Syrian foreign policy has been largely influenced by two philosophies—pan-Arabism and Syrian nationalism. At times these two doctrines have been mutually supporting; at other times they have conflicted. Neither has been able to dominate totally.

Pan-Arabism was the dominant philosophical force in the Syrian approach to foreign relations in the early years of independent Syria. It appeals for the union of all Arabs, emphasizing cultural affinity, opposition to the "Zionist expansion" in Israel, and resistance to Western imperialism. Syrian pan-Arabism developed along two lines—Islamic Arab nationalism as envisioned by the Sunni urban majority who dominated Syria at independence and Baathist ideological Arab socialism. These two forces dominated Syria until the late 1950s. They carried Syria into the union with Egypt and rejected formal alliances with non-Arab states, whether the Soviet Union or the West. Nevertheless, the Baathists felt philosophically more at ease with the socialist states than with the West.

As with Arab nationalism, there were two trends in Syrian nationalism. The first was exemplified by those who believed in the union of geographical Syria. This tendency was best expressed by the PPS, but that party's fortunes have faded. The other strain of Syrian nationalism identified with the Syrian Arab Republic. As the Syrian people have become increasingly accustomed to thinking of Syria as existing within its current geographical limits, loyalty to the Syrian Arab Republic has grown, and this perception of Syrian nationalism has increasingly gained favor. These "little Syria" nationalists began to gain dominance during the union with Egypt. Few Syrians had realized the extent to which they identified with their own government in Damascus until it became evident that Egyptian policy was not necessarily in the Syrian interest. Syrian nationalism was the banner around which anti-union forces rallied, leading to the breakup of Nasser's United Arab Republic.

The revolution of 1963, which brought the Baathists to power, was in effect a turning away from narrow Syrian nationalism in favor of broader Arab national goals. By this time, however, Syrian nationalism was firmly rooted even within the Baath party. The 1966 Baathist coup was a victory for the Syrian nationalists within the party and led to the exile of the old-line Arab nationalist Baathists, including Aflaq and Bitar. When al-Assad took power in 1970, he moved Syria even further away from Arab nationalism in favor of Syrian self-interest.

The ascendancy of either Syrian national views or Arab national views did not mean that the other philosophy was totally disregarded. The difference was in emphasis. Each continued to influence Syrian policy and the Syrian people. For instance, in 1976, despite the outcry from the other Arabs, al-

Assad could send his troops into Lebanon and fight pitched battles with the Palestinians because Syria's basic national interests were threatened by events in Lebanon. Nevertheless, this policy of ignoring the other Arabs could not be sustained over time; therefore, Damascus welcomed the opportunity to return to the Arab fold under the standard of Arab unity and Arab nationalism following the October 1976 Riyadh Summit.

No matter which philosophical tendency took precedence at a specific time, Syrian foreign policy has been dominated by two related issues—Israel and Syria's roles in Arab politics. The question of the fate of the Palestinians and the future of Israel is of greater importance to the Syrians than to other Arabs for several reasons. First, the peoples of Palestine and Syria share a common ancestry. Palestinian Arabs and Syrian Arabs have been buffeted throughout history by the same forces. Therefore, the plight of the Palestinians is deeply felt. Second, the Syrian people have the feeling that they are in competition for geographical Syria. Israeli occupation of Palestine, which was cut out of Syria by the Europeans, is seen as only a first step in Israeli expansion. Israeli occupation of Golan in 1967 and Israel's actions in Lebanon have more recently reinforced for the Syrians most of their fears of sinister Israeli intentions.

After the Israel issue, the most serious foreign policy question is that of Syria's role in the Arab world. Since independence, the Syrians have been committed to pan-Arabism. The Syrians perceive that Damascus must play a leading role in effecting Arab unity. This view has brought them into sharp conflict with all of their Arab neighbors at one time or another. Although these differences have been intense, they can be put aside very quickly if necessary.

Syria's relations with the great powers have been colored by the Arab-Israeli conflict, Syrian anti-imperialism, and the political philosophy of their leaders. As a result, the Damascus regime continues to find more in common with the socialist countries than with the West. Nevertheless, under al-Assad, Syria has attempted to improve relations with the United States and Europe. This action has provided not only a Western balance against Soviet attempts to dominate Syria but an economic balance as well.

Bibliography

A good place to begin looking more deeply into the politics and government of Syria is in one of several general studies. *Syria: Modern State in an Ancient Land* (Boulder, Colo.: Westview Press, 1983), by John Devlin, is a perceptive analytical study of the general Syrian scene. Tabitha Petran's *Syria* (New York: Praeger Publishers, 1972), one of the general survey books in the Nations of the Modern World Series, is also an excellent introduction with some very good sections. Other works that provide a good introduction to the history of Syria include A. L. Tibawi's *A Modern History of Syria Including Lebanon and Palestine* (New York: St. Martin's Press, 1969), and Anne Sinai and Allen Pollack's *The Syrian Arab Republic* (New York: American Academic Association for Peace in the Middle East, 1976). The latter is a collection of essays on Syrian history, government, ideology, the economy, and population that provide a wealth of information. The essays themselves are uneven, however.

Several more scholarly specialized works delve into particular aspects of the Syrian experience. In *The Struggle for Syria* (New York: Oxford University Press, 1965), Patrick Seale analyzes the regional and internal factors leading to the union with Egypt in 1958. At times, however, the wealth of detail is overwhelming. Gordon H. Torrey, in *Syrian Politics and the Military: 1945–1958* (Columbus: Ohio State University Press, 1964), looks at the same period but with an eye more keenly focused on competition within the Syrian military and between the military and traditional landowning and commercial elites. In *Syria Under the Ba'th, 1963–66: The Army-Party Symbiosis* (New York: Halsted Press, 1972), Itamar Rabinovich analyzes the crucial period of Baathist rule following the 1963 coup and the very special relationship between the party organization and the military. Umar F. Abdallah, in *The Islamic Struggle in Syria* (Berkeley: Mizan Press, 1983), provides a valuable analysis of the Muslim fundamentalist movement in Syria. The author's sympathy toward the fundamentalists is apparent. Regarding Syria's policy toward Lebanon, Adeed Dawisha's *Syria and the Lebanese Crisis* (New York: St. Martin's Press, 1980) is the best single study.

Two of the many articles on Syria are worth special note. Moshe Maoz's "Attempts at Creating a Political Community in Modern Syria," *Middle East Journal* 26, no. 4 (1972), pp. 384–404, is an excellent place in which to begin to understand the ebb and flow of independent Syria. Michael H. Van Dusen, in "Political Integration and Regionalism in Syria," *Middle East Journal* 26, no. 2 (1972), pp. 123–136, provides the best short study on the problem of regionalism and the ways in which it affects the Syrian nation. At the same time, the author analyzes the means by which national leaders have used their position to enhance personal influence in their traditional regional power base.

12

Hashimite Kingdom of Jordan

M. Graeme Bannerman

Historical Background

The Kingdom of Jordan is another of the successor states of the Ottoman Empire. The territory east of the Jordan River, however, has a reputation dating back several millennia of being the crossroads between the Mediterranean to the west, the Orient to the east, and Arabia to the south. The ancient biblical kingdoms of Gilead, Amman, Moab, and Edom were largely located in present-day Jordan. Because of its relatively remote though strategically important location, the area was usually the last conquered and the first abandoned as the great ancient empires ebbed and flowed. Egyptian, Hittite, Assyrian, Persian, Greek, Roman, and Byzantine soldiers all occupied the region.

Of all the peoples of antiquity, the Nabataean Arabs were probably the most direct ancestors of modern Jordanians. Shortly after 800 B.C., the Aramaic-speaking inhabitants of Petra, southeast of the Dead Sea, created their kingdom along the key north-south trading routes, maintaining their independence until conquered by the Romans under Pompey in 64 B.C.

It is in sociological terms that the Islamic conquest of the area has had the greatest impact. The battle of Yarmuk in northern Jordan in A.D. 636 expelled the Christian Byzantines and laid the groundwork for the establishment of Islam as the religion of the majority of Jordanians. At various times, the area was ruled from Damascus, Baghdad, Cairo, Jerusalem, and Istanbul. Under Ottoman rule, southern Jordan was governed as part of the Hijaz, whereas the north was included in the Damascus governate.

Like the countries of the rest of the Levant, the modern Jordanian state emerged as a result of the collapse of the Ottoman Empire in World War I. Arab tribesmen under the leadership of Amir Faysal, son of Sharif Husayn (al-Hashim) of the Hijaz (now Saudi Arabia) and advised by the famous Lawrence of Arabia, marched northward against the retreating Ottoman forces. When Faysal's army defeated the Ottomans and conquered Aqabah and Amman, the tribes east of the Jordan quickly joined the Arab revolt against Istanbul. By the end of the war, nearly all of current Jordan was in Hashimite hands. Nevertheless, Jordan's destiny was determined by other forces. Under the terms of the secret Sykes-Picot Agreement of May 1916, the Levant had already been divided into British

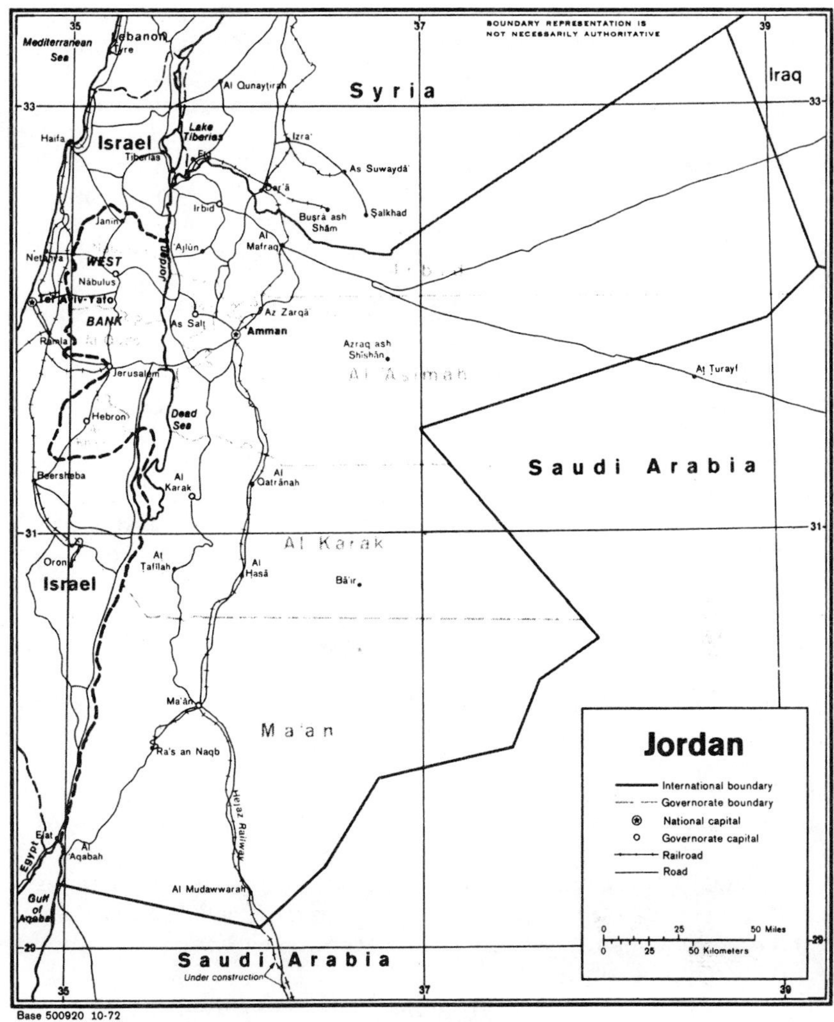

and French spheres. What is now Lebanon and Syria came under French control, whereas Palestine eastward to Iraq was given to the British. At that time, few considered the area east of Jordan to be a separate entity. To the Arabs it was part of greater Syria, which included the present states of Israel, Jordan, Lebanon, and Syria; to the British and the European Zionists, it was an integral part of Palestine.

Amir Faysal, who attended the 1919 Paris Peace Conference, pressed for the complete independence of the Levantine Arabs, basing his arguments on President Woodrow Wilson's Fourteen Points promoting self-determination for all people. Arab leaders also contended that in wartime they had been promised an independent state that included Transjordan and Palestine. Faysal failed, however, to win his point against British and French imperial aspirations and Zionist demands for a homeland. Nevertheless, the Arabs were prepared to assert their independence without European acquiescence. In March 1920 a group of Arab nationalists convened the General Syrian Congress in Damascus and declared the independence of Syria (including Jordan and Palestine) and Iraq. The decision was opposed by Britain and France, and, in the following month at the San Remo Conference, the Levant was divided in accordance with the Sykes-Picot framework while ignoring the Arab declarations and British promises. Palestine, including what is now Jordan, was effectively separated from Syria. In July 1920 an Arab force was defeated by the French, for the time being destroying Arab hopes for political independence in the Levant.

The status of Jordan remained unclear at that time. The British felt some obligation to the Hashimites for unkept wartime promises and feared a possible worsening of Anglo-French relations if Arab attacks on Syria were launched from Jordan. Amir Abdallah, the brother of King Faysal of Syria, was in Jordan organizing the tribes to strike at the French in Syria. The British, realizing such an attack was not in their best interest, offered Abdallah (who was very popular with the Jordanian tribes) the opportunity to be the amir of Transjordan. In this way, Anglo-French difficulties were limited and British promises to the Hashimites were partially met. Abdallah accepted the British offer because an emirate in Jordan was a tangible gain and he had little chance of displacing the French from Syria.

The establishment of a governmental system for the new emirate took much time and effort on the part of the British. Being politically cut off from Syria, with whose government its people had been traditionally associated, Transjordan lacked a national identity and had practically no economic base. The few Arab administrators in Jordan were those who had fled from the French in Damascus and were generally more concerned with reasserting Arab control in Syria than with making Jordan an independent, self-sufficient state. On the economic side, less than 3 percent of the land was under cultivation, and, with virtually no other economic assets in the country, the new government was heavily dependent on British economic support.

Thus, when Britain recognized Transjordan as a self-governing state on May 15, 1923, Amir Abdallah was in no position to run a country. National borders were ill-defined. His father's kingdom of the Hijaz to the south was collapsing before the followers of Ibn Saud, and he lacked the resources to assist his father or to protect his own interests. His nation, moreover, was totally dependent on British subsidies. Therefore, though recognized as self-governing, Jordan was, in fact, governed by the British.

The British were primarily interested in maintaining stability. The prospect of chaos and anarchy—or worse, some rival power assuming control of Transjordan—forced London to take a more active interest in the fledgling country than it might otherwise have done. The British goal was to establish an effective local administration and thus reduce what was considered a drain that the British treasury could ill afford. British policy, therefore, was to provide British officials to train a pro-British local administration and military force that would become financially and politically independent while remaining friendly to London.

With the assistance of a small but devoted group of British officials, Transjordan under Amir Abdallah made slow but steady progress toward true independence. At first the administration was simple. Abdallah ruled with the advice of a small executive council. British officials handled defense, foreign affairs, and finance.

A major step toward real independence came with a new treaty in 1928 between the British and Abdallah that gave greater authority to the amir and his officials. Under the agreement, however, London retained the right to oversee finance and foreign policy, and British officers still controlled the Arab Legion. In the same year, the Organic Law of 1928 was promulgated. This law took the first move toward a representative government by providing for a legislative council to replace the old executive council.

In the early 1930s progress toward independence continued as Transjordan gained the right to send consular representatives to other Arab countries. In May 1939 the legislative council was converted to a council of ministers, or cabinet. Although actual rule continued to rest with the amir and the British, a loyal opposition composed of Arab nationalists evolved during the 1930s. Their most prominent vehicle for dissent was the Istiqlal (Independence) party, which was also active in Palestine and Syria.

Throughout the period, Amir Abdallah demonstrated ambitions greater than just ruling a small desert kingdom. He envisaged a broader role for his dynasty, and, as a direct descendant of the Prophet, he possibly even dreamed of reestablishing the caliphate. His immediate ambitions were directed at regaining the Hijaz from the Saudis and at reestablishing the Arab kingdom of his brother Faysal in Syria.

During World War II, Transjordan played an influential role in inter-Arab affairs. The Arab Legion, as Transjordan's British-led army was called, helped suppress the pro-German revolt of Rashid Ali in Iraq. Moreover, Abdallah was instrumental in the formation of the Arab League. The Arab League was the first concrete step toward pan-Arab unity, and Abdallah envisioned the reunification of the Arabs under the Hashimites. His wholehearted cooperation with the British stemmed in part from the hope that his cooperation would help him become ruler of an independent Arab state composed of Syria, Lebanon, Palestine, and Transjordan—and subsequently of Iraq as well.

Abdallah's amibitions proved unrealistic, for opponents to such a scheme included the Zionists, the Syrian nationalists, the Lebanese Christians, the Saudis, the Egyptians, and the French. Thus, Abdallah had to be satisfied with achieving total independence for Transjordan and his recognition as king. In 1946 Transjordan and the United Kingdom reached a new agreement whereby the Organic Law of 1928 was replaced by a constitution and Abdallah was recognized as king of Transjordan. Two years later, London agreed to continue paying a subsidy in return for British access rights to two military bases.

The rising crisis in Palestine became the dominant concern of the fledgling state. Abdallah's policy toward Palestine differed from that of other Arab states. In fact, he met secretly with Zionist leaders, including Golda Meir, in an attempt to work out some modus vivendi with the emerging Jewish state. His position appears to have been based on a sense of realism and on a deep commitment to Transjordan's vital links with Palestine. Nevertheless, when Israel declared its independence, the Arab Legion occupied areas of Palestine adjacent to Jordan that had been allocated to the Arabs in the United Nations Partition Plan of 1947. Although some of this territory was lost, Abdallah's forces were the most successful of the Arab armies. When the fighting halted, the Arab Legion held perhaps 20 percent of Palestine, including the old city of Jerusalem.

On April 24, 1950, Abdallah unilaterally annexed the portion of Palestine—called the West Bank—held by his forces and changed the name of his nation to the Kingdom of Jordan. This action unequivocally altered not only the history of the country but its political, social, and economic structure as well. The total number of Palestinians, including refugees from Israeli-held areas, and the inhabitants of Jordan's newly acquired West Bank (annexed Palestine) outnumbered the Transjordanians. More important, most other Arabs joined the Palestinians in believing that Abdallah had betrayed them by annexing part of Palestine. Indeed, only Pakistan and Britain ever formally acknowledged the annexation. Jordan became a pariah among the Arab states, with only the fellow Hashimite regime in Iraq offering support.

The annexation of the West Bank was for Abdallah the natural outgrowth of his greater Syrian policy. In the same vein, he alone among the Arab rulers extended full citizenship rights to the Palestinians. However, he was detested by the Palestinians for what they perceived to be his self-serving action and his betrayal of their cause to obtain Palestinian national rights. The other Arabs opposed him as much for his greater-Syrian ambitions as for his role in Palestine. The Arab League so vehemently opposed the annexation that Jordan was nearly expelled. An agreement was reached with the Arab League when Jordan agreed that it was merely holding the West Bank in trust, and Abdallah promised that he would forego any separate nonaggression pact with Israel. The Palestinians, however, never forgave him. While he was praying in Jerusalem on July 20, 1951, he was assassinated by a vengeful Palestinian nationalist.

The smooth transition of power from Abdallah to his oldest son, Talal, was a reflection of the stability of the Hashimite state, primarily based on the loyalty of the British officers and the Arab Legion. Under Talal, a new constitution was promulgated in January 1952. Talal, however, had a long history of mental illness and under his doctor's advice abdicated in favor of his son Hussein, who was still a minor. A regency council of three was formed to govern for several months until the young Hussein reached maturity and assumed the throne in May 1953.

Political Environment

The Land

The 95,594 square kilometers (ca. 36,900 square miles) that constitute the Hashimite Kingdom of Jordan form part of the north Arabian plateau that Jordan shares with its neighbors: Syria to the north, Iraq to the east, and Saudi Arabia to the south. There are no natural frontiers between Jordan and its Arab neighbors. The western border of Jordan is the Great Rift Valley, through which the Jordan River flows. From an average of 600 to 900 meters (2,000 to 3,000 feet) on the plateau, the landscape plummets to well below sea level in the valley. The Great Rift Valley also includes the Dead Sea and the Gulf of Aqaba to the south, and extends into east Africa. Jordan's only coastline is a 19-kilometer (12-mile) stretch on the Gulf, including the port of Aqaba. Beyond the Great Rift Valley lie Israel and the West Bank highlands.

Rainfall is the most important climatic determinant. More than four-fifths of Jordan is desert or semidesert receiving less than 10 centimeters (4 inches) of rain annually. Prevailing westerly winds draw winter rains to the northern areas of the country; but in the south, dry winds from the Sahara are the rule. Consequently, Jordan's population is concentrated in the northwestern corner of the East Bank and on the West Bank where rainfall, averaging about 30 to 41 centimeters (12 to 16 inches) annually, permits some farming. All of Jordan's major cities—Amman, Irbid, Zarqah, and the West Bank towns—are concentrated in this area. Some attempt has been made to expand the area of settlement and cultivation. Of particular note are the reforestation projects north of Amman and the East Ghor irrigation canal project in the Jordan River valley. Moreover, plans have been discussed for years to dam the Yarmuk River, which forms a portion of the borders between Jordan and Israel, and Jordan and Syria. These plans could enhance the supply of water available for irrigation, but political problems have blocked the project. Already, the smaller Zarqah River is being used to provide water for the lower Jordan valley. Available water is limited, however.

Jordan is also poor in minerals and fuels. It has no commercially exploitable oil. There are small manganese ore and copper deposits near the Dead Sea. Phosphates, located at Wadi al-Hasa, are the only large earners of foreign currency other than tourism and the remittances from Jordanians working abroad.

The People

Although most Jordanians are of Arab heritage, they may be roughly divided into two principal groups: Palestinians and East Bank Jordanians. Palestinians are those who lived in the British mandate of Palestine and who have been under Jordanian sovereignty since 1948. These include both the refugees who fled from the Israelis and the inhabitants of the West Bank. By 1967 these Palestinians constituted perhaps two-thirds of the entire population of Jordan. Throughout the period of Jordanian sovereignty over the West Bank, a continuous migration from the West Bank to the east occurred. Amman's population grew from 30,000 in 1948 to 250,000 in 1961 to 350,000 just prior to the 1967 war to more than 750,000 in 1983. At the same time, the West Bank proportion of the total Jordanian population declined from 62 percent in the late 1940s to 47 percent in 1961. As a result of the 1967 war, another 200,000 to 250,000 Palestinian refugees entered the East Bank. Palestinians now constitute more than half of the total East Bank Jordanian population. Forty percent still live in the United Nations Relief and Works Agency (UNRWA) camps. The remaining 60 percent are more assimilated into the general population.

Since 1948 Jordan alone among the Arab states has given full citizenship to all Palestinians. No official distinction was made between Palestinians and East Bank Jordanians. Palestinians were afforded the same political and economic opportunities as all Jordanians. Because of their industry and their generally higher level of education, the Palestinians have played a preponderant role in many aspects of Jordanian society, despite their traditional antipathy for the monarchy. In particular, they have dominated the fields of education, medicine, and the civil service.

Between 1948 and 1967 the Palestinians were gradually assimilated into the rest of Jordanian society. Even the Jordan Arab Army (as the Arab Legion was renamed), the backbone of support for the monarchy, witnessed a growing number of Palestinians in the officer corps. The 1967 Arab-Israeli war, resulting in Israeli occupation of the West Bank, slowed the trend but did not stop it entirely. Many of the present business and government leaders on the East Bank are of Palestinian origin.

The East Bank Jordanians are, nevertheless, the rock upon which the Hashimite monarchy has been built. Most East Bankers are Sunni Muslims, although a small Christian minority is also present. Among the Palestinians, the percentage of Christians is higher. Most East Bank Jordanians are members of several hundred Arab tribes. Although today a majority have settled and live in Amman or in the agricultural regions to the northwest of the capital, the bedouin tradition is still strong. Bedouin values and virtues continue to have an important influence on society. Those who continue to live a nomadic life and those who have settled in towns maintain these values. In Jordan, more than any other state of the Fertile Crescent, the tribal elements provide a disproportionate number of recruits for the military and are guaranteed representation in government, thus influencing government policy.

Two minority elements on the East Bank—the Christians and the Circassians—have also provided backing for the Hashimites. Jordan's Christian population is urban and has lived in the area for centuries. Most are the descendants of early converts to Christianity, whereas others have allegedly descended from the crusaders. In any case, they are predominantly Greek Orthodox and Greek Catholic.

The Circassians settled in Jordan in the last decade of the nineteenth century. They were part of the approximately 1 million Muslims who fled the Caucasus when the Russians captured it from the Ottomans, and were given land by the Ottoman sultan in what is now Israel, Jordan, and Syria. The Circassians are Sunni Muslims and generally have been accepted by their Arab neighbors. Although they did come into conflict with unruly bedouins from time to time, they have been traditionally loyal to the monarchy and have held very senior positions in the government. They are particularly numerous in the armed forces as well as in the police force. Circassians are divided into two major groups—the Adigah and the Chechen. Both are guaranteed representation in Parliament.

Although rivalries have existed among the bedouin tribes, between the bedouin and the Circassians, and between the nomads and the villagers, the East Bank

Jordanians are united in their support for the monarchy and resistance to Palestinian domination of Jordan. In recent years, some have even welcomed the loss of the West Bank. These elements stress their belief that the political benefits to Jordan from the loss of the West Bank outweigh the economic liabilities.

Economic Conditions

Despite harsh climatic conditions, Jordan remains primarily an agricultural country. About 40 percent of the work force engages in agriculture, forestry, and herding, contributing perhaps a quarter of the gross domestic product (GDP) and 50 percent of the exports. Agricultural production, however, is very erratic owing to political events and to the unreliability of rainfall. For instance, since 1967 cereal production has varied from 297,000 tons in that year to 56,000 tons in 1973. Several dams have been constructed and several more are planned in order to better utilize scarce water for agricultural production.

Prior to 1967 the country appeared to be well on its way to becoming economically self-sufficient. The loss of the West Bank was a harsh blow to Jordan's economy, however. Before 1967 the West Bank accounted for 60 to 80 percent of the country's agricultural land, 75 percent of the GNP, 40 percent of the government's revenue, and nearly 33 percent of its foreign currency income. The hope for self-sufficiency has all but vanished.

Jordan's small industrial and mining sector was not severely hurt by the loss of the West Bank. The nation's oil refinery, the national power plant, and the important phosphate mines are on the East Bank. In addition, most of the larger manufacturing facilities are located between Amman and Zarqah. These include textiles, leather, batteries, food processing, brewing and bottling, and cigarette manufacturing. Although progress is being made in developing resources, Jordan's economic potential remains modest.

Although possessing no oil of its own, Jordan has indirectly benefited from the rapid rise in the price of oil during the 1970s. Subsidies from Arab oil-producing states and remittances from Jordanians working abroad have helped to transform Amman. Real GDP rose at an average annual rate of 11.7 percent, industrial production increased by 16.6 percent, and construction increased 23.8 percent annually during the same period.

With the economic slowdown in the oil industry during the 1980s, the Jordanians have seen a decline in their growth rates to less than 5 percent of those of the mid-1980s. Remittances from workers abroad have held fairly constant, as Jordanian workers were not as heavily involved in construction and other sectors of the Arab Gulf economies, which have been most drastically reduced. Subsidies from the Arab states have been cut in half, and further funding for military purchases is questionable. Consequently, the Jordanians have had to borrow in the international market, thus raising concerns about future debt service problems.

Political Structure

Jordan is a constitutional monarchy. The current constitution, promulgated in 1952 during the brief reign of King Talal, gave increased authority to Parliament.

Nevertheless, ultimate authority over the legislative, executive, and judicial branches was retained by the monarch.

Executive power is primarily vested in the king. He appoints the prime minister and members of the cabinet and has the power to dismiss members of the cabinet. Power to dismiss the prime minister is vested in the Parliament. When the Parliament is suspended, the king assumes this responsibility. The king's considerable powers include the right to sign and promulgate laws, veto legislation, issue royal decrees (with the consent of the prime minister and four cabinet members), approve amendments to the constitution, command the armed forces, and declare war. In addition, he appoints and dismisses judges.

The question of royal succession is also addressed in the constitution. The throne is guaranteed through the eldest male in direct line from King Abdallah. Should there be no direct male heir, the eldest brother becomes king. On occasion, the king has altered this formula by decree. In 1965 Hussein changed the order of succession by removing from the line of succession the two sons he sired by marriage to an English woman. He also placed his more competent brother Hassan ahead of Muhammad, the second eldest brother. If a king is either a minor or incapacitated for more than four months, a regent or regency council is established.

The council of ministers is empowered to perform necessary operational matters in the absence of a royal decree. The council, which consists of the prime minister and a variable number of ministers, shares executive responsibilities with the monarch. The cabinet's area of responsibility includes all affairs of state in implementing the policies of the king and prime minister. Its members can be appointed and dismissed by the king, but the entire cabinet can be brought down by a vote of no confidence in the lower house of the legislature.

Under the constitution, Jordan has a bicameral national assembly. The lower house, known as the House of Representatives, is elected by popular vote. Since 1973 women have had the right to vote. Representatives are elected for four-year terms. Minority rights are protected. Since the 1928 constitution, Circassians have been guaranteed representation. The current constitution provides not only for Circassian but also Christian and bedouin representation. The sixty members of the lower house are elected from three bedouin districts and fourteen regular districts. Each bedouin district selects one representative from the local tribes. The other fifty-seven representatives are elected from the fourteen regular districts—seven on the West Bank and seven on the East Bank. Seats are distributed within these districts in order to guarantee representation by Christians and Circassians. In Amman, for instance, there are eight representatives—two Christians, one Circassian, and five Arab Muslims.

The upper house is called the Senate. This body is appointed by the king and cannot be more than one-half the size of the lower house. The prime minister originates legislation and submits proposals to the lower house. The approval of the Senate is necessary only when the lower house accepts a proprosal. Should only one of the houses of Parliament pass a bill, the two meet together to resolve their differences.

The loss of the West Bank in 1967 brought into question the representation of the residents of those areas in Parliament. The decision of the Arab states at

Rabat in 1974 giving the Palestine Liberation Organization sole responsibility for the destiny of the West Bank further clouded the future of West Bank representation in Parliament. Subsequently, King Hussein dissolved Parliament. This action appears to have been a result of his inability to challenge the Rabat decision and his unwillingness to accept it by organizing a purely East Bank Parliament.

By October 1983, King Hussein determined that circumstances had changed, and he announced his decision to recall Parliament. The Jordanians determined that it was in their best interest once again to increase their influence on the West Bank and to open the political system to Jordan's increasingly prosperous and well-educated society. Further delay in recalling Parliament, moreover, raised the possibility that a quorum could not be attained. As it was not possible to hold elections on the West Bank, the constitution had to be amended to permit elections for the East Bank and West Bank vacancies to be filled by a vote of Parliament. Parliament was reconvened in the spring of 1984 following bi-elections on the East Bank.

Jordan is divided into eight regional provinces, each administered by a governor who is appointed by the king. Loyalty to the monarch is the key element in each appointment. Five of the governorates—Amman, al-Balqa, Maan, Irbid, and Karak—are on the East Bank, and three—Jerusalem, Nablus, and Hebron—are on the West Bank. The governors have extensive local powers, including the right to void the election of a village mayor. This is important, for despite the extensive power of the central government and the governors, the village is the basic political unit for most Jordanians or, in the case of the bedouin, the tribe. Since independence, a major goal of the central government has been to enable the king to enhance his direct contact with the villagers. The government has had some success on the East Bank. On the West Bank, where much of the Jordanian bureaucracy was removed following the 1967 Arab-Israeli war and the remainder became associated with the Israeli military government, contact with the king has once again become the prerogative of the mayors, or *mukhtars* (headmen). The former Jordanian members of Parliament, governors, and officials on the West Bank have lost much influence. The mayors, in contrast, make visits to Amman and have direct contact with King Hussein and his ministers. Moreover, the mayors are recognized by the Israelis and other Arabs as the effective leaders of the West Bank.

There are three sources of law: Shari'a (Islamic law), European codes, and tradition. The Jordanian constitution and the Court Establishment Act of 1951 created a judiciary to reflect these sources of law. Three categories of courts were outlined in the constitution: regular civil courts, religious courts, and the special courts. The civil courts system, which is heavily based on Western law, has jurisdiction in all cases not specifically granted to the others. The religious court system has responsibility for personal status and communal endowment. Shari'a courts have responsibility for the Muslims, whereas the various Christian sects have their own councils. The special courts have responsibility for tribal questions and land issues. The king retains the right to appoint and dismiss judges and to pardon offenders.

Political Dynamics

Despite the trappings of constitutional democracy, true political power in Jordan rests with the king. His primary support comes from the army. The legislature is as powerful as the monarch allows it to be. Although there is little doubt that Hussein, as Abdallah before him, believes in the benefits of a more representative government, he continues to concentrate power in his own hands.

The Army

The role performed by the Jordanian army in the political arena would be difficult to overemphasize. Some authors have stated that Jordan was created by the army.[1] It has been recruited primarily from the East Bank Jordanian population, whose loyalty to the king has been beyond question. Only twice—in the mid-1950s confrontation with the Arab nationalists and in the 1970 clashes with the Palestinians—has the throne been seriously threatened. On each occasion, new and less-reliable elements had increased their influence within the army. The alteration in the composition of the armed forces made the army more susceptible to political pressures, which permitted antiregime elements to attempt to undermine the military's support for the king. Both attempts failed.

The Arab Legion, as created by the British, was a small elite corps composed primarily of tribal elements. These tribesmen were loyal to the king and supported Jordan's traditional close ties with the British. With the coming of the Palestine War of 1948, the narrowly recruited elite force had to be rapidly expanded. Increasingly large numbers of East Bank townspeople were brought into the army, including the anti-Hussein conspirator, Ali Abu Nuwar.

The changing composition of the armed forces was such that regional political influences came to have a significant impact on elements within the army. By the early 1950s, British power and influence were receding throughout the Middle East in the face of a rising tide of Arab nationalism. This nationalist sentiment, which developed a decidedly anti-European cast following the overthrow of the Egyptian monarchy, found many sympathetic ears in the Jordanian army. Some even blamed the Hashimites' close ties with the West as a key factor behind Jordanian and Arab military setbacks. As relations soured between the United States and Egypt over Cairo's purchase of Czechoslovakian arms and the U.S. failure to build the Aswan Dam, President Nasser's brand of Arab nationalism gained influence in Jordan at the expense of the British and Hashimite loyalists.

Pressure on Hussein to join the pro-Western, anticommunist Baghdad Pact came from London and Washington, and from his cousin, King Faysal, in Baghdad. Hussein was forced to determine whether his primary interest lay in allying more closely with the West or with the Arab nationalists and Nasser. Although the Baghdad Pact was widely denounced as a "tool of the West" and a form of "neocolonialism," Hussein, in late 1955, decided to maintain his ties with Britain and Iraq. Flying in the face of popular wishes and growing Arab nationalist influence in the army, his prime minister, Hazza al-Majali, announced in early December that Jordan intended to enter the alliance. Riots broke out in

Amman. After three days, order was restored by the Jordanian army, but the incident drove the young Hussein into the arms of the nationalists.

Jordan did not join the Baghdad Pact, al-Majali was replaced as prime minister, and, on March 1, 1956, General John Bagot Glubb (Glubb Pasha), commander of the Arab Legion, and his British staff were dismissed. The king attempted to ameliorate a hostile British reaction by emphasizing that he had made the decision on his own without pressure from the other Arab states, but such assertions were not convincing. Al-Majali had visited Syria, Saudi Arabia, and Egypt in the month prior to the dismissals, and these governments had encouraged Jordan to stay out of the Baghdad Pact.

The king, for his part, had made a daring move by aligning himself with the Arab nationalists. He was greatly influenced by the rising tide of Arab nationalist sentiment in the armed forces. Following Hussein's dismissal of the British, his popularity at home and throughout the Arab world was never higher. His move also appears to have been calculated to use this popularity to solidify his political position. To draw on this strength within the army, Hussein appointed a nationalist officer, Abu Nuwar, to command the army and to complete the transition. He officially changed the army's name to the Jordanian Arab Army.

Although the Arab nationalists both at home and abroad were supportive of the king's action, they were never loyal to him. The tenuous nature of his alliance became evident the following year. Believing that his destiny was more closely tied with the other Arabs than with the West, Hussein attended an Arab solidarity conference in January 1957. By an agreement signed at the conference, Egypt, Syria, and Saudi Arabia guaranteed the payment of a subsidy if Jordan terminated its relations with the British. In March the Jordanians abrogated their treaty with Britain, resulting in the withdrawal of the last British garrisons from Jordan and the termination of the British subsidy. Hussein's Arab allies, however, failed to replace his losses. (Saudi Arabia made one quarterly payment; Syria and Egypt contributed nothing.)

By cutting his ties with the British, Hussein had left the monarchy open to a direct challenge from the Arab nationalists. In April 1957 Abu Nuwar and a group of nationalist officers attempted to control the political process by vetoing the king's choice of prime minister. Some have termed Abu Nuwar's action an attempted coup. Hussein met the challenge by addressing his bedouin troops directly. They sided with him against the nationalists, forcing Abu Nuwar into exile. Henceforth, the influence of the Arab nationalists in the army was diminished.

With army loyalty ensured, the only internal group able to threaten the monarchy was the Palestinians. Until the mid-1960s, however, the Palestinians had almost no effective organization and little in the way of a political program. Convinced that they were powerless to regain their lost homeland by themselves, they were compelled to look to the Arab states as the only force capable of confronting Israel. As time went on without any apparent success, a few Palestinians began to assert that they must rely on themselves and that the struggle was theirs rather than that of the Arab states. In the early 1960s, some Palestinians began to organize into commando groups, such as al-Fatah and the

Popular Front for the Liberation of Palestine (PFLP). Although the commandoes launched a few generally ineffective raids into Israel, they failed to persuade the majority of Palestinians that the Palestinian people could achieve their goals without relying on the Arab states.

This attitude changed dramatically after the June 1967 Arab-Israeli war. Israel's humiliation of the Egyptian, Syrian, and Jordanian armies convinced most Palestinians not only that the Arab states were inept but also that they did not care about the Palestinians. The popularity of the commandos soared, and groups like al-Fatah had to turn away recruits. This growth in commando strength provided the Palestinians with a military force capable of challenging the Jordanian army. In addition, the loyalty of some elements of the army was questioned. After twenty years of Jordanian citizenship, many Palestinians had entered the military. The Palestinian percentage in the military did not equal their majority *status* in the general population and they were not in key positions, but the Palestinians nevertheless played a significant role.

As a result of the new Palestinian influence, combined with the devastating economic impact created by the loss of the West Bank, King Hussein faced the most serious crisis of his reign. More than half the population of the truncated Jordanian state was Palestinian. The army was discredited, but the prestige of the commandos was high: They were the heroes of the Palestinians. The commandos from the Jordanian territory made terrorist attacks, each raid enhancing the popular mystique of the guerrillas while leaving the Jordanian army to absorb the retaliatory blows of the Israeli Defense Forces. The Palestinians adopted a no-compromise attitude toward the Israelis and the Jordanians. They demanded that Jordan not interfere in their raids. When Jordanian authorities arrested a group of terrorists who had launched rockets against the Israeli port of Eilat, a threatened confrontation with the commandos forced their release.

More than any other incident, the battle of Karameh illustrated the rising tide of fedayeen popularity. In March 1968 the Israelis struck at the Karameh refugee camp on the East Bank of the Jordan, a key center for cross-river Palestinian raids. The Israelis severely damaged the village, but they were not able to intimidate the fedayeen. With the aid of Jordanian army resistance, the fedayeen stood and fought, inflicting numerous casualties upon the Israeli troops. Despite the crucial role of Jordanian artillery, the battle was widely viewed as a great victory for the commandos, in contrast to the previous failures of the army.

The overwhelming popularity of the fedayeen, particularly al-Fatah, enabled the guerrilla organizations to assume de facto control of Palestinian camps and neighborhoods throughout Jordan. With the military assistance and training provided by other Arab states, they virtually became a state within a state, challenging the sovereignty of the king. In November 1968, a three-day battle between the fedayeen and the army was the first in a series of clashes. Each concluded with some Jordanian concession to the Palestinians, for Hussein's greatest fear was that continued fighting could lead to civil war.

By the summer of 1970, an all-out confrontation between the monarchy (supported by the East Bank Jordanians) and the Palestinians seemed inevitable. The fedayeen appear to have made two serious tactical errors. The first was the alienation of the Jordan Arab Army, as a result of their having criticized the ability of its soldiers and their moral fiber. The disciplined Jordanian troops were subjected to taunts and insults, creating a large reservoir of ill will. These actions weakened support for the commandos even among the Palestinians in the military. Second, the Palestinians ignored the differences between Palestinian interests and those of the East Bank Jordanians. As a result, King Hussein had the large East Bank Jordanian population and the army clamoring for him to suppress the "arrogant" fedayeen.

The conflict came to a head in September 1970 (called "Black September" by Palestinian groups). For the next ten months the Jordanian army chipped away at Palestinian strongholds, ultimately destroying them. At times, such as in late September 1970, the fighting was very intense. Jordan's action alienated most of the other Arab states. Syria sent 200 tanks across the Jordanian border, but heavy losses, logistical difficulties, and the threat of Israeli intervention forced the Syrians to withdraw. Interestingly, although Baghdad strongly condemned Hussein, Iraqi forces in Jordan did not intervene. Libya broke relations and transferred its annual subsidy from the Hashimite government to the commandos. Kuwait ended its economic assistance. The bitterness toward the Jordanians led Palestinian nationalists to sever their ties to the Hashimites, who were widely considered, next to the Israelis, the greatest enemies of Palestinian nationalism. Despite the criticism of the other Arabs, Hussein's confrontation with the commandos was a tremendous victory for the monarchy. Thousands of Palestinian fighters fled or were killed or captured. The authority of the king, supported by the Jordanian army, was once again unchallengeable.

Political Parties

Political parties currently have little influence on the decisionmaking process. They have been officially banned since 1957. Prior to that time, King Hussein had allowed parties to function freely, with the hope that Jordan's government could develop into a constitutional monarchy. The Baath, Nationalist, Liberal, Communist, Muslim Brotherhood, and other parties were all active in the mid-1950s. The majority of these were ideological or sectarian, without a wide popular base. Many were antimonarchy.

As tensions rose in Jordan with the increasing influence of the Arab nationalists, the political parties criticized Jordan's pro-Western policies and, sometimes, the king. In 1956 the Arab nationalists won the parliamentary election. Their leader, Sulayman Nabulsi, a West Bank Palestinian, became prime minister. Nabulsi, who was closely associated with Abu Nuwar, pushed for greater ties with Nasser and other Arab nationalist states. When the nationalists overstepped the bounds of loyal opposition in 1957, conspiring with Abu Nuwar against the monarchy, the king exercised his power. He not only removed Nabulsi from power but banned all political parties as well.

The king has attempted to maintain at least the idea of popular representation despite the ban on political parties. Elections have been held periodically. Candidates are chosen by the government, however, thus limiting true popular representation. As a result, several other mechanisms have been created to make the government more responsive to the people. In 1971 the Jordanian National Union was established as the nation's sole authorized political organization. It failed to win widespread support, however, Democracy has not taken root, and Jordan remains a monarchy with only the thinnest veneer of representational government. Influence on the political process in Jordan, therefore, remains with those who can influence the king. Members of the ruling family, close advisers, traditional leaders, and, of course, the military continue to fill this role.

Foreign Policy

In the more than thirty years since independence, Jordan's relative influence in regional affairs has diminished. Whereas in 1950 Jordan was a regional power that could thwart the will of its fellow Arab states by annexing the West Bank, and the Hashimite monarchy could rival the Saudi monarchy, this is no longer the case. The decline has been the result of the diminution of the relative military strength of the Jordanian armed forces and of Jordan's economic base with the loss of the West Bank on the one hand, and the rise of other powers in the Arab world on the other. Consequently, Jordan's regional influence is less than before, and its foreign policy objectives have become increasingly limited.

In formulating its foreign policy, Jordan now finds itself more and more watchful of the policies of others. The preservation of the monarchy and the status of East Bank Jordanians appear to be its primary goals. Until the 1974 Rabat summit meeting, in which the Arab states recognized the Palestinian Liberation Organization as the representative of the Palestinian people, regaining the West Bank was of great importance. Since then, the Amman government has adopted a more ambivalent attitude. Some have even argued that regaining the West Bank would cause too many problems and therefore should not be attempted.

To achieve even its limited goals, Jordan necessarily seeks outside support from two principal sources—the West and other moderate Arabs. Jordan's Western connection originated in the mandate era and the close treaty ties between Britain and the kingdom following independence. As the British influence and ability to intercede in support of the monarchy declined, the United States replaced the United Kingdom as the principal Western ally. In spite of some differences with Washington and considerable criticism from other Arabs, King Hussein has maintained this relationship because it has been in Jordan's best interest. The West provided a needed subsidy, arms, and some political support. Finding another source of assistance appeared to require unacceptable changes in the Jordanian government.

The Jordanians have also had to seek support from the moderate Arabs. Whereas in the early 1950s the Jordanians were rivals of the Saudis, Amman has now become increasingly dependent on Saudi economic and political support. The economic support keeps the Jordanian economy afloat and helps purchase needed military equipment. The political support helps provide an umbrella from Jordan's sometimes tumultuous relations with its neighboring Baathist regimes in Syria and Iraq. In some respects, Jordan has become a buffer that protects the Arabian peninsula monarchy from the turmoil of the Fertile Crescent.

Despite the loss of influence and the decline in the military prowess of the Hashimite kingdom, the monarch and his East Bank supporters have displayed a remarkable willingness to tolerate abuse from fellow Arabs when it has been necesary to assert basic Jordanian interests. In 1970, for instance, the Jordanian army crushed the Palestinians and thwarted a Syrian invasion while ignoring the cries of fellow Arabs. Amman has also had to establish a working relationship with the Israelis because economic ties between East and West Bank Arabs have continued and the Jordanian Arab Army is no longer a match for the Israelis.

More recently, the Jordanians have continued their independent course even in the face of considerable opposition from Syria. The Jordanians have been ardent supporters of Damascus's arch rival, the Baathist regime in Baghdad. Similarly, the Jordanians are among the most effective supporters of the relatively moderate forces within the PLO, which are led by Yasir Arafat. Attempts to undermine Arafat have been strenuously opposed by the Jordanians. Using their influence, Amman has attempted to convince the Palestinians that their aspirations will be addressed only through negotiations with Israel. At the same time, King Hussein has displayed his willingness to break with the Arab consensus. This could never be more clearly illustrated than with his reestablishment of full diplomatic relations with Egypt, even though Cairo continued to adhere to the Camp David agreement and to maintain diplomatic relations with Israel.

Notes

1. P. J. Vatikiotis, *Politics and the Military in Jordan: A Study of the Arab Legion, 1921–1957* (London: Frank Cass & Co., 1967).

Bibliography

There are several good books on Jordan that offer a general understanding of history and government while providing a background for further study. Raphael Patai's *The Kingdom of Jordan* (Princeton, N.J.: Princeton University Press, 1958) and Ann Dearden's *Jordan* (London: Robert Hale, 1958) are now somewhat out of date, but they remain important doorways to an understanding of Jordan. Anne Sinai and Allen Pollack present a series of informative articles in *The Hashimite Kingdom of Jordan and the West Bank* (New York: American Academic Association for Peace in the Middle East, 1977). Owing to the wide range of topics and authors, however, coverage here is uneven. Nevertheless, many of the articles are excellent, and a great amount of information is available. A more recent work, *Jordan: Crossroads of Middle Eastern Events* (Boulder: Westview Press, 1983), by Peter Gubser, presents a brief but complete discussion of Jordanian society, economy, politics, and history. Though sympathetic to the Hashimites, this book is objectively analytical in approach.

Important sources of information about Jordan are the autobiographies and studies by British and Jordanian people who have contributed to the development of Jordan. Most notable are the memoirs of King Abdallah, *Memories of King Abdallah of Transjordan* (London: Jonathan Cape, 1950). Former commander of the armed forces, Glubb Pasha, has also written several books on Jordan. All contribute to a better understanding of the kingdom. In particular, *A Soldier with the Arabs* (New York: Harper, 1958) is a necessity if one is to truly appreciate the Jordanian army and its traditions. Former Arab Legion Commander Frederick G. Peake's (Peake Pasha) *A History of Jordan and Its Tribes* (Coral Gables: University of Miami Press, 1958) remains a classic discussion of the Jordanian tribes.

Scholars, too, have provided several excellent works on aspects of Jordanian history, politics, and society. In *Politics and the Military in Jordan: A Study of the Arab Legion, 1921–1957* (New York: Praeger Publishers, 1977), P. J. Vatikiotis analyzes the role of the military in creating and supporting the Hashimite regime. Reeva S. Simon, in his well-documented "The Hashemite Conspiracy: Hashemite Unity Attempts, 1921–1958," *International Journal of Middle East Studies* 5, no. 3 (1974), pp. 314–327, discusses the aspirations of the Hashimite regimes of Iraq and Jordan to establish a larger Arab state under their leadership. Detailed studies of social and political structure on the local level can be found in Richard T. Antown's *Arab Village: A Social Structural Study of a Transjordanian Peasant Community* (Bloomington: Indiana University Press, 1972) and Peter Gubser's *Politics and Change in al-Karak* (London: Oxford University Press, 1973). Gubser presents an excellent study of the function of political power at the local level. The author is a keen observer and offers detailed insight into the Jordanian political system. Finally, the most significant recent study is *Jordan: The Impact of Social Change on the Role of the Tribes*, Washington Paper No. 108 (New York: Praeger Publishers, 1984), by Paul A. Jureidini and R. D. McLawin. The main thesis of this book is that the tribes of Jordan, which have provided the principal pillar of support for the Hashimite Kingdom, are losing their cohesion and influence in contemporary Jordan. A shift in loyalty from the person of the king to the state is also occurring.

13

State of Israel

Bernard Reich

Israel is a product of Zionism (the Jewish national movement). Since biblical days, Jews of the Diaspora (Jewish communities outside Israel) have hoped that they would return to Zion, the "Promised Land." Over the centuries Zionism developed spiritual, religious, cultural, social, and historical concepts linking Jews to the land of the historical Jewish states in Israel. The political variant of Zionism that saw the establishment of a Jewish state as a logical consequence of Zionism developed in the nineteenth century partly as a result of political currents then prevalent in Europe, especially nationalism and anti-Semitism. There was also a revival of Zionism in Eastern Europe and Russia. Groups such as the "Return to Zion" movement, whose goal was immigration and settlement, were established to alleviate the problems of the Jewish communities in Europe through the development of settlements in Palestine.

Historical Background

In 1897 Theodor Herzl, a Viennese journalist who had proposed establishing a self-governing community for the Jewish people in his book *Der Judenstaat* (The Jewish State), organized a conference at Basle, Switzerland, to assemble prominent leaders from the major Jewish communities and organizations throughout the world. This assembly shaped a Zionist political movement and established the World Zionist Organization (WZO). The Basle Program, which became the cornerstone of Zionist ideology, enunciated the basic aim of Zionism: "to create for the Jewish people a home in Palestine secured by public law."

World War I enabled the Zionist movement to make important gains. The WZO had developed into an organized and worldwide movement. With the aid of Dr. Chaim Weizmann, a prominent Zionist leader and chemist who contributed to the British war effort, the Zionist organization secured the Balfour Declaration (1917) from the British government, stating that "his Majesty's Government view with favour the establishment in Palestine of a national home for the Jewish people." By the end of the war,

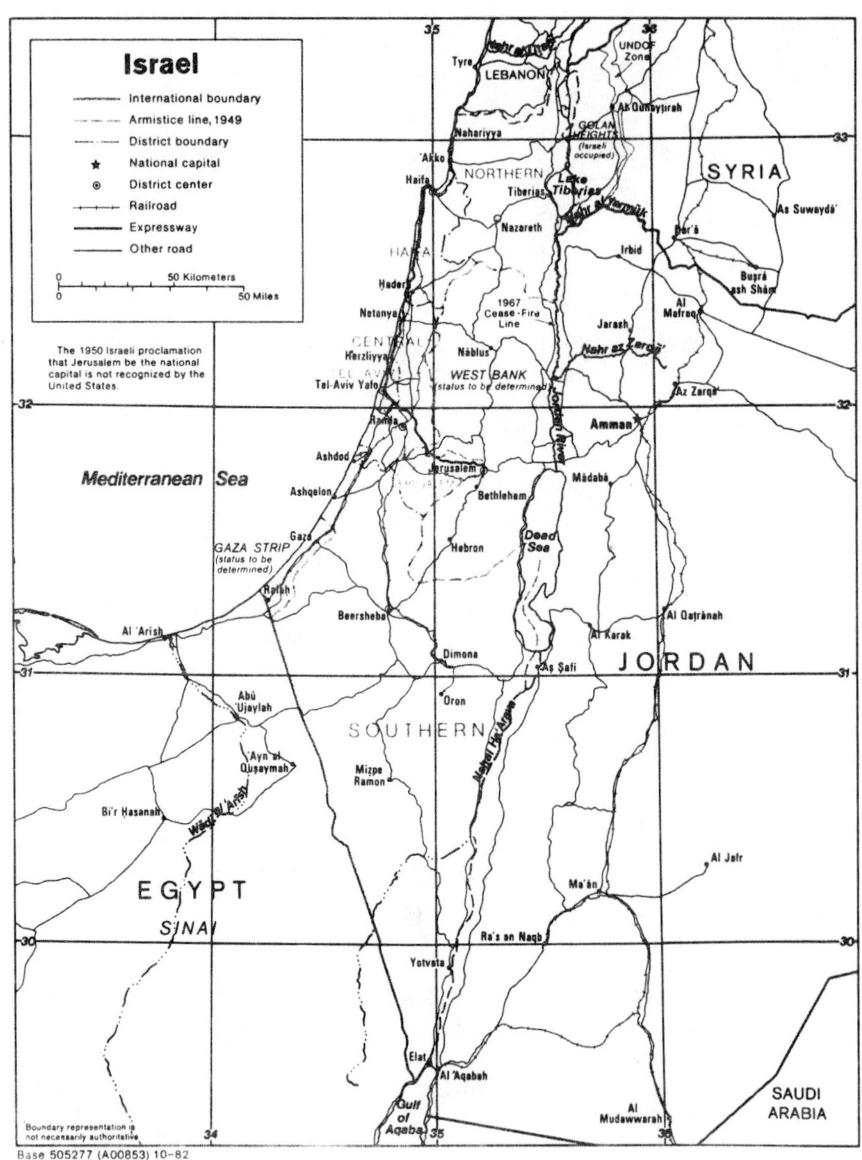
Israel
International boundary
Armistice line, 1949
District boundary
National capital
District center
Railroad
Expressway
Other road
50 Kilometers
50 Miles
The 1950 Israeli proclamation that Jerusalem be the national capital is not recognized by the United States.
Tyre
LEBANON
UNDOF Zone
GOLAN HEIGHTS (Israeli occupied)
Nahariyya
'Akko
Haifa
NORTHERN
Tiberias
Lake Tiberias
Nazareth
SYRIA
As Suwaydā'
Irbid
Hadera
Netanya
1967 Cease-Fire Line
Jarash
Al Mafraq
CENTRAL
Herzliyya
Nāblus
WEST BANK (status to be determined)
Tel-Aviv Yafo
Az Zarqā'
Amman
Jordan River
Ashdod
Jerusalem
Mediterranean Sea
Ashqelon
Bethlehem
Mādabā
Gaza
GAZA STRIP (status to be determined)
Hebron
Dead Sea
Rafah
Beersheba
Al Qaṭrānah
Al 'Arish
Al Karak
Dimona
Aş Şafi
JORDAN
Abū 'Ujaylah
Oron
SOUTHERN
'Ayn al Quşaymah
Mizpe Ramon
Bi'r Ḩasanah
Al Jafr
EGYPT
SINAI
Ma'ān
Ra's an Naqb
Yotvata
Elat
Al 'Aqabah
Gulf of Aqaba
Al Mudawwarah
SAUDI ARABIA
Boundary representation is not necessarily authoritative
Base 505277 (A00853) 10-82

British control had replaced Ottoman rule in Palestine. The Palestine mandate was allocated to Great Britain by the Allied Supreme Council on April 25, 1920, and was confirmed by the Council of the League of Nations on July 22, 1922. Between 1920 and the termination of the mandate in May 1948, British control of Palestine was exercised by a high commissioner and an executive council composed of senior British officials. Autonomous Arab and Jewish communal groups were established, and each was granted powers of self-government within the framework created by British Orders-in-Council and the regulations of the mandate system.

During the mandate period, the Jewish community in Palestine (Yishuv) established institutions for self-government and procedures for implementing political decisions. All significant Jewish groups belonged to the organized Jewish community with the exception of the ultra-orthodox Agudat Israel, which refused to participate. Agudat Israel opposed Zionist policies because of its belief that only by the hand of God, not man, could Israel be properly reestablished. By secret ballot the organized Jewish community chose the Assembly of the Elected (Asefat Hanevcharim) as its representative body. It met at least once a year, and between sessions its powers were exercised by the National Council (Vaad Leumi), which was elected by the assembly.

The mandatory government entrusted the National Council with the responsibility for Jewish communal affairs and granted it considerable autonomy. The executive committee of the National Council—through a number of self-created departments concerned with education, culture, health, social welfare, and religious affairs—acted as the administering power for the Jewish community. The council also controlled the clandestine recruitment and military training of Jewish youth in the defense force (Hagana), which after independence formed the core of Israel's defense forces. The General Federation of Labor (Histadrut), founded in 1920, coordinated labor-related matters and engaged in social welfare and economic endeavors. Political parties were established, and they contested the elections for the various political posts. The political elite filled several roles in the Zionist movement, the Hagana, and the Histadrut, and in other political institutions; it was also involved in relations with the British as the mandatory power and the promotion of Jewish immigration and settlement in Palestine.

Prototypical political institutions, founded and developed by and for the Jewish community, laid the foundation for many of Israel's public bodies and political processes. The party system was initiated, and proportional representation was instituted. Not only were procedures established and tried but, more important, the masses and the elite gained experience in the functioning of political institutions. Several of the semigovernmental organizations that were created (most notably the Histadrut and the Jewish Agency) continued to play important roles after Israel's independence. These contributed to the growth of a highly developed system of Zionist political parties and the consequential prevalence of coalition executive bodies in the Zionist movement and the local organs of Palestine Jewry.

The National Council functioned concurrently with the internationally recognized executive of the Jewish Agency for Palestine.[1] Weizmann, as president of the WZO, negotiated with leading representatives of Jewish organizations and communities throughout the world for their participation in the work of the Jewish Agency. In August 1929 these negotiations culminated in the establishment of a new body, the Jewish Agency for Palestine, popularly referred to as "the Expanded Jewish Agency." The agency included Jews and Jewish organizations sympathetic to the idea of a Jewish national home but not ideologically committed to Zionism. It took over the activities—such as fundraising and maintaining liaison with foreign governments—designed to build a national home in which concerned Jews everywhere could participate. The agency conducted negotiations with the Palestine mandatory government, the United Kingdom, and the League of Nations. It also sought accommodation with the Arabs but was unsuccessful.

Throughout much of the mandate period, the Jewish and Arab communities of Palestine were in conflict over the future of the territory. Unable to find a solution to satisfy these conflicting views, and because of the heavy cost in men and money, the British conceded that the mandate was unworkable and turned the problem over to the United Nations, which placed the Palestine issue before its General Assembly in April 1947. The United Nations Special Committee on Palestine (UNSCOP) was created to examine the issues and to submit proposals for the solution to the problem. The committee recommended that the mandate be terminated and that the independence of Palestine be achieved without delay; however, it was divided over the future of the territory. The majority recommended partition into a Jewish state and an Arab state linked in an economic union, with Jerusalem and its environs established as an international enclave. The minority recommended that Palestine become a single federal state, with Jerusalem the capital, and with Jews and Arabs enjoying autonomy in their respective areas. On November 29, 1947, the United Nations General Assembly adopted the majority recommendation (the Partition Plan) over Arab opposition (they favored the minority report) by 33 votes to 13, with 10 abstentions.

The situation in Palestine deteriorated rapidly. Disorders reminiscent of those of the 1920s and 1930s broke out in all parts of the country. As the end of the mandate approached, these degenerated into a virtual civil war. Israel declared its independence on May 14, 1948, and General Sir Alan Gordon Cunningham, the last British high commissioner, departed. Armies of the Arab states entered Palestine and engaged in open warfare with the defense forces of the new state. The United Nations secured a truce, and the military situation was stabilized in 1949 by a series of armistice agreements between Israel and the neighboring Arab states. The United Nations Truce Supervision Organization (UNTSO) was established to oversee the armistice. No general peace settlement was achieved.

The provisional government of Israel, which was formed at the time of independence and recognized by the major powers, was new in name only. It had begun to function de facto following adoption of the partition resolution, and it drew on the experience gained by the Jewish community in Palestine during the mandatory period. Shortly after the partition vote, the United Nations established a Palestine commission to effect a transfer from the mandatory power to the proposed Arab and Jewish states. That commission had to work exclusively with the Jewish community because neither the Arabs nor the British would cooperate. As early as March 1948 a temporary National Council of State, chosen from the National Council and Jewish Agency Executive, assumed control in many areas. On May 14, the new provisional government proclaimed Israel's independence, repealed the British mandatory restrictions on immigration and the sale of land, and converted the Hagana into the Israel Defense Forces (IDF).

The provisional government had three elements: a state council that acted as parliament; a cabinet elected by the state council from among its members; and a president elected by the state council. David Ben Gurion, chairman of the Jewish Agency and leader of the dominant political party, Mapai (Israel Labor party), was selected as prime minister and minister of defense and Chaim Weizmann was elected president. The National Council of the mandate period formed the basis of the state council; the executive of the National Council became the cabinet; and the presidency was entirely new. The provisional government directed the war against the Arab states, levied taxes, established administrative agencies, and conducted essential public services. It functioned from May 14, 1948, until early 1949. At its session just prior to the national elections of January 25, 1949, the state council adopted a transition ordinance transferring its authority to a constituent assembly and convened on February 14, 1949. That assembly, which later declared itself the First Knesset (Parliament), was a unicameral chamber composed of 120 members representing 12 of the 24 parties that contested the January 1949 elections.

Political Environment

Israel's special role as the world's only Jewish state has had a manifold effect on its political system. Israel is concerned that all Jews who wish to immigrate are free to do so and is interested in the well-being of Jews everywhere. The encouragement of Jewish immigration has left its mark on every aspect of Israeli life. The commitment to unfettered Jewish immigration was articulated initially in Israel's Declaration of Independence, which proclaimed that "the State of Israel will be open to the immigration of Jews from all countries of their dispersion." It was reaffirmed in the Law of Return of July 5, 1950 (which provided that "every Jew has the right to come to this country as an 'oleh' [Jew immigrating to Israel]") and has been reinforced by the programs and actions of successive Israeli governments. Encouraging the ingathering of exiles has received overwhelming support in Parliament and from the Jewish population, and it has been implemented almost without regard to the economic costs and social dislocations caused by the rapid and massive influx of people.

Israel's commitment to immigration results from its view of its mission as the emissary of the exiled and scattered Jewish people—it is an outward expression of a bond of faith between Israel and world Jewry. It removes Jews from areas of distress and thus serves to meet the needs of world Jewry. Immigration serves Israel's needs by providing the manpower necessary for Israel's security and development.

Several problems, some of them highly significant, have resulted from this policy. Unlike the period of the mandate when immigration was selective and severely limited by British-imposed restrictions, Israel has admitted whole communities virtually without regard to their economic usefulness or its own absorptive capacity. Initially the immigrants were the remnants of European Jewry; but during the nascent years of Israel's independence, the Jewish communities of Muslim states of the Middle East and North Africa arrived in large numbers. The Jews of Yemen (about 45,000) and Iraq (about 123,000) were brought to Israel by airlifts, popularly known as "Operation Magic Carpet" and "Operation Ali Baba." Between 1919 and 1948, about 90 percent of the Jewish immigrants came from Europe or other Western countries. Since 1948, immigration has been overwhelmingly non-Western (see Table 13.1).

After the Six-Day War in 1967, immigrants again came mainly from the West and the Soviet Union. But Jewish immigration has been declining since the early 1970s and in recent years has exceeded emigration only slightly. This decline has resulted from a number of factors, including a waning Zionist ideology and the decrease in Israel's attraction for immigrants given the problems posed by security and difficult economic conditions. Few large sources of immigration are left, and the Soviet Union's Jewish community remains unable to depart. Nevertheless, in late 1984 and early 1985 a massive airlift brought thousands of Falashas (Jews of Ethiopia) to Israel in a complicated effort known as Operation Moses.

Geographically and demographically, Israel is an Oriental country; culturally, socially, and politically it is Western in nature and orientation. The early Zionists laid the foundations for an essentially European culture in Palestine and subsequent immigration accelerated the trend of Westernization. The Occidental immigrants developed the Yishuv structure of land settlement, trade unions, political parties, and education in preparation for a Jewish national state that was Western in orientation. Future immigrants had to adapt themselves to a society that had formed these institutions, and this presented a problem for those who were part of the immigration from non-Western countries.

Massive immigration of Jews from the states of the Middle East and other parts of Asia and Africa has resulted in an influx of large numbers of people whose societal and cultural traditions are akin to the Oriental populations among whom they lived for generations, and different from those of their Western co-religionists. Their customs, practices, and attitudes are those of the East rather than the West. Family loyalty is strong; concepts of responsibility very often do not transcend the family. Suspicion of government and all of its ramifications is great; resistance to taxation, rationing, and other controls is prevalent. Partially because of their lack of

TABLE 13.1 Immigration to Israel

Period	Total	Last Continent of Residence				
		Asia	Africa	Europe	America & Oceania	Not Known
1919–1948[a]	482,857[b]	40,895	4,041	377,381	7,754	22,235
1948–1951[c]	686,739	237,352	93,951	326,786	5,140	23,510
1952–1954	54,065	13,238	27,897	9,748	2,971	211
1955–1957	164,936	8,801	103,846	48,616	3,632	41
1958–1960	75,487	13,247	13,921	44,595	3,625	99
1961–1964	228,046	19,525	115,876	77,537	14,841	267
1965–1968	81,337	15,018	25,394	31,638	9,274	13
1969–1971	116,484	19,700	12,065	50,558	33,891	270
1972–1974	142,755	6,347	6,821	102,763	26,775	49
1975–1979	124,827	11,793	6,029	77,167	29,293	545
1980–1982	46,750	5,368	3,732	23,869	13,596	185

[a]Up to May 14, 1948

[b]Includes about 11,000 illegal immigrants and about 19,500 tourists who remained in Israel

[c]From May 15, 1948

Source: Israel, Central Bureau of Statistics, *Statistical Abstract of Israel 1983,* no. 34 (Jerusalem, 1983), pp. 137–138.

education and experience, relatively few members of the Oriental community have succeeded in achieving responsible government posts, although the numbers are growing. Their living conditions and standards are generally lower than those of the Occidental community, and a relatively small proportion attend Israel's universities.

Numerous difficulties have beset efforts to settle and absorb the masses of immigrants. Economic, social, and cultural assimilation of the immigrants in a short span of time would have been a formidable undertaking for a small country even under the most favorable conditions. In Israel, this has been attempted despite the obstacles posed by limited resources, defense needs, and the composition and character of the new immigration. Israel has been obliged to undertake the training or retraining of the immigrants for gainful employment and to provide housing, schooling, and medical facilities. Although the material problems have not yet been fully solved, they are well defined, and manifold activities are directed toward their solution.

The nonmaterial problems, which are essentially those of cultural and social acclimation, are more complex and their resolution will require time. Although the basic religious tradition of the Jewish population is an asset because it provides a common core of values and ideals, there are major differences in outlook, values, frames of reference, levels of aspiration, and various other social and cultural components. Army service, which emphasizes education as well as the experience of common living and working and of learning the Hebrew language, facilitates acculturation and encourages evolution in the direction of a unified, multicultural society. Despite these efforts, the full integration of immigrants into Israel's society remains the state's greatest social problem.

The Arabs of Israel (i.e., those who have lived in Israel since its independence, or their offspring, and who are Israeli citizens and not the Arabs in those areas occupied by Israel during the June War) are confronted by problems qualitatively different from those facing Jewish immigrants. Following Israel's independence, and as a result of the ensuing war between Israel and the Arab states, a large number of Arabs who had lived in the part of Palestine that is now Israel fled and took up residence in Arab states, either as refugees or members of their permanent populations. The Arabs who chose to remain in Israel—and who numbered about 700,000 in 1985—form Israel's Arab community.

After the 1949 armistice agreements, activities of the Arab community were regarded primarily as concerns of Israel's security system, and most of the areas inhabited by the Arabs were placed under military control. A military government was established in these districts, and special defense and security zones were created. Israel's Arabs were granted citizenship with full legal equality but were forbidden to travel into or out of security areas without permission from the military. Military courts were established in which trials could be held in closed session. With the consent of the minister of defense, the military commanders could limit individual movements, impose restrictions on employment and business, issue deportation orders, search and seize, and detain a person if it were deemed necessary for security purposes.

Those who argued in support of the military administration saw it as a means of controlling the Arab population and preventing infiltration, sabotage, and espionage. Furthermore, it was contended that the very existence of the military administration was an important deterrent measure. As evidence developed that the Israeli Arabs were not disloyal, pressure for relaxation and then for total abolition of military restrictions grew in the Knesset and in public debate. The restrictions were gradually modified, and on December 1, 1966, military government was abolished. Functions that had been exercised by the military government were transferred to relevant civilian authorities.

The major long-term problem for Israel's Arab minority is its social integration. Although Israeli Arabs vote, sit in the Knesset, serve in government offices, have their own schools and courts, and prosper materially, they face difficulties in adjusting to Israel's modern Jewish- and Western-oriented society. Most of the major factors facilitating Jewish integration are not operative with regard to the Arab minority. The Arabs tend to live in separate villages and in separate sections of the major cities. They speak Arabic, attend a separate school system, and do not serve in the army. Centuries of foreign control have had their effect on the basic political attitudes of the Arabs—despotic rule, violence, and extortion have engendered an attitude of suspicion and mistrust toward government.

The Arab and Jewish communities in Israel have few points of contact, and those that exist are not intimate; they are separate societies that generally continue to hold stereotypical images of each other—images often reinforced by the schools, the media, social distance, and, most significant, by the tensions and problems created by the larger Arab-Israeli conflict in its numerous dimensions. There is mutual suspicion and antagonism, and there is still a Jewish fear of the Arabs—a result of wars and terrorism.

Successive Israeli governments have sought to bring about a more complete integration of its Arab citizens into the life of the country and to foster their economic, social, and cultural advancement. However, the problem is complex and continuing efforts are needed.

Over time the Arab community has become increasingly politicized. Israel's Arab population has long enjoyed legal equality, has participated in parliamentary elections and in local government, and has had its own state-supported educational and religious institutions. But below the surface equanimity, Israeli Arabs were discontented with a perceived second-class status resulting from various forms of unofficial discrimination. In the wake of the October War and with the increased international standing of the Palestine Liberation Organization (PLO) and the emphasis on Palestinian participation in the efforts to resolve the Arab-Israeli conflict, the Arabs of Israel seemed to become more restive and more politically aware. In the spring of 1976, Israel's Arabs participated in their first general protest and staged the most violent demonstrations in Israel's history. The riots, whose extent and ferocity surprised both Israeli Arabs and Jews, grew out of a general strike, centered in Nazareth, that was organized to protest land expropriations in Israel's northern section. The government had adopted a five-year plan to increase the number of Jewish settlers in Galilee and had expropriated lands, some of which were Arab-owned. The Arabs protested that, despite compensation, their land should not be expropriated to provide land for Jewish settlers. The expropriation served as a catalyst; the initial demonstrations escalated and eventually became broader and more general in their focus, incorporating complaints about Arab second-class status and adding other issues to the list of grievances.

Although there has been growing political action among Israel's Arabs, they still remain relatively inactive. They have failed to form a significant independent Arab political party that could appeal to the Arab voter, represent the Arab minority in the quest for Arab rights, and express its opinions and views. Given the absence of important Arab political parties, the Communist party in its various incarnations has played an important role in the articulation of the Arab perspective and in promoting Arab positions. No Arab leaders of national stature have appeared on the scene, although some local leaders are relatively well known nationally. Despite increased political awareness and activism, the Arabs have failed to organize on a mass communal basis to improve their position and status. The Arab issue has been of little prominence on the political scene; there has been little ethnic strife between the Arab minority and the Jewish majority. Social and political improvements do seem to have facilitated political organization and political action, and have raised expectations and stimulated further political demands. Nevertheless, it is uncertain whether the political quiescence that has characterized Israel's Arabs will continue, in light of their growing political awareness.

Religion and the State

Israel's Jewishness is a basic element underlying its political system. However, the overwhelmingly Jewish character of the state ensures agreement neither on the appropriate relationship between religion and the state, on that between the religious and secular authorities, nor on the methods and techniques to be employed by religious authorities. Since independence, Israel has had to come to terms with the concept of its "Jewishness" and the definition of "who is a Jew," and thus it has had to address the question of the roles to be played by religious forces and movements within the state. The conflict between secular and religious perspectives on these and related matters has been a continuing characteristic of Israel. One faction insists on the primacy and enshrinement of Jewish religious values while the other seeks to focus on more secular themes, thus limiting the role of religion in the state. A large group remains uncommitted. A compromise among these views has characterized the situation since Israel's independence.

"Who is a Jew" has been at the center of a religion-state controversy in Israel and has had theological, political, and ideological overtones with specific practical dimensions. Secular and religious authorities and ordinary citizens have faced the question in connection with issues of immigration, marriage, divorce, inheritance, and conversion as well as in matters related to registration to secure identity cards and in the official collection of data and information. The question relates to the application of laws such as the Law of Return, the Nationality Law, and others passed by the Parliament, as well as those relating to marriage and divorce and their interpretation by secular and religious authorities. As a result, it has become essential to determine who is a Jew and to decide who would make such a determination, utilizing which criteria. Over time a number of celebrated instances relating to this question have arisen.

Although Israel's government is secular, it takes into account the requisites of that segment of the population that observes religious tradition. The Ministry of Religious Affairs is concerned with meeting Jewish religious requirements, such as the supply of ritually killed (kosher) meat, rabbinical courts, and religious schools (Yeshivot), as well as with meeting the religious needs of the non-Jewish communities that enjoy religious autonomy. These functions are noncontroversial; few dispute the duty of the government to meet the religious requirements of the people. Nevertheless, there is sharp and recurrent controversy concerning the extent to which religious observance or restriction is directly or indirectly imposed on the entire Jewish population. The observant community, through its own political parties and through its membership in government coalitions, has been able to secure government agreement to establish separate school systems, to exempt their young women from army service, and to curtail almost all business and public activity on the Sabbath. Thus, the less observant Jews of Israel often argue that they do not possess religious freedom because of governmental acquiescence to demands of the observant Jewish groups, such as restriction of public services on the Sabbath and the limitations placed on the role of non-Orthodox Judaism in Israel.

Israel utilizes a modified millet system derived from the period of Ottoman control. The various religious communities and religious authorities exercise jurisdiction in litigation involving personal status and family law, and apply religious codes and principles in their own judicial institutions. Matters that are secular concerns in other states often are within the purview of religious authorities; even though there is no established religion, all religious institutions have a special status and authority granted by the state and are supported by state funds.

The political reality of Israel has required coalition governments from the outset. That same reality has necessitated inclusion of political parties of the religious community in virtually all cabinets as coalition partners that have control of the Ministry of Religious Affairs and usually also of the Ministry of the Interior. As a consequence, the religious parties have been given substantial political power and, hence, the ability to enforce many of their demands and perspectives concerning the role of religion in the Jewish state. As a further consequence, state support of religious authority, including the maintenance of the Sabbath and Jewish dietary restrictions, have become a feature of the state, as have numerous other factors of a more minor nature. As a result of cabinet participation and control of important ministries, the religious minority has been able to exert significant influence on the nature, functioning, and decisionmaking of the system. The religious parties became particularly prominent following the accession to office of Menachem Begin and the Likud in 1977, and the coalition agreements by which the 1977 and 1981 governments were established reflected the desire and ability of the religious parties to press for substantial concessions. The role of religion in Israel's everyday life clearly remains a major social and political issue.

Economic Conditions

Israel's economy has undergone substantial change since independence, and the economic well-being of its people has improved significantly. Israel remains something of an economic "miracle" belying the pre-independence prophecies that its troubled economy could not long endure. Instead, this country, virtually bereft of natural resources and faced with substantial burdens imposed by massive immigration and by Arab hostility, had achieved a relatively prosperous economic level by the 1980s. The standard of living in Israel and the productivity of its labor force are comparable to those in such West European countries as Italy and the United Kingdom; its life-expectancy levels are among the highest in the world; and it has maintained extensive social service for its population. These achievements are matched by similar statistics in other sectors.

Israel's small size (about 20,700 square kilometers, or 8,000 square miles) and lack of mineral and water resources profoundly affect its economy. The lack of domestic energy resources makes its economy sensitive to international oil developments—a dependence exacerbated in the late 1970s, when Israel returned the oil fields in Sinai and offshore in the Gulf of Suez to Egypt (Israel had been the main party responsible for developing oil fields) and had to resume purchasing large quantities of oil on the world market. Since 1979 Israel's oil imports have contributed significantly to its large balance-of-payments deficit, with oil imports costing more than US$1 billion a year.

Extensive irrigation and intensive farming methods have dramatically increased agricultural production for both domestic consumption and export. The amounts of irrigated land and of agricultural exports rose substantially between 1948 and the 1980s. Agricultural exports, though still substantial, have accounted for a declining percentage of total exports as Israel has developed its industrial base.

Some of Israel's achievements, particularly in the area of industrial development, can be traced to a significant investment program financed from outside sources, including U.S. government aid (both loans and grants), the sale of Israeli bonds, investments, and German reparations and restitution payments. At the same time, donations from the world Jewish community in support of Israel-based philanthropies have helped reduce the government's burdens in the social-welfare sector, thereby permitting the use of scarce funds for economic projects. This capital inflow has been complemented by an efficient economic machinery utilizing new industrial techniques and Israel's substantial and well-endowed human-resource base.

The various methods of raising capital have permitted Israel to pursue a policy of rapid economic and demographic expansion despite the lack of natural resources. Israel has maintained growth rates in real gross national product (GNP) exceeding 9 percent for prolonged periods. From 1950 to 1972, real output grew at an average annual rate of nearly 10 percent, and output per worker more than tripled.

During the initial twenty-five years, the state and its citizens undertook massive housing construction, built new towns, established new agricultural settlements, developed a modern agricultural system, modernized industry, constructed a national road network, and created a new economic and social infrastructure. A social-welfare system to include government aid for the disadvantaged as well as education and health schemes were created. These developments occurred despite the allocation of substantial resources to defense.

The rapid increase in population and economic output has been accompanied by significant increases in the standard of living. Real per capita income has increased steadily since 1948 and in 1984 was equivalent to approximately US$5,500. Government expenditures have consumed a large portion of the GNP, and in 1978 the government received in taxes nearly one-half of the total GNP. Yet even this high level of tax revenue was insufficient to fund the budget, requiring the government to finance the deficit by borrowing from Israel's central bank—in effect printing money, an inflationary activity. Israel has had double-digit inflation since at least the 1970s, and triple-digit inflation began in 1979. In 1980 inflation was 131 percent; in 1982, 120.4 percent; and in 1983, 145.6 percent. At the time of the July 1984 Knesset elections, the inflation level was estimated at a 400 percent annual rate.

Government-sector demand has been high in recent years, despite attempts by a succession of finance ministers to implement austerity plans, and private demand has also been substantial. The results include high inflation; large deficits in the current account, with Israel importing more goods and services than it exports; and constant devaluations of the local currency (originally the pound, or lira, and now the shekel). All in all, foreign capital inflows have allowed Israel to "live beyond its means."

During the Labor party's domination of Israel's political life from independence until 1977, socialist and economic policies, pursued in a mixed economy, were adapted to the special circumstances of Israel. The government played a central and decisive role in the economy, aided by semigovernmental institutions such as the Jewish Agency, the United Israel Appeal, the Jewish National Fund, and the Histadrut. The government owned and operated the railroads, the postal service, and the telephone, telegraph, and broadcasting facilities in addition to the usual government public works such as road and irrigation projects; there was also substantial government investment in public corporations in areas such as oil, electricity, and fertilizers.

The system was altered in 1977, when the Likud government came to power. By October of that year, the Likud government was ready to inaugurate its new economic plan, which sought to modify substantially the existing socialist system and to replace it with a free-enterprise approach. The goal was to check inflation, cut the foreign trade deficit, raise the growth rate, and promote foreign investment. The new economic policy would also remove some of the vast bureaucratic holds on the economy and some of the government-imposed controls instituted over the previous three decades. Virtually all foreign currency regulations were eliminated, and arbitrary exchange rates for the Israeli pound were abandoned, leaving it to find its own level on international exchanges. The pound continued to depreciate, and its devaluation was expected to promote a flow of dollars and other foreign currency into the country. A new value-added tax of 12 percent was also imposed. It was hoped that these new policies would increase exports by making Israeli products less expensive and decrease imports (and consumption generally) by making imports more expensive, by leaving less money in the hands of the Israeli consumer, and by encouraging greater productivity. The overall goal was to eliminate the government from the economy and to apply free-market principles. Although there were important changes in the economy, the basic problems remained and, in some instances, grew.

The 1984 Knesset election campaign focused substantial attention on Israel's economic situation, and the economy became an early priority for the national unity government installed in September 1984. In its basic guidelines presented to and approved by the Parliament, the new government pledged to reduce the balance-of-payments deficit, check inflation, renew economic growth while maintaining full employment, strengthen the export and productive sectors of the economy, and reduce the proportion of public and administration services. To achieve these goals the government noted that it would reduce public, civilian, and defense expenditures and curb private consumption. It would also seek a variety of other objectives, including increased national saving and taxation system reform. It pledged itself to expand the infrastructure to service and promote high-technology enterprises; to bolster agriculture and agricultural exports; to encourage tourism; and to provide housing for new immigrants, younger Israelis, and large families.

In keeping with its stated policies, the government soon instituted an austerity plan that included cuts in military expenditures, increases in taxes, charges for public services, and reductions in food subsidies. Arrangements were also concluded for initial freezes in wages and prices, and a temporary ban on imports of luxury products was instituted. The new government took the problem seriously and launched a series of steps to respond to the economy's various problem areas.

Israel continues to face balance-of-payments, inflation, and debt-management difficulties in its economy, largely as a result of the country's strong commitment to security. The demands of Israel's defense sector are a major element in its economic concerns. The continuation of the Arab-Israeli conflict and the consequent security requirements imposed by Arab hostility have necessitated large and continuous defense expenditures that have imposed a substantial burden.

In recent years Israelis have become more aware of economic issues and there seemed to be little confidence that the government, or its potential successors, could deal effectively with the crucial economic problems facing the country. At the same time, because the average Israeli was well insulated from the effects of poor economic management thanks to a widespread system of indexing, inflation, unemployment, and trade deficits were subjects for academic discussion rather than everyday concerns of the population. The Israeli economy has been in trouble, but the Israelis' economic well-being was barely affected—at least as the Israelis perceived it. Many Israelis did not see much difference between the economic policies and programs of Labor (socialism) and Likud (capitalism), despite the ideological differences each sought to portray. A major test for future Israeli governments will be their ability to create public awareness of the problems facing the country and to gain public confidence in their ability to deal effectively with the salient economic issues.

Political Structure

Constitutional Consensus

Israel's system of government is based on an unwritten constitution. The first legislative act of the Constituent Assembly in February 1949 was to enact a "Transition Law" (Small Constitution) that became the basis of constitutional life in the state. Administrative and executive procedures were based on a combination of past experience in self-government, elements adapted from the former mandatory structure, and new legislation. According to the Small Constitution, Israel was established as a republic with a weak president and a strong cabinet and Parliament. It was anticipated that this document would be replaced in due course by a more extensive one.

The First Knesset devoted much time to a profound discussion of the constitutional issue. The major debate was between those who favored a written constitution and those who believed that the time was not appropriate for imposing rigid constitutional limitations. The latter group argued that a written constitution could not be framed because of constantly changing social conditions resulting from mass immigration and a lack of experience with independent governmental institutions. There was also concern about the relationship between state and religion and the method of incorporating the precepts and ideals of Judaism into the proposed document.

The discussion of these issues continued for over a year and on June 13, 1950, the Knesset adopted a compromise that has indefinitely postponed the real issue. It was decided in principle that a written constitution would ultimately be adopted, but that for the time being there would not be a formal and comprehensive document. Instead, a number of fundamental or basic laws would be passed dealing with specific subjects, which may in time form chapters in a consolidated constitution. By 1985 Israel had adopted eight Basic Laws dealing with various subjects: The Knesset (1958); The Lands of Israel (1960); The President (1964); The Government (1968); The State Economy (1975); The Army (1976); Jerusalem, The Capital of Israel (1980); and The Judiciary (1984). The Basic Laws provide a definitive perspective of the formal requirements of the system in each specific area of activity, thereby providing a framework for governmental action.

Several areas of consensus, together with the extant fundamental laws, define the parameters of Israel's political system. Those disavowing allegiance to these Jewish-Zionist ideals constitute little more than protest groups. Israel's self-definition as a Jewish state is perhaps the most significant area of agreement, although there is a divergence of views on some of its tenets, their interpretation, and their implementation. Accord centers on the goals or purposes of Israel, such as the "ingathering of the exiles." Consensus has also been reached on the principle that Israel should be a social-welfare state in which all share in the benefits of society and have access to essential social, health, and similar services, although there are conflicting views regarding the scope and method of implementation of this principle. Foreign and security policy constitutes another area enjoying wide consensus because of its overriding importance in light of continuing Arab hostility and the resultant conflict, although there is discord concerning methods and techniques of implementation of agreed goals.

Political Institutions

The president, the government (cabinet), and the Knesset perform the basic political functions of the state within the framework provided by Israel's constitutional consensus.

The president is elected by the Knesset for a five-year term and may be reelected for no more than two consecutive terms. He is head of state, and his powers and functions are essentially those of a representative character. In the sphere of foreign affairs these include signing instruments that relate to treaties ratified by the Knesset, appointing diplomatic and consular representatives, receiving foreign diplomatic representatives, and issuing consular *exequaturs.* In the domestic sphere, he has the power to grant pardons and reprieves and to commute sentences. Subsequent to nomination by the appropriate body, he appoints judges, *dayanim* (judges of Jewish religious courts), *qadis* (judges of Muslim religious courts), the state comptroller, the president of the Magen David Adom Association (Red Shield of David—Israel's Red Cross), and the governor of the Bank of Israel, as well as other officials as determined by law. He signs all laws passed by the Knesset, with the exception of those relating to presidential powers, and all documents to which the state seal is affixed. Official documents signed by the president require the countersignature of the prime minister or other duly authorized minister, with the exception of those for which another procedure is laid down, as in the case of the judges.

The president's powers and functions relating to the formation of the government fall into a different category. After consultation with representatives of the parties in the Parliament, the president selects a member of the Knesset to form a government. Although anyone may be chosen, traditionally the member has been the leader of the largest party in the Knesset. Until now this formal discretion has not been accompanied by any real choice because the political composition of the Knesset has clearly determined the selection. Nevertheless, situations are conceivable in which different party combinations might gain the support of the Knesset. Were this to occur, the president would fulfill a crucial political role in determining the person chosen to form a cabinet. The president also receives the resignation of the government. Another aspect of the presidential role that could have considerable political significance is his public position—his visits throughout the country, his speeches, and his formal opening of the first session of each Knesset.

The member of Parliament entrusted by the president with the task of forming the government establishes a cabinet, generally with himself as prime minister and a number of ministers who are usually, but not necessarily, members of the Knesset. The government is constitutionally instituted upon obtaining a vote of confidence from the Parliament. The cabinet is collectively responsible to the Knesset, reports to it, and remains in office as long as it enjoys the confidence of that body. A government's tenure may also be terminated by ending the Knesset's tenure, by the resignation of the government on its own initiative, or by the resignation of the prime minister.

The Knesset is the supreme authority in the state. It is a unicameral body of 120 members elected by national, general, secret, direct, equal, and proportional suffrage for a term not to exceed four years. Voters cast their ballots for parties, rather than individual candidates, although each party presents the voter with a list of up to 120 names—its choices for Knesset seats. After ballots are cast, seats in the Knesset are determined. Those party lists that have received at least 1 percent of the total number of valid votes cast can be represented in the Knesset. Any list failing to obtain this minimum of 1 percent does not share in the distribution of mandates, and its votes are not taken into account when determining the composition of the Knesset. The distribution of seats among the party lists is determined by dividing the number of valid votes obtained by all the lists that secured the minimum percentage (1 percent) by the number of Knesset members (120), and the result is set as the quota for each Knesset seat. Each list receives the nearest whole number of seats thus determined, and the remaining seats are allocated by a complicated formula that generally benefits the larger parties, under the terms of the Bader-Ofer Amendment of 1973.

The main functions of the Knesset are similar to those of most modern parliaments. They include expressing a vote of confidence or no-confidence in the government, legislating, participating in the formation of national policy, and supervising the activities of the governmental administration. The Knesset must also approve the budget and taxation, elect the president of the state, recommend the appointment of the state comptroller, and participate in the appointment of judges. It is divided into a number of committees, each responsible for a specific area of legislation. Many of the Knesset's activities are performed in these committees. With some minor exceptions the ratio of committee memberships is generally proportional to that of the party's representation in the Knesset as a whole.

Judicial authority is vested in religious as well as civil courts. The latter include municipal and magistrates' courts for civil and criminal actions, district courts for appeals from the lower tribunals and matters beyond the jurisdiction of a magistrate, and the Supreme Court. The Supreme Court cannot review legislation passed by the Knesset, but it has the power to invalidate administrative actions and interpret statutes it regards contrary to the law. Each major community has its own religious courts that deal with matters of personal status. Rabbinical courts have exclusive jurisdiction over Jews in marriage and divorce, and they may act on alimony, probate, succession, and other similar questions with the parties' consent. The Christian ecclesiastical courts have exclusive authority over marriage, divorce, alimony, and confirmation of wills, and they may judge other similar matters if the parties agree. The Muslim courts have exclusive jurisdiction in all matters of personal status. The judicial appointment procedure seeks to discourage political influence, and judges enjoy tenure subject only to good behavior.

Two other institutions unique to the Israeli system are significant elements of the political structure. The Histadrut and the Jewish Agency, although technically extragovernmental, perform governmental functions, and their personnel often attain positions of responsibility within the government. The Histadrut is of greater significance than the usual trade union organization and is unique in that it combines trade unionism, economic enterprise, cultural and social activities, and social welfare. It is one of the largest employers in Israel and has engaged in overseas projects in support of Israel's foreign policy. The Jewish Agency for Israel represents the World Zionist Organization and acts on behalf of Jews throughout the world who are concerned with Israel's development, Jewish immigration and settlement, and the cultural and spiritual ties and cooperation among the Jewish people. The agency has been responsible for the organization of Jewish immigration to Israel; the reception, assistance, and settlement of these immigrants; care of children; and aid to cultural projects and institutions of higher learning. It fosters Hebrew education and culture in the Diaspora, guides and assists Zionist youth movements, and organizes the work of the Jewish people in support of Israel.

Political Dynamics

Political life is intense in Israel, and political parties play a central role in the social and economic—as well as political—life of the country. Israel's political system is characterized by a wide range and intensity of political and social viewpoints, which are given expression not only in political parties but also in newspapers and a host of social, religious, cultural, and other organizations. Numerous minority and splinter factions freely criticize the government. This diversity has been most apparent in the existence of multiple parties contesting parliamentary elections (and in the factions within most of the major parties) and in the various coalition governments that have been characteristic of Israel since its inception (see Tables 13.2 and 13.3).

Political parties are overwhelming in their presence—virtually all political life is organized in and through the parties, which are crucial for the political socialization of Israelis as well as for the policymaking of the state. Because Israelis vote not for individuals but for parties, it is the party that determines where individuals will be placed on the election list and thus who will represent it in Parliament and in government. Individuals or groups of individuals, no matter how prominent, have not done well when divested of the support of the established parties. In the several instances in which there has been notable success (such as the Democratic Movement for Change, or DMC, in 1977), it has tended to be ephemeral in nature. Electoral campaigns are controlled by the parties that make the decisions, wage the campaigns, and spend the money. In the final analysis, the voter focuses on the party; the party member looks to it for fulfillment of his or her needs; and the politician needs its leaders and machinery to ensure his or her political future.

Israel's political parties and the blocs they have formed have undergone numerous mergers, splits, disagreements, and reconciliations as a result of ideological differences, policy disagreements, and personality clashes. Large numbers of parties have contested the 120 seats in the Parliament, and many have been successful in winning representation in it. For example, in 1977 twenty-three parties sought parliamentary representation, and thirteen were successful. In 1981 thirty-one parties sought seats, and initially ten were represented. In 1984 twenty-six political parties sought Knesset mandates, and fifteen were successful. The large number of parties, reflecting Israel's political fragmentation, is a result of the proportional representation system compounded by personal and ideological differences as well as by the intensity of views held by segments of Israel's polity on numerous issues.

Israel's complex party structure demonstrates various dimensions of cleavage, but socioeconomic, religious-secular, and foreign policy–national security issue areas tend to be the most significant. Israel's parties have economic views ranging from Marxism through liberal socialism to free enterprise. There are also different views concerning the role of government in economic (and, consequently, social) policy. The role of religion has differentiated those who seek to make Jewish religious law a central factor in state activity from others who have sought to enhance the secular nature of the system and those who have worked to eliminate virtually all vestiges of religious influence. Views of the ultimate extent of the state and the

TABLE 13.2 Political Parties and Knesset Election Results (1949–1961)

	1949		1951		1955		1959		1961	
Party	%	Seats	%	Seats	%	Seats	%	Seats	%	Seats
Mapai (Israel Workers)	35.7	46	37.3	45	32.2	40	38.2	47	34.7	42
Mapam (United Workers)[a]	14.7	19	12.5	15	7.3	9	7.2	9	7.5	9
Ahdut Haavoda (Unity of Labor)[b]	—	—	—	—	8.2	10	6.0	7	6.6	8
Herut (Freedom)	11.5	14	6.6	8	12.6	15	13.6	17	13.8	17
General Zionists	5.2	7	16.2	20	10.2	13	6.2	8	—	—
Progressives	4.1	5	3.2	4	4.4	5	4.6	6	—	—
Liberal[c]	—	—	—	—	—	—	—	—	13.6	17
United Religious Front[d]	12.2	16	—	—	—	—	—	—	—	—
Mizrahi (Merkaz Ruchani—Spiritual Center)	—	—	1.5	2	—	—	—	—	—	—
Hapoel Hamizrahi (Workers of the Spiritual Center)	—	—	6.7	8	—	—	—	—	—	—
National Religious (Mafdal)[e]	—	—	—	—	9.1	11	9.9	12	9.8	12
Agudat Israel (Association of Israel)[f]	—	—	—	—	—	—	—	—	3.7	4
Poalei Agudat Israel (Workers of the Association of Israel)[f]	—	—	—	—	—	—	—	—	1.9	2
Torah Religious Front[g]	—	—	3.6	5	4.7	6	4.7	6	—	—

Arab Democratic List	1.7	2	2.4	3	1.8	2	—	—	—	—
Arab Progress and Work	—	—	1.2	1	1.5	2	1.3	2	1.6	2
Arab Farmers and Development	—	—	1.1	1	1.2	1	1.1	1	—	—
Arab Cooperation and Brotherhood	—	—	—	—	—	—	1.2	2	1.9	2
Communist	3.5	4	4.0	5	4.5	6	2.8	3	4.2	5
Sephardim	3.5	4	1.8	2	—	—	—	—	—	—
Fighters List	2.1	1	—	—	—	—	—	—	—	—
Women's International Zionist Organization (WIZO)	1.2	1	—	—	—	—	—	—	—	—
Yemenites	1.0	1	1.2	1	—	—	—	—	—	—

[a]Formed 1948—Hashomer Hatzair, Ahdut Haavoda, Poalei Zion.

[b]Formed by merger of Poalei Zion (Workers of Zion) and smaller socialist Zionist groups. Included in Mapam 1949 and 1951.

[c]Formed 1961—merger of General Zionists and Progressives.

[d]Elected as follows: Hapoel Hamizrahi, 6; Mizrahi, 4; Agudat Israel, 3; Poalei Agudat Israel, 3.

[e]Merger—Mizrahi and Hapoel Hamizrahi.

[f]In Torah Religious Front until 1961 elections and again in 1973 elections.

[g]Joint list Agudat Israel and Poalei Agudat Israel.

TABLE 13.3 Political Parties and Knesset Election Results (1965–1984)

Party	1965 %	1965 Seats	1969 %	1969 Seats	1973 %	1973 Seats	1977 %	1977 Seats	1981 %	1981 Seats	1984 %	1984 Seats
Mapai (Israel Workers)	IA		IA		IA		IA		IA		IA	
Mapam (United Workers)[a]	6.6	8	IA		IA		IA		IA		IA	
Ahdut Haavoda (Unity of Labor)[b]	IA		IA		IA		IA		IA		IA	
Alignment (Mapai and Ahdut Haavoda)	36.7	45	—	—	—	—	—	—	—	—	—	—
Rafi (Israel Labor List) (Reshimat Poalei Israel)[c]	7.9	10	IA		IA		IA		IA		IA	
Israel Labor[d]	—	—	IA		IA		IA		IA		IA	
Maarach (Alignment of Israel Labor and Mapam)	—	—	46.2	56	39.7	51	24.6	32	36.6	47	34.9	44
State List[e]	—	—	3.1	4	—	—	—	—	—	—	—	—
Gahal (Gush Herut Liberalim)[f]	21.3	26	21.7	26	—	—	—	—	—	—	—	—
Independent Liberals[g]	3.8	5	3.2	4	3.6	4	1.2	1	—	—	—	—
Shlomzion[h]	—	—	—	—	—	—	1.9	2	—	—	—	—
Free Center[i]	—	—	1.2	2	—	—	—	—	—	—	—	—
Likud[j]	—	—	—	—	30.2	39	33.4	43	37.1	48	31.9	41
National Religious (Mafdal)[k]	9.0	11	9.7	12	8.3	10	9.2	12	4.9	6	3.5	4
Agudat Israel (Association of Israel)[l]	3.3	4	3.2	4	—	—	3.4	4	3.7	4	1.7	2
Poalei Agudat Israel (Workers of the Association of Israel[l]	1.8	2	1.8	2	—	—	1.4	1	—	—	—	—
Torah Religious Front[m]	—	—	—	—	3.8	5	—	—	—	—	—	—
Tami	—	—	—	—	—	—	—	—	2.3	3	1.5	1
Morasha (Heritage)[n]	—	—	—	—	—	—	—	—	—	—	1.6	2
Shas (Sephardi Torah Guardians)[o]	—	—	—	—	—	—	—	—	—	—	3.1	4
Arab Progress and Work	2.0	2							—	—		
Arab Cooperation and Brotherhood	1.4	2	—	—	—	—	—	—	—	—	—	—
Alignment-affiliated Arab and Druze lists	—	—	3.5	4	2.4	3	—	—	—	—	—	—
United Arab List	—	—	—	—	—	—	1.4	1			—	—

New Communists (Rakah) (Reshima Komunistit Chadasha)[p]	2.3	3	2.8	3	3.4	4	—	—	—	—	—	—
Israel Communists (Maki) (Miflaga Komunistit Israelit)[p]	1.1	1	1.2	1	—	—	—	—	—	—	—	—
Democratic Front for Peace and Equality (Hadash)[q]	—	—	—	—	—	—	4.6	5	3.4	4	3.4	4
Moked[r]	—	—	—	—	1.4	1	—	—	—	—	—	—
Flatto-Sharon	—	—	—	—	—	—	2.0	1	—	—	—	—
Citizens' Rights Movement (Ratz)	—	—	—	—	2.2	3	1.2	1	1.4	1	2.4	3
Democratic Movement for Change (DMC) (Dash)[s]	—	—	—	—	—	—	11.6	15	—	—	—	—
Shinui	—	—	—	—	—	—	—	—	1.5	2	2.6	3
Haolam Hazeh	1.2	1	1.2	2	—	—	—	—	—	—	—	—
Shelli (Shalom Lemaan Israel—Peace for Israel)[t]	—	—	—	—	—	—	1.6	2	—	—	—	—
Progressive List for Peace	—	—	—	—	—	—	—	—	—	—	1.8	2
Telem[u]	—	—	—	—	—	—	—	—	1.6	2	—	—
Ometz (Courage to Cure the Economy)	—	—	—	—	—	—	—	—	—	—	1.2	1
Yahad[v]	—	—	—	—	—	—	—	—	—	—	2.2	3
Kach[w]	—	—	—	—	—	—	—	—	—	—	1.2	1
Tehiya[x]	—	—	—	—	—	—	—	—	2.3	3	4.0	5

IA: In Alignment

[a]Formed 1948—Hashomer Hatzair, Ahdut Haavoda, Poalei Zion.

[b]Formed by merger of Poalei Zion (Workers of Zion) and smaller socialist Zionist groups.

[c]Formed 1965—Ben Gurion splinter group from Mapai.

[d]Formed 1968—merger of Mapai, Rafi, Ahdut Haavoda.

[e]Ben Gurion splinter group from Israel Labor. Later part of Likud (in 1977 as part of La'am).

[f]Formed 1965—merger of Herut and majority of Liberal party.

[g]Minority of Liberal party not joining in merger with Herut.

[h]Joined Likud after 1977 election.

[i]Formed 1968—splinter group from Herut.

[j]Formed 1973—merger of Gahal, State List, Free Center, Greater Israel Movement. La'am—formed within Likud 1976—part of Free Center (Merkaz Hofshi), State List (Reshima Mamlachtit), Greater Israel Movement (Hatnuah Leeretz Israel Hashlemah).

[k]Merger—Mizrahi and Hapoel Hamizrahi. Elected as follows: Hapoel Hamizrahi, 6; Mizrahi, 4; Agudat Israel, 3; Poalei Agudat Israel, 3.

TABLE 13.3 (continued)

[l]In Torah Religious Front until 1961 elections and again in 1973 elections.
[m]Joint list Agudat Israel and Poalei Agudat Israel.
[n]Splinter from NRP and Poalei Agudat Israel.
[o]Sephardi split from Agudat Israel.
[p]Split of Communist party in 1965 resulted in formation of Rakah and Maki.
[q]Formed 1977—Rakah and some Israel Black Panthers.
[r]Israel Communist party and Tchelet Adom (Blue-Red) Movement.
[s]Formed 1976—Shinui (Change), Democratic Movement, Free Center, Zionist Panthers, various individuals. Led by Yigael Yadin. Split September 1978.
[t]Formed 1977—merger of Moked, Haolam Hazeh, independent socialists, and some Black Panthers.
[u]Led by Moshe Dayan.
[v]Led by Ezer Weizman.
[w]Led by Rabbi Meir Kahane.
[x]In 1984 Tehiya-Tzomet.

role of Zionism have divided groups (for example, the Communists) that oppose the concept of a Zionist state from others that have supported the notion of a binational entity or a truncated Jewish state, and from others that favor an exclusively Jewish-Zionist state in the whole of Palestine—both east and west of the Jordan River. Foreign policy issues are currently less divisive than they were in the early days of the state. When the Soviet Union was an ardent suitor of the new Jewish state, it facilitated the adoption of pro-Soviet foreign policy stances by political groups with a Marxist orientation, such as Mapam. At the same time, parties of the right (such as the General Zionists and Herut) advocated a Western orientation. Soon, however, the choice was unrealistic, and since the early 1950s a pro-Western orientation has dominated Israeli thinking.

Particular special interest groups have created parties to represent their views and to secure their interests more effectively. These parties have reflected a wide spectrum of perspectives and concerns, ranging from the ethnic and social goals of the Arab parties and parties seeking to represent Yemenites and Sephardim to the more practical attempts of some groups to promote narrower goals such as revocation of income tax. Individual and personal factors have also played a role in party formation. Individuals with ambitions or personal concerns, ranging from animosity toward other political figures to a desire to achieve a particular status, have established their own parties to contest Knesset elections; this was the case in 1977 with Shmuel Flatto-Sharon, who sought election and the accompanying parliamentary immunity as a means of avoiding extradition for trial in France. Historical developments, mostly during the pre-independence period, and personal differences among the political elite have been important elements in fostering party proliferation.

Israel's political parties may be categorized into parties of the left, parties of the center-right, and the religious parties. There are also various particularistic parties that tend on the whole to be small and short-lived.

On the left are the socialist parties, of which the major element is the Israel Labor party (Mifleget Haavoda Haisraelit). This party formally came into being in 1968 as a result of the merger of three labor parties: Mapai, Ahdut Haavoda, and Rafi. Mapai (an acronym for Mifleget Poalei Eretz Israel, or Workers Party of the Land of Israel), the Labor party's major component, was founded in 1930 by a merger of Ahdut Haavoda and Hapoel Hatzair. Under the leadership of David Ben-Gurion, it became the most prominent and important party in the Yishuv and, later, in independent Israel.

Prior to statehood, Mapai's role was virtually unchallenged. Mapai continued its dominant role following statehood, and in elections for the Knesset it consistently obtained the largest single percentage of votes until the 1977 election. It was the dominant member of all government coalitions, and ordinarily its members held the important portfolios of prime minister, defense minister, foreign minister, and finance minister. Its role in the Jewish Agency and in the Histadrut was also significant. The continuing role of Mapai as the most important member of the Parliament and of the cabinet, and its status in the Jewish Agency and Histadrut, was the basis for its unique position in the Israeli system. The party, as one of the political institutions of the country, was identified with the state in the minds of many voters. In addition, because of its long tenure of office, it permeated the governmental administrative, economic, and other institutions of Israel.

The Labor party was dominant and remained the single most important factor in Israeli politics until the 1977 parliamentary elections, although it began to lose support in the 1970s. Disillusionment with its weakening leadership, particularly at the time of the Yom Kippur War of 1973, combined with scandals and with economic and social problems to raise significant doubts about the efficacy of its governmental role. Labor lost its dominance in 1977 and failed to regain it in the 1981 and 1984 elections, although its leader, Shimon Peres, became the prime minister in the government of national unity in September 1984.

On the extreme left of the political spectrum is the Communist party, which has undergone a number of permutations over the years since its founding in the mandate period. The party's membership and voting support is overwhelmingly Arab, but its leadership has become increasingly divided between Jews and Arabs. The party, known as Rakah (Reshima Kommunistit Chadasha, or New Communist List), is pro-Moscow and strongly anti-Zionist. It is legal, competes in the political system, and wins seats in the Parliament, but it is isolated in Israeli political life; that is, it does not join the government and is seen as a perennial and reflexive opponent of government policy.

On the right of the political spectrum are a number of parties at whose core lies Herut (Freedom), formed by Menachem Begin as an independent political party in 1948. Herut's origins go back to the 1920s and Vladimir Zeev Jabotinsky's establishment of the Zionist Revisionist movement. The Revisionist movement undertook numerous activities during the mandate, including the organization of illegal immigration to Palestine and the establishment of the Irgun. When the Israeli government forced the Irgun to dissolve, Menachem Begin created the Herut party to carry on the work of the Irgun and the Jabotinsky-Revisionist ideology, and Herut became the representative of the Revisionist movement in Israel. Begin remained the leader of the party, and of the Likud bloc that it dominated, until his retirement from public life in 1983.

In 1965 Herut was joined by the former General Zionists in the Liberal party to form the parliamentry bloc Gahal (an acronym for Gush Herut Liberalim—the bloc of Herut and the Liberals). Likud (Unity) was formed in 1973 as a parliamentary bloc by the combination of Gahal and La'am (Toward the People), and Begin retained his dominant role.

On the extreme right are two parties formed in recent years. First, Tehiya (Renaissance) was created in response to the Camp David Accords and the Egypt-Israel Treaty, which its founders saw as inimical to Israel's interests in that both relinquished territories important for Israel's security and made other concessions deleterious to Israel's future. Second, Kach, headed by Rabbi Meir Kahane, focuses on the need to make Israel Jewish by ousting the Arabs from both Israel and the West Bank and the Gaza.

Parties with a religious orientation have played a major role in Israel's political life. At the core are the National Religious party and Agudat Yisrael (or Agudat Israel), although their centrality has increasingly been challenged in recent years. The National Religious party (NRP, or Mafdal—for Miflaga Datit Leumit) was founded in 1956 by Mizrahi (Spiritual Center) and Hapoel Hamizrahi (Workers of the Spiritual Center) as a religious party seeking to combine religious concerns and a moderate socialist orientation in economic matters within a Zionist framework. Agudat Israel (Association of Israel) is an ultra-Orthodox party focusing its attention on the religious nature of the state and seeking to have Israel function in accordance with the principles of the Torah.

Divisons within the ranks of the religious movements have become more pronounced in recent years, eclipsing the NRP-Agudat split. Within each party are differences over issues and leadership, but broader discord within the Orthodox religious community has led to new religiously based parties, some of which were offshoots of existing ones. Numerous factions, each with its own leadership and agendas, compete to secure loyalty and votes as well as program goals and political patronage. In the 1981 election this competition led to the creation of Tami and in 1984 to the formation of new parties that also were successful in securing seats in the Knesset: Morasha (Heritage) was created by a splinter group from NRP that joined with Poalei Agudat Israel; and Shas (Sephardi Torah Guardians) was a Sephardi split from Agudat Israel.

Notwithstanding these and other areas of discord, the religious parties have a major common denominator—their effort to represent the interests of Israel's Orthodox community. They share a loyalty to traditional religious Judaism and realize the need to organize and mobilize the religious community to prevent secular intrusion into the religious domain and to ensure perpetuation of religious values and life-styles. In part because of these concerns, the parties have created communal and educational frameworks to draw together those Jews who are faithful to the Orthodox perspective. They may differ in their approaches to secular society and in their views of Zionism, but they agree that there must be no contradiction of *halachah* (Jewish religious law) and that Orthodox religious interests must be preserved and enhanced.

Over the years a number of political parties have been created with focuses and concerns not readily categorized into right, left, and religious groupings. Some have been of consequence; others have had fleeting roles. The more significant of these parties have been near the center of the political spectrum. The Liberal party (Hamiflaga Haliberalit) was established during the Fifth Knesset by a merger of the General Zionist party (Hatzionim Haklaliyim) and the Progressive party (Hamiflaga Haprogressivit). The Independent Liberal party (Haliberalim Haatzmaim) was formed in 1965 by the Progressive faction in the Liberal party. The Citizens' Rights Movement (CRM, or Hatnuah Lezhuiot Haezrach) was founded in 1973.

The Democratic Movement for Change (DMC, or Hatnuah Hademocratit Leshinui) was formed in 1976, under the leadership of Yigael Yadin, to contest the 1977 election. It was not a typical political party: Its membership cut across the spectrum of political ideologies and party affiliations, and its main theme was electoral reform and the revitalization of Israel's political system. It focused on the mismanagement and corruption of the Labor-led coalitions of Israel. Yadin brought to the party a reputation based on a "nonpolitical" (and hence "clean") past; he had been chief of staff of the army as well as a distinguished professor and archaeologist popularly known for his work at Masada.

The multiplicity of parties, the diversity of views they represent, and the proportional-representation electoral system have resulted in the failure of any one party to win a majority of Knesset seats in any of the eleven elections between 1949 and 1984, thus necessitating the formation of coalition governments. Prior to the national unity government formed in 1984, only twice have the coalitions been truly broad based—and these were established in times of national stress: the provisional government formed at independence and the government of national unity formed during the crisis preceding the 1967 war and maintained until the summer of 1970. The 1984 national unity government was unique in that it was based on a principle of power sharing between Labor and Likud, the two major political blocs.

Notwithstanding these factors, all of the coalitions have proved remarkably stable, for a number of reasons. Israel had only six prime ministers during its first three decades of independence: David Ben-Gurion (1948–1953, 1955–1963), Moshe Sharett (1954–1955), Levi Eshkol (1963–1969), Golda Meir (1969–1974), Yitzhak Rabin (1974–1977), and Menachem Begin (1977–1983). Yitzhak Shamir (1983–1984) and Shimon Peres (1984–) came to office following Begin's resignation and the Knesset election of 1984, respectively. Although there have been a number of cabinet changes, most have been essentially formal. They occurred following the election of a new Knesset, the choice of a president, the retirement of David Ben-Gurion, his return to public life, his second retirement, the 1967 crisis and war, the death of Levi Eshkol, the retirement of Golda Meir, the retirement of Menachem Begin, and so forth. The personal stabilizing influence of Ben-Gurion, Moshe Sharett, Levi Eshkol, and Golda Meir during their respective tenures as prime minister and the preponderant strength of Mapai and the Labor party were important factors in maintaining stability. After the 1977 election Menachem Begin played a similar stabilizing role in the governments he headed, until his resignation in 1983. The rigorous discipline of Israel's parties has curbed irresponsible action by individual Knesset members. Continuity of policy has also been enhanced by the reappointment of many ministers in reshuffled cabinets and by the longevity in office of bureaucratic officeholders.

The formation of a governing coalition is an arduous and complex task involving numerous factions and individuals in tough bargaining for political power and prestige. Coalition partners understand their political value and exact high political prices (usually measured in power to secure policies and patronage) for their participation in a government coalition. Thus, all governments and their programs have been compromises in terms of personnel, positions, and policies.

The coalitions constructed since independence have involved a multiplicity of parties, with Labor as the dominant party between 1949 and 1977, and Likud dominant between 1977 and 1984. Yet despite the clear supremacy of one coalition member, the smaller parties often tend to be powerful because of their importance to the government's continuation in office. Nevertheless, the major portfolios have always been retained by the dominant coalition party, except in the case of the government of national unity established in 1984. Thus, Mapai/Labor and Likud held the portfolios of prime minister, defense minister, foreign minister, and finance minister while allocating less central positions to the other parties in the coalition.

The requirements of coalition government have placed limitations on the prime minister's ability to control fully the cabinet and its actions. The prime minister does not appoint a minister; he or she reaches accord with the other parties, and they select the occupants of the several portfolios who share in the cabinet's collective responsibility for governing Israel. Similarly, the prime minister cannot dismiss any of the ministers.

Despite party proliferation and general political diversity, Israel's political life has been dominated by a relatively small and cohesive Jewish elite that has been mostly homogeneous in background. Most of its leaders were European in origin, arrived in Israel during the Second Aliyah (1904–1914), and were personally acquainted with one another, if not close friends. The political elite has been predominantly civilian in character and background. The military generally is not regarded as part of the political elite, although it is consulted on matters relating to national defense and plays a role in the decisionmaking process on security-related issues. The armed forces generally are excluded from politics, although retired senior military officers increasingly have been co-opted into the political elite, partly as a consequence of decisions to include highly visible and publicly acclaimed figures in the ranks of the parties. Religious elements have had a somewhat similar position. They have exerted a strong influence in the cabinet and Knesset as political parties because of their role in cabinet formation. The rabbinate is not considered part of the political elite, and the religious establishment generally does not intervene in politics.

The IDF is virtually unique in the Middle East in that it does not, as an entity, play a role in politics, despite its size, budget, and importance. Individual officers and senior commanders have secured important positions in the Israel Defense Forces, but they have done so as individuals, when not on active service and without the backing of the military as an institution. It has only been after their retirement that such military men as Generals Moshe Dayan, Yigal Allon, Yitzhak Rabin, Yigael Yadin, Ezer Weizman, Haim Bar Lev, and Ariel Sharon have played a key role in political life. They have attained position and power by working within the bounds of the political system and by joining political parties, not through their utilization of the military in opposition to the system. Their military reputations and popular prestige enhanced their chances for, but did not ensure, significant political careers. The officer corps has not, and probably could not, become closely aligned with one political faction or party, and active-duty officers are prohibited from engaging in political activities. The IDF performs the tasks of the traditional army—defense of the state—and does so in an apolitical fashion. It has not been seen as a threat to the regime, and there has never been any consideration of a military coup. Civilians continue to control the military and do so by virtue of their dominant positions within the Israeli system, not because they control the military itself.

New Dimensions in Politics

The turmoil in the political process and political life of Israel at the time of the Yom Kippur War set in motion forces that subsequently affected the political process. The change from euphoria before the war to uncertainty after it accelerated political change and facilitated the replacement of personalities and the alteration of policies. These effects were not obvious in the elections for the Eighth Knesset and local authorities, held at the end of December 1973. Golda Meir was charged with creating a new government and did so in early 1974, only to resign a month later, primarily because of dissension within the Labor party that centered on the question of political responsibility for lapses at the outset of the war.

This situation set the stage for the selection as prime minister of Yitzhak Rabin, former chief of staff, a hero of the 1967 war, and former ambassador to the United States, as well as the scion of a prominent labor-movement family. Rabin's government represented a departure from the past and ushered in a new era in which some of Israel's best-known names and personalities moved from the focus of power. Leadership had begun to be transferred from the immigrant-founder generation to the native-born sons. Golda Meir's singular role gave way to the representation of diverse views in Israel's three-man shuttle-diplomacy negotiating team (Rabin, Yigal Allon, and Shimon Peres) and in their coterie of advisers.

The protest movements and new political parties resulting from the Yom Kippur War have had varying degrees of success in establishing themselves in the political structure. They developed initially in response to perceived mismanagement during the war and focused on the need for political reform. Among the resultant parties was the Democratic Movement for Change, which secured sizable representation in the Knesset in 1977 and joined the Likud-led coalition in the fall of that year. It later split into several smaller groups and disintegrated by the time of the 1981 Knesset elections. Yigael Yadin, its founder and titular head, retired from politics to return to academic-scholarly pursuits.

In a more general sense, many of the forces set in motion by the October War and its aftermath seemed to coalesce in such a way as to tangibly affect the situation when Israel's electorate went to the polls in May 1977.

They gave the largest number of votes to the Likud, led by Menachem Begin, and Labor lost a substantial number of seats compared to its showing in 1973. Many of Labor's lost mandates went to the newly established DMC, but Likud also gained additional members. Thus ended was Labor's dominance of Israeli politics, which had begun in the Yishuv period. Israel therefore chose a new regime, and the Likud, under Begin's leadership, emerged as the leading political force.

Israel's 1977 elections were seen as a new political "earthquake" reflecting and foreshadowing substantial change. Menachem Begin and the Likud now formed the government and took control of Israel's bureaucracy. The parties constituting the Likud bloc (especially Begin's Herut) had been serving as the opposition since independence, with the exception of their joining the "wall-to-wall" government of national unity during the 1967 war crisis and remaining in it until their withdrawal in 1970, when they vocally opposed the government and criticized its programs, politics, and leadership. As a consequence of the 1977 election, Likud became the ruling coalition responsible for establishing and implementing programs and policies for Israel. It sought to implement its own program within the broad ideology developed decades earlier by Vladimir Jabotinsky. Once in power as prime minister, Begin found in Jabotinsky a source of inspiration and a guide for concrete policy, and he worked toward the implementation of Jabotinsky's vision.

The 1981 Knesset election was not conclusive in identifying a popular preference for Likud or Labor. The electorate virtually divided its votes between the two blocs but awarded a majority neither of votes nor seats in the Parliament, and coalition politics continued to characterize the system. President Yitzhak Navon granted the mandate to form the new government to Begin, and he succeeded in forming a Likud-led coalition that subsequently received the endorsement of the Knesset. The election highlighted the political dimension of the ethnic issue when Likud secured the majority (probably some 70 percent) of the Oriental Jewish vote, following a pattern foreshadowed in the 1977 election.

Extensive Oriental support for Begin and the Likud in 1981 can be seen as a desire to achieve change through support of a party and government perceived as sympathetic to the Oriental plight. Begin's popularity in the Oriental community was a direct result of previous Oriental failures, his courting of the community even as opposition leader, and his responsiveness during his first administration. This support of Begin and Likud, an apparent identification of a political "home," to a significant degree came in lieu of an effective independent Oriental political organization that had not arisen and remained successful in previous years, although both Tami (in 1981 and 1984) and Shas (in 1984) were able to draw some voters to their Oriental-based political movements. Likud was widely seen as the party to assist the Oriental community in emerging from its second-class status.

The second Begin government (1981–1983) came to office with a narrow margin in the Parliament, but the prime minister was able to maintain that control despite the traumatic events associated with the war in Lebanon and major economic problems. Begin, personally, was a popular politician with strong charismatic appeal to broad sections of the populace, and he was an able and skilled political leader, in much the same manner as David Ben-Gurion and Golda Meir had been. He remained popular and powerful until his resignation from office in the fall of 1983. His foreign minister, Yitzhak Shamir, a relative newcomer to politics, replaced him. The short-lived Shamir government, officially endorsed by the Knesset in October 1983, was virtually the same as its predecessor in personalities and policies. Shamir pursued a policy of continuity to the extent possible.

In the spring of 1984 the Parliament called for new elections, and in July the Eleventh Knesset was chosen. A new phase of leadership by more conventional individuals was launched—a phase of "politics without charisma." The 1984 campaign lacked the sense of vibrancy that might have been created by a figure able to generate interest in the election process and in the issues facing Israel. Begin's refusal to emerge from his self-imposed retirement brought to an end the period of "father figures." It was thus left to Yitzhak Shamir (Likud) and Shimon Peres (Labor Alignment) to lead the lackluster politicians who vied for the voters' approval, and the results, in part, reflected their inability to entice the noncommitted voters to full participation. Labor was unable to capitalize on Likud's misfortunes, including the retirement of Begin (and his remaining in seclusion throughout the campaign), the Lebanese quagmire, and the economic problems (reflected in the oft-quoted figure of 400 percent inflation). Shamir proved able to retain much of Likud's electoral support, avoiding what many thought (and the polls earlier predicted) would be a Labor victory by a substantial margin.

Fifteen of the twenty-six political parties that contested the 1984 election secured the necessary 1 percent of the valid votes cast to obtain a seat in the Parliament. The two major blocs were relatively close—the Labor Alignment secured 44 seats and the Likud secured 41 seats—whereas the remaining parliamentary seats were not distributed in any clear pattern that would facilitate the forming of a new government. The 1984 election results seemed partly to reflect a small but perceptible shift to the right in the electorate as a whole. The Labor Alignment and its closest parliamentary allies secured about the same number of seats as they had had in the outgoing parliament. Although Likud appeared to lose some of its mandates, Tehiya gained seats, and Kach's mandate resulted from a move to the right of a sufficient number of voters to gain the minimum percentage required for a seat. The vote of the Oriental Jewish community seemed to play a role in Kahane's victory, as well as in the move to the right of the soldiers' vote and in the securing of the four seats gained by the Sephardi Torah Guardians, apparently at the expense of the more European-dominated "establishment" Agudat Israel (which lost half of its seats) and Tami. The Oriental vote could, once again, be associated with Likud and its allies to the right.

In a major sense, the results of the election were inconclusive. No party secured a majority, but, then, none had ever done so in previous elections.

This time, however, no party or grouping became the obvious choice to form the next government. Each had natural allies and opponents, but there was little room for maneuver in forming a coalition. Every significant perspective seemed to secure a place in the Parliament, and most were represented by about the same number of members of Parliament as their ideological opponents. Israelis appeared to be divided on many of the key issues facing the country, whether in the foreign policy, political, economic, social, or religious arenas; between those who supported Likud and those who supported Labor; and among a host of smaller parties with their own particular agendas and conceptions of Israel's future.

The division in the Israeli body politic proved to be the main factor that led to, and complicated the formation of, the government of national unity that was approved by the Knesset in September 1984. The negotiations leading to the formation of this new government were lengthy and complex, and at its base was a complicated series of compromises and concessions, including the division of the prime minister's position between Shimon Peres for the first twenty-five months of the tenure of the governments and Yitzhak Shamir for the remaining twenty-five months of the coalition's life. The government inaugurated a new experiment in Israeli politics.

Foreign and Security Policy

The primary objectives of Israel's foreign and security policy are the quest for peace through negotiations with the Arab states and the assurance of security in a region of hostility through an effective defense capability. The goals of peace and security derive from the continuing conflict with the Arab states—a conflict that remains the preeminent problem confronting Israel. It affects all of Israel's policies and activities, both domestic and foreign and in every area of concern and application. Israel recognizes that peace and cooperation with the neighboring Arab states is vital for the long-term survival and development of the Jewish state, and this objective remains the cornerstone of its foreign policy.

Israel's preoccupation and preeminent concern with peace, national survival, and security are the consequences of the country's geostrategic situation, particularly the conflict with its Arab neighbors. During its first thirty-four years of existence, it fought six wars with the Arab states and the Palestine Liberation Organization, and it remains at war with all of the Arab states but Egypt. Six wars, countless skirmishes and terrorist attacks, and incessant, vituperative rhetoric, as well as the Holocaust and Arab hostility during the mandate period, have all left their mark on Israel's national consciousness. Israel spends, on a continuing basis, a major portion of its budget and GNP on defense and defense-related expenditures and has, by regional standards, a sizable standing army and reserve force. Its military power is substantial but not unlimited, constrained by its own demography and economy as well as by international factors.

The centrality of the Arab threat derives from the fact that Israel is perhaps unique among states in having hostile neighbors on all of its borders, with the exception, since 1979, of Egypt. This threat is perceived not as an aberration of history but, rather, as history's latest manifestation. The Israelis retain a clear view of Arab hostility, which has been modified significantly only by the actions of President Anwar Sadat of Egypt.

Israel's quest for peace with the Arab states dates back to its very establishment. The armistice agreements of 1949 were meant to facilitate a transition to "permanent peace in Palestine." The Israelis tended to be hopeful, but negotiations were not begun and Israel soon became preoccupied with the need for security.

The June War of 1967 substantially modified the content of the issues central to the dispute and generated change in the Israeli system and in Israeli perceptions. The realities of Arab hostility, the nature of the Arab threat, and the difficulties of achieving a settlement became more obvious. However, the issues of the conflict changed with the extent of the Israeli victory: Israel occupied the Sinai peninsula, the Gaza Strip, the West Bank of the Jordan River, the eastern sector of the city of Jerusalem, and the Golan Heights. Israel adopted the position that it would not withdraw from those territories until there were negotiations with the Arab states leading to peace agreements that recognized Israel's right to exist and accepted Israel's permanent position and borders. Throughout the period between the June War (1967) and the October War (1973), the focal point in the Middle East was the effort to achieve a settlement of the Arab-Israeli conflict and to secure a just and lasting peace. In these attempts, based on United Nations Security Council Resolution 242 of November 22, 1967, the regional states, the superpowers (and lesser powers), and the main instrumentalities of the international system were engaged. Israel focused its attention on peace and security objectives and developed positions concerning the occupied territories, the Palestinians, and related questions, thus providing the base for the post-October War policy. Although some of the interwar efforts were promising, peace was not achieved and there was little movement in that direction. Instead, the October War erupted and created a new environment for the quest for peace and the development of Israeli foreign policy. Israel's position in the international community deteriorated with the outbreak of the fighting. Israel was condemned by various states, and some severed diplomatic relations.

During the course of the war and immediately afterward, Israel's ties with most of the remaining states of Black Africa were broken. Many of them linked the rupture of relations with Israel's refusal to withdraw from the occupied territories. Except for South Africa, no major African state publicly backed Israel or offered assistance. To most Israelis this fact symbolized not only the injustice of the international community but also the success of Arab oil blackmail and the failure of Israel's program of international cooperation. Israel had provided many of these African states with technical assistance, which the Africans had lauded publicly for promoting African development. Israel retained relations with only five African states: South Africa and four black states—Malawi, Lesotho, Botswana, and Swaziland.

Then, later in November 1973, the Organization of African Unity Ministerial Council noted the "expansionist designs of belligerent Israel" and denounced the country.

The ruptures with Africa were a disappointment, but a shift in the attitudes and policies of the European states was perhaps more significant. Israel's international isolation was compounded by the unwillingness of the European allies of the United States to allow the use of their facilities and/or airspace for the shipment and transfer of supplies to Israel during the war. Portugal was an exception and allowed the use of the Azores, thereby forcing the United States to establish special systems for the resupply of Israel. The Europeans were reluctant to be associated with the U.S. effort and were concerned with the reduction of Arab oil shipments to them. On November 6, the nine members of the European Economic Community adopted a joint communiqué on the Middle East clearly aimed at placating the Arabs. It called on Israel to withdraw from occupied Arab territories and to recognize the rights of the Palestinians.

Japan, which receives from 80 to 90 percent of its oil from the Middle East and much of that from the Arab states, also began to modify its policy. The Japanese, who had hitherto adopted and maintained a posture of neutrality in the Arab-Israeli conflict, now seemed to shift to a more pronounced pro-Arab position. They called for implementation of United Nations Resolution 242 (1967) and stressed the Arab interpretation of the resolution, calling on Israel to withdraw from all Arab territories. They also increased their contributions to the United Nations for aid to Palestinian refugees and offered development loans to several Arab states.

The war thus increased Israel's dependence on the United States. No other country could or was prepared to provide Israel with the vast quantities of modern and sophisticated arms required for war or for the political and moral support necessary to negotiate peace. Nevertheless, Israel was concerned that the United States might withdraw its support from Israel and that it might utilize its leverage to effect changes in Israel's position. In addition, there were questions about the U.S. role on such matters as the cease-fire, the peace negotiations, and the terms of a Middle East settlement.

In the wake of the October War, modifications of Israel's policy were relatively minor, and there were no dramatic shifts in objectives and content. The primary goals remained: the achievement of an Arab-Israeli settlement and the assurance of security in the interim. This constancy resulted, in part, from Israel's collective conception of its fundamental international position—and the limited policy options that flowed therefrom—which was not substantially altered. Israel's view of itself as geographically isolated and lacking dependable allies, its geographical vulnerability, and its need to acquire and produce arms for self-defense were reaffirmed by the October War. Israel believed that it won a military victory and that its strategic concepts were vindicated.

Israel recognized the dangers inherent in its increased isolation in the international community and in its increased dependence on the United

States. In the wake of the war it attempted to reaffirm and reestablish the ties that had been disrupted as a result of the conflict and attendant use of the Arab oil weapon. Israel launched an intensive effort to restore its traditionally close relations with the states of Europe; yet with Israel's increased economic and military needs and diplomatic isolation, its relationship with the United States became more central. After the October War, as before, the United States remained critical to Israel's security, to the search for peace in the Arab-Israeli zone of the Middle East, and to the continued prosperity of the Jewish state. However, there was an ambivalence and an uneasiness in Israel's postwar policy, which sought to solidify the support and aid of the United States while reducing Israel's dependence on that nation.

The 1977 elections that brought Begin and Likud to power brought changes in some policy sectors and reconfirmed others. The Begin government maintained Israel's focus on the goal of establishing a peace that would include the end of war, full reconciliation and normalization, and an open border over which people and goods could cross without hindrance. On the question of occupied territories, the new government could rely on a general consensus opposing a return to the armistice lines of 1949, thus ruling out total withdrawal, although there was disagreement concerning the final lines to be established and the extent of compromise on territorial retention. The focus of territorial disagreement was the West Bank. There was a substantial difference between the Begin-Likud view, which opposed relinquishing any territory, and the compromise views articulated by Labor and others to Likud's left. The Labor governments between 1967 and 1977 had generally tried to limit settlements to those that could serve a security function and had sought to avoid conflict between the settlements and the local Arab populations. Thus, settlements generally were established in areas with relatively small Arab populations. The Begin government altered that policy. Rather than restricting settlements in Judea and Samaria to those that were primarily security oriented, it supported settlement as a natural and inalienable Jewish right in that area. The broadest and most articulate consensus continued to revolve around the question of a Palestinian state and the PLO: In short, Israel's refusal to negotiate with the PLO and its opposition to the establishment of an independent Palestinian state on the West Bank and in the Gaza Strip were reaffirmed.

Israel's national consensus focused on the need for peace, and the main obstacle appeared to be the continuing Arab unwillingness to accept Israel and to negotiate with it. This unwillingness was modified as a result of Anwar Sadat's November 1977 initiative, which led to his visit to Israel and to the inauguration of direct negotiations between Israel and Egypt. The negotiations that followed Sadat's visit to Jerusalem culminated in the Camp David summit meeting of September 1978 at which Israel, Egypt, and the United States agreed to two frameworks for continued negotiations. The primary objective of post–Camp David negotiations was to convert the frameworks into peace treaties. Despite substantial U.S. efforts to secure the involvement of other Arab states, especially Jordan and Saudi Arabia, none agreed to participate in the negotiations or to encourage the peace process. The parties concentrated their initial efforts on the Egypt-Israel Peace Treaty, and a treaty was concluded and signed at the White House on March 26, 1979.

The Egypt-Israel Peace Treaty was a significant accomplishment that represented a first step toward a comprehensive Arab-Israeli settlement and regional stability. A long and complex process was necessary to resolve fully the Arab-Israeli conflict, and negotiations to that end could involve only Egypt and Israel since the other Arab states and the Palestinians refused to participate. In May 1979 Israel and Egypt, with the participation of the United States, began negotiations concerning a comprehensive peace and full autonomy for the inhabitants of the West Bank and Gaza. The negotiations proceeded slowly and were periodically suspended. The failure of the parties to reach agreement reflected their wide divergence regarding the translation of the concept of full autonomy from paper to reality. Substantial agreement was reached on peripheral and essentially technical matters, but central problems (such as those concerning security) remained unresolved. Egypt and Israel could agree neither on the extent of powers of the self-governing authority to be established nor on a number of related questions.

Nevertheless, parallel to the autonomy talks, the process of normalization of relations between Egypt and Israel moved ahead on schedule and without major disturbances. Normal relations officially began in early 1980 after Israel had completed most of its withdrawal from the Sinai Peninsula, the borders between the two states were opened, and direct communications links were inaugurated.

The peace process was soon overshadowed by the sixth Arab-Israeli war—the war in Lebanon in 1982. The continued presence in Lebanon of missiles that had been moved there by Syria in the spring of 1981 remained an Israeli concern, as were the PLO attacks against Israeli and Jewish targets worldwide, despite a U.S.-arranged cease-fire in the summer of 1981. On June 6, 1982, Israel launched a major military action against the PLO in Lebanon (called "Operation Peace for Galilee"), which sought to remove the PLO military and terrorist threat to Israel and to reduce the PLO's political capability. The military objective was to ensure security for northern Israel, to destroy the PLO infrastructure that had established a state within a state in Lebanon, to eliminate a center of international terrorism, and to eliminate the PLO from Lebanon so that its territory would not serve as a base of operations from which Israel could be threatened. But the political objectives were not so precise: Primarily there was the goal of weakening the PLO so that its influence would no longer be as significant politically, but there was also the hope that a new political order in Lebanon might lead it to consider becoming the second Arab state to make peace with Israel. In many respects the results were ambiguous. Israel's northern border was more secure, but the Israeli troops who remained in Lebanon until the summer of 1985 became targets of terrorists and others, and numerous casualties resulted. The costs of the war, however they might have been measured, were high. Externally, Israel's military actions caused concern and dismay in many quarters, including the United States, and its international isolation was increased. What achievements were accomplished occurred primarily in the military realm—the PLO was defeated, and its military and terrorist infrastructure in Lebanon was destroyed. The political achievements were less tangible. Despite some losses, the PLO remained the primary articulator of Palestinian views, and Arafat soon rebounded to his preeminent position in the organization. Although an agreement between Israel and Lebanon calling for Israeli withdrawal and for the normalization of relations between them was concluded in May 1983, it was soon unilaterally abrogated by the government of Lebanon.

Menachem Begin's tenure as prime minister brought peace with Egypt and significantly reduced the military danger to the existence of Israel by neutralizing the largest Arab army with whom it had fought five wars. Operation Peace for Galilee led to debate and demonstration within Israel but did not expand the peace domain for the Jewish state. The government of Prime Minister Yitzhak Shamir, endorsed by the Knesset in October 1983, proposed continuity in principles and policy, but its brief tenure was not highlighted by major developments in the quest for peace. The national unity government installed in September 1984 highlighted the importance of peace in its governmental program. It restated the elements of Israel's national consensus on the elements of peace and identified its objectives as "continuing and extending the peace process in the region and consolidating the peace with Egypt." It also called on Jordan to begin peace negotiations.

The Search for Friends and Allies

Israel's broader approach to foreign policy began to take shape once it became clear that peace would not follow the armistice accords that marked the end of its War of Independence. Israel directed its attention beyond the circle of neighboring Arab states to the broader international community in an effort to establish friendly relations with the states of Europe and the developing world, especially Africa and Latin America, as well as the superpowers, and to gain their support in the international arena. These relationships were seen not only as having a positive effect on the Arab-Israeli conflict but also as generating bilateral political and economic advantages that would help to ensure Israel's deterrent strength through national armed power and through increased international support for its position. At the outset it also held a strongly positive view of the United Nations, fostered by that organization's role in the creation of the state. With the increasingly large anti-Israel majority in the United Nations, and given this majority's virtually automatic support for Palestinian and Arab perspectives, Israel's views have changed markedly, and the United Nations is regarded as an unhelpful factor in the quest for peace and security. Israel has sought to maintain positive relations with Europe based on the commonality of the Judeo-Christian heritage and democratic tradition and the memories of the Holocaust; its approach to the developing world, which began in earnest in the late 1950s, has focused on Israel's ability to provide technical assistance in the development process. Despite the substantial efforts made in these sectors, however, the centrality of the Arab-Israeli conflict has enlarged and enhanced the role of the superpowers, particularly the United States, in Israeli eyes.

Israel's leaders recognized early on the crucial role that the great powers would play in ensuring the country's defense and integrity. In the euphoric days following independence, many believed that nonalignment in the cold war was possible and that Israel could establish and maintain friendly relations with, and secure support from, both East and West (the Soviet Union and the United States), although most realized that Israel's long-term interests lay in the West. Nonalignment was in accord with Israel's perception of its national interest and seemed to be a realistic assessment in light of the policies and activities of both powers in the period following World War II, when Soviet and U.S. support for Israel and the competition between them was seen as auguring well for the new state.

In keeping with that perception, Israel's government, upon attainment of statehood, proclaimed a policy of noncommitment (nonidentification) in the East-West conflict. Although Israel noted that in the ideological struggle between the democratic and communist social orders it had chosen democracy, it was nonaligned and not identified with any bloc in the cold war. This was a policy facilitated by Soviet actions in support of the new state when the Soviet Union voted for the partition plan of 1947, accorded de jure recognition to Israel shortly after its independence, supported its applications for membership in the United Nations, and gave it moral, political, and material support. However, soon after the end of the War of Independence, various factors contributed to Israel's shift to a pro-Western orientation, including ideological sympathies, the large size and importance of Western Jewry, and Soviet abandonment of a policy of support for Israel and denial of loan requests, coupled with a relatively constant flow of economic aid from the U.S. government and the American Jewry. Israel's support for the United Nations' resolutions and actions concerning the invasion of Korea was seen in the Soviet bloc as an unfriendly act.

Relations between the Soviet Union and Israel deteriorated rapidly in the period from 1949 to 1953, and Israel's foreign policy relinquished belief in Soviet friendship and support as a realistic policy alternative. Soviet support for, and expanded relations with, the Arab states by the mid-1950s tended to confirm this perspective. Soviet economic and military assistance to the Arab world, the Soviet bloc's rupture of relations with Israel in 1967, and the continuation of that break have led Israel farther into the Western camp, although it continues to seek the restoration of ties to the Soviet Union and its allies.

The United States and Israel

The complex and multifaceted "special relationship" with the United States that had its origins prior to the establishment of Israel has focused on the continuing U.S. support for the survival, security, and well-being of Israel.

At the outset, U.S. policy was based on humanitarian considerations associated with the plight of European Jewry, but by the 1970s political and strategic considerations had become dominant. U.S. policy on arms supplies evolved from "embargo" to "principal supplier," and arms became an important tool of U.S. policy to reassure Israel and to achieve policy modification. The two states developed a diplomatic-political relationship that focused on the need to resolve the Arab-Israeli dispute; but, although they agreed on the general concept, they often differed on the precise means for achieving the desired result. The relationship became especially close after the Six-Day War, when a congruence of policy prevailed on many of their salient concerns. Nevertheless, the two states often held differing perspectives on regional developments and on the dangers and opportunities they presented. No major ruptures took place, although significant tensions were generated at various junctures.

Israel's special relationship with the United States—which revolves around a broadly conceived ideological factor, is based on substantial positive perception and sentiment evident in public opinion and official statements, and manifests itself in political-diplomatic support and in military and economic assistance—has not been enshrined in a legally binding document joining the two states in a formal alliance. Moreover, the exact nature of the United States' commitment to Israel remains imprecise. Israel has no mutual-security treaty with the United States, nor is it a member of any alliance system requiring the United States to take up arms automatically on its behalf.

Nevertheless, the United States is today an indispensable, if not fully dependable, ally. In one way or another, it provides Israel with economic (governmental and private), technical, military, political, diplomatic, and moral support. It is seen as the ultimate resource against the Soviet Union; it is the source of Israel's sophisticated military hardware; it is central to the Arab-Israeli peace process.

Over nearly four decades the United States and Israel have established a special relationship replete with broad areas of agreement and numerous examples of discord. The two states maintain a remarkable degree of parallelism and congruence on broad policy goals. Nevertheless, there was, is, and will continue to be a divergence that derives from a difference of perspective and overall policy environment.

Notes

1. The term *Jewish Agency* first appeared in international usage in the mandate entrusting the administration of Palestine to the British government. In article 4

the WZO was recognized as "an appropriate Jewish Agency . . . for the purpose of advising and cooperating with the administration of Palestine in such economic, social, and other matters as may affect the establishment of the Jewish National Home and the interests of the Jewish population in Palestine, and, subject always to the control of the administration, to assist and take part in the development of the country." The agency was expected to "take steps in consultation with His Britannic Majesty's Government to secure the cooperation of all Jews who are willing to assist in the establishment of the Jewish National Home."

Bibliography

Bernard Reich, in *Israel: Land of Tradition and Conflict* (Boulder, Colo.: Westview Press; London and Sydney: Croom Helm, 1985), provides an overview of the country's geography, demography, history, economics, politics, and foreign policy. Howard M. Sachar's *A History of Israel: From the Rise of Zionism to Our Time* (New York: Alfred A. Knopf, 1976) and Noah Lucas's *The Modern History of Israel* (New York and Washington, D.C.: Praeger Publishers, 1975) provide histories of Israel that antedate independence. The mandate period is discussed in J. C. Hurewitz's *The Struggle for Palestine* (New York: W. W. Norton, 1950) and Christopher Syke's *Crossroads to Israel* (Cleveland and New York: World Publishing, 1965). Shlomo Avineri's *The Making of Modern Zionism: The Intellectual Origins of the Jewish State* (New York: Basic Books, 1981) and Walter Laqueur's *A History of Zionism* (New York: Holt, Rinehart & Winston, 1972) provide a comprehensive history and examination of the Zionist movement, its origins, and diverse ideological trends. Amos Elon's *Herzl* (New York: Holt, Rinehart & Winston, 1975) is a biography of the Zionist movement's founder, and Ben Halpern's *The Idea of the Jewish State*, 2d ed. (Cambridge: Harvard University Press, 1970) is a sympathetic study of the origins and development of the Zionist idea.

A brief introduction to various aspects of Israeli society and to Jewish history and values may be found in the Israel Pocket Library (Jerusalem: Keter Books, 1973 and 1974), a series of fifteen paperback volumes containing material from the *Encyclopedia Judaica*. The titles are *Anti-Semitism, Archaeology, Democracy, Economy, Education and Science, Geography, History from 1880, History Until 1880, Holocaust, Immigration and Settlement, Jerusalem, Jewish Values, Religious Life and Communities, Society*, and *Zionism*. The series also has a *Cumulative Index*. Efraim Orni and Elisha Efrat, in *Geography of Israel*, 3d rev. ed. (Jerusalem: Israel Universities Press, 1971), provide a detailed examination of all facets of Israel's geography.

The constitutional and legal parameters of the political system are considered in Emanuel Rackman's *Israel's Emerging Constitution, 1948–51* (New York: Columbia University Press, 1955), which deals with the problems involved in the development of a constitution; in Henry E. Baker's *The Legal System of Israel* (Jerusalem: Israel Universities Press, 1968); and in *Fundamental Laws of the State of Israel* (New York: Twayne Publishers, 1961), edited by Joseph Badi. An important study of the Parliament is Asher Zidon's *Knesset: The Parliament of Israel* (New York: Herzl Press, 1967), which is complemented by Eliahu S. Likhovski's *Israel's Parliament: The Law of the Knesset* (Oxford: Oxford University Press, 1971).

The basic features and issues of the political system are described and analyzed in the following works: Joseph Badi, *The Government of the State of Israel: A Critical Account of Its Parliament, Executive, and Judiciary* (New York: Twayne Publishers, 1963); Marver H. Bernstein, *The Politics of Israel: The First Decade of Statehood* (Princeton, N.J.: Princeton University Press, 1957); Leonard J. Fein, *Israel: Politics and People* (Boston: Little, Brown & Co., 1968); Yehoshua Freudenheim, *Government in Israel* (Dobbs Ferry, N.Y.: Oceana Publications, 1967); and Oscar Kraines, *Government and Politics in Israel* (Boston: Houghton Mifflin, 1961). Gad Yaacobi's *The Government of Israel* (New York: Praeger Publishers, 1982) provides unique insights into the political process by a leader of the Israel Labor party who has served as a member of the Knesset and as a cabinet minister. In *Israeli Democracy: The Middle of the Journey* (New York: The Free Press; London: Collier Macmillan, 1982), Daniel Shimshoni examines the ways in which public policies were formed in Israel until 1977.

Various aspects of Israeli politics are discussed in the following more specialized studies: Alan Arian, *The Choosing People: Voting Behavior in Israel* (Cleveland and London: Case Western Reserve University Press, 1973); Alan Arian, ed., *The Elections in Israel—1969* (Israel: Jerusalem Academic Press, 1972); Howard R. Penniman, ed., *Israel at the Polls: The Knesset Elections of 1977* (Washington, D.C.: American Enterprise Institute for Public Policy Research, 1979); Dan Caspi, Abraham Diskin, and Emanuel Gutmann, eds., *The Roots of Begin's Success: The 1981 Israeli Elections* (London and Canberra: Croom Helm; New York: St. Martin's Press, 1984); Yuval Elizur and Eliahu Salpeter, *Who Rules Israel?* (New York: Harper & Row, 1973); Eva Etzioni-Halevy, *Political Culture in Israel: Cleavage and Integration Among Israeli Jews* (New York and London: Praeger Publishers, 1977); Peter Y. Medding, *Mapai in Israel: Political Organization and Government in a New Society* (Cambridge: Cambridge University Press, 1972); Lester G. Seligman, *Leadership in a New Nation: Political Development in Israel* (New York: Atherton Press, 1964); and David M. Zohar, *Political Parties in Israel: The Evolution of Israeli Democracy* (New York, Washington, D.C., and London: Praeger Publishers, 1974).

Studies of the salient domestic political and social issues tend to be relatively few in number. Among the more reliable are S. N. Eisenstadt's *Israeli Society* (New York: Basic Books, 1967), Judith T. Shuval's *Immigrants on the Threshold* (New York: Atherton Press, 1963); and Alex Weingrod's *Israel: Group Relations in a New Society* (New York: Praeger Publishers for the Institute of Race Relations, 1965). Israel's economy is examined by David Horowitz in *The Economics of Israel* (Oxford: Pergamon Press, 1967). The relationship of religion and the state is discussed in the following: Joseph Badi, *Religion in Israel Today: The Relationship Between State and Religion* (New York: Bookman Associates, 1959); Gary S. Schiff, *Tradition and Politics: The Religious Parties of Israel* (Detroit: Wayne State University Press, 1977); Charles S. Liebman and Eliezer Don-Yehiya, *Civil Religion in Israel: Traditional Judaism and Political Culture in the Jewish State* (Berkeley, Los Angeles, London: University of California Press, 1983); and Oscar Kraines, *The Impossible Dilemma: Who Is a Jew in the State of Israel?* (New York: Bloch Publishing Co., 1976). Yigal Allon's *The Making of Israel's Army* (New York: Bantam Books, 1971) and Amos Perlmutter's *Military and Politics in Israel: Nation-Building and Role Expansion* (London: Frank Cass and Co., 1969) consider the role of the military. For a general overview of the IDF, its background, and its development, see Edward Luttwak and Dan Horowitz's *The Israeli Army* (New York: Harper & Row, 1975). Jacob M. Landau, in *The Arabs in Israel: A Political Study* (London: Oxford University Press, 1969), presents a comprehensive survey and analysis of the role of the Arabs in Israel. An alternative perspective is provided by Sabri Jiryis's *The Arabs in Israel* (New York and London: Monthly Review Press, 1976).

Israel's international relations are discussed in Theodore Draper's *Israel and World Politics: Roots of the Third Arab-Israeli War* (New York: The Viking Press, 1968) and in *Israel and the United Nations*, the report of a study group set up by the Hebrew University of Jerusalem (New York: Manhattan Publishing Company, 1956). Ernest Stock's *Israel on the Road to Sinai, 1949–1956* (Ithaca, N.Y.: Cornell University Press, 1967) is an incisive study of Israel's foreign policy from 1948 to the Sinai campaign, with a sequel on the June 1967 war. Walter Eytan, a ranking Israeli diplomat, has written *The First Ten Years: A Diplomatic History of Israel* (New York: Simon & Schuster, 1958). Israel's international cooperation program is discussed in these books: Leopold Laufer, *Israel and the Developing Countries: New Approaches to Cooperation* (New York: The Twentieth Century Fund, 1967); Shimeon Amir, *Israel's Development Cooperation with Africa, Asia, and Latin America* (New York: Praeger Publishers, 1974); and Michael Curtis and Susan Aurelia Gitelson, eds., *Israel in the Third World* (New Brunswick, N.J.: Transaction Books, 1974). Michael Brecher's *Decisions in Israel's Foreign Policy* (New Haven: Yale University Press, 1975) and *The Foreign Policy System of Israel: Setting, Images, Processes* (New Haven: Yale University Press, 1972) provide a comprehensive approach to Israel's foreign policy process and examine some major decisions. Meron Medzini, editor of *Israel's Foreign Relations: Selected Documents, 1947–1979,* 5 vols. (Jerusalem: Ministry for Foreign Affairs, 1976–1982), provides the major documents of Israel's foreign policy from its inception through 1979.

Nadav Safran, in *Israel: The Embattled Ally* (Cambridge: Belknap Press of Harvard University Press, 1981), provides coverage of Israel's domestic scene as it affects foreign policy. Yehoshafat Harkabi, in *Arab Strategies and Israel's Response* (New York: Free Press, 1977), and Gabriel Sheffer, ed., in *Dynamics of a Conflict: A Re-examination of the Arab-Israeli Conflict* (Atlantic Highlands, N.J.: Humanities Press, 1975), deal with aspects of the Arab-Israeli conflict and Israel's position and perspective. Bernard Reich's *Israel and Occupied Territories* (Washington, D.C.: U.S. Department of State, 1973) focuses on the problem of the territories occupied by Israel in the 1967 war, and Gershon R. Kieval's *Party Politics in Israel and the Occupied Territories* (Westport, Conn.: Greenwood Press, 1983) provides a more detailed analysis of Israel's policy. Bernard Reich, in *Quest for Peace: United States–Israel Relations and the Arab-Israeli Conflict* (New Brunswick, N.J.: Transaction Books, 1977), deals with Israel's relations with the United States in the context of the efforts to resolve the Arab-Israeli conflict. Bernard Reich's *The United States and Israel: Influence in the Special Relationship* (New York: Praeger Publishers, 1984) examines Israel's crucial links with the United States.

Books by and about senior Israeli policy and decisionmakers offer valuable insights into the past and present of Israel. Among the numerous works of this genre, the following are of particular interest: Menachem Begin, *The Revolt* (New York: Nash, 1981); Eitan Haber, *Menachem Begin: The Legend and the Man* (New York: Delacorte Press, 1978); David Ben-Gurion, *Israel: A Personal History* (New York: Funk and Wagnalls; New York and Tel Aviv: Sabra Books, 1971) David Ben-Gurion, *Rebirth and Destiny of Israel* (New York: Philosophical Library, 1954); David Ben-Gurion, *My Talks with Arab Leaders* (Jerusalem: Keter, 1972); Michael Bar-Zohar, *Ben-Gurion: The Armed Prophet* (Englewood Cliffs, N.J.: Prentice-Hall, 1968); Moshe Dayan, *Story of My Life: An Autobiography* (New York: William Morrow, 1976); Moshe Dayan, *Breakthrough: A Personal Account of the Egypt-Israel Peace Negotiations* (New York: Alfred A. Knopf, 1981); Abba Eban, *Autobiography* (New York: Random House, 1977); Terence Prittie, *Eshkol: The Man and the Nation* (New York: Pitman, 1969); Teddy Kolleck and Amos Killeck, *For Jerusalem—A Life* (New York: Random House, 1978); Golda Meir, *My Life* (New York: G. P. Putnam's Sons, 1975); Shimon Peres, *David's Sling: The Arming of Israel* (London: Weidenfeld & Nicolson, 1970); Matti Golan, *Shimon Peres: A Biography* (New York: St. Martin's Press, 1982); Yitzhak

Rabin, *The Rabin Memoirs* (Boston: Little, Brown & Co., 1979); Ezer Weizman, *On Eagles' Wings* (New York: Macmillan, 1979); Ezer Weizman, *The Battle for Peace* (Toronto, New York, London: Bantam Books, 1981); and Chaim Weizmann, *Trial and Error* (New York: Schocken, 1966).

The government of Israel is a prolific publisher of high-quality materials that would serve the interested reader well. Among these, the *Israel Government Year Book* and *Statistical Abstract of Israel*, both issued annually, are particularly valuable.

14

The Palestinians

Aaron David Miller

The origins of a distinct Palestinian national identity and claim to the area that now comprises Israel, the West Bank, and Gaza is a relatively recent development. Apart from the period of the Israelite kingdoms (roughly from the eleventh to the ninth centuries B.C.), historic Palestine never existed as an independent and sovereign entity. The term itself—*Filastin* in Arabic—was derived from the ancient Philistine people and adopted by the Romans to describe the province of Judea after the suppression of the last Jewish revolt in the second century A.D. Throughout the centuries Palestine remained a loosely defined geographic and administrative concept. Indeed, the modern revival of the area as a distinct political and national entity was almost entirely a result of the interaction among European imperial politics, Zionism, and Arab nationalism in the late nineteenth and early twentieth centuries.

Even the area's geographic identity was never precisely fixed. Throughout history, the borders of Palestine shifted. During King David's time, historic Palestine may have included all of present-day Jordan and Lebanon. Under the Romans, the area was reduced in size and comprised three administrative units stretching to the southern part of modern Jordan. Although the Muslim conquerors of the seventh century basically preserved a similar administrative framework, the Ottomans did not.[1] By the late nineteenth century, parts of Palestine were included in the Ottoman *vilayets* of Beirut and Sham. The remainder was divided into the two *sanjaks* of Acre and Nablus, with a separate administrative unit for Jerusalem. It was not until the post–World War I era that the core area of historic Palestine, now mandated to Britain, came to correspond roughly to the modern state of Israel, the West Bank, and Gaza. In 1922 the area east of the Jordan River was detached from the Palestine Mandate to lay the foundation of the present Hashimite Kingdom of Jordan. In 1948 the West Bank was occupied

The views expressed in his chapter represent those of the author alone and do not necessarily reflect those of the Department of State or any other U.S. Government agency.

by Jordan, leaving for the new Israeli state a narrow coastal strip, the Galilee area, and the Negev desert. During the 1967 war, Israel occupied the West Bank, Sinai, the Gaza strip, and the Golan Heights.

During the first nineteen centuries of the modern era—roughly, the time between the Roman and British occupations—historic Palestine underwent many political and economic changes. As a bridgehead between Asia and Africa, the area became a route of trade and conquest for invading armies. It also became a pawn of empires, including the Greek, Roman, Persian, Byzantine, Mamluk, and Ottoman. Each left its own legacy and influence. From the perspective of our story, however, it was the Muslim conquest in the seventh century that was destined to change the area in important ways. Significant Christian and Jewish communities continued to exist. The majority of the population, however, was eventually converted to Islam and adopted the Arabic language and culture. Moreover, Palestine was to become more open to the influences of the Arabic-speaking hinterland.

Well before the nineteenth century, then, Palestine had become an area inhabited predominantly by Arabic-speaking Muslims. Although statistics for the early period are not reliable, by 1880 residents of Palestine probably numbered a half-million, with the Arab population constituting about three-quarters of this total. The population was largely Sunni Muslim, traditional, and agricultural. As some scholars have pointed out, there were cultural, religious, and geographic attachments to the idea of *Filastin* but no defined sense of political or national community. Arab residents would have described themselves as members of a family, a *hamula* (extended clan), or a village, as a part of a religious community, even as subjects of the Ottoman Empire, but not as Palestinian nationals.

Moreover, Arab society was characterized by traditional divisions that would later hinder the development of a national identity and political movement. First and foremost, social and political organization hinged on affiliations with family and village. The importance of these bonds cannot be overestimated. Although family associations provided a durable and rooted environment at the local level, they would later complicate organization at the national level. The peasants (*fellahin*) even lacked a strong sense of class consciousness.[2] Most villages were divided into *hamulas*, each protected by a prominent landowning family in exchange for the clan's political allegiance.

These divisions were also reflected in the Christian and Muslim elites. A handful of leading Muslim families vied for political and economic influence. Moreover, a professional middle class, dominated largely by Christians, began to emerge. Common Muslim and Christian opposition to Zionism could not eliminate the tensions between them. Christian Arabs, divided into competing sects themselves, were wary of the pan-Islamic trends in Arab political life. Muslims were often resentful of a successful Christian professional class and were suspicious of their ties to the British and French.[3] Finally, divisions persisted not only between rural and urban areas but also among towns and among prominent families within the urban areas. One of the most prominent of these rivalries, that between the Husaynis and Nashashibis of Jerusalem, would have a significant influence on the development of the Palestinian national movement.

The Emergence of the Palestinian National Movement, 1917–1948

By the late nineteenth and early twentieth centuries, important forces that would later change the political attitudes of Palestinian Arabs had begun to intrude into this traditional world. The Arab national movement, initially based on a general desire to promote Arab cultural and literary achievements and to secure equality and political rights for the Arabic-speaking inhabitants of the Ottoman Empire,[4] began to influence political attitudes. There was little in this movement, dominated largely by Christian Arabs who were influenced by Western ideas of patriotism and nationalism, that focused on a separate Palestinian identity, much less that separated Palestinian Arabs from their neighbors or from the Ottoman Empire. Nor was the Great Arab Revolt against the Ottomans enough to shake the traditional loyalties of most Muslims. Indeed, until the collapse of the Ottoman Empire itself, most remained loyal to the idea of the Ottoman state.

It was neither the heavy-handed policies of the Ottoman Turks nor the ideas associated with European nationalism, however, that generated increasing political activity among the Arabs of Palestine and laid the basis of their national movement. What accelerated this process was the emergence of a Zionist movement backed by Britain and committed to Jewish immigration into Palestine and to the establishment of a national home there. In 1880 the members of the Jewish community in Palestine numbered roughly 35,000. By 1900 the community had risen to 50,000 members and, by 1914, to at least 80,000. These immigrants were not traditional Jews content to study and pray. Largely of Eastern European origin, they were labor socialist and egalitarian in outlook and possessed different language and customs certain to be regarded with suspicion by the more traditional local population. Although these early years witnessed some Jewish-Arab cooperation, and in some instances overlapping economic interests, it quickly became clear that their objectives were destined to collide.

Increasing Jewish immigration coincided with two other trends that would help to crystallize a particularist Palestinian identity. First, the Arabs were alarmed that the Zionists were receiving the active support of the greatest European power, Great Britain. Not only did the British appear to be actively promoting the idea of a Jewish national homeland as outlined in the Balfour Declaration of 1917, but they seemed to be hostile and insensitive to Arab nationalist aspirations. Second, the collapse of the Syrian-Arab nationalist movement and government in Damascus in 1920 forced the Arabs of Palestine to become more self-reliant and independent. Until the early 1920s, political activists had looked to Syrian nationalists as their primary source of inspiration and guidance. At the first national congress held in Jerusalem in 1919, the delegates had argued that Palestine was an Arab country that should be allied with Syria, although pro-Britain pan-Arabist elements disagreed.[5] In any event, when French forces pushed the Arab nationalists out of Damascus, the Palestinian Arabs began to look inward and develop their own campaign to oppose the British and Zionists. During these years Palestinian nationalists intensified their efforts to lay specific claims to Palestine based on the historical continuity of Arab settlement and their majority status there. The concept of *Filastin* as a political idea became increasingly prominent as Palestinian Arabs began to clarify their own thinking. In 1920, at the National Congress in Haifa, an Arab Executive Committee was formed to coordinate nationalist activities.

By the late 1920s, the Palestinian national movement was becoming increasingly frustrated and radicalized. The Wailing Wall riots of 1929, sparked by conflict over access to the Muslim and Jewish holy places, were exploited by the Haj al-Amin al-Husayni, the Mufti of Jerusalem, to unify the movement and to attract the support of Arab states. Concerned about increasing Jewish immigration (by 1936 Jews constituted 28 percent of the entire population), the Palestinian Arabs saw Zionism as a force that threatened to transform their entire way of life. Moreover, by the mid-1930s the fact that other nationalist movements in the region were beginning to realize their potential only heightened the Palestinians' frustration that it was the Zionists, not themselves, who might be next in line for independence.

This frustration and militance, embodied in the continuing rise of the Mufti, culminated in the Arab strike and rebellion of 1936–1939—the longest anticolonial revolt in the East during the interwar period.[6] Although the British succeeded in quelling the revolt, the turn to armed struggle and terrorism forced London to acknowledge the depths of Arab grievances and to reconsider support for the idea of partitioning Palestine into Jewish and Arab states. Not coincidentally, this rethinking occurred at a time when Britain feared that a rising fascist Germany and Italy might exploit anti-British sentiment in the East and undermine British colonial interests. The British White Paper of 1939, though rejected by the Arabs, drastically limited Jewish immigration into Palestine and cut land purchases.

Moreover, the revolt sparked renewed interest in Palestine among the Arab states and elevated the Palestinian cause to a new level in inter-Arab and British-Arab politics. There is little doubt that the active diplomatic intervention of key Arab states played an important role in forcing British concessions. Nonetheless, the involvement of the Arab states also foreshadowed a potential conflict of interests between regimes with their own political and territorial agendas on the one hand, and a divided Palestinian nationalist movement on the other. This conflict, exacerbated by the virtual dependence of the Palestinian movement on the support of Arab regimes after 1948, remains one of the most serious challenges facing the Palestinians today.

Whatever short-term gains the Palestinian Arab revolt achieved, it left their community divided, exhausted, and leaderless. This decline in Palestinian fortunes came at a time when the Zionists, galvanized by the threat of Hitler's Germany, were preparing themselves to respond to their greatest challenge. Between 1939 and 1945 the institutions created by the Jewish community of Palestine over the past decade and a half began to mature in their fight to combat British restrictions on Jewish immigration into Palestine. With the full revelation of Hitler's campaign to exterminate European Jewry, the Zionists intensified their campaign to secure support for a Jewish homeland as Zionist resistance groups launched terrorist and guerrilla attacks against British occupation authorities and prepared themselves for a military showdown with the Arabs. Although the Palestinian Arabs sought to mobilize as well, they were now almost entirely dependent on a self-interested and unorganized Arab world. Growing international support for a Jewish state, embodied in the November 1947 United Nations General Assembly resolution supporting the partition of Palestine, revealed that the Palestinians were being overtaken by events beyond their control. The establishment of the state of Israel in May 1948, which had been preceded by almost a year of undeclared civil war between the Arabs and Jews, would deepen Palestinian dependence on the surrounding Arab states.

From Refugees to National Revival, 1948–1984

The first Arab-Israeli war spelled disaster for the Palestinian Arab population. Caught up in the chaos of civil war and the Arab attack, without effective leadership, and terrified by reports of Israeli massacres at Palestinian villages like that of Deir Yassin, thousands of Palestinians fled their homes to take refuge in Arab-controlled areas and neighboring states. The events of 1947–1949 represented the *al-naqba* (disaster) in every sense of the word. By 1949 fewer than half of the estimated pre-1947 Palestinian population of 1.3 million remained in their original homes.[7] This dispersal affected most aspects of Palestinian life. Although family and village ties provided a remarkable degree of stability, it is difficult to overestimate the negative social and political impact of the 1948 war. Economically, the refugees were stripped of their land and professions as agrarians, and were relegated initially to the economic margins of the Arab societies in which they now lived. The refugees lacked the skills to accommodate themselves to the urban areas near which most of the refugee camps and shanty towns were located. This process paradoxically led to a broadening of occupations as the Palestinians sought to improve their status through education, but it also created a tremendous dislocation—forcing thousands to rely on UN services and the international dole. The UN-supported and privately owned refugee camps reinforced the ambiguous nature of their predicament. Many Palestinians believed that the camps had been designed to contain and control them, yet thousands found security and identity there and strength in their family, clan, and village associations.

The dispersal of the refugees also had a significant impact on their political activity and organization. With their leadership discredited as a result of the war and given the total collapse of an already divided national movement, it was inevitable that the Palestinians would become dependent on their Arab hosts and be tempted to follow their lead. The Arab states had already played the major role in the military struggle against Israel, and now they vied for control of Palestinian national politics. The regimes, which were not unsympathetic to the Palestinian cause, recognized the emotional pull of the issue in domestic and regional politics. Still, the Arab states were determined to ensure that the Palestinians neither threatened their internal security nor dragged them into an untimely or unwanted war with Israel. Moreover, the Palestinian issue quickly became a contentious one in the inter-Arab competition for influence. In September 1948 the Arab Higher Committee, now under Egyptian auspices, created the Government of All Palestine based in Gaza. Within two months, Transjordan had assembled a group of pro-Jordanian Palestinians in Jericho to support a union of Palestine and Transjordan—a move that would presage King Abdallah's formal annexation of the West Bank in 1950.

That the Palestinians lacked the resources to create an independent and credible national movement during the 1950s did not mean that they had lost their attachment to Palestine. Indeed, one of the paradoxes of the war and dispersal was a strengthening of the Palestinians' sense of identity. Ironically, both Israel and the Arab regimes were ultimately responsible for helping to create a strong national consciousness. The often hostile reception accorded the refugees by the Arab countries only reinforced their separate status. In their art, literature, and music, the idea of *Filastin* and a land lost remained strong. And in their politics, the Palestinians, though prevented from organizing a separate and independent Palestinian national movement, expressed their commitment to regaining their homeland in the pan-Arab, Baathist, or even Islamic fundamentalist trends sweeping the Arab world.

It was from this diaspora—the most embittered and alienated of the refugees—that a new national leadership would emerge. Unlike their parents, the members of this younger generation, well educated and politically aware, were not content to reminisce about Palestine; on the contrary, they were determined to organize in an effort to liberate their land. During the 1950s two different trends emerged that would lay the foundation of the present-day PLO. The first, embodied in the Arab Nationalists Movement founded by Dr. George Habbash, a Greek Orthodox medical student from Lydda, emphasized the importance of Arab unity and later the transformation of Arab society into a revolutionary force as the sine qua non for the liberation of Palestine. The second, represented by the Palestine National Liberation Movement—Fatah—was organized by a group of Palestinian students, among them a young engineering student named Yasir Arafat. This group pushed a more straightforward nationalist and conservative line emphasizing the importance of Palestinians taking action in defense of their own interests. Both groups would stress the centrality of the armed struggle in pursuit of their objectives.

Out of this complex environment of increasing Palestinian activism and the Arab states' desire to control the Palestinian cause came the PLO.

Created in 1964 largely at the initiative of Gamal Abdul Nasser to harness the Palestinians' militant spirit and to counter Syria's support for the Fatah organization, the PLO was nonetheless a reflection of mounting pressure to do something for the Palestinian cause. The PLO was Egyptian controlled and led by a pro-Egyptian Palestinian attorney, Ahmad Shukairy. Yet these years also witnessed the creation of the institutions—the Palestine National Assembly, the Executive Committee, and the Palestine Liberation Army—that would provide the basis for the future Palestinian national movement. Moreover, it was an Egyptian-backed organization that accelerated the efforts of the more militant groups to establish their credibility. Within a year after the PLO was created, Fatah had launched its first military operation against Israel.

Only after 1967, however, did the Palestinian national movement emerge as a credible and popular force in Palestinian and Arab politics. Israel's humiliating defeat of the Arab states during the June 1967 war not only discredited traditional Arab leadership but pushed aside the old Palestinian leadership as well. The Arabs' inability to strike effectively at Israel and the empty rhetoric emanating from Cairo and from Shukairy himself only reinforced the Palestinian conviction that Arab regimes were incapable of protecting their own interests against Israel, let alone furthering Palestinian goals. More important, the Palestinians' call for armed struggle embodied in the activities of the "fedayeen" (literally, those who sacrifice themselves) generated a powerful appeal for an Arab world that needed inspiration in the wake of the 1967 debacle. The fact that the Palestinian resistance movement's military activities were often inept and poorly organized and that their rhetoric was overblown was not as important as the act of the resistance itself. In 1968, after Palestinian fighters had engaged and inflicted casualties on a much larger Israeli force at Karameh in Jordan, their popularity soared. By 1969 Arafat's Fatah organization and Habbash's Popular Front for the Liberation of Palestine (PFLP) laid claim to the leadership of the PLO and gave it a much more militant and independent direction.

In the next decade and a half the PLO developed from a marginal organization controlled by the Arab states to a relatively independent national movement with broad support among the Palestinians, the Arab states, and much of the international community. Although the PLO failed to achieve any of its territorial aims, it did provide a symbol of national identity and pride for Palestinian refugees and persuaded key Arab states to recognize its status as the legitimate representative of the Palestinian people at the Rabat Summit in 1974. Meanwhile, the PLO had begun to develop a range of institutions to serve the diaspora communities that supported it. In Lebanon, where the Palestinians developed their main base of operations after being expelled from Jordan in 1970–1971, the PLO offered a variety of services including security for the refugee camps. The Palestinian Red Crescent, SAMED (which is the PLO's economic arm), and various educational and social agencies provided a focus of economic and political activity for the refugees. Paradoxically, the development of these services and the PLO's autonomous status in Lebanon created a state-like structure that invariably generated tensions with a range of Lebanese groups, particularly Maronite Christians. The Syrians also became concerned about the PLO's independent status and its alliance with the Muslim left. And the Israelis saw the development of the PLO's military capabilities as a political and security threat. Indeed, it was the PLO's military infrastructure in southern Lebanon that provided the justification for Israel's 1982 invasion.

The Palestinians and Their Politics

Although the PLO made considerable progress in establishing a focus of authority for a dispersed community and in creating a national movement with which Palestinians could identify, serious divisions persisted. The historical cleavages within the Palestinian community were difficult to overcome and were reflected in the ideological and organizational differences that divided Palestinian politics at the local and national levels. It was no coincidence, for example, that the leaders of two of the more militant PLO groups—George Habbash of the PFLP and Naif Hawatmeh of the Democratic Front for the Liberation of Palestine (DFLP)—were Christians who saw in the secular and supranational approach a way to equalize their status with the majority Muslim population. Family, class, and regional differences would also come into play. Palestinians who remained in their homes in Israel and the West Bank had a much different outlook from that of the refugees who found themselves beyond the borders of Palestine. Indeed, the PLO, a product of the Palestinian diaspora, has always faced the challenge of trying to reconcile its interests with those Palestinians living inside Israel, the West Bank, and Gaza.

These differences are exacerbated by the Palestinian community's dispersal throughout the Arab world. Today the world's estimated 4.3 million Palestinians are concentrated in Israel, the West Bank, Gaza, Jordan, Syria, Lebanon, and the Gulf region. Almost 1.4 million Palestinians are still registered as refugees with the United Nations Relief and Works Agency (UNRWA), and an estimated 700,000 still live in refugee facilities in Jordan, Syria, Lebanon, and the Israeli-occupied West Bank and Gaza. Although the conditions of each of these communities vary according to the political environment of the host government and the way each regime has dealt with the Palestinian issue, this geographic dispersal presents perhaps the greatest obstacle to creating a unified and independent political movement capable of mobilizing the resources of the Palestinian community.

Only in the Hashimite Kingdom of Jordan, where over a million Palestinians reside today, are Palestinians granted citizenship en masse. They do not require official work or residential permits, and they can travel on Jordanian passports. Many of the refugees who arrived in 1948 assimilated successfully into Jordanian society. Some have achieved high political office, including that of foreign minister, prime minister, and defense minister, although Palestinians have traditionally been underrepresented in the Jordanian government. Palestinians also did extremely well in business and in the professions, and they predominate today in most sectors of the Jordanian economy. To be sure, there is considerable tension between native East Bank Jordanians and the Palestinians. Indeed, many Jordanians, particularly those in the military and security services, remain wary of the Palestinians for political and security reasons. And many Palestinians continue to feel like second-class citizens.

Nonetheless, Palestinians were integrated into Jordan in a way unparalleled elsewhere in the Arab world, and they developed a strong stake in Jordan and a respect for King Hussein. Those who arrived after 1967, among them many of the 200,000 Palestinians who now live in refugee camps and shantytowns, are more susceptible to the militant nationalism of the PLO, but even they have no intention of directly challenging the Jordanian establishment. Palestinians in Jordan and thousands more working on Jordanian passports in the Gulf states have little incentive in undermining the economic gains they have achieved. Still, there is no guarantee that the strong Palestinian stake in the stability of Jordan will continue. Much will depend on economic prosperity, the degree to which Palestinian nationalist aspirations can be fulfilled, and the extent to which their desire for greater participation in Jordan's political system can be accommodated.

The Palestinians' experience in Lebanon represents the other extreme. Although perhaps 100,000 of Lebanon's Palestinians (out of an estimated total of some 350,000) were granted citizenship and were able to play important roles in banking, business, and other professions, life for the majority was extremely harsh. Lebanon's loose, laissez faire economic system allowed many to circumvent officially imposed restrictions on employment, but the need for work permits, political and social discrimination, and a constant security threat created an extremely difficult situation. Unlike the Hashimites, Lebanon's ruling elite, particularly the Maronite Christians, had no stake in assimilating poor and predominantly Muslim refugees whom they considered a threat to their political and economic dominance. The majority of the Palestinian population remained refugees located in poor neighborhoods and in UNRWA-sponsored and privately owned camps.

By the early 1970s, as the PLO entrenched itself in Beirut and southern Lebanon, the Maronites saw a potential alliance developing with their Muslim rivals. Moreover, PLO raids into Israel resulted in costly Israeli retaliation. The 1975–1976 Lebanese civil war, which undoubtedly was accelerated by the Palestinian presence, not only resulted in a bloody confrontation with the PLO's traditional ally Syria but laid the foundation for a Maronite-Israeli alliance that would ultimately facilitate Israel's June 1982 invasion. Today, Lebanon's Palestinians remain on the economic and political margins—still at odds with the Lebanese Christians and Muslims and more vulnerable and dependent than ever before.

In Syria, where almost 250,000 Palestinians reside, the refugees have fared considerably better. In contrast to Lebanon, Palestinians in Syria are eligible for government jobs and service in the army. Most Palestinians are granted equal rights with other Syrian citizens, although economic opportunities are often limited by a tightly regulated economy. As chief defender of the Palestinian cause, Syria has a political stake in not trying to integrate the refugees and to keep their cause alive and tightly controlled. As with other Syrian citizens, the Palestinian political activities are closely monitored inasmuch as Damascus seeks to control any independent nationalist leadership.

Finally, in the years following the 1948 war, a large number of Palestinians made their way into the Gulf area in search of security and economic opportunity. In Kuwait, for example, the Palestinian community numbers 400,000—constituting roughly 60 percent of the total population and a highly disproportionate share of the civil service and professional establishment. Throughout Saudi Arabia (with an estimated Palestinian population of 120,000) and the Gulf region, citizenship for Palestinians is difficult to acquire and their activities are closely monitored. Relatively small Palestinian populations are also found in the United Arab Emirates (50,000) and Qatar (20,000).

The diffuse nature of Palestinian political organization, geographic dispersal, and traditional divisions within the Palestinian community are invariably reflected in their national politics and in the institutional embodiment of Palestinian nationalism, the PLO. Traditionally described as an umbrella organization, the PLO comprises a variety of institutions that have provided political coordination for the eight fedayeen groups and have offered social and economic services to Palestinians not only in Lebanon but throughout the Middle East. Although the PLO is a highly decentralized organization, these institutions have come to constitute a quasi-state structure. Moreover, they have helped to create the image that the PLO is not simply a political organization or large bureaucracy but a "government in exile" complete with an army, treasury, cabinet, parliament, and diplomatic corps. The most important of these institutions—those responsible for setting PLO policy and administering the organization—were created in 1964 and have been reshaped by the fedayeen groups that took over the PLO in the late 1960s. The PLO's social and economic infrastructure was created later—largely in an effort to create bonds with the Palestinian community and to respond to the needs of the refugees in Lebanon, where the PLO was based between 1970 and 1982.

In 1964 the Arab League summit authorized the creation of the Palestine Liberation Organization. Ahmad Shukairy, the Palestinian representative to the League, drafted a charter that became the PLO's basic political document and a constitution that laid out the rules and regulations of the organization. The constitution describes the operation of most of the political institutions mentioned below. It is important to keep in mind, however, that the actual operation of these institutions often owes more to political trading, maneuvering, and consensus politics than to fixed constitutional practice.

At the highest level, the PLO's constitution provides for a Palestinian National Assembly, more commonly referred to as the Palestinian National

Council (PNC). This body is the "supreme authority" of the PLO and is charged with the responsibility for drafting its policies and programs. Theoretically, members are to be elected either by the Palestinian people or through a procedure devised by the PLO's Executive Committee. In practice, the PNC's 400-plus members are nominated and chosen through a more informal process of negotiation influenced by the fedayeen groups, trade unions, associations, and independents. Although roughly one-quarter of the PNC members are official representatives of various guerrilla groups, the majority of members usually support one faction or another.

The PNC has been described as the PLO's parliament in exile and has provided a forum to endorse important shifts in PLO policy. Moreover, only the PNC by a two-thirds majority can change the PLO's charter, or covenant. The fact that the covenant has been amended only once (in 1968) indicates how sensitive its maximalist tenants are and how complex a PNC amendment process could be. Two-thirds of the PNC membership must be present to constitute a quorum, although decisions are to be taken by a majority vote. As the seventeenth PNC session held in Amman demonstrated, however, the regulations can be shaped to fit political needs. Arafat's Fatah organization orchestrated the Amman session and has historically exerted the key influence in PNC meetings. But the PNC is not a rubber stamp; moreover, it has provided the forum for bitter inter-Palestinian controversy and debate. Although its members are to be elected once every three years and it is authorized to meet in regular sessions, internal Palestinian rivalries and external pressures have resulted in irregular meetings. Since 1974 the PNC has convened five times. The last and perhaps most controversial PNC session held in Amman in November 1984 was boycotted formally by six of the PLO's eight fedayeen groups based in Damascus.

The PNC elects the PLO's Executive Committee (EC)—the body charged with the daily administration of the organization's affairs and, in fact, its most important decisionmaking organ. The Executive Committee, chaired by Arafat since 1969, is in charge of the PLO's various political and military departments and is authorized to implement decisions taken by the PNC. Like the PNC, the EC, with anywhere from eleven to fifteen members, functions on a consensus principle. Representatives are drawn from the most important of the fedayeen groups and from "independents" who are usually aligned with one PLO faction or another. Although a majority vote is theoretically sufficient to carry a decision, the EC operates with a view toward achieving the broadest possible support for PLO policies and thus tries to accommodate various factions and their constituencies. Nonetheless, as a result of its size and control over the PLO's resources, Fatah has played the most important role in the EC. Since 1983 the de facto split within the PLO and Fatah's almost complete domination of the EC have reinforced this trend.

In 1973 a Central Committee now composed of some sixty members was created to serve as a link between the PNC and the EC when the larger body was not in session. The Central Committee includes all the members of the EC as well as representatives of other PLO-affiliated organizations. Although it has little power to set policy in its own right, it has served to reinforce decisions taken by the EC in an effort to convey the impression of broader support in the Palestinian community at large.

The PLO's constitution also provides for a Palestine National Fund (PNF) to be administered by the EC. The PNF, which until 1984 was based in Damascus and has since moved its offices to Amman, is funded primarily by contributions and subsidies from Arab governments. A "liberation tax" (roughly 5 to 7 percent of annual income) is also levied on Palestinians throughout the Arab world. The PNF's budget is administered through the EC and approved by the PNC. It is important to note, however, that each of the PLO's constituent groups has its own financial patrons and resources.

In addition to the guerrilla and terrorist operations undertaken by the various PLO fedayeen groups, the constitution provided for the creation of a Palestine Liberation Army (PLA). Although the PLA was theoretically meant to operate through an independent command supervised by the EC, it was from the beginning controlled by the Arab states who financed, equipped, and trained it. The PLA was initially divided into three brigades sponsored by Egypt, Syria, and Iraq. By the late 1970s it had fallen almost completely under Syrian control. The dispersion of Palestinian fighters in the aftermath of the 1982 Israeli invasion has further deepened the PLO's dependency on the Arab states that closely monitor its military activities. Finally, to provide security for the refugee camps and to try to defuse potential conflicts among the fedayeen groups, the PLO created a Palestine Armed Struggle Command (PASC) in 1969. Originally designed to coordinate military action among the various fedayeen groups, the PASC developed a constabulary function, issuing identity cards and policing refugee camps.

Although the PLO's military and political institutions generally receive the most attention, it should also be noted that the organization has developed a complex infrastructure to serve the social, economic, and educational needs of its Palestinian constituents. These institutions were clearly established with political purposes in mind—to help the PLO penetrate every dimension of Palestinian life and to forge a new sense of national identity. Yet they also were designed to meet the basic needs of Palestinians who could not get a satisfactory level of services from their host governments or from international organizations. Most of these institutions matured during the twelve years the PLO was based in Lebanon.

One of the most important of these institutions is SAMED, which provides much of the economic infrastructure for the Palestinian community. Initially created in Jordan as a welfare organization dedicated to the needs of those killed in the service of the Palestinian cause, SAMED developed into an economic organization divided into three basic sectors: agriculture, light industries, and film processing. SAMED's work force, which numbers between 5,000 and 8,000 employees (the majority of them female), produces a wide variety of consumer products from kitchenware to suitcases.

Equally important is the Palestinian Red Crescent Society (PRCS), created by Fatah in 1968 to attend to the needs of its own fighters and expanded to serve the general Palestinian population. The PRCS has concentrated its attention on Palestinians in Lebanon, although it has also established hospitals and clinics in a number of Arab countries. In addition, it maintains a social department that includes health education and vocational training.

Finally, the PLO provides a range of cultural and artistic programs and educational and research facilities. One of these, the Palestine Research Center established in Beirut in 1965, was tasked with collecting information relating to the Palestinian movement and has played an active role in research and writing on the Palestinian issue. The Center publishes *Shu'un Filastiniyya* (Palestinian Affairs).

The existence of these institutions within the PLO structure, however, does not suggest that the organization is highly centralized and controlled. Historically, political power within the PLO was concentrated not in a set of overarching institutions but in the various constituent fedayeen groups that constituted the organization. This decentralized structure has had important consequences for the development of the PLO's tactics and strategy. By 1969 (the year Arafat assumed chairmanship of the PLO's Executive Committee and Fatah moved to unite the PLO), the corporate identities of the various groups were already becoming established. Groups such as the PFLP and DFLP emerged as independent organizations with revolutionary and secularist outlooks, in contrast to Fatah's more conservative nationalism. Other groups such as Saiqa and the Arab Liberation Front (ALF) were directly controlled by Syria and Iraq. Most of these groups had their own bureaucratic structures and institutions to serve their constituents. All presented obstacles to Fatah's efforts to unify and dominate the PLO and shape its policies.

As the largest and wealthiest group, Arafat's Fatah organization emerged as the driving force within the PLO. Fatah itself has been a decentralized organization, but it has had a more stable leadership, a broader Palestinian, Arab, and international constituency, and more fighters under arms than any other Palestinian group. In fact, those who created the organization in the late 1950s have been together longer than any other ruling Arab elite. Indeed, Fatah has had considerable success in controlling the PLO's most important decisionmaking bodies. With the all but formal split within the PLO in the years following Israel's 1982 invasion, Fatah's influence and power have increased.

Nonetheless, the smaller groups have historically been able to influence the PLO's tactics and strategy to an extent well beyond that suggested by their size. Groups such as the PFLP, DFLP, and Saiqa derive their influence from several sources. First, the presence of these factions helped to demonstrate the PLO's claim that the resistance movement is a heterogeneous one encompassing broad currents of the Palestinian community. Establishing the "democratic" nature of the organization is a key element in maintaining the PLO's image as the most representative and legitimate Palestinian movement. In this respect, the smaller groups have exploited the organization's fear of fragmentation and can wield considerable power to advance their own interests.

Second, groups such as the PFLP and DFLP, led by charismatic and committed leaders pushing radical ideologies, served as the resistance movement's ideological conscience. They cannot compete with Fatah for control over the PLO's day-to-day operations. Yet over the past two decades they have been instrumental as guardians of the PLO's maximalist goals—preventing serious slippage and serving to check Arafat's inclination to test the waters of political compromise. Third, smaller groups have access to independent resources provided by their various Arab and international patrons, resources that have given them a freedom of action and a capability to set into motion events that affect the PLO as a whole. Thus, in both Black September 1970 and Black June 1976, the PFLP played a leading role in triggering confrontations with Jordan and Syria that quickly embroiled the PLO.

Finally, some of these groups have emerged as forces in their own right. The PFLP-GC (the latter term stands for "General Command"), though now tainted by its subservience to Syria, acquired a reputation for its military operations. The DFLP is known for its political sophistication and organizational skills. And the PFLP, with its history of charismatic leadership under George Habbash, revolutionary commitment, and sensational terrorist operations, has emerged as Fatah's main organizational and ideological rival.

This loosely organized style, preserved primarily to accommodate various Palestinian and Arab interests in an effort to keep the organization together, was reflected in the PLO's institutions. Decisionmaking was consensual in nature, and even Fatah itself was divided into smaller factions that had to be accommodated. Organs such as the PLO's Executive Committee (responsible for running the PLO on a day-to-day basis) and the Palestine National Council functioned not by majority vote but by consensus. Although this principle was essential to organizational unity, it resulted in an organization that had extreme difficulty formulating a decisive military or political course of action. This difficulty was particularly evident in the area of political strategy, in which the PLO's position on negotiations and accommodation with Israel evolved too slowly to keep ahead of fast-moving developments. The PLO's need to adhere to the maximalist goals embodied in its covenant, in an effort to appease militant Palestinians or Arab patrons, has prevented the PLO from responding decisively, let alone initiating pragmatic steps to further its territorial goals. This problem is highlighted by the diverging interests between the Palestinian diaspora and the Palestinian community on the West Bank. How to reconcile the dreams and organizational interests of the PLO with the West Bankers' pragmatic desire to end the Israeli occupation constitutes perhaps the greatest challenge the Palestinians will confront in the years ahead.

The Palestinians and the Arab World

While the Palestinians tried to cope with the divisions that hampered their national movement, they also had to deal with their dependence on Arab states. To a large extent this dependency was self-imposed. From the first stirrings of Palestinian national consciousness, the Arabs of Palestine looked for support to the Arab states that surrounded them. Over the past half-century, Arab regimes have backed the Palestinian cause financially, equipped its military forces, and argued the PLO's case in world capitals.

This support, however, has come at an enormous price. Without an independent base of operations and access to resources of their own, Palestinians had little choice but to defer to Arab regimes whose timetables and agendas did not always coincide with their own. This is not to suggest that these states, particularly those on the confrontation line with Israel, had no genuine commitment to the Palestinian cause. Indeed, the Palestinian issue holds a powerful and emotional appeal for an Arab world that still ideally likes to define itself by what it shares in common rather than by what divides it. To the Arab world, the displacement of Palestinian Arabs by Jews supported by a Christian West became a popular and shared grievance that served to rally nationalists, Baathists, fundamentalists, and Marxists around a powerful issue that the regimes simply could not ignore.

This emotional commitment, however, coexisted with a number of more practical concerns that made conflict between the Palestinians and the Arab regimes almost inevitable. First, the Palestinians had to deal with regimes that were status quo powers—that is, powers more interested in enhancing their own state sovereignty than in chasing the dream of trying to liberate Palestine. But regardless of how conventional the PLO has now become, it is committed to a revolutionary change in the status quo—the creation of another state in a volatile area. It is not that, say, Egypt, Jordan, or Syria are opposed to helping the Palestinians realize their national aspirations, but that they are determined to ensure that this process of self-determination is compatible with and perhaps subordinate to their own national interests.

Second, Arab states such as Lebanon, Jordan, and Syria play host to large and potentially hostile Palestinian populations that could present enormous security problems as well as challenges to their own political legitimacy. In two states, Jordan and Lebanon, the Palestinian factor has already caused serious difficulties. No regime can now afford to allow the PLO to operate independently inside its borders or to drag it into an unwanted war with Israel. Thus, these states are placed in the somewhat anomalous position of trying to support the idea of Palestinian rights and self-determination abroad while denying their own constituents and Palestinians those same rights at home.

Third, the Palestinian issue and the PLO have become pawns in an inter-Arab competition for influence in the region. The importance of a regime's support for the Palestinian cause in validating its Arab nationalist credentials and protecting and furthering its interests in the region cannot be overestimated. In fact, the Palestinian cause becomes both an advantage and a liability for some states. Nasser, for example, exploited the Palestinian cause in his bid for regional hegemony, whereas Saudi Arabia's close ties with the West, particularly the United States, make it vulnerable to Palestinian charges of dealing with Israel's primary ally. In the hands of opposition elements or rival regimes, the Palestinian issue offers a powerful weapon with which to attack the establishment.

The Arab states' ambivalence toward the Palestinian issue has only exacerbated the Palestinians' dilemma of trying to harness Arab power without becoming appendages of a particular regime's foreign policy. Although the PLO has retained considerable leverage in its efforts to maneuver through the maze of inter-Arab rivalries, it has often found itself locked in bitter controversy with the Arab regimes. Indeed, it is no coincidence that with the exception of Egypt, every other state that shares contiguous borders with Israel has at one time or another engaged in bloody confrontations with the PLO. The fact that the PLO, particularly Arafat's Fatah organization, has tried to maintain ties with all these regimes is a testament to its adaptability. Nonetheless, this balancing act has been extremely costly as the PLO's political strategy is pulled in different directions by powerful and competing forces.

Although the Palestinians have had important contacts and relationships with a wide range of Arab states—Iraq, Kuwait, Saudi Arabia, and Algeria—four Arab regimes have figured most prominently in the PLO's tactics and strategy. Not coincidentally, all of these states share contiguous borders with Israel and have lost territory in Arab-Israeli wars. Three host large Palestinian populations. Yet all share one common problem: how to discharge their commitment to the Palestinian cause while protecting their own national interests. For the Palestinians and the PLO, the challenge is even more acute: how to take advantage of Arab support while maintaining their independence. These dilemmas continue to characterize Palestinian-Arab state relations to this day.

Throughout the 1950s and 1960s Palestinians looked to Egypt as their primary source of political and moral support. The association was a natural one. Under Nasser, Egypt quickly emerged as the leading proponent of pan-Arabism and champion of Palestinian rights. Nasser's stirring rhetoric and his support for fedayeen operations from Gaza became a source of inspiration for Palestinians across the political spectrum. Indeed, by the late 1950s Nasser's picture had replaced that of the Mufti in many Palestinian homes. Nasser sought to manage the Palestinian issue and keep the Palestinian national movement well-heeled; he also helped to elevate their cause to a new level in inter-Arab politics.

By the 1960s, however, with the collapse of the Egyptian-Syrian unity scheme and the creation of an Egyptian-controlled PLO, Palestinian and Egyptian interests began to diverge. Fatah drew closer to Syria, which provided support for its operations before the 1967 war. Moreover, the

Arab defeat in 1967 paved the way for a greater divergence of interests between Cairo and the PLO. Israel's crushing defeat of the combined Arab armies convinced militant Palestinians that Egypt was in no position to take effective military action on their behalf. In fact, the loss of Egyptian territory persuaded Nasser to consider a political strategy to regain Sinai. Nasser also saw the rising popularity of the fedayeen as a challenge to his personal prestige and their call for armed struggle as a potential threat to Egyptian interests. Indeed, Nasser's 1969–1970 war of attrition against Israel could not hide the fact that PLO-Egyptian interests were diverging. Nasser's acceptance of a U.S. initiative to end the war and to negotiate for the return of Arab territory alarmed the PLO and confirmed suspicions that Egypt was thinking seriously about a separate deal.

Nasser's death in September 1970 paved the way for a major crisis in PLO-Egyptian relations. It was clear in the wake of the October 1973 war and Anwar Sadat's decision to participate in the U.S.-sponsored disengagement agreements with Israel that Egypt had begun to pursue a course that might be difficult for the PLO to accept. Sadat never intended to betray the Palestinian cause, but he appeared determined not to permit the PLO or the Syrians to interfere with what he believed to be Egypt's pressing problems—the return of Sinai and economic development. Sadat's decision to travel to Jerusalem in November 1977, his agreement to the Camp David Accords a year later, and the signing of the Egyptian-Israeli peace treaty in March 1979 brought the PLO's relations with Egypt to a new low.

It would take nothing less than Sadat's death, an Israeli invasion of Lebanon, and a major Syrian-PLO crisis to pave the way for a reconciliation between Arafat and Sadat's successor, Hosni Mubarak. Arafat's surprise meeting with Mubarak in December 1983 in the wake of the PLO's expulsion from Lebanon by Syrian-backed PLO groups seemed to indicate that the rapprochement might be mutually beneficial. For Arafat, who needed allies to help counter the Syrians and to support his political strategy, Egypt seemed to be a natural ally. And for Mubarak, determined to reintegrate Egypt into the Arab world, the Palestinian issue offered a useful bridge. Finally, supporting the Palestinian cause and identifying closely with the PLO would allow Egypt to counter criticism that it was maintaining its peace treaty with Israel at the expense of Palestinian and Arab interests.

Nowhere are the contradictions and tensions of Arab state–Palestinian relations better illustrated than in the roller-coaster-like course of Syrian-Palestinian relations. Although since the 1960s Damascus has been one of the most consistent patrons of a militant Palestinian nationalism, it has tried to ensure that Palestinian interests remain compatible with, if not subordinate to, Syrian national concerns. Until the mid-1970s, Arafat and Fatah were able to avoid a dangerous dependency on Syria—maneuvering in a multipolar Arab world while attempting to find a middle ground amid the competing and conflicting interests and objectives of Egypt, Jordan, Syria, and Iraq.

Syria's intervention in Lebanon in 1976 and the growing split with Egypt in the wake of the October 1973 war created, at least for Arafat, a unipolar environment in which Damascus emerged as the preeminent Arab patron of Palestinian nationalism. Syrian forces in Lebanon, control over PLO supply lines, and influence with other Palestinian and Lebanese groups gave Assad formidable leverage. Egyptian President Anwar Sadat's decision in 1977 to go to Jerusalem, the Iran-Iraq War in September 1980, and deteriorating relations with Jordan further sharpened Syria's isolation and increased Assad's determination not to lose control over the Palestinian card. Arafat continued to broaden his relations with Iraq, Jordan, and Saudi Arabia, but none of these states had the resources to compete with Syria's leverage over the PLO. In November 1980, in the chill of the Jordanian-Syrian cold war, Assad pressured Arafat to boycott the Arab summit at Amman—the first such gathering the PLO had missed since its creation.

In the aftermath of the PLO's withdrawal from Beirut, Arafat apparently had an opportunity to reduce his dependence on Damascus and to broaden the PLO's ties to Jordan and Egypt. Damascus had provided limited support for the PLO during the Israeli invasion and had itself taken a beating from the Israelis on the ground and in the air. Thus, it was badly discredited among many Palestinians. Moreover, as diplomatic efforts intensified to get the PLO out of Beirut and to make progress toward President Reagan's September 1 initiative, the Saudis, Jordanians, and Egyptians—not the Syrians—were expected to play leading roles. Finally, the withdrawal of PLO forces from Beirut and the relocation of Arafat's headquarters to Tunis seemed to give him additional maneuvering room vis-à-vis Damascus. The Palestinian National Council resolutions in February, though intentionally ambiguous, appeared to give Arafat an opportunity to explore the possibilities of cutting a deal with Jordan's Hussein.

Over the recent past, as Arafat began to cooperate more closely with King Hussein, Syrian-PLO relations have deteriorated even further. Syria's support for the mutiny within Fatah in the summer of 1983, Arafat's expulsion from Damascus, and Syria's role in pushing Arafat out of Tripoli in December opened up a new rift in Syrian-PLO relations. The convening of the PNC in Amman almost a year later and the Arafat-Hussein agreement of February 1985 further narrowed the prospects for reconciliation. Syria's Palestinian allies responded with acts of terrorism against Palestinian and Jordanian officials while Syria tried to exploit the de facto split between groups such as the PFLP and DFLP based in Damascus and Fatah based in Tunis.

As with Egypt and Syria, the Jordanian-Palestinian relationship is a study in both cooperation and competition. Jordan has territorial and demographic ties to Palestine that make it a vital issue in Jordanian domestic and foreign policy. Nonetheless, Jordan's control of the West Bank and the presence of over a million Palestinians on the East Bank have generated a level of interest in the Palestinian issue unparalleled elsewhere. For the PLO as well, Jordan, in the light of these same factors, has occupied a prominent place in its tactics and strategy. Indeed, trying to find a way to reconcile Jordan's security and sovereignty with Palestinian national and territorial ambitions has remained the central dynamic in Palestinian-Jordanian relations over the past four decades.

This dilemma has resulted in a relatively intense degree of competition and cooperation between the Hashimite kings and the Palestinian national movement. Abdallah set out to integrate Palestinians into his kingdom but also to subordinate any separate Palestinian identity within a Hashimite framework. Although Abdallah believed that incorporating the West Bank, including Jerusalem, increased his stature and prestige and gave the Hashimites a greater role to play in Arab affairs, the fact remains that it also created numerous problems. Incorporating thousands of better-educated and relatively urbanized Palestinians into a basically traditional East Bank environment laid the basis for serious strains. Abdullah's 1951 assassination in Jerusalem by a young Palestinian follower of his rival the Mufti reflected how dangerous the Hashimite involvement had become.

Abdallah's West Bank policies created a difficult legacy for his grandson King Hussein, who ascended the throne in 1953. It was clear even before Fatah laid claim to the leadership of the PLO in 1969 that Jordanian and Palestinian interests were almost certain to collide. Hussein had tried to curtail fedayeen activity from Jordan into Israel well before the 1967 war. Nonetheless, with Jordan's defeat and the loss of the West Bank in 1967, Hussein was in no position to confront the fedayeen. Having ensconced themselves in Jordan following the Israeli occupation of the West Bank, the fedayeen began to step up cross-border operations. Indeed, both the PFLP and DFLP saw great utility in laying the groundwork for a direct challenge to the monarchy. By mid-1970 the Jordanian army had already clashed with the fedayeen on several occasions, thus setting the stage for the events of September 1970.

Black September constituted a watershed in Jordanian-Palestinian relations. King Hussein's crackdown on the fedayeen ended their autonomous military and political presence in Jordan and established a precedent that every Arab regime has continued to respect: The Palestine movement would not be permitted to challenge the authority of an established Arab state. Although the conflict was sparked by the PFLP's hijacking of several international jetliners, two of which were flown to the Jordanian desert, Hussein clearly used the incident to move boldly against the Palestinians.

Although the king's campaign against the guerrillas in 1970–1971 and the smashing of the PLO's independent infrastructure in Jordan would end the Palestinians' military threat to Jordan, the Palestinians would continue to pose a threat to Hashimite interests. The challenge derived neither from the PLO's military prowess nor from the terrorist campaign it pursued against Jordanian interests in the wake of Black September. The real problem for the Hashimites was much more subtle, linked as it was to the increasing popularity and legitimacy of the PLO both within the Arab world and on the West Bank. Hussein could not afford to allow another force, particularly one that contained elements dedicated to his demise, to provide a focus for Palestinian nationalism on the West Bank, let alone for Palestinians on the East Bank. Yet by 1974 Yasser Arafat was already a rival to the king on both sides of the Jordan River. Hussein's 1972 federation plan for uniting both banks of the Jordan led to further isolation within the Arab world and opposition from Palestinians. Moreover, the Rabat decision of 1974 undermined Hussein's hopes and plans for an active and assertive Jordanian-brokered solution to the Palestinian problem.

Since 1975 the basic theme in Jordanian-PLO relations has revolved around Hussein's efforts to contain and co-opt Palestinian nationalism and to ensure that the PLO does not interfere with Jordan's political and security interests. Paradoxically, much of this effort has been made in the context of an improving relationship between Arafat and Hussein—particularly after 1979, when the PLO chairman visited Amman for the first time in nine years. Unlike Abdullah, Hussein did not believe he could eliminate Palestinian nationalism by suppressing and subordinating it to a larger Jordanian national identity. The king believed that there was room to accommodate a separate Palestinian identity within a Jordanian framework. This framework, outlined in Hussein's concept of a confederation with the West Bank, would enable him to maintain his political and security interests and to defuse the force of Palestinian irredentism. It is this objective that Hussein sought in his February 1985 framework agreement with Yasser Arafat.

The origins of the Palestinians' relationship with Lebanon go back to the influx of refugees who moved north across the Israeli border in the wake of the 1948 war. Yet, it was not until the 1960s and 1970s that Lebanese-Palestinian relations began to affect local and regional politics in dramatic ways. During these years the Palestinian resistance movement began to operate in southern Lebanon against Israel and by the early 1970s had established a base of operations there. In the wake of the PLO's expulsion from Jordan, Palestinian guerrillas began to search for another base from which to organize politically and to launch guerrilla and terrorist operations. Lebanon, with a weak central authority and a large Palestinian population augmented by the influx of 1967 refugees, appeared to provide an ideal location. Not only did the Palestinian refugees require protection and organization against a variety of hostile Lebanese elements, but Lebanese society, itself in the process of political and social change, seemed to offer a number of possible Muslim allies who might welcome Palestinian support in their own challenge to the system. By the late 1960s, the Palestinians had already engaged in bloody clashes with the Lebanese Army. These confrontations resulted in the 1969 Cairo accords, which were designed to restrict Palestinian military activity but in reality merely formalized their presence in southern Lebanon.

By the mid-1970s the Palestinians had become deeply embroiled in Lebanese politics, alienating the Christian community and threatening the internal power balance. PLO groups were natural allies for the Muslims and the Druze, who sought to challenge the established order. Although Fatah initially tried to stay out of the 1975 Lebanese civil war, other groups such as the PFLP believed that their independence and survival depended on an alliance with the Muslims and the Druze against the Maronites. As the Palestinian-Muslim alliance threatened to disrupt the balance of power and to turn the tide against the Christians, Syria moved to restore the status quo. Syria's June 1976 intervention on the side of the Maronites brought the PLO into direct conflict with one of its traditional allies. Moreover, Syrian involvement narrowed Palestinian political and military operations, although it did not restrict the PLO's ability to operate in southern Lebanon. Indeed, by March 1978, following a PLO terrorist attack in Israel that left over thirty dead, Israel launched what would be the first of two invasions of Lebanon to crush PLO military capabilities.

Although the PLO had more freedom in Lebanon than in any other environment in which the Palestinians had ever operated, the Lebanese base proved to be a quagmire. The Palestinians were trapped between the Lebanese who resented their presence, the Syrians who sought to control their independence, and ultimately the Israelis who moved in June 1982 to destroy the PLO as a political and military force. The armed struggle may have had political and psychological value in the late 1960s, but by the 1980s it had become a drain on Palestinian resources and a poor substitute for a political strategy. It is ironic that the most effective military weapon the PLO had ever developed against Israel—long-range artillery and multiple katyusha rockets—precipitated an invasion that cost the organization its most valuable asset: a relatively independent base.

The Palestinians and Israel

The Palestinians have tried to contend with the challenges posed by a divided political community and a dependence on Arab states, but they have also had to deal with Israel. The process has been a complex one. For the Palestinians in the diaspora and for the PLO, the relationship with Israel has been primarily confrontational. For the Palestinians who remained in their homes in 1948 or the West Bankers who came under Israeli control in 1967, the situation was not so harsh, nor were their choices so stark. To varying degrees, these communities were also adversely affected—either in the case of Israeli Arabs, by economic and social discrimination, or in the case of West Bankers, by military occupation. Nonetheless, they were spared much of the wrenching trauma of the uprooting of 1948. Moreover, as a consequence of their interaction with Israel, they were direct beneficiaries of a variety of social, economic, and political benefits. These circumstances tended to produce a much more pragmatic view of Israel and the Israelis and a more realistic appreciation of what was possible in any future accommodation. Both the Palestinians in Israel and the occupied territories increasingly identified with the PLO and chafed under Israeli settlement and land-expropriation policies. Yet, despite their subordinated status, they remained less embittered and alienated than those Palestinians who found themselves scattered throughout the Middle East.

For the PLO, which reflected the national sentiments of the diaspora Palestinians, the lack of credible military options against Israel has always been obvious. Throughout the 1960s and early 1970s the PLO sought to pursue a policy of armed struggle against Israel consisting primarily of cross-border terrorist and guerrilla attacks, internal sabotage, and international terrorism. Although these tactics had political and psychological value within the Palestinian movement and helped gain the PLO's attention within the region and abroad, they had a counterproductive effect on Israel and exacerbated relations with the PLO's Arab allies. Moreover, these attacks steeled the resolve of the Israelis, who viewed the Palestinians and their cause in exclusively military terms. Most Israelis consider the PLO a terrorist organization and oppose a PLO role in negotiations or in any future settlement. Moreover, the PLO's involvement in international terrorism also cost it dearly in the West—particularly in the United States, where the image of Palestinian masked gunmen killing Israeli athletes at the 1972 Olympic games in Munich remains a powerful one. However justified terrorism may have been to alienated Palestinians, it left in its wake a public relations nightmare for their cause.

Nevertheless, the Palestinians have increasingly fared much better in the political arena. In the wake of the 1973 war, the PLO began a campaign, symbolized by Arafat's 1974 address to the United Nations to gain diplomatic recognition. The PLO obtained official observer status at the United Nations, the only nongovernment entity to do so; in 1975 it was admitted to the nonaligned movement, and in 1976 to the Group of 77 developing nations. By 1977 the PLO had become a full member of the Economic Commission for West Asia, and in the fall of 1980, Arafat addressed the UNESCO General Conference at Belgrade. In the meantime, the Political Committee of the Council of Europe had met with a PLO delegation. In 1981 the Soviet Union, which had officially recognized the PLO in 1978 as the sole legitimate representative of the Palestinians, extended formal diplomatic recognition to the organization.

Palestinians residing in Israel proper and in the Israeli-controlled West Bank and Gaza fared much better in many respects than those in the diaspora. Of these three groups, the situation of Israel's Arab minority, now numbering close to 700,000 (about 16 percent of the Israeli population), was by far the best. Those Palestinians who remained in their homes were spared much of the trauma of the uprooting; moreover, although they lived under special security restrictions until the mid-1960s, they were eventually granted citizenship under Israeli law. Many enjoyed the social and economic benefits and services of a rapidly developing modern state and achieved a higher standard of living than that of the Palestinians on the West Bank and Gaza. Moreover, Israel's Palestinian Arabs began to play an active role in Israeli politics, voting in higher percentages than most Israelis.

Nonetheless, citizenship and equal status under the law could not prevent the de facto social and economic discrimination that affected this community. Lack of employment and educational opportunities at the higher levels, isolation from the mainstream of Israeli society, and constant Israeli suspicion of their loyalties have led to frustration and alienation. Moreover, the issue of Israeli land expropriation in the Galilee made many Palestinians more receptive to identification with the Palestinian nationalists on the West Bank and outside Israel. Over the past decade many have come to identify with the PLO, although they are torn between their Palestinian nationalist identity and the stake they have developed in the Israeli state. This rapidly growing and increasingly politicized community will present Israel with a complex problem, whether or not a solution to the broader Palestinian problem can be found.

In Gaza, the situation of the Palestinian population has been much worse. In 1949 the 100,000 new refugees in the area lived in overcrowded and squalid conditions, primarily in UN-sponsored facilities. Egypt, which occupied the area in 1948, had its own economic problems and possessed neither the resources nor the incentive to develop the area. Industry was almost nonexistent, and per capita income was one of the lowest in the world. Paradoxically, however, unemployment and an increasing population led UNRWA to train and sponsor Palestinians, many of whom were sent abroad for their education.

Israel's occupation of the Gaza strip in 1967 led to an improvement in the economic situation as Palestinian workers found employment in Israel and benefited from an increase in the standard of living, wages, and social services. Nonetheless, Gaza, with its overcrowding, became a hotbed of Palestinian nationalism and, between the years 1969 and 1972, presented Israel with a significant security problem. Today's Gaza Strip, given its estimated population of 450,000, remains one of the highest-density population centers in the world. Moreover, unlike the West Bank, Gaza lacks a diversified indigenous leadership. Social and political organization remains highly stratified, with a few prominent families such as the Shawa clan dominating the area's economic and political life.

The 800,000 Palestinians who currently reside on the Israel-occupied West Bank have fared much better than those in Gaza. Under King Abdullah, the Jordanians sought to integrate the West Bank, to ensure its economic dependence on the East Bank, and to subordinate a separate Palestinian national identity within a Hashimite framework. Palestinians from the West Bank were represented in Parliament and appointed to cabinet-level positions. Municipal town councils functioned with relative autonomy under the control of conservative pro-Jordanian elites. Nonetheless, political and economic power was concentrated in Hashimite hands as the Jordanians pursued a determined policy of preventing the emergence of an independent West Bank political or economic infrastructure that could challenge East Bank control. By 1966 the gross national product of the West Bank was only one-third of the total GNP of both Banks, even though its population was almost half of the total. West Bank economic life revolved almost entirely around agriculture, tourism, UNRWA-supported activities, and worker remittances from abroad.

The Israeli occupation in 1967 transformed the political and economic environment of the West Bank. Under the Jordanians, political life was highly conservative and traditional. Political and social life among the elites revolved around a small number of influential families who dispensed patronage and acted as middlemen between the local population and the authorities. Even with the rise of a more politicized middle class, the West Bank was remarkably free of the more progressive forces such as political parties, students, and trade unions that acted as agents of political change elsewhere.

The effects of the West Bank's contacts with Israel, particularly the increase in the standard of living and employment opportunities in Israel, increased the leverage of a salaried middle class that was capable of acting independently of the traditional elite. Moreover, the prestige and power of the pro-Jordanian notables were undermined as a result of the 1967 war and the increasing popularity of the PLO. The impact of these changing attitudes was demonstrated most clearly in the 1976 municipal elections, in which a group of younger and more nationalist mayors replaced traditional figures. The Jordanians, primarily through their financial leverage, continued to assert considerable influence. Yet the West Bankers, though still divided along regional and family lines, were increasingly influenced by a new Palestinian nationalism reflected in the activities of the new mayors—Basam Shaka of Nablus, Fahd Qawasmeh of Hebron, Muhammed Milhem of Halhul, and Karim Khalaf of Ramallah—and in the rising popularity of the PLO.

The emergence of a Likud government in 1977 committed to incorporation of the West Bank into Israel proper accelerated the process of alienation and radicalization on the West Bank, although it also increased the difficulties of political organization. Likud's strong-arm policies in the occupied territories combined with traditional divisions in West Bank society prevented the emergence of an all-area leadership, even though these tactics could not diminish West Bank support for Palestinian nationalism or for the PLO. In 1980 the bombing attacks against West Bank Mayors Shaka and Khalaf and the exile of Milhem and Qawasmeh created a leadership vacuum. Yet it was one that neither the Israelis nor the Jordanians could fill. West Bankers, alienated by increasing settlement activity, land expropriation, and hardline security policies, refused to associate with the Camp David autonomy negotiations or the Israeli-proposed village leagues. Even though many politically aware West Bankers became increasingly frustrated with the PLO's inability to adopt practical steps to help end the Israeli occupation, the organization, particularly Arafat's Fatah group, remained the symbol of their national identity. Through both intimidation and respect, the PLO strengthened its veto power over the political future of West Bank Palestinians.

The increasing politicization of West Bankers over the past ten years, however, could not change basic realities. The West Bank, predominantly Sunni Muslim and rural, remains a highly conservative environment divided along family, village, and class lines. These divisions, as well as Israel's occupation policies, have prevented the emergence of a coordinated national leadership willing and able to speak on behalf of the entire area. The National Guidance Committee formed in the years following the Camp

David Accords tried to fulfill this function, but it was undermined by Israel and viewed with considerable suspicion by both the PLO and Jordan.

It is unlikely that the West Bankers by themselves will be able to take the political or military initiative to change their situation. In a decade and a half of Israeli rule, the Palestinians on the West Bank have been unable to make the security costs of the occupation too high for Israel to bear. Despite the radicalization of many and the potential for increasing violence in the years to come, strong pragmatism and adaptability continue to characterize their day-to-day attitudes. Whether these qualities become relevant to the political process, however, will probably depend less on the West Bankers themselves than on the interests and competing agendas of Israel, Jordan, and the PLO.

Notes

1. Yehoshua Porath, *The Emergence of the Palestinian Arab National Movement, 1918–1929* (London: Frank Cass, 1974), pp. 4–6.
2. Rosemary Sayigh, *From Peasants to Revolutionaries* (London: Zed Press, 1979), pp. 30–39.
3. Ann Moseley Lesch, *Arab Politics in Palestine, 1917–1939* (Ithaca, N.Y.: Cornell University Press, 1979), p. 61.
4. Yehoshua Porath, "The Palestinian-Arab Nationalist Movement," in Michael Curtis et al., *The Palestinians: People, History, Politics* (New Brunswick, N.J.: Transaction Books, 1975), pp. 121–127.
5. Porath, *The Emergence of the Palestinian-Arab National Movement*, pp. 89–92.
6. James Jankowski, "Egyptian Responses to the Palestine Problem in the Interwar Period," *International Journal of Middle Eastern Studies* 12 (1980), pp. 1–28.
7. Don Peretz, "Palestinian Social Stratification—The Political Implications," in Gabriel Ben-Dor, ed., *The Palestinians and the Middle East Conflict* (Ramat Gan, Israel: Turtledove Publishing, 1979), pp. 403–427.

Bibliography

The most comprehensive study of the origins of the Palestinian movement is Yehoshua Porath's two-volume study, *The Emergence of the Palestinian Arab National Movement, 1918–1929* (London: Frank Cass, 1974) and the *Palestinian Arab National Movement: From Riots to Rebellion, 1929–1939* (London: Frank Cass, 1977). Ann Moseley Lesch's *Arab Politics in Palestine, 1917–1939: The Frustration of a Nationalist Movement* (Ithaca, N.Y.: Cornell University Press, 1979) is an excellent but less detailed treatment of the same period. Neville Mandel's *The Arabs and Zionism Before World War I* (Berkeley: University of California Press, 1976) provides a very readable account of Arab reaction to early Zionist endeavors. And Barry Rubin's *The Arab States and the Palestine Conflict* (Syracuse, N.Y.: Syracuse University Press, 1981) deals with the Arab states and the Palestinians before 1948. For a study of the impact of the 1948 war on the Palestinian population, see Ibrahim Abu Lughod, ed., *The Transformation of Palestine* (Evanston, Ill.: Northwestern University Press, 1971).

The Palestinian national movement and the PLO have been the subjects of numerous studies. Among the best and most objective are William B. Quandt, Fuad Jabber, and Ann Mosely Lesch, *The Politics of Palestinian Nationalism* (Berkeley: University of California Press, 1973); Bard E. O'Neill, *Armed Struggle in Palestine: A Political-Military Analysis* (Boulder, Colo.: Westview Press, 1978); Helena Cobban, *The Palestinian Liberation Organization: People, Power, and Politics* (London: Cambridge University Press, 1984); and Aryeh Y. Yodfat and Yuval Arnon-Ohanna, *PLO: Strategy and Tactics* (New York: St. Martin's Press, 1981). More personalized and partisan accounts of the PLO and Palestinian cause can be found in Abu Iyad, *My Home, My Land: A Narrative of the Palestinian Struggle* (New York: Times Books, 1981); Abdallah Frangi, *The PLO and Palestine* (London: Zed Books, 1982); and Edward W. Said, *The Question of Palestine* (New York: Times Books, 1979).

For more specialized accounts of various aspects of Palestinian politics, see Yehoshafat Harkabi, *The Palestinian Covenant and Its Meaning* (London: Vallentine, Mitchell, 1979); Galia Golan, *The Soviet Union and the Palestinian Liberation Organization* (New York: Praeger Publishers, 1980); and Gabriel Ben-Dor, ed., *The Palestinians and the Middle East Conflict* (Ramat Gan, Israel: Turtledove Publishing, 1978).

For an economic and social study of the Palestinian movement, see Rosemary Sayigh, *Palestinians: From Peasants to Revolutionaries* (London: Zed Press, 1979); see also Joel S. Migdal, ed., *Palestinian Society and Politics* (Princeton, N.J.: Princeton University Press, 1980), and Khalil Nakleh and Elia Zureik, eds., *The Sociology of the Palestinians* (London: Croom-Helm, 1980). On the Palestinians in Jordan, see Shaul Mishal, *West Bank, East Bank* (New Haven: Yale University Press, 1978). For various accounts of the Palestinian experience on the West Bank, see Moshe Ma'oz, *Palestinian Leadership on the West Bank* (London: Frank Cass, 1984); Rafik Halabi, *The West Bank Story* (New York: Harcourt Brace Jovanovich, 1982); and Ann Mosely Lesch, *Political Perceptions of the Palestinians on the West Bank and the Gaza Strip* (Washington, D.C.: Middle East Institute, 1980).

15

Arab Republic of Egypt

Bernard Reich
Sally Ann Baynard

Historical Background

Throughout recorded history the civilization of the Nile Valley flourished as a result of a combination of plentiful water, good soil, and climatic conditions contributing to a long growing season. The Nile River also provided swift, efficient, and cheap transportation and became the focal point of both ancient and modern civilizations. In ancient days a series of great kingdoms, ruled by pharaohs, developed in the valley and made important and long-lasting contributions to civilization in the fields of science, architecture, politics, and economics. These ancient kingdoms provided a base for the development of the modern Egyptian political system. Throughout its history Egypt has remained essentially a united entity, ruled by a single government, in part because of its need for overall planning for irrigation and agricultural production.

After the sixth century B.C., Egypt fell under the influence of Persia, Greece, Rome, and the Byzantine Empire. Beginning with the Persian conquest in 525 B.C., Egypt was ruled for nearly twenty-five hundred years by alien dynasties or as a part of a foreign empire. This foreign domination left its imprint. Christianity was brought to the Nile Valley and, in A.D. 639 Arab invaders from the east entered Egypt. They converted Egypt into the Arab and Islamic society that it has remained ever since. The period of Arab political domination, however, was broken at various times by other powers, notably the Mamelukes (1252–1517) and the Ottomans (1517–1882). This legacy of foreign control has been a matter of concern to Egyptian nationalists and has been a significant factor in the Egyptian political culture and world outlook.

In some respects, the most significant external influence came after the Ottoman Turks gained control of Egypt and made it a province of the empire in 1517. That initial Ottoman influence was modified by the Napoleonic invasion of 1798 and the developments that followed, which introduced an unrest and assisted the transition from the military feudalism of the past to a new system. The Western impact, the important reforms of Muhammad Ali (1805–1849), known as the founder of modern Egypt, and the construction of the Suez Canal

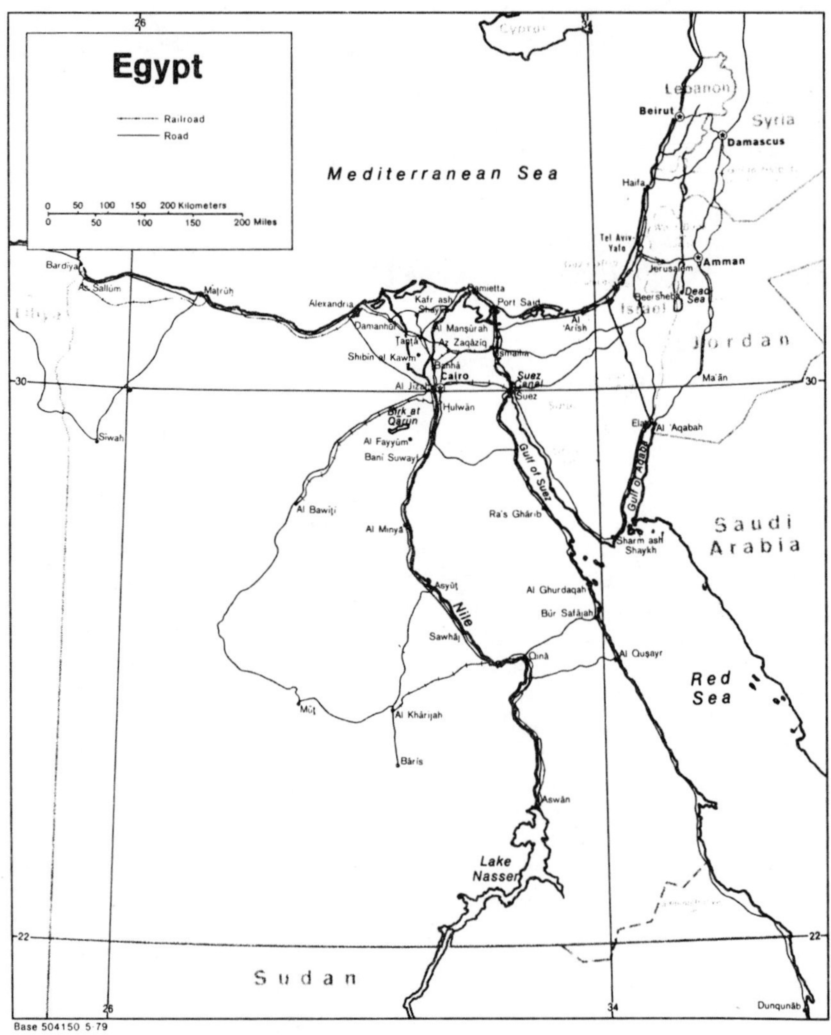

in the mid-nineteenth century all contributed to the development of the modern Egyptian state.

Muhammad Ali was neither an Egyptian nor an Arab, but an Albanian who came to Egypt from Kavalla (Macedonia) as an army commander in charge of a unit of the Ottoman army sent to deal with Napoleon. In 1805 the Ottoman sultan appointed him governor of Egypt with the title of pasha. Muhammad Ali brought significant change to the country and, to a large degree, established its independence from the Ottoman sultan. Under the former's control, Egypt began to develop the elements of a modern state and a more European cultural orientation. Muhammad Ali launched an ambitious series of domestic projects designed to improve the economy and general condition of the state. Agricultural production was improved and reorganized, and a program of industrialization was inaugurated. He forced Egyptian products into the European market and encouraged the production of cotton. Turks were replaced with Egyptians in the administration. He stressed education and sought to improve its quality. He created a modern national army, organized on European lines, that gained substantial experience in various areas of the Middle East during his reign. He created the base for a modern political system and the conditions for the rise of Egyptian nationalism.

Although European powers had been interested in Egypt for some time, the opening of the Suez Canal to world navigation and commerce in 1869 vastly increased great-power interest in Egypt. England, the greatest sea power of the time, was particularly concerned with the canal because it provided a shorter and more efficient link in its lifeline of the British Empire, which stretched from London to the Far East and included east Africa and the Gulf area. Problems associated with the canal's operation and Egypt's financial mismanagement provided the framework for the British occupation in 1882, although other European powers had also been concerned about the financial situation of Egypt. Foreign creditors, anxious about the funds they had entrusted to Khedive Ismail, pressed their respective governments for relief and assistance. As a result, Egyptian finances were controlled by foreign creditors and Ismail was deposed in 1879. Popular opposition formed against the khedive, his court, and the foreign powers. Khedive Tawfiq, who succeeded Ismail, ruled a country that was heavily taxed and was under British and French financial supervision and political control.

In response to this situation, Colonel Ahmed Arabi led a group of Egyptian nationalists who protested British and French interference in the sovereignty of Egypt and opposed the lack of indigenous political participation in Egypt. They sought constitutional reform, liberalization of Egyptian political participation, and an end to foreign interference in the affairs of Egypt. The British and French supported the khedive. In July 1882 British forces landed in Egypt and crushed the Arabi revolt. Although they were originally to leave after the restoration of order, British forces remained in Egypt until the mid-1950s and real control over the affairs of state resided in British hands for the next seven decades, thereby giving Britain control over the canal. The khedive (and later king) remained the titular authority, but the British representatives (under various titles) were the final authorities on the affairs of state.

World War I added a new dimension to the commercial and strategic importance of the Suez Canal for England and the West. In December 1914 Britain proclaimed Egypt a British protectorate, and the title of khedive was changed to that of sultan.

Opposition to the British intensified during World War I. Exasperation and frustration characterized the Egyptian nationalist movement. There had been some hope engendered by such events as the Arab revolt against the Ottoman sultan and such declarations as Wilson's Fourteen Points. Within Egyptian society there emerged the beginnings of nationalistic ideas of a political nature that were to spearhead the movement to remove British control and establish Egyptian control over the country. In this post–World War I context a new political organization developed, al-Wafd al-Misri ("the Egyptian Delegation"). Under the leadership of Saad Zaghlul and later Nahas Pasha, al-Wafd al-Misri sought independence from the British and self-rule in Egypt. The Wafd hoped to present its position to the great powers at the postwar conferences—especially at the Paris Peace Conference, where the fate of the Ottoman territories was to be determined. British opposition to Egyptian independence effectively prevented the Wafd from achieving its goal, and the period until 1952 is replete with Egyptian nationalist efforts to end British domination of the country. The Wafd remained the most important political party in Egypt until its abolition following the 1952 revolution. Throughout the period it opposed British imperialism and sought Nile unity with the Sudan as a part of Egypt.

In the aftermath of World War I Egyptian opposition to British rule became increasingly hostile. In the face of such pressure, the protectorate was terminated and in February 1922 the British unilaterally proclaimed Egypt a constitutional monarchy. However, the British reserved their freedom of action on four matters: the Sudan, the defense of Egypt against foreign intervention, the security of the canal (i.e., the communications line of the British Empire), and the protection of foreign interests and minorities. In March, Sultan Fuad became the king of Egypt. Thus, by 1922 Egypt had become technically an independent country with its own king and in alliance with England (which provided assistance in defense and related matters). A constitution was developed and promulgated in April 1923, launching a new experiment in government and politics. A Parliament was elected and a government was formed. Domestic politics began to operate, and rivalries between power blocs and political institutions began to develop. Local politics reflected a good deal of the rivalry between the king on the one hand and the government and Parliament on the other (both of the latter generally dominated by the Wafd, which opposed both the king and the British). Many of the concerns of Egyptian society were not effectively dealt with because the main political forces were in conflict with each other. Fortunately, there was more agreement on the question of the British position in Egypt. All elements of Egyptian society generally agreed that the British should leave and that full control should be vested in Egyptian authorities.

British influence, however, remained paramount. British troops and officials were stationed in Egypt, mostly but not solely concerned with the canal and the security of the imperial communications system. Through them, the British were able to influence political activity and policy decisions. British-Egyptian negotiations continued, on a somewhat sporadic basis, during much of the period until 1936. At that time a new Anglo-Egyptian treaty was written that altered but did not terminate the British role. On many of the key issues little changed and British influence remained significant, although its formal trappings were modified.

World War II provided an important milestone in the political development of Egypt. Its territory was used as a base of Allied operations, but local sentiment was generally against England as the hated occupier. The war, however, sapped British strength and financial resources, and Britain was soon forced to reconsider its position throughout the Middle East, setting the stage for a major political realignment throughout the area, especially in Egypt and Palestine.

After World War II Egypt became involved in two related matters that laid the foundation for the Egyptian revolution. The first was the creation of Israel following the British withdrawal from the Palestine mandate in 1948, which Egypt opposed and which, in turn, led to the Arab-Israeli War of 1948–1949 in which the armed forces of Egypt performed poorly. The corruption and inefficiency of the government of King Farouk (whose rule began in 1936) were later cited as major causes for the poor performance of Egyptian military forces against the new state of Israel. The war was probably the most important single event in Egypt's political development prior to the 1952 revolution. It helped to complete the rupture between the army and the king, and increasingly ruthless police actions were instituted by the government in response to the political disorganization and turmoil that followed the war. Egypt's economic crisis also worsened as mismanagement and corruption became rampant.

The second issue was the continuing opposition to the British role in Egypt and the desire of the nationalists, often led by the Wafd, to reduce or eliminate the British position and control. Negotiations to revise the 1936 treaty, especially those relating to the questions of the Sudan and the canal, were unsuccessful. Clashes between the British and Egyptian nationalists became increasingly frequent. On October 15, 1951, the government of Egypt under Prime Minister Nahas Pasha abrogated the 1936 treaty and proclaimed Farouk king of Egypt and the Sudan.

An impasse had been reached in the relations between King Farouk and politicians (especially the Wafd) that deadlocked the processes of government and made ruling impossible. Political chaos and the breakdown of public order were indications of the problems. Deterioration in relations with England exacerbated the situation and led to a military overthrow of the alien dynasty.

This provided the backdrop to the Egyptian Revolution of 1952. Disturbances broke out, and mobs attacked foreign establishments in Cairo. The British objected, and clashes between British troops and Egyptians soon intensified. January 26, 1952, a day of violence, came to be known as "Black Saturday" and was followed by the ouster of Nahas Pasha and the proclamation of martial law.

The Egyptian Revolution (1952)

By 1952, King Farouk's government was viewed by Egyptian nationalists as incompetent, corrupt, and unable to deal effectively with either the British or the problem of Israel. The obvious solution in the minds of many younger military officers (and like-minded civilians) was to change the country's leadership in order to improve Egypt's ability to respond to these threats.

On July 23, 1952, members of a small clandestine military organization known as the Free Officers launched a coup d'état that established a new system of government. Farouk was forced to abdicate and left the country on July 26, 1952.

The 1952 coup was swiftly and efficiently executed. The military controlled the major instruments of force, and there was no significant opposition to their actions. The guiding hand of the new system was the Revolutionary Command Council (RCC), whose titular head was a senior military officer, General Muhammad Naguib, one of the few successful Egyptian officers in the 1948 war.

The immediate concern of the RCC was to dismantle the corrupt structures of the monarchy and to create a new political order that would institute major social change. The Free Officers, however, were somewhat naive in their approach to government. Since the ouster of Farouk was the major objective of the coup, the Free Officers did not have a careful and articulated plan for the ordering and functioning of Egyptian life after the coup. Their basic goal was to end political corruption and inefficiency and to prevent further humiliations such as the Arab-Israeli War of 1948–1949 and the British control of Egypt. Moreover, the Free Officers had not sufficiently determined how to achieve the long-term goals of ousting the British from Egypt (especially the canal zone) and securing the linkage with the Sudan. No formal ideological position was articulated, although a brief six-point statement of position and goals was advocated. The regime declared its opposition to colonialism, imperialism, and monopolies, and also asserted its support for social justice, a strong military, and a democratic way of life. Theirs was a program that any Egyptian nationalist could endorse.

Immediate decisions were essential to ensure the functioning of the system and to provide an overall perspective. It was agreed that Farouk would abdicate and would be permitted to leave Egypt and live in exile. The constitutional monarchy was preserved at first, and a regency council was established to preside in the name of Farouk's infant son, Fuad II; a general purge of corrupt officials was instituted; and land reform was to be a major program of the RCC. At this time, the RCC intended to return Egypt to a civilian government as soon as possible.

After a period of some uncertainty concerning the organization and structure of the government, the RCC decided that the changes they envisaged were simply not possible within the existing political system. In December 1952 the 1923 constitution and the parliamentary form of government were suspended. The following January General Naguib announced that all political parties had been banned and their funds confiscated, and that constitutional government would not operate for a three-year transition period. In February an interim constitution was proclaimed that provided the terms for the operation of the government during this time. This constitution noted that the people were the source of all authority but also that all power was clearly vested in the RCC, which would act in all crucial capacities throughout the transition period. With the abolition of political parties, the RCC created a new political organization called the National Liberation Rally to replace the banned political parties.

In June 1953 the RCC moved to the next step in the conversion of the political scene. The monarchy was abolished. A republic, with Naguib as both president and prime minister, was declared. The main structural changes were now in place, permitting the processes of government to function within a new framework.

The Emergence of Nasser

The most crucial factor in this period was the emergence of Gamal Abdul Nasser as the primary force of Egyptian national life. Nasser appeared in the public view rather slowly. When the Free Officers overthrew Farouk, attention was focused on General Naguib as the titular and apparent head of the new regime; therefore, Nasser appeared to be little more than another colonel in the RCC. Slowly his role as the guiding force behind the revolution began to clarify, and Nasser emerged as the victor of a power struggle within the RCC, making his primary role apparent to the outside observer. The struggle for control between Nasser and Naguib went through several stages, culminating in the ouster of Naguib on November 14, 1954, and in his being placed under house arrest. Thus Nasser's dominant position was secured within the system, allowing him to become the undisputed leader of Egypt and, later, of the Arab world.

Political Environment

Egypt's social and economic structure is closely linked to the Nile River, which has traditionally been an important source of revenue and a central factor in daily life. Traditionally and currently, wealth is most often measured in land ownership and control of agricultural production. Egyptian society has been based to a significant degree on the peasants, the *fellahin,* who constitute the vast majority of the Egyptian population. The *fellahin* are the backbone of the Egyptian system, even if they are relatively deprived economically and educationally, as well as in terms of life expectancy, wealth, health, literacy, and most of the other measures of achievement in society. Both Nasser and Sadat traced their roots and publicized their connection to this group. In addition to the *fellahin* are the traditional wealthy, upper-class landowners and the middle-class city-dwellers. The traditional supporters of the king and members of the court also came from the upper class. Since the 1952 revolution, however, the growing bureaucracy and the military officer corps have increasingly improved their status and power within the system.

At the time of the revolution Egypt was a poor country facing a host of social and economic problems: low per capita income, unequal income distribution, disease, early death, low life expectancy, and a low literacy rate. Agriculture was the dominant sector of the economy and this required the use of Nile water for irrigation. Industry was a minor factor and was significantly limited by poor natural and mineral resources and by the lack of sufficiently trained workers.

The Egyptian Revolution of 1952 was launched to deal with a political issue, but almost as crucial were the substantial economic and social problems of Egypt, which were among the earliest problems tackled by the regime. There was a two-class system—a very rich upper class and very poor lower class, with the latter vastly larger than the former. The upper class of bankers, businessmen, merchants, and landlords controlled the wealth of the country and dominated its political institutions. It could and did prevent the adoption of reform measures that would diminish its economic and/or political control. Much of Egypt's land was concentrated in the hands of relatively few absentee landowners. The poor were mostly landless peasants who constituted more than 75 percent of the population. Furthermore, they were illiterate and had little opportunity to improve their situation. Their health standards were deplorable and they had no political influence. Education and employment were severely limited. This disparity between the landowning rich and the poor peasantry was further compounded by overpopulation, exacerbated by the high birth rates of the poor. The population growth rate surpassed that of agricultural production increases. Moreover, the possibility of food production keeping pace with population growth was limited by lack of control of the water resources of the Nile.

One of the goals of the revolution, announced shortly after the takeover by the Free Officers, was the achievement of social and economic justice through elimination of the corrupt system and the monopoly of wealth. Although lacking a specific ideology and well-developed programs for implementing these goals, the new government attempted to raise the standard of living of the average Egyptian, especially of the fellahin of the Nile Valley, and to reduce the poverty and disease that had permeated Egyptian society for so long.

Agriculture

Egypt is the gift of the Nile and has been dependent on that single main source of fresh water for the thousands of years of its recorded existence. There is a narrow strip of poor land along the Mediterranean coast where some crops can be grown on land when there is minimal rainfall. Except for this area, virtually all agriculture is dependent on irrigation from the Nile. The land made inhabitable and cultivable by the river constitutes a small portion of Egypt's overall landmass (about 4 percent); therefore, agricultural production, despite the rich soil and the favorable climate, has been limited, although it is the main occupation of, and provides the livelihood for, most Egyptians.

The limited agricultural production does not provide sufficient food for Egypt's increasingly large population. Despite efforts to control it, Egypt's population growth rate has hovered at about 3 percent per year since the revolution. At this rate of portending growth, Egypt's population will number approximately 60 to 70 million by the year 2000—a population beyond Egypt's projected capacity to feed, clothe, house, and employ.

Agrarian reform became the first and most significant domestic effort of the regime, demonstrated by the Agrarian Reform Law of September 1952. It limited individual landholdings to less than two hundred feddans (approximately two hundred acres) and reduced the rents paid for lands while increasing agricultural wages. In an effort to redistribute existing agricultural land and to divide the wealth of the country more equitably, some lands were expropriated (with compensation) and redistributed. Because land redistribution diminished the power of the major landowners, it was also a partially political act. As a result of shifting wealth from the upper class to the lower class, the technocrats and army officers became part of the new upper class of Egypt.

Related to the Agrarian Reform Law were other measures of considerable importance, of which the Aswan High Dam was among the most significant. The purpose of the dam was to improve Egypt's economic system by increasing the already high productivity levels of the Nile Valley lands through an improved irrigation system. The dam was designed to increase water storage capacity, to prevent devastating floods, to add cultivable land, and to create substantial additional hydroelectric capacity. The dam also had symbolic value as an achievement of the revolution.

The completion of the Aswan High Dam has had mixed results. Many of the anticipated benefits have been realized. There has been a significant increase in the cultivated area of Egypt and in net agricultural output; flood control has also helped to lead to productivity gains; additional electrical power, primarily for industrial use, has been made available; and navigation along the Nile, which is utilized as a major transportation artery in Egypt, has been improved and a fishing industry has been developed in Lake Nasser. However, there are some problems. For example, silt has been trapped behind the dam in Lake Nasser. More chemical fertilizer is thus needed because the soil is no longer replenished in the flooding process. Salinity has increased in the northern portion of the river and in some of the land formerly flood-drained. Other chemical and biological changes have also affected the river and its role in Egyptian life.

Other Economic Sectors

The 1952 revolution was of little immediate consequence to the Egyptian economy. The land reforms resulted in some redistribution of land and wealth, but the economy continued to be based on private enterprise. Some restrictions were placed on the economy, but these were directed mainly toward foreign trade and payments. By the end of the 1950s government attitudes had shifted to favor public participation in, and direct regulation of, the economy; and in 1961 a series of decrees nationalized all large-scale industry, business, finance, and virtually all foreign trade. Private enterprise and free trade were replaced by Arab socialism, which was proclaimed the basis of the economic system. In practice, this meant establishing a mixed economy with a large public sector (including all foreign trade) and with the remaining private economic activities subject to various kinds of direct controls. Prices were regulated, and a resource allocation was determined by administrative action and decision.

The system derived its socialist character mainly from the fact that all big business was controlled by the government. Modern manufacturing, mining, electricity and other public utilities, construction, transport and communication, finance, and wholesale trade were primarily owned by the government, whereas most retail trade, handicrafts and repair, housing, professional services, and agriculture were privately owned. The government imposed some control on agricultural production through its control of the irrigation system and through the compulsory participation in government-sponsored agricultural cooperatives. Control was also exercised over the distribution of capital goods, raw materials, and semimanufactures as well as over prices and wages.

By 1962 the Egyptian economy and the context in which it functioned had changed considerably. Ownership of the main branches of the economy had been transferred to the government. The wealth remaining in private hands was essentially real estate and that, too, was carefully controlled. Government budgets accounted for about 60 percent of the GNP. Inequality of wealth and income had been greatly reduced, largely through a process of agrarian reform, higher taxation, the extension of social services, and by a series of nationalizations and sequestrations. The role of foreigners in the economy had been substantially reduced and, in some sectors, terminated. Industry had made substantial progress—accounting for more than 20 percent of the GNP—and continued to increase its proportion.

Efforts to improve the economic system were severely hampered by the losses suffered in the 1967 Arab-Israeli war. As a consequence of that conflict, Egypt lost substantial revenues from the closure of the Suez Canal, the loss of the oil fields in the occupied Sinai Peninsula, and the loss of tourism. All three elements had been important to Egypt's earning of foreign exchange for its development and for the purchase of needed imports. The lost revenues would have helped to reduce Egypt's foreign debt.

In the wake of the 1973 October War the situation began to change. The canal was reopened (1975) and the Sinai oil fields were later returned to Egyptian control. The improved tranquility resulting from the Sinai disengagement agreements (1974 and 1975) and the peace treaty (1979) with Israel also helped to improve tourism and commercial investment in Egypt. Increased donations and contributions to Egypt, especially from the oil-rich Arab states of the peninsula and Gulf (which have been contributing huge amounts of money per year since 1967) enlarged Egypt's economic potential for development. The October War tended to have positive results for the Egyptian economy. The war involved the oil-rich Arabs in the process of a settlement and created an aura of stability and tranquility that fostered domestic, regional, and international involvement in the Egyptian economy.

The war also gave way to the announcement of a new approach to economic matters generally referred to in Egypt as the "opening"—the economic open-door policy. In a 1974 working paper, President Anwar Sadat set forth a statement of Egypt's long-term economic and social objectives. He discussed the successes of the revolution, including the emancipation of women, the establishment of many public-sector enterprises, the Agrarian Reform Law, and advances in education and other social services. He also identified some of the shortcomings in Egypt's existing economic employment in the public sector and excessive interference by government ministries in the operation of the economy; moreover, he called for a change in the philosophy of planning and in the implementation of government policy. Decentralization was deemed essential, as were efforts to make Egypt's administrative machinery responsive to innovation and to interested foreign investors. In general, the opening sought to unite Arab and Western (especially U.S.) capital, technology, and expertise with Egyptian labor and Egyptian and Arab markets to help rejuvenate the Egyptian economy. To a great extent, this opening depended on regional and domestic stability and represented a shift from the previous situation in which there was a heavy reliance on Soviet-bloc technology and markets and on isolation from Western technology, markets, and hard currency.

Poverty and ignorance remain important problems for Egypt. The heavy dependence on agriculture has made the Nile and its control a major interest of the government and a focal point of many of its programs. The government has worked to develop sources of revenue other than agriculture and has also attempted to increase the land area under cultivation. Economic problems, and especially the availability of food, are often exacerbated by the population growth rate. Egypt's main dilemma is its population, the density of which is one of the highest in the world. In part this density results from the fact that only a very small portion of the country's total landmass is inhabited, owing to the lack of water and cultivable land in the broad desert regions that constitute much of the landmass of the country. Improved health conditions and reduced death rates only add to the increasing population burden.

From World War II until 1961 Egypt held substantial foreign-exchange reserves. In 1962 the foreign-exchange reserves were exhausted, and Egypt entered a period of severe foreign-exchange crises that still exists.

Egypt continues to have an underdeveloped, labor-surplus economy, a high annual import bill, and increasing labor pools owing to the high birth rate. The country still suffers from high defense expenditures that, in the late 1960s and early 1970s, were often between 20 and 25 percent of the GNP. These expenditures increased the need for external financial support in the form of loans, grants, and subsidies.

Thirty-four years after the Egyptian Revolution, many of the socioeconomic problems facing the country were quite similar to those that had prevailed at the time of the coup: Egypt remained a poor and developing country; it was densely populated; and its birth and population growth rates continued to be high. A very high, though declining, proportion of the population continued to work in agriculture. Unemployment and disguised unemployment remained problems facing the government. Migration to the cities, for employment and housing, tended to create problems for the major cities while the increasing numbers working abroad constituted a brain drain that adversely affected economic development. Despite the considerable expansion of educational and health facilities, endemic diseases were widespread and illiteracy remained at a relatively high level. Clearly, Egypt was faced with the need to develop new approaches and to achieve new accomplishments in the socioeconomic area.

Political Structure

Egypt's political system has experimented with several variations in the search for a permanent structure. With Nasser at its head, the RCC exercised primary responsibility for the functioning of the system and the establishment of government policy. During the transition period a number of outstanding problems, including the position of England in Egypt and the canal zone, were finally resolved. Then, in 1956, Nasser formally inaugurated a new system that consolidated power in his own hands.

On January 16, 1956, a new constitution was proclaimed in which extensive powers were concentrated in the hands of the president. The constitution also established a single political party, the National Union, which replaced the Liberation Rally. A National Assembly was to perform the legislative function.

The political party and the Parliament, as well as most other instruments of government, remained under the control of Nasser, who was elected president by more than 99 percent of the vote in 1956. In the same year martial law was terminated, political prisoners were released, and other changes occurred. The RCC members became civilians (with the exception of General Abdul Hakim Amer, who was minister of defense) and joined various agencies of the government. A plebiscite formally approved a new constitution. A National Assembly election awaited the termination of the Suez crisis (i.e., until 1957). The new system created a strong presidency and seemed to ensure that, with all members of Parliament belonging to a single political party, Parliament would be docile and subservient while the president exercised virtually all significant powers in the system. But the new system was short-lived.

In February 1958 Egypt joined Syria to form the United Arab Republic (UAR). The union of these two dissimilar and geographically noncontiguous political units into a single state called for the creation of a new political structure. A strong president was to be assisted by ministers appointed by and responsible to him. A single legislative house was to be created. The provisional constitution of the new UAR was proclaimed and Nasser became president. Nasser received nearly all the votes cast in the presidential election on February 21, 1958. The president was assisted by vice-presidents, a cabinet of ministers, the National Assembly, and regional councils. Both Egyptians and Syrians were represented in the institutions of government, but much of the actual governing was by decree of Nasser and his chief advisers and aides—especially General Amer, who held much of the responsibility for and control of the Syrian region. In September 1961, Syria, disenchanted with Egyptian domination and Nasser's growing socialism, severed ties with the UAR and reestablished its independence. Egypt continued to be known by the name "United Arab Republic" until it became the Arab Republic of Egypt (ARE) in 1971.

With the termination of the United Arab Republic of Egypt and Syria in 1961, there was an intensification of Nasser's socialist programs in Egypt. A new governmental system was again devised and implemented soon thereafter, with a clear socialistic focus. Socialistic measures adopted in the early 1960s included further agrarian reform, progressive tax measures, nationalization of business enterprises, and, in general, increased governmental control over the economy. A new charter and constitution were created, and a new political organization, the Arab Socialist Union (ASU), was formed. Elections for Parliament took place. A new constitution was adopted in 1964 that provided the framework for the remainder of the Nasser tenure.

A new phase in Egyptian politics began with the death of Nasser on September 29, 1970, and his replacement by Anwar Sadat.

Sadat's consolidation of control was followed by changes in the political structures and processes of politics. On September 11, 1971, Egypt's permanent constitution was approved by general referendum. It was designed to embody the goals and principles of the revolution and to form the basis of the government's policy. It is similar to its predecessor in continuing the strong presidential system extant in Egypt since the revolution. According to the constitution, the president of the republic is head of state. He is empowered to declare a state of emergency in the case of national danger, subject to a referendum within sixty days. Legislative power is vested in the National Assembly, composed of at least 350 members, at least half of whom must be workers and farmers. The president may appoint up to 10 members. The president may object to laws passed by the National Assembly within thirty days of their passage, but the assembly has the right to override his objection by a two-thirds vote. The president has the power to appoint vice-presidents and the prime minister and his cabinet, and is supreme commander of the armed forces. Although the constitution increased the powers of the National Assembly, dominant authority remained with the president, who has the right of temporary rule by decree. The constitution includes guarantees of freedom of expression, as well as assurance of freedom from arbitrary arrest, seizure of property, and mail censorship. Press censorship is banned except in periods of war or emergency. The Arab Socialist Union was declared the only authorized political party, although this dictate was subsequently modified by legislation. Islam was declared the state religion, although freedom of religion was guaranteed.

In 1976 Sadat initiated what appeared to be a move toward a multiparty system when he announced that three ideological "platforms" would be organized within the ASU. The centrist group—the Egyptian Arab Socialist Organization—had Sadat's personal support and won a vast majority of the seats in the 1976 parliamentary election. Sadat refused to allow independent parties to be formed, and the three organizations never took root as genuine vehicles of political participation. Only after the violent clashes over increased prices of basic commodities in January 1977 did Sadat permit parties to be formed. The opposition by these parties was too much for Sadat to bear, however, and he soon clamped down on such groups as the New Wafd party and the leftist National Progressive Unionist party.

In July 1978 Sadat created the National Democratic party (NDP) and later permitted a leftist party to organize as an official opposition. Both the Egyptian Arab Socialist Organization and the Arab Socialist Union were abolished in April 1980. An Advisory Council was established to serve the functions of the old ASU Central Committee, and in the September 1980 elections for that council, Sadat's new NDP won all 140 seats, with the 70 remaining posts appointed directly by the president. Sadat, like Nasser before him, wanted to create a political organization but was unable to tolerate the loss of political control that would have accompanied the trend by which such organizations would become genuine vehicles for mass participation.

Sadat's assassination in October 1981 changed very little about Egyptian domestic politics. Hosni Mubarak left the basic structure unaltered. He allowed the New Wafd to participate in the 1984 parliamentary elections, but the NDP won handily and some opposition parties failed to get sufficient votes to secure even one seat in the assembly. Despite all the changes, Egypt remained a strong presidential system with a facade of one-party rule.

Political Dynamics

Nasser ruled Egypt from 1954 until his death in 1970. He was the first Egyptian since the pharaohs to control Egypt for any long period. During his tenure he captured the attention and imagination not only of the Egyptian people but also of the Arab world, as well as of much of the developing and nonaligned Third World and other portions of the international community. Egypt ended British control, established a republican form of government, and began extensive political change. In an effort to alter and ameliorate the centuries-old Egyptian social and economic systems, reforms were inaugurated.

Nasser succeeded in nationalizing the Suez Canal. He was able to thwart the objectives of Israel, England, and France in the 1956 Sinai War and was able to turn defeat into achievement—if not victory—with the aid of the United States and the Soviet Union. He secured arms and aid for the Aswan High Dam from the Soviet Union and its bloc allies after the United States proved unwilling to provide the military, technical, and economic aid essential to these projects. In the realm of Arab unity Nasser realized achievements (and failures), but he tended to symbolize Arab accomplishment for many of the ordinary citizens of the Arab world.

Nasser's accomplishments in the 1950s were soon followed by difficulties. The United Arab Republic dissolved in 1961, Egypt became unsuccessfully involved in the civil war in Yemen in the early 1960s, and there were feuds with other Arab states and challenges to Nasser's role as Arab world leader. The 1967 Arab-Israeli war proved disastrous and resulted in the loss of the Sinai Peninsula, the closure of the Suez Canal, and the loss of a substantial portion of Egypt's military capability.

Despite these reverses Nasser was still the preeminent Egyptian and Arab, the most influential figure in the Middle East, and a focal point of regional and international attention. Nasser's role extended beyond that designated in the constitution. He exercised unwritten powers by virtue of his unique standing in the system, his accomplishments, and his charismatic appeal to the peasantry that formed the backbone of Egypt. He controlled all the main instruments of violence and of power—including the army, the secret police and intelligence agencies, and the Arab Socialist Union—and dominated the cabinet and the National Assembly. At the time of his death, Nasser's central role and his charismatic appeal to the overwhelming majority of Egyptians raised doubts about a successor's ability to replace Nasser as the undisputed leader of Egypt and the Arab world. Nasser's death in September 1970 marked the end of an era in modern Egyptian history, and no figure was clearly identified as his successor. Anwar Sadat became president and was later formally elected to that position, securing approximately 90 percent support in a national referendum.

The problem of succession foreshadowed a power struggle, for the clear and unopposed succession by any one individual was not ordained. Nasser had not prepared an elaborate institutional legacy that would ensure orderly succession. Under the terms of the constitution, and by the terms of Nasser's legacy, Sadat was to succeed as president. But virtually all observers regarded him as little more than an interim leader to be followed by a powerful successor once the behind-the-scenes struggles had been played out among the contenders. Among the possible successors were Ali Sabri (who had headed the ASU and was apparently favored by Moscow because of his pro-Soviet leanings) and various other high-ranking officials of the Nasser state. The struggle began as soon as Sadat formally succeeded to the presidency.

Sadat sought to consolidate his position but did not make a major overt move until May 1971, when he purged the government of senior officials who opposed him. This group included Ali Sabri, then vice-president, as well as the minister of war, the head of intelligence, and various other senior officials. These officials were later tried for high treason.

Sadat proclaimed 1971 as a year of decision that was to result in war or peace in the Arab-Israeli conflict, but the year ended with no substantial movement toward achievement of this objective. By 1972 Sadat had become an object of ridicule and cruel jokes, which raised doubts about his leadership. It was in partial response to domestic criticism and to the concerns and complaints of the military that he decided to terminate the role of the Soviet advisers in Egypt in 1972. Sadat soon began to prepare for the October War because he saw little progress toward a political settlement of the conflict with Israel. The beginning of the war in October 1973 and its successes (despite the final outcome and the potential for military disaster) strengthened Sadat's position and enhanced his prestige in Egypt and in the broader regional and international systems. The world's attention was once again drawn to the Arab-Israeli conflict, and Sadat began to press the United States for assistance in resolving the issue. Further, he secured support for his position from the more moderate Arab states. This took the immediate form of the Arab "oil weapon" during the 1973 war and of financial assistance afterward. Sadat was able to place Israel on the defensive internationally and to secure further international support for the Egyptian and Arab positions.

In April 1974 Sadat produced a document called the October Working Paper, which discussed the new era ushered in by the October War. It called for extensive reform and change in Egypt and suggested that the lot of the average Egyptian would improve. It embodied his concept of the philosophy and guidelines appropriate to the new era Egypt had entered. It also sought to provide a framework for Egypt's economic and social development in light of the impact of the October War.

By the 1980s domestic tension in Egypt had grown, although Sadat's grip on power was in no way diminished. Confessional conflict had occurred between the large Coptic Christian minority and the Islamic fundamentalists, and Sadat placed restrictions on both. In the years after 1979 it became clear that there was a growing diversity of opinion among Egyptians, especially over Sadat's controversial foreign and economic policies. Opposition politicians were able to capitalize on the fact that little economic improvement had been achieved and that Sadat's peace with Israel had left Egypt isolated in the Arab world. Sadat continued to pursue his course. The years 1980 and 1981 were marked by increasingly violent opposition—and Christian-Islamic fundamentalist clashes—as well as by repressive reactions by the Sadat government.

Severe repression of Sadat's opposition began in September 1980 with the formerly tolerated leftist party, but the major move was made almost a year later, in September 1981, when the government arrested more than 1,500 Egyptian political figures of all political persuasions. Certain religious groups were banned and their newspapers closed. A number of Muslim Brother leaders were arrested, and Sadat dismissed the Coptic leader, Pope Shenuda III. Many fundamentalist mosques were taken over by the government, and the security appartus began to clamp down on universities. Foreign journalists who had criticized Sadat were expelled along with the Soviet ambassador and other Soviet diplomats.

On October 6, 1981, Sadat was assassinated by Muslim fundamentalists. A state of emergency was declared, and the National Assembly nominated Vice-President Hosni Mubarak to succeed Sadat. Although the assassins were quickly arrested, conflict broke out in Asyut between the security forces and the fundamentalists. The anti-Sadat demonstrations were limited in scope and were soon quelled. A presidential referendum was held, and Mubarak was sworn in as president on October 14, 1981.

Although Mubarak cracked down on the religious extremists associated with Sadat's assassination, he released many of the other political figures whom Sadat had arrested a month before his death. Over the years since his accession to power, it has become clear that the difference between Mubarak and Sadat is principally one of style. Whereas Sadat emphasized foreign policy, Mubarak has concentrated on domestic politics and the economy. The battle against corruption started from the top under Mubarak and Sadat's brother, and some of his closest associates were taken to court for corrupt practices. Unlike Sadat, Mubarak and his family had maintained a low profile and lived modestly.

Despite the release of many political detainees, Mubarak has kept a close rein on Egyptian politics. The state of emergency was renewed annually long after the emergency following Sadat's death had passed. Mubarak has not yet put his own mark on Egyptian politics, but it is clear that he continues to be constrained by the same kind of economic and political problems that faced Sadat and Nasser before him. Tensions with Egyptians who favor Islamic government have become an increasingly pressing problem for Mubarak, who continues to choose the middle road between the secular and religious approaches to government. He has at times attempted to placate the Islamic fundmentalists but, at other same times, has clamped down on them when their protests threatened to erupt publicly.

Foreign Policy

Napoleon once labeled Egypt "the most important country" because of its central location, which provided a key to Africa and the Middle East. In the post–World War II period Egypt has become perhaps more significant. The Suez Canal is a prime artery for oil. Egypt is a leading state in the African, Islamic, Arab, and nonaligned Third World nations. It is also the primary state for the establishment of peace or the waging of war in the Arab-Israeli conflict. It has been courted by both the United States and the Soviet Union, each in pursuit of its own interests in the region and in the broader international community.

Egypt is the leading state of the Arab world in a number of other respects. Its population and military forces are the largest. It has been the leader of the Arab world in communications (publishing, arts, literature, movies) and other spheres. Egypt has been, and remains, influential throughout the Arab world; much of the Arab world's activity focuses on or takes its lead from Egypt.

In the nineteenth century and the early part of the twentieth century Egypt spearheaded Arab contact with the Western world and helped to develop the intellectual bases for Arab, as well as Egyptian, nationalism. It was a leader in the establishment of the Cairo-headquartered Arab League. Further, its Suez Canal was an important strategic-economic asset.

After the 1952 revolution Egypt emerged as an important Third World—neutralist and nonaligned—power, and Egypt and Nasser were increasingly looked to for leadership in the Arab world and beyond. Nasser's concept of three circles of foreign policy provided some indication of the spheres in which Egypt was influential: Arab, African, and Islamic as well as Third World spheres of policy and activity.

Egypt's foreign policy was virtually nonexistent prior to the 1952 revolution. Major and assertive foreign policy positions developed only after the revolution and essentially seemed to be reactive—responding to events as they developed. Nasser's foreign policy focused, in the first instance, on the need to eliminate the British colonial presence in the canal zone and in the Sudan. In the second instance, there was the problem of Israel. It is in these contexts that relations with the United States and the Soviet Union emerged.

Initial successes were achieved with the agreement on the withdrawal of the British from their positions in Egypt and the resolution of the Sudan problem (although the Sudan eventually chose independence rather than union with Egypt). On February 12, 1953, England and Egypt signed the Agreement on Self-Government and Self-Determination for the Sudan, which provided for the latter's transition to self-government and its choice between linkage with Egypt or full independence. The Suez question was settled in an agreement of October 19, 1954. That agreement declared the 1936 treaty to be terminated and provided for the withdrawal of British forces from Egyptian territory within a period of twenty months.

Relations with the superpowers were different. Although the United States was initially helpful to the new regime and provided technical and economic assitance, as well as some assistance in the negotiations with the British, there were difficulties concerning Nasser's requests for arms. Further, U.S. Secretary of State John Foster Dulles viewed Egypt's increasingly close ties with Communist China and the Soviet Union with suspicion. The Baghdad Pact, conceived and sponsored by the United States, was not viewed positively by Nasser, who saw it as a threat to Arab independence and autonomy. Raids on Israel by fedayeen and counterraids by Israel into Gaza sparked, in Nasser's view, a need for arms for defense, and his quest led him to closer links with the Soviet bloc, thus further straining ties with the United States. The Dulles decision that the United States would not fund the Aswan High Dam was a major blow to the plans of the new regime, which decided to continue building and to secure the necessary funding and assistance from alternative sources. The Soviet Union was prepared to assist in the construction and to provide some financial assistance. But in Nasser's view a more demonstrable act was needed. And so, in July 1956, he nationalized the Suez Canal and stated that the proceeds of the canal revenues would go to the construction of the dam.

The crucial exchanges between Nasser and the United States set the tone for the less-than-cordial relationship that followed. While the U.S.-Egyptian relationship deteriorated, the Soviet role in Egypt (and elsewhere in the Arab world) improved. The Soviet assistance for the Aswan Dam project and the supply of arms essential to the continued stature and satisfaction of the Egyptian military and, ostensibly, to the defense of Egypt against Israel were elements that helped to ensure the positive Soviet-Egyptian relationship.

Nasser's nationalization of the Suez Canal and the securing of Soviet arms via Czechoslovakia contributed further to the deterioration of the U.S.-Egyptian relationship. On the other hand, Soviet-Egyptian relations improved during this time. Then came the Sinai-Suez War of 1956, when Israel, France, and England joined in an effort to unseat Nasser and restore the canal to Western control while destroying Egypt's military capability (especially its ability to use the newly acquired arms). The United States opposed the effort and exerted considerable pressure on its three friends to withdraw from Egyptian territory. In assisting the Nasser regime the United States won much goodwill in the Arab world, especially Egypt. But this goodwill was soon dissipated when the United States became involved in the 1958 Lebanese crisis and opposed the Egyptian position.

The Kennedy administration witnessed a minor reversal of this negativism, as the style and sometimes the substance of the new regime began to be welcomed in the Arab world and important gestures by Kennedy were viewed with favor in Cairo. But, with the death of Kennedy and the establishment of President Lyndon Johnson's position on foreign policy, the relationship began to deteriorate once again. By the time of the June War of 1967, relations between the two states were poor; the war itself was a catalyst that precipitated the break of diplomatic relations. The relationship between the United States and Egypt remained antagonistic until the October War, and until President Richard Nixon and Secretary of State Henry Kissinger established the policy that led to a rapprochement between the two states and the growth of a cordial relationship in virtually all the bilateral spheres. This relationship involved, for example, state visits by Sadat to the United States in 1975 and 1977 and a 1974 state visit by Nixon to Egypt, and other high-level meetings between responsible officials in both states.

Relations with the Soviet Union were somewhat different. Beginning in the mid-1950s, Soviet economic and technical assistance were important elements in the Aswan Dam project and in Egypt's economic development. Military assistance was another element in the developing relations of the two states. Because Nasser felt that Egypt required arms to maintain the regime and to ensure proper capability in dealing with the problem of Israel, the Soviet Union became a major factor inasmuch as it was prepared to provide arms under terms of cost and payment acceptable to the Egyptians. The Egyptian military soon had a Soviet arsenal. Soviet equipment provided the arms essential for the

Egyptian armies in the 1956, 1967, 1969–1970, and 1973 wars. But, despite the consummation of a treaty of friendship in 1971, the Soviet role in Egypt proved to be increasingly problematic from the perspective of many members of the senior Egyptian military.

The rift between Egypt and the Soviet Union became more obvious after the accession of Sadat and his consolidation of power. The disassociation began when the Soviet Union attempted to influence the choice of Nasser's replacement after his sudden death in 1970. With Sadat's consolidation of his position following the arrest of his major opponents, the relationship with the Soviet Union deteriorated further as the Soviet Union and its Egyptian clients began to differ on various aspects of the situation and the approach to the Arab-Israeli problem. There appeared to be constraints placed on Egyptian military plans and activities. There were disagreements concerning the Soviet refusal to provide Egypt with the desired offensive military equipment. There were tensions between Egyptian and Soviet military officers in Egypt, and these events culminated in the expulsion of Soviet advisers in July 1972. After the October War Egypt complained that the Soviets were lax in resupplying the Egyptian military forces. In addition, Egypt increasingly turned to the West, especially the United States, and Sadat articulated the view that Kissinger and the United States held the crucial cards for peace in the region and could also become the source of essential economic and technical assistance for Egypt.

There were increased Soviet limitations on arms supply to Egypt, difficulties over the repayment of the Soviet debt owed by Egypt, and a growing realization that the United States—not the Soviet Union—could aid the quest for peace. Despite improved relations during the months that followed the ouster of Soviet advisers in 1972, the Soviet-Egyptian relationship has not returned to its former levels—especially since the 1973 war, when the improved relationship between Egypt and the United States began to supplant some of the elements of the Soviet-Egyptian dealings of previous times. Egyptian leaders had recognized that their primary concerns of recovering territory captured by Israel during the 1967 war, resolving the Arab-Israeli conflict, and promoting the development of Egypt had not been attained through the Soviet connection; moreover, there was the growing view that a Western (i.e., U.S.) linkage was more appropriate.

At the heart of Egypt's foreign policy lay questions more closely related to developments in the region. Nasser believed that Egypt's destiny was to lead in three circles: the Arab, the Islamic, and the African. In his *Philosophy of the Revolution*, Nasser argued that Arab unity had to be established, for it would provide strength for the Arab nation to deal with its other problems. Arab unity was a consistent theme during the period of his tenure (after 1954) and a source of some interest in his policy to outsiders. He argued that Egypt led by Nasser should lead to a united Arab world. He saw Egypt as the state that had to fulfill that role, and in his pursuit of foreign policy he sought to achieve the various goals of leadership involved in his three circles. Sadat retained that general theme but focused much of his foreign policy attention on the question of the Arab-Israeli conflict and the future of the Palestinians. In the final analysis Egypt continues to be the primary country for resolution of the Arab-Israeli conflict—it must be the leader if war is contemplated and is similarly crucial if there is to be peace.

A main theme of Egyptian policy has continued to be its leadership role in the Arab world. Developed as a pan-Arab or Arab nationalist role in the 1940s and 1950s, it acquired added dimensions with Nasser's increasing interests in the Arabian peninsula and the Gulf region in the 1960s. Increasingly, Egypt became the Arab leader in the conflict with Israel and the effort to deal with Israel's role in the Middle East. After the ouster of the British from Egypt and the nationalization of the Suez Canal, the first significant issue for Nasser was the tripartite (Israel-England-France) invasion of Egypt in 1956. Subsequent Israeli evacuation of the Sinai (under U.S. pressure and international cajoling) temporarily relegated the issue to the background and permitted Egypt to turn to issues elsewhere, such as the union with Syria—1958–1961—and the Yemen civil war in the early 1960s. But in 1967 the focus of Egypt's attention was again drawn to the Arab-Israeli issue, and the June War of 1967 returned this question to the central position it has occupied since. After the June War the main, if not sole, issue of Egypt's foreign policy remained the question of the Arab-Israeli conflict and the effort to accomplish Israeli withdrawal from the territories occupied in that conflict. Guiding the Egyptian position after the June War was the Khartoum summit resolution of September 1967. At that time the Arab states pledged their joint military, political, and diplomatic activity to achieve Israeli withdrawal from occupied Arab territory; and further, they articulated their position that there could be no negotiation, no recognition, and no peace with Israel and that the rights of the Palestinians had to be restored. These commitments and beliefs provided the framework for Egyptian policy until after the October War of 1973, which modified the environment for approaches to the Arab-Israeli conflict.

Following the October War, Sadat began to alter his foreign policy approach in an obvious manner. He began with the assumption that the key to both his domestic and foreign policy problems lay in closer ties with the United States and a tenuous relationship with the Soviet Union. He believed that the United States could admonish Israel to relinquish territories occupied in the 1967 war and could provide technical and economic assistance for Egypt's economy and social development at home. The U.S. option seemed to be the logical approach diplomatically and politically and also would be helpful for economic reasons. Regional tranquility seemed to be an essential ingredient in Sadat's approach to Egypt's problems.

The postwar approach began in the months following the war. In January 1974, Kissinger achieved a first-stage disengagement agreement separating Israeli and Egyptian forces along the Suez Canal and in Sinai. Relations between Egypt and the United States began to improve dramatically as relations with the Soviet Union continued to deteriorate. After further and substantial effort, a second-stage disengagement between Israel and Egypt, known as Sinai II, was signed in September 1975 and provided for further Israeli withdrawals and the return to Egypt of important oil fields in Sinai.

Nixon visited Egypt in June 1974, and Sadat later visited the United States (October/November 1975). Sadat saw only gains in his dealings with Washington.

In the wake of the Sinai II agreement, Egyptian policy took on a new cast. Sadat seemed to be interested in maintaining the role of the United States as the power to help attain peace by changing Israel's policies. The situation was slowed, however, by regional developments such as the civil war in Lebanon and by the U.S. presidential elections. The conclusion of the elections in November 1976 and the winding down of the Lebanon conflict set a new process in motion. During the initial months of President Carter's administration there was substantial movement toward the establishment of a process to lead toward peace or at least toward a Geneva Conference designed to maintain the momentum toward a settlement. But the movement toward a settlement seemed to slow substantially by October of that year, thus leading to Sadat's decision to "go to Jerusalem" and to present his case and the Arab position directly to the Israeli Parliament and people. In so doing he set in motion a new approach to the Arab-Israeli conflict in which direct Egypt-Israel negotiations became, for the first time, the means to peace in the Middle East. The direct negotiations were continued at the Cairo Conference and Ismailia Summit of December 1977 and in lower-level contacts over the ensuing months. Then, in September 1978, Sadat met with President Carter and Israeli Prime Minister Begin for the Camp David Summit, which provided a framework for peace between Egypt and Israel and, ultimately, for a broader arrangement between Israel and the other Arab states. On March 26, 1979, Sadat signed the Egypt-Israel Peace Treaty in Washington. Implementation of the treaty, which normalized relations between the two states, proceeded as scheduled and diplomatic relations were established. At the same time, various contacts were made, including tourist and communications links. These actions led to Egypt's isolation in the Arab world, which refused to accept Sadat's argument that the treaty and peace with Israel were in the best interests of the Palestinians and the other Arabs. Failure to achieve substantial progress toward implementation of the other Camp David framework, which provided for arrangements for the West Bank and Gaza, further complicated Egypt's and Sadat's position. Despite U.S. involvement and effort, the talks were suspended.

Sadat's assassination in October 1981 raised questions about Egypt's foreign policy direction, particularly its arrangements with Israel. President Mubarak reaffirmed and built upon the policies he inherited from Sadat, emphasizing negotiated solutions to the Arab-Israeli conflict, maintenance of the peace with Israel, and close and positive relations with the United States. The peace treaty's provisions were implemented on or ahead of schedule. Although he has insisted on maintenance of the peace with Israel, he has also been critical of Israel at times. He sharply criticized Israel's June 1982 invasion of Lebanon and withdrew his ambassador from Israel following the Sabra and Shatila refugee camp massacres in September 1982, although Egypt's embassy has remained in Tel Aviv just as Israel's embassy has remained in Egypt. Nevertheless, he has worked to reduce Egypt's Arab world isolation by gradually restoring and improving relations with the Arab states. He has succeeded in improving ties with the more moderate Arab states (Jordan restored diplomatic relations in September 1984), and Egypt was readmitted to the Islamic Conference in early 1984. Mubarak also shrewdly utilized the opportunity presented by the Iran-Iraq War to improve his ties with several Arab moderate states, in part through offers of assistance to Iraq. He has also sought to improve Egypt's international standing through increased participation in regional and international forums.

Relations with the United States have remained positive since their restoration in 1974 and have improved following the Camp David summit and the Egypt-Israel Peace Treaty. The personal chemistry between Sadat and Jimmy Carter was an important factor in this development. Mubarak has been able to broaden and strengthen the relationship since his accession to office. Numerous exchanges of visits between U.S. and Egyptian officials (including regular trips by Mubarak to Washington) have allowed the dialogue on Middle Eastern and other issues to continue. U.S. economic and military assistance to Egypt rose to several billion dollars a year in the 1980s and was provided in various areas of activity. Strategic cooperation, including joint military exercises, has improved the relationship, as has Mubarak's support for the September 1, 1982, U.S.-Middle East peace initiative.

Bibliography

A review of the background of modern Egypt and the nature of its people is essential to an understanding of its political culture. Two works are particularly important in this regard. Henry A. Ayrout's *The Egyptian Peasant* (Boston: Beacon Press, 1963) focuses on the fellah, whereas William Lane's *Manners and Customs of the Modern Egyptians* (New York: E. P. Dutton, 1923) surveys much of Egyptian society and culture.

The historical background of modern Egypt is considered in Robert O. Collins and Robert L. Tignor, *Egypt and the Sudan* (Englewood Cliffs, N.J.: Prentice-Hall, 1967); Peter Mansfield, *The British in Egypt* (New York: Holt, Rinehart & Winston, 1971); and Nadav Safran, *Egypt in Search of Political Community: An Analysis of the Intellectual and Political Evolution of Egypt, 1804–1952* (Cambridge: Harvard University Press, 1961). David S. Landes, in *Bankers and Pashas: International Finance and Economic Imperialism in Egypt* (Cambridge: Harvard University Press, 1958), provides an account of Egyptian-European commercial relations in the nineteenth century, with emphasis on the Suez Canal. Jamal Mohammed Ahmed, in *The Intellectual Origins of Egyptian Nationalism* (London: Oxford University Press, 1960), provides an introduction to nationalism as it developed in Egypt.

General studies of Egypt focusing on the period since the revolution include Anouar Abdel-Malek, *Egypt: Military Society—The Army Regime, The Left, and Social Change Under Nasser* (New York: Random House, 1968) (translated by Charles Lam Markmann); R. Hrair Dekmejian, *Egypt Under Nasir: A Study in Political Dynamics* (London: University of London Press; Albany: State University of New York Press, 1972); Harry Hopkins, *Egypt: The Crucible—The Unfinished Revolution in the Arab World* (Boston, Mass.: Houghton Mifflin Co., 1969); Jean and Simone Lacouture,

Egypt in Transition (New York: Criterion Books, 1958) (translated by Francis Scarfe); Tom Little, *Modern Egypt* (London: Ernest Benn, 1967); Peter Mansfield, *Nasser's Egypt*, rev. ed. (Baltimore, Md.: Penguin Books, 1969); Amos Perlmutter, *Egypt: The Praetorian State* (New Brunswick, N.J.: Transaction Books, 1974); Georgiana G. Stevens, *Egypt: Yesterday and Today* (New York: Holt, Rinehart & Winston, 1963); P. J. Vatikiotis, ed., *Egypt Since the Revolution* (New York and Washington, D.C.: Praeger Publishers, 1968); Keith Wheelock, *Nasser's New Egypt: A Critical Analysis* (New York: Praeger Publishers, 1960); Donald N. Wilber, *United Arab Republic: Egypt—Its People, Its Society, Its Culture* (New Haven, Conn.: Human Relations Area Files Press, 1969); John Waterbury, *Egypt: Burdens of the Past, Options for the Future* (Bloomington: Indiana University Press, 1978); John Waterbury, *The Egypt of Nasser and Sadat* (Princeton, N.J.: Princeton University Press, 1983); Panayotis J. Vatikiotis, *Nasser and His Generation* (New York: St. Martin's Press, 1978); Mohamed Heikal, *Autumn of Fury: The Assassination of Sadat* (New York: Random House, 1983); Raymond Baker, *Egypt's Uncertain Revolution Under Nasser and Sadat* (Cambridge: Harvard University Press, 1978); Elie Kedourie and Sylvia G. Haim, eds., *Modern Egypt: Studies in Politics and Society* (London: Frank Cass, 1980); and John Waterbury, *Hydropolitics of the Nile Valley* (Syracuse, N.Y.: Syracuse University Press, 1979).

An understanding of revolutionary Egypt is facilitated by the works of its three presidents: Mohammed Naguib's *Egypt's Destiny: A Personal Statement* (Garden City, N.Y.: Doubleday, 1955); Gamal Abdul Nasser's *Egypt's Liberation: The Philosophy of the Revolution* (Washington, D.C.: Public Affairs Press, 1955); Anwar el-Sadat's *Revolt on the Nile* (New York: The John Day Co., 1957); and Anwar el-Sadat's *In Search of Identity: An Autobiography* (New York: Harper & Row, 1978).

Anthony Nutting, in *Nasser* (New York: E. P. Dutton, 1972), and Robert St. John, in *The Boss: The Story of Gamal Abdel Nasser* (New York, Toronto, London: McGraw-Hill, 1960), provide biographical studies of Nasser.

Studies of particular aspects of politics of Egypt include Iliya Harik, *The Political Mobilization of Peasants: A Study of an Egyptian Community* (Bloomington: Indiana University Press, 1974); Christina Phelps Harris, *Nationalism and Revolution in Egypt: The Role of the Muslim Brotherhood* (The Hague: Mouton, for The Hoover Institution on War, Revolution, and Peace, 1964); James B. Mayfield, *Rural Politics in Nasser's Egypt: A Quest for Legitimacy* (Austin: University of Texas Press, 1971); Nissim Rejwan, *Nasserist Ideology: Its Exponents and Critics* (New York: John Wiley and Sons, 1974); P. J. Vatikiotis, *The Egyptian Army in Politics: Pattern for New Nations?* (Bloomington: Indiana University Press, 1961); and Malcolm Kerr and El Sayed Yassin, eds., *Rich and Poor States in the Middle East: Egypt and the New Arab Order* (Boulder, Colo.: Westview Press, 1982).

Egyptian foreign policy has not engendered many full-length studies. Nevertheless, several works provide a useful beginning: *Egypt and the United Nations*, report of a study group set up by the Egyptian Society of International Law, prepared for the Carnegie Endowment for International Peace (New York: Manhattan Publishing Co., 1957); Charles D. Cremeans, *The Arabs and the World: Nasser's Arab Nationalist Policy* (New York: Praeger Publishers, for the Council on Foreign Relations, 1963); and A. I. Dawisha, *Egypt in the Arab World: The Elements of Foreign Policy* (New York: John Wiley & Sons, 1976). More specific themes are considered in Karen Dawisha's *Soviet Foreign Policy Towards Egypt* (New York: St. Martin's Press, 1979), Alvin Z. Rubinstein's *Red Star on the Nile* (Princeton, N.J.: Princeton University Press, 1977), and Ismail Fahmy's *Negotiating for Peace in the Middle East* (Baltimore: Johns Hopkins University Press, 1983).

Finally, Bent Hansen and Karim Nashashibi, in *Foreign Trade Regimes and Economic Development: Egypt* (New York: National Bureau of Economic Research,

1975); Charles Issawi, in *Egypt in Revolution: An Economic Analysis* (London: Oxford University Press, for the Royal Institute of International Affairs, 1963); Robert Mabro, in *The Egyptian Economy, 1952–1972* (London: Oxford University Press, 1974); Patrick O'Brien, in *The Revolution in Egypt's Economic System: From Private Enterprise to Socialism, 1952–1965* (London: Oxford University Press, 1966, issued under the auspices of the Royal Institute of International Affairs); Khalid Ikram, ed., in *Egypt: Economic Management in a Period of Transition* (Baltimore: Johns Hopkins University Press for the International Bank for Reconstruction and Development, 1980); and Alan Richards, in *Egypt's Agricultural Development, 1800–1980: Technical and Social Change* (Boulder, Colo.: Westview Press, 1982), provide valuable studies of Egypt's economy and the problems facing economic planners in the coming decades.

16

Democratic Republic of Sudan

Sally Ann Baynard
Bernard Reich

The Sudan is the largest country in Africa (consisting of some 2,506,000 square kilometers, or 967,500 square miles), bounded on the north by Egypt; on the east by the Red Sea and Ethiopia; on the south by Kenya, Uganda, and Zaire; and on the west by the Central African Empire, Chad, and Libya. The dominant geographical feature of the Sudan, as in Egypt, is the Nile; the White Nile flows from the great lakes region of Africa, and the Blue Nile originates in the highlands of Ethiopia. The two branches join at Khartoum and form the Nile, which winds through desert for the next 1440 kilometers (900 miles) until it reaches the Egyptian border north of Wadi Halfa.

The Sudan has a population estimated at 21.8 million in 1985, and its density varies widely. The population is not of uniform stock. In the 1956 census 572 tribes were registered. However, approximately 40 percent are of Arab stock and mainly centered in Khartoum and the northern provinces of the Sudan. In the south, the people belong to Nilotic and Nilo-Hamitic groups. The most important southern tribes are the Dinka, the Shilluk, the Nuer, and the Zande. Tribes of origin similar to many southern Sudanese are found in Ethiopia, Uganda, and the Congo. In the northern provinces the population is almost entirely Muslim, and in the south, tribal religions and Christianity prevail.

Historical Background

Bilad al-Sudan was the name given by medieval Muslim geographers to the region south of the Sahara and Egypt. Since the end of the nineteenth century, the term has been used in a more restricted sense to refer to the territories south of Egypt, which were part of the Anglo-Egyptian condominium from 1899 to 1956.

The history of the modern Sudan begins in the nineteenth century. Muhammad Ali, the Ottoman sultan's viceroy in Egypt, coveted Sudan because of its wealth—especially the precious metals and slaves—as well as

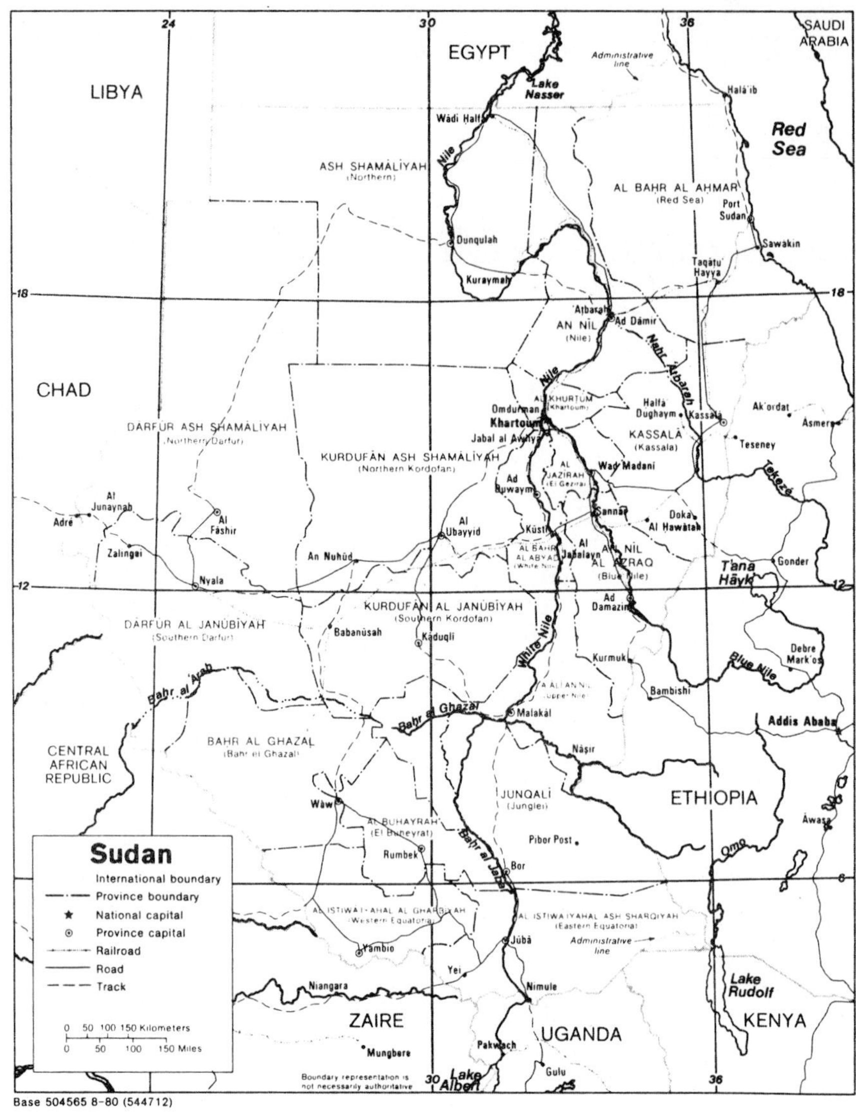

for prestige and strategy. Between 1820 and 1822 his expeditionary forces conquered and unified the north-central areas of the country. During the reign of the Khedive Ismail (1863–1879) the provinces of Darfur, Bahr al-Ghazal, and Equatoria, as well as the Red Sea port of Suakin, were brought under Egyptian control. But local leaders challenged the Egyptians and a rebellion grew out of a fanatical Islamic-revivalist movement. Its leader, Muhammad Ahmad ibn-Abdallah, claimed to be the Mahdi ("divine leader" or "Guided One"), chosen by God. He sought to oust the Egyptians and to establish a religious state. In August 1881 the Mahdi's followers, the Ansar, defeated the troops sent against them. Later they took the initiative and, in 1882–1883, conquered most of Kordofan, Darfur, and the Bahr al-Ghazal. In 1885 the Mahdi's troops conquered Khartoum, and, after his death later that year, his successor, the Khalifa 'Abdallahi, ruled until the end of the Mahdist state.

In 1896 the British government decided to reconquer the Sudan in order to reimpose Egyptian control over what was described as Egyptian territory temporarily occupied by Mahdist rebels. The expeditionary force of British and Egyptian troops took Khartoum in Egypt's name in 1898, and by the end of that year the remaining Mahdist forces were defeated, the Khalifa 'Abdallahi was killed, and the Sudan was reconquered.

The foundations of the new regime in the Sudan were laid by an agreement signed by Britain and Egypt in January 1899, establishing their joint rule—the Anglo-Egyptian Condominium—over Sudan. The condominium agreement stressed the position attained by Britain through its participation in the reconquest of the Sudan, and gave Britain de facto control despite official pretense that it was a joint government with Egypt. The British established a colonial regime headed by a governor-general, appointed by the Egyptian khedive on the recommendation of the British government, with full military and civilian control. The governor-general, who held both executive and legislative powers, was always British. He proclaimed, made, altered, or abrogated all laws, orders, and regulations. In 1943, however, the British started a gradual transition to partial autonomy by establishing an Advisory Council for the northern Sudan. In 1948 a Legislative Assembly was established for all of the Sudan. The transfer of power was slow and caused friction with Egypt, which regarded the Sudan as part of a united Nile Valley whose political future was linked to Egypt, and which objected to any form of Sudanese self-rule under British tutelage.[1]

The 1952 revolution in Egypt marked a turning point for the Sudan. The Free Officers agreed to grant the Sudanese the right of self-determination, as they were eager to secure the British ouster from Sudan as soon as possible. The Free Officers also hoped that the Sudanese would choose to link themselves with Egypt. Late in 1952 the Free Officers concluded an accord with the Sudanese parties, and on February 12, 1953, Egypt and Britain signed an agreement concerning the future of the Sudan. A transition period of three years was established to prepare for self-determination, which would allow the Sudanese to decide the future of the Sudan: independence or union with Egypt. During the transition period the administration would be transferred to the Sudanese and elections would be held under international supervision. British and Egyptian troops would be evacuated as soon as the Sudanese Parliament decided that "Sudanization" was completed and the time for self-determination had come. Two international commissions were to assist in that transition. Elections took place in November 1953, and Ismail al-Azhari's pro-Egyptian National Unionist party (NUP) won an absolute majority. In January 1954, al-Azhari became the first prime minister of the Sudan.

Sudanization of the administration was considered completed in August 1955, and the Sudanese Parliament demanded the evacuation of British and Egyptian troops. This evacuation was accomplished by November 1955. Parliament and the government also demanded a simplification of the complicated constitutional procedure originally prescribed for self-determination, and in the end it was agreed that the Sudan's future would be decided by a vote in Parliament. It was now quite clear that al-Azhari and his supporters had changed their minds about a union with Egypt and preferred complete independence. A resolution to that effect was unanimously adopted by Parliament on December 19, 1955, and on January 1, 1956, the Sudan became formally independent.

Political Environment

The Problem of the Southern Sudan

From independence until the early 1970s, and starting again in 1983, the Sudan has been engulfed in what has been termed "the southern Sudan problem." This problem, amounting at its worst to outright civil war, has caused significant casualties, prevented economic development both in the north and in the south, and threatened the political unity of the country.

The south was composed of three of the nine original provinces of the Sudan: Bahr al-Ghazal, Upper Nile, and Equatoria. This area differs from the northern part of the country in many significant ways: ethnicity, religion, geography, history, language, climate, and resources. The northern Sudanese are predominantly Muslim and oriented to the Arab world, whereas the southerners are more closely related ethnically and historically to non-Arab Africa and are mostly animists or Christians (the latter being in the minority). In addition to ethnic, historical, religious, and geographical factors, the two areas of the Sudan are also distinguished from one another by language and climate. Although some tribal languages survive in the north, virtually all northern Sudanese speak Arabic. Although it is not as widely spoken as the Arabic in the north, English is the lingua franca of the south. Climatically, the north has little rainfall and must rely on arid agricultural techniques, whereas the south has significant rainfall and other water resources and thus a greater agricultural potential. Oil has accentuated north/south differences as all oil finds to date have occurred in areas of the southern Sudan adjacent to the north; in addition, political conflicts over the location of a planned refinery have helped create the conditions for an outbreak of renewed civil violence.

Many of the factors separating the two areas were compounded by official policies—initially by that of the British, who insisted on ruling the southern Sudan as a separate entity. Although this policy may have been designed to protect the relatively less developed southern region, it retarded national unity. Policies of Sudanese governments since independence have also fostered regional differences. Notwithstanding a decision made following the Juba

Conference of 1947 to create a united Sudan, southerners have remained suspicious of northerners, who had carried out massive slave raids in the nineteenth century and who, in general, to this day retain patronizing attitudes toward southern Sudanese.

Even before independence, civil conflict broke out. In August 1955 an armed insurrection, which started with an army mutiny by southerners, led to the first Sudanese civil war, which in turn lasted until 1972 and left thousands of Sudanese (mostly southerners) dead, many areas of the south devasted, and the national treasury drained.

The governments of the Sudan from 1956 through 1958 were unable to resolve (and remained relatively indifferent to) the southern conflict. Under General Ibrahim Abboud, who came to power in November 1958, the southern Sudan issue was treated primarily as a military problem. The objectives of the regime were to foster national integration and unity by pursuing a policy of Arabization and Islamization in the southern provinces. A heavy-handed administration and military action against the rebels and their supporters did little to improve the situation. Missionaries were expelled in 1964 because the administration believed that they compounded the problem. Many southerners saw these efforts as confirming their belief that a separate state was the only real solution to the southern Sudan problem.

The unresolved issue of the civil war was one of the factors in the demise of the Abboud regime. The financial costs of the war had weakened the economy, and student protests over the southern conflict triggered the confrontations that became the October 1964 Revolution. The transitional civilian governments that replaced Abboud were concerned about the situation in the south but more interested in the power struggles in Khartoum. In the south, personal, tribal, and religious divisions soon emerged in disputes over tactics and objectives. The main debate revolved around separatism or federalism. In March 1965 the Round Table Conference on the South was convened in Khartoum to establish a constitutional framework acceptable to all sides—the first genuine effort to resolve the issues involved in the problem of the southern Sudan. The southern leadership and its main political organization—the Sudan African National Union (SANU)—split, and the position of the northern politicians was fragmented by party politics. The conference itself ended in virtual deadlock. When the Mahjoub government achieved power in June 1965, it was disillusioned by the failure of the Round Table Conference and alarmed by the deteriorating security situation in the south, so it gave the southern army commands a free hand to destroy the Anya Nya. A series of bloody reprisals for Anya Nya harassment followed, numerous civilians lost their lives, suspected Anya Nya villages were burned, and indiscriminate killing in Wau and Juba caused a mass exodus to the bush. The pattern of Anya Nya raids and army reprisals destroyed orderly administration throughout most of the southern provinces, and village life often fell apart as people fled across the borders to refugee camps or scattered into the forests and swamps. Alongside a tribal identity, a "southern" identity was rapidly developing. By January

1971, however, a semblance of order had been restored, as most of the politicians and the majority of the Anya Nya commanders accepted a former Sudan army lieutenant, Joseph Lagu, as leader both of the Anya Nya and of a new Southern Sudan Liberation Movement (SSLM). It was Lagu's SSLM that, throughout 1971, continued a dialogue with the Sudan government on proposals for "regional autonomy" and that eventually reached agreement on the ending of the rebellion and on a new structure of southern self-government in March 1972.

In June 1969 the new government declared its policy of solving the southern Sudan problem by granting regional autonomy to the southern provinces, and a ministry for southern affairs was created to implement the policy. Some southerners were appointed to positions of responsibility, and governmental funds were allocated for development and reconstruction in the south. The crucial event occurred in March 1972 with the conclusion of the Addis Ababa Agreement, which, *inter alia*, provided for the return and rehabilitation of Sudanese refugees abroad, the reintegration of Anya Nya rebels into the Sudanese armed forces, and the establishment of administratively autonomous institutions for the southern provinces. Hostilities ceased. Then began the difficult task of integrating the south into the political and economic life of the country while permitting the region to retain a large measure of autonomy. Under the provisions of the 1972 accord, the internal affairs of the southern provinces are administered by an autonomous regional government with its parallel structure of ministries, government agencies, and civil servants. Both the annual and the development budgets of the southern region are subsidized by the national government. The theme of national unity also stresses the reduction and regulation of the ethnic, sectarian, and political cleavages that characterized public life in the Sudan in the past. Elections for the Regional People's Assembly were held in November 1973. Subsequently, the assembly elected Abel Alier as president of the High Executive Council (on the nomination of President Nimeiri), and other members of that council were appointed. In the 1978 elections General Joseph Lagu was elected president of the High Executive Council.

The reconciliation between the Nimeiri government and the southern Sudanese proved to be only temporary. Nimeiri was unwilling to allow the southern regional government to exercise true autonomy. As his rule became increasingly authoritarian after 1971, Nimeiri gave the southern Sudanese as little opportunity for genuine political participation as he gave the northerners. The trigger for the outbreak of civil war was Nimeiri's announcement that the southern region was to be redivided into three regions (as the northern Sudan had been), in contravention of the 1972 Addis Ababa Agreement, which had required a referendum in the south to precede any changes in the political arrangements reached at the end of the war. As in 1955, the rebellion began with a mutiny: Southern soldiers and officers, ordered to be moved to the north, deserted with their arms and equipment.

Two other factors played a major role in escalating the incidents of violence into outright civil war. The discovery of oil in the northern part of the southern region and the plans of the government to locate the refinery for this oil at Kosti in the northern Sudan infuriated southerners. They were already suspicious of Nimeiri by this time and had witnessed long-standing traditions of exploitation at the hands of the north.

The event that may have made civil war inevitable was Nimeiri's decision in September 1983 to implement Islamic law in the Sudan. Early statements by the government noted that Islamic punishments would not be meted out to non-Muslims, but by 1984 several non-Muslim southerners had suffered hand amputation for theft in Khartoum. It was never made clear whether Islamic law would be applied in the south, but the fact of its application to non-Muslim southerners in Khartoum, the timing of the decisions, and Nimeiri's apparent insouciance with regard to southern sensitivities all convinced politically active southerners that the time had come to return to the bush in rebellion.

By 1984 the civil war had resumed and, as before, had a profound influence on political and economic events in Khartoum. By the middle of 1984 work had stopped on two important projects. Attacks on Chevron oil installations and on the huge Jonglei Canal project (designed to increase water flow in the Nile by bypassing the Sudd) in 1983 and 1984 brought work to a halt. The military leaders of the new rebel movement were from the large tribes (such as the Dinka) and were better educated and equipped than those in the 1955–1972 conflict. There appeared to be few prospects for reconciliation. Southern leaders had trusted Nimeiri and his colleagues in 1972, and their trust had been betrayed. They were unlikely to take this route again, and religious, political, and economic issues between north and south became more stark than ever before.

Although the southern conflict did not directly bring about the fall of the Nimeiri government on April 6, 1985, it accentuated the existing economic and political problems that Nimeiri had not resolved. The civil war remains the single most pressing difficulty of the new government. Without an end to the domestic conflict, no economic progress can be made as oil exploration and production are dependent upon an end to the violence in the southern Sudan. Unsuccessful negotiations were held in late 1985 and the new regime is clearly intent upon reaching an accord with the southerners. Most of the foreign policy initiatives of the new government have seemingly been aimed, indirectly, at the civil war: Rapprochement with Libya and Ethiopia were essential if the government wanted to stop these neighboring states from resupplying the southern rebels and providing them with cross-border sanctuaries and training facilities. No regime in Khartoum has lasted more than four years without resolving the smoldering southern conflict. If the new regime does not succeed in bringing about this resolution, no other economic or political progress is likely: The drain on the treasury, the debilitating effects of the conflict on politics in Khartoum, and the disruption of the Sudan's relations with its neighbors are too great to be borne for an extended period.

Economic Issues

A major traditional economic problem of the Sudan is its heavy dependence on a single cash crop, cotton, which is its main source of income as well as its primary export. The Sudan is first and foremost an agricultural and pastoral country. Agriculture is a significant element in the country's gross domestic product (GDP) and employs a substantial segment of the population, whereas manufacturing industries and minerals contribute very little to the GDP. The share of extra-long staple cotton in the exports of the Sudan reaches more than 70 percent in some years. Such dependence on one major export crop, with wide fluctuations in price and quantity exported, has caused political as well as economic instability. Fortunately, the oil that has been discovered in the Sudan, though it is of low quality and appears to be a relatively small deposit, presents some potential for future energy self-sufficiency.

The Sudan has never enjoyed economic prosperity, despite its abundance of arable land and potentially plentiful water supply. Traditional problems, such as overdependence on a single cash crop, labor shortage, and brain drain, have been compounded by a crushing external debt, a sinking standard of living, unfulfilled development hopes, and virtual bankruptcy as a result of the economic crisis of the 1980s.

The Sudan has a low per capita income. The average population density is also low, and no significant population pressure is exerted against available resources. As one of the few developing countries that is underpopulated, the Sudan often suffers a labor shortage, particularly during the cotton-picking season. This shortage has been aggravated by the departure of skilled laborers to the Gulf states and Saudi Arabia. Transportation and other infrastructural elements are inadequate and number among the important problems in the economy—problems that have been aggravated by civil war. Finally, perhaps one of the most striking features of the Sudanese economy is the dominant role that is played by the public sector in all important economic activities. The government owns the majority of modern capital establishments in the economy.

The availability of water is the governing factor for agriculture in the Sudan. The cultivable land is estimated to be about 200 million feddans (one feddan = 0.4152 hectare, or 1.038 acres), but only about 8 percent of this cultivable land is being utilized in agriculture, and fewer than 4 million feddans are under irrigation. Half of this area is accounted for by the Gezira scheme, the large irrigated agricultural project located in the triangular area south of the confluence of the White and Blue Niles at Khartoum.

Prior to the Nile Waters agreement of 1959, distribution of water between the Sudan and the UAR was governed by the Nile Waters agreement of 1929, which allocated 4 billion cubic meters (5.2 billion cubic yards) to the Sudan. However, with the 1959 agreement and the construction of new dams, the problem of securing sufficient water to extend the area under irrigation in the Gezira scheme has been solved. The Sudan is now entitled to draw 18.5 billion cubic meters (24.2 billion cubic yards) at the Aswan High Dam, or the equivalent of about 20.5 billion cubic meters (26.8 billion cubic yards) in the Sudan, and the way has been opened for considerable expansion and diversification of irrigated agriculture, in part because of other projects designed to achieve more efficient use of the Nile waters. In spite of the significant role played by irrigation, the rainlands are more important. With the exception of cotton and some other less important crops, the Sudan's foodstuffs and most exported agricultural products come from the rainlands, and the nation is self-sufficient in the essential foods.

The main cereal crop is sorghum (durra). It is the most important staple food and is grown mainly in the rainlands. Normally the Sudan produces enough for domestic consumption, but the dependence upon rainfed agriculture leaves the region vulnerable to drought. By early 1985 the famine that had begun to prevail in Ethiopia and other Sahelian states had also become evident in the Sudan. The situation was aggravated by the presence of almost a million refugees, many fleeing starvation in their own homelands. By mid-summer of 1985 as many as 8 million Sudanese faced famine, especially in the western provinces of Darfur and Kordofan, where average daily food supplies averaged far less than half the required amount. Western nations, relief organizations, and the United Nations began to airlift emergency supplies, but not in the volume needed to prevent widespread malnutrition and starvation.

The ginning of cotton encouraged the beginning of industry in the Sudan early in the twentieth century. With the exception of soap, soft drinks, and oil pressing, large industries that manufacture import substitutes began operation only after 1960. The government has encouraged industrialization by various means. The Approved Enterprises (Concessions) Act of 1959 gave generous concessions to infant industries. The Organization and Promotion of Industrial Investment Act of 1967 has been even more generous to industry. In addition, the Industrial Bank, which was established in 1961, assists in the financing of private industrial enterprises, providing nearly two-thirds of the capital required. In 1972 the Ministry of Industry introduced new legislation to encourage industrial investment. The 1972 industrial act was amended in 1974, and an agricultural act was promulgated in 1976 to encourage foreign investment in the agricultural sector.

The Sudan's main exports are primary agricultural products, and since the establishment of the Gezira scheme in 1925, cotton has dominated the Sudan's exports, although groundnuts and gum arabic have become increasingly important export products. The major imports are vehicles, transport equipment, machinery, appliances, and textiles. Perhaps an even more striking change has occurred in the pattern of suppliers and buyers. The United Kingdom used to be the largest seller and buyer from the Sudan (30–40 percent before independence). In 1973 only 3.4 percent of the Sudan's exports went to the United Kingdom, and only 10 percent of imports were bought from the United Kingdom. Trade with socialist countries increased between independence and the communist-supported coup attempt in 1971 as a result of several bilateral agreements. But their share in the Sudan's trade has, with the exception of the People's Republic of China, drastically declined since that 1971 effort. Trade with the Arab countries has been expanding in recent years and exports to them have reached about 10 percent, but imports from these countries form a smaller percentage. The Arab countries are a good market for the Sudan's animal exports.

Although the Sudan endured—and recovered from—severe economic problems in the 1956–1958 period and again in the early 1960s, its economy was in extremely poor shape by 1985. In the 1970s, when economic development was stressed, government agenices were permitted to borrow freely from foreign governments and commercial banks, insofar as the Bank of Sudan (the central bank) remained unaware of the extent of the nation's debt. Between 1982 and 1985 estimates of the Sudanese external debt rose from about US$3 billion to about US$9 billion, a sum substantially beyond the Sudan's ability to pay. Foreign lenders repeatedly rescheduled debt payments in the early 1980s, but by 1985 this measure had brought little relief. The austerity program initiated by the Nimeiri government in late 1984 and early 1985, combined with the occurrence of a coup d'état in April 1985, gave the government that came to power in that same month a little breathing space on economic issues—but these issues will continue to be a major obstacle for the foreseeable future.

Political Structure

On April 6, 1985, the government of Ja'far Muhammad al-Nimeiri was overthrown in a military coup led by the minister of defense. The coup was triggered by uncontrollable riots and demonstrations in the capital, led and carried out by a broad segment of the politically active population: intellectuals, students, trade unionists, and professionals. The newly established structure of government was to be temporary, inasmuch as the military rulers had reached agreement with the broad coalition that had led the demonstrations against Nimeiri for a one-year transitional period in which a new constitution would be drawn up and a democratic government formed.

The 1973 constitution was suspended and virtually all organs of the Nimeiri government were dismantled following the coup. On April 9, 1985, General Abdel Rahman Siwar al-Dhahab, who had led the coup, announced the formation of a Transitional Military Council (TMC), composed of fifteen officers, with General Siwar al-Dhahab as the chairman. Siwar al-Dhahab was also vested with the power to conduct "affairs of sovereignty" and to exert legislative authority during the transitional period. Agreement on the formation of a military/civilian cabinet (Council of Ministers) was reached between the TMC and the group that had spearheaded the demonstrations—the Assembly of National Forces for the Salvation of the Sudan (National Front). The National Front was composed of disparate political groups, including elements of the professional unions, the Umma party, the National Unionist party, the Arab Socialist Baath party, the Sudanese Communist party, and the Muslim Brotherhood. On April 22, 1985, a fifteen-member cabinet was named. Two posts—ministers of defense and interior—were reserved for military and police officers, respectively, and the remaining posts were given to civilians named by the National Front, including that of the prime minister, Dr. Al-Jazouli Dafa'allah, who had been head of the powerful physicians' union. Another major legal change at this time was the affirmation of the provisions of the 1972 Addis Ababa Accord.

With the government structure in such a state of transition, it was not at all clear what shape Sudanese politics might take in the future. Under Nimeiri all parties had been banned, except for the government-created party, the Sudanese Socialist Union. Within a few weeks of the April 6 coup, no fewer than forty political parties and groups had announced their existence. None of these parties was banned and all shades of political opinion were allowed free expression, from Communists on the left to Muslim fundamentalists on the right.

The major parties of the pre-Nimeiri period appear to have undergone greater fission than ever before, and no clear consensus has emerged as to the form of government the Sudan should have. The TMC announced that an elected constituent assembly would undertake the creation of a new constitution. Given the continuing insurgency in the south, it remains impossible to hold elections in most of the southern Sudan—and yet to hold an election without southern voting (as was done in the 1965 elections) would express an unacceptable degree of despair over the resolution of the conflict.

Political Dynamics

The political parties of the Sudan at the time of independence did not differ from one another very dramatically on ideological grounds. All of the major parties (i.e., those excluding the southern parties, the small Communist party, and the Muslim Brotherhood) claimed to favor nonalignment, democracy, and socialism of some sort. The NUP of Prime Minister al-Azhari differed from its greatest rival, the Umma party, only in its greater intimacy with Egypt. Shortly after independence, the NUP split as the leader of the Khatmiyya sect withdrew his support. The portion of the NUP that had split off—not to reunite until 1967 when the Democratic Unionist Party (DUP) was formed—was the nucleus of a new party, the People's Democratic party (PDP), which included the most pro-Egyptian elements of the old NUP.

In mid-1956 the two religious leaders, Abdel Rahman al-Mahdi of the Ansar (Umma party) and Ali al-Mirghani of the Khatmiyya (PDP), joined forces in a coalition government that lasted for almost one and a half years. This coalition was a cynical association at best, formed by the two rival patriarchs for the sole purpose of excluding al-Azhari from power. Agreeing on nothing, the coalition accomplished nothing, except the reelection of its members in the February 1958 elections. Although the two groups did not differ significantly on ideology, they disagreed sharply on the form of a permanent constitution (presidential or parliamentary), on the Sudan's relationship with Egypt, and on the question of accepting aid from the United States. The issue of U.S. aid divided not only the two parties but the internal leadership of the PDP as well.

After winning a joint election victory in February 1958, the government showed signs of tension. The economic situation had deteriorated because of a poor cotton crop, there was dissension over a U.S. aid proposal, and Umma party Prime Minister Abdallah Khalil felt threatened not only by rumors of a planned coalition between his current coalition partner (the PDP) and the opposition NUP but also by the fact that he was in danger of losing the leadership of his own party. He suspected that Ansar leader and Umma patron Abdel Rahman al-Mahdi planned to replace him with his own son. Under these conditions, the prime minister, who had once been an officer, turned to the army and asked its commander to take over the reins of government.

General Ibrahim Abboud thus came to power in a handover rather than a takeover. Parties were abolished, the Parliament was dissolved, and the constitution (which comprised only a temporary set of rules in any case) was suspended.

A Supreme Council of the Armed Forces ruled the country from November 1958 until October 1964. All power and authority was vested in Abboud, as president of the council, but he gave broad latitude to his cabinet ministers, especially the foreign minister, and was also strongly influenced by the chief justice. Although there was no progress made toward constitutional rule and no genuine, mass political participation during the Abboud period, the council's rule was a benign dictatorship by any standards. Abboud did not seek power; then, when it became apparent that a popular revolution, uniting disparate political groups, sought removal of military rule, he bowed out.

Progress during the Abboud period was chiefly economic in the sense that development planning began during these years. What foundered, however, was the regime's attempt to reach a military solution to the civil war and to forcibly Islamize the south. The drain on the treasury of accelerated military action in the south was a major factor in the economic downturn of 1963 and 1964 that helped stir popular resentment. The southern conflict also provided the trigger for mounting unrest to become revolution as the popular demonstrations in October grew out of discussions of the southern problem at Khartoum University.

The transitional government that succeeded Abboud was made up of such diverse elements as the traditional parties, the Muslim Brotherhood, assorted leftists, and the Communist party of the Sudan. The left (especially the communists) had been the organized strength behind the October Revolution and played a major role in the first transitional cabinet (from November 1964 to February 1965), but the traditional parties gradually began to edge the leftists out of positions of power.

The transitional government put much emphasis on the problem of the southern Sudan and tried—unsuccessfully—to solve it with the help of southern leaders. Freedom of the press was restored, and the ban on political parties was rescinded. In June 1965 elections were held in which all parties except the PDP participated. Since no party won an absolute majority, a coalition was formed between the Umma party, with 76 seats, and the NUP, with 53 seats. Muhammad Ahmad Mahjoub (Umma) became prime minister and al-Azhari (NUP) permanent chairman of the Presidential Council.

In the Umma, a right wing (under the leader of the Mahdiyya Order, the Imam al-Hadi al-Mahdi) supported Premier Mahjoub, whereas younger elements followed the imam's nephew, Sadeq al-Mahdi. Sadeq al-Mahdi became prime minister after a vote of no-confidence forced Mahjoub to resign in July 1966. The new government, also a coalition of the Umma and the NUP, was able to improve the economic situation and promised to deal with the question of southern Sudan by providing a degree of regional autonomy. However, as the NUP withdrew its support, the government was defeated in the assembly. Mahjoub again became premier, supported by a coalition of the NUP, the Imam al-Hadi al-Mahdi faction of the Umma, and the PDP. In December 1967 the PDP and the NUP merged to form the Democratic Unionist party (DUP).

Elections took place in April 1968. The Democratic Unionist party won 101 seats, Imam al-Hadi al-Mahdi's faction of the Umma 36 seats, and Sadeq al-Mahdi's faction 30. The two former groups formed a government under Mahjoub. Its position was undermined by disputes between the coalition partners and by reports that the two wings of the Umma had reunited and were about to reestablish their conservative rule.

On May 25, 1969, a group of army officers staged a bloodless coup converting the state to the Democratic Republic of the Sudan. The Constituent Assembly, the Presidential Council, and the transitional constitution were abolished. All political parties and organizations were also abolished and their leaders were arrested. The new regime proclaimed a policy of Sudanese socialism. The state would participate in the economy to a greater extent while maintaining full freedom for foreign aid and local capital.

In the first twenty-six months of the new government, all legislative, executive, and judicial authority was vested in the Revolutionary Command Council (RCC), consisting of nine officers and one civilian. Jaafar Muhammad Nimeiri, whom the younger officers had selected to lead the coup only shortly before it was initiated, was chairman of the RCC. Until the RCC was disbanded in 1971, he was no more than first among equals. The officers had come to power with the cooperation of the Communist party of the Sudan (CPS), but most of the officers were only vaguely leftist. Although they had come to power proclaiming socialism, it took some months before the new government began to implement some socialist measures, nationalizing some foreign businesses and confiscating some local enterprises. After overcoming a threat from the right—specifically, from the Ansar in March

1970—tensions erupted between the RCC and the CPS. In November 1970 three officers were expelled from the RCC; two were communists. In July 1971 a coup led by the three former RCC members, supported by the CPS, almost succeeded in toppling the government. After three days Nimeiri and his colleagues were brought back to power in a countercoup. The leaders of the failed coup were executed after hasty trials, the leftists were purged from the government, and the CPS was almost destroyed.

The RCC members agreed to disband after the 1971 coup and in October Nimeiri became president following a one-man presidential referendum. Within one year, all but one of his former RCC colleagues had been dismissed or had left the government. Between 1971 and 1976 Nimeiri cemented his hold on the government, establishing political institutions and organizations but retaining clear command over the whole system.

Neither the 1973 constitution, which granted broad powers to the president, nor the People's Assembly, nor the Sudanese Socialist Union (the political party) provided for popular participation in government. In 1975 and 1976 there were serious coup attempts. In the 1976 attempt some of Ansar leader Sadeq al-Mahdi's forces were infiltrated from Libya. Although this attempt failed, Nimeiri agreed in the following year to a "reconciliation" with some of his political opponents. Sadeq al-Mahdi, other former party leaders, and the leader of the Muslim Brotherhood were brought into the government on terms that were not made public. The next year Sadeq al-Mahdi left, claiming that the reforms he had anticipated had not been carried out. The strength of the Ansar was diminished, the Muslim Brothers remained in government, and Nimeiri was left in a stronger position than before.

Having rejected leftism following the abortive 1971 coup, Nimeiri proclaimed national unity and economic development as the guiding principles of his regime from 1972 on, particularly after reaching accord with the southern Sudanese in 1972. He moved away from the socialist measures of 1969–1971 and sought Western investment and aid. By 1978, however, having tried both left and right, Nimeiri took up a new element in his political thinking, as reflected in his book entitled "Why the Islamic Path?" Nimeiri had never been religious, but within five years his new religious sentiments began to take political shape.

A master tactician, Nimeiri had played off against one another all of the potent groups and individuals in Sudanese politics, but as the mid-1980s approached he was running out of room to maneuver. His June 1983 decision to redivide the southern Sudan into three provinces had precipitated outbreaks of violence in the south. The economy was in dire straits. Nimeiri's health had been precarious, and his popularity in the northern Sudan had sunk to an all-time low.

In September 1983 Nimeiri declared that Islamic law would be implemented as the law of the Sudan, and over the succeeding months specific steps were taken to put this decision into practice. Alcohol was banned and its possession made punishable by flogging. Although all criminals had been amnestied at the onset of Islamicization, repeat offenders were soon suffering amputation. The entire political system, though it remained authoritarian, began to take on an Islamic tone; yet prominent Sudanese Muslims criticized the impropriety or illegality of the steps taken. As manifestations of public dissent and strikes by doctors, professors, bank workers, and others multiplied in the spring of 1984, Nimeiri declared a state of emergency on April 30. At the same time, he fired all judges and magistrates and established "courts of decisive justice" manned by new law graduates to dispense swift new Islamic penalties.

The president stepped back a bit from some of these measures in September 1984, suspending the new courts, backpeddling on the redivision of the south, and ending the state of emergency. Efforts to Islamicize continued, however, as taxes were replaced with Islamic *zakat* (almsgiving), throwing the already crumbling economy into a tailspin. Any hopes that Nimeiri might compromise on Islamicization were dashed in January 1985 when, for the first time in history, a Sudanese citizen was executed for criticizing the government. Moderate religious leader Mahmoud Muhammad Taha, a devout intellectual in his 70s, was hanged for heresy and for criticizing Islamic law. In March 1985 Nimeiri dismissed all Muslim Brothers from the government, giving credence to the view that Nimeiri's Islamic policy had been carried out not at the behest of the Brotherhood but, rather, because of Nimeiri's own desire to do so and at the urging of a group of Sufis close to the president.

Dissent mounted and by early April the capital was disrupted by strikes and demonstrations. The day Nimeiri was to return from a visit to Washington he was removed by a junta headed by the minister of defense, whom he had appointed only a few weeks before. The senior commanders, clearly worried about the unpredictable results of continued unrest, apparently took over to preempt such a move by younger officers of a more radical persuasion.

The officers who took over the government in April 1985 did not do so with great enthusiasm and were, in general, a fairly conservative group. Their declared intent to return the country to civilian, democratic rule appeared to be sincere. It remains to be seen, however, whether the forty-some parties operating in Khartoum will be able to submerge their differences long enough to compromise on a format for elections. If the civilians are unable to agree, either the military commanders may decide to stay in power, or, as the one-year transitional period draws to a close, a sovereignty council may be created to assume the role of chief of state.

Other than the future shape of politics and government, the April 1985 regime is faced with the gravest economic and security problems. Experience has shown that the southern rebellion cannot be resolved by force alone—by either side. If the government cannot reach agreement with the rebels, not only will the war continue to drain the economy but also oil production cannot be restarted. If the economy remains in its present critical condition—with deteriorating living standards, shortages of basic commodities, and the threat of starvation in the hinterland—the situation will not be conducive to reasoned political compromise. The regime has little in its favor except for the widespread optimism among those Sudanese who appear still to be rejoicing in the removal of a government that almost all segments of society had come to hate.

Foreign Policy

Several factors have influenced Sudanese foreign policy since independence. First, the primacy of domestic politics has guaranteed in almost all regimes that foreign policy would serve as little more than a tool of domestic power struggles. Second, Sudanese foreign policy remains very much influenced by geopolitical considerations. These include the importance of relations with such powerful neighbors as Egypt and Ethiopia, porous borders with eight countries, and unstable neighbors. The relationship with Egypt is especially significant. No Sudanese government can ignore the link with Egypt, which has strong ties to Sudanese political factions. Every Egyptian government since Sudanese independence has sought influence in the Sudan, and every Sudanese government has looked to Egypt (sometimes unwillingly) as its most important foreign relationship.

The Sudan falls into both the African and Arab regions. It became an Arab League member upon independence and was one of the founding members of the Organization of African Unity in 1963. Relations with the nations of Africa other than the Sudan's immediate neighbors were unimportant to regimes in Khartoum prior to 1969, and even then, African relationships have never been as important to Sudanese policymakers as Arab ties. Among the neighboring states, Ethiopia has always been next most important to the Sudan (after Egypt) because of its size, its position upstream on the Blue Nile, its historical links with the Sudan, and the Ethiopian civil war, which is of many years standing. Ethiopia and the Sudan have held one another in a mutual hostage situation off and on for years, with Ethiopia threatening the Sudan by harboring (and sometimes arming and training) southern rebels and the Sudan doing the same with the Eritreans. Fundamentally, there is a strong affinity between the two nations, although this is often disguised by different ideologies and divisive disagreements over borders and refugees. Uganda is perhaps the next most important of the African neighbors, and, as in the case of Ethiopia, its long civil agony has burdened the Sudan with thousands of refugees. The Chadi civil war has also been costly for the Sudan. Relations with Kenya, the Central African Republic, and Zaire have been peaceful in recent years.

Libya presents no intrinsic threat to the Sudan because the very small adjacent areas of the two countries are virtually uninhabited, and hundreds of miles of trackless desert separate major cities and installations of the two nations. Libya, in alliance with Chad and/or Ethiopia, poses a more serious concern: Libya's resources and hostility, in combination with the other two states' long, porous borders near important areas (oil installations in the west near Chad and the major dams in the east near Ethiopia), could be ominous.

From independence up to 1967, Sudanese foreign policy was indistinct. The unstable coalitions of the 1956–1958 period were unable to agree on a common foreign policy and therefore proclaimed little more than nonalignment (despite friendly relations with the West). Under General Abboud foreign policy was more geared to economic needs than to political links. The Sudan sought during this regime to maximize foreign aid and investment and to avoid high-profile political statements. Foreign policy went through a very brief radical phase under the transitional governments following the October Revolution of 1964, but when parliamentary government resumed in June 1965, foreign policy returned to business as usual.

Foreign policy might have remained ambivalent, but it was galvanized by the 1967 Arab-Israeli war. The Sudan mobilized during the war and broke diplomatic relations with the United States and Britain. Following the war, the government in Khartoum moved closer to the Arab states than ever before and exerted efforts to bring the quarreling Arab nations together, culminating in the convening of the 1967 Arab League summit in Khartoum. At the same time, and in the same vein, the Sudan began to pursue better relations with the Soviet bloc. Although the Sudan had always had normal relations with the Soviets, Sudanese governments had remained fundamentally pro-Western. This situation began to change in 1967, although the big shift would not come until May 1969.

The May 1969 coup d'état fundamentally changed Sudanese foreign policy. Ideology had never played a large role in policymaking until this time. The young officers followed the lead of their civilian foreign minister, Babikir Awadallah (who, in the early days, was their prime minister as well). Babikir Awadallah saw all foreign policy through the lens of the Arab-Israeli conflict, thus prompting not only an alignment of the Sudan with the radical states of the Arab world but also its attempts to join an ephemeral unity effort with Egypt and Libya—the Federation of Arab Republics. Common cause was also found with the African radical states. The Soviet Union and its allies were invited to involve themselves in the Sudanese military and intelligence units, and relations with the West (especially the United States and the United Kingdom) deteriorated.

The communist coup attempt in July 1971 radically altered the direction of Sudanese foreign policy. Nimeiri and his colleagues believed that the Soviets had known of the plans of the Sudanese communists and felt betrayed by their erstwhile ally. The Sudanese ambassador in Moscow was recalled, and the Sudan stopped just short of breaking diplomatic relations. Between 1971 and 1976 the Sudan went through a transitional phase of foreign policy. Its relations with China, Yugoslavia, and Romania (the Warsaw Pact maverick in foreign policy) thrived and its relations with the West slowly improved; its relations with the Soviets returned only slowly to normal, and even then exhibited an undercurrent of suspicion. In the Arab and African arenas the Sudan moved during the 1971–1976 period toward a renewal of its friendships with the conservative states, without relinquishing its radical cohorts of the 1969–1971 period.

After implementing Islamic law in September 1983, Nimeiri seemed to become less interested in foreign policy. Although he still routinely denounced the Soviets, all his rhetorical fire was directed to the internal arena. In 1984 and 1985 he began criticizing the United States for the slowness of its economic aid; he also expressed open resentment of U.S. criticism of Islamicization in the Sudan. Reports of suspended U.S. aid in late 1984 were later denied by both nations, but in the last months of the Nimeiri regime both the United States and Egypt were clearly worried about the course of events in Khartoum.

The overthrow of Nimeiri brought dramatic changes in foreign policy as the new government sought both to distance itself from its predecessor and to chart a foreign policy course that would aid resolution of the civil war. Within only weeks of taking power, General Siwar al-Dhahab initiated a reconciliation with both Ethiopia and Libya, and diplomatic relations were soon reestablished with both neighboring states in addition to "normalized" ties with the Soviet Union. Although the United States was openly concerned about this move, the normalization was clearly tied to the new regime's desperate efforts to end the civil war. A cutoff of Libyan and Ethiopian aid to the southern rebels was essential if the war was to be ended, and an end to the war was the necessary precursor to any economic improvement.

Relations between Egypt and the Sudan have remained close under the new regime. The new chief-of-state, General Siwar al-Dhahab, comes from a family with historical links to Egypt as members of the Khatmiyya sect, and it is likely that Mubarak has been personally reassured by the Sudanese that the improved ties with Qaddafi do not signify a deterioration in relations with Egypt. Although Prime Minister al-Jazuli noted that some of the agreements made with Egypt by Nimeiri were abrogated, it has become clear that he was referring to the superficial "integration" agreements (which both sides discounted generally anyway) and not to the fundamental relationship itself.

Ties with Saudi Arabia are likely to improve, as recently suggested by the increased Saudi aid for petroleum purchases by the new regime. Nimeiri had become an embarrassment even to such Islamic conservatives as the Saudis, who were disturbed at the vacillation of his policies over the years and the endemic corruption of his regime.

As the Sudan grapples with the important decisions to be made regarding a new constitution and the transition from military rule, and as it struggles to end its civil war, its foreign policy issues are likely to remain secondary. In fact, those issues will become a priority only when, as in the past, foreign relationships begin to affect the important domestic problems of politics and finance.

Bibliography

John Obert Voll and Sarah Potts Voll, in *The Sudan: Unity and Diversity in a Multicultural State* (Boulder, Colo.: Westview Press; London and Sydney: Croom

Helm, 1985), offer a comprehensive survey of the modern Sudan. The Sudan's history is considered in P. M. Holt and M. W. Daly, *The History of the Sudan from the Coming of Islam to the Present Day*, 3d ed. (Boulder Colo.: Westview Press, 1979); Mekki Abbas, *The Sudan Question: The Dispute over the Anglo-Egyptian Condominium, 1884–1951* (New York: Praeger Publishers, 1952); Robert O. Collins and Robert L. Tignor, *Egypt and the Sudan* (Englewood Cliffs, N.J.: Prentice-Hall, 1967); Richard Hill, *Egypt in the Sudan 1820–1881* (London: Oxford University Press, 1959); P. M. Holt, *The Mahdist State in the Sudan, 1881–1898: A Study of Its Origins, Development, and Overthrow* (London: Oxford University Press, 1958); Mekki Shibeika, *The Independent Sudan* (New York: Robert Speller, 1959); A. B. Theobald, *The Mahdiya: A History of the Anglo-Egyptian Sudan, 1881–1899* (London: Longmans, Green, 1951); and Gabriel Warburg, *The Sudan Under Wingate: Administration in the Anglo-Egyptian Sudan 1899–1916* (London: Frank Cass, 1971). Also useful is *Documents on the Sudan, 1899–1953* ([n.p.], Egyptian Society of International Law, 1953).

K. M. Barbour's *The Republic of the Sudan: A Regional Geography* (London: University of London Press, 1961) provides a discussion of the geography of the Sudan.

H. C. Jackson's *Behind the Modern Sudan* (London: Macmillan & Co.; New York: St. Martin's Press, 1955) focuses on the problems of administration of the Sudan during the condominium period.

Muddathir 'Abd al-Rahim's *Imperialism and Nationalism in the Sudan: A Study in Constitutional and Political Development, 1899–1956* (London: Oxford University Press, 1969) provides an overview of the preparations for Sudan's political independence.

Peter K. Bechtold's *Politics in the Sudan: Parliamentary and Military Rule in an Emerging African Nation* (New York: Praeger Publishers, 1976) is an excellent study of Sudanese politics and policy since independence.

General surveys of all aspects of Sudan include Harold MacMichael, *The Sudan* (New York: Praeger Publishers, 1955), which covers the period to 1953; and Harold D. Nelson et al., *The Sudans: A Country Study* (Washington, D.C.: Government Printing Office, 1983), which focuses on the postindependence era.

The southern Sudan problem is considered from different perspectives in Oliver Albino, *The Sudan: A Southern Viewpoint* (London: Oxford University Press, for the Institute of Race Relations, 1970); Joseph Oduho and William Deng, *The Problem of the Southern Sudan* (London: Oxford University Press, for the Institute of Race Relations, 1963); Cecil Eprile, *War and Peace in the Sudan, 1955–1972* (London: David & Charles, 1974); Robert O. Collins, *The Southern Sudan, 1883–1898: A Struggle for Control* (New Haven: Yale University Press, 1962); and Dunstan M. Wai, ed., *The Southern Sudan: The Problem of National Integration* (London: Frank Cass, 1973). Former Prime Minister and Foreign Minister Mohamed Ahmed Maghoub has written *Democracy on Trial: Reflections on Arab and African Politics* (London: Andre Deutsch, 1974).

17

Socialist People's Libyan Arab Jamahiriya

Bernard Reich
Sally Ann Baynard

Libya is situated in North Africa, bordered by the Mediterranean Sea in the north, by the Arab Republic of Egypt and the Sudan in the east, by Niger and Chad in the south, and by Tunisia and Algeria in the west. It has an area of about 1,774,150 square kilometers (685,000 square miles), more than 90 percent of which is desert. Libya is composed of three distinct geographical units: Tripolitania, in the west, with an area of about 248,640 square kilometers (96,000 square miles); Cyrenaica in the east, with an area of about 699,300 square kilometers (270,000 square miles); and Fezzan in the south and southwest, with an area of about 826,210 square kilometers (319,000 square miles).

Libya's small population of approximately 3.7 million (1984 estimate) contrasts with its large land area. Overall population density is only about 3.5 persons per square mile, but 90 percent of the people live in less than 10 percent of the total area, primarily along the Mediterranean coast. More than a quarter of the population is urban, mostly concentrated in the two largest cities, Benghazi and Tripoli. The majority of the population is of Arab origin, descending from the two great bedouin tribes of Beni Hilal and Beni Suleim, who came originally from the Arabian peninsula and entered Libya in the eleventh century. Berbers are descendants of the original inhabitants of North Africa and are now found only in the oases of Jalo and Auguila and in the mountain regions of Tripolitania. The Tuaregs live in the southern oases of Fezzan. Virtually all Libyans are Sunni Muslims, predominantly Senussi.[1]

Historical Background

In the earliest days the area that is now Libya was visited by Phoenician sailors who established trading posts along the coastline. Later the Greeks landed. Subsequently, the control of part of the area fell to Alexander the

Great and later to the Egyptian kingdom of the Ptolemies. Rome annexed Cyrenaica and Tripolitania, both becoming part of the Roman Empire. Eventually Pax Romana prevailed, and Libya enjoyed a long period of prosperity and peace. A period of decline began in the middle of the fourth century. In the seventh century Arab invaders arrived from Egypt, and most of the Berber tribes embraced Islam. The Arabs who swept across North Africa in the seventh century ruled for 900 years, interrupted by the Normans, the Spaniards, and the Knights of St. John. They were finally replaced in 1551 by the Ottoman Turks, who ruled until 1911. Italy declared war on the Ottoman Empire in September 1911; Italian troops landed in Tripoli in early October and later that month in Benghazi.

The Italian conquest was not accomplished without difficulty, despite a Turkish-Italian treaty in October 1912 by which sovereignty was conceded. In World War I, the Senussis, who had opposed Turkish rule, were led against Italy by the movement-founder's grandson (Muhammad Idris el-Mahdi el-Senussi) with Turkish support. Senussi strength was centered in Cyrenaica. Resistance against Italian control continued until 1931 although, by 1932, Fascist rule had subdued all opposition. In 1934 Italy adopted the name "Libya" (used by the Greeks for North Africa west of Egypt) as the official name of its colony consisting of Cyrenaica, Tripolitania, and Fezzan. Colonization along the coast included the settlement of Italian peasants and consolidation of Italian control. World War II interrupted Italy's plans, and by the end of 1942 British and French forces had swept the Italians out of the country. In 1947 Idris returned to Cyrenaica from exile in Egypt. The Italian legacy was of little value. Education had been neglected before the war and stopped after 1940; Libyan participation in the colonial government had been discouraged, and training for self-rule had been ignored. However, Idris and his supporters had sided with the British and were promised, at minimum, freedom from Italy. The form this freedom should take, however, became the subject of great-power rivalry. A British military administration was installed in Tripolitania and Cyrenaica, while the French governed Fezzan.

The machinery for settling the country's future was contained in the Italian Peace Treaty of 1947, which provided that the future of Italy's former colonies should be decided by Britain, France, the Soviet Union, and the United States, with the stipulation that if no agreement was reached the question would be taken to the United Nations. Each of the powers proposed alternative plans for the area, and it was decided that a four-power commission should ascertain the wishes of the Libyans. In 1948, after visiting Libya, the commission ended in disagreement on many of the specifics; however, they reached accord on the view that the Libyans wanted independence but were not yet ready to rule themselves. By the summer of 1948, it was clear that the four powers were unable to agree and the matter went to the United Nations, where it was debated in the General Assembly in the spring of 1949. Initial sentiment seemed to favor the postponement of independence and the establishment of some form of trusteeship. But

Libya

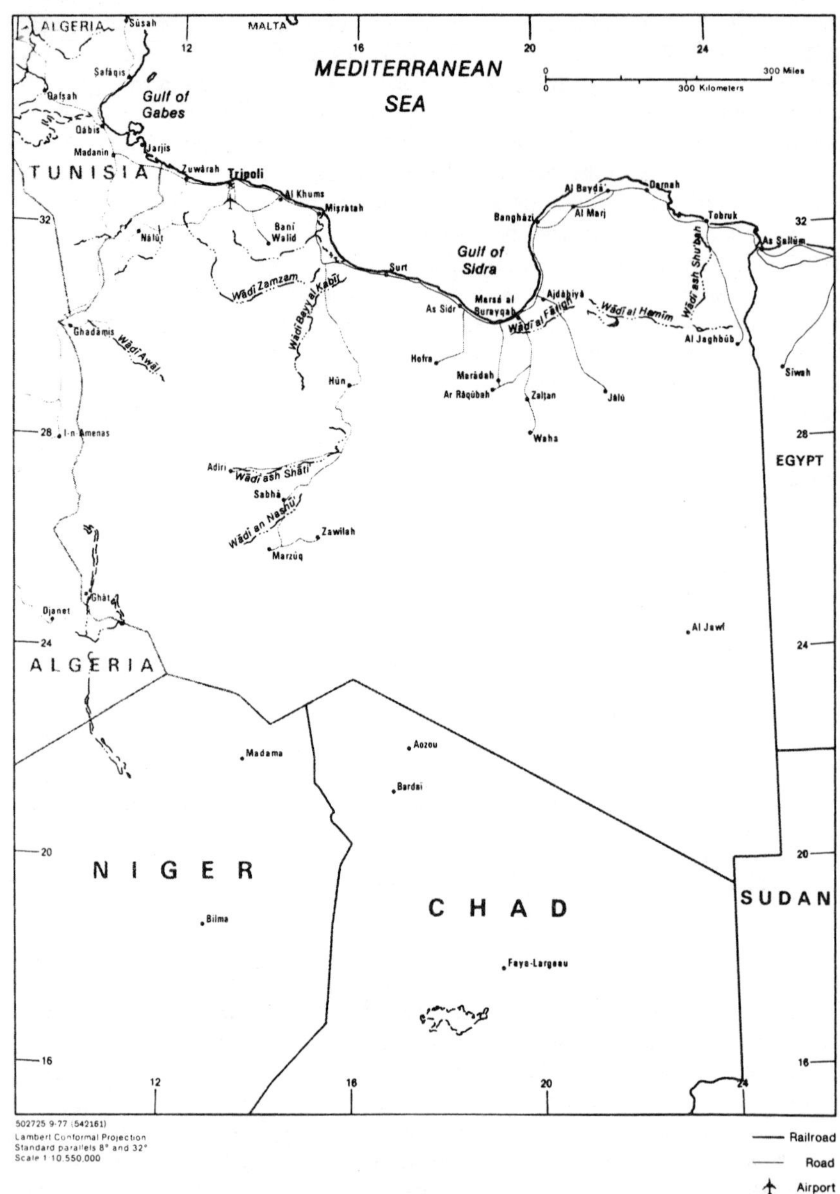

502725 9-77 (542161)
Lambert Conformal Projection
Standard parallels 8° and 32°
Scale 1:10,550,000

Railroad
Road
Airport

agreement could not be reached on this approach, and support for independence increased. On November 21, 1949, the General Assembly adopted a resolution that Libya (composed of the three territories) should become an independent state no later than January 1, 1952.

The assembly resolution allowed approximately two years in which Libya was to be prepared for independence. British and French administration continued during much of the period as Adrian Pelt, the United Nations commissioner appointed to assist in the transition to independence, helped to prepare the institutions of self-government. Pelt was assisted by an international advisory council composed of representatives of several United Nations members and a committee of twenty-one Libyans (seven from each region). A constituent assembly was convened in December 1950, but it encountered difficulties in its efforts to devise a constitution and establish institutions of government. The main issue was the rivalry between the three provinces. Tripolitania sought a unitary system, since it had the greatest population and area, whereas Cyrenaica and Fezzan insisted on status and representation equal to that of Tripolitania. The matter was eventually resolved by establishing Libya as a federation in which substantial autonomy was given to each of the three component units. Libya became independent on December 24, 1951, as the United Kingdom of Libya, composed of Fezzan, Cyrenaica, and Tripolitania, with Idris I as its monarch.

Political Environment

Economic and Social Issues

The main economic and social problems facing Libya are related and tend to reinforce each other. Primarily, Libya faces a lack of both human and natural resources (except for oil). In the early days following independence, the problem was far more acute, for oil had not yet been discovered in commercial quantities. In addition, the Italian legacy was of limited value and had an essentially negative effect. At the time of independence, at least 90 percent of the population was illiterate and no significant educated elite existed. The best agricultural land was held by Italian settlers and there was no indigenous economic infrastructure. Furthermore, the substantial amounts of capital required for development were not internally available. These deficiencies were partially overcome by outside assistance. The need for capital was partially met by grants from the United States and the United Kingdom, while large-scale technical aid was made available by the United States and the United Nations. Other countries, notably Italy, also provided some assistance. Although petroleum revenues became available as a source of development financing, and foreign capital assistance became less necessary, the need for outside technical services continued because of the lack of sufficient numbers of Libyans with the education or skills essential to the management of the expanding economy. To overcome the shortage of qualified personnel, Libya recruited foreign experts in industry, aviation, agriculture, and planning and development through the United Nations and its specialized agencies and from various governments. Libyans also studied abroad on government fellowships to acquire and refine their knowledge in technical and administrative fields.

Libya's natural-resource base remains weak, despite abundant petroleum. Mineral resources—other than petroleum and gas—are either nonexistent or not yet proven. Libya is essentially an immense desert with scattered settlements—coastal strips, oases, and the northern plateaus. This factor limits the country's economic development, since the cost of the infrastructure needed to link these various areas is considerable.

The Libyan economic predicament can be better understood in relation to the following background. Before the oil era, economic development appeared to be an almost impossible task: The paucity of both human and natural resources, the constraints on agricultural progress, and the peculiarities of the geography all seemed to pose insuperable obstacles. Petroleum has eliminated a single, although important, constraint on Libya's economic development—the availability of finance. All other constraints still operate today and are likely to restrict the pace of economic development for many years. Since petroleum is a depletable resource, it may not, according to some estimates, sustain for more than two decades the level, or the rate of growth, of income to which Libya has become accustomed. The old predicament was how to break away from the vicious cycles of poverty and backwardness. The present predicament is how to use petroleum wealth in ways that will achieve the old objective—a decisive escape from the constraints of backwardness. Through this achievement the government hopes to prevent economic and developmental stagnation, a fall in incomes, or even the recurrence of poverty after the oil era.

Libya's major resource before the discovery of petroleum at the end of the 1950s was agriculture. This sector still retains its importance, not as a major source of income or of exports but as a large employer. However, water supply is scarce, and in areas where the main source of water is rainfall, the supply is very irregular. Irrigation projects have not achieved levels necessary for agricultural self-sufficiency.

The nature and prospects of the Libyan economy changed drastically with the discovery of important petroleum reserves about 1960. Libya distinguished itself in the history of the petroleum industry as the country in which exploration, development, and production proceeded at very fast rates. Indeed, the first major petroleum discovery was made by ESSO on June 10, 1958 (in the Zelten field), less than four years after the granting of the concessions; and the first exports left Libya's shores on September 12, 1961, little more than two years later. The discovery of the Zelten field was rapidly followed by others. The discoveries in 1959–1960 further revealed that Libya had important petroleum reserves and that very large supplies would soon become available. Libya's position was strengthened even further after the June 1967 Middle East War because, with the closing of the Suez Canal, Libyan petroleum exports to Europe had a significant comparative advantage over petroleum from the Gulf area, which had to be either transshipped or routed around Africa. Production and exports continued to increase at a fast rate. In the late 1960s Libya became increasingly concerned with conservation, partly because it began to realize that the life of its reserves at the current rates of production might prove to be too short in relation to the span of time desired for economic development. Thus, in 1972 and 1973 Libya's petroleum production dipped below the level attained in 1968 and was one-third less than the 1970 peak. These lower rates of production—some 2–2.5 million barrels a day—are close to the optimum rate for Libya, given the nature of its petroleum reserves, the characteristics of the country's petroleum fields, world petroleum prices, Libyan domestic revenue needs, and the time horizon of economic development. Petroleum, Libya's greatest mineral resource, is also its major industry and has become the dominant commodity in its foreign trade.

Apart from petroleum, Libya's exports are chiefly agricultural products, although such exports have decreased by almost 50 percent since 1960, partly because local consumption has increased and partly because migration to the cities has decreased production. About 30 percent of Libya's farm products are exported: Agricultural exports include peanuts, citrus fruits, castor beans, almonds, and some wine. Before the discovery and exploitation of petroleum, the agricultural sector employed 70 percent of the labor force and constituted 30 percent of the gross domestic product (GDP).

Other than agriculture and petroleum, Libya's few industries consist largely of government-owned facilities, services, and processing plants, which mostly produce for the Libyan market. The most important government-owned facilities are the public utilities, public works departments, and port and harbor services.

After the 1969 revolution, the Revolutionary Command Council (RCC) redirected the economy toward rapid economic development, a more equal distribution of income and services, greater government economic control, and independence from foreign influence. Among the most important policies of the regime have been those designed to manage and deal with the problems attendant upon a lack of natural and human resources. Managing the petroleum resources of the state and the revenues to be derived therefrom became a major government policy. The revenues, in turn, were to be used to effect some improvement in the human-resource base. An improvement in the literacy of the population was sought through compulsory and free elementary education. Secondary schools, universities, and adult and technical education have also become more widely available. Improvement in health standards and other elements designed to improve the personal situation of the population also contribute to this improved resource base.

The government has made large investments in roads, ports, airports, and communications designed to tie the dispersed population together and to connect Libya to the outside world. It has also embarked upon an ambitious program in health, education, and welfare services designed to reach the villages. In addition, the government has provided generous loans for the development of low-cost housing, small businesses, and industry. Responding to a shortage of private capital, the new regime has set up a variety of government corporations and agencies designed to meet a wide range of needs. Because of a shortage of skilled Libyan manpower, foreigners, in significant numbers, have necessarily been brought into the government bureaucracy, schools, hospitals, irrigation and agricultural management, construction projects, and oil production.

The RCC generally intensified the government's role in the economy. Progressive assertion by the government of its right to determine prices and quantities of petroleum exports was accompanied by eviction of the remaining Jews and Italians; by nationalization of the country's banking, insurance, and petroleum-marketing companies; and by expansion of the participation and control of industry and commerce by Libyans and Libyan-owned firms. On July 21, 1970, all remaining Italians (about twenty thousand) were expelled after their assets were confiscated. The properties of non-resident Jews were also confiscated. In December 1971 the government nationalized the production and exporting facilities of the British Petroleum Company, and in the spring of 1972 it nationalized the pharmaceutical trade. The government's role in the economy is now overwhelmingly predominant. Mineral rights are vested in the state, as are water rights. The basic infrastructural facilities—highways, communications, ports, major airlines, major airports, and electric power capacity—are directly or indirectly owned and operated by the government. After expulsion of the Italians the government became a major landowner. It directly controlled the money market and, through its exchange control mechanism, it controlled the movements of foreign trade (except in the petroleum industry) and that part of domestic trade that had its origins or its destination in foreign trade.

Libyan government expenditures have not kept pace with the rapid rise in petroleum revenues. The resulting surplus has led to the growth of large Central Bank reserves of foreign exchange and gold. From mid-1973 to 1976 these reserves were in excess of $3 billion.

The government has a budget for ordinary expenditures and a separate development-plan budget. In addition, there are special allocations for subsidies, foreign aid, and much of the country's military outlays, which also come from petroleum revenues. By law, 15 percent of petroleum revenues must be set aside as reserves each year, and 70 percent of the remainder must be devoted to development.

The first Libyan five-year plan, in which communications and public works were given priority, was ratified in 1965 and extended in 1968. A revised five-year plan was instituted in 1969 by the Idris regime, which placed more emphasis on agriculture, transport, and housing as well as on local government. The second plan was replaced by a three-year development plan (1972–1975) following the 1969 revolution and economic policy shift. The revised plan was modified again in 1973 to allow yearly allocations to be added. The five-year plan for 1976–1980 envisaged a total expenditure of about $24 billion. It stressed the development of agriculture, educational facilities, transportation, housing, electrification, and industrial projects outside the petroleum sector.

Industrialization has been limited because of small domestic markets, uneven distribution of population, lack of skilled manpower, and few natural resources other than petroleum. The largest industrial projects are directly connected with the petroleum sector, including refining and liquefaction of natural gas. A growing number of small manufacturing establishments produce a variety of consumer goods, including food products. Increasing amounts have been allocated for industrial products in the development budgets. In addition, there are plans for a petrochemical industry based on natural gas, a resource that is currently underused.

Political Structure and Dynamics

The Kingdom of Libya

The constitution of the United Kingdom of Libya remained in effect and guided the government of the state until 1963, when it was replaced by a revised document establishing a unitary system.

The 1951 constitution established the United Kingdom of Libya as a constitutional monarchy under Muhammad Idris el-Mahdi el-Senussi. Sovereignty was vested in the nation but entrusted to Idris and his male heirs by the people. Islam was declared the religion of the state and Arabic its official language. Executive power was granted to the king, whereas legislative power was shared by the king and Parliament. King Idris was to exercise his executive power through an appointed prime minister and cabinet or council of ministers, whereas legislative power was vested in a Parliament, which he convened and could adjourn (for up to thirty days) or dissolve. The king sanctioned and promulgated all laws and made the necessary regulations through the relevant ministries for their implementation. In "exceptional and urgent circumstances" when Parliament was not in session, the king was permitted to issue decrees, subject to confirmation by Parliament when it convened. He could veto legislation, and his veto could be overridden only by a two-thirds vote of both the Senate and the House of Representatives. The king was supreme commander of the armed forces; he could proclaim a state of emergency and martial law, declare war, and conclude peace, with the approval of Parliament. In addition, he appointed senators, judges, and senior public servants. The king was supreme head of state, "inviolable" and "exempt from all responsibility."

The cabinet was appointed and dismissed by royal decrees on the prime minister's recommendation. Although the cabinet was selected by the king, under article 86 the cabinet members were collectively responsible to the lower house of Parliament, and each was individually responsible for the activities of the ministry that he headed. A vote of no-confidence by Parliament could force the resignation of any or all ministers. The cabinet was responsible for the direction of all of the internal and external affairs of the state.

Parliament consisted of two chambers. The Senate had twenty-four members (eight from each province), one-half of whom were appointed by the king. The others were elected by the legislative councils of the provinces. Each served for eight years and could be reappointed or reelected. The House of Representatives consisted of deputies elected by popular suffrage on the basis of one deputy for every twenty thousand inhabitants or any fraction of that number exceeding half (although each province was required to have at least five members). The deputies served for a maximum of four years. Parliamentary sessions were called by the king in November. During sessions, a bill could be introduced by the king or by one of the chambers; it had to be adopted by both chambers and ratified by the king before becoming law. However, only the king and the House of Representatives could initiate bills involving the budget.

The federal government exercised legislative and executive powers as described in article 36 of the constitution, which provided a detailed listing of areas for the exercise of its power. In other areas there were provisions for joint powers between the federal and provincial governments. The provinces were to exercise all powers not assigned to the federal government by the constitution. Each province was to have a governor (*wali*) appointed and removed by the king and representing the king in the province. An executive council and a legislative council would be established in each province.

The state was essentially an artificial creation of the United Nations following the failure of the four great powers to agree on the disposition of the Italian colonies of Tripolitania, Cyrenaica, and Fezzan. The three areas of Libya had been separate ones with no common historical tradition. They were geographically separated until Italy formally combined them as Libya in 1934. Population was concentrated in several areas, widely separated, and had no significant transportation links or other elements to tie the regions together or to provide a sense of identity or unity. Although the years of Italian rule and settlement generated a strong animosity toward the invader, Libyan society was unable to produce a well-organized nationalist movement. Italian occupation was terminated by the Allied armies, not by armed Libyan resistance or the activities of a Libyan nationalist movement. After the Axis armies were driven out during World War II, the areas under British and French military control were separately administered. The federal system established at the time of independence was a device to hold the disparate areas together.

The original adoption of the federal system was a necessary compromise in the drafting of the constitution and was expensive and cumbersome. Scarce human resources were divided into four governments rather than concentrated in the central government, whose control of the country and its policies was thereby weakened. The system also presented obstacles to the national economic development effort as each of the provinces approached many of the economic issues independently, with varying requirements and regulations governing trade and related economic factors.

Friction between Tripolitania and Cyrenaica plagued Libya from the beginning of the federal system. Tripolitania had strongly favored a unitary state, whereas Cyrenaica and Fezzan advocated federalism. Rivalries between Tripolitania and Cyrenaica frequently developed into conflicts between provincial and federal authorities, but the king and his government were in firm control. Nationalist elements, mainly in Tripolitania, disagreed with the king's conservative regime and his pro-Western policy.

The federal structure was abolished in 1963 and replaced by a unitary system that established the authority of a unitary government with jurisdiction over all matters within the state. The country's name was changed to the Kingdom of Libya, with Idris I remaining the monarch. The provinces surrendered administrative and financial decisionmaking to the national government, whose authority was exercised through ten administrative districts, each headed by a *wali*.

The shift from the federal to a unitary system in 1963 did not alter the government greatly because much of the structure established in 1951 remained intact at the national level. The major changes in the constitution related to the federal elements contained in the 1951 document. The division of powers between the federal governments was replaced by ten administrative districts, for each of which a *wali* was appointed, dismissed, or transferred by the council of ministers and empowered to execute the policies of the government in his district. The powers of the *walis* were more limited than those of the governors under the 1951 constitution. All matters except those dealing exclusively with local affairs were under the direction of the national government. One of the more significant changes in the federal government occurred in the provisions relating to Parliament. As a result of the 1963 constitution, the king was empowered to appoint all of the senators and could increase their number. Elections for members of the House were opened to universal suffrage. Before this change was instituted, the system had been based on the fragmentation of power among the palace, the organs of the federal government, the organs of the provincial governments, and other centrifugal powers, including certain religious institutions. However, King Idris I and his loyal supporters remained the focal points of power.

King Idris was the strongest single source of power in the Libyan political system. He determined the policies, which were implemented by his ministers, whom he appointed and dismissed at will. The will of the king prevailed when it was expressed. Often he did not appear to be involved in the daily activity of the government and allowed the prime minister and cabinet to implement policies as they deemed appropriate so long as they retained the confidence of Parliament and stayed within the broad policy outlines established by the king. The king's dominant position in the political system was the result of many factors: his role in Libyan history as leader of the resistance against Italian domination; his personality; the respect he commanded from Libyans in general; his role as a quasi-religious leader of the Senussi sect; his constitutional powers; and the nature of the system itself. Because the system was torn by centrifugal forces, he was able to maintain the balance among these forces, thereby preserving internal stability and order as well as his own special position and role.

Idris's long experience as the head of the Senussi gave him a position of veneration throughout the nation, and he was particularly adept at manipulating Libyan politics. The political circle he led was centered in the palace and in the special ties to Cyrenaica—not in the populace. Political expression was limited, and political parties were prohibited. The ministers were closely linked to and dependent on the monarchy, despite the provisions of the constitution that stated that they were collectively and individually responsible to the lower house of Parliament. In fact, their positions and policies were determined by the king. In the governmental structure the only significant potential alternative power center was the House of Representatives. It consisted of elected members, and its vote of confidence was essential to the continuation of a cabinet in power. It was the only place in which policies were publicly discussed, evaluated, and frequently criticized, and it provided a forum for the opposition to express its views. But its power was limited by constitutional and political restrictions. In theory, the king shared the right of legislation with the House and the Senate, and he was the ultimate arbiter in any dispute between the House and the cabinet. Moreover, elections were often controlled to ensure smooth relations between the House and the cabinet.

The king gradually consolidated his power, playing people against each other, maneuvering disparate factions and cliques to suit his purposes, and imposing limitations on various organs of the state. He often trespassed in areas beyond his constitutional limits and even meddled in purely administrative matters. He carefully sought to have the cabinet subordinated to the palace, and the Parliament to the cabinet. The provinces gradually weakened and became subordinated to the cabinet. Despite opposition to his policies and programs, the king controlled the Libyan political system with a firm hand, and political development was stifled.

The Revolution of 1969

On September 1, 1969, a bloodless military coup d'état overthrew the government of King Idris (who was out of the country at the time). There was little resistance, even by elements thought to be loyal to the king (such as the police and the tribes). Although the king made an attempt to secure British assistance to restore his position, he was unsuccessful and eventually renounced the throne. The monarchy was abolished, and a Revolutionary Command Council of twelve young military officers proclaimed a Libyan Arab Republic and vested supreme authority for all government and public affairs in itself. All legislative functions were to be executed by the RCC. The constitution and Parliament were abolished, the government was dismissed, and the ban on political parties was continued.

The RCC proclaimed a republic opposing imperialism and favoring the establishment of a revolutionary, socialist, and progressive Libyan state. The basic tenor and approach of the new regime became clear in the RCC's proclamation of September 1, 1969:

> In the name of God, the Compassionate, the Merciful, O great Libyan people: . . . your armed forces have destroyed the reactionary, backward, and decadent regime. . . . In one terrible moment of fate, the darkness of ages—from the rule of the Turks to the tyranny of the Italians and the era of reaction, bribery, intercession, favoritism, treason, and treachery—was dispersed. Thus, from now on, Libya is deemed a free, sovereign republic under the name of the Libyan Arab Republic—ascending with God's help to exalted heights, proceeding in the path of freedom, unity and social justice, guaranteeing the right of equality to its citizens, and opening before them the doors of honorable work—with none terrorized, none cheated, none oppressed, no master and no servant, but free brothers in the shadow of a society over which flutters, God willing, the banner of prosperity and equality. . . . Stand together against the enemy of the Arab nation, the enemy of Islam, the enemy of humanity, who burned our holy places and shattered our honor. Thus will we build glory, revive our heritage, and revenge an honor wounded and a right usurped.[2]

The regime that came to power had certain clear objectives and developed an ideology, albeit often unfocused and confused. Their immediate problem was to create a functioning political system. Much of the period since the revolution has reflected this dual effort—formulating a coherent ideology and constructing a functioning political structure to promote the ideology. Both have undergone substantial evolution.

The RCC sought to move Libya in new directions after the revolution. Its motto became "freedom, socialism and unity," and it sought to take strong measures to achieve these ends. The definition and meaning of these three concepts and the policies designed to achieve them were increasingly provided by Muammar Qaddafi, who emerged as the main power of the new regime shortly after the revolution. He has continued to exercise authority despite numerous modifications in the structures and procedures of government.

Qaddafi articulated a world view known as the third theory, a philosophy in which he advanced an alternative to Marxist socialism and Western capitalism. In his view, the Quran, in which all wisdom is to be found, provides for an egalitarianism that is the basis of socialism and provides the Islamic content of Qaddafi's socialism. A recurring theme in public statements has been a comparison between capitalism and communism and exhortations that Libyan socialism is not akin to that of Lenin or Marx. Rather, according to Qaddafi, "it is the socialism of the true faith. It is the socialism which springs from the heritage and beliefs of this people."[3] Socialism will thus provide for social justice within the system, and all will be able to share in the benefits of society. He sought to free Libya from poverty and backwardness, from injustice and oppression, and from foreign elements and influences. He also strove to build Arab unity by linking

Libya with other Arab states. In the final analysis, he saw these elements as mutually supportive and increasingly leading to the attainment of the designated goal of unity.

In support of the regime's ideology, a series of measures aimed at Arabization and Islamization of Libya were instituted. As early as September 1969, the RCC ordered the use of Arabic for all signs, tickets, and other documents. Subsequently, Libya insisted on passports being written in Arabic rather than the internationally accepted English or French. Efforts were made to increase the use of Arabic in regional and international forums. Libya's Italian community was warned about its colonialist past soon after the revolution. In July 1970 the property of the Italian and Jewish communities in Libya was confiscated.

Although the basic elements of the ideology were identified soon after the revolution took place, the machinery and policy necessary to achieve the goals were more difficult to develop. At first the RCC—the group of officers who staged the revolution and continued to run it—was the supreme governing body. Muammar Qaddafi soon emerged as the leading figure of the council, its chief spokesman and ideologist.

Qaddafi was born in 1942 in a bedouin tent in the Libyan desert of a not well-to-do family belonging to a small tribe, originally of Berber origin. He attended local elementary and secondary schools, where his education was Arabic and Islamic, and many of his teachers were Egyptian. He focused on the study of history and apparently was influenced by the major historical events of the time: the creation of Israel, the Egyptian Revolution of 1952, and the invasion of Egypt by Israel, England, and France in 1956. His education and his family background provided the basis for his strong and devout Muslim beliefs and his austere and simple life-style and puritanical code of personal conduct and morals. He maintained much of his bedouin ethics and code of action. During his formative years he was influenced not only by events but by the needs of his people. He saw the monarchy as reactionary and under foreign influence, and Libyan society as backward. He viewed the changes in Egypt as beneficial and adopted Nasser as his hero and the Egyptian Revolution as a model for change in Libya. The military academy and a military career appeared to be a logical avenue for upward mobility, political activity, and revolution that would change the system. Qaddafi entered the academy in 1961 and prior to his graduation met many of his future colleagues in the RCC. After graduation he served in the army, rising to the rank of captain (at age twenty-seven) at the time of the 1969 overthrow of Idris. He was made commander-in-chief of the armed forces in October 1969 and became chairman of the RCC.

Initially, the RCC formed a government under Dr. Mahmud S. al-Maghrebi, who was not an RCC member. But, in January 1970 Qaddafi became prime minister with his chief aide, Abdel Salem Jalloud, as second in command. Internal strife within the junta was suppressed, and, in December 1969, a conspiracy led by the ministers of defense and the interior, which attempted to overthrow the regime, was foiled.

Government activities were managed by a cabinet appointed by the RCC, chiefly composed of civilian technocrats but with RCC members holding such critical cabinet posts as prime minister, minister of defense, and minister of the interior. From the beginning, the RCC functioned as a closed system of authority with supreme power. Power was concentrated in the hands of the RCC, and it was strongly supported by the armed forces and by the general population. Within the RCC the decisionmaking process was informal and appeared to be in accord with traditional Arab approaches to decisionmaking (rather than Western-style formal and institutionalized procedure), which involved elite consensus rather than formal votes. The consensus resulting from discussion and debate also helped to reinforce unity rather than to accentuate division within the ruling group. Within the RCC, loyalty to Qaddafi seemed to be maintained because of the strong agreement among its members concerning the goals of the revolution—Arab nationalism and the improvement of the condition of the average Libyan.

Control over the government has increasingly resided in Qaddafi, although, in contrast to the monarchy, he has attempted to promote greater popular participation in government. An early effort was undertaken in June 1971 with the establishment of the first significant postindependence political party—the Arab Socialist Union (ASU)—its character clearly patterned after the model of the Egyptian ASU, developed under Nasser. The Libyan ASU was to be the vehicle of Arab nationalism and would facilitate political socialization and participation. The party was to be based on an alliance of the "active popular forces," which included peasants, workers, soldiers, intellectuals, and nonexploiting capitalists; and peasants and workers were to constitute not less than 50 percent of the members of any branch of the party. The structure provided for provincial congresses, which would elect committees from which the RCC would appoint a national congress. The ASU provided a rudimentary political organization, which took root, although, in general, the results were disappointing to the RCC leadership.

In a speech at Zouara in April 1973, Qaddafi launched an attack on the shortcomings of the revolution's domestic progress and the reluctance of the people to contribute to national development. He proclaimed as a new stage in the revolution a program of five principles: the suspension of all laws then in force and their replacement by Shari'a (Islamic law); repression of all adversaries of the revolution (especially communists); the arming of the masses so that they could attain the objectives of the revolution; the purging of the administration and administrative reform; and a cultural revolution directed against everything contrary to the Quran and the promotion of pure Islamic thought. Popular committees came into existence in schools, businesses, industrial enterprises, and public institutions. They were ostensibly created to oversee the administration of those bodies in the public interest.

Qaddafi moved ahead with the attempt to construct a political system. In January 1976 a "Green Book" appeared in which he elaborated the principles of popular government, expounded his political ideas, voiced criticism of political parties and parliamentary assemblies, and stressed the necessity for popular participation in government. The publication of the Green Book coincided with the meeting of an elected national congress in Tripoli in January 1976 that considered establishing a new political system in Libya.

On March 3, 1977, a General People's Congress of elected representatives changed the country's name to the Socialist People's Libyan Arab Jamahiriya, proclaimed the establishment of people's power, and vested all power in the General People's Congress. Colonel Qaddafi, as secretary-general of the General Secretariat of the General People's Congress, continued to be chief of state. The People's Congress replaced the Revolutionary Command Council, which was abolished as the supreme authority, but former RCC officers were named members of the secretariat and served in an advisory capacity. The General People's Congress Committee, which replaced the Council of Ministers, was composed of cabinet officers appointed by the secretariat and was headed by Abdulati Ubaydi (Obeidi) who was thus de facto head of government. The cabinet ministers were made responsible for day-to-day operations of their ministries. There were local congresses at the village or neighborhood level, labor syndicates, unions, and professional associations. The Arab Socialist Union (ASU) remained the sole political party. The March 1977 Congress decreed that the country's legal codes would henceforth be based upon the Quran.

Despite the new names and structures and the formal end of the RCC, the political system continued to be dominated by the officers who joined with Qaddafi to overthrow the king in 1969. Throughout the late 1970s and early 1980s organizational structures in Libya continued to be replaced by "people's committees" or "people's bureaux." Often these new bodies contained some of the former administrators of the institutions they replaced. Although high-level decisionmaking remained in the hands, and under the control, of Qaddafi and his closest lieutenant, Abdel Salem Jalloud, there clearly was greater popular participation in many lower-level government organizations.

Foreign Policy

King Idris followed a pro-Western foreign policy. Treaties signed with Britain (July 1953) and the United States (September 1954) provided for the maintenance of military bases and forces in Libya, in exchange for development grants and budgetary subventions. An agreement with France (August 1955) provided for communications facilities in the southwestern desert areas. Close ties were also maintained with Turkey and Greece. Within the Arab League, which Libya joined in 1953, Libya supported the conservative bloc despite internal pressures for closer ties with Egypt. After the 1967 Arab-Israeli war, Libya committed itself, along with Saudi Arabia and Kuwait, to provide subsidies to Egypt and Jordan as compensation for war losses.

Under internal and external pressure for the liquidation of foreign bases, the government publicly supported the early evacuation of these bases but took few practical steps in that direction. In June 1967 the government officially requested Britain and the United States to liquidate their bases as soon as possible and the process of liquidation was begun. But the matter became urgent only after the revolution.

In the African arena, Libya was a founding member of the Organization of African Unity (1963) and generally supported its anticolonialist resolutions and policies. Efforts were also made to establish closer economic cooperation among the Maghrib states. Discussions concerning this cooperation were held with Tunisia, Algeria, and Morocco.

Qaddafi regarded the coup of September 1969 as the starting point of Libyan independence. The RCC gave priority to removing the foreign bases, eliminating the vestiges of imperialism, and supporting the Arab cause. Shortly after the overthrow of Idris, the regime approached the United States and England to secure the removal of their bases. Agreement was soon reached, and the British bases at Tobruk and al-Adam, as well as the U.S. base, Wheelus Field, were evacuated in the spring of 1970. The new government vigorously sought to unite with other Arab states in a pan-Arab federation as a means of achieving Arab unity. The obvious first partner was Egypt, for geographical and ideological reasons as well as because of Nasser's prestige and Qaddafi's efforts to emulate Nasser, who was his idol. Although Nasser was wary of such a union, Sadat was less cautious and saw it as a means of strengthening Egypt's domestic and regional position.

After the Arab summit conference of December 1969, Qaddafi, President Nasser of Egypt, and President Ja'far Nimeiri of the Sudan met in Tripoli for discussions that resulted in the Tripoli Charter of December 27, 1969. The three leaders reaffirmed faith in the objective of Arab unity, announced their intention to work toward some form of unity, and agreed to meet at periodic intervals for planning. Following Nasser's death in September 1970, Qaddafi, Sadat, and Nimeiri announced on November 8, 1970, that a tripartite federal union would be formed. Syria, under al-Assad, was accepted into the federal plan and, after further meetings, Qaddafi, Sadat, and al-Assad simultaneously announced from their respective capitals on April 17, 1971, the formation of a federation by Libya, Egypt, and Syria. The Sudan did not formally accede. The three heads of state signed the draft constitution of the new federation in Damascus on August 20, 1971, and the document received overwhelming approval by the electorate of the three countries in the referendum of September 1, 1971. To Qaddafi and the RCC, formation of the federation was a major step toward the goal of unity of the Arab nations.

In 1972 Qaddafi suggested fusion of Egypt and Libya, and on August 2, 1972, the Benghazi Declaration was issued over the signatures of Qaddafi and Sadat. Libya and Egypt were to be merged subject to approval by popular referendums of both countries by September 1, 1973. There was to be a single capital, Cairo, and one president elected by universal suffrage, who in the first instance would be Sadat. In order to give detailed shape to the union, some three hundred Egyptians and Libyans, in equal numbers, spent months in a series of committee meetings. But the differences between Egypt and Libya presented thorny problems. Reservations from the Egyptian side grew stronger, and eventually some Libyans also became concerned. The referendums of September 1, 1973, never occurred and union with Egypt was not established. Following the October 1973 war, relations between the two countries deteriorated rapidly with accusations and counteraccusations often voiced—including Egyptian accusations that Qaddafi was plotting to overthrow the Sadat regime and was financing the assassination of Sadat.

The failure to unite with Egypt was followed by an effort to link Libya and Tunisia into a single "Islamic Arab Republic." In January 1974, Tunisia and Libya announced the formation of a union following talks between President Bourguiba and Qaddafi. The plan called for a single state, the Islamic Arab Republic, with a single constitution, a flag, president, and army, and legislative, judicial, and executive authorities. A referendum would be held in Tunisia and in Libya to verify popular approval. But opposition within Tunisia emerged and the plans were aborted.

In 1984 Qaddafi inaugurated yet another unity scheme, this time with King Hassan of Morocco. Perhaps in reaction to talk of unity among Algeria, Tunisia, and Mauritania, and capitalizing on King Hassan's concern with retaining control of the former Spanish Sahara, Qaddafi's newest plan of unity did not produce any immediate tangible results greater than those yielded by earlier projects.

Under Qaddafi, the Libyan government has been uncompromising in its stance toward Israel and has become a major supporter of the Palestinians. Qaddafi has condemned Zionism as an aggressive nationalism, has sought Israel's elimination from the Middle East, and opposes all forms of Arab-Israeli negotiations. Despite his rhetoric and support for the Palestinians, Qaddafi has not played a practical role in the Arab confrontation with Israel. He has provided financial, moral, and political support to the PLO, but during the October 1973 war Libya sent no troops to the battle area and its military contribution was essentially confined to the transfer of aircraft to Egypt. It also played a minor role in the use of the oil weapon in 1973–1974, following the lead of Saudi Arabia. Libya has worked to counter Israeli influence in Black Africa by offering aid and assistance in the expectation that relations with Israel would deteriorate.

As Egyptian President Anwar Sadat moved closer to a peace treaty with Israel in the late 1970s, Libya became a leader of the "rejection front" of the Arab states that denounced any political settlement with Israel. After the signing of the Egypt-Israel Peace Treaty in March 1979, Libya was a leader in the move to expel Egypt from the Arab League and has remained as firmly opposed to Mubarak's quiet foreign policy as it was to Sadat's more flamboyant approach.

The volatility of foreign policy under Qaddafi has prevented the development of close and stable relations with other Arab states, and relations with most of the major powers have also been turbulent. Relations with the United States have deteriorated while military and economic ties with the Soviet Union, once anathema to the regime, have increased. The United States has been the object of verbal attack, and there have been few important areas of cooperation between the Libyan and U.S. governments. The October War was followed by increased contacts between the Libyan and Soviet governments and the development of military supply links. Libya's relationship with the Soviet Union remains close. Sophisticated Soviet equipment has been provided to Libya and was used in its interventions in Chad in the 1980s.

Qaddafi has long sought a leading role in Africa and has become deeply involved in the politics of the Organization of African Unity (OAU). Qaddafi's hopes of becoming OAU president for the 1982–1983 period were dashed when the organization virtually disintegrated over the questions of the Sahara and the Chad civil war. In addition, there have been accusations by conservative African nations concerning Libyan aid to various subversive movements in Africa.

Increasingly, Qaddafi has sought to have Libya associated with "revolutionary" causes and movements. He has been active in various regions in support of coups and in the funding and training of guerrilla groups and opposition political movements. He has been implicated in efforts to assassinate rival leaders and opponents to his regime and in support of terrorist groups and movements. At the same time, he has been involved in military ventures in Uganda in 1979 in support of Idi Amin and in Chad since 1980. These and similar activities have strained Libya's relations with many of the European states and with the United States. Relations between the United States and Libya have deteriorated since the 1969 coup because of Libya's support of international terrorism and subversion against Arab and African governments. In 1972 the United States recalled its ambassador, who has not returned. Controls on the shipment to Libya of military equipment and civilian items that might serve military purposes were imposed in the 1970s. In 1981 the Libyan People's Bureau (functioning as the Libyan embassy) in Washington was closed by the United States. In the same year a clash between Libyan and U.S. aircraft resulted in the shooting down of two Libyan planes. Subsequently, the United States took additional measures to reduce the U.S. commercial presence in Libya, to reduce tourism and travel to that country, and to limit the connections between the two states. During the Reagan administration, United States–Libyan relations have remained at the lowest level consistent with the maintenance of diplomatic relations.

The described patterns of established Libyan policy have been further intensified over time. Qaddafi's primary attention remains focused on the need to ensure "justice for the Palestinians" and to acquire a credible political-diplomatic and military capability for Libya.

Notes

1. The Senussi are a religious order or brotherhood intent on practicing a purified Islam. They have a strong inclination toward Sufism, and the tenets of their sect (*tariqa*) include work, unity, and organization. The order was founded by Sayid Muhammad Ben Ali al-Senussi, the grandfather of King Idris, in 1843.

2. Text as published in *Middle East Journal* (Spring 1970), p. 203.

3. Text in *Middle East Journal* (Spring 1970), p. 207.

Bibliography

John Wright, in *Libya* (New York: Praeger Publishers, 1969), provides a general history of Libya, especially of the period from 1911 to 1951. E. E. Evans-Pritchard, in *The Sanusi of Cyrenaica* (London: Oxford University Press, 1949), provides an important study of Libya's main religious order and its role in the country's development. Henry Serrano Villard, the first U.S. minister to Libya after independence, gives a general overview in *Libya: The New Arab Kingdom of North Africa* (Ithaca, N.Y.: Cornell University Press, 1956). The United Nations commissioner in Libya, Adrian Pelt, describes the transformation of Libya from an Italian colony to an independent state in *Libyan Independence and the United Nations: A Case of Planned Decolonization* (New Haven: Yale University Press, for the Carnegie Endowment for International Peace, 1970). Majid Khadduri, in *Modern Libya: A Study in Political Development* (Baltimore: Johns Hopkins University Press, 1963), considers the monarchy in detail. And Salaheddin Hassan's, "The Genesis of the Political Leadership of Libya 1952–1969: Historical Origins and Development of Its Component Elements" (Ph.D. dissertation, George Washington University, Washington, D.C., 1973) is a study of Libya's political elite in the period of the monarchy.

General surveys of Libya include J. A. Allan, *Libya Since Independence: Economic and Social Development* (London: Croom Helm, 1982); Omar L. Fatahly and Monte Palmer, *Political Development and Social Change in Libya* (Lexington, Mass.: Lexington Books, 1979); Harold D. Nelson, *Libya: A Country Study*, 3d ed. (Washington, D.C.: American University, Foreign Area Studies, 1979); John K. Cooley, *Libyan Sandstorm* (New York: Holt, Rinehart & Winston, 1982); Marius Deeb and M. J. Deeb, *Libya Since the Revolution: Aspects of Social and Political Development* (New York: Praeger Publishers, 1982); and Benyamin Neuberger, *Involvement, Invasion and Withdrawal; Qadhdhafi's Libya and Chad, 1969–1981* (Tel Aviv: Shiloah Center for Middle Eastern and African Studies, Tel Aviv University, 1982). Ruth First, in *Libya: The Elusive Revolution* (Middlesex, England: Penguin Books, 1974); and Henri Habib, in *Politics and Government of Revolutionary Libya* (Montreal: Le Cercle du Livre de France, 1975), assess the revolutionary regime of Qaddafi.

Libya's economy is surveyed in *The Economic Development of Libya*, the report of a mission organized by the International Bank for Reconstruction and Development at the request of the government of Libya (Baltimore: Johns Hopkins University Press, for the International Bank for Reconstruction and Development, 1960), and in Rawle Farley's *Planning for Development in Libya: The Exceptional Economy in the Developing World* (New York: Praeger Publishers, 1971). A plan for the economic and social development of Libya is detailed in Benjamin Higgins, *The Economic and Social Development of Libya* (New York: United Nations Technical Assistance Programme, 1953).

J. A. Allan, in *Libya: The Experience of Oil* (Boulder, Colorado: Westview Press, 1981), examines Libya's major resource and its effects on the development of the state.

Finally, biographical data on Qaddafi are available in Mirella Bianco's *Gadafi: Voice from the Desert* (London: Longman Group, 1975), and Frederick Muscat's *My President, My Son* (Malta: Adam Publishers, 1974). *Thus Spoke Colonel Moammar Kazzafi* (Beirut: Dar Al Awda, 1974) contains the texts of interviews with Qaddafi in which his views are clarified.

18

The Maghrib: An Overview

John P. Entelis
Mark A. Tessler

North Africa constitutes a unique world of its own, however much it may share in culture, religion, language, and history with the rest of the Middle East. This chapter provides an introduction to that unique world and to the following three chapters on its constituent countries. The distinctiveness of this area is in great part related to its relative geographical isolation. The Arab invaders in the seventh century A.D. named it *jazirat al-maghrib* (islands of the west). It is a virtually self-contained region, bounded by the Mediterranean Sea to the north, the Atlantic Ocean to the west, the Sahara to the south, and 300 miles of desert running to the Mediterranean between Tripolitania and Cyrenaica to the east. The term *North Africa* came into being during the more than 130 years of European colonial rule and today is used by the peoples of the Maghrib themselves in referring to Morocco, Algeria, and Tunisia. Despite the existence of three separate, independent political entities, the entire region is characterized by cultural unity and ethnic and religious homogeneity.

Historical Background

The indigenous Berber society of North Africa has been subjected to recurring foreign invasions and influences. The first conquest occurred around 1200 B.C. and lasted nearly a thousand years, bringing the Phoenicians and Carthaginians to the region. Roman domination followed, becoming firmly established with the destruction of Carthage in 146 B.C. and lasting for 650 years. Then came two centuries of Vandal and Byzantine rule. The whole of the Maghrib was brought under Arab control by A.D. 710, initiating 1,200 years of Arab-Islamic predominance. Direct Arab rule by the Eastern caliphate over the Maghrib was terminated by the end of the eighth century, however, leaving the three states of North Africa to develop their own autonomous sociopolitical forms, at the local level at least. Turkish hegemony was established over Algeria and Tunisia in the middle of the sixteenth century and continued in modified form until the nineteenth century, after which European occupation occurred.

None of these successive invasions managed to destroy totally the underlying fabric of Berber culture, although the coming of the Arabs and Islam in the mid-seventh century did affect Berber society deeply. In the 300 years following conquest of the Maghrib by the forces of the Arab-Islamic world, a confused pattern of political rule, new social forms, and religious movements emerged. This period saw the assimilation of Islam by North Africa's masses, who in turn were trying to adapt the religion to local needs. Formal political authority was almost always external and was exercised in the name of Islam. Yet Berber nationalism and social organization remained strong and contributed to the development of a unique Maghribi personality.

The eleventh century witnessed the emergence of the first of three indigenous empires in the Maghrib. During the next four centuries, these empires established the foundation for the three North African states that were later to emerge with their own identities and histories. The Almoravid Empire (1042–1147) was established by Berber-speaking nomads from Mauritania and the western Sahara. The Almoravids constituted the first dynasty to unify Morocco, and at one time their rule extended as far east as Algiers. They established a historic link between the Maghrib and Muslim Spain lasting 250 years, bringing enormous benefits to the former and extending the life of the latter. The Almoravids also eliminated all heretical sects and imposed, with a permanent imprint, the Malikite school of Islam, named after Malik ibn Anas, an eighth-century religious leader of Medina.

The second major indigenous empire was that of the Almohads (1147–1269), sedentary Berbers of the High Atlas Mountains and direct successors to the Almoravids. In the fashion of their predecessors, the Almohads were inspired by the visionary leadership of a puritanical religious teacher, ibn Tumar (1076–1130). The most significant political contribution of the Almohads was probably the unification of the Maghrib under a single North African dynasty for the first and only time in history. The empire ranged from Agadir in Morocco to Tripoli.

The dissolution of the Almohad Empire in 1269 was followed by the emergence of three separate Berber kingdoms: the Hafsids in Tunis; the Zayanids in Tlemcen, in what is now Algeria; and the Merinids in Fez, in present-day Morocco.

Under the Merinids, Fez prospered, making it equal to any town in the world in civility, culture, and refinement. Tunis under the Hafsids became the uncontested capital of Tunisia and an important commercial center. It was also one of the foremost centers of learning in the Maghrib. The famous historian ibn Khaldoun studied at the Zitouna Mosque in Tunis.

The Zayanids ruled over a society that was essentially tribal, yet urban and civilized life also developed in their realm. The Zayanid state, like the Merinid and to a lesser extent the Hafsid, profited from the administrative and artistic skills of Andalusian refugees in creating the rudiments of an administration and in embellishing the capital with mosques and schools. During the Zayanid period, Tlemcen became known as the "pearl of the Maghrib" and, for the first and only time, was the capital of an independent state.

The power and vitality of these separate Berber empires had begun to decline by 1500. From the north, the Iberian powers intervened in North Africa and established coastal enclaves. From the east, the Ottomans extended their sovereignty to Algeria and Tunisia in the mid-sixteenth century, although they never fully controlled the Algerian countryside and never conquered Morocco. By the end of the eighteenth century, political and social stagnation in the Maghrib was so advanced that it set the stage for the full-blown intervention of European powers, beginning with the French conquest of Algeria in 1830.

European colonial rule in the Maghrib varied according to the metropole (France or Spain), the time of occupation, and the nature of the territory occupied. Nevertheless, the overall process was remarkably similar in all three countries. Over 90 percent of the population of the Maghrib was colonized by France. Only northern Morocco escaped this pattern, having been administered as a Spanish protectorate. French administrators and colonial settlers sought to implant the civilization of the metropolitan country. However, they remained outsiders and assumed a privileged position vis-à-vis the native population.

French colonization was intense and far-reaching, more so in Algeria and less in Morocco but pervasive throughout. French rule lasted 132 years in Algeria (1830–1962), 75 years in Tunisia (1881–1956), and 44 years in Morocco (1912–1956). Algeria suffered the bulk of North Africa's European settler population. At their height, in 1955, Europeans constituted 13 percent of the total Algerian population. There were also many settlers in Tunisia and Morocco, where they made up 8 percent and 6 percent of the population, respectively. Settlers appropriated 27 percent of Algeria's arable land (more than 7 million acres), 21 percent of Tunisia's arable land (2 million acres), and 7 percent of that in Morocco (2.5 million acres).

Juridically, Algeria was an integral part of France, whereas Tunisia and Morocco, as protectorates, preserved substantial elements of their indigenous precolonial governments, albeit in emasculated form. Protectorate status should not be misunderstood. In both countries, French administrators controlled the policymaking process in internal as well as external affairs. Under the nominal authority of the native head of state (the *bey* in Tunisia and the *sultan* in Morocco), French directors, supervised by the resident general, established administrations that in effect were carbon copies of modern French ministries. The protectorate was not without benefit, however, for it did help ensure the survival of traditional elites and institutions, especially in Morocco.

The colonial experience in all three countries brought a shift from tribal forms of solidarity to more differentiated social structures. It caused increasing differentiation, the erosion of tribal units, rural exodus, and the emigration of thousands of North Africans to Europe.

It may be helpful to our subsequent country-by-country analysis to identify three analytically distinct forms of colonialism in North Africa. Segmented colonialism, best represented by the experience of Morocco, involves limited yet highly visible economic domination. This domination does not destroy the indigenous political and cultural order. The case of Tunisia represents instrumental colonialism, which involves more intense economic exploitation and does not hesitate, when necessary, to intervene in other sectors of society. Finally, total colonialism, as experienced by Algeria, is characterized by unrestrained domination of a society at all levels, based upon the negation of its social, cultural, political, and economic order.

The period of colonial rule also witnessed the rise of nationalism in North Africa. In fact, Maghribi nationalism began in part as a direct reaction to Western colonial rule. Although influenced by the revival of Arab political consciousness, which made itself felt in the mid-nineteenth century, the form of this nationalist expression was largely European in ideology, terminology, and structural organization, with French leftist political thought particularly influential. Because of this origin, North African nationalism has continued to display tendencies that sometimes conflict. That is, traditionalist, religious, and purely Arab components vie with modernist, secular, and bilingual elements, resulting in an ideological cleavage that has yet to be resolved in a manner satisfactory to both masses and elites.

The nationalist response to colonialism was relatively similar throughout the Maghrib. Three distinct ideological tendencies are discernible, and, by independence, each was present in all three North African countries, although their functional weight and the timing of their emergence were not identical in Algeria, Tunisia, and Morocco. First, there were the liberal assimilationists—sons of the old, traditional elite who admired and imitated the colonial rulers, assimilated some of their styles and values, accepted their rules of the game, and attempted to engage in a dialogue. Liberals were particularly influential during the early and middle years of colonialism in Algeria and Tunisia.

A second elite group was composed of traditionalists who assumed a nationalistic-scripturalist orientation. This perspective was advocated by the learned, scholarly, and urban families, which had historically constituted a distinctive high-status group. They called for a reaffirmation of national, cultural, and religious integrity in the face of Western colonial domination. During the period of colonialism this group was also the first to call for the maintenance of a national personality, usually by stressing the use, revision, and celebration of the Islamic heritage (scripturalism) and by emphasizing Arabism as a language, culture, and common history (nationalism).

A third group was composed of populists. Trained in European schools and environments, these individuals sought to generate in their own societies the liberal trends formed in Europe through bourgeois revolutions. At the same time, they rebelled against the colonial status quo and appealed for mass mobilization against foreign domination. Unlike the traditionalists, the populists had a broader base of support, higher levels of education, and a more cosmopolitan outlook. And unlike the assimilationists, they were determined to attack and oppose colonial domination. In essence, the populists were secularists with a modernizing view of political change, who, while profoundly marked by a nationalist ideology and political activism, were influenced by Europe, which represented a model for their own growth. Thus, although they were militant in their struggle against France, they tended to be somewhat reconciliatory once in power.

A fourth category of elite types has emerged in the post-independence period. Emanating essentially from the radical intelligentsia and workers, this most recent nationalistic group calls for mass mobilization and the radical restructuring of indigenous society. Its members have tended to view the infrastructure of dependency of their societies much more seriously than their predecessors had done. This orientation has only recently appeared, however, and even today its influence is indirect.

The Land and the People

Although the transition from the green vegetation of the Mediterranean to the barren desolation of the Sahara is nowhere exactly the same, the topography of the Maghrib follows a general pattern: coastal valleys and plains, followed by mountains, high steppes, more mountains, and finally desert. The most noteworthy geographical element is the long and basically continuous chain of the Atlas Mountains, which forms a horizontal backbone extending across the entire length of the three countries from southwest Morocco to northeast Tunisia. Filled with steep valleys and narrow gorges, this mountain chain cuts off the desert to the south from the more fertile areas north and west of the mountains.

The descendants of the original inhabitants of North Africa are the Berbers, who currently number about 6 million and are found predominantly in Morocco and Algeria. The Berbers' principal distinguishing characteristic is their individualistic language, Berber. The percentages of Berberophones in Algeria and Morocco are estimated to be as high as 25 to 40 percent, respectively. Tunisia, because of its historical proximity to the Arab east, is today virtually devoid of non-Arabic speaking Berbers. For all practical purposes, Tunisian Berbers have been thoroughly Arabized in their cultural identity.

Aside from the original Berber inhabitants and the Arabized Berbers, the Arabs have made the most important contribution to the demography of the Maghrib. They arrived in North Africa beginning in the mid-seventh century, and over a period of several hundred years managed to transform the Berber-populated Maghrib into an integral part of the Arab-Islamic world. In terms of culture, language, and religion, the Arabs profoundly and permanently affected North African society.

Europeans have also helped shape the society of North Africa. Despite their relatively brief presence in the Maghrib and their relative isolation from the native population, the Europeans induced profound changes. However, with political independence, the mass exodus of Europeans (French, Spanish, and Italian people) and indigenous Jews, and the long-term process of Arabization and Islamicization, the Maghrib of today is ethnically, culturally, and religiously homogeneous.

Compared to states farther east, the Maghrib is religiously more unified, with the Malikite school of orthodox or Sunni Islam predominating. There are no indigenous Christian minorities and, except for the Kharijites of Jerba and the Mzabites of Algeria, no major Islamic sects. Indigenous Jews, once numerous, now constitute an insignificant and steadily diminishing minority. Because of this religious uniformity, Islam is an important common denominator throughout North Africa, mitigating differences of tribe, language, and life-style. Notwithstanding different policies toward religion and religious practice adopted by the various political leaders of the Maghrib, Islam is designated as the state religion in each of the three constitutions. The Algerian and Tunisian presidents must be Muslims, and in the Moroccan constitution the king is given the title "commander of the faithful."

Despite the predominance of Islam as a social, cultural, and ideological force, traditional Islamic institutions have declined significantly in importance, especially in Tunisia and Algeria. This decline can be attributed to modernization and the increased power of the central state apparatus. It is also in part the result of Islamic reformist movements that influenced the Maghrib in the late nineteenth century.

Modernization has also resulted in the decline of the old religious elite (the ulama). Even the direct involvement of reformist ulamas in the pre-independence nationalist struggle, as in Algeria, was not enough to salvage their prestige or retrieve their position.

Yet, in the Maghrib, as elsewhere in the Muslim world, a re-Islamicization of politics has occurred during the last decade. Referred to by various labels—Islamic resurgence, popular puritanism, Islamic fundamentalism, militant Islam, and Muslim radicalism—this Islamic resurgence has assumed national and even transnational significance, with widespread implications for state and society in North Africa. This new trend differs markedly from traditional mysticism and saintly worship, long associated with North African rural life. It also differs from the official and reformist Islam of the state, in which the recasting of transcendant religious values in modern form has increasingly worn thin.

No doubt the experience of revolutionary Iran, where Muslim militants took over power in 1979, has had an impact on North Africa. Yet the rise of populist Islam in the three countries of the Maghrib has more to do with local considerations than with any external experience, however appealing or galvanizing. Specifically, a deep alienation has developed among the disadvantaged and dislocated members of the population. These North Africans believe that their cultural integrity and economic well-being have been sacrificed for the sake of state-led policies that have failed to promote economic development and/or have increased the gap between rich and poor.

Alienation has been reinforced by other factors. On the one hand, the governments of Morocco, Algeria, and Tunisia espouse Islamic principles but have nonetheless pursued policies of secular development, based on industrialization, mass education, and bureaucratization. The result has been an ideological gap between principle and practice, with neither secular ideology (nationalism or socialism) nor state-sponsored religion (official Islam) providing the kind of psychological palliative necessary for people experiencing the stress of rapid social change. On the other hand, partial and incomplete social mobilization at the level of the individual has left its mark, too. Education, urbanization, and other aspects of modernization have not improved conditions for many North Africans. As a result, sacrifices made in the name of modernization have produced widespread frustration and resentment, which in turn have inspired a reactionary return to a familiar cultural tradition—Islam.

North Africa's high degree of ethno-religious uniformity does not rule out internal diversities. For example, the Maghrib is geographically fragmented into distinct demographic areas that do not complement each other. Important linguistic and cultural divisions also persist. These disharmonies are reflected in the principal patterns of life supported by the region. Several distinct rural patterns can be identified in the Maghrib, including the pure nomads of the desert; the seminomads of the steppe-desert; the sedentary Berberophone mountaineers, who cover all of the Rif and most of the Atlas Mountains in Morocco and the Kabylia Mountains in Algeria; a large block of tribes and loosely organized groups, found in the coastal plains and hills of Morocco and in eastern Algeria, who are only now settling on the land; and, finally, the authentic village life of North Africa, found in the old, settled areas of northeast Tunisia and along the *sahel* of the country's eastern shore. It is here that one finds the highest degree of rural sophistication in the Maghrib.

Those living on the land have been affected by demographic and economic forces that have shifted populations away from the countryside and into towns and cities. These forces are breaking down the delicate balance of the rural economy, wherein products of the pasture are traded for those of the town and village. They are also causing societies to become importers rather than exporters of foodstuffs.

North African urban life, like its rural counterpart, is diverse. First, there are the traditional Islamic cities such as Fez, Tunis, Tetuan, and Tlemcen. These are old cities whose elites constitute an indigenous bourgeoisie. The best tradition of eastern Arab-Islamic culture is to be found in these cities. A second group consists of such coastal port towns as Algiers, Tangier, Oran, and Bejaia, which possess no distinctive quality but simply reflect the pattern found among most Mediterranean port cities. They are normally separated from their own culture and society and stand out as peninsulas detached from the heartland in a physical and spiritual sense. A third urban type, quite distinct from the previous two, comprises the strategic regional centers that were founded for economic or political purposes. Constantine in eastern Algeria is a good example. Finally, many new towns like Kenitra, Annaba, Skikda, Bizerte, and Casablanca were created to serve European needs. Smaller cities, such as Setif in Algeria, were established for security reasons or to exploit natural resources.

Urbanization in North Africa must be distinguished from urbanism. Changing economic conditions and the growth of population in the countryside have resulted in large-scale internal migrations to towns and cities. Thus, the movement into urban conglomerations owes more to demographic and economic pressures in the rural areas than to the growth of opportunities and attractions in the towns. Once in the city, rural migrants rarely become transformed into "modern" people exhibiting the traits associated with urbanism, such as a cosmopolitan outlook and receptivity to change. They are simply relocated from one physical space to another without necessarily undergoing a qualitative change in outlook or behavioral patterns. Moreover, they are often crowded into urban slums, where the physical conditions are scarcely better than they had been in the rural areas. This overlapping process of overurbanization and underurbanism in the Maghrib represents but one part of a larger phenomenon occurring through the Middle East.

Bibliography

For obvious historical reasons, research and writing on the three North African states of Algeria, Morocco, and Tunisia have been dominated by French scholarship and French-language literature. In recent years, however, more and more first-rate publications on the Maghrib have appeared in English. Students can now rely entirely on the English-language literature for an introductory understanding of North African society and politics. This select bibliography lists only English-language materials, including both original works and translations. Many additional bibliographical citations can be found in the books listed.

North Africa's pre-Islamic history is presented in lively and interesting form by Paul MacKendrick, in *The North African Stones Speak* (Chapel Hill, N.C.: University of North Carolina Press, 1980), whereas the history of the pre-independence period, with concentrations on precolonial and colonial North Africa, is provided in Jamil M. Abun-Nasr, *A History of the Maghrib* (Cambridge: Cambridge University Press, 1975); Charles-André Julien, *History of North Africa—Tunisia, Algeria, and Morocco: From the Arab Conquest to 1830* (New York: Praeger Publishers, 1970); and Abdallah Laroui, *The History of the Maghrib: An Interpretive Essay* (Princeton, N.J.: Princeton University Press, 1977)—the latter two being translations of original French-language works. The colonial Maghrib and the period of the national independence struggles, involving both general as well as country-specific analyses, can be found in Jacques Berque, *French North Africa: The Maghrib Between Two World Wars* (London: Faber and Faber, 1967); John K. Cooley, *Baal, Christ and Mohamed: Religion and Revolution in North Africa* (New York: Holt, Rinehart & Winston, 1965); Alal al-Fassi, *The Independence Movements in Arab North Africa* (New York: Octagon Books, 1970); Charles F. Gallagher, *The United States and North Africa: Morocco, Algeria, and Tunisia* (Cambridge, Mass.: Harvard University Press, 1963); David C. Gordon, *North Africa's French Legacy, 1954–1962* (Cambridge, Mass.: Harvard University Press, 1964); and Lorna Hahn, *North Africa: Nationalism to Nationhood* (Washington, D.C.: Public Affairs Press, 1960).

Studies devoted to comparative analyses of the three North African political systems include John P. Entelis, *Comparative Politics of North Africa: Algeria, Morocco, and Tunisia* (Syracuse, N.Y.: Syracuse University Press, 1980); Richard M. Brace, *Morocco, Algeria, Tunisia* (Englewood Cliffs, N.J.: Prentice-Hall 1964); Manfred Halpern, *The Politics of Social Change in the Middle East and North Africa* (Princeton, N.J.: Princeton University Press, 1963); Elbaki Hermassi, *Leadership and National Development in North Africa: A Comparative Study* (Berkeley and Los Angeles: University of California Press, 1972); Clement Henry Moore, *Politics in North Africa: Algeria, Morocco, and Tunisia* (Boston: Little, Brown, 1970); and I. William Zartman, *Government and Politics in Northern Africa* (New York: Praeger Publishers, 1963).

A systematic comparative study of elite politics in the Maghrib can be found in I. William Zartman et al., *Political Elites in Arab North Africa* (New York: Longman, 1982). A comparative analysis of political and economic performance with some useful original interpretations is that of Richard Lawless and Allan Findlay, eds., *North Africa: Contempoary Politics and Economic Development* (London: Croom Helm, 1984). Samir Amin's *The Maghrib in the Modern World: Algeria, Tunisia, Morocco* (Baltimore: Penguin Books, 1970) is explicitly leftist in orientation, with a focus on the political economy of North African development. Sizable portions of Michael C. Hudson, *Arab Politics: The Search for Legitimacy* (New Haven, Conn.: Yale University Press, 1977), and James A. Bill and Carl Leiden, *Politics in the Middle East* (Boston: Little, Brown, 1979), deal with North African political systems in a comparative way.

Diverse social, economic, political, and anthropological themes are treated in several excellent anthologies and edited books on North Africa: Leon Carl Brown, ed., *State and Society in Independent North Africa* (Washington, D.C.: The Middle East Institute, 1966); Michael Brett, ed., *Northern Africa: Islam and Modernization* (London: Frank Cass, 1973); Ernest Gellner and Charles Micaud, eds., *Arabs and Berbers: From Tribe to Nation in North Africa* (Lexington, Mass.: Lexington Books, 1972); Ernest Gellner and John Waterbury, eds., *Patrons and Clients in Mediterranean Societies* (London: Duckworth, 1977); and I. William Zartman, ed., *Man, State, and Society in the Contemporary Maghrib* (New York: Praeger Publishers, 1973). The book by Robert Montagne, *The Berbers: Their Social and Political Organisation* (London: Frank Cass, 1973), is a translation of a 1931 study that remains one of the best accounts of Berber sociopolitical organization.

Two reference works in English are particularly useful. They are Wilfrid Knapp's *North West Africa: A Political and Economic Survey* (London: Oxford University Press, 1977); and *The Middle East and North Africa*, an annual volume published in London by Europa Publications. Also of use to the introductory student is Lois A. Aroian and Richard P. Mitchell, *The Modern Middle East and North Africa* (New York: Macmillan, 1984).

The international politics of North Africa has yet to receive adequate book-length treatment in English. A recommended start is that of Richard B. Parker, *North Africa: Regional Tensions and Strategic Concerns* (New York: Praeger Publishers, 1984). First-rate selective surveys may be found in A. L. Udovitch, ed., *The Middle East: Oil, Conflict and Hope* (Lexington, Mass.: Lexington Books, 1976); John Waterbury and Ragaei El Mallakh, *The Middle East in the Coming Decade: From Wellhead to Well-Being?* (New York: McGraw-Hill, 1978); John Waterbury, "The Soviet Union and North Africa," in Ivo J. Lederer and Wayne S. Vucinich, eds., *The Soviet Union and the Middle East: The Post World War II Era* (Stanford, Calif.: Hoover Institution Press, 1974); Charles F. Gallagher, *The United States and North Africa* (Cambridge, Mass.: Harvard University Press, 1963); Clement Henry Moore,

Politics in North Africa (Boston: Little, Brown, 1970); and I. William Zartman, *Government and Politics in Northern Africa* (New York: Praeger Publishers, 1963). Of related significance is L. Carl Brown, *International Politics and the Middle East* (Princeton, N.J.: Princeton University Press, 1984).

The leading English-language scholarly journals treating the Maghrib on a regular basis are the *Middle East Journal*, *The Maghreb Review*, and the *International Journal of Middle East Studies*.

19

Kingdom of Morocco

Mark A. Tessler
John P. Entelis

Historical Background

Until 1894 Morocco remained viable under the rule of a strong and effective sultan, Mulay Hassan (1873–1894), who, among other things, maintained internal order and kept the country's finances on a relatively sound footing thanks to a flourishing export trade. Moreover, Hassan obtained the diplomatic assistance of Britain in his attempt to impede the annexationist ambitions of France and Spain. Relatively immune from outside intervention, the dynamic sultan built up an army, reestablished the authority of the Alawi Sharifian Empire, which had been established in 1666, and restored financial order.

After his death, however, the country fell into immediate difficulties, largely owing to the mismanagement of Hassan's son and successor, Abd al-Aziz (1894–1908), a young and weak ruler. The monarchy was forced to borrow heavily and quickly incurred a largely external debt. No longer able to resist European pressures and creditors, the country's internal sovereignty began to be questioned. The intrigues and maneuvers of the foreign agents who advised Abd al-Aziz poorly on financial matters virtually sealed the fate of Moroccan autonomy. By 1908 Morocco was in general revolt against Abd al-Aziz, who was accused of having abandoned the country to foreigners and foreign financial interests.

Abd al-Aziz's successor, Mulay Hafid, further indebted Morocco in a futile attempt to salvage the country from the enormous sums it owed. At the same time, dissident tribes in Fez besieged him and he turned to France for military, political, and economic assistance. The conditions under which France agreed to intervene on his behalf were exorbitant—nothing less than relinquishment of Moroccan political independence, which, indeed, had been formalized by the Treaty of Fez, signed by France and Morocco on March 30, 1912. The treaty formally established Morocco as a French protectorate; moreover, it granted France sole responsibility for all reforms, national defense, foreign policy, and economic and financial affairs.

It took nearly one-quarter of a century for France to pacify Morocco completely. Early opposition was particularly vigorous in the Anti-Atlas Mountains. More-

over, of the three Maghribi states, only Morocco maintained a "continuity of resistance." After the tribal battles and countryside wars subsided, an urbanized version of nationalist resistance immediately emerged, committed to the same goal of eventual freedom.

Under French protection, the basic structure of the sultan's government was retained; indeed, the feudal elements in Moroccan society were encouraged and the great families maintained their powerful positions. Official decrees and legislation were signed by the sultan and promulgated in his name, leaving him at the center of public life as at least the nominal source of authority in the country. Furthermore extensive European colonization in Morocco came late, since actual pacification of the country was not achieved until the 1930s.

Unlike French colonialism in Algeria, colonialism in Morocco left domestic, political, and social institutions intact. Thus, traditionally privileged classes were preserved, especially the commercially and culturally dominant Arab bourgeoisie in the cities of Fez and Rabat and the Berber tribal notables of the countryside. Similarly, internal social evolution was modest. On the one hand, the traditional elite was not infused with fresh blood by upwardly mobile lower-status groups. On the other, few of these elites either received a modern French education or gained access to modern administrative and professional careers as, for example, had some Tunisians.

Although the traditional elite of Morocco—the great bourgeois families from Fez and elsewhere—desired independence and possessed an Islamic-nationalist orientation, they eventually capitulated to French demands and reluctantly accepted their status. They remained frustrated, however, and after 1926 their ranks were joined by a small group of populists—young men, usually from leading urban families, who had received a modern education and were frustrated and embittered by the French presence. Disaffection also emerged during this period among skilled urban craftspeople, who were beginning to suffer because of strong competition from manufactured goods introduced by the colonialists. Frustrated traditional elites, radicalized younger elites, and disaffected lower-middle-class elements constituted a powerful nationalist front with an urbanized focus.

The movement toward nationalism gained momentum in 1930, when the Berber decree (*dahir*) of May 16 was issued from Rabat. The decree established a separate system of customary law tribunals in Berber-populated parts of the country and was part of a French effort to isolate the rural areas from the growing nationalism of the cities. Empowered to deal with civil matters these tribunals created an artificial division between the Arabs and the Berbers by removing the latter from the national system of Muslim jurisprudence.

Incipient nationalist forces representing traditionalists like Allal al-Fassi as well as westernized intellectuals like Ahmad Balafrej immediately and vigorously protested the decree, and their protests soon attracted the skilled craftspeople and shopkeepers of the towns to their cause. Although French authorities sought to dilute the implications of the *dahir*, the damage had already been done. Nationalist consciousness quickly spread, especially among Morocco's youth.

In May 1934 the Kutla al-'Amal al-Watani, or Comité d'Action Marocaine, was formed as the first overtly nationalist party in the country. The Comité worked peacefully, but unsuccessfully, for reforms within the framework of the protectorate. But with the French dissolution of the Comité in 1937, there was no effective political organization to lead the nationalist movement until the formation of the Istiqlal (Independence) party in 1943. The Istiqlal demanded full freedom for Morocco and a constitutional form of government under Sultan Muhammad Ben Yussuf (Muhammad V), who supported the nationalist movement.

After World War II, the Istiqlal was joined by two other parties—the Democratic Independence party (PDI), a splinter party from the Istiqlal, and the Communist party, which had very little support. The Istiqlal had strong support in the towns and a tacit alliance with the throne. It was challenged by powerful rural chieftains allied with the French, by some traditionalist elements in the cities, and by the heads of some religious brotherhoods.

During the late 1940s the Istiqlal transformed itself from an elite to a mass party, with independence as its primary objective. As the alliance between the

Istiqlal and the monarchy became more overt and began to challenge French hegemony in the country, colonial authorities exercised their power in response. In August 1953, the sultan was exiled and replaced by a more docile relative. The French had miscalculated, however. The deportation catalyzed the nationalist movement into an all-out fight for freedom and independence. Moreover, reactions at the popular level were totally unanticipated; the king was a martyr and a saint in the eyes of the masses, and an incipient guerrilla war soon broke out.

A relatively quick political settlement was achieved, thereby preventing the occurrence of widespread violence, and the return of Muhammad V from exile in November 1954 marked the virtual end of colonial rule in Morocco. On March 2, 1956, the former French-controlled regions of the west and south were joined with the Spanish-controlled areas of the north and east, and the country was formally declared independent.

The monarchy emerged as the major beneficiary of independence at the expense of the national elite, which was relegated to a secondary role. Indeed, Morocco is unique in the Middle East and North Africa in that its struggle for independence revolved around the capture, revival, and renovation of this traditional political institution. The masses, who had not been politically educated, revered the king for his mystical religious qualities, or *baraka*. The diverse forces of modern nationalism looked to him to satisfy their demands for a national government. The king was thus the one leader whose right to rule rested on sufficiently diverse modern and traditional grounds to satisfy virtually all sectors of nationalist opinion.

At the time of independence Morocco enjoyed a sufficient level of national unity, institutional stability, and effective political leadership to give it a promising future. Political parties, with the Istiqlal in the predominant position, provided necessary cadres for the new government. The urban resistance was incorporated into the police, and the Army of Liberation, which was one of the last groups to recognize the monarchy's independence, was absorbed into the Royal Armed Forces (FAR). Other civil servants were recruited among former employees of the ministries under the protectorate and among newly trained Moroccan youth. Over this diverse and heterogeneous group King Muhammad V ruled as arbitrator and symbol of Moroccan unity.

On the surface it appeared that political life in Morocco might move toward a European model of constitutional democracy based on a competitive multiparty system. Political freedom, although circumscribed, was nonetheless real and exercised. Yet, within five years of independence, both the national and the political unity that had existed during the anticolonialist struggle disappeared. The sharing of power between the king on the one hand and the Istiqlal and other nationalist leaders on the other broke down. Muhammad V was unwilling to become a constitutional figurehead, and the Istiqlal leadership was unwilling to accept the secondary role that the king had envisioned for it.

The Istiqlal also quickly began to show signs of internal strain, which hampered its attempts to reduce the political predominance of the monarch. Tension between the conservative and radical wings of the party reached a breaking point in 1959, when Prime Minister Abdallah Ibrahim of the Istiqlal joined a group of young, secular-minded intellectuals and trade-union leaders to form a new left-wing party, the National Union of Popular Forces (UNFP). The UNFP charged the traditional leadership elements of the Istiqlal with undue caution, compliance with the dictates of the royal household, and indifference to meaningful social and economic reform. Moreover, the new party called for election of a popular assembly to write a democratic monarchical constitution. In its pusuit of social and economic goals, the UNFP worked closely with the large Union of Moroccan Labor (UMT).

Although this fragmentation of the nationalist elite was the result more of dissension within the Istiqlal than of machinations by the palace, it enabled the king to manipulate the diverse factions that emerged; it also explains, in part, the current king's control of the political elite. The breakup of the Istiqlal thus contributed heavily to the course of politics in independent Morocco. The influence of the Istiqlal and the UNFP was also limited in substantial measure by their urban orientation and the fact that neither had much appeal among Morocco's rural masses.

Meanwhile, Muhammad V had been developing the institution of the Monarchy. His son, Hassan, was made acting head of state whenever the king was out of the country, and in 1957 Hassan was officially designated crown prince. Thus established was the principle of primogeniture, which was later formally institutionalized in the 1962 constitution. The power of the throne was further consolidated when the police and the army, under the direct control of the king, intimidated, harassed, and generally repressed the political activities of an increasingly vocal and oppositional UNFP.

In May 1960 the king, impatient with partisan politics and resentful of the increasing criticism leveled at monarchical institutions, dismissed the government of Abdallah Ibrahim and his cabinet of predominantly UNFP ministers. He appointed himself prime minister and made the crown prince his deputy. For all practical purposes, Hassan was given effective executive power, thereby setting in motion a process of direct monarchical involvement in partisan politics.

In February 1961 King Muhammad V died following routine surgery, and, on March 3, Hassan II ascended the throne. French-educated, with a law degree from Bordeaux, Hassan II pursued a policy that consolidated power in his own hands and reduced the political role of the existing parties. The young king, however, lacked Muhammad V's charisma and the advantage of being a nationalist hero. In the absence of genuine popular appeal and personal standing, Hassan's attempts to strengthen and consolidate his authority over national affairs led to serious political conflicts.

The new king's first government was essentially composed of individuals chosen more for their personal loyalty than for any program or policy they represented. This criterion was consistent with Hassan's view that the role of political parties is to organize support for the monarchy rather than to represent segments of the electorate in the formulation of public policy.

With a minimum of consultation but in keeping with his father's public promise, King Hassan introduced a constitution that was approved in a national referendum in December 1962. Largely inspired by de Gaulle's Fifth Republic, this new national document formally established a constitutional monarchy with guaranteed personal and political freedoms. Yet the constitution's principal provisions solidified the king's own power at the expense of theoretically representative and freely elected legislative organs—namely, the directly elected House of Representatives and the indirectly elected (and hence more easily controlled) Chamber of Counsellors. The king could also dissolve the legislature and was granted unlimited emergency powers for those times in which constitutional institutions were in danger of impairment or dissolution.

The first national elections under the 1962 constitution were held in May 1963. Hassan encouraged the creation of parties unquestionably loyal to the throne, including the Front for the Defense of Constitutional Institutions (FDIC) and a conservative Berber party, the Popular Movement (MP). The FDIC sought to mobilize the parties and men who had participated in the nationalist movement from outside, or even in opposition to the Istiqlal, and who would support the monarchy for its own sake or for the sake of personal advantage.

The FDIC was a weak and hastily formed coalition and was unable to project a truly nationalist image. It failed to win the majority that the king believed would confirm his authority to rule. In the following months, repressive action was therefore taken against both opposition parties—the Istiqlal and the UNFP. Several Istiqlal deputies were arrested for protesting against corruption and mismanagemenet of the election, and in July 1963 many UNFP leaders were arrested in connection with an alleged coup plot.

In this atmosphere, the king was unable to establish a loyal and effective government. The next two years witnessed a succession of cabinets, none of which commanded strong parliamentary support. The FDIC itself underwent an internal split, further diminishing Hassan's political standing. Finally, on June 7, 1965, following a series of demonstrations, strikes, and bloody riots in Casablanca, Hassan invoked the emergency power granted under article 35 of the constitution and personally assumed full legislative and executive power.

These actions, however, failed to halt the process of political and social unrest that had been set in motion at the death of Muhammad V. The disappearance and alleged assassination of the popular UNFP leader, Mehdi Ben Barka, in Paris in October 1965 by agents of the Moroccan government further accelerated the split between the throne and independent political forces. Other disturbances followed, including union demonstrations and strikes by workers and students. In retaliation, the police seized newspapers and made mass arrests. For the next five years (1965–1970), political activity in Morocco virtually disappeared.

In July 1970 the king unexpectedly announced that a new constitution would be submitted for a national referendum later that month. Although no single event precipitated the return to constitutional government, it had become increasingly apparent that the monarchy, relying principally on security forces and the army for support, had isolated itself and jeopardized its legitimacy among a normally supportive mass public. Thus the king, taking advantage of a period of relative calm, sought to open a new era of cooperation with political parties.

Critics complained that they had not been consulted about the new constitution and charged that it merely legalized the king's excessive power. Nevertheless, despite opposition from the main political parties, trade unions, and major student organizations, the new constitution was approved. Immediately thereafter, in August 1970, elections for a new single-chamber legislature were held.

The Istiqlal and the UNFP, which had joined together in the National Front (Kutla Wataniya) to oppose ratification of the new constitution, tried to organize a boycott of the parliamentary elections. In both instances, the Kutla's efforts were futile in the face of the regime's campaign to arouse popular support. By opposing the constitution and the elections, however, it deprived the king of a meaningful popular mandate. The regime was forced to continue relying on an array of loyal "independent" politicians, the loyalty and effectiveness of internal security forces, and ultimately the army.

The palace's orchestrated attempts at power balancing and its elimination of effective opposition failed to prevent attempts by army and air force officers to assassinate the king in July 1971 and August 1972. Indeed, discontent over Hassan's autocratic rule and corruption among many of his associates helped to bring on the attempted coups. Hassan emerged unscathed in both instances, however, and was more determined than ever to suppress elements he perceived to be dangerous. In a series of trials in 1973 and 1974, authorities handed down death sentences and imprisonments in connection with guerrilla operations in the countryside, which were supposedly masterminded by UNFP leaders and supported by Colonel Muammar Qaddafi of Libya. The UNFP itself was officially banned in March 1973.

Between the two assassination attempts, during the spring of 1972, the king announced a third "new" constitution. Executive power was to be vested in the government and an assembly, and two-thirds of the latter's membership was to be elected by universal suffrage, as compared to half under the 1970 constitution. The National Front, caught unprepared by the new initiative, urged a boycott of the constitutional referendum. It then accused the government of rigging the balloting, in which the constitution was ratified by an overwhelming margin. With the split between the palace and opposition elements as wide as ever, the new cabinet appointed in April was substantially similar to its predecessor. Elections for the new Parliament were postponed indefinitely.

Following the August 1972 coup attempt, the king approached the opposition parties and asked for their cooperation, but, in return for their participation in the government, the Istiqlal and the UNFP demanded concessions that Hassan was unwilling to make. They insisted upon far-reaching reforms, including measures to curtail some of the king's powers and to guarantee political freedom.

Once the king felt confident that his control of the military had been reestablished, he ignored the demands of the opposition parties, which were themselves in disarray. By spring 1972, old divergences between the Istiqlal and the UNFP had reemerged, ending the Kutla's already loose coalition. Moreover, within the UNFP itself, tactical and ideological differences that had earlier divided the Ibrahim Ben-Siddiq (Casablanca) and Abderrahim Bouabid (Rabat) wings of the party led to a formal rupture in July 1972. The latter faction, which became dominant, reconstituted itself as the Socialist Union of Popular Forces (USFP), whereas the Casablanca group retained its old name and gradually declined in influence.

These developments assisted the king in his efforts to retain authority. They also enabled him to present himself as the supreme political arbiter within Morocco's pluralist social order. In a manner that was to become a central element in his astute political style, Hassan combined his skill in manipulating and outmaneuvering the often squabbling opposition parties with liberalization measures that created the impression of change and progress. This combination, along with his willingness to suppress dissent when necessary, has helped the king monopolize power during the twenty-four often-turbulent years since his ascent to the throne.

In 1973 King Hassan undertook another set of programs and policies designed to put critics on the defensive and to increase popular support for the monarchy. Among other things, he announced plans for the "Moroccanization" of parts of the economy over the next two years; and, at the same time, he reinforced his traditional support in the rural areas by ordering that nationalized foreign-owned land (mostly French) be distributed among the peasantry. In addition, Hassan introduced an ambitious five-year development plan (1973–1977) that called for annual economic growth of 7.5 percent.

The king also undertook several foreign policy initiatives, both substantive and symbolic, that had primarily domestic rather than international objectives. In fact, Hassan has often used external challenges to diffuse domestic unrest and to mobilize the population under the banner of national unity. For example, in 1973 the king derived significant domestic political capital from his strong stand in a fishing dispute with Spain. In addition, Moroccan troops were dispatched to the Syrian and Egyptian fronts during the October 1973 Arab-Israeli war in order to enhance Hassan's image as a defender of the Palestinian and Arab national causes.

The king expanded this strategy and scored a major political victory in 1974 and 1975 by reasserting his country's historic claim to the Western Sahara, which, at the time, was controlled by Spain. In November 1975 he organized the "Green March," in which approximately 350,000 civilians assembled on Morocco's border with the Sahara and staged a symbolic walk into the disputed territory. These events mobilized popular support from all segments of society and raised Hassan's political fortunes enormously. Moreover, since both the Istiqlal and the USFP supported "reintegration" of the Sahara, opposition parties were placed on the defensive in their conflict with the king.

The king's initiative yielded further dividends when Spain agreed in 1976 to relinquish the Sahara to Morocco and Mauritania. Further, since the northern two-thirds, which Morocco was to receive, contained large deposits of phosphate, the victory portended economic benefit as well as political gain. Indeed, Morocco is the world's largest exporter of phosphates even without the Sahara, and a rise in the world price of the mineral in 1974 had relieved some of the financial pressure on the kingdom and added an economic dimension to Hassan's newly enhanced position.

In 1976 and 1977 Hassan, with his political circumstances vastly improved, permitted the resuscitation of political life. Press censorship was lifted, political detainees were released, elections for provincial assemblies and municipal councils were held in 1976, and a year later the long postponed parliamentary elections finally took place. After nearly seven years of royal dictatorship, these moves were received with enthusiasm in Morocco; but they were not associated with a reduction in monarchical authority. Hassan sought to capitalize on his success in the Sahara and other areas—a success he was confident would result in an electoral victory. He also sought to reestablish a state of political normalcy, in which opponents could be either co-opted or contained and in which his own preeminent position would be more secure.

The result of the 1977 elections was indeed a landslide victory of the monarchy over the opposition and leftist groupings. The Rassemblement National des Indépendants (RNI), a loosely organized front of independent candidates whose only platform was "unconditional loyalty" to the king, won 81 of the 176 seats contested for the new Chamber of Representatives. Thirty-three additional seats were won by right-wing parties, who declared their intention of working with the independents. Thus the monarchy was assured a large and comfortable majority. The Istiqlal made a reasonable showing, winning a respectable 45 seats and reaffirming, in the process, its potential for organizational and electoral strength. The same could not be said, however, of the leftist USFP, which suffered a humiliating defeat, gaining only 16 seats in the new chamber. Even the party's popular leader, Abderrahim Bouabid, was unsuccessful in his bid for a seat in Parliament.

Despite the success of candidates loyal to the king, most observers believed the elections were relatively free from government interference and saw them as an important step on the road to democracy. The Istiqlal, in opposition since the early 1960s, thus agreed to enter the ruling coalition. Further, the USFP acknowledged that its losses were in substantial measure due to the popularity of the king in the wake of the Green March, and the party agreed to participate in parliamentary life as a "loyal and constructive" opposition. In the wake of these developments, the king achieved his goal of reviving parliamentary life and, at the same time, enhancing his own dominant position.

Political tranquillity did not last long. Problems reappeared in the late 1970s and have intensified during the 1980s. Several interrelated factors are responsible.

First, rebels claiming to represent the indigenous population of the Western Sahara have opposed Morocco's annexation of the territory. Known as the Popular Front for the Liberation of Saguiat el-Hamra and Rio de Oro, or Polisario Front, the guerrillas have been supported by Algeria and Libya and have engaged Morocco in a costly war, in its ninth year at the time of this writing. Polisario's successes led Mauritania to abandon its portion of the former Spanish colony in 1978. Moroccan forces sustained heavy losses through 1981, with estimates of FAR soldiers killed totaling around 150 a month. More recently, Morocco has enjoyed a position of military superiority; but, even so, the maintenance of its positions in the Sahara has proved enormously expensive. With approximately 100,000 troops in the disputed territory and a massive program of both military and civilian construction, the country is spending on its Saharan campaign an amount equal to 40–45 percent of the annual state budget.

Second, the economy has been harmed by other factors. Particularly devastating has been a severe drought, which began in the mid-1970s and has yet to abate completely. The drought has not only diminished the contribution of agriculture to GDP but has also driven hundreds of thousands of destitute peasants out of the rural areas and into urban slums. Morocco has also been hurt by a substantial decline in the world price of important exports, especially phosphates. The overall result has been an alarming growth in foreign indebtedness, sharply reduced investment in development projects, and steadily increasing poverty.

In the face of growing economic difficulties, public discontent reemerged in 1978 and 1979. On the one hand, there were complaints about the objective conditions of poverty. Unemployment as approximately 35–40 percent, for example. It was even higher among the young. There was also a marked increase in such poverty-related problems as crime and alcoholism. On the other hand, discontent was intensified by inequality and corruption. With access to wealth determined largely by family or political connections, the elite continued to prosper, despite the economic crisis. Over 50 percent of the national income was consumed by the richest 10 percent of the population. In addition, although the Saharan war contributed heavily to the nation's economic burden, some individuals were actually benefiting from the conflict, making huge profits on contracts for supplies and construction. Hassan himself acknowledged in a 1977 speech that "we are heading for a society in which the rich will be very rich and the poor will be very poor."

Signs of discontent included labor unrest in the form of strikes and protest demonstrations and the emergence of militant Islamic groups opposed to the established political order. In response to these challenges, the king began to retreat from the political reforms of the mid-1970s. The events of 1981 were particularly important. First, the king asked the nation to postpone for two years the parliamentary elections scheduled for that year. Although he claimed to be awaiting a resolution of the Saharan conflict, Hassan's decision was heavily influenced by the declining popularity of his government. Second, major riots broke out in Casablanca. Roving bands from the city's slums attacked banks, car dealerships, and other symbols of authority and privilege. Police almost lost control in some areas. They occasionally fired into the crowds, killing, in all, at least 200 youthful protestors, possibly many more. Third, the rioting was followed by numerous arrests, including those of trade-union leaders and even members of Parliament belonging to the USFP.

Pressure mounted through 1983 and the first half of 1984. In January 1983 there were reports of a military plot against the king. Senior officers were arrested, and General Ahmed Dlimi, commander of Morocco's forces in the Sahara, was killed in a bizarre car accident. It is widely believed that Hassan's supporters arranged the "accident." The military had grown to over 200,000, and the regime was becoming increasingly concerned about political consciousness and discontent within its ranks, especially among younger officers. Following Dlimi's death, Hassan fragmented the FAR command structure.

In 1983 Hassan again postponed the parlimentary elections rescheduled in 1981. Elections for provincial and prefectural assemblies were postponed as well. Elections for municipal and rural councils did take place, but these were accompanied by serious irregularities, thus rendering meaningless the victory of Hassan's supporters. On the contrary, the elections deepened public alienation and cynicism. Widespread intimidation and fraud accompanied the balloting. Many also complained about interference in candidate registration and campaign procedures.

January 1984 brought new and more widespread rioting, followed by another crackdown. The disorders began with strikes and protests by students in Marrakesh, who were sometimes joined by adults from poorer neighborhoods. Student-based protests also flared in Agadir, Safi, and Kasbah-Tadla in the south and in Rabat and Meknes in central Morocco. Trouble then spread to five northern cities, where adults participated heavily in riots of much greater intensity. The same economic and political grievances were everywhere apparent, and some protestors carried banners denouncing Hassan personally. At least 150 persons had been killed by the time order was restored.

Arrests followed. The International League of Human Rights put the figure at 1500–2000, which is consistent with the government's own reports. The League also monitored the detention and trial of prisoners, reporting that it found no instances of torture but considered many sentences "exorbitant." Some individuals were condemned to life in prison. Verdicts handed to Islamic militants were especially harsh. They included thirteen death sentences, the first for political crimes since 1972.

It was expected that the fall of 1984 would bring even more tension. Legislative elections were scheduled for September, but there were fears that these would be either postponed again or, as in the local elections of 1983, blatantly rigged. Concern was also fueled by the announcement in early summer of major cuts in the educational budget. The proposed austerity measures would eliminate as many as 40,000 secondary-school places—a situation that most assumed would spark new protests when the school year began.

Events unfolded in an unexpected way, however. The biggest surprise was the announcement on August 13 that Hassan and Colonel Muammar Qaddafi of Libya had agreed to a union between their countries. Another surprise was that the initiative had come from Hassan. The two North African leaders, long bitter rivals, met in Oujda in Western Morocco and decided to form the "Arab-African Union." This union is a loose federation rather than a unified state to which the participants would surrender sovereignty. Nevertheless, the agreement calls for a presidency that rotates between the two heads of state, an executive committee to carry out presidential directives, a permanent secretariat with an annual budget and offices in Rabat and Tripoli, and mutual defense obligations.

Hassan's rapprochement with Qaddafi had been in the making for over a year. The Libyan colonel visited Rabat in June 1983, at which time Hassan exchanged acceptance of Libya's involvement in Chad for an end to Qaddafi's support of the Polisario.

Hassan hopes the agreement with Libya will reduce opposition from the Polisario in the Sahara, even though the situation will not change dramatically so long as the rebels continue to receive support from their principal backer, Algeria. Another goal is to reduce domestic opposition from militant Muslim movements. Although the fundamentalists do not view Libya's revolution as truly Islamic, Qaddafi is identified with Islam in the popular mind and the union thus gives Hassan another opportunity to associate himself visibly with the religion.

Direct economic benefits are the most central element in Hassan's political calculus. At a time when opportunities for Moroccan workers are diminishing in Europe, he anticipates a new employment market for his citizens in oil-rich and underpopulated Libya. Thousands of Moroccans worked there in the early 1970s. Morocco also hopes to buy Libyan oil at preferential prices. Energy costs represented 28 percent of the country's import bill in 1983. Finally, Morocco looks to increased trade and investment. The two countries concluded several major commercial agreements early in 1984, and Moroccan exports to Libya have already increased dramatically.

The union with Libya also figured in Hassan's foreign policy calculations, and here a major goal was to counter a challenge from Algeria. Morocco and Algeria are rivals for leadership in the Maghrib; in addition, Algeria is the Polisario's principal backer. In 1983 Algeria appeared to line up support against Morocco by concluding a treaty of Fraternity and Concord with Tunisia and Mauritania, and rapprochement with Qaddafi was part of Hassan's response. The union sought to outflank Algeria by joining its neighbors to the east and west. Hassan hoped that this action would put pressure on the regime in Algiers, causing it to cease efforts to isolate Morocco and to reduce assistance to the Polisario. Morocco also hoped that the treaty would push Tunisia, which is concerned about Libya's growing military buildup, toward a position of neutrality in regional politics. If successful, an improvement in Morocco's position in the Maghrib would also most likely enhance the king's stature at home.

The Moroccan electorate overwhelmingly endorsed the union in a referendum later in August; and, although such plebiscites do not necessarily constitute a true indication of popular sentiment, preliminary reaction did appear to be highly favorable. All of Morocco's political parties, including the opposition, also endorsed the union. They organized hundreds of public meetings during the two-week campaign preceding the referendum. Finally, the palace claimed to have received thousands of letters and telegrams endorsing the treaty. Thus, the union with Libya was successful in achieving its short-term goals. It diverted attention from the immediate problems, raised hopes of economic benefit, and boosted the popularity of the king.

This change in the public mood and in the popularity of Hassan's government was enhanced by the resuscitation of parliamentary life in the fall of 1984. Morocco's twice-postponed parliamentary elections were finally held in September 1984. Provincial and prefectural elections were held in August. Equally significant, the elections appear to have been reasonably fair. There were some complaints, but they were not excessive. In addition, Hassan released 354 political prisoners shortly before the balloting. Finally, the new Parliament will be more representative and will contain a greater diversity of views than those of the recent past. This is not to say that the assembly and government will be independent of the palace. But, in the short run at least, the new Parliament may increase public confidence in national political institutions, thus both enhancing the legitimacy of Hassan's government and buying time with which to address other problems.

Two-thirds of the seats in Parliament are chosen by direct suffrage, the remainder by provincial and prefectural assemblies. In 1984 twelve political parties competed for representation, fielding 1,366 candidates for the 199 seats popularly elected within Morocco. Five seats were chosen by direct suffrage among the Moroccans living abroad, including 450,000 Moroccan laborers in France. These results did not undermine the dominance of politicians loyal to the king, but they did produce a few significant changes.

In the same year the leftist USFP, the largest opposition party and a victim of electoral interference in the past, doubled its representation in Parliament. It won 17 percent of the popular vote, ranking third among the parties. The USFP's improved showing indicated tolerance of dissent during the election and portended more political diversity in the new Parliament. Another development was the poor performance of the Istiqlal, Morocco's oldest party and the foundation of the nationalist movement prior to independence. The PI ranked fifth with only 12 percent of the popular vote, although its position improved in the indirect balloting. Finally, the biggest winner was the Union Constitutionelle (UC), a new party formed in 1983. It received 27 percent of the vote in both the popular and the indirect balloting. UC leaders are closely aligned with the king. Moreover, since the party is not highly institutionalized and has no secure electoral constituency, it is particularly dependent on ties to the palace. Nevertheless, it is a party of the moderate center, with many young technocrats in its ranks. The UC's success occurred largely at the expense of electoral fronts controlled by conservative barons with years of participation in patrimonial politics.

Table 19.1 shows the number of seats occupied by each political party in the new Parliament. It also shows the number won in the popular voting and the number selected by regional assemblies in the indirect balloting. Finally, it shows the number of seats held by each party in the Parliament elected in 1977.

In the wake of the union with Libya and election of a new Parliament, the political situation within Morocco was calm at the conclusion of 1984. Moreover, with political life revived and his critics on the defensive, King Hassan enjoyed a much more secure domestic position.

At the time of this writing, it remains to be seen whether Hassan's government will be able to use this respite to deal meaningfully with pressing economic and political problems. Morocco must work to reduce the gap between rich and poor and to share more equitably the nation's economic burden. It must also continue to open up political life. Despite the success of the 1984 elections, democracy is not present if it depends on the monarch's mood, on his calculations about whether liberalism or repression is the most effective way to contain challenges and maintain political supremacy. Finally, Morocco must bring to an end the long and costly war in the Sahara.

If no progress is made on these issues, Morocco can be expected to begin another cycle of challenge, response, and challenge again. The reforms and

TABLE 19.1 Seats Occupied by Each Political Party in the New Moroccan Parliament, 1977 and 1984

	1984			1977
	Direct Vote	Indirect Vote	Total	Total
Rassemblement National des Independants (RNI)	39	22	61	141
Parti National Democratique (PND)	15	9	24	—
Union Constitutionelle (UC)	56	27	83	—
Mouvement Populaire (MP)	31	16	47	44
Istiqlal (PI)	24	17	41	49
Union Socialiste des Forces Populaires (USFP)	35	1	36	16
Total	204	102	306	264

liberalization of the mid-1970s were a welcome response to years of mounting tension. Nevertheless, in the absence of attention to underlying problems, the momentum they generated soon dissipated and public discontent followed by repression soon reemerged. The fall of 1984 again brought hopes of movement toward progressive change. However, as occurred a decade earlier, these hopes will soon fade unless a fundamental political change takes place.

Political Environment

Political Culture

One feature of Moroccan political culture is distrust. This is visible both in the attitude of the masses toward their leaders and in relations among political elites. Power is viewed as a coercive instrument rather than as a basis for cooperative action. Colonial repression reinforced the native distrust of authority and made the development of a cooperative conception of power difficult to achieve. The forced imposition of a modern and impersonal administration further reinforced this tendency.

Conspiritorial politics have also characterized post-independence Morocco. Political authority and power are derived only secondarily from formal political roles and offices, and the system thus lacks accepted rules by which decisions are cooperatively reached. Political life is instead dominated by patterns of patrimonialism and clientelism, wherein power and influence are determined primarily by personal associations and political connections. What keeps the system intact is the overriding desire of its elite members to defend their positions by maintaining a stable equilibrium, containing but not destroying their rivals and resisting change that might overwhelm the system's absorptive capacity. Such attitudes often lead to political stalemate, another feature of Moroccan political life.

An emphasis on patron-client relationships produces a group orientation, which has always existed and continues to play an important role in Morocco's political culture and behavior. It is within this group framework that one can best understand the almost continuous process of alliance building and alliance maintaining, which involves both elites and nonelites. A political culture dominated by norms of clientelism and patrimonialism encourages others to defend themselves through the formation of alliances; a politician must always be alert to rivals who might outmaneuver and isolate him by offering more to his clients or rendering superior service to his patrons. Nonelites in this system defend themselves and obtain resources by acquiring the protection of a more powerful individual, who in turn shares in the authority and resources of his own patrons to the extent that he has the loyalty of many clients to deliver.

A peculiar irony of this system of cleavages, with its high degree of tension and conflict, is that it has inhibited the creation of nationwide consensus. Primary loyalty is to smaller political groupings. Except for political beliefs predicated upon Islamic principles, which still have meaning among many of the masses, it seems doubtful that a broadly based nationalist ideology could be established in such a fluid milieu. The various political groupings display no commitment to a comprehensive political program, focusing almost entirely on short-term tactical objectives. Thus it is almost meaningless to talk about political ideology in Morocco today, despite the extensive use of ideological slogans by alienated intellectuals, dissident university students, and disaffected opposition politicians.

Economic Conditions

Agriculture is the key to the economic well-being of a large proportion of Morocco's citizens. Nearly 70 percent of the population derives its living directly or indirectly from the soil.

Despite the country's congenial climate and varied soils, Morocco's agriculture is confronted with a number of serious problems. Predominant among these are the increasing lack of water as one moves from northwest to southeast and the year-to-year unpredictability of rainfall. Primitive methods of cultivation, a lack of understanding about the use of fertilizers and insecticides, and an absence of the means to acquire them also contribute to low yields on the vast majority of farms. An additional problem is the fragmentation of land holdings resulting from traditional Muslim inheritance law. This fragmentation has created large numbers of minute, irregularly shaped, and often widely scattered plots, adding to the inefficiency of cultivation.

Traditional agriculture accounts for about 85 to 90 percent of the total land under cultivation. Much of the agricultural land in the traditional sector is devoted to grazing, however, and average yields per acre of cultivated land are less than half those in the modern sector. The traditional sector supports about 1.5 million families, who, even in good years, consume most of what they produce.

Only about 10 to 15 percent of total agricultural land is farmed by modern methods, but this proportion includes some of the most fertile land in the country and accounts for over 85 percent of commercial agricultural production, including almost all of the citrus fruit, fresh vegetables, wine, soft wheat, and other cash crops. As of 1978 these agricultural products accounted for 36 percent of merchandise exports, although agriculture's share of exports had declined from over 50 percent in the early 1960s. Much of the land in the modern and export-oriented agricultural sector is controlled by wealthy landlords, and some of the production in this sector has historically benefited from subsidized credit provided by the government.

The development of Moroccan agriculture since 1956 has been characterized by conservatism, coupled with an emphasis on technical progress rather than on social change. Despite occasional imaginative projects and the redistribution of 400,000 hectares of nationalized foreign-owned land, the government has been unable either to restructure the agricultural sector or to overcome the obvious problems of poverty and unemployment in the rural farming areas. As a result, agriculture's contribution to the gross domestic product declined from 23 percent to 1960 to 19 percent in 1979. Finally, the country has been affected by a severe drought, which, at the time of this writing, has persisted for almost a decade. The drought has further diminished agricultural production and increased rural poverty, driving hundreds of thousands of destitute peasants out of the countryside and into urban slums.

Mineral resources are also important. Morocco's most promising source of overall economic growth is its phosphate industry, especially during the period since its acquisition of major deposits in the former Spanish Sahara. Major investments in the expansion of production were undertaken during 1975–1977, and by 1978 the sale of all minerals accounted for 41 percent of merchandise exports. There was also a windfall from higher world phosphate prices in the mid-1970s. On the other hand, phosphate prices have declined sharply in the last few years; in addition, Morocco has been hurt by a quadrupling of petroleum prices, a resource that Morocco must buy abroad and whose share of imports almost tripled between 1978 and 1982. Therefore, despite the importance of phosphates in the Moroccan economy, the country has a serious and steadily worsening balance-of-payments problem.

Manufacturing remains relatively unimportant. It accounted for 16 percent of GDP in 1960, and, despite occasional attempts by the government to stimulate investment in this sector, it increased little during the ensuing two decades. Some progress has been made in the manufacture of clothing and textiles, which by 1980 accounted for 11 percent of merchandise exports.

Demographic factors also contribute to Morocco's economic problems. The population is increasing at a rate in excess of 3 percent per year, thereby erasing any short-term gains in the agricultural and industrial sectors. In addition, the job market is expanding much more slowly than is the demand for jobs. As a result, unemployment ranges from 20 to 30 percent in the cities and probably averages 40 percent in the rural areas. It is even higher among the young. Including underemployment, the figure could be as high as 50 percent, and in all probability it will continue to rise.

An aspect of Morocco's economic situation that has particular implications for social and political stability is the ever-widening discrepancy between society's wealthy few and its impoverished masses. At present consumption levels, it is estimated that 10 percent of the Moroccan population absorbs 50 percent of the nation's wealth and that, despite calls for a more equitable distribution, the gap will get larger rather than smaller. Concurrently, economic expectations continue to rise among all sectors of the population, causing increased frustration and a growing potential for political unrest.

Political Structure

According to the provisions of the 1972 constitution, Morocco is a constitutional, democratic, and social monarchy, and Islam is the official state religion. The constitution provides for equality under the law and guarantees freedom of movement, speech, opinion, and assembly. Amendments to the constitution may be initiated by either the king or the legislature, but such initiatives require approval by popular referendum.

The power and authority of the state are highly centralized in the person of the king. He is the supreme civil and religious authority—the "commander of the faithful"—as well as commander-in-chief of the armed forces. The crown is inherited and usually transmitted to the eldest son, although another son may be designated should the king so desire. The king appoints all important officials, including the premier and the cabinet. He promulgates legislation passed by the legislature and has the authority to dissolve the legislature, to submit legislation for popular referendum, to declare a state of emergency during which he may rule by decree, and to sign and ratify treaties. He presides over the cabinet, the Council for National Development and Planning, and the Supreme Judicial Council.

The 1972 constitution vests legislative authority in a unicameral House of Representatives, whose members are elected for a four-year term. The legislature's constitutional powers include the right to initiate constitutional amendments, authorize declarations of war, and approve extensions of a state of emergency beyond thirty days. The king may request that the legislature reconsider legislation before giving his assent. He may also dissolve the House by decree and call for new elections, but he cannot dissolve the succeeding House for a year. Elected regional assemblies also exist at the provincial and prefectural levels.

Judicial and administration institutions reflect both French and Spanish influences. The country is administratively divided into nineteen provinces and two urban prefectures, Casablanca and Rabat. The provinces are further divided into seventy-two administrative areas and communes. Each of the administrative regions is headed by a governor, who is appointed by the king and responsible to him. On April 12, 1976, the king appointed governors to three administrative provinces in the former Spanish Sahara.

The judicial system is headed by a Supreme Court composed of four chambers: civil, criminal, administrative, and social. In 1965 a special court was established to deal with corruption among public officials. All judges are appointed by the king with the advice of the Supreme Judicial Council. Moroccan courts administer a system that is based on Islamic law but strongly influenced by the French and Spanish legal systems. A separate system of courts administers the religious law of Morocco's Jewish citizens.

Political Dynamics

Morocco's constitutional system, like that of its neighbors to the east, provides only a glimpse of the actual configuration of power in the state. Morocco's King Hassan has, to date, successfully consolidated power by manipulating competing groups and rival factions and, when necessary, by eliminating them altogether. Although systems of consultation and advice exist within the broader structures of power, including those mandated by constitutional provisions, there are no formal systematic procedures that would force the ruler to accept advice.

Moroccan political life is dominated by a group of approximately 1,000 men who constitute the country's political elite. Leaders of the various political parties and other formal and informal groups and associations, including chief representatives of labor unions, economic organizations, and agricultural interests, speak for and control most who are politically active. These political parties, pressure groups, and regional interests are in fierce competition for influence and patronage. However, although institutionalized pluralism seems to prevail, political life is in fact dominated by the monarchy, whose authority and power—despite serious social and political buffeting in recent years—remain unequaled in the country. Although the other institutions, including political parties, labor unions, and rural interests, compete with and attempt to limit the king's freedom of action, he remains at the center of politics in Morocco. The king relies on his traditional legitimacy to retain the support of the masses. In addition, however, monarchical supremacy has, to a considerable degree, depended upon existing social pluralism and divisions among the elite. King Hassan skillfully employs his control of royal patronage to balance and dominate the segmented political elite.

The sources of the monarchy's power and prestige are diverse yet interdependent. The king's moral authority is primarily based on his role as spiritual leader, or imam, of the Islamic community. Concurrently, he is a member of the Alawite dynasty, formally accepted as legitimate ruler by the same Islamic community in Morocco for over 300 years. Because of his noble religious ancestry and the attendant supernatural qualities ascribed to him, the Moroccan king satisfies the aspirations of rural Muslims who seek the miraculous qualities inherent in the monarch's personal charisma, or *baraka*. Regardless of what the more modernized sectors of society may think of the king, he is deeply venerated by the rural masses, who view him as a *sharif* (descendant of the Prophet) and as a dispenser of God's blessing.

The monarchy also represents the symbolic leadership of the nationalist struggle. In the minds of the masses, national independence and political unification are intimately associated with monarchical authority—however limited the king's actual involvement in the pre-independence nationalist movement may have been.

The king's power and prestige are further enhanced by the fact that he is the nation's most prominent dispenser of patronage and the ultimate source of spoils in the system. The palace has a very real command over Moroccan commercial activities as well as over the distribution of patronage, both of which it uses to sustain the king's secular clientele and to build his secular alliances. Indeed, these commercial and patronage resources are the king's most effective levers of political control.

As we have seen, Moroccan society consists of numerous segments that have historically related to one another by tension and conflict. Thus one of the most important political roles in the country has been that of arbiter among conflicting groups. This role has also helped to make the monarch the pivotal center of Morocco's disparate and factionalized political arena. The king uses his role as arbiter in two ways: He promotes continued fragmentation by protecting and rewarding the various parties that show him allegiance, and he enhances his own influence by keeping the fortunes of these groups dependent on his favors. Accordingly, the king seeks to preserve the system of factionalism but will move against any party or faction that grows too strong. His success in maintaining such a balance lies, as mentioned, in his ability to appeal directly to the masses and in his control over patronage and economic resources, as well as in the segmented character of Moroccan society.

If all else fails, power and control can be maintained by the king's loyal lieutenants. An executive staff, the intelligence and security branches of the Ministry of the Interior and the Ministry of National Defense, as well as a once-again loyal army and officer corps all assist in the maintenance of royal authority throughout the kingdom.

The past and current success of royal control has therefore centered on the ability of the king to manipulate the elite while maintaining broad political support from the rural masses. As long as the elite remains small, socially and educationally homogeneous, and politically fragmented, the system has fairly good prospects for maintaining power. However, the size of the elite and the balance of its component parts cannot be guaranteed in the future. On the contrary, rapid population and educational growth will inevitably threaten the equilibrium at all social levels, including that of the elite. The implications of this long-term demographic process for the monarchy's hegemonic role are, of course, obvious. Over time, Morocco will have to broaden the base of participation in the political process if it is to maintain political stability. Yet, if it does so, there is the danger that an expanded political class will overwhelm the resources of the patronage system controlled by the palace, thereby exceeding its absorptive capacity and destablizing the political system from within.

The present system can also be expected to come under pressure from nonelite sectors of society. Economic and political grievances, which are growing among the masses, may ultimately erode the legitimacy accorded to the monarchy and become the most salient dimension of public attitudes toward authority. Such pressures have already made themselves felt, in the rioting of 1981 and 1984, for example. Though limited to the urban poor, these disturbances are a strong indication that the masses are beginning to demand greater accountability from the king and his government, and that they may no longer respond to symbolic appeals based on historic or religious criteria.

Morocco has developed a multiparty system. Yet, since the early 1960s, the outcome of party competition either at the polls or in Parliament has not decisively affected the composition or policies of the king's government. The centralized role of the monarchy, the king's tactic of playing one party against the other, and the pervasive infighting that occurs within most parties all combine to place severe limits on the autonomy of political parties.

Though none of Morocco's political parties is autonomous, there are important differences among them with respect to both structure and influence. The Rassemblement National des Indépendants (RNI), which held an absolute majority in the assembly elected in 1977, is more of an informal electoral front than an institutionalized political party. It is dominated by rural notables and men from leading urban families who are long-time associates of the king, and its platform is based principally on "unconditional loyalty" to Hassan. The RNI split in 1981, with rural elements breaking away to form a separate faction, the Parti National Democratique (PND). The RNI and PND fared less well in the 1984 election.

As reported earlier, a new party, the Union Constitutionelle (UC), was the major victor in 1984. The UC is more of a centrist party than either the RNI or the PND, and its cadres, for the most part, are younger than those of the other two. In the 1984 election it made a special attempt to appeal to youth and presented itself as a movement committed to addressing social and economic problems. Nevertheless, although its leader was a trade unionist early in his political career, the party was created with strong backing from the king, and, like the RNI and PND, it lacks a grass-roots base and is highly dependent on the palace for legitimacy and support.

The Mouvement Populaire (MP) bears some resemblance to the parties mentioned earlier. It is dominated by conservative rural notables tied to the palace and does not have an independent platform or ideology. At the same time, as the party of leading Berber families in the north and central mountain regions, it is much older and has a secure electoral base. The party was established in 1957 by men who had led resistance to French colonialism in the rural areas.

Only two parties are highly institutionalized and have an appeal that does not depend on an ability to extract favors from the palace. These are the Istiqlal (PI) and the Union Socialiste des Forces Populaires (USFP). Formed during the anticolonial struggle against France, the PI is the party of Moroccan nationalism, and, under the direction of its founding father and venerable leader, Allal al-Fassi, it was a major political force in the years after independence. Al-Fassi died in 1973. The PI did reasonably well in the 1977 balloting, largely because of its historic role, its long-time advocacy of Morocco's claim to the Sahara, and its organizational strength in urban areas. The PI's weaknesses include a lack of appeal in the countryside and a conservative ideology that many Moroccans regard as outdated. These factors contributed to the party's poor showing in 1984.

The USFP traces its origins to a faction that broke with the Istiqlal in 1959, after charging the latter's leadership with being too conservative. As its name suggests, the USFP is a socialist-oriented party of the left. Its support comes principally from the trade-union movement, from other working class elements and the urban poor, as well as from Morocco's small community of intellectuals. The party's symbolic hero and political ideologue was Mehdi Ben Barka, an original founder of the splinter group. Because of his opposition to the king, Ben Barka was kidnapped by Moroccan security agents in France in 1965 and subsequently killed. The USFP is the principal and most long-standing opponent of the governments formed by the king, although it has occasionally joined the ruling coalition temporarily for tactical reasons. The USFP did poorly in the 1977 elections and was the victim of electoral interference in the local elections of 1983. It did better in the balloting of 1984, however, with its appeal apparently increased by growing economic and social problems.

Finally a number of minor, weakly organized, independent and pro-monarchy parties round out the political party system.

The Moroccan military, once viewed as a staunch pillar of the monarchy, has on occasion represented the most serious threat against that monarchy. This was particularly true after the July 1971 and August 1972 attempted coups and, more recently, following the discovery of a plot and the arrest of senior officers in January 1983. Although King Hassan has apparently been able to reestablish control of the armed forces, the prospect that they will remain indifferent to the profound social dislocations occurring in the society can never be a certain one. To this scenario must be added the changing social background and educational levels of new army recruits and younger officers, who are less committed to patrimonial attachments and the power of local and national patrons, including the king. Adding further to the political significance of the military, which grew to over 200,000 men in the wake of the war in the Sahara, is the dramatic increase in its functional weight.

Other important political institutions include the National Union of Moroccan Students (UNEM) and various labor unions. Since the 1960s the UNEM has been extensively involved in extralegal and radical activities directed against the regime and its incumbents, most of whom are viewed with hostility, contempt, or indifference. Either through this and other organizations, or simply as individuals, students have expressed a wide range of political, social, economic, and educational grievances.

The Moroccan trade-union movement acquired skill, conviction, and solidarity as a result of its struggles against colonial repression. Until 1960 the Union of Moroccan Labor (UMT) was Morocco's sole labor and trade-union confederation. In that year, the Istiqlal organized a rival union, the General Union of Moroccan Workers (UGTM), but the UGTM was unable to compete with the UMT for political influence. More recently, in the later 1970s, the new Democratic Workers Confederation (CDT) a socialist-oriented union with ties to the USFP, overtook the UMT in prominence and militancy. The union's protest activities helped to bring about the disturbances in Casablanca of June 1981, and a number of CDT leaders were arrested following the riots.

Despite the UMT's historic role and the CDT's occasional success in opposing the regime, the political and economic climate in Morocco remains hostile to the development of a vigorous and independent labor movement. Three particular factors inhibit such development. First, the high level of unemployment makes the unions insecure and vulnerable to sudden, unplanned changes in membership, recruitment, financial support, and organizational solidarity. Second, the unions are subject to harsh pressure and blandishments from the government. Finally, very serious differences exist between trade-union interests and those of the politicians. In addition, the constant factor of monarchical manipulation accentuates divisions instead of fostering unity in the labor movement, just as it has with the opposition political parties.

Foreign Policy

Foreign policy decisions in Morocco are made by the narrow strata of incumbent political elites that revolve around the authority of the monarch. While pluralistic tendencies are evident in certain sectors of Moroccan domestic life, no such pluralism exists in the articulation, deliberation, and implementation of foreign policy. Overall, Morocco's foreign policy objectives are to enhance King Hassan's domestic prestige and to protect the status of the political elite; to generate international support for the country's struggle to reintegrate the Western Sahara; to cultivate close economic, technical, and military ties with France and the United States; and to maintain a symbolic association with the Afro-Arab world.

Morocco's continuing strong ties to France are in part a response to geopolitical and economic realities and in part a function of historical conditioning. They are also a reflection of the elites' close affinity with French culture, language, and civilization. These latter characteristics are not shared by the population at large or even by a great portion of its educated classes, a fact that highlights the discontinuity between elite and mass political culture. As a result, there is some uncertainty as to what extent the Moroccan people share in their government's strong pro-Western orientation, including its warm and friendly relations with the United States.

France and the United States have rewarded Morocco's "moderation" in world affairs by becoming the predominant suppliers of military aid and substantial contributors of economic assistance to post-independence Morocco. France remains Morocco's closest trading partner and provides the country with extensive technical, financial, and educational aid, for which there is an urgent need. Relations with the Soviet Union are cordial and developing, and the USSR is a major purchaser of Moroccan phosphates.

Morocco also identifies with the aspirations of the Arab world, including the call for Arab unity, opposition to Zionism, pride in a common cultural, religious, historical, and linguistic heritage, and a desire to assert an authentic Arab identity. In addition, Morocco's ties to the Arab world have been an important source of economic assistance. Saudi Arabia in particular has provided Morocco with considerable aid in recent years, helping to offset the high cost of the war in the Western Sahara. At the same time, however, Morocco is less intensively involved in inter-Arab affairs than are the states of the Arab East.

As discussed earlier, Morocco's relations with its North African neighbors are more ambivalent, although, like the other states of the Maghrib, Morocco continues to profess a generalized commitment to eventual North African unity.

Relations with Algeria have long been marked by ideological and territorial disputes, as well as by competition for leadership in the Maghrib. Furthermore, the two countries have been at odds over the Western Sahara for the last decade. Algeria is the principal backer of the Polisario Front, the guerrilla organization fighting Morocco for control of the former Spanish colony.

Relations with Tunisia are more amicable. Both regimes share similar international orientations and are closely aligned with the West. Both also share similar development policies, especially in the crucial area of private foreign investment. On the other hand, relations have cooled somewhat in the last few years, because of Tunisia's growing ties to Algeria and what Morocco perceives as Tunisia's neutrality in the Saharan war.

Until recently, Libya and Morocco have been enemies. Libya's Colonel Qaddafi was blamed by Moroccan authorities for supporting various plots against the crown in the early 1970s. In the late 1970s Morocco was disturbed by Libya's extensive assistance to the Polisario. However, King Hassan and Colonel Qadaffi effected a rapprochement in 1983, thus leading, as discussed earlier, to a loose union between the two countries in 1984. Some of Morocco's Western allies fear that the union will increase the international legitimacy of Qaddafi, whom they distrust, and offer the Libyan leader new opportunities to meddle in Moroccan affairs. Thus far, however, the union has been popular in Morocco and has improved rather than weakened the domestic position of Hassan's government.

Because the monarchy's legitimacy is questioned by many disaffected elements of the middle class, and also because of growing economic and political discontent among the masses, foreign policy initiatives are often undertaken to mobilize support for the monarchy and to distract attention from pressing domestic problems. Such was the case with the "Green March" into the Western Sahara in 1975 and the union with Libya in 1984. Other actions include participation in the 1973 Arab-Israeli war and Hassan's decision in 1977 to send Moroccan paratroop units to Zaire to support President Joseph Mobutu's struggle with secessionist forces.

Bibliography

The history of pre-independence Morocco, including the precolonial, colonial, and nationalist phases, is systematically analyzed in the following works: Allal al-Fasi, *The Independence Movement in Arab North Africa* (New York: Octagon, 1970); Douglas E. Ashford, *Perspectives of a Moroccan Nationalist* (Totowa, N.J.: Bedminster Press, 1964); Stephane Bernard, *The Franco-Moroccan Conflict, 1943–1956* (New

Haven, Conn.: Yale University Press, 1968); Robin Bidwell, *Morocco Under Colonial Rule: French Administration of Tribal Areas, 1912–1956* (London: Frank Cass, 1973); Edmund Burke, *Prelude to Protectorate in Morocco: Precolonial Protest and Resistance, 1860–1912* (Chicago: University of Chicago Press, 1976); Ross Dunn, *Resistance in the Desert: Moroccan Responses to French Imperialism, 1881–1912* (Madison: University of Wisconsin Press, 1977); John P. Halstead, *Rebirth of a Nation: The Origins and Rise of Moroccan Nationalism, 1912–1944* (Cambridge, Mass.: Harvard University Press, 1967); and Alan Scham, *Lyautey in Morocco: Protectorate Administration, 1912–1925* (Berkeley: University of California Press, 1970).

Islam's importance in Moroccan political and social life receives exceptional scholarly treatment by Clifford Geertz, in *Islam Observed: Religious Development in Morocco and Indonesia* (New Haven, Conn.: Yale University Press, 1968); Dale F. Eickelman, in *Moroccan Islam: Tradition and Society in a Pilgrimage Center* (Austin: University of Texas Press, 1976); and Ernest Gellner, in *Saints of the Atlas* (Chicago: University of Chicago Press, 1969).

A number of important sociological and anthropological themes in Moroccan life are conscientiously treated in Kenneth Brown, *People of Sale* (Cambridge, Mass.: Harvard University Press, 1976); Daisy Hilse Dwyer, *Image and Self-Image: Male and Female in Morocco* (New York: Columbia University Press, 1978); David Hart, *The Ait Atta of Southern Morocco: Daily Life and Recent History* (Boulder, Colo.: Westview Press, 1984); Bernard Hoffman, *The Structure of Traditional Moroccan Rural Society* (The Hague: Mouton, 1967); Vanessa Maher, *Women and Property in Morocco: Their Changing Relation to the Process of Social Stratification in the Middle Atlas* (London: Cambridge University Press, 1974); Gavin Maxwell, *Lords of the Atlas: The Rise and Fall of the House of Glaoua, 1893–1956* (New York: Dutton, 1966); Paul Rabinow, *Symbolic Domination: Cultural Form and Historical Change in Morocco* (Chicago: University of Chicago Press, 1975); David Seddon, *Moroccan Peasants: A Century of Change in the Eastern Rif, 1870–1970* (Folkestone, England: Dawson, 1981); and John Waterbury, *North for the Trade: The Life and Times of a Berber Merchant* (Berkeley and Los Angeles: University of California Press, 1972).

The most reliable analyses of Moroccan political development and institution building are Douglas E. Ashford's *Political Change in Morocco* (Princeton, N.J.: Princeton University Press, 1961); Mark Tessler's "Morocco: Institutional Pluralism and Monarchical Dominance," in I. William Zartman et al., eds., *Political Elites in Arab North Africa* (New York: Longman, 1982); I. William Zartman's *Morocco: Problems of New Power* (New York: Atherton Press, 1964); I. William Zartman's *Destiny of a Dynasty: The Search for Institutions in Morocco's Developing Society* (Columbia: University of South Carolina Press, 1964); and John Waterbury's *The Commander of the Faithful: The Moroccan Political Elite—A Study in Segmented Politics* (New York: Columbia University Press, 1970). The last is probably the best work in any language on the nature of elite politics in Morocco. Also highly instructive is the book by Hassan II, King of Morocco, entitled *The Challenge: The Memoires of King Hassan II of Morocco* (London: Macmillan, 1978).

Aspects of the war between Morocco and the Polisario in the Western Sahara are carefully documented and discussed by John Damisk, in *Conflict in Northwest Africa: The Western Sahara Dispute* (Stanford: Hoover Institute Press, 1983); Tony Hodges, in *Western Sahara: The Roots of a Desert War* (Westport, Conn.: L. Hill, 1983); and Virginia Thompson and Richard Adloff, in *The Western Saharans: Background to Conflict* (London: Croom Helm, 1980).

Local government, public administration, planning, and aspects of economic development are the concern of Douglas E. Ashford, *Morocco-Tunisia: Politics and*

Planning (Syracuse, N.Y.: Syracuse University Press, 1965); Douglas E. Ashford, *National Development and Local Reform: Political Participation in Morocco, Tunisia, and Pakistan* (Princeton, N.J.: Princeton University Press, 1967); and John W. Behen, *The Economic Development of Morocco* (Baltimore: Johns Hopkins University Press, 1966).

Rom Landau, in *Hassan II: King of Morocco* (London: George Allen & Unwin, 1962), and Rom Landau, in *Morocco Independent* (London: George Allen & Unwin, 1961), portray sympathetic accounts of King Hassan II and his regime.

General surveys of Morocco include Nevill Barbour's *Morocco* (New York: Walker, 1965); Lorna Hahn and Mark I. Cohen's *Morocco: Old Land, New Nation* (New York: Praeger Publishers, 1966); and Vincent Monteil's *Morocco* (New York: Viking Press, 1964). Finally, an indispensable reference work is the *Area Handbook for Morocco* (Washington, D.C.: Government Printing Office, 1965).

20

Democratic and Popular Republic of Algeria

John P. Entelis

Historical Background

The initial French conquest of Algeria in 1830 was relatively easy, but another four decades passed before all of Algeria was pacified under French control. The French colonial implantation was massive. By the end of the first fifty years of French occupation, the Algerian Muslims had lost not only their freedom but also their land. The French authorities offered French settlers free transportation, land, seed, and livestock, and their products were imported duty-free into France. By 1851, over 150,000 Europeans had settled in Algeria, and after the 1870 Franco-Prussian War, Algeria's political status was closely linked to metropolitan France.

A governor-general was appointed by Paris and empowered to legislate by decree. He was thus able to control the application of, or to withhold altogether, metropolitan legislation. Moreover, as the European settlers gained strength, they were able to exert vast influence on the machinery of government. They could determine policies, influence the enactment and execution of laws, and control the appointment of high officials of the administration.

The political and personal status of native Algerian Muslims was likewise deeply affected. By 1900 Algerian Muslims had been reduced from relative prosperity to economic, social, and cultural inferiority. Three million inhabitants had died, tribes had been disbanded, and the traditional economy was radically altered during prolonged "civilizing" campaigns. In particular, the production of wine for export replaced the traditional production of cereals for domestic consumption. Virtually all of Algeria's traditional economic structure and land-use practices were dislocated as a consequence of French colonial policy, with its property laws, sequestrations of land after the early revolts, expropriations, forestry laws, regulations concerning pasture lands, and a host of other measures that were either forced upon the administration or inspired by its policy of giving preferential considerations to the interests of the Europeans.

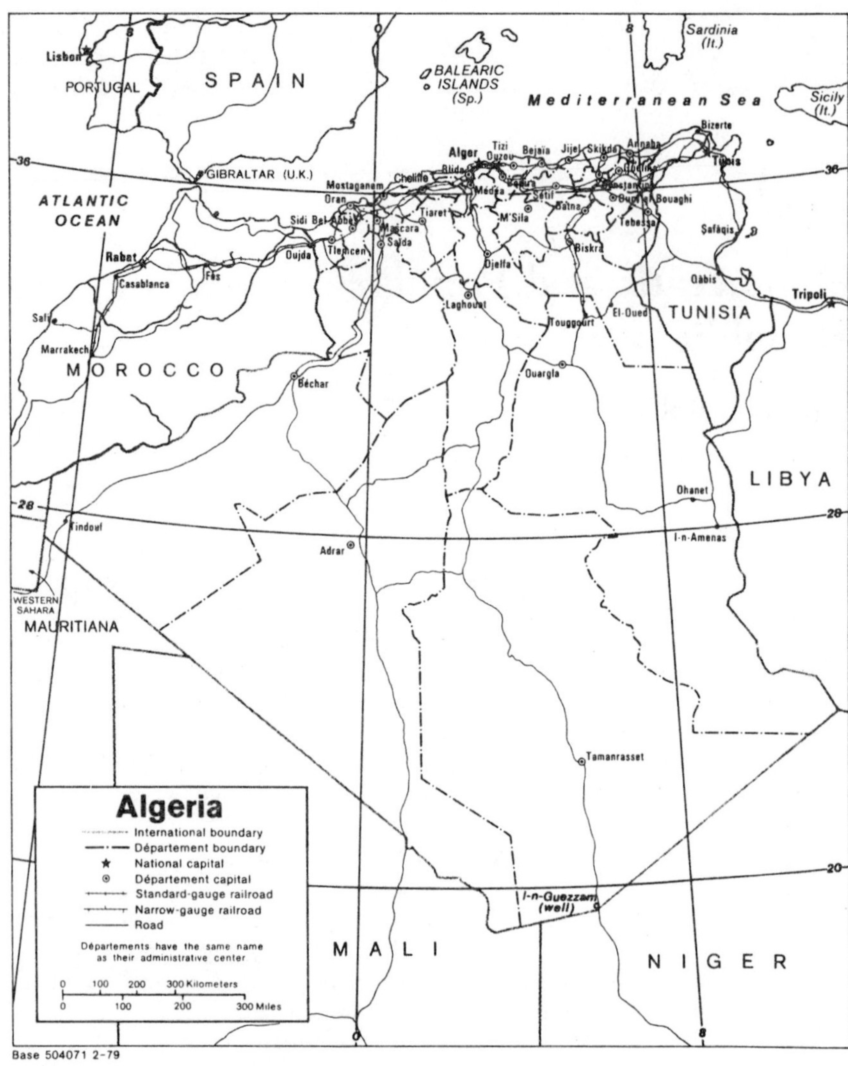

The intermittent attempts at incremental political and social reforms designed to benefit the native Algerians were inconsequential. As long as the settler population controlled Algeria, Paris-inspired reform legislation was doomed.

In reaction to the policy of total colonialism adopted by the French, an Algerian national movement appeared. It can be divided into four distinct historical periods. From 1830 to about 1870 traditional Algerian nationalists resisted colonial rule. They were typified by Amir Abd al-Kadir who led a heroic but futile revolt. By 1870 Algerian society had been so dislocated that an indigenous Algerian political and national identity all but ceased to exist. The period from 1920 to 1954 witnessed the rise of a new, urban-based nationalism and the gradual shift from collaboration with the French to radical opposition. The fourth period, 1954 to 1962, marked the Algerian Revolution, a time of violence and brutality on both sides that culminated in formal independence in July 1962.

The Algerian Revolution erupted when all hope of an evolutionary settlement was destroyed by blunders of postwar French policy and the opposition of French settlers to any concessions to Muslim nationalist aspirations. For the angry young nationalists who formed the backbone of the revolution, the various reformist efforts of the previous period had become irrelevant. In early 1954 the Revolutionary Committee for Unity and Action (CRUA) was organized by dissidents from the earlier movements, ex-soldiers in the French army who had gained valuable experience in the Indochinese campaigns, and miscellaneous groups of dedicated and desperate men who were unafraid of—indeed, they invited—violence and dangerous risks. The nine so-called historic chiefs who had formed the CRUA shared four basic experiences. All were radical militants of peasant and working-class background; all were ex-French army soldiers; all were members of the Organisation Spéciale (OS), the nationalist organization that had been founded in the late 1940s by Ahmad Ben Bella and Hocine Ait Ahmed; and all had served time in French prisons.

After several months of preparation during the summer of 1954, military organization was established and the country divided into six *wilayas*, or districts. On November 1, the National Liberation Front (FLN), with its fighting arm the National Liberation Army (ALN), issued a proclamation calling on all Algerians to rise and fight for their freedom. The revolution had begun.

In September 1958 the FLN constituted itself into a government, the Provisional Government of the Algerian Republic (GPRA), which negotiated independence after 1958. A final accord on a cease-fire was reached at Evian, France, on March 19, 1962, and formal independence was declared on July 3, 1962.

Independence was achieved despite the military impotence of the revolutionaries and the serious divisions existing within the FLN. These splits were basically caused by the fact that there had been neither an incontestable leader, a political organization, nor an articulated ideology before the revolution. Yet, although the country lay exhausted and prostrate from the draining ordeal of a savage eight-year guerrilla war, and the structure of state and society was virtually decimated by the hasty retreat of frightened colons, Algeria finally emerged free and in control of its own political destiny after 132 years of French colonial rule.

The superficial unity that marked the FLN's military and diplomatic efforts broke down immediately after independence, and a vicious struggle for power among contending groups began. The three major contestants for power were the Algerian provisional government, the *wilaya* commands, and the army of the frontier or external army (ALN), based in Morocco and Tunisia during the revolution. At issue were wartime misdemeanors, ideology, ethnic and clan ties, loyalties to specific individuals, and competing perspectives on the nature of post-independence Algerian society. At stake was political predominance in the state.

The first round in the struggle was fought on the eve of independence at the Tripoli (Libya) congress of the FLN national council in May 1962. Factionalism and deep-seated antagonism among all the principal nationalist leaders quickly surfaced. The purpose of the Tripoli meeting was to elect a political bureau to assume control of the FLN and to devise a political and economic program, which later became the official policy of independent Algeria.

When the competing factions returned to Algeria, Ben Bella, with the military support of the ALN chief of staff, Colonel Houari Boumedienne, was able to gain the initiative and establish his authority over party and nation.

On September 20, 1962, elections for the National Assembly were held. All powers of the GPRA were transferred to the new assembly, and formal proclamation of the Democratic and Popular Republic of Algeria was made. Six days later, the assembly elected Ben Bella premier and empowered him to form a government. He immediately formed a cabinet that included Boumedienne as defense minister. Others were chosen from the Algerian Army (ANP) and Ben Bella's personal and political associates.

Once the new government had consolidated its position, it set about addressing the severe economic plight of the country, caused in great part by the sudden and massive exodus of the Europeans. The latter included virtually all the entrepreneurs, technicians, administrators, teachers, doctors, and skilled workers in the country. After factories and shops closed and farms ceased operations, over 70 percent of the population was left unemployed. In March 1963 Ben Bella, overwhelmed by the catastrophic economic situation and unguided by any particular socialist ideology, signed into law several decrees ("the March Decrees") that legalized the takeover of extensive agricultural and industrial properties abandoned in the colon exodus and instituted the system of *autogestion*, or workers' management.

Autogestion was conceived as an economic system based on workers' management of their own affairs through elected officials and cooperation with the state through a director and national agencies. The state's function was to guide, counsel, and coordinate their activities within the framework of an evolving national plan. *Autogestion* was seen as a stage in the transformation from a colonial to a socialist economy. The severe shortage of qualified personnel and the inability of workers and peasants to fully comprehend the principles of self-management made this experiment in socialism more a myth than a reality.

Ben Bella's style of rule did not instill confidence among a war-weary population. He quickly attempted to increase his personal standing and power. In April 1963 he took over the position of general secretary of the FLN. Subsequently, he engineered the passage of a constitution creating a presidential regime with the FLN as the sole political party. In September 1963 he was elected president for a five-year term. He also assumed the title of military commander-in-chief while becoming head of state and head of government.

This consolidation of personal power and apparent move toward dictatorial government aroused opposition and the reemergence of factionalism. Farhat Abbas, the president of the assembly and the leading spokesman for a more liberal policy, resigned from the presidency and was subsequently expelled from the FLN. In the Kabyle, where discontent was accentuated by Berber regionalism, sporadic disturbances broke out and a revolt had to be quashed by police action and political compromise.

In April 1964 the long-awaited First Congress of the FLN was held in Algiers to sort out the ideological differences among various competing groups within the ruling establishment. Toward this end the Algiers Charter, as it came to be called, was formally adopted. The charter defined the relationship between the state, party, and army, and supported traditional Islamic principles as theoretical guidelines for Algerian socialism and the policy of *autogestion*.

The Congress, however, precipitated the feud between Ben Bella and Boumedienne. Ben Bella attempted to strengthen the leftist organizations in the hope that they would help him against the army, while Boumedienne tried to unify the army against Ben Bella by resolving the conflict between the former *wilaya* leaders and the newer officers of the ANP.

Ultimately, Ben Bella lost. Despite his numerous efforts to institutionalize the revolution and its socialist ideology, his popularity among the masses, and his status as one of the "historic chiefs" of the revolution, he was never able to overcome the many rivalries, challenges, and controversies that faced his regime. In addition, his ouster of the traditional leaders, his repeated political attacks on the workers union (UGTA), his failure to make the FLN an efficient mass party, his suspicion of plotters behind every door, and his increasingly dictatorial tendencies alienated many political leaders and interest groups. Furthermore, Ben Bella's constant improvisation in policy offended even his closest supporters. Once the army turned against him, he was left virtually powerless and vulnerable, and in June 1965 he was ousted from power.

The military takeover hardly caused a ripple in Algerian society. The constitution was suspended, and power was smoothly and efficiently transferred to Boumedienne and a twenty-member Council of Revolution, which was designated as the supreme political body. Boumedienne was named prime minister and minister of defense, and Abdelaziz Bouteflika continued as foreign minister. According to the council, the aims of the new regime were to reestablish the principles of the revolution, to remedy the abuses of personal power associated with Ben Bella, to end internal divisions, and to create an "authentic" socialist society based on a sound economy.

For his base of support, Boumedienne relied on the veterans of the war of independence (*mujahidin*), the ALN officers, and a new class of young technocrats—a reflection of his more somber and low-key style of authority. The shy, introverted Boumedienne was a reformist and an organizer who stressed the need for planning and reflection, and was wary of radical change. During the first two years of his rule, he initiated no bold new initiatives. He made little attempt to resuscitate national political life, and the Algerian National Assembly remained in abeyance while the FLN was moribund.

Despite Boumedienne's cautious administration, opposition against him began to crystallize among left-wing ministers, the UGTA, the students, and some sections of the army—notably the former *wilaya* leaders. This group favored the syndicalist approach to socialism embodied in *autogestion* to the more centralized and technocratic system being developed by Boumedienne. They also feared that collegial rule was being supplanted by a dictatorship of Boumedienne and the small group around him.

On December 14, 1967, Colonel Tahar Zbiri, army chief of staff and a prominent former *wilaya* leader, launched an armed uprising in the countryside. It was quickly and efficiently suppressed by forces loyal to Boumedienne, but other groups, especially dissident students, continued to demonstrate their opposition to the new regime by striking and staging street demonstrations. There were reports of guerrilla activity in the Aurès and Kabylia regions, and on April 25, 1968, an unsuccessful attempt was made to assassinate Boumedienne.

Between 1968 and 1972, however, the regime managed to consolidate its power, thereby enabling it to initiate bold policies of development in the industrial, agricultural, and political fields. The second stage of the reform of governmental institutions, for example, was put into operation in May 1969, when the government held elections for the *wilaya* popular assembly (APW). Both the earlier February 1967 APC (communal popular assembly) elections and the May 1969 APW elections clearly indicated how Boumedienne envisioned the organization of the Algerian state and its political institutions. Specifically, his idea was to implement a system of decentralized local government counterbalanced by a single centralized party, the FLN, and a well-established administration.

It was also during this period that the regime gave priority to the development of heavy industry, particularly of the petroleum and gas industry. At the end of 1971 a major attempt was also made at agrarian reform in order to improve the lagging agricultural sector, which had received only secondary attention in the attempt to boost industrial productivity.

In the political sphere, the lack of political representation and popular participation in the first five years of Boumedienne's rule, despite the creation of local and *wilaya* assemblies, led him to reassess the status of the nation's political institutions, particularly its single-party governing structure, the FLN. The regime's successful creation of a stable political environment had been achieved at the expense of public participation in the political process. The FLN had been allowed to become moribund and overly bureaucratized. Thus, on June 19, 1975 (the tenth anniversary of his ascent to power), Boumedienne announced the preparation of a national charter and constitution that would provide for political institutions that were to be either created or reactivated.

In May 1976 Boumedienne submitted the charter to public debate. The extensive and surprisingly candid discussions at party gatherings, trade-union meetings, and assemblies of the burgeoning peasants' association reflected widening public participation in political life while reaffirming the power of Boumedienne and his regime.

On June 27, 1976, the new National Charter was overwhelmingly approved by a referendum. The charter represents an ideological inventory of Algeria's socialist history and charts the direction the country intends to pursue. It also delineates the popular and institutional basis of the future Algeria, giving renewed prominence to the FLN as the nation's only authentic representative of the people's will. Emphasis is also placed on the participatory role of citizens in a socialist society.

In November 1976 Algerians again went to the polls and overwhelmingly approved a new constitution that recreated the National Popular Assembly (Assemblée Populaire Nationale, or APN) and restored the country to constitutional rule for the first time since the July 1965 suspension of the 1963 constitution promulgated under Ben Bella. The new constitution was a lengthy document, containing a preamble and 199 articles; it ushered in what has become known as the Second Algerian Republic (the first republic lasted from 1963 to 1965). In theory, the National Charter and the new constitution signaled the return of constitutional government, but since Boumedienne personally led and encouraged the public debate that favored both new documents, the votes approving them were in fact votes of confidence in the man himself and his personal system of rule.

A month after approval of the constitution, Boumedienne, the only candidate on the ballot, was overwhelmingly elected president of the republic. According to the constitution, Boumedienne, as president, officially became head of state, head of government, commander-in-chief of the armed forces, head of national defense, and nominally the head of the FLN—all of which significantly enhanced an institutional power that was already well-fortified by his support from the military.

Finally, as provided for in the new constitution, elections for the new National Popular Assembly were held on February 25, 1977. Although all of the candidates were chosen by the FLN, there was a certain amount of debate over the choices between the grass-roots militants and the party leadership. The representatives elected to a five-year term of the new assembly included six government ministers, diplomats, army officers, peasants, industry and office workers, civil servants, and party workers, several of whom were women. Emphasizing that the new assembly was composed of a majority of peasants and workers, government officials described the APN as the final step in the construction of a socialist state that began a decade earlier with local elections.

On April 27, 1977, the assembly formed a new government. The president remained firmly in control, however, since all twenty-four ministers and three secretaries of state were considered to be the "president's men"—loyal, obedient, and, for the most part, competent. Since Boumedienne did not designate a prime minister—a constitutional role of his office—he further enhanced the presidential prerogative within Algeria's political system.

In addition to creating the important institutional and participatory bases of Algerian political life, Boumedienne's main accomplishments as leader of Algeria during the years of his tenure included stabilizing the nation's leadership, consolidating government control over the economy, introducing comprehensive economic planning, capitalizing on petroleum and gas revenues, and generally aiming at rapid industrialization.

Boumedienne's sudden illness in November 1978 and his death a month later from a rare blood disease left Algeria without a designated successor. As stipulated in the constitution, National Assembly President Bitah assumed interim responsibilites as chief of state while a special congress of the FLN was convened to select a candidate. The congress's choice of Colonel Chadli Benjedid—a senior military officer—as presidential candidate and secretary-general of the party reflected the preeminence of the military office corps as a predominant political force in Algerian political life.

After pursuing a cautious policy of "change within continuity" in the immediate years following Boumedienne's death, Chadli Benjedid undertook a number of wide-ranging initiatives that enabled him to consolidate his power and take full control of the state, party, and military apparatus on the eve of his reelection to the presidency in early 1984. As a result, the process of "de-Boumediennization" has virtually been completed, with Chadli's men and policies now firmly in place. This process has been achieved through a combination of liberalization measures, policy shifts, coercive pressures, changes in key personnel, and modifications of the rules of the game.

Popular measures implemented almost immediately after Chadli's assumption of power in 1979 included the elimination of the much-hated exit visa, which had been required of all citizens and foreign residents alike for travel abroad; the release of politically innocuous prisoners, such as Ben Bella, who had been placed under house arrest following the 1965 coup; the return of noted exiles, such as Tahar Zbiri, who had conspired to overthrow Boumedienne in 1967; the lifting of controls against certain dissidents at home, such as Ferhat Abbas and Benkhedda, who had come out in 1976 against Boumedienne's foreign policies (especially Algeria's relation with Morocco); and the implementation of a massive anticorruption drive directed against well-known public figures who governed under Boumedienne, such as Abdelaziz Bouteflika, who had been the country's long-term foreign minister from 1963 to 1979, as well as against numerous other high-ranking officials and their subordinates. Aside from opening up what had become an increasingly oppressive and corrupt society, these measures enabled the new regime to eliminate loyalists of the previous government whose devotion to Chadli was uncertain.

Also important were the many policy shifts that Chadli undertook in the economic, administrative, and foreign policy realms. Almost all large state enterprises, for example, accused at once of being overly centralized, inefficient, and parasitic, were broken up into smaller, more manageable parts. Similarly, "super" ministries were reduced in number—the purpose being to make them more accountable but also more controllable through "divide and rule" among potentially ambitious bureaucrats who might envision the use of ministerial or subministerial authority to accumulate power into their own hands. Other changes included the opening up of the Algerian economy to certain types of limited foreign investment, the expansion and revitalization of the country's private sector in both agriculture and consumer industries, the diversification of arms purchases away from the Soviet Union and toward such Western manufacturers as Britain and the United States, and the lowering of Algeria's once highly visible profile in global and Third World affairs.

Yet none of these "liberalizing" efforts has been allowed to challenge the regime's central authority. Accordingly, the regime—when necessary—has used sweeping coercive measures to put down uprisings, demonstrations, and other forms of antistate behavior. In this regard, the government has come down hard on university students, Islamic fundamentalists, and ethnic Berbers who have challenged the education, religion, and language policies of the regime. In almost each instance, however, a firm response has been quickly followed by a conciliatory gesture aimed at appeasing discontented groups. In combination, the carrot-and-stick approach has managed to effectively control and contain the limited antigovernment actions that the country has experienced in recent years.

Numerous personal shifts have occurred since 1979 that have also succeeded in firming up Chadli's power. These shifts have taken place in all the key institutions of the state, such as the cabinet, the National Assembly, the Political Bureau and Central Committee of the FLN, the military, and the directorships of the nationalized companies. Through elections, reductions in numbers, forced retirements, and movements to symbolic but politically insignificant positions at home and abroad, Chadli's regime has virtually eliminated all serious contenders to his increasingly "sultanic" authority. Finally, in both the armed forces and the political party Chadli has changed certain rules—especially the powers of appointment—to ensure that "his people" are placed in decisive positions.

A frontal assault on the sluggish, corrupt-ridden, and bloated bureaucracy that had made the Algerian economy so inefficient these many years, despite the existence of ample hydrocarbon reserves, has now been undertaken without fear of challenge or opposition. To the initial call for "A Better Life" that constituted the motto of the extraordinary party congress in 1980 has now been added "Discipline and Hard Work to Guarantee the Future," an objective advanced at the fifth FLN Congress in December 1983. Efficiency, accountability, and productivity are the hallmarks of the "new" Algeria. In order to counteract unemployment, low food production, rapid population growth, and overurbanization, the current regime has reoriented its domestic development away from heavy industry (except for energy) toward agriculture, light industry, consumer goods, and the social services (i.e., housing, education, and health care). The mistakes of the past—which include unrealistic concentration on heavy industry, excessively rigid socialism, and the loss of private business initiative—have all been recognized, and attempts are now being made to correct them.

In the five-year period from Chadli's uncontested election to the presidency in February 1979 to the renewal of his five-year mandate in January 1984 (with over 95 percent of the popular vote in both instances), Algeria has evolved away from the ideological militancy and economic austerity of the Boumedienne era into a more "liberalized" phase of decentralization, deconcentration, and (limited) democratization, which have become the salient features of the current regime. Through a series of broad measures in virtually all sectors of politics and economics, Chadli Benjedid has taken the Algerian ship of state toward a different, more pragmatically oriented direction in clear distinction to the volatile "romanticism" of Ben Bella and the heavily ideological orientation of Boumedienne. Thus, a full two decades after independence Algeria's revolution has been institutionalized, with Chadli's no-nonsense, business-like demeanor representing a new style of governance.

Political Environment

Political Culture

As elsewhere in the Maghrib, elite political culture markedly differs from mass political culture in Algeria. The masses continue to identify unswervingly with Islam and its religious symbols. It is only in the relatively small "modernized" sector of the population and its even smaller elite component that one finds elements of a more secular political culture and ideology.

Algerian political culture reflects the impact of traditional cultural values, assimilated Western political ideologies, and historical experiences—especially the revolutionary war. A conflictual political culture has emerged in which hostility and mistrust between elite groups predominate. Algerian politicians often behave somewhat like their Moroccan counterparts: as if they are constantly maneuvering and scheming to acquire more power. Further, they expect others to behave in a similar manner.

One immediate consequence of this behavior is the personalization of political differences, such that personal rivalries and personal clashes substitute for legitimate political discourse. Another is the distrust of any form of political opposition, thus leading Algerian politicians to view any form of public political disagreement as illegitimate and harmful to the political process.

Despite these attitudes, the current regime has begun to encourage and even articulate the need for "legitimate" dissent and the free expression of opposing opinions. Such a trend was evident earlier under Boumedienne as, for example, when the animated debates over the National Charter became remarkably open and candid.

Paradoxically, another and altogether inconsistent aspect of Algerian political culture is the strong feeling that political relations must be based on equality and reciprocity. This sentiment has its origins in the traditional Islamic concepts of *shura* (consultation) and *ijma'* (consensus), which were central to decision-making in the Islamic state. The most noteworthy expression of the Algerian's demand for equality is found in the notion of collegial rule and in the rejection of the idea of a "cult of personality." Ben Bella's adherence to this "cult" was the most damning accusation made against him. In contrast, Boumedienne's rule emphasized collegiality and consultation, albeit among a narrow group of political advisers, technocrats, and military men. In his later years Boumedienne personally assumed extensive decisionmaking authority (which his successor has also maintained for himself), thereby undermining the tendency toward collegiality within the political elite that had been gaining strength in the period immediately after Boumedienne's death.

The mixture of distrust and egalitarianism in Algerian political life is often explained by the so-called individualistic nature of the Algerians themselves—that is, by their distrust for those who have power and their demand for an equal share of influence. Yet this individualism, manifested at times by a kind of public rebellion and sporadic violence, belies an underlying pressure to conform to rigorous traditional social codes that must be obeyed and to a public opinion that must be respected. As a result, attitudes toward the power role of government are characterized by fundamentally inconsistent behavioral patterns. On the one hand, the colonial and war experiences have exerted a particularly profound impact on the elites' perception of the "proper" role of government. They engendered a belief in the need for a strong centralized state with respect to economic development and organization. On the other hand, Algerian political culture contains a strong current of populism, as reflected by the principles and practices of *autogestion* in the first years of independence.

Algerian populism reflects a belief in the supremacy of the will of the people. It places justice and morality above all other norms and emphasizes the importance of a direct relationship between the people and their leaders, in which intermediary institutions and mediating structures play only a minor role.

Apart from Algerians' perceptions of the role of government in society, their concept of the greatest social and political good is embodied in the concepts of nationalism and socialism. Although there appears to be more attachment of the rhetoric and symbolism of these two concepts than to their substance, they have assumed sacrosanct status among the political elite. The statist policies of the Algerian ruling elite are in fact justified by nationalist terms, wherein the state is viewed as having a right to intervene in many areas of national life. Yet there remains a genuine commitment to the welfare of the masses as well as to the idea of socialist mass political participation and administrative decentralization.

Other elements of political culture and ideology in Algeria include a belief in a continuing revolution, Arab unity, and the resurrection of an Algerian Arab-Islamic culture through Arabization and under the guidance of a mass-mobilization political party. The Islamic component of socialism remains a salient feature of contemporary ideology. Algerian socialism is linked to the world of Islam, which constitutes the "heart, mind, and soul of the Algerian consciousness." The relationship between socialism and Islam, reflected in earlier ideological documents, is reaffirmed in both the National Charter and the new constitution, which explicitly extol Islamic socialism as the road to political, economic, social, and cultural salvation.

In practical terms, the duality of Islamic and socialist ideological content in Algerian political thought has permitted incumbent leaders to sustain a conservative—indeed, puritanical—policy in the areas of personal, religious, and moral affairs while simultaneously pursuing a radical modernization policy involving rapid and sweeping economic growth, the use of advanced technology and scientific know-how, and dependence on Western secularists for administrative, organization, and financial expertise. Inevitably, the coexistence of Western secular ideas of revolutionary socialism and French republicanism and traditional Islamic political ideology have created unavoidable tensions and contradictions within Algerian political culture.

At the same time, Islamic socialist ideology enables the government not only to reject Western secularism and to identify with other "radical" Arab states but also to reject certain aspects of local tradition thought to impede social progress. Through numerous government-controlled propaganda organs and the communications media, the regime has continued to advance a socialist program primarily aimed at developing the economic strength of the state, raising the standards of living of its rural and urban populations, and providing a framework for rapid industrialization and agrarian reform. Even the much-heralded liberalization reforms instituted by Chadli Benjedid in order to revitalize the long-neglected private sector have not fundamentally altered the country's basic socialist orientation.

Economic Conditions

In the decade following independence, Algeria nationalized all major foreign business interests as well as many private Algerian companies. Nationalization ranged from the assumption of a controlling interest in some cases to complete takeover in others. Today the Algerian economy is almost totally government-controlled. State enterprises and government agencies control much of the foreign trade, almost all of the major industries, large parts of the distribution and retail systems, all public utilities, and the entire banking and credit system.

The commitment to what has come to be called state capitalism evolved out of the radical nationalism of the Boumedienne group. The members of this group were convinced that true national independence could be realized only through control of natural resources, especially hydrocarbons, and through rapid industrial development—objectives that, in the context of world capitalist domination, could be achieved only through nationalization and state control of the economy.

Since the late 1960s industrial development has been given priority over agricultural development, and within the industrial sector most investment has gone into basic industries. This strategy has been justified by two arguments. First, continued dependence on the export of raw materials and agricultural products would prevent Algeria from achieving the type of economic independence deemed necessary to make political independence truly meaningful. Second, not only could Algeria's petroleum and gas resources finance industrialization, but they could be also used to develop a petrochemical industry that would be the foundation of the entire strategy of industrialization.

It was believed that, over time, industrialization would lead to the creation of numerous jobs, thereby somewhat offsetting the country's chronic unemployment and underemployment problems. In the short run, however, employment generated by the new capital-intensive industries could only marginally alleviate the unemployment problem, especially since Algeria has one of the world's highest population growth rates. Thus, in November 1971 the Charter of the Agrarian Revolution proclaimed the government's intent to profoundly change the economic and political cast of the traditional sector of Algerian agriculture, and there has been a gradual shift in the severe investment imbalance between the industrial and agricultural sectors.

Algeria's emphasis on industrialization was reflected in its first four-year plan (1970–1973), which marked the first real effort at a comprehensive economic policy. The plan allocated 45 percent of total capital investment to the establishment of a capital-intensive industrial sector that was to be the basis of economic growth. Only 15 percent went to agriculture, whereas 40 percent of investment was allocated to social and economic infrastructure. The investment strategy was called "planting Algeria's oil," thereby using petroleum revenues to create a strong industrial base. At the same time, an agrarian revolution policy, as it was called, aimed at improving efficiency through land reform and a system of cooperatives. The program was not only undercapitalized but, owing to resistance from the rural population, it failed to increase agriculture's percentage of the GNP, which in fact declined from 13 percent in 1969 to 9 percent in 1973.

The second four-year plan (1974–1977) attempted to remedy the apparent imbalances and malfunctions of the first plan without jeopardizing the heavy emphasis on rapid industrialization. The new plan, nevertheless, placed more emphasis on developing consumer industries that create jobs, fighting regional economic disparities, encouraging small and medium-sized industries, and promoting land reform. The 1974–1977 plan also placed a major emphasis on housing, an area that was conspicuously neglected in the first plan.

Still uncertain is how much new investment in agriculture will improve the poorest parts of the countryside (in contrast to the state and self-managed farms), and, in particular, how much success the authorities will have in coping with the intractable problems associated with rural economic and social development.

By the time Chadli Benjedid assumed power in 1979, many of the shortcomings associated with Boumedienne's centralized development strategy had become evident. Such a strategy, based as it was on heavy industrialization, had created dualistic economic structures, threatened Algiers and other coastal cities with hyperurbanization, caused intolerably high unemployment in both the rural and urban areas, exacerbated income inequalities despite theoretical salary ceilings, and so neglected domestic food production that it increasingly failed to meet the country's needs. The new government gave priority to alleviating these problems and to deferring further heavy industrial investment until a later date.

Algeria's substantial foreign debt, contracted mainly to pay for industry, was also causing concern, particularly since it implied an unwelcome vulnerability to pressure from overseas. Following nearly two years of debate, the FLN, at its extraordinary session in June 1980, put forth a new five-year plan (1980–1984) that was intended to overcome many of these problems.

"Toward a Better Life" became the principal theme of the FLN special session. It was meant to signal the shifting away from the previous emphasis on heavy industry to a concern for the social needs of the people, notably in the areas of education, health, and housing, and on developing food and consumer industries. These policies and other proposals put into effect since the extraordinary session in 1980 did not mean that Algeria's socialist structure was being dismantled or that the country was forfeiting its revolutionary commitments. Algerian officials have repeatedly assured their people and foreign observers that this self-induced internal revolution was not to be interpreted as a return to "liberal" society, "in the sense that society as a whole would be made to suffer for the sake of the individual." In the words of the general-secretary of the Planning and Regional Development Ministry, "the main lines of the Plan were meant to follow the options and political orientations already chosen for the country's development strategy. Algeria remains committed to creating a modern, stable and independent economy which is capable of generating its own internal development." And despite the decisions to halt construction of more liquified natural-gas plants, to slow investment in other heavy industries, and to channel more funds into agriculture, light industry, and public services, the secretary-general indicated that it was "vital for Algeria's economy to continue the development of basic industries in the future. For this reason a high rate of investment would be maintained in both basic and consumer industries. This represented about 40 percent of Algeria's gross national product which, although less than the 55 percent of the last few years, was still very high." These and other statements confirm the notion that Chadli's "Toward a Better Life" policies have not meant liberalization or democratization; instead, decentralization and deconcentration as ways to more effectively utilize Algeria's human, natural, and industrial resources have become the touchstone of the new directive. The tilt toward pragmatism resulting from the disenchantment with centralized development planning has been viewed as an issue of management and administration, not one of politics.

The government has also increased the scope for private-sector growth. In a speech in May 1982 Chadli encouraged Algeria's small but energetic private sector to expand in the retail, housing, and tourism industries. It is estimated that Algeria's private sector accounts for a third of the economy. In addition to the half of farming that is privately owned, trade is wholly in private hands. The same is true of approximately half the country's building and textile firms. The government wants the private sector's help in creating jobs and tapping savings for investment. At present, private fortunes are often stashed away or smuggled abroad. Some 95 percent of all investment is provided by the state. New laws are seeking to pinpoint the areas that private industry can invest in without fear of interference. The criterion governing private-sector development is that private companies should not be allowed to occupy a "strategic" position in any industry—either by being the sole source of supply of a key component or by being jointly able to exert a monopoly over price. Some planners have gone so far as to say that private industry "is an ally of the revolution." One should be careful not to exaggerate the importance of this development, however, for Algeria remains essentially a socialist state—whatever critics may think of its socialist pretensions in other areas of state behavior.

The government is also acting to establish more joint-venture companies with foreign concerns. In particular, Western businesses are being given tax holidays to encourage them to invest in consumer-goods industries, housing, and electronics. Yet most foreign businesses remain wary of the Algerian market. For example, although such companies can repatriate profits worth up to a quarter of their investment, they still must pay stiff taxes.

The agricultural sector has been severely neglected in the past, with disastrous consequences. In theory, Algeria should be able to feed itself. In practice, it imports half of its grain, is the world's biggest importer of eggs, and ships huge amounts of meat and dairy products. Chadli's development plan envisions the building of twenty dams for irrigation. Farmers, who have suffered under state-run collectives, are being given more credits and encouraged to till small plots that they could eventually own. In addition, a new agricultural bank has been established at Blida, and steps are being taken to break up the two thousand *autogestion*, or self-managed, state farms into several thousand smaller units. These and other measures being recommended will require time before any substantial results can be seen.

It is not yet certain whether all these highly publicized efforts at streamlining the Algerian economy in response to accumulated social grievances are part of a broader, more permanent shifting of the system from a center-down to a bottom-up strategy of development. As early as 1971, for example, the Boumedienne regime had begun a campaign against poor governmental performance, which it said was caused by excessive centralization. The government then mobilized party ideologues, representatives of the mass organizations within the FLN (UGTA, UNPA, UNFA, and so on), and the state-controlled mass media to push for decentralized planning and administration. Yet, by the time of Boumedienne's death in late 1978, little of a concrete nature had been accomplished given that the decentralization effort remained stuck at the level of rhetoric.

Chadli's team was quick to support the principle of decentralization but began to act only after political power had been effectively consolidated. Clearly, many of the components necessary for a viable, local level–oriented decentralization process are already in place. Land reform, better structures for communal decisionmaking, private-sector incentives, industrial restructuring, regional development, priority given to projects for basic needs rather than export-based production, and other policies favoring peripheral and rural areas already can be seen, if only in embryonic form. Recently, a significant step was taken in administrative reorganization when, in December 1984, the government approved a measure increasing the number of *wilayas* from 31 to 48. As a major factor in impelling local economic development, the increase in regional units can only benefit the public inasmuch as it will make the administration more accessible and accountable.

The theme of "Discipline and Hard Work to Guarantee the Future" marked the FLN's fifth party congress held in December 1983. Among its many objectives was the continuation of the government's efforts at streamlining the economy so as to make it more efficient and responsive to populist needs. The broad outline of the next five-year plan was also discussed. It was given concrete meaning at the twelfth session of the FLN's Central Committee, which convened in May 1984, and was officially approved by the cabinet in early July 1984. On balance, the 1985–1989 plan reflects the government's determination to shift economic priorities from state-centered to society-centered needs. Other principal features of the new plan include increasing the degree of horizontal integration of Algerian industry by promoting intersectoral exchanges, developing import-substitution manufacturing, and improving storage facilities and the distribution system, problems that have long plagued Algerian bureaucracy.

In order to tackle the serious problem of overurbanization in the major coastal cities, projects are to be implemented that will stimulate new industrial development in the High Plateaux and the south. It is hoped that this measure will decongest already overpopulated cities, and that the setting up of family-planning clinics throughout the country will arrest the uncontrolled birth rate. Continuing the programs begun in the previous plan, the new development scheme will emphasize social and communications infrastructures, especially housing and rail transport. A priority issue that has already caused controversy and may yet give authorities political problems in the future is the decision reflected in the plan to reorient secondary and higher education in order to meet more closely the economy's evolving manpower demands and employment possibilities. However, attempts to limit enrollment in certain popular professions such as medicine and law, as well as efforts to keep students at regional rather than urban universities so as to achieve more regionally balanced growth, have already created anxiety and concern among many of the nation's youth.

It will be some time, however, before the whole package of reform measures originally introduced by the Chadli government and spelled out in the two five-year plans will be adopted in any comprehensive or integrated fashion. The hydrocarbon industry, for example, continues its financial domination of the economy. The focus on industrial investment has not been significantly lessened but merely supplemented by new policy orientations. Yet the time frame within which an objective evaluation could be made is still too small, for the Algerians tend to think of policy implementation as a protracted process—one accomplished over a long period of time. Nonetheless, the path to subnational policy initiation and follow-through comes into conflict with Algeria's historic urge for "organic unity" and its need for central direction and close supervision. It is thus too early to decide whether an effective transformation of elite political culture has taken place or whether mere managerial tinkering explains the current push toward decentralization.

In the meantime, society's multiple dilemmas continue to mount, with the problem of an unproductive and deteriorating agricultural sector causing particular alarm. Not only has domestic food production fallen severely short of satisfying the basic food needs of Algeria's 22 million people, but the drain on human and financial resources has been enormous as well, thus obstructing the overall effort at achieving an integrated and self-sufficient development.

What was initially a peasant revolution has ironically culminated in a form of vigorous state capitalism, using modern large-scale techniques and small-scale local plants. The process of industrialization, however, has tended to bifurcate society into isolated poles of growth and stagnation that will require more than money or goodwill to overcome. Finally, Algeria's state capitalism has created and sustained a new elite. This economic system has put a premium on centralized control of the whole economy and on nationalization of the means of production. Thus, economic power has come to be concentrated in the hands of the state officials who control the national enterprises.

Political Structure

The 1965 coup suspended the National Assembly and constitution established under Ahmad Ben Bella. During the next ten years, Algerian political life was strongly centralized under the Council of the Revolution and the council of ministers, both headed by Boumedienne. In the absence of a constitution, the council of ministers became responsible for the day-to-day administration of the government and thus became the effective executive and legislative body. The FLN (Algeria's only party organization) and other national-level institutions were allowed to atrophy so that Boumedienne's vision of a strong, secure, centralized government could evolve without the challenge that such organizations could present. Boumedienne believed that institutional development could emerge only via a systematic process of political education.

In accordance with this strategy, communal elections first took place in 1967 and were renewed every four years (1971, 1975, 1979, 1983). Likewise, *wilaya* (regional) elections were held in 1969 and every five years thereafter (1974, 1979, 1984). However, these local and regional assemblies (in 1984, 700 and 48 in number, respectively) remain largely administrative in nature and have no significant political authority.

Despite the regime's claim that the assemblies were created with the objective of instituting a greater measure of self-government at the local level, they actually strengthened national political control. For example, although the elections permit choices among candidates—there are, according to the system, three times as many candidates as seats to be filled—the majority of the candidates are nominated by the FLN. There is also no party competition nor do candidates engage in an electoral contest, as campaigning is the work of FLN notables and ministers. The result is politically lethargic and administratively marginal local-level associations that depend on the central authorities for guidance and animation.

Either because the system of assemblies had succeeded sufficiently or failed altogether, Boumedienne began, in the early 1970s, to call for greater politicization of the masses by advocating renewed involvement in the FLN as the sole ideological and institutional organ of the socialist revolution. In mid-1976, he personally directed the revival of constitutional politics in the form of public debates that preceded the voting on the National Charter. The nationwide referendums that approved the National Charter and constitution in June and November 1976, respectively, represented the formal reestablishment of constitutional government.

The 1976 constitution, with amendments introduced in 1979, states that the republican nature of the state cannot be altered and that the state religion is Islam. It reaffirms the socialist system and the territorial integrity of the country and guarantees freedom of expression and assembly. The document also reaffirms state control of the means of production, land reforms, free medical care, worker participation in industry, and campaigns against corruption and nepotism. It guarantees that so-called nonexploitative private property of artisans, small farmers, and traders who derive their income from their own work will be respected. The constitution also guarantees the "liberation of women and their full participation in the political, economic, social and cultural life of the nation."

Executive powers are vested in the president of the republic, who is elected for a five-year term by direct, adult suffrage and can be reelected for an unlimited number of terms. Although the day-to-day administration of government is the responsibility of the council of ministers, the president is empowered to enact laws by decree when the legislature is not in session.

In each of the three presidential elections that have taken place under the new constitution—Boumedienne in 1976 and Chadli Benjedid in 1979 (following Boumedienne's death in late 1978) and 1984—the single FLN candidate has received over 95 percent of the popular vote. These overwhelming electoral endorsements have bathed the presidential office with populist legitimacy, thereby enabling the incumbent to act decisively and authoritatively.

Constitutional prerogative already concentrates virtually all important powers in the executive branch of government. Article 3 of the constitution, for example, identifies eighteen separate presidential powers and prerogatives. The president is the guarantor of the constitution, commander-in-chief of the country's armed forces, and head of the Supreme Court; he presides over the Council of Ministers, makes appointments to high military and civilian positions, concludes and ratifies international treaties, and appoints and recalls all Algerian ambassadors. In brief, both the constitution and the National Charter confirm the president's power to determine Algeria's domestic and foreign policies.

In addition, the president holds the top leadership post in the FLN along with the defense ministry—hence the highly centralized and powerful presidential system of government in Algeria.

The National Popular Assembly (Assemblée Populaire Nationale) is the country's unicameral legislature with members being elected by secret, direct, and universal suffrage for a period of five years. The first APN elections held in well over a decade took place in early 1977 with 783 FLN-sponsored candidates vying for the then 261 available parliamentary seats. The second such elections occurred in 1982 under more liberalized conditions that allowed, for the first time, non-FLN candidates to compete for parliamentary seats in the expanded 281-member body. The electoral results saw a major turnover in the incumbents, with nearly half the parliamentarians being newcomers and "only" 197 winning seats under the FLN banner. Earlier local elections in December 1979 for 703 communal assemblies saw newcomers winning more than 80 percent of the seats. It is still too early in the young history of Algeria's political institutions to determine whether the revitalized APN will be permitted to act as a forum for serious political debate or whether it will simply serve as the regime's bureaucratic rubber stamp.

Technically, the state's principal policymaking organ is the National Liberation Front, Algeria's sole legal political party as designated by article

95 of the constitution. Through its Political Bureau and Central Committee the FLN draws up policy, which is then put before the National Assembly in the form of bills for enactment into law. The Council of Ministers is given the responsibility of putting policies and laws into effect. To better coordinate the policymaking (FLN) and executive (cabinet) functions, the president of the republic is automatically designated secretary-general of the FLN.

Political Dynamics

Politics in post-independence Algeria has been characterized by a stable system of rule, with power concentrated among relatively few individuals situated within select institutions. Although the incumbent elites remained relatively unchanged during the Boumedienne years (1965–1978), significant alterations in the top political elites and within the state's political institutions have taken place since the mid-1970s. The turnover of personnel in upper leadership positions has been particularly pronounced in the early 1980s.

As we have seen, the series of nationwide participatory efforts (National Charter, constitution, etc.) were preceded by a number of carefully prepared local and regional assembly elections and followed by a systematic series of conventions of the various national organizations (UGTA, UNJA, etc.). A party congress of the National Liberation Front was convened in January 1979 following Boumedienne's death, and a single presidential candidate was selected (Chadli Benjedid) and confirmed a month later by the electorate in a national election. Local (1983), regional (1984), party (1983), legislative (1982), and presidential (1984) elections have been renewed since the 1979 FLN convention—all according to specific constitutional and statutory provisions.

This accelerated pace of political activity following nearly a decade of authoritarian single-man rule at the national level reflects the growing importance of institutional life and the concurrent deemphasis of informal, patron-client, and personalized politics at the highest levels of power. This is not to say, however, that the historically pervasive influence of informal politics or the importance of clientelist, personal, and other face-to-face ties has been completely eradicated from Algerian political life. Nonetheless, such behavior has now been incorporated into more formal and regularized settings under closer public scrutiny.

The peaceful transfer of power from Boumedienne to Benjedid attests in part to the credibility and effectiveness of the various institutional arrangements put into place by Boumedienne and his colleagues during the last decade of his life. Particularly significant has been the emergence of a powerful and interlocking technocratic system, with its tripartite mobilizational, managerial, and military components working collectively to ensure a relatively effective and unchallenged operation of the state.

Effective power is concentrated in the hands of a technocratic elite whose claim to authority is based on the modern skills that its members possess and for which there is a high value in the society. Algeria's technocratic system consists of three major units: the military, the party, and the government-administration. Although they have very different internal characteristics, they are united in an overriding new allegiance to the state and its developmental objectives. Most of them share a common background in the National Liberation Army (ALN) and its experience in the revolutionary war. In the decade following his consolidation of power in 1968, Boumedienne depended on this triumvirate to maintain and aggrandize power as well as to erect his socialist state using the crucial technical skills that this group possesses. For the better part of the 1968–1978 period, however, these elements were unevenly aligned, with the FLN reduced to a minor, functionary role while the military and the administrative elite were elevated to dominant positions.

Initially, with the elimination of the past political elite and the establishment of an internal cohesion within the army's structure of authority, the new Boumedienne regime sought to strengthen its hold on the economy and administration by recruiting civil servants and technicians in such a way that the congruence between military and managerial elites was maximized. Yet, to a certain extent, this congruence was achieved at the expense of the single party, which was left in the hands of faithful party hacks such as Ahmed Kaid, who, while they did not lack enthusiasm, loyalty, and "personality," were clearly second-rate relative to the educational and technical standards used to recruit and maintain the military and administrative elites.

The balancing of forces began to take place in the mid-1970s, when Boumedienne, at the time of the tenth anniversary of his 1965 coup d'état, launched a campaign to revitalize political life at the national level through the formulation and implementation of a National Charter and a new constitution followed by presidential and legislative elections all organized under the political guidance of the FLN. The acid test came rather suddenly with Boumedienne's passing, as the single party, in its formal structure and statutory language at least, was significantly enhanced in power and prestige such that its Political Bureau and Central Committee replaced the dissolved Council of the Revolution as the country's "supreme political body."

The Military

Until such time as the party tests and sustains its theoretically defined political clout, however, the military remains the most decisive elite group in Algerian politics today. This has been the case since the time that the old dissensions between the conventional nationalist army (ALN) and the *mujahidin* or *wilayists* (i.e., those who fought in the interior of the country during the revolutionary war) were resolved in favor of the former, renamed the Algerian People's Army (ANP) in 1963.

The military's claim to privileged status is not limited to the obvious fact that it monopolizes the nation's coercive instruments of force. Nor is it based entirely on the fact that Boumedienne was the wartime chief of staff and later the defense minister who provided the critical support that brought Ben Bella to power and subsequently engineered his overthrow in a military coup. Equally important has been the fact that the military continues to possess a revolutionary mystique; that it was instrumental in establishing law and order from the chaos that followed independence; that it possesses the special skills of organization and management that have enabled society to stabilize and develop; that it has become directly involved in local rural affairs, thus gaining popular support at the mass level; and, finally, that it has continued to adhere firmly to the notion that it alone is the guardian of the revolution. In fact, the military has thus far played a guardian role, directly involving itself in politics only when the situation required, as it did in 1962 and 1965. In each instance of direct army intervention, the military followed a policy of "returning to the barracks" to observe the political process carefully, with a discreet but always present eye.

In addition to its explicitly military functions, the army is heavily involved in a variety of civic-action and educational projects. It is thus directly involved in the state-building process—an involvement that further enhances its already wide appeal among the rural masses. Its representation in all elite political institutions, including the Council of Ministers, the National Assembly, and the FLN, permits the military to monitor all political activities directly. Military elites are also active participants at the local and regional levels. At the local level, for example, army officers collaborate with the communal administration, often providing goods and services and dispensing favors that the party is unable or unwilling to provide. At the intermediate level, the heads of the country's military districts function in capacities as regional governors with more influence than the heads of the forty-eight APWs. Finally, the qualitative and quantitative improvement in manpower and equipment since the 1967 Arab-Israeli war, when Soviet military assistance and training accelerated noticeably, has made Algeria a power in regional Arab and North African affairs, thus further enhancing the military's domestic standing among elites and masses alike. In the 1980s the diversification of arms purchases, including advanced U.S. transport aircraft and British missiles, along with the further professionalization of the army through military training agreements with the United States and other Western powers, have added to the Algerian officer corps a power, prestige, and pride that have carried over into the society at large.

The Administrative Elite

The administrative elite constitutes a second important component of the Algerian political system. In fact, with the increasing industrialization and complexity of Algerian society, the administrative elite may eventually replace the military as the paramount voice in policymaking. This category includes the civil service, whose activities extend beyond the actual administration of the country into the substantive functions of various other ministries and their local networks, as well as a more narrowly defined new class of technocrats who have the authority and responsibility for the planning, development, operation, and expansion of the nation's industrial complex, particularly the petrochemicals industry. The largest and most prestigious of all the state-owned industries is SONATRACH, the huge Algerian state petroleum combine that has recently been broken up into several constituent parts without, however, losing importance in the national economy.

The administrative elite has expanded so rapidly since the Boumedienne takeover that it has tended to divide into component groups. In fact, ever since the technocratic revolution began in the late 1960s, bureaucratic politics within the ministerial and presidential councils have been conducted primarily among the competing administrators. This administrative group constitutes an important subelite within the larger ruling elite and has been the most noticeable recipient of new class status, including conspicuous wealth and other tangible signs of social advantage. Furthermore, unlike the military and party elites, the administrators manage programs that exert a major influence on the country's development and its political dynamics.

The Party

Although the role of the FLN in achieving national independence was a decisive one, the party was not able to maintain its power and prestige after independence. The factionalism that had been suppressed in the name of national unity during the revolution quickly reappeared as the party leaders vied with one another for positions of power. The quality of FLN leadership at the local level declined, and in many cases individual party officials seemed more intent on achieving personal advancement than on building up the party as an effective peacetime organization.

For their part, the heavy hands of the state and the army have not allowed the party any independent political activity. The party is unattractive to young people with an educated and intelligent interest in politics because they are required, as members, to be conformists. Most debilitating has been the virtual powerlessness of the party as a dispenser of even the most minor favors and services. For the better part of Boumedienne's thirteen-year rule, the FLN was anything but a vanguard party; indeed, its role was simply to propagate others' policies or to defend others' candidates. Consequently, the influence and role of the FLN has been negligible.

Despite its shortcomings, the party remains the predominant institutional medium for the expression of popular will. It remains subordinate, however, to the military and administrative elites. At the time it was thought that this inferior status might have undergone a transformation in the aftermath of the fourth party congress held in early 1979 to select a new presidential candidate and following the logical growth of authority and prestige that the FLN had achieved as part of the former president's prodigious effort to revitalize the party via an array of mobilizational campaigns. These campaigns were intended to gain support and legitimacy for the Charter and constitution, both of which institutionalized the FLN as an integral force in national politics. Clearly it was Boumedienne's intention to create a viable national political organization that would permit popular participation in the political life of the state, thereby maintaining the populist quality of the regime. As he told an assembly of mayors back in early 1973, when he initiated his campaign to reactivate party life: "A revolution needs revolutionaries and the socialist revolution socialist militants. Whoever has faith in the revolution and its objectives must join the party. Otherwise he can have no place at any level of responsibility."

Given their new responsibilities, power, and resources, the party elites in 1979 firmly believed that Algeria would soon be transformed into an effective single-party system. However, by 1984 Chadli's manipulation of the critical party organs of the Political Bureau and Central Committee had reduced the FLN to a passive bureaucracy—a mere receptacle of dead ideas headed by a "oui-oui" functionary.

Various other national organizations remain subordinate to the FLN: the workers union (UGTA), the farmers organization (UNPA), the Youth Association (UNJA), the organization of former resistance fighters (ONM), the women's association (UNFA), and the newly formed (May 1983) union of small merchants and artisans (UNPCA). None of these organizations have any significant power or authority. The student union is the only group that has sought to challenge centralized authority and assert its own view; and it was finally suppressed in 1971 after a series of student boycotts, strikes, and demonstrations. It has not been revived and is conspicuously absent from the list of national organizations included in the party section of the National Charter. Its activities have been incorporated into the more docile and politically inefficacious UNJA. At the UNJA's youth congress held in January 1979, however, more radicalized elements known as "Pagsistes" managed to achieve several positions of leadership in the UNJA, with the potential of transforming it into a meaningful representative of independent student interests. Pagsistes were also elected in March 1979 to the executive commission and national secretariat of the UGTA. Finally, the Parti de l'Avant-Garde Socialiste (PAGS) is a party of opposition devoid of legal standing and heir to the principles of the defunct (1962) Parti Communiste Algérien (PCA). It is as constant and continuous in its criticism of the current regime as it was of the former one, especially following the onset of the agrarian revolution in 1971. It has also been active in the various committees of the Volontariat, a national service organization for youth and students.

Chadli Benjedid's regime has been much less tolerant of the Pagsiste presence in these and other national organizations than its predecessor had been. At the last congresses of both the UNJA (May 1982) and the UGTA (April 1982), for example, left-wing influence was sharply curtailed, as was demonstrated by the election of a new secretary-general of the labor union (Belakhdar) and the reelection of a noncontroversial incumbent as the secretary-general of the youth movement (Noureddine Djellouli). As with virtually all aspects of the party apparatus, the militantly socialist and leftist tendencies associated with former FLN coordinator Mohammed Salah Yahiaoui have been permanently displaced.

The most volatile and potentially disruptive category of oppositional forces comprises the partially educated, inadequately trained, monolingual Arabists with strong traditional and religious ties who are rapidly swelling the ranks of the urban unemployed. Since at least one or more decades must pass before the country's program of capital-intensive selective industrialization will have a meaningful impact on the national employment picture, especially on its minimally skilled and unskilled sectors, the potential for excessive, if not revolutionary, demands seems great. The facts that nearly 65 percent of the country's population is under eighteen years of age and that the net annual birth rate is over 3 percent combine to aggravate an already precarious situation.

Moreover, these groups seem most vulnerable to psychologically inspired and culturally motivated religious appeals, insofar as their bleak economic futures are ensconced within an anomic sociopsychological environment in which family ties are disintegrating, sexual frustrations are increasing, crime and other expressive forms of personal disaffection are mounting, and a general social malaise is imposing itself on all of Algeria's burgeoning urban conglomerations. Inasmuch as a socialist revolution is theoretically already in place and both communism and capitalism in their "pure" forms remain unacceptable, only a religious Islamic revolution can successfully alleviate the growing sense of social isolation and personal alienation so evident among this current generation of youth and young adults. To a much greater degree than the ineffectual political opposition abroad, these "disruptive dropouts" constitute a direct threat to the system's social stability and an ominous, indirect threat to its political viability.

Foreign Policy

Algerian foreign policy has been strongly influenced by the revolutionary experience of the nearly eight-year war of independence. The revolution left a legacy of emotional extremism, verbal excess, and diplomatic abrasiveness in the conduct of foreign affairs. To these have been added the Algerian predisposition to suspicion, which is inherent in the political culture and nurtured by a clandestine guerrilla life and the internal rivalries of post-independence politics.

Despite the country's modest natural and human resources and limited military capabilites of global standards, Algeria sees itself playing a major role in world politics. In geopolitical terms the country's leaders have described Algeria as the core state of the Maghrib, on the borders of the Mediterranean, with a dual attachment of the African and Arab worlds and, thus, ideally located at the crossroads of three continents. Using its position as a major producer of oil and natural gas, Algeria has also taken a leading role in the so-called north-south dialogue between the major Western industrialized countries and the developing countries of the Third World. Algerian nationalization of its own petroleum industry and the policies it has been able to pursue as a member of the Organization of

Petroleum Exporting Countries (OPEC) are the most important ways in which Algeria has sought to be an exemplar to the rest of the Third World.

Emotionally and ideologically, Algeria's revolutionary heritage has brought it into a kind of spiritual communion with those nations that had similar experiences—notably, Yugoslavia, Cuba, and Viet Nam. One practical consequence of this revolutionary ardor has been the emergence of Algiers as a center for any number of Black African liberation movements, and even of fringe revolutionary groups in Latin America, the Middle East, and other parts of the world, although in recent years it has tended to discourage revolutionary "renegades" such as America's Black Panther party from establishing a political presence in the capital.

Boumedienne, unlike his predecessor, somewhat reduced the verbal encouragement for violent revolutionary activities, especially when these may have jeopardized advantageous economic relationships. Yet, given the mythology of the success of the revolution—a mythology continually being shaped into a central pillar of the new national tradition, certain predominant principles of foreign policy have remained throughout the postindependence period. These principles are nonalignment in the global struggle between the USSR and the United States, identification with the Third World, promotion of revolutionary independence movements and wars of national liberation directed against colonialism and imperialism, advocacy of African and Arab unity, an unswerving support of the Palestinians in their struggle against Israel and Zionism, and strong logistical and diplomatic backing for the Polisario guerrilla movement in its attempt to establish an independent Sahrawi Arab Democratic Republic (SADR) in the former Spanish Sahara, which is currently being occupied and administered by Morocco.

Despite nuanced changes in style and approach, Chadli Benjedid has remained faithful to the principles and foreign policy orientation established by his predecessor. Such an orientation—although more radical in words than deeds—has brought Algeria into conflict with its ideologically different neighbors. Its geopolitical competition with Morocco, especially, has led to serious disagreements involving direct armed conflict in 1963 and indirect military engagement through Algeria's support of Polisario in the Saharan war. Even after the settlement of the dispute in the Western Sahara, serious disagreement will remain, given the fundamental dissonance in attitude, style, and ultimate objectives of the two countries.

Although Tunisia's espousal of Western values and its particularly close ties with France and the United States make it ultimately suspect by Algerian decisionmakers, relations have improved markedly in recent years. Territorial disputes between the two countries have been resolved in favor of Algeria and its petroleum and gas interests. A Treaty of Friendship and Harmony was signed between the two countries in March 1983, thus formalizing a new and harmonious relationship that had been evolving since Chadli's accession to power. The treaty emphasized the historic "community of destiny" of the Maghribi world and invited other states to membership in an eventual political union—an invitation quickly and formally taken up by Mauritania in December 1983. The conclusion of a "unity" treaty between Morocco and Libya in mid-1984 has given urgency and greater significance to the Algeria-Tunisia-Mauritania arrangement.

A paradoxical feature of Algerian foreign policy is that, despite its revolutionary rhetoric, austere manner, and radical posturing, Algeria maintains direct and continuing contacts with a wide variety of different regimes. Algeria's wide range of contacts qualifies it as one of the few countries in the Third World to advocate and successfully maintain an independent position in international affairs. For example, it has been able to sustain a close military assistance relationship with the Soviet Union while simultaneously developing an extensive economic relationship with the United States. In fact, in 1976 the United States became Algeria's main trading partner, supplanting France. More dramatically, Algeria became the key negotiating party involved in the release in January 1981 of the fifty-two American diplomats held hostage at the United States Embassy in Tehran, Iran.

Despite the legacy of bitterness engendered by the revolution, Algeria still maintains close bilateral relations with France, reinforced by economic, cultural, and trading ties. At the same time, Algeria is highly sensitive to any suggestion that its independence is being undermined by its relations with France or any other power. Moreover, foreign policy rhetoric is never allowed to interfere with foreign trade dealings and international business transactions, which Algeria conducts in a highly businesslike and efficient manner, all seemingly designed to enable others to understand that its commerce and its foreign policy rhetoric are matters distinct from one another.

Bibliography

Probably the most comprehensive analysis of the complexities and dynamics of the Algerian revolutionary war fought against France from 1954 to 1962 is that of Alistair Horne, *A Savage War of Peace: Algeria, 1954–1962* (New York: Penguin Books, 1979). Paul Henissart's *Wolves in the City* (London: Rupert Hart-Davis, 1971) is a fascinating and chilling account of the last destructive, anarchic days of French colonial rule in Algeria. Martha Crenshaw Hutchinson, in *Revolutionary Terrorism: The FLN in Algeria, 1954–1962* (Stanford, Calif.: Hoover Institution Press, 1978), formulates an analytical model of terrorism that she then applies to the case of the wartime FLN. More standard accounts of that bloody struggle for independence include Edward Behr, *The Algerian Problem* (London: Hodder and Stoughton, 1961); Michael K. Clark, *Algeria in Turmoil* (New York: Grosset & Dunlap, 1960); Richard M. Brace and Joan Brace, *Algerian Voices* (Princeton, N.J.: D. Van Nostrand, 1965); Richard M. Brace and Joan Brace, *Ordeal in Algeria* (New York: D. Van Nostrand, 1960); Joan Gillespie, *Algeria* (New York: Praeger Publishers, 1960); David Gordon, *The Passing of French Algeria* (New York: Oxford University Press, 1966); and Alf Andrew Heggoy, *Insurgency and Counterinsurgency in Algeria* (Bloomington: Indiana University Press, 1972). Brief analyses of the Algerian Revolution are included in Eric R. Wolf, *Peasant Wars of the Twentieth Century* (New York: Harper & Row, 1969), and John Dunn, *Modern Revolutions* (Cambridge: Cambridge University Press,

1972). Frantz Fanon, in *The Wretched of the Earth* (New York: Grove Press, 1963), and Frantz Fanon, in *A Dying Colonialism* (New York: Grove Press, 1967), provide philosophical and highly ideological insights into the origins, causes, and consequences of the revolutionary war and its impact on natives and colonialists alike. Fanon's credo on the need for the violent transformation of man, state, and society remains a central theme in the writings of many Third World revolutionary leaders. The impact of the Algerian war on French society and politics is competently treated by Tony Smith, *The French Stake in Algeria, 1945–1962* (Ithaca, N.Y.: Cornell University Press, 1978).

Pierre Bourdieu's *The Algerians* (Boston: Beacon Press, 1962) provides an outstanding socioanthropological insight into the colonialist system and the destructive effect it had on Algerian people and society. Thomas L. Blair's *The Land to Those Who Work It: Algeria's Experiment in Workers' Management* (Garden City, N.Y.: Anchor Books–Doubleday, 1970), Ian Clegg's *Workers' Self-Management in Algeria* (New York: Monthly Review Press, 1971), and Marnia Lazreg's *The Emergence of Classes in Algeria: Colonialism and Socio-Political Change* (Boulder, Colo.: Westview Press, 1976) focus on specific socioeconomic themes and issue areas. Sid-Ahmed Baghli, in *Aspects of Cultural Policy in Algeria* (Paris: UNESCO, 1977), devotes his study to cultural policy in the Boumedienne period.

Although over a decade old, William B. Quandt's *Revolution and Political Leadership: Algeria, 1954–1968* (Cambridge, Mass.: MIT Press, 1969) remains the most authoritative study of Algerian political development at the elite level. The critical roles being played by military and other elites in independent Algeria are comprehensively analyzed in I. William Zartman's "The Algerian Army in Politics," in Claude E. Welch, Jr., ed., *Soldier and State in Africa* (Evanston, Ill.: Northwestern University Press, 1970); I. William Zartman's "Algeria: A Post-Revolutionary Elite," in Frank Tachau, ed., *Political Elites and Political Development in the Middle East* (New York: Schenkman, 1975); and John P. Entelis's "Algeria: Technocratic Rule, Military Power," in I. William Zartman et al., *Political Elites in Arab North Africa* (New York: Longman, 1982). David Ottoway and Marina Ottoway, in *Algeria: The Politics of a Socialist Revolution* (Berkeley: University of California Press, 1970), and Jean Leca, in "Algerian Socialism: Nationalism, Industrialization, and State-Building," in Helen Desfosses and Jacques Levesque, eds., *Socialism in the Third World* (New York: Praeger Publishers, 1975), describe and evaluate Algeria's socialist experiment. Arslan Humbaraci's *Algeria: A Revolution that Failed—A Political History Since 1954* (New York: Praeger Publishers, 1966) provides an informative, although at times biased, generally political history of the country since the early 1950s.

The political dynamics of the post-independence Algeria are treated in the following works: John P. Entelis, *Algeria: The Revolution Institutionalized* (Boulder, Colo.: Westview Press, 1986); John P. Entelis, *Comparative Politics of North Africa: Algeria, Morocco, and Tunisia* (Syracuse, N.Y.: Syracuse University Press, 1980); Henry F. Jackson, *The FLN in Algeria: Party Development in a Revolutionary Society* (Westport, Conn.: Greenwood Press, 1977); John R. Nellis, *The Algerian National Charter of 1976: Content, Public Reaction, and Significance* (Washington, D.C.: Georgetown University Center for Contemporary Arab Studies, 1980); and Hugh Roberts, "The Politics of Algerian Socialism," in Richard Lawless and Allan Findlay, eds., *North Africa: Contemporary Politics and Economic Development* (London: Croom Helm, 1984).

The best analyses of Algerian foreign policy are found in Robert A. Mortimer, "Global Economy and African Foreign Policy: The Algerian Model," *African Studies Review* 27, no. 1 (March 1984), pp. 1–22; Robert A. Mortimer, "Algeria and the

Politics of International Economic Reform," *Orbis* 21, no. 3 (Fall 1977), pp. 671–700; and Robert A. Mortimer, *The Third World Coalition in International Politics*, 2d ed. (New York: Praeger Publishers, 1984). The best reference work on Algeria is Harold D. Nelson, ed., *Algeria: A Country Study*, 3d ed. (Washington, D.C.: Government Printing Office, 1979). Two excellent annotated bibliographies dealing exclusively with Algeria are Alf Andrew Heggoy's *Historical Dictionary of Algeria* (Metuchen, N.J.: Scarecrow Press, 1981) and Richard I. Lawless's *Algeria* (Santa Barbara, Calif.: CLIO Press, 1980).

21

Republic of Tunisia

John P. Entelis
Mark A. Tessler

Historical Background

The French colonial experience in Tunisia, while not benign, brought less social disruption than occurred in neighboring Algeria. Under the Treaty of Ksar Said, signed on May 12, 1881, and also known as the Treaty of Bardo, the bey of Tunis agreed to a "voluntary limitation" of the external sovereignty of Tunisia for a "temporary but indefinite period." France was empowered to act in a sovereign manner in all external Tunisian affairs and in matters relating to the defense of the country. In 1883, under the terms of the Treaty of La Marsa, the French gained control over Tunisia's domestic affairs. Although the traditional hierarchy of the bey's government was preserved, a separate parallel French administration was established and quickly acquired all effective control in the state. The bey was reduced to a figurehead, with real power passing to the French resident-general.

Although no large-scale colonialization occurred, as it had in Algeria, the French administration placed the European settlers' interests first and subjected Tunisia to so-called reforms that were clearly not in the interest of the Muslim population. Administrative offices were, in theory, open to both Tunisian and European civil servants, but in practice all major posts were occupied solely by the French until after World War I. In addition, as land was bought by settlers, the dispossessed rural Muslim population sank into a destitution similar to that experienced by its Algerian counterpart. On the other hand, the French settler population remained much smaller than its counterpart in Algeria, never exceeding 7 percent of the total Tunisian population. It also penetrated the country's economic and commercial life with far less intensity. For example, the fertile and commercially prosperous area of the Sahel, along the central-eastern coast of the country, was left largely in Tunisian hands.

The French colonial experience in Tunisia also featured some relatively positive elements. In particular, it intensified the process of modernization that had already been under way for several decades. During the reign of Ahmed Bey (1837–1855), for example, the system of taxation was revised, slavery was

Tunisia

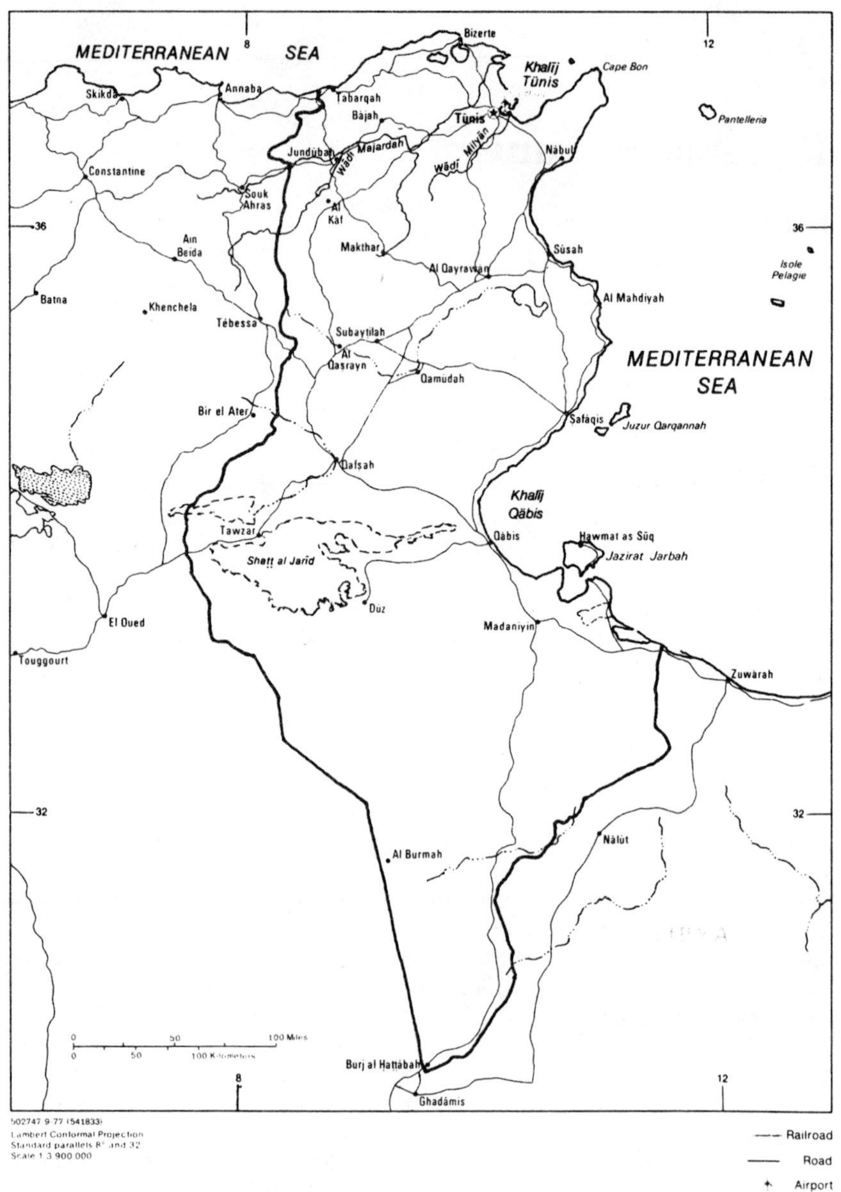
MEDITERRANEAN SEA
8
12
Bizerte
Khalīj Tūnis
Cape Bon
Skikda
Annaba
Tabarqah
Bājah
Tūnis
Pantelleria
Jundūbah
Wādī Majardah
Wādī Milyān
Nābul
Constantine
Souk Ahras
Al Kāf
36
Aïn Beida
Makthar
Sūsah
Isole Pelagie
Al Qayrawān
Batna
Khenchela
Al Mahdiyah
Tébessa
Subaytilah
Al Qasrayn
MEDITERRANEAN SEA
Qamūdah
Bir el Ater
Şafāqis
Juzur Qarqannah
Qafsah
Khalīj Qābis
Tawzar
Qābis
Ḩawmat as Sūq
Jazīrat Jarbah
Shaţţ al Jarīd
Dūz
El Oued
Madaniyīn
Touggourt
Zuwārah
32
Nālūt
Al Burmah
0 50 100 Miles
0 50 100 Kilometers
Burj al Ḩaţţābah
Ghadāmis
502747 9-77 (541833)
Lambert Conformal Projection
Standard parallels 8° and 32
Scale 1:3,900,000
Railroad
Road
Airport

abolished, military installations were established, and the production of armaments was commenced. In addition, important experiments were made in the area of education, designed to acquaint Tunisians with the ways of Europe. In the 1870s, on the eve of the French invasion, Kheireddine Pacha, premier of Tunisia under Ahmed's successor, expanded reformist activities. The administration of justice was reorganized, and development projects were initiated. Kheireddine himself considered the expansion of modern education, as exemplified by the creation of Sadiki College, to be his most important accomplishment.

These reforms did not strengthen Tunisia enough to enable it to repel the invasion of the French in 1881. Rather, because local government was relatively ordered and effective, the French were able to rule by discreet and indirect means. The French military presence, so pronounced in Algeria and Morocco, was virtually absent in Tunisia.

France's contribution to Tunisia's modernization was perhaps greatest in the field of education. Despite certain qualitative limitations, the French-instituted bilingual system of Arabic and French language instruction, which was discouraged in Algeria and never really developed during the brief protectorate period in Morocco, enabled Tunisia's educated elite to learn bilingual cultural and language skills, reinforced by university training in France. These skills were used to great advantage in the nationalist struggle for independence and in the subsequent modernization of the country.

Tunisia was the first of the three North African countries to be influenced by modern nationalism. In 1905 the Young Tunisian movement was established by members of the young Europeanized professional middle class of Tunis. Borrowing from the Young Turk movement of the decaying Ottoman Empire, the Young Tunisians represented the reformist and liberal aspirations of the first generation of North African nationalists. The demands they made were for better education, a combination of French and Arab cultures, and access to government by Tunisians. But they commanded neither national support nor a mass following, and their demands were framed within the limits of the protectorate. Most sought to modify but not to overthrow French colonial rule, and some even welcomed the French as allies in their struggle to modernize and reform traditional institutions and practices.

The achievement of at least nominal independence in eastern Arab countries after World War I and the example of the nationalist movement in Egypt inspired Tunisians with a greater national consciousness. The Liberal Constitutional party, more popularly known as the Destour (the Arabic word for constitution), was organized in February 1920. The party's founder, Shaykh Abdelaziz al-Thaalibi, was also one of the founders of the prewar Young Tunisian movement.

The emergence of the Destour party marked a new moment in Tunisian nationalism—that of traditionalistic anticolonialism. In contrast to the bicultural orientation of the Young Tunisians, the Destour called for greater emphasis on Arab culture and Islam and criticized the French for introducing an alien cultural order, one they declared to be "superfluous" in Tunisia. Composed primarily of middle-class urbanites, the Destour lacked the force of a mass movement and functioned as an essentially bourgeois pressure group. Nevertheless, the party provided an ideological foundation for opposition to French colonialism, and, over the next decade, it recruited many well-educated young men who were eventually to take control of the nationalist movement. In March 1934 these young men broke away to form the Neo-Destour party.

The principal force behind the new party's creation was a thirty-one-year-old French-educated lawyer, Habib Bourguiba, who eventually led Tunisia to independence and, in the process, earned the label "father of his country." In his socioeconomic background, education, and professional training, Habib Bourguiba exemplified the entire Neo-Destour leadership.

Bourguiba was born of middle-class parents in 1903 at Monastir in the Sahel and was educated as a lawyer at the Sorbonne. Like many of his generation who were trained in French universities in the 1920s, he adopted a populist mode of nationalist consciousness. Bourguiba and his contemporaries inherited from the Young Tunisians a strong faith in liberal France and in its economic and cultural innovations, and from the old Destour they stole the banner of anticolonialism. What they reacted against was not the actual French presence but, rather, the relationship of subordination it implied.

Unlike the members of old Destour, the Neo-Destourians were secular nationalists. Nevertheless, as they turned to the masses throughout the country for support, they were not opposed to using Islamic symbols as instruments of political mobilization. The Neo-Destour was committed to both national independence and modernization via extensive grass-roots organization and political education. Unchallenged as it was by other nationalist groups, occasional French attempts at repression, exile of leaders, and other paralegal means of suppression failed to impede the party's efforts to construct a mass movement.

The nationalist movement did not resort to violence in Tunisia until 1954, when groups of guerrillas, or *fellaghas,* began to operate in the countryside, thereby paralyzing nearly seventy thousand French troops. With its hands full in Algeria, Morocco, and Indochina, the French government under the premiership of Pierre Mendès-France finally offered full internal autonomy to Tunisia in June 1955. Less than a year later, on March 20, 1956, Tunisian independence was formally declared.

Post-independence politics in Tunisia have been dominated by two overwhelming forces: the charisma and popular appeal of Habib Bourguiba, the country's only president for almost thirty years of independence; and the political supremacy of the Destourian Socialist party (PSD) over all other national organizations and governmental institutions. Despite his regime's increasingly authoritarian cast in recent years, the "Supreme Warrior" provided national unity and political stability in the years following independence. Indeed, it is not an exaggeration to credit Bourguiba's authoritarian presence and manipulative skills with the evolution of Tunisia into a relatively stable, effective, and developed polity.

There are six distinct historical phases in post-independence Tunisia. In the first period, 1955–1959, Bourguiba overcame internal challenges and consolidated his position. On June 3, 1955, he signed a convention with France proclaiming Tunisia's internal autonomy. The secretary-general of the party, Salah Ben Youssef, denounced the autonomy convention with France as a "step backward" and openly attacked Bourguiba. Instead, Ben Youssef called for immediate Tunisian independence within the framework of pan-Arabism. Ben Youssef had the support of strongly religious and conservative groups, as well as of urban elements that sympathized with his espousal of a radical Arab nationalism drawing inspiration from Nasserism in Egypt. On the other hand, Bourguiba, who represented moderation and an attachment to specifically Tunisian (as opposed to broader Arab-Islamic) virtues and possibilities, had the support of educated, Western-trained elites from the Sahel and Tunis.

In the bitter and personal confrontation that took place between these two charismatic leaders, Bourguiba prevailed because of the overwhelming support of the party and the crucial backing of the trade-union movement, headed by Bourguiba's ally, Ahmed Ben Salah. Ben Youssef organized a guerrilla insurrection in the south, but this was quashed with the help of French troops. He then fled to Libya in 1956 and was later assassinated in 1961 in Frankfurt, Germany. Although Ben Youssef's opposition failed, it constituted a severe challenge to Bourguiba and the Neo-Destour, and one of its legacies is that it helped to crystallize the authoritarian manner in which the new regime often exercised power.

The termination of the Ben Youssef challenge and the granting of political independence in March 1956 did not completely eliminate internal differences. A conflict between Bourguiba and his former supporter, Ben Salah, subsequently emerged. Bourguiba's political objectives were to unify the party on the broadest possible base, to secure for it a virtual monopoly of power, and to avoid risking national unity or foreign investment by radical economic change. Ben Salah, on the other hand, envisioned the General Union of Tunisian Workers (UGTT) as the national instrument for social and economic transformation. He also spoke of the nationalization of all resources and proclaimed the need for a socialist approach to development. Ben Salah was removed as head of the union and replaced by Ahmed Tlili, who shared Bourguiba's liberal and reformist political philosophy.

Thus, in the first years of autonomy and independence, Bourguiba was able to establish his supremacy not only in the party but also in the formal machinery of the state. In April 1956 he became prime minister, leading a government in which sixteen of the seventeen ministers belonged to the Neo-Destour. In July of the following year, Bourguiba became head of state as well, when his government abolished the powerless and unpopular monarchy of the bey and proclaimed Tunisia a republic.

A new constitution, promulgated in June 1959, established Tunisia as an Islamic republic within the greater Maghrib, with Arabic as its official language. In confirming the paramount authority of the president, the constitution declared the government responsible to the president rather than to the legislature. In the strong presidential system that emerged, Bourguiba simply replaced the bey as chief of state while simultaneously remaining at the head of the only effective political party. It is significant that the most important reform legislation enacted during this period was introduced by presidential decree and passed without legislative review.

On November 8, 1959, Tunisia held its first elections under the new constitution. President Bourguiba ran unopposed, and all ninety National Assembly candidates were backed by the Neo-Destour. Thus, by 1959 Bourguiba and his Neo-Destour party had placed their indelible imprint on the Tunisian political system.

The second period, 1960–1964, was highlighted by a series of internal and external crises and by the regime's gradual shift from reliance on the private sector to reliance on the public sector as the vanguard of economic development and modernization. In July 1961 fighting broke out between Tunisian and French troops over the Tunisian demand for France's evacuation of the large naval base at Bizerte, on Tunisia's northern coast. After nearly two years, the French departed in March 1963. The confrontation enhanced the prestige and popularity of Bourguiba in the eyes of his own people and the world community. Nonetheless, an assassination plot against Bourguiba was discovered in December 1962. Several junior army officers, including former officers in the bey's forces, a member of the presidential guard, and a former military commander, were arrested, convicted, and executed. Following attempts to expand its influence among students and workers, the Tunisian Communist party was banned in the subsequent year. Finally, relations with Algeria were strained as a result of charges that the newly independent country had aided Youssefists in the coup attempt.

In the economic realm, Bourguiba's policies seemed noticeably inadequate. During the first half-decade of independence, they had proved unsuccessful both in attracting significant foreign investment and in preventing a serious general decline in the economy. As a result, the government turned to state planning. Its goals were to encourage economic growth, to break up the rigidities of social stratification, to equalize opportunities, and to increase social mobility. Toward this end, in May 1964, the Tunisian National Assembly enacted legislation authorizing the expropriation of all foreign-owned land.

The nationalization legislation also signaled a new political commitment to socialism. In October 1964 the Neo-Destour party officially changed its name to the Destourian Socialist party (PSD) in order to emphasize this commitment. A month later there were new elections. Bourguiba again ran unopposed, and the PSD, which was the only party to present candidates, won all the seats in the National Assembly.

During the 1964–1969 period, the chief issue dominating internal politics was the effort to collectivize agriculture. Agrarian policy was enacted by the minister of finance and planning, Ahmed Ben Salah, who had returned to government in 1961 after a five-year absence. Ben Salah, now fully backed by Bourguiba and the party, formulated an ambitious ten-year plan of economic development and reform, based almost completely on state control and initiative in industry and agriculture. The core of Ben Salah's scheme was a system of agricultural cooperatives. The cooperative system was to be developed primarily on the large nationalized French estates in the north of the country but was also to involve the small landholdings of many Tunisian farmers.

Many peasants opposed incorporation into the new cooperatives. The cooperative scheme was also seen as a threat by larger Tunisian landowners, and, since many of these individuals wielded influence in government circles, opposition soon became more directly political. Finally, mismanagement became an issue as productivity levels remained low, despite large subsidies. As a result, in September 1969 Ben Salah was shifted to the Ministry of Education and his agricultural plans were abandoned. He was later arrested and in May 1970 was sentenced to ten years of hard labor on assorted charges of financial mismanagement and other abuses and irregularities. He escaped to Europe in February 1973 and remains a critic of the regime. More important, the socialist orientation he had introduced to the nation was abandoned.

Bourguiba was chronically ill during this period and frequently out of the country for treatment. In fact, the ouster of Ben Salah was in part the result of a struggle for power among Ben Salah and other political elites who sought to position themselves to succeed Bourguiba. The Ben Salah affair also brought a serious challenge to Bourguiba, in that the president was indirectly implicated because of the political support and warm personal encouragement he had earlier given to Ben Salah. Nevertheless, the president's control of the party and the government remained secure, as reflected in the 1969 presidential and National Assembly elections. Moreover, within a few years Bourguiba had regained his health sufficiently to return to active participation in political life.

The 1970–1974 period witnessed a brief reemergence of liberalism as Bourguiba sought to reestablish his popularity and prestige and to stabilize the country's economic and political systems. Several former high government officials were reappointed to important positions in the party and the government. These included Ahmed Mestiri, the leader of a Tunis-based liberal and social democratic faction; Habib Achour, who returned as head of the UGTT; Muhammad Masmoudi, who became minister of foreign affairs; and Bahi Ladgham, who served briefly as prime minister before being replaced by Bourguiba's close ally and a respected economist, Hedi Nouira.

The government's sensitivity to charges of authoritarianism was clearly demonstrated at the 1971 PSD Congress in Monastir, where the regime's characteristic balance between authority and liberalism tipped toward liberalism and reconciliation. Discussion was free and open, and democratic in spirit and practice. Bourguiba, however, chose his own men for key positions in the party's political bureau, ignoring the general sentiment at the congress in favor of movement toward competitive politics.

The experiment in liberalism lost its momentum in the years that followed, and at the PSD Congress of September 1974, also held in Monastir, it came to an end. The delegates unanimously acclaimed Bourguiba as party president for life and called for a constitutional amendment to make him president for the duration of the republic. The Congress also established a system by which the president named the members of the party's political bureau. In December 1974 the new National Assembly voted by acclamation to permit Bourguiba to remain president for life "as an exceptional measure and in recognition of services rendered." The measure made the premier, Hedi Nouira at this time, the automatic successor in the event of the president's death or incapacity.

The expectation that Tunisia's increasing political sophistication would eventually lead to a multiparty political system was, for the time being at least, rejected by Bourguiba and his party deputies. Although basic political order had been maintained and popular support for the regime continued, power was exercised in an increasingly authoritarian manner, especially against students and other outspoken leftist critics of the regime.

The period that followed, 1975–1979, was marked by two interrelated trends. First, the PSD continued to become more politically and ideologically monolithic and, at the same time, lost much of its early effectiveness as a vehicle of mass mobilization. Second, important new political actors emerged, some of whom operated within the established political system and some of whom challenged the dominant political order from without. The overall result was a weakened PSD and an increasingly heterogeneous and conflict-ridden political environment.

Bourguiba and his new prime minister, Hedi Nouira, showed little interest in the policies of social and cultural reform that had been a hallmark of Tunisian political life until the fall of Ben Salah. In addition, with concern for social mobilization diminished, they placed much less emphasis on popular participation in the grass-roots activities of the PSD. Proclaiming that they were *evolutionaries*, not revolutionaries, Bourguiba and Nouira devoted themselves to expanding the private sector of the economy, dismantling most of the nation's remaining cooperatives, and aggressively encouraging foreign investment.

Under these conditions, the machinery of the PSD was permitted to atrophy. Mass political activity diminished sharply, and the party lost much of its dynamism at the local level. As efforts to foster popular awareness and participation had virtually ceased, most local PSD committees now did little more than dispense patronage in order to retain the support of area notables. Moreover, although political freedoms had been limited in the past, the new regime was even less tolerant of dissent and more narrowly tied to a single ideological tendency. Bourguiba showed little inclination to rehabilitate former opponents or to encourage a diversity of views among those willing to work within the PSD, something that had not always been the case in the past.

New political actors and challenges to the government emerged in this political environment. Ben Salah established the socialist-oriented Movement of Popular Unity (MUP) from his European base. He accused Bourguiba and Nouira of favoring the privileged classes and of ceasing to work for the Tunisian people. The MUP was banned in Tunisia, however, and in 1975 and 1976 many leftists sympathetic to Ben Salah were arrested. Then, in the summer of 1977, thirty-three members of the MUP were arrested and tried for threatening state security and defaming the president.

The liberals, who had helped to oust Ben Salah and had been a major force within the PSD in the early 1970s, fared somewhat better. But their fate, too, reflected the regime's continued opposition to political pluralism. Led by Ahmed Mestiri, former minister of the interior, the liberals formed the Movement of Social Democrats (MDS) in 1976, declaring that a single-party regime was "no longer adapted to the needs and aspirations of the people." The June 1978 request by Mestiri and the liberals for authorization to establish an independent social democratic party was denied, however. The MDS was permitted to publish newspapers in Arabic and French, although these were sometimes temporarily shut down for criticizing the government.

The political force that challenged the government more seriously was the General Union of Tunisian Workers, the labor confederation that had been an ally of the PSD after independence and was now led by Habib Achour. Following the strikes in 1976, the government and the UGTT in 1977 negotiated a "social contract" that gave industrial workers pay raises linked to inflation. But labor unrest continued, and the government was especially disturbed by the presence at demonstrations of many unemployed young people, most of whom were not UGTT members. Some government officials argued that disturbances were an understandable response to economic and social dislocations; but Nouira took a hard line and Bourguiba supported him, leading to a major cabinet reshuffle. The government also harassed the union and encouraged attacks on some of its offices.

The UGTT's response came in January 1978. First, Achour resigned his position on the PSD political bureau and central committee. Then the union challenged the government directly by calling a general strike for the 26th. Although not encouraged by the UGTT, extensive rioting in Tunis and several other cities accompanied the strike, demonstrating the anger of the urban poor. At least one hundred persons were killed as the army moved in to restore order. Hundreds more were arrested, including Achour and thirty other UGTT leaders, all of whom were charged with subversion. Thereafter, January 26th, 1978, became known as Jeudi Noir, or Black Thursday. Achour was sentenced to prison and, after Bourguiba pardoned him in 1979, remained under house arrest until 1981. The UGTT, for its part, moderated opposition to the government and appointed a new secretary-general.

Militant Islamic groups emerged in the 1970s, constituting yet another faction of the increasingly complex and conflict-ridden political scene. An early Muslim group was the Association for the Protection of the Koran, founded in 1970 and granted legal status as a cultural group. The dominant faction by the late 1970s was the more explicitly political Mouvement de la Tendance Islamique (MTI), which was denied legal status by the government. One manifestation of the Islamic tendency's opposition to the government was its attack during Ramadan 1977 on a union-supported Sfax café frequented by nonbelievers. Although most militant Islamic leaders counseled against such violence, they nonetheless spoke out forcefully in opposition to the regime and its policies. For example, Hassan Ghodbani, the young imam of an important Tunis mosque, stated in 1979 that "we stand against Bourguiba's pretension of being the Supreme Combattant. No one is greater than another unless he is God." Even though the government by the mid-1970s had become more conservative, it was visibly concerned about growing popular support for anti-establishment Islamic groups. By the early 1980s it had arrested many MTI leaders.

The current period, which began in 1980, has finally seen some halting movement toward the creation of a multiparty political system. More important, however, have been the continuation and intensification of political trends that emerged in the middle and late 1970s. The PSD remains dominant although its vitality and institutionalization continue to erode. At the same time, the emergence of rival groups and new challenges has contributed further to the complexity of the political scene. Finally, deepening public anger over political and economic grievances has brought new violence, of a scope and intensity unprecedented in Tunisia and the effects of which are still being felt.

Early in 1980 Prime Minister Nouira suffered a stroke. Bourguiba replaced him with Mohammed Mzali, a former minister of education, and Mzali's government moved tentatively in the direction of political liberalization. Indeed, such movement had begun in 1979. Even though Nouira and the PSD had formally rejected the idea of a multiparty system, the National Assembly in that year amended the electoral code to permit two candidates to compete for each seat in parliamentary elections. In 1980 Mzali released most political prisoners. He also brought into his cabinet a member of the MDS and several former ministers who had lost their positions in 1977 for opposing Nouira's hard line against labor. Early in 1981 amnesty was granted to all members of the MUP except Ben Salah, who remained in exile.

At a special PSD Congress in April 1981, Bourguiba declared that non-PSD candidates would be permitted to participate in legislative elections, scheduled for November, and that any group receiving 5 percent of the vote would be recognized as a political party. Furthermore, in July the Tunisian Communist party (PCT) was officially recognized and exempted from the 5 percent rule. The PCT and the MDS both presented candidates in the 1981 elections, as did a Tunis-based faction of the MUP. Sometimes known as MUP-2, the new faction distanced itself from Ben Salah's group in Europe and was headed by Mohammed Bel Hadj Amor. Only the MTI was excluded from the limited opening given to groups seeking to challenge the PSD. None of these factions won even a single seat in Parliament, however. The PSD, now operating with UGTT in an electoral front, won 95 percent of the popular vote and all 136 seats in the assembly.

The MDS and Amor's faction of the MUP were recognized by the government in November 1983, thus continuing the trend toward political pluralism. But some within the PSD opposed this trend, and, in any event, many observers saw relatively little substance in what had been accomplished. Noting the weakness of groups outside the PSD, as well as claims of irregularities in the 1981 balloting, some concluded that Mzali was not seriously interested in multiparty politics. He was seen instead as pursuing a strategy designed not only to improve Tunisia's public image but, more important, to undermine rivals for leadership inside the PSD. Among his major opponents for influence within the party were Driss Guiga, minister of the interior and an opponent of multiparty politics, and Mohammed Sayah, a former PSD secretary-general who had supported Nouira's hard line in 1978. Mzali's position as heir apparent was also challenged by

Bourguiba's wife, Wassila, who has used her influence on behalf of several of the prime minister's rivals.

The result of these developments was an increasingly complex and uncertain political scene. New actors had appeared, but the PSD remained dominant and had yet to permit movement toward genuine power-sharing. Moreover, inside the PSD, Mzali and others were increasingly absorbed in intraparty battles. Some charged they were neglecting the nation as a consequence. Finally, although Bourguiba remained politically active, he turned 80 in 1983 and his advancing age added to the existing concern over the country's political future. One outcome of this situation was continuing political drift. Another was growing popular frustration, which had already been visible in the Black Thursday disturbances of 1978 and which manifested itself dramatically in widespread public rioting in late 1983 and early 1984.

The new disturbances began in the oases of the south, which are among the poorest communities in Tunisia. They were sparked by the government's announcement on December 29 of a rise in the price of semolina. On New Year's day a rise in the price of bread was announced as well, and this in turn brought a new wave of rioting. Disturbances now broke out in major towns in the south, including Kasserine, Gafsa, Mitlaoui, and Gabes. By January 3 rioting had also occurred in Sfax, the country's second largest city, and in Tunis, as well as in other urban centers. Order was not restored until January 5, by which time security forces had killed over 150 persons and wounded hundreds more.

At the height of the rioting, thousands of students, workers, and unemployed slumdwellers roamed the streets, shouting antigovernment slogans and attacking symbols of authority and wealth. Thousands more shouted encouragement from open windows and rooftops. Protestors attacked cars and buses, tore up street signs, looted and set fire to shops, and, in some areas, attacked public buildings. They also fought police and military units, which had brought in tanks, armored personnel carriers, and even helicopters to repulse the rioters.

The immediate cause of these "bread riots" was removed on January 6, when Bourguiba went on television to announce that price rises would be rescinded. After a week of mounting violence, the price rollback brought spontaneous popular celebrations and the country gradually returned to normal. Nevertheless, the scope and intensity of the rioting showed that public anger was based on much more than the price of bread. Indeed, the most intense anger appeared to be directed not only at the government but also at the consumption-oriented middle and upper classes, population categories perceived to be prospering at a time when the economic circumstances of the masses were steadily deteriorating and the government was asking the poor to tighten their belts even more.

Although dramatic changes probably will not occur until Bourguiba dies, Tunisians are waiting to see what kind of political system emerges from this environment. If the PSD remains moribund but continues to impose itself and preside over a hollow pluralism, there will be difficulty ahead. Popular frustration will continue to mount, and one or several of the party's institutional rivals may challenge the government by extralegal means. Whether this challenge occurs or not, the political scene will be tense. Alternatively, if the PSD permits genuine competition for power, the years ahead could bring progressive political change. One result would be the evolution over the course of several elections of an effective multiparty system, in which the PSD would be one of several major parties. Another result might be continued PSD dominance, but that would require the party to rejuvinate itself and demonstrate its leadership ability in an arena where voters have meaningful alternatives.

Political Environment

Tunisia's political culture has been influenced by a distinct and historically legitimized tradition of national unity, which also gives the country an important advantage in the quest for nation building. There are both geopolitical and demographic dimensions to this unity. With respect to the former, the geographical basis of modern Tunisia appeared in its rough outlines in Roman times, and, with few exceptions, the area has been ruled as a unified whole since that time. The various dynasties that governed the country possessed centralized and cohesive administrative networks that, for the most part, extended to the whole of the territory. Thus, even though such dynasties were often nominally subservient to the authority of a foreign power, such as the Ottoman sultan, Tunisia's borders remained constant and the state gained legitimacy in the eyes of those living within it.

The demographic dimension is based on the absence of significant ethnic and cultural cleavages. Virtually all Tunisians are Arabs and Sunni Muslims. In contrast to Algeria and Morocco, Tunisia's Berber-speaking population today numbers no more than 2 to 3 percent. Until recently Tunisia had a flourishing Jewish community; but Jews, too, never exceeded 3 percent of the population. Finally, Tunisia has historically had far fewer tribal divisions than other countries in the Maghrib. All of these factors give the Tunisian population a degree of homogeneity that is not only rare in today's world but, despite some vestigial regionalism, also frees it from the problems of ethnic and cultural pluralism that plague so many developing societies.

Bourguiba and the Neo-Destour brought to independent Tunisia a specific set of beliefs about modernization and development. These included a commitment to balancing Tunisia's Arab and Islamic legacy with what they called the country's Mediterranean personality. Drawing inspiration from Tunisian history dating back to the country's incorporation into the Carthaginian and Roman empires, this process involved, after 1956, a simultaneous commitment on the part of the ruling elite both to increased Arabization and to the construction of a genuinely bicultural (Arabo-Islamic and Franco-European) normative order.

Bourguiba and his associates also placed great emphasis on the role and responsibilities of the individual citizen in promoting national development. This emphasis was reflected in the particular importance attached by the regime to education and social mobilization. Formal and informal socialization processes were set in motion, with a view toward fostering new values and behavior patterns among the populace. The president's goal was to carry out a "psychological revolution" that would transform people and, in the process, restructure social and human relationships in a way that would make modernity possible. As defined by Bourguiba himself, the objective was to make each Tunisian "a good citizen, capable of initiative, eager to learn and cooperate, so the battle against underdevelopment will be won."

The concept of guided democracy was another component of Bourguiba's political philosophy. Until the country's psychological revolution is accomplished and the nation possesses an enlightened and politically mature citizenry, a dedicated, competent, and progressive-minded elite must assume leadership and exercise control of the state.

The kinds of policies and programs that characterized Tunisia during the first decade and a half of independence reflected these values and objectives. They gave the country a reputation for innovation, bold reform, and progressive social engineering that has not entirely faded, despite the fact that, as discussed, the ideological character of Tunisian political life has narrowed and become more conservative during the last decade or so. Moreover, these policies and programs helped to shape a post-independence generation of educated Tunisians, whose political weight is only beginning to be felt and whose contribution to the nation's political culture will become visible in the years ahead.

The reforms introduced by the regime touched on many areas. In 1956 a new Personal Status Code was enacted. Designed, in part, in the context of a larger campaign to promote women's emancipation, it replaced Quranic law in the areas of marriage, divorce, and childbearing. The code made Tunisia the first Arab country to outlaw polygamy. In 1956 and 1957 the government nationalized Muslim landed estates (*habous*), arguing that they were controlled by religious leaders who failed to encourage their rational exploitation. These lands were later redistributed, taking account of the rights of both traditional beneficiaries and nonowning tenants. In 1958 a new bilingual educational system was put in place. Attention was given to the increased use of Arabic, but, from the third grade on, French was the language of instruction of many subjects. The newly established University of Tunis taught most of its courses in French, although plans were also laid for increased Arabization in higher education. In 1960 Bourguiba began a campaign against the traditional observance of Ramadan, the Muslim holy month during which believers fast from sunrise to sunset. He argued that fasting during Ramadan decreased economic productivity. He also claimed to be respecting Islamic principles, given that Muslims are not required to fast during periods of war and, as the president insisted, that Tunisia was engaged in a war against underdevelopment.

The Neo-Destour was an effective political organization during these years, involving the masses in its programs of change. Members of the party's approximately 1,250 territorial and professional units met often to discuss national problems and raise public awareness. The party performed important regulatory and distribution functions at the local level too, helping citizens to solve personal problems and dispensing patronage. All of these activities built loyalty to the political system and helped to foster popular support for its reforms. The party claimed to have 400,000 active members by 1965, and auxiliary organizations, such as the National Union of Tunisian Women and the National Union of Tunisian Students, were also active in mobilizing and politicizing the populace.

A major effort was made in the field of education, with annual allocations in this area regularly absorbing 25 to 30 percent of the state budget. In the decade following independence, literacy climbed from 15 to 35–40 percent, the proportion of primary school-aged children attending class grew from 25 to 60–70 percent, and the proportion completing high school rose from 3 to almost 30 percent. As indicated, the explicit goals of this investment in education were to create a human-resource base for development, to train a loyal and politically responsible citizenry, and to instill in the nation's youth a respect for Arab-Islamic civilization free from blind obedience to outmoded traditions.

As a result of these efforts, Tunisia by 1960 was third among Arab countries in the proportion of children attending school. By 1965 it had moved into second place, behind Lebanon. The regime also took care to see that women as well as men shared in the expansion of education. The proportion of girls in school rose steadily during this period, climbing from less than 30 percent at independence to over 40 percent a decade later. Programs were also set up to offer vocational training to students who terminated their education without completing high school; and, again, professional development centers were set up for both men and women.

Although serious opposition was not tolerated in this dynamic but centralized political environment, Bourguiba's exercise of power during these early years was neither totalitarian nor directed primarily at personal rather than national advancement. The president consulted widely on important policy matters and permitted senior officials to exchange ideas vigorously. He also addressed the people in countless speeches and rehabilitated former opponents willing to work with him in the party. Meaningful competition sometimes existed at nonelite levels too, as local officials struggled with one another and with the party hierarchy. Finally, there was at least some validity (though exaggerated) to the government's claim that its opposition was directed principally at those who opposed change in order to preserve their privileges and at the reactionaries who threatened the nation's revolution. Thus, despite some absues of power, the government was genuinely committed to far-reaching social change and was highly popular with the masses.

A political counterculture began to emerge in the 1970s, accompanying and reinforced by changes in the ideological orientation of the top elite and the increasing authoritarianism of the government. These new trends, one expression of which is growing public support for militant Islamic movements, reflect the unfulfilled expectations of an increasingly mobilized populace and the intensification of economic problems and inequities. Even younger Tunisians, educated and socialized during the reformist period that followed independence, are in many cases losing faith in the vision and strategy of modernization articulated by Bourguiba and the Neo-Destour. This is particularly true of young people whose social origins are modest and of those whose education did not go much beyond primary school. Among the complaints of such individuals are these: (1) A bicultural orientation limits opportunities for advancement among persons from traditional milieux whose familiarity with the French language and culture is limited, and (2) rapid modernization intensifies competition for jobs and status and increases the relative deprivation of those who are unable to seize the new opportunities being created.

Conscious of the declining popularity of Western-inspired images and symbols, the ruling elite in recent years has sought to invoke Arab and Islamic symbols as a means of buttressing its rule. For the most part, the Bourguibist system has managed to integrate successfully Tunisia's Arab-Muslim identity with a secular, although not necessarily Western, notion of Tunisian nationalism. Nevertheless, with the fading of the political norms that prevailed in Tunisia in the 1950s and 1960s with the rise throughout the Arab world of popular opposition to models of development based on either capitalism or socialism, and with Tunisia's first post-independence generation now reaching adulthood and entering the mainstream of national life, Tunisian political culture is at present in a time of transition.

Economic Conditions

From 1956 to 1961 the government pursued a liberal economic, laissez-faire policy. However, the results of private investment and initiative were disappointing, largely owing to the exodus of the resources Tunisia most needed—capital and skills—as the French departed.

In 1961 the Tunisian leadership, faced with a deteriorating economic situation, assigned Ben Salah the task of developing a planned economy, with strict controls ensuring protected internal markets as well as a fixed exchange rate and currency regulation. A ten-year developmental perspective (1962–1971) was then drafted, the objectives of which were to implement Destourian socialism, especially its development component. The first three-year (1962–1965) and four-year (1966–1970) plans set goals in four broad categories: (1) decolonization; (2) reform of economic structures, including industrialization; (3) human development, including education, the training of cadres, and the fight against illiteracy and unemployment; and (4) the generation of internal investment, designed to lessen the dependence on foreign assistance. Most of Ben Salah's objectives were unrealistic, however, since they required expenditures and investment disproportionate to the economic capability of the country.

The most distinctive feature of Tunisian economic policy in the 1960s was the promotion and imposition of a system of agricultural and commercial cooperatives. The intention was that cooperatives should not only play an important political and social role in the development of the country but also contribute to the solution of economic problems. Yet the socialist experiment was discontinued in 1969, mainly because of economic mismanagement and widespread opposition to agricultural cooperatives among the rural middle class.

Tunisia's experiment in socialism was replaced by the reestablishment of liberal economic policies. The new regime of Prime Minister Nouira emphasized the need for greater foreign private investment, in part as a means of creating much-needed employment. An April 1972 law, for example, gave major fiscal advantages to foreign companies producing primarily for export, and a 1974 law provided for similar incentives based on the number of jobs created. In its effort to attract foreign enterprises, Tunisia emphasized the availability of cheap labor and the relative absence of social conflict. Most of Nouira's economic policies have remained in force under the Mzali regime.

Economic performance improved in the 1970s. Aggregate GDP increased about 7 percent annually between 1973 and 1976 and even more between 1977 and 1980. Some gave credit to the laissez-faire orientation of the Nouira government and its pursuit of foreign investment. Others argued that Tunisia was benefiting from earlier investments in education and reform. They also pointed out that in the 1970s Tunisia had begun to benefit from the sale of petroleum resources, which by 1980 accounted for over half of total exports. Growth rates declined after 1980. Nevertheless, with per capita income now exceeding US$1,000, the country's overall economic position is far better than it was at the end of the Ben Salah era.

Despite these gains, however, Tunisia faces serious economic problems. First, aggregate growth notwithstanding, productivity is low as evidenced both in the structure of exports and imports and in the distribution of the GDP. With the exception of textiles, which account for about 14 percent of sales abroad, major exports are raw materials. Two sectors are dominant. One is based on phosphates, the price of which has been depressed in recent years. But the more important sector is petroleum, the price of which is also declining and whose importance for Tunisia will diminish further because of limited reserves. Indeed, unless new discoveries are made, the country will be a net importer of petroleum by 1990. Other sources of foreign currency are tourism and remittances from Tunisians working abroad. Neither source is indicative of productive capacity, however; nor does either produce enough additional revenue to keep Tunisia's foreign debt from climbing.

On the domestic side, the position of manufacturing in GDP has increased only slightly, from 8 percent in 1961 to 14 percent in 1983. Even more discouraging is an almost 50 percent decline in the relative position of agriculture during this period, from 24 to 13 percent of GDP. As a result, Tunisia must spend increasing sums for the importation of food stuffs. Petroleum also accounts for a considerable share of imports, since the country exports high-quality crude and then purchases refined products of lesser quality for domestic use.

Second, growth rates are offset by population increases and rising expectations. The population has been growing by about 2.6 percent a year, meaning that 55 percent of the country's citizens are under the age of 20 and the number of job-seekers is increasing every year. Because conditions in the countryside drive hundreds of thousands of people into urban slums, the annual urban growth rate exceeds 4 percent. As a result, unemployment is about 20 percent. It is even higher among young people, and the situation is getting worse; the government has chronically fallen short of its targets for the expansion of employment opportunities. Other problems are a growing shortage of adequate housing, poverty that requires the government to spend precious resources on subsidies for basic commodities, and aggregate needs that require using foreign-currency reserves to import food and energy.

Third, the distribution of available resources is highly skewed. The gap between rich and poor, though not as large as in some developing countries, has increased appreciably in recent years. On the one hand, luxurious villas and apartment complexes are multiplying in some areas, as are other visible signs of wealth and consumption. On the other, poverty is growing too, with an increasing divide between regularly employed workers who are protected by trade unions and social legislation and those who work on an intermittent or seasonal basis, in the informal sector, or perhaps not at all. The former group received substantial pay raises following the strikes and disturbances of 1978. Members of the latter group, whose material conditions are deteriorating, feel powerless and resent the fact that the nation's economic burden is not distributed equitably.

Government economic policy addresses some of these problems, but success, to date, has been limited. For example, investment in agriculture has increased, with the goal of improving both self-sufficiency in food production and economic opportunities in the rural areas. Nevertheless, owing partly to the onset of drought in 1982, the projected growth in the agricultural sector has not been realized. The current plan also allocates more resources for manufacturing, in order to create jobs and increase exports. Again, however, targets have not been met.

Finding the money to implement economic policies is another major problem. The loss of oil revenues, currently projected for 1990, will be a major blow to the economy. Tunisia could also be hurt by a reduction in opportunities for its citizens to work in France and Libya, the consequences of which would be heightened unemployment as well as reduced revenues. The current development plan proposes increased revenues from tourism, phosphates, and foreign investment, but it is unlikely that these revenues will be sufficient to meet Tunisia's needs.

Political Structure

Tunisia's major political institutions—the presidency, the cabinet, the National Assembly, and the PSD—all bear the unmistakable imprint of Habib Bourguiba, who is both head of government and head of the party. The president exercises great power. He is guardian of the constitution and has the authority to appoint his government, which is directly responsible to him. He drafts the general policy of the country and controls its execution. The president is also designated commander-in-chief of the armed forces and makes all military appointments. Finally, with the agreement of the National Assembly, the president has the authority to ratify treaties, declare war, and make peace.

The president's initiative to draft legislation has priority over that of National Assembly members. He also ratifies legislation and has the power of veto, subject to a two-thirds overriding majority that, during the time the post-independence constitution and assembly have been in existence, has never been invoked. According to the constitution, the president may convene special sessions of the Parliament, issue orders in council when the assembly is in recess (constitutionally limited to six months of the year), and take exceptional measures in times of crisis. Though presidential tenure was originally limited by the constitution to three five-year terms, a constitutional amendment passed by the National Assembly in December 1974 named Habib Bourguiba president for life.

In all his functions the president is assisted by a cabinet, and since the mid-1970s Bourguiba has increasingly left the running of day-to-day government affairs to the cabinet and the prime minister. The latter is appointed by the president and responsible only to him. In the event of the death or incapacity of the president, the prime minister succeeds him until new presidential elections are held. With Bourguiba's advancing age and faltering health, in-fighting among the prime minister and various cabinet ministers has intensified in recent years.

Legislative authority is constitutionally exercised by the people through a unicameral National Assembly, the members of which are directly elected for five-year terms coinciding with those of the president. The assembly must meet at least twice a year for sessions of not more than three months each, although additional sessions may be called by the president or a majority of assembly members. The president can dissolve the assembly and request new elections in response to a vote of censure against him, but he must resign if the newly elected assembly confirms the vote censure.

Since independence, there have been five elections for the National Assembly, all won by PSD candidiates. The party controls individual candidacies through its political bureau, which drafts the lists after consulting with the leaders of national organizations. Because the assembly is dominated by the PSD, it has not commanded much respect or attention either as a forum for serious political discussion or as a source of meaningful legislation.

In terms of regional and local government, Tunisia is divided into thirteen governorates, or provinces. Each is headed by a presidentially appointed governor, who is assisted by either an appointed government council or an elected municipal council. Provinces are subdivided into delegations, communes, and *cheikhats*.

The PSD remains dominant at all levels, and, at present, formal party and governmental structures legitimize leaders and policies to a greater extent than they function as effective mechanisms for representative participation in the political process. In recent years, however, an increasing number of new political actors and organizations have emerged on the scene, thus expanding the scope and complexity of political life.

Opposition parties with legal status include the liberal and social democratic MDS; the socialist-oriented MUP-2, a Tunis-based offshoot of Ben Salah's party; and the Tunisian Communist party (PCT). All three remain weak, however, with no representation in the assembly and little grassroots organization. Ben Salah's MUP-1 is still banned, but there is speculation that Ben Salah himself might be granted amnesty and permitted to return to Tunisia. Several of his former associates retain positions of influence within the PSD.

The most serious challenges to PSD dominance come from labor and the Islamic Tendency Movement. UGTT was weakened early in 1984 by a split leading to the formation of the National Union of Tunisian Workers (UNTT). Composed primarily of white-collar workers, UNTT is progovernment in orientation. It was further affected by a power struggle between its president, Habib Achour, and its secretary-general, Taieb Baccouche. At present, however, Achour is in the dominant position, and, as was the case in the late 1970s, he is opposing the government on economic issues. Achour has also discussed the possibility of forming a Tunisian Labor party, which would operate in association with UGTT.

The release of detained MTI members in 1984 brought speculation about a change in the political status of the militant Islamic movement. Mzali met with MTI leader Abdel Fateh Morou, and some reports indicate that he was prepared to grant the MTI legal status and to make Morou minister of religious affairs. Bourguiba is said to have rejected the plan, however. Whether these reports are accurate or not, the government is clearly concerned about the Islamic movement's growing strength, and the MTI, for its part, is seeking ways to make its influence felt.

A final institution that may play an increasingly important political role is the small and traditionally apolitical military. But its circumstances are changing. First, it has been politicized by use in domestic disturbances. Second, its officer corps is being altered. That is, professional soldiers educated before independence are retiring, and younger officers tend to be more politically conscious and ideological. In addition, some officers are now of modest social origin and highly sensitive to political and economic disparities. Third, the government in 1980 responded to the military's call for a major program of expansion and modernization, thereby increasing the functional weight of the army.

Political Dynamics

The cult of personality that has long dominated Tunisian political life leaves uncertain the degree to which the "party-government" created by Bourguiba and his contemporaries will endure his passing. Given the relatively sophisticated level of political awareness and experience extant among many of the society's educated elites, both in and out of power, a significant change in the existing political order in the period following Bourguiba's demise would not be surprising.

The major structures of government—including the National Assembly, the PSD and its political bureau and national congress, and the cabinet—have long been little more than appendages to Bourguiba's system of personal rule. Assisting the president have been two groups of ruling elites found in both party and government. The old guard is composed of long-time associates of the president who participated in the pre-independence struggle and who attained their positions through long years of party service. Then there is a second category of younger men brought into government by Bourguiba because of their specialized education, technical skills, and modernist outlook. Neither group, however, has been allowed to achieve an independent base of power strong enough to challenge Bourguiba's rule.

Bourguiba developed his preeminent role in the political process by deftly manipulating and controlling his political subordinates. Particularly effective has been the way dissidents have been removed from office, even forced into exile, but later rehabilitated and returned to positions of responsibility. Thus, there has generally been an atmosphere of insecurity among the members of the political elite as they struggle for presidential favor while never really knowing when their political fortunes may turn.

This system of political "musical chairs" is a trademark of Bourguiba's style. The Tunisian leader's ability to engineer these purges while maintaining his authority over both the government and the PSD can be explained only in terms of his own enormous charisma, his prestige as the father of his nation, his deftly developed skills as a political tactician, and the continuing availability of talented individuals who have managed the affairs of state and party in effective style.

The ensconcement of patrimonial leadership was accomplished through the instrument of the PSD. Important decisions within the party originate at higher levels and are transmitted down the party hierarchy to the branches. The latter enjoy considerable latitude in expressing local grievances, provided they are not of such a nature as to embarrass, compromise, or threaten the regime; but policy is not discussed at branch level—it is explained and received.

The upper levels of the party hierarchy have been transformed into docile sounding boards for the government. The party's representative organs, such as the national congress and the national council, are hardly ever convened; when they do meet, they demonstrate little independence, aiming simply to express solidarity and approval. The political bureau itself, supposedly the party's executive decisionmaking body, has been reduced under the impact of presidential government to a ceremonial role and, like other party organs, limited to advisory functions.

In the last few years, especially since the rioting of early 1984, the inadequacies of this top-heavy political system have become increasingly clear and the Tunisians have begun to think about the character of political life that will emerge in the post-Bourguiba era. Many Tunisians believe that Bourguiba's brand of single-party rule performed critical functions in the years following independence, helping to shape the identity and political culture of the country and leading the nation's struggle for modernization and development. More recently, however, the structure of the political system appears to be geared to the exigencies of an earlier era, and many of its top leaders appear to be self-interested and self-absorbed.

The PSD has lost most of its former dynamism and, with this, much of its popular support. Its ideological elan is gone, and its institutional structure has atrophied. The 1984 disturbances revealed these weaknesses. Out of touch with the masses, party leaders were unable either to anticipate the public's reaction or to prepare the populace to accept a rise in the price of bread and semolina. Once the price rise had been decided upon, moreover, party cadres disappeared from view and made no attempt to calm the public.

At present, two questions dominate the Tunisian scene and the future will depend heavily on how they are resolved. First, who will lead the PSD and emerge as Bourguiba's heir? Second, what will be the relationship between the PSD and other national political institutions?

A struggle for power within the PSD has been under way for several years, with Mzali's opponents trying to diminish his influence and the prime minister seeking to remove challengers from important positions. The disturbances of January 1984 intensified this struggle, forcing a showdown between Mzali and Driss Guiga, minister of the interior. Supported by Bourguiba's influential wife, Wassila, Guiga was Mzali's most important rival for PSD leadership. Nevertheless, Mzali succeeded in laying much of the responsibility for the rioting on the interior minister. Guiga was forced to resign and later, having fled the country, was tried in absentia for high treason and sentenced to prison. Mzali thereafter removed a number of other officials who had been associated with Guiga.

Despite these changes, Mzali's position is far from secure. He has been unable to remove some officials formerly associated with Guiga. Moreover, the upper echelons of the PSD contain other challengers. Mzali's most important rival at present is probably Mohammed Sayah, former PSD executive secretary and Bourguiba protégé. Sayah's influence had declined in recent years, and he was serving as ambassador to Italy at the time of the 1984 riots. But he was brought back in the wake of the disturbances and, with direct access to the president and many friends in high places, his influence is considerable.

Given that Bourguiba was hospitalized late in 1984, one is led to consider that the president's health may also influence the outcome of this struggle for power. The president has strongly supported his prime minister, officially designating him as his successor in a major policy speech in early 1985. This formal public declaration has not dampened concern, however, and the struggle to control the PSD remains intense, absorbing the energies of Mzali and other senior officials and contributing to a mood of uncertainty in the country.

A second political issue preoccupies Tunisians. Will moves toward pluralism continue, and, if so, will they assume proportions capable of changing the character of political life? Guiga was staunchly opposed to multiparty politics, and, for this reason, advocates of political liberalism are not unhappy about his demise. Sayah, whose fortunes are ascending, is also believed to favor PSD dominance. Mzali favors some interparty competition but, thus far, has not permitted the kind of competition that might lead to a reduction in the PSD's power.

On the other hand, with the number and strength of rival political actors increasing, the future may not be determined by the PSD alone. The UGTT, the MTI, and the military are all political forces that, potentially, have the ability to challenge the PSD. Any might be able to force the present government to accept additional and more genuine interparty competition, or even to press for other, more dramatic political changes.

Foreign Policy

Tunisian foreign policy has thus far been the creation of Habib Bourguiba, whose views on foreign affairs have been greatly influenced by his links to France. As a product of Western liberal thinking, Bourguiba has shunned radical and extremist policies. He has consistently assumed a moderate, pro-Western stance on East-West issues, generally remaining suspicious of the communist bloc and of those Afro-Arab leaders who have sought communist friendship in the form of military aid agreements and tacit military-political alliances.

During the cold war, it was therefore natural for Tunisia to turn to the United Sates as a countervailing force to the power of the Soviet bloc. When decolonization disputes during the 1960s undermined Franco-Tunisian cooperation, the United States also became Tunisia's principal supplier of economic assistance.

Tunisia, however, has consistently demonstrated a close affinity to France, with whom it maintains extensive cultural, educational, and commercial ties. Although the United Sates is perhaps regarded as the world's preeminent military power, Bourguiba and his generation of Gallicized elites consider France the most influential cultural, intellectual, and "spiritual" force. Economic and military ties between the two countries have increased since the mid-1970s.

Despite the importance of its close ties to the United States and France, Tunisia has sought to avoid compromising its nonaligned status. It continues to maintain proper diplomatic and economic relations with all the major states of the communist world and its a member in good standing of the Third World. The country's receipt of significant economic and technical aid from numerous international organizations, petroleum-exporting Arab states, Soviet bloc countries, China, and most Western industrialized states reflects its general acceptance by the world community.

Tunisia's major foreign policy problems have arisen from ideological, political, territorial, and economic disputes with its neighbors. Tunisia's pro-Western orientation has brought it into conflict with both Algeria and Libya. Its failure to implement the hastily announced January 1974 merger with Libya strained relations between the two countries and led to Libyan economic retaliation, political subversion, and military threats. Tunisia stands in sharp ideological contrast to the puritanical, fundamentalist, and fervently Arabist Libya of Colonel Qaddafi. Given the profound differences in style, temperament, and political orientation, tensions are likely to remain, although rapprochements have ocasionally surfaced between Qaddafi and Bourguiba.

Relations with Algeria, historically cool but correct, have warmed in recent years, in part as a result of Tunisia's desire to find a regional counterweight to Libyan pressure and in part owing to the increased moderation of Algeria's present leadership. Thus, Tunisia and Algeria, along with Mauritania, signed a Treaty of Fraternity and Concord in 1983. Tunisia has long regarded Morocco as its closest ally in the Maghrib, but its own improved relations with Algeria and its neutral position on the conflict in the Sahara have somewhat diminished the importance of this relationship.

Tunisia has worked to reestablish its credentials as a loyal member of the Arab community. During the 1960s Bourguiba alientated most of Tunisia's Arab "brothers" by advocating the then unthinkable recognition of, and negotiations with, Israel. Aware of the strong emotional identification of Tunisia's population with the Arab cause, the Tunisian leadership has since been careful to maintain its solidarity with the Arab world, primarily through consistent—though largely rhetorical—support of the Palestinians. In 1979 Tunisia deepened its involvement in inter-Arab politics by becoming host to the League of Arab States, which left its Cairo base in protest of Egypt's signing of the Camp David Accords and a peace treaty with Israel. At the present time, the secretary-general of the Arab League is a Tunisian.

In conclusion, Tunisian foreign policy goals have been modest, its techniques eminently practical and realistic, and its results undramatic though very beneficial to the country in terms of economic assistance. Given Tunisia's small size, limited resources, and military vulnerability, Bourguiba has managed to establish a respectable position for Tunisia in world affairs.

Bibliography

Tunisia's colonialist experience is sensitively treated by a Jewish "native son," Albert Memmi, in *The Colonizer and the Colonized* (Boston: Beacon Press, 1967). Several works deal with Tunisia's political history from the precolonial period through independence, such as L. Carl Brown's *The Tunisia of Ahmad Bey: 1837–1855*, (Princeton, N.J.: Princeton University Press, 1974); Charles F. Gallagher's "Tunisia," in Gwendolyn M. Carter, ed., *African One-Party States* (Ithaca, N.Y.: Cornell University Press, 1962); Nancy E. Gallagher's *Medicine and Power in Tunisia: 1780–1900* (New York: Cambridge University Press, 1983); Wilfred Knapp's *Tunisia* (London: Thames and Hudson, 1970); Leon Laitman's *Tunisia Today: Crisis in North Africa* (New York: Citadel Press, 1954); Dwight L. Ling's *Tunisia: From Protectorate to Republic* (Bloomington: Indiana University Press, 1967); *Tunisia 54* (New York: Negro University Press, 1969); and Nicola Ziadeh's *Origins of Nationalism in Tunisia* (Beirut: Khayat's, 1962).

As one of the few instances of evolutionary political development in the Third World, Tunisia has received its share of scholarly attention. Themes such as modernization, social change, and political development are intelligently treated by Douglas E. Ashford, in *National Development and Local Reform: Political Participation in Morocco, Tunisia, and Pakistan* (Princeton, N.J.: Princeton University Press, 1967); Willard A. Beling, in *Modernization and African Labor: A Tunisian Case Study* (New York: Praeger Publishers, 1965); L. Carl Brown, in "The Tunisian Path to Modernization," in Menahem Milson, ed., *Society and Political Structure in the Arab World* (New York: Humanities Press, 1973); Ghazi Duwaji, in *Economic Development in Tunisia: The Impact and Course of Government Planning* (New York: Praeger Special Studies, 1967); and Charles Micaud, with Leon Carl Brown and Clement Henry Moore, in *Tunisia: The Politics of Modernization* (New York: Praeger Publishers, 1964).

Prospects for political institutionalization with special reference to Tunisia's single-party system are the concern of Clement Henry Moore, *Tunisia Since Independence: The Dynamics of One-Party Government* (Berkeley and Los Angeles: University of California Press, 1965); Clement H. Moore, "Tunisia: The Prospects for Institutionalization," in Samuel P. Huntington and Clement H. Moore, eds., *Authoritarian Politics in Modern Society: The Dynamics of Established One-Party Systems* (New York: Basic Books, 1970); Lars Rudebeck, *Party and People: A Study of Political Change in Tunisia* (New York: Praeger Publishers, 1969); and Russell P. Stone, "Tunisia: A Single-Party System Holds Change in Abeyance," in I. William Zartman et al., *Political Elites in Arab North Africa* (New York: Longman, 1982).

Sociological, cultural, and psychological studies of Tunisia may be found in Jean Duvignaud, *Change at Shebika: Report from a North African Village* (New York: Pantheon Books, 1970); Mark A. Tessler, "The Tunisians," in Mark A. Tessler, William M. O'Barr, and David H. Spain, eds., *Tradition and Identity in Changing Africa* (New York: Harper & Row, 1973); Russell Stone and John Simmons, eds., *Change in Tunisia: Essays in the Social Sciences* (Albany: State University of New York Press, 1976); and Rafik Said, *Cultural Policy in Tunisia* (Paris: UNESCO, 1970). Finally, *Tunisia: A Country Study* (Washington, D.C.: Government Printing Office, 1979) provides comprehensive reference material on the country.

Contributors

John Duke Anthony is president of the National Council on U.S.-Arab Relations and previously of the Middle East Educational Trust. He has taught at Johns Hopkins School of Advanced International Studies and has served as a visiting professor at a number of other institutions. His publications include *The Middle East: Oil, Politics and Development; The Sultanate of Oman and the Emirates of Eastern Arabia;* and *Arab States of the Lower Gulf: People, Politics, and Petroleum.*

M. Graeme Bannerman is staff director of the U.S. Senate Foreign Relations Committee. He previously served in the Department of State where he was an analyst and a member of the Policy Planning Staff with responsibility for the Near East and South Asia. He has a Ph.D. in Middle East history and has taught at the American University of Beirut, Georgetown University, and George Washington University.

Sally Ann Baynard received her Ph.D. in political science with a Middle East Studies focus from the George Washington University and has taught Middle East politics and international relations at the College of William and Mary and Georgetown University. She has published a number of articles on Sudanese politics and foreign policy.

John P. Entelis is professor of political science and co-director of the Middle East Studies Program at Fordham University. He is the author of numerous publications on the comparative and international politics of the Middle East and North Africa, the most recent being *Algeria: The Revolution Institutionalized* (Westview, 1986). Dr. Entelis has taught at the University of Algiers and the University of Tunis as a Senior Fulbright Professor.

George S. Harris is director of the Office of Research and Analysis for the Near East and South Asia in the Bureau of Intelligence and Research of the Department of State. He has taught at the School of Advanced International Studies of Johns Hopkins University and at George Washington University. Among his publications are *The Origins of Communism in Turkey* (1967); *Troubled Alliance: Turkish-American Problems in Historical Perspective, 1045–1971* (1972); and *Turkey: Coping with Crisis* (Westview, 1985).

John A. Hearty was a Peace Corps volunteer in Tunisia and has visited the Gulf area. He is a Ph.D. candidate in the Department of Political Science at George Washington University, where he specializes in the politics of the Middle East and works as a management consultant at United Communications Group.

David E. Long is in charge of the Near East and South Asia sections in the Office of Counter Terrorism and Emergency Planning of the Department of State. He was formerly executive director of the Center for Contemporary Arab Studies at Georgetown University.

David McClintock is associate professor of political science at North Carolina State University where he teaches a course on politics of the modern Middle East. He served twenty-two years as a U.S. Foreign Service officer and was stationed in Lebanon, Jordan, and Yemen. He was principal officer of the U.S. Diplomatic Mission in Yemen from 1970 to 1972.

Aaron David Miller is a member of the Department of State's policy planning staff. During 1982–1983 he was a Council on Foreign Relations Fellow where he completed his most recent book, *The PLO and the Politics of Survival.* His articles have appeared in the *New York Times, Los Angeles Times, Washington Quarterly, Current History,* and the *Jerusalem Quarterly.*

Bernard Reich is professor of political science and international affairs, director of the Middle Eastern Studies Program and former chairman of the Department of Political Science at George Washington University in Washington, D.C. He has written numerous books and articles on various aspects of the politics and international relations of the Middle East. His most recent books are *The United States and Israel: Influence in the Special Relationship* (1984) and *Israel: Land of Tradition and Conflict* (Westview, 1985).

Mark A. Tessler is professor of political science at the University of Wisconsin-Milwaukee and faculty associate of the Universities Field Staff International. Among his publications are *Tradition and Identity in Changing Africa* (1973), *Arab Oil: Impact on the Arab Countries and Global Implications* (1976), *Political Elites in Arab North Africa* (1982), and *The Evaluation and Application of Survey Research in the Arab World* (1986).

Index